Tax Law
Volume I

The International Library of Essays in Law and Legal Theory
Series Editor: Tom D. Campbell

Schools

Natural Law, Vols I & II *John Finnis*
Justice *Thomas Morawetz*
Law and Economics, Vols I & II *Jules Coleman and Jeffrey Lange*
Critical Legal Studies *James Boyle*
Marxian Legal Theory *Csaba Varga*
Legal Reasoning, Vols I & II *Aulis Aarnio and D. Neil MacCormick*
Legal Positivism *Mario Jori*
American Legal Theory *Robert Samuel Summers*
Postmodernism and Law *Dennis Patterson*
Law and History *David Sugarman*
Law and Language *Fred Schauer*
Sociological Theories of Law *Kahei Rokumoto*
Rights *Carlos Nino*
Law and Psychology *Martin Lyon Levine*
Feminist Legal Theory, Vols I & II *Frances Olsen*
Law and Society *Roger Cotterrell*
Contemporary Criminological Theory *Francis T. Cullen and Velmer S. Burton Jr.*

Areas

Criminal Law *Thomas Morawetz*
Tort Law *Ernest J. Weinrib*
Contract Law, Vols I & II *Larry Alexander*
Anti-Discrimination Law *Christopher McCrudden*
Consumer Law *Iain Ramsay*
International Law *Martti Koskenniemi*
Property Law, Vols I & II *Elizabeth Mensch and Alan Freeman*
Constitutional Law *Mark V. Tushnet*
Procedure *D.J. Galligan*
Evidence and Proof *William Twining and Alex Stein*
Company Law *Sally Wheeler*
Privacy, Vols I & II *Raymond Wacks*
Lawyers' Ethics *David J. Luban*
Administrative Law *D.J. Galligan*
Child Law *Harry D. Krause*
Family Law, Vols I & II *Harry D. Krause*
Welfare Law *Peter Robson*
Medicine and the Law *Bernard M. Dickens*
Commercial Law *Ross Cranston*
Environmental Law *Michael C. Blumm*
Conflict of Laws *Richard Fentiman*
Law and Religion *Wojciech Sadurski*
Human Rights Law *Philip Alston*
European Community Law, Vols I & II *Francis Snyder*
Tax Law, Vols I & II *Patricia D. White*
Media Law *Eric Barendt*
Labour Law *David L. Gregory*
Alternative Dispute Resolution *Michael D.A. Freeman*

Legal Cultures

Comparative Legal Cultures *Csaba Varga*
Law and Anthropology *Peter Sack*
Hindu Law and Legal Theory *Ved Nanda*
Islamic Law and Legal Theory *Ian Edge*
Chinese Law and Legal Theory *Michael Palmer*
Russian Legal Theory *W. Butler*
Common Law *Michael Arnheim*
Japanese Law and Legal Theory *Koichiro Fujikura*
Law and Development *Anthony Carty*
Jewish Law and Legal Theory *Martin P. Golding*
Legal Education *Martin Lyon Levine*
Civil Law *Ralf Rogowski*
African Law and Legal Theory *Gordon Woodman and Akintunde Obilade*

Future Volume
Cumulative index

Tax Law
Volume I

Edited by

Patricia D. White

The University of Utah College of Law

NEW YORK UNIVERSITY PRESS
REFERENCE COLLECTION

Manufactured in Great Britain

First published in the U.S.A. in 1995 by
NEW YORK UNIVERSITY PRESS
Washington Square
New York NY 10003

Library of Congress Cataloging-in-Publication Data
Tax law / edited by Patricia D. White.
p. cm. – (International library of essays in law and legal theory. Areas: 24)
Includes bibliographical references.
ISBN 0-8147-9281-2
1. Income tax–Law and legislation–United States. 2. Income tax–United States. 3. Taxation–United States. I. White, Patricia D. II. Series.
KF6369.A2T275 1994
343.7305'2–dc20
[347.30352] 94–21391
CIP

Contents

Acknowledgements

The editors and publishers wish to thank the following for permission to use copyright material.

Blackwell Publishers for the essay: Richard A. Epstein (1986), 'Taxation in a Lockean World', *Social Philosophy and Policy*, **4**, pp. 49–74.

Commerce Clearing House, Inc., Chicago, for the essay: Walter J. Blum (1982), 'Revisiting the Uneasy Case For Progressive Taxation', *Taxes*, **60**, pp. 16–21.

Florida Tax Review for the essay: Paul R. McDaniel and James R. Repetti (1993), 'Horizontal and Vertical Equity: The Musgrave/Kaplow Exchange', *Florida Tax Review*, **1**, pp. 607–22.

The Harvard Law Review Association for the essays: William D. Andrews (1974), 'A Consumption-Type or Cash Flow Personal Income Tax', *Harvard Law Review*, **87**, pp. 1113–88. Copyright © 1974 by The Harvard Law Review Association. Boris I. Bittker (1967), 'A "Comprehensive Tax Base" as a Goal of Income Tax Reform', *Harvard Law Review*, **80**, pp. 925–85. Copyright © 1967 by The Harvard Law Review Association. Richard A. Musgrave (1967), 'In Defense of an Income Concept', *Harvard Law Review*, **81**, pp. 44–62. Copyright © 1967 by The Harvard Law Review Association. Alvin C. Warren, Jr. (1975), 'Fairness and a Consumption-Type or Cash Flow Personal Income Tax', *Harvard Law Review*, **88**, pp. 931–46. Copyright © 1975 by The Harvard Law Review Association.

National Tax Association-Tax Institute of America for the essays: Henry Aaron (1969), 'What is A Comprehensive Tax Base Anyway?', *National Tax Journal*, **22**, pp. 543–9; Louis Kaplow (1989), 'Horizontal Equity: Measures in Search of a Principle', *National Tax Journal*, **42**, pp. 139–54; Richard A. Musgrave (1990), 'Horizontal Equity, Once More', *National Tax Journal*, **43**, pp. 113–22.

Stanford Law Review and Fred B. Rothman & Company for the essays: Barbara H. Fried (1992), 'Fairness and the Consumption Tax', *Stanford Law Review*, **44**, pp. 961–1017. © 1992 by the Board of Trustees of the Leland Stanford Junior University. Mark Kelman (1983), 'Time Preference and Tax Equity', *Stanford Law Review*, **35**, pp. 649–80. © 1983 by the Board of Trustees of Leland Stanford Junior University.

University of California Press for the essay: Joseph Bankman and Thomas Griffith (1987), 'Social Welfare and the Rate Structure: A New Look at Progressive Taxation', *California Law Review*, **75**, pp. 1905–67.

Patricia D. White (1990), 'Realization, Recognition, Reconciliation, Rationality and the Structure of the Federal Income Tax System', *Michigan Law Review*, **88**, pp. 2034–96. © Patricia D. White.

The Yale Law Journal Company and Fred B. Rothman & Company for the essay: Alvin Warren (1980), 'Would a Consumption Tax Be Fairer Than an Income Tax?', *Yale Law Journal*, **89**, pp. 1081–124.

Every effort has been made to trace all the copyright holders, but if any have been inadvertently overlooked the publishers will be pleased to make the necessary arrangements at the first opportunity.

Series Preface

The International Library of Law and Legal Theory is designed to provide important research materials in an accessible form. Each volume contains essays of central theoretical importance in its subject area. The series as a whole makes available an extensive range of valuable material which will be of considerable interest to those involved in the research, teaching and study of law.

The series has been divided into three sections. The Schools section is intended to represent the main distinctive approaches and topics of special concern to groups of scholars. The Areas section takes in the main branches of law with an emphasis on essays which present analytical and theoretical insights of broad application. The section on Legal Cultures makes available the distinctive legal theories of different legal traditions and takes up topics of general comparative and developmental concern.

I have been delighted and impressed by the way in which the editors of the individual volumes have set about the difficult task of selecting, ordering and presenting essays from the immense quantity of academic legal writing published in journals throughout the world. Editors were asked to pick out those essays from law, philosophy and social science journals which they consider to be fundamental for the understanding of law, as seen from the perspective of a particular approach or sphere of legal interest. This is not an easy task and many difficult decisions have had to be made in order to ensure that a representative sample of the best journal essays available takes account of the scope of each topic or school.

I should like to express my thanks to all the volume editors for their willing participation and scholarly judgement. The interest and enthusiasm which the project has generated is well illustrated by the fact that an original projection of 12 volumes drawn up in 1989 has now become a list of some 60 volumes. I must also acknowledge the vision, persistence and constant cheerfulness of John Irwin and the marvellous work done by Mrs Margaret O'Reilly and Sonia Hubbard.

TOM D. CAMPBELL
Series Editor
The Faculty of Law
The Australian National University

Introduction[1]

The title of these volumes promises rather more than two volumes can possibly deliver. Part of the reason is that taxes come in so many forms. Governments seek to raise revenue in a variety of ways and for myriad reasons. Among the kinds of things which have historically been taxed are property, wealth, income, transactions, specified activities and status. The schemes which governments have selected for implementing their revenue raising choices have also varied in complexity. In some countries, such as the United States, some of them have been enormously complex and technically difficult. Another reason why the title 'Tax Law' is necessarily overbroad is that tax law of whatever kind is essentially statutory. Even among common law countries there is less in the way of shared principles in the tax realm than in many other areas such as tort, contract or criminal law.

As a consequence of all of this statutory variety and complexity, tax scholarship has evolved in a curiously insular fashion. Predictably, perhaps, there has been less in the way of discussion across international borders in the tax area than in many other spheres of legal theory. Indeed a review of the footnotes of most of the articles which have appeared in major American, Canadian and British law reviews in recent years shows a remarkable lack of cross-fertilization. This insularity is not solely geographic, but separates disciplines as well. Most noteworthy has been the relatively distinct evolution of tax scholarship within the fields of law and economics. Both lawyers and economists have written extensively about a wide variety of tax topics, but most lawyers do not know the economics literature well nor economists the legal literature. With a few important exceptions, scholars in the two disciplines do not publish in the same journals and do not respond to each other's work.

Somewhat surprisingly, perhaps, philosophers and political theorists have been largely omitted from contemporary discussions of tax theory. Occasional bows are made in the direction of John Rawls or Robert Nozick, but legally trained tax theorists have not shown much interest in the kind of foundational justificatory questions that philosophers might help them with, while the technical details of tax law doubtless inhibit those in other disciplines from focusing directly on issues of taxation.

In selecting the essays for these volumes, I have not sought to portray tax scholarship in either an interdisciplinary or an international light. Instead, my aim has been to present essays which reflect the tenor of American tax theory scholarship in the legal arena over the past few decades. Income tax has dominated these discussions and thus is preeminently the subject of these volumes. I include here the work of some economists, ones who have both participated in and importantly influenced discussion within the community of legal scholars. I make these choices because I take the overall purpose of these volumes to be a reflection of significant debate as it has actually occurred.

Chapter 1 in this collection is Richard A. Epstein's 'Taxation in a Lockean World', chosen because it begins near the beginning: it seeks to explore the justification for a government's taxing its citizenry by asking what limitations ought properly to be placed on the sovereign's ability to tax. Epstein presumes a somewhat Lockean social contract wherein, in exchange for a similar promise by others, the citizen surrenders to the state his unrestricted freedom to behave as he chooses. He describes a bargain wherein the loss of liberty can be justified only if the collective gain outweighs the sum of the individual losses. Arguing from within this framework, Epstein defends several limiting principles. Ideally, equity would demand that each person's tax burden be proportional to the benefit he receives from the government. This goal can best be approached if taxes are levied upon cash and cash equivalents at the time of their receipt, and if rates are flat rather than progressive. Epstein's paper is rare in the American legal tax literature in beginning where it does, but the principles which it defends are central to the very rich debates which characterize this literature at its best. The subsequent 14 essays in this volume exemplify this richness.

The decision about *what* to tax is central to any government's scheme of taxation. In the US the federal income tax accounts for roughly 60 per cent of the government's total tax receipts (and about 90 per cent if employment taxes are excluded). One might imagine, therefore, that there is some clearly defined notion of 'income' which is by common consensus subject to taxation. Such an inference would be wrong on at least two counts. Even though there is a statutory system of revenue assessment and collection in place which succeeds fairly well in demarking some items as income and hence subject to taxation, and others as different from income and hence not subject to taxation, significant debate has been provoked. This concerns whether it is possible to give a theoretical definition of income and whether it is either useful or desirable to enshrine such a definition as the standard to which an income tax system should aspire and be held.

The idea that a touchstone concept of income can be systematically defined and used as a normative tool in the design of a tax system comprises the heart of the debate of the next three papers. Boris Bittker's 'A "Comprehensive Tax Base" as a Goal of Income Tax Reform' takes the pragmatic approach characteristic of all of his work. Bittker argues that the Haig-Simons definition of income favoured by economists is not clear enough to serve as a normative standard for the income tax system. Moreover, he argues, no such definition is needed. Tax provisions do and ought to encompass more than judgments about whether they conform to a theoretical definition of income. For example, they reflect judgments about how best to stimulate economic growth, about how best to encourage socially useful behaviour, and about administrative efficiency.

The next two chapters, both by distinguished economists, were written in response to Bittker. Richard Musgrave develops the view that a basic concept of income is not only desirable but necessary in an equitable income tax system. Horizontal equity demands that like taxpayers be treated alike; thus a common standard must exist by which similarity can be determined. He acknowledges that equity is not the only appropriate normative goal of a tax system, and that sometimes other goals may conflict with and even override its requirements. He argues, however, that this does not obviate the need for a uniform standard by which to determine what the demands of equity are.

In 'What is a Comprehensive Tax Base Anyway?', Henry Aaron takes something of a middle position. He argues that it is possible to devise a theoretically precise definition of income (which would be somewhat different from the Haig-Simons definition) but that, in practice, such a definition could not be consistently applied. Nonetheless, he acknowledges the usefulness of the notion of a comprehensive tax base as a standard to which to refer in making *ad hoc* judgments about individual provisions. It helps in asking the right questions and in thinking clearly about answers.

The Haig-Simons definition of income has formed the traditional starting point in considering how to describe the ideal base of the income tax. Roughly, that definition equates a taxpayer's taxable income with the combination of his consumption during some period and the increase or decrease in his net worth during that same period. The next several essays examine whether income so conceived *should* form the base of the tax system or whether it would be fairer simply to tax a taxpayer's consumption during the relevant period – thus eliminating his savings from his tax base. This alternative conception of the desirable tax base has come to be called a 'consumption' tax. Unlike an income ideal, a consumption ideal does not reflect differences in the form of taxpayers' savings. The tax base only includes amounts consumed. It would not, for example, favour the accumulation of wealth in the form of appreciation in the value of property already owned over its accumulation through the saving of currently-acquired cash or assets.

Although early arguments for taxation based on consumption can be found in Thomas Hobbes and John Stuart Mill, and although the idea gained currency in economists' circles considerably earlier than it did in American legal literature, William Andrews's 'A Consumption-Type or Cash Flow Personal Income Tax' (published in 1974 and reprinted here as Chapter 5) is the paper which sparked a debate which has been central to legal academic discussions of tax policy over the last 20 years. The debate has spread from learned journals to the back rooms of Congress and the editorial columns of the *Wall Street Journal*. Although the US has yet to enact any form of a federal consumption tax, the seeds of the idea are firmly planted in the legislative consciousness.

Andrews's paper challenges the adequacy of the income ideal in the context of the taxation of individuals by arguing that it does not deal satisfactorily with savings. He spells out the difficulties he perceives and then develops a consumption ideal which he argues is better suited to dealing with a taxpayer's savings in a fair and simpler manner which is also administratively practical. He argues that even if a pure income tax, unencumbered by practical difficulties, could be implemented, a pure version of a consumption-type tax would be fairer.

This last claim is the focus of the next two essays, both by Alvin Warren. In 'Fairness and a Consumption-Type or Cash Flow Personal Income Tax', Warren examines Andrews's argument that a consumption ideal would yield a fairer tax because it 'ultimately imposes a more uniform burden on consumption, whenever it may occur, than does an accretion-type tax'.[2] Warren argues that, by reducing the after-tax return on invested savings, a tax based on an income ideal *would* indeed change the relative positions of taxpayers who differ in their preferences about whether to save now or in the future but that a tax based on a consumption ideal is unable to achieve any systematic redistributive effect among taxpayers of different wealth. It is not obvious, in Warren's view, which of these consequences an equitable tax system would be best advised to avoid. Warren further develops this theme in 'Would a Consumption Tax Be Fairer Than an Income Tax?' (Chapter 7). Here he argues that a comparison of the equity of a consumption-type tax with that of an income-type tax is indeterminate so long as the choice is conceived as an abstract comparison of the consumption ideal and the income ideal independent of considerations of how wealth ought to be treated. Considerations of wealth raise many issues; indeed, wealth should never be ignored in thinking about how best to construct a fair tax base.

Another objection to Andrews's claim that a tax based on a consumption ideal is inherently fairer than one based on an income ideal is explored in Mark Kelman's imaginative piece,

'Time Preference and Tax Equity' (Chapter 8). Kelman, like Warren, exploits the fact that Andrews does not give a systematic account of what the concept of 'fairness' might entail when applied to a tax scheme. Kelman examines both Andrews's claim that an income tax is less fair than a consumption tax because it does not distinguish between people who consume in the present and those who save and thus defer consumption, and also Warren's suggestion that the saving taxpayer might in fact be better off because of the interest earned on his savings. Kelman argues that the question of whether a fair tax system would distinguish between the current consumer and the saver is a complicated one which depends on one's conception of the 'origin' of interest. He spells out four quite different accounts of what interest might represent. Three of these conceive of interest as having essentially psychological roots, while the fourth views it purely as a function of market forces. In Kelman's view, no one view is obviously superior to the other three.

Finally, Barbara Fried's recent essay, 'Fairness and the Consumption Tax', is an ambitious contribution to the debate concerning the relative fairness of consumption and income taxes. Fried analyses the argument made by consumption tax proponents that it is unfair to tax unconsumed returns to capital. This argument apparently comes in three versions, each resting on a different concept of fairness. These three concepts are mutually inconsistent, yet each version of the argument ultimately rests on the claim that an income tax is likely to 'disadvantage savers relative to consumers, as compared to the respective positions of such parties in a no-tax world'.[3] She concludes, first, that it is not even clear that a tax on income from capital does favour spenders relative to savers and, second, that certainly the case has not yet been proved that it would be unfair if it did.

The design of a tax system requires more, of course, than the choice of a tax base. Another essential feature is a rate structure which determines what proportion of an individual's tax base the taxing entity will seek to collect. A system's rate structure can be more or less complex and/or systematic, but a complete description of it would focus on the effective tax burdens imposed on taxpayers, taking into account all exemptions, preferences, credits and other adjustments built into the system.

There are an infinite number of rate patterns which a system could employ, but academic discussion (for no very good reason that I can think of) has focused almost entirely on three: rate structures which are progressive, proportionate and regressive. Under a progressive tax, the percentage of the tax base claimed by the government increases as the tax base increases; under a proportionate tax, the rate does not vary with the size of the tax base, while under a regressive scheme the rate varies inversely. Since a regressive rate structure is widely thought to be unfair, it has been given considerably less attention than the other two.

Without doubt, the most influential analysis of the relative merits of progressive and proportionate rate patterns in American legal literature was written in 1952 by Walter J. Blum and Harry Kalven, Jr. Their article, 'The Uneasy Case for Progressive Taxation', was first published in the *Chicago Law Review* and has since been republished as a monograph (and hence is ineligible for inclusion here). Blum and Kalven note the broad and strong intuitive appeal of a principle of progressivity; they then proceed – meticulously, systematically and critically – to examine the foundations of this idea and the justificatory arguments which might be made on its behalf. As its title suggests, their piece concludes inconclusively with the following observation:

> [T]he theory of progression is a matter of major importance for taxation. The adoption of progression necessarily influences the positive law of taxation more than any other factor. But in the end it is the implications about economic inequality which impart significance and permanence to the issue and institution of progression. Ultimately a serious interest in progression stems from the fact that a progressive tax is perhaps the cardinal instance of the democratic community struggling with its hardest problem.[4]

Despite, or perhaps because of, its careful irresolution, Blum and Kalven's essay did not spawn a large body of serious scholarship plumbing the deep issues associated with the choice of a rate structure. It is itself the classic discussion and has importantly shaped the views of tax scholars in the four decades since being written. The short piece by Walter Blum in this collection (Chapter 10) is included largely in recognition of the central role that Blum and Kalven's original paper has played in people's thinking about rate structures. Blum's 1981 paper, 'Revisiting the Uneasy Case for Progressive Taxation', focuses briefly on four features which were characteristic of the US economic situation at that time and explores the implications of a progressive rate structure for each.

In 1987 another pair of legal scholars published an ambitious paper seeking to examine the underpinnings of progressivity. In Chapter 11 entitled 'Social Welfare and the Rate Structure: A New Look at Progressive Taxation', Joseph Bankman and Thomas Griffith argue that any rate structure must both presume and be measured by a theory of distributive justice. They criticize Blum and Kalven's method of analysis for not being grounded in such a theory of distributive justice and for treating proportionate taxation as if it were a natural default position rather than one which, no less than progressive taxation, requires affirmative justification. Bankman and Griffith concentrate on what they call 'welfarist' theories of distributive justice – those which measure the goodness of a social state by the well-being of its citizens. They evaluate the benefits and costs of progressivity using the tools of a branch of economics known as optimal taxation. Through the use of economic models, optimal taxation purports to be able to provide a means of calculating a tax rate structure in which, under a given theory of distributive justice, revenues would equal expenditures and social welfare would be maximized. The rate structures produced by optimal tax models will vary significantly according to the assumptions made about a variety of different features concerning the structure of the economic system and the determinants of individual utility. Nonetheless, Bankman and Griffith argue, using plausible assumptions about these two features, optimal tax models suggest that, under any 'welfarist' theory of distributive justice, the optimal tax is progressive but not characterized by graduated rates.

The concept of horizontal equity is often cited as an appropriate goal for any tax system, regardless of its rate structure. Horizontal equity is the requirement that equals be treated equally. The next three essays address the normative status of horizontal equity. The first of these, 'Horizontal Equity: Measures in Search of a Principle', by Louis Kaplow, argues that the principle in fact has no normative content independent of that of vertical equity. Vertical equity is the requirement that there be 'appropriate' differentiation among unequals. Kaplow's analysis concludes that compliance with vertical equity ensures compliance with horizontal equity, and that horizontal equity does not provide an adequate measure by which a tax system should be judged. In Chapter 13, 'Horizontal Equity, Once More', Richard Musgrave takes the position that horizontal equity does have independent normative content. He argues that, whereas the requirements of vertical equity vary significantly depending on the view of distributive justice presumed by the tax system, the requirements of horizontal equity remains unchanged. Paul McDaniel and James Repetti respond to the debate in 'Horizontal and Vertical Equity: The Musgrave/Kaplow Exchange' (Chapter 14). They take the position that neither horizontal nor vertical equity has any normative content independent of an underlying theory of distributive justice. Indeed, they conclude that, in all probability, neither principle serves as a useful standard for analysing a tax system's provisions.

The normative choices which a government makes in the design of its tax system must necessarily comply with the strictures of the structural requirements, if any, which logically underlie *any* tax system. I conclude this volume with an essay of my own, 'Realization, Recognition, Reconciliation, Rationality and the Structure of the Federal Income Tax System', which seeks to isolate and articulate the underlying structure on which the content of the tax law hangs. I argue that by examining the necessary structure of a tax system (apart from its particular content or goals), we can better understand the role played by its most characteristic features.

Together the contributions in this volume cover a considerable range. My essay, like Epstein's, is unusual in the American legal tax literature in beginning where it does. We are both exploring the *foundations* of the taxing enterprise, his paper in asking whether taxation can be justified as a matter of political theory, and mine in asking whether there is a conceptual structure undergirding all systems of taxation – a sort of metaphysics of tax. The 13 papers in between represent the best of contemporary mainstream debate about what to tax and how to do so fairly.

Notes

1 I benefited in the selection of essays for these volumes from suggestions made by Jeffrey Lehman and Lawrence Zelenak. My research assistant, David Wood, was unfailingly helpful. Work on this volume was supported by the University of Michigan Law School's Cook Endowment for faculty research.
2 Andrews, Chapter 5, p. 171 quoted in Warren, Chapter 6, p. 196.
3 Fried, Chapter 9, p. 287.
4 Blum and Kalven (1952), 'The Uneasy Case for Progressive Taxation', *University of Chicago Law Review*, **19**, at 417, 520.

References

Blum, Walter and Kalven, Harry (1952), 'The Uneasy Case for Progressive Taxation', *University of Chicago Law Review*, **19**.
Blum, Walter and Kalven, Harry (1953), *The Uneasy Case for Progressive Taxation*, Chicago: The Law School, The University of Chicago.
Chirelstein, Marvin A. (6th edn, 1991), *Federal Income Taxation*, Mineola, N.Y.: Foundation Press.
Goode, Richard (1964), *The Individual Income Tax*, Washington, D.C.: Brookings Institution.
Graetz, Michael (1979), 'Implementing a Progressive Consumption Tax', *Harvard Law Review*, **92**.
Groves, Harold (1974) in D. Curran (ed.), *Tax Philosophers: Two Hundred Years of Thought in Great Britain and the United States*, Madison: University of Wisconsin Press.
Gunn, Alan (1979), 'The Case for an Income Tax', *University of Chicago Law Review*, **46**.
Hobbes, Thomas (1947) in M. Oakeshott (ed.), *Leviathan*, Oxford: Basil Blackwell.
Kaldor, Nicholas (1955), *An Expenditure Tax*, London: Allen & Unwin.

Mill, John Stuart (1909) in W.J. Ashley (ed.), *Principles of Political Economy*, London and New York: Longman, Green and Co.

Mirrlees, James A. (1971), 'An Exploration in the Theory of Optimum Income Taxation', *Review of Economic Studies*, **38**.

Musgrave, Richard A. (1959), *The Theory of Public Finance; A Study in Public Economy*, New York: McGraw-Hill.

Nozick, Robert (1974), *Anarchy, State, and Utopia*, New York: Basic Books.

Pechman, Joseph A. (1957), 'Erosion of the Individual Income Tax', *National Tax Journal*, **10**.

Pigou, Alexandre (3rd edn, 1942), *A Study in Public Finance*, London: Macmillan.

Rawls, John (1971), *A Theory of Justice*, Cambridge, MA: Harvard University Press.

Simons, Henry C. (1938), *Personal Income Taxation*, Chicago: University of Chicago Press.

Stiglitz, Joseph (1982), 'Utilitarianism and Horizontal Equity: The Case for Random Taxation', *Journal of Public Economics*, **18**.

U.S. Dept. of the Treasury (1977), *Blueprints for Basic Tax Reform*, Washington, D.C.: Government Printing Office.

Utz, Stephen G. (1993), *Tax Policy, An Introduction and Survey of the Principal Debates*, St. Paul, Minn.: West Publishing Co.

[1]

Social Philosophy & Policy Vol. 4 Issue 1 ISBN 0625–0525

TAXATION IN A LOCKEAN WORLD*

BY RICHARD A. EPSTEIN

'Tis true governments cannot be supported without great charge, and it is fit everyone who enjoys a share of the protection should pay out of his estate his proportion for the maintenance of it. But still it must be with his own consent, i.e., the consent of the majority giving it either by themselves or their representatives chosen by them. For if any one shall claim a power to lay and levy taxes on the people, by his own authority, and without such consent of the people, he thereby invades the fundamental law of property and subverts the end of government. For what property have I in that which another may by right take when he pleases to himself.[1]

I. LIBERTY AND TAXATION

One constant refrain of political and constitutional history treats taxation as an inherent and indispensable power of the sovereign. In one sense that proposition seems to be a self-evident truth: if the sovereign is without resources, then it cannot carry out any mission, however defined. It must atrophy and die. Taxes are to the state as food is to the body. Yet in another sense the proposition is one that leads to anxiety and disquiet. *Pace* Locke, the institutions of representative government do not work as smoothly as we might hope. Taxation is the power to coerce other individuals to surrender their property *without* their consent. In a world – a Lockean world – in which liberty is regarded as a good and coercion an evil, then taxation authorizes the sovereign to commit acts of aggression against the very citizens it is supposed to protect. The two sides of the dilemma are thus complete. A world without taxation is a world without government; a world with taxation is a world with institutionalized coercion, where the citizen is made the servant instead of the master of the sovereign. Liberty and

* An earlier version of this paper was presented at a conference on "Taxation and Liberty" organized by Alvin Rabushka and held in Santa Fe, New Mexico in September 1985, at the law and economics workshop at the University of Toronto earlier that month, and at the Washington University Business School in January. I should like to thank Walter Blum, James Buchanan, Joseph Isenbergh and William Niskanen for their valuable comments on earlier drafts of this paper.

[1] John Locke, Of Civil Government (Second Treatise) ¶140, 142.

sovereignty are in conflict. With the tension unresolved, we are left only with the unhappy choice between anarchy and totalitarianism.

One central question for any political theory is how to escape the horns of this dilemma. More precisely, the question is how to preserve the power of taxation while curbing its abuse. The most promising line of inquiry, I believe, is to show that taxation, while an inherent power of the sovereign, is a *limited* one as well. This involves applying the general principles of limited government to the program of taxation. This effort to find that middle course invites a set of inquiries that are avoided with both extreme positions. What are the limitations upon the sovereign power to tax? And how do they preserve the liberties of the citizens so taxed? That question itself has two separate parts: first, what is the *substantive content* of the limitations that should be imposed and, second, what are the *institutional arrangements* that give these limitations a fair chance of success?

The failure to answer either of these questions in definitive form has led to the modern consensus that veers too far in the direction of untrammeled state power to tax. The first part of the conventional wisdom is that democratic political institutions are the prime source of protection against abuse of the power of taxation. The risk of exploitation is reduced because no single individual is given the power to tax without being accountable to the public at large, which can voice its collective objection to oppressive taxes at the polls, a check to which all politicians pay homage. Within the American system at least, however, the second part of the consensus answer specifies only weak constitutional restrictions upon the power to tax. Taxes can be struck down if they rely upon a suspect class or limit a preferred individual freedom. An income tax of 10 percent on whites and 20 percent on blacks, or vice versa, is invalid because it relies upon a racial classification. A special onerous tax upon magazines and newspapers is invalid as an infringement of the freedom of speech. These limitations upon the power to tax still leave the legislature enormous discretion with respect to the objects and the level of taxation; and they have done nothing to limit the vast proliferation of special provisions in the Internal Revenue Code that have proved remarkably resistant to intelligent reform nor, in earlier days, to question a steeply progressive tax with top marginal rates that nominally exceeded ninety percent. A clear theory of individual rights and limited government points to more robust constitutional limitations upon the power to tax than the political consensus now accepts.

Both the objects of taxation and the rates are covered by my analysis, which links the modern themes of tax equity to the general theory of political obligation. The paper proceeds as follows. Section II outlines the basic political justification for taxation. Section III explains the basic taxation bargain that this theory calls forth. Section IV then shows how that bargain can be applied to technical questions of both the tax base and the rate structure. Section V gives a brief account of the possible constitutional limitations upon the government's power to tax.

II. THE ORIGINAL POSITION

The American tradition of government has been heavily influenced by Lockean social contract theory. The central question for Locke is how one is to move from a world with a large number of separate and autonomous individuals into a world with a single sovereign able to maintain political order, all the while protecting both liberty and property against government domination. In the Lockean view, all individuals are endowed with rights of personal liberty and rights to acquire property,[2] rights that control against theft, aggression, and fraud. Yet in the absence of any state the only remedy available to these individuals is self-help, whereby force resists or combats force. The weakness in this system lies not in its basic conception of entitlements. Locke himself accepts the set of entitlements that has in fact shaped both the civil and criminal law of virtually all civilized societies. I know, for example, of no one who defends murder, rape, or theft. Similarly, no one thinks that the right of self-defense should be abolished as a matter of first principle, even if they think that the existence of an organized police force calls for pragmatic restrictions upon its use.

The difficulties of the Lockean view lie in the vagaries of its enforcement. It is one thing to believe in the right of self-defense. It is quite another to determine who is the aggressor and who is the victim. To allow every person to make that determination for himself invites in private affairs what is so common in international relations: aggression under the pretext of defense. Similarly, there are limits to the right of self-defense even when the use of force is justified: once the peril has ceased the further use of force is excessive and outside the boundaries of the original justification. But, again, these limits are neither self-defining nor self-enforcing.

[2] There are difficulties in Locke's account of the original position, which treats all external things as being owned in common while each individual has exclusive ownership of his own person. Locke himself thought that his labor theory of value explained why any individual could take land or other property from the original common pool. But his theory is subject to the criticism that the private ownership it creates is subject to a lien for the benefit of the public at large, for otherwise the individual acquirer gets more than his labor has added. Locke's case would have been made more forcefully if he had taken the basic position of both the common and the Roman law – that all external things are unowned in the original position – for then first possession need not defeat any prior claims. The original no-ownership rule has a utilitarian simplicity, for there is little need to worry about a monopoly over natural resources when each person owns his own labor. For a defense of the common law solution, see Richard A. Epstein, Takings: Private Property and the Power of Eminent Domain, Chs. 2 & 20; and *Possession as the Root of Title*, 13 Ga. L. Rev. 1221 (1979).

The state offers a practical way to escape these enforcement difficulties by providing a single umpire whose decisions bind both contestants. Adjudication and public force replace self-help. Difficulties beset the implementation of the plan by the formation of government. Sovereignty sounds like an abstraction, but the power is always in the hands of natural persons ("real people") who may use their monopoly of force as a cloak for aggression against the very persons whose liberty and property they are sworn to protect. *Quis custodiet custodies?*, "Who guards the guardians?" is still the most probing question ever asked in political theory. In light of the manifold disasters of this and every other century, one could almost wish for a world without organized government on the commendable theory that random assaults offer a smaller risk than organized terror. But that solution is simply not in the cards. The void created by the lack of central authority will be filled by some desperado who will then disarm all his rivals. The practical choice therefore is not the choice between government and no government; the consistent anarchist will lose all (hypothetical) wars to the determined statist. The only set of feasible choices therefore are on the second order questions: what kind of state, with what kind of governors, minimizes the abuse of centralized power?

The options are limited and the risks are high, but on balance the best answers seem to come from the cross between the natural rights and the utilitarian tradition that together have inspired contract theories of the state and constitutional theories of limited government. Ideally, one can conceive of a (hypothetical) bargain calling for the universal renunciation of force by all persons, present and future. That agreement promises enormous gains to all the parties to it.[3] The theory of the state fleshes out the terms of that agreement.

The agreement is not real, so how can the argument proceed? Certain individuals might think themselves better off in a world that does tolerate the war of all against all, because they think that this is one war they can win. One person, therefore, might wish to hold out against the multitude. The greater the number of persons, the more likely that one of them will respond in this way. The theory of natural rights is designed to counter just this possibility by noting that the *baseline* against which "being better off" is measured gives to each person only his natural rights to liberty and property, and not the fruits acquired by theft, aggression, or deception.[4] The impulse

[3] The metaphor of bargain has been used to describe other situations in which coercive forced exchanges are designed to overcome common pool problems. Bankruptcy is one such example; see, e.g., Jackson, *Bankruptcy, Non-Bankruptcy Entitlements, and the Creditors' Bargain*, 91 Yale L.J. 857 (1982).

[4] See Frank Michelman, *Ethics, Economics, and The Law of Property*, 24 NOMOS, Ethics, Economics and the Law 3 (1982) for a vision of the world without such a baseline; and the brief rejoinder by Harold Demsetz, *Professor Michelman's Unnecessary And Futile Search For The Philosopher's Touchstone*, *id.* 41.

behind that intuition comes from two sources: the first is the self-evident belief that individual autonomy is a primary and indisputable good, and the second is that the overall level of human satisfaction and happiness is greater in a world without aggression than in a world with it.

Even if the baseline can be set as Locke would set it, the operation of the state cannot rest on actual or tacit consent. Instead, the justification for the state depends upon the *network of forced hypothetical exchanges* needed to overcome the persistent problems of collective action: holdouts and free-riders flourish in a world of high transaction costs.[5] Armed with that (inchoate) realization, the Lockean solution was simple and correct. It postulated a world in which, as a first approximation, every individual was required to surrender his right to use force to the state in exchange for the like promise of every other individual to so refrain. In such a world, the gains from being free of risk of aggression are worth more than the unqualified rights of self-help they replace. The risk of aggression of course remains, and self-help (now subject to judicial scrutiny and review) remains for emergencies where state intervention cannot be timely. Starting from the original set of entitlements, the formation of the state looks very much like a Pareto-superior move in which some natural rights are surrendered in exchange for the greater protection of the natural rights that are retained. Taxation is the form of surrender, and security is the good received in exchange. In the modern language of welfare theory, one distribution of rights is Pareto-superior to another so long as one person is better off in the first world than in the second, and no one else is worse off.[6] The formation of the state appears to satisfy this social welfare condition. Indeed, one can go further and argue that a more stringent requirement is satisfied as well. The gains of organized society cannot be captured solely by a small few. State protection is general so that each person shares in the social gains, roughly pro rata, in accordance to the value of his original endowments. Insisting that the surplus be divided in this unique way increases the definiteness of legal rights, which in turn reduces the danger of wealth loss from factional struggle.[7] In principle, no person can object to the second world in which the use of sovereign power leaves him better off than he was with his natural endowments. Similarly, no person can be allowed to stand outside the compact, for then the entire arrangement will unravel; for without universal compliance, the monopoly of the state is lost and the regime of self-help,

[5] See, generally, Russell Hardin, Collective Action (1982) for an account of these difficulties.

[6] See, e.g., Coleman, *The Economic Analysis of Law*, 24 NOMOS, Ethics, Economics and Law, Ch. 4 (J. Pennock & J. Chapman eds. 1982).

[7] In contrast, note that a per capita division of the gain from public expenditures may require explicit cash transfers between members of the society. Who is to pay and who is to collect is far from evident. The pro rata position is designed to avoid the social losses that would follow from any effort to redistribute the surplus by direct transfer payments.

with all its deficiencies, will emerge anew. The reconciliation of liberty and coercion is found in the stipulation for a return benefit, unobtainable through voluntary agreement, that exceeds in value the losses of liberty and property entailed by the formation of the state.

III. THE TAXATION BARGAIN

The task of governance does not end with a simple statement of the theory that justifies sovereign power. A Lockean theory leaves the state with functions to discharge – the keeping of order. The state must have the resources to discharge them. These funds could in principle come from voluntary contributions, but that prospect is bleak. Just as voluntary agreements could not form the state, so they cannot fund its continued operations; free riding endures. Everyone has the incentive to let other persons pay the private costs of the public good. The system is then in fundamental disequilibrium, for the state must have the resources it cannot command. Taxation from all is the only viable source of revenue to restore the equilibrium implied by the simple proposition that the state must have a secure revenue base. The question is distribution and incidence of the tax in question. At this point, one might expect that Locke himself would discuss in some detail the nature and the sources of the tax, but apart from his keen sense that taxation should be proportionate to the property protected,[8] he veers away from the issue.

Yet so great is the power of his theory of the state that it does more than account for the existence of the power of taxation. It also provides a blueprint for the closer analysis of the particular rules that limit the exercise of the taxing power. That such limitations are needed seems evident given the constant temptations for self-aggrandisement in politics. Even if all individuals abandon the use of force, they still remain political actors able to resort to influence and intrigue. The modern theory of public choice makes it abundantly clear what everyone who has heard of factions has known intuitively all along. There is a constant pressure for special interest legislation that is fundamentally at odds with the Pareto-superior pattern of forced exchanges appropriate for state initiation. In its place are efforts to achieve implicit transfers of property and wealth from one group to another. In the effort to skew the gains from collective life, taxation can be, and has been, used as a weapon of confiscation.[9] The Lockean theory of government calls for the use of coercion only to create a larger pie with all persons sharing in the gain. In practice, resort to governmental power often leads to a

[8] See note 1, *supra*.

[9] See Epstein, *Taxation, Regulation and Confiscation*, 20 Osgoode Hall L.J. 433 (1982).

smaller pie. Some individuals will obtain larger slices; otherwise nothing will drive the process. But others necessarily will be left with far less than they had before the government program was placed in operation. The standard Pareto measures are systematically violated.[10] There is no possibility that all will be allowed to share pro rata in the social gain. Democratic processes may make it more difficult to form a winning coalition; and they are certainly superior to despotic rule. But they do provide a new arena for abuse that cries out for institutional control. What form should the taxation bargain take?

A. Tax neutrality. A sound tax is designed to interfere as little as possible with the ordinary decisions that individuals would make in the investment and consumption of their capital and labor. On the Lockean theory, the sphere of individual autonomy should be invaded as little as possible in order to secure the maintenance of public order. In the original state of nature no individual can pass judgment on what others decide to do with their liberty or property unless the use of force or fraud is involved. The creation of a system of government should strive not to reduce the scope of permissible individual choice from what it was before. Accordingly, no person or group should be able to use the tax system to change the pattern of preferences of other individuals. If A ranks a set of (noncoercive) alternatives 1 to n before taxation, then A's ranking of those alternatives should remain 1 to n, without alteration, after the tax is imposed. So, too, with all other persons. If subsidies and penalties are generally forbidden, then they are forbidden not only by direct regulation, but by taxation as well.

The postulate of tax neutrality immediately follows.[11] Tax neutrality is a principle that recognizes that before a system of taxation is imposed, individuals order their preferences in a discrete and particular way. The ideal of tax neutrality simply provides that the system of taxation, as far as possible, should preserve the relative priorities that individuals attach to various activities. The function of the state is to protect liberty and property. It is not to aid one group or another in skewing the uses to which individuals put their natural endowments. Observing the principle does more than keep the relations between taxpayer activities constant. It also keeps their relative wealth constant as well, so that an increase for one is matched by a

[10] I explore some of these tensions in Richard A. Epstein, Takings, at Ch. 2, 12, and 18; *Toward a Revitalization of the Contract Clause*, 51 U. Chi. L. Rev. 703 (1984); and *Why Restrain Alienation?*, 85 Colum. L. Rev. 770 (1985).

[11] Here tax neutrality must be kept distinct from the idea of "revenue neutrality" that has been prominent in recent discussions of tax reforms. Revenue neutrality provides that the total revenue collected by the state should not be decreased by any substantive principles of tax reform. But it does not tell us how to decide the soundness of one basic structure against another. As a matter of first principle, once the right structure is worked out, the tax rates should be set so as to provide funds sufficient to discharge the public obligations.

proportionate increase for others. If tax neutrality could be perfectly achieved, the laws would act as a prism which magnified equally all preexisting endowments. The nature of private activities would not change, nor would the relative endowments of private persons.

The desirability of tax neutrality also follows from the more overtly economic view of the subject. In a well functioning economy, every actor should have to face the full opportunity costs of his private decisions. Where private rights in labor and property are well-defined, that normally will be the case. A system of taxation that imposes differential taxes necessarily subsidizes some activities and penalizes others, thereby distorting relative prices and, in consequence, private decisions on consumption and investment. Likewise, if taxation were allowed to make some persons better off and others worse off, struggles would arise between persons who would want to funnel wealth through the tax system and those who would want to keep it out of the system. These resource losses would reduce the likelihood that any tax imposed will be Pareto-superior, for some persons could and would emerge net losers when the tax system incorporated subsidies for a select few and correlative penalties for the rest of us.

Many modern (political) debates on tax reform appear to assume that the level of wealth is independent of the distribution of the tax burden. Too often the question of "fairness" in tax legislation is taken to mean that the distribution of tax burdens has no allocative effects. Nothing could be further from the truth. Taxes can create distortions that reduce wealth. The question is how to minimize these distortions. A sound tax, which funds only needed public goods, will always be subject to some evasive response by private parties. But these are minimized by a system that does not seek to reshape basic preferences and that tries to insure that every public expenditure is worth more to every party taxed than the revenues that are lost. Tax neutrality represents one constraint on government policy that is designed to keep government activity as close as possible to the Pareto ideal.

B. Costs of administration. Any tax system costs money to administer, costs which are incurred both by the state and by private parties. These costs are incurred in order to bring about a simple transfer of wealth between two sides. The smaller their sum, the greater the fraction of the social product that is left for use in either public or private hands. In general, simple rules are far easier to administer when mass transactions are at issue. A tax system that demands extensive information to implement is inferior to one that has greater ease of operation by depending upon reliable and measurable facts on the public record. If the costs of collection are high, it increases the likelihood that the taxation (and its associated expenditure) will not meet the requirements of a proper Pareto-superior forced exchange.

C. Rent-seeking. Taxation should be made as invulnerable to political pressures and manipulation as possible. The dangers of faction and abuse of power tend to unfairly skew the terms of forced exchanges. Again, there is nothing unique about taxation. The general theory of property rights makes it clear that the opportunity for political, rent-seeking behavior is greatest where property rights are ill-defined. Taxation can easily be fitted into the general model of property rights, for any tax creates a *lien* for the benefit of the state upon the assets of all its citizens. Talk of a "tax lien" is no loose or florid analogy. Taxes are "floating liens" (parallel to those obtained by many private lenders) that the state may quickly convert into a fixed lien against particular property when taxes are unpaid. That lien can then be foreclosed and the property sold to satisfy the underlying obligation.[12]

The characteristics of the floating lien influence the operation of the system. The greater the freedom state officials have in specifying the contours of the floating lien, the greater the resource losses the tax system will create. Again, the theory of property rights accounts for this result. Ill-defined rights confer discretion upon public officials. Discretion in turn means that there is greater uncertainty in the income stream of all individuals taxed, which typically implies a welfare loss since most persons are risk averse. Discretion also creates a common-pool problem not dissimilar to that which applies to fisheries or oil and gas. It is one thing for A, B, C, and D each to owe $25; it is quite another thing for A, B, C, and D to owe jointly $100. In the first situation (that of separate debts in equal amounts) the obligations are well-defined, and the persons involved cannot shift by political action the burden of their obligations to others. In the second situation these obligations are ill-defined, and each person is tempted to spend real resources (up to $25) to deflect some or all of the common debt to others. Those strategic expenditures in the aggregate produce dead weight social losses, which threaten the integrity of the taxation bargain: when taxation shrinks the social pie it cannot be a Pareto-superior forced exchange, no matter what the final distribution of rights.

IV. IMPLEMENTING THE BARGAIN

It now remains to consider the extent to which both substantive and institutional rules can implement these primary features of the taxation bargain. I believe that they can. In some cases, the theory points to very clear results, while in others the question of trade-offs (chiefly between adminis-

[12] Hence the demand for the pro rata distribution of the surplus. See Coleman, *The Economic Analysis of Law*.

trative costs and incentive effects) is far more vexatious. What follows is an effort to apply the basic theory to some of the central features of a sound system of taxation.

A. Cash or kind? The first proposition is that taxes should normally be collected in cash, not kind. With virtuous governments and virtuous individuals, the choice in the form of taxation might seem unimportant. The right assets will move from private to public hands but only in ways that surmount the standard public goods problems. But as ever, the choice of institutional form depends critically upon the ability to resist the full panoply abuses, both public and private, that arise when information is imperfect, the costs of monitoring are positive, conflicts of interest are rampant, and the temptation to siphon off public resources for private benefit is pervasive.

In this imperfect world, the monetary tax has major operational advantages. From the side of the individual taxpayer, the imposition of a strict monetary obligation allows him to decide which resources to sell or mortgage in order to pay the tax. In general we can expect that the individual will preserve from the taxing authorities those assets to which he attaches the highest subjective valuation, that is, those in which his value in use is greater than the market value.[13] As all persons are in the same position with respect to the tax obligation, each person is able to appropriate the entire surplus value to himself, which in turn reduces the likelihood that the wrong resources will be taken for public use. The upshot is that it is more likely that the operation of the system will be Pareto-superior, with a pro rata division of the surplus, than will a system that allows the government to select the assets to be taken from each individual.

The constraint that taxes be paid in money also imposes an important limitation upon the discretion of government officials. If the government were allowed to impose taxes in kind (say 25 percent of the goods owned by the taxpayer), individual taxpayers would have powerful incentives to influence the choice of assets taken by the government. Government officials might (improperly?) threaten to take assets with high subjective values in order to increase the opportunities for obtaining bribes.[14] Thus, if one's home is worth $25,000 in the open market, but $35,000 subjectively to the taxpayer, the ability to take the home instead of cash creates the opportunity for bribes between one dollar and $9,999. Side payments in that amount

[13] On the importance of subjective value generally, see Timothy Muris, *Cost of Completion or Diminution in Market Value: The Relevance of Subjective Value*, 12 J. Legal Stud. 379 (1984).

The question of subjective value plays an important role in the law of eminent domain, on which I have written generally; Richard A. Epstein, Takings: Private Property and the Power of Eminent Domain (1985).

[14] On this process generally, see Benson & Baden, *The Political Economy of Governmental Corruption: The Logic of Underground Government*, 14 J. Legal Stud. 391 (1985).

would leave both the official and the private party better off, but would result in large systemic social losses. These opportunities for game playing are not restricted to the immediate relationship of taxpayer and public official, for it is possible to envision deals in which bribes are paid to induce tax collectors to levy against the key assets of a business rival or a political opponent.

The possibilities for abuse do not stop when the specific assets are taken into government hands. The management and sale of unwanted assets must proceed on a gigantic scale, and offer ample opportunities for negligence, corruption, favoritism, and abuse. Even if these forces could be banished from public life, the administrative costs of the system would still be very high. A simple rule that all taxes be paid in cash provides a powerful and workable constraint upon both public and private misbehavior.

It is easy to overlook the importance of these institutional arrangements in dealing with matters of taxation. Robert Nozick has argued, for example, that "Taxation of earnings from labor is on a par with forced labor."[15] His conclusion is true if the only relevant political inquiry is whether or not taxation involves the use of coercion. A pure libertarian could therefore condemn taxation and forced labor with equal vigor.[16] Yet once *any* forced exchanges are admitted into the system, then Nozick has only answered the first question: Is there a taking of private property? He does not begin to answer the question of whether some greater benefit is provided in return. On that question the differences between taxation and forced labor, which are widely understood intuitively, become critical. The problems of private evasion and public abuse just mentioned make it clear that a system of ordinary taxation is more apt to generate Pareto-superior taxes than a system of forced labor. The differences here are as substantial as those between a system of conscription (a tax in kind on some individuals) on the one hand and a volunteer military force paid for by general tax revenues. Nozick's categorical condemnation of all coercion provides no framework for ranking alternative systems of taxation or, indeed, any government action, in any responsible way.

There are, of course, some limits to the principle that the government's sole source of resources should be monetary taxation. While taking labor is generally unwise, taking property may not be. Simple taxation may not work, for example, when holdout problems threaten to block the acquisition of specific land for a public highway. Occasionally, the eminent domain power to take property must be invoked. But as with taxation, the object of the law is to implement Pareto-superior forced exchanges with a pro rata division of

[15] Robert Nozick, Anarchy, State and Utopia 169 (1974).

[16] Nozick has some sense of the point for he notes that he equivocates by the use of the phrase "on a par with," which may mean simply "is" or is "a kind of"; *id.* at 169, note*. Yet he never explores any of the functional reasons that make for the differences.

the surplus. In principle, the eminent domain power should strive to work toward a distribution of benefits and losses identical to that achieved by a well-functioning tax. The compensation requirement operates to insure a return of benefits to the individual equal to the value of the property surrendered, which are then augmented by his pro rata share in the social surplus (if any) generated by the government activity. Eminent domain is far more expensive to operate than ordinary taxation. The in-kind nature of the appropriation calls forth an elaborate network of protections for private parties, not the least of which is the right to a judicial determination of the value of the property taken. Yet here, litigation is so expensive and valuation so controversial that much abuse remains.[17] A well run society subordinates the use of eminent domain to the use of taxation.

B. The Comprehensive Tax Base. The Lockean theory offers guidance on the appropriate base for taxation. The ends of government are to protect a person in all his "life, liberty and estates," so that presumptively everything of value protected by government is subject to taxation. That intuition is captured in the two standard definitions of income, those of Haig and of Simons, which today generally guide theoretical discussions of taxation. Haig's definition of personal income was "the money value of the net accretion to one's economic power between two points in time."[18] Simons' definition made more explicit the place of consumption in the general picture: "Personal income may be defined as the algebraic sum of (1) market value of rights exercised in consumption and (2) the change in value of the store of property rights between the beginning and end of the period in question."[19] Both these comprehensive definitions are required by the Lockean theory, for both advance tax neutrality by preventing distortions in the prior patterns of individual preferences.[20] To be sure, the definition does not answer every question about the proper base for taxation. There is, for example, a debate over whether casualty losses for nonbusiness property

[17] One obvious point is that the government normally need not compensate the owner anything for the legal and business costs incurred when condemnation takes place. See, e.g., Bodcaw v. United States, 440 U.S. 202 (1979). For the complications in setting the right rule, see Ayer, *Allocating the Costs of Determining "Just Compensation,"* 21 Stan. L. Rev. 693 (1969), and Epstein, Takings: Private Property and the Power of Eminent Domain, Ch. 4 (1985).

[18] Haig, The Federal Income Tax 7 (R. Haig ed. 1921).

[19] H. Simons, Personal Income Taxation 50 (1938). Professor Bittker has observed that Simons regarded Haig's definition "as interchangeable with his own." See B. Bittker, *A "Comprehensive Tax Base" As a Goal of Income Tax Reform*, 80 Harv. L. Rev. 925–932 (1967). It is not clear why Simons chose to measure consumption by market value instead of subjective value. For a discussion of the difficulties with subjective variations, see *infra* at section (c).

[20] Simons was no stranger to political theory; see his *Some Reflections on Syndicalism*, 52 J. Pol. Econ. 1 (1944), reprinted in H. Simons, Economic Policy for a Free Society (A. Director ed. 1947).

should provide a deduction to their owner.[21] While it might be thought that the casualty deduction for personal property compromises the rate base, the opposite conclusion seems correct.[22] The destruction of property is a net decrease in wealth, which cannot be regarded as consumption. Hence, by the Haig–Simons definition it reduces income and thus functions as a deduction against income from other sources. Similar but more difficult questions arise with, for example, medical deductions and charitable contributions.[23] But these definitional problems can be given plausible answers, and in any event cannot be allowed to obscure the important agreement over many different kinds of income – wages, interest, royalties, rents, dividends, capital appreciation – now reached by the tax system,[24] and which under any view compromise the huge bulk of any tax revenues.

Finding the appropriate definition of income can be regarded either as an end in itself or as the start of a more complex inquiry into tax policy. In theory, it should clearly be the latter. Once the comprehensive definition of gross income is established, the issue is whether there is any deviation from the original tax base that satisfies dual constraints of Pareto superiority and pro rata division of the gain. A moment's reflection should indicate that further refinement is not only possible, but strictly necessary.[25]

The most vivid illustration is imputed income, that is, income which comes from the productive use of one's talent or property without the interposition of any market transaction, such as a sale or a salary. The consumption of home grown food and the value of services about the home are two common illustrations. In principle, all imputed income falls within the taxation base, as the principle of tax neutrality opposes any differential tax cost on market income that will bias individuals toward nonmarket uses

[21] Internal Revenue Code (I.R.C.), § 165(c)(3).

[22] Epstein, *The Consumption and Loss of Personal Property under the Internal Revenue Code*, 23 Stan. L. Rev. 454 (1971).

[23] See William D. Andrews, *Personal Deductions in an Ideal Income Tax*, 86 Harv. L. Rev. 309 (1972).

[24] See I.R.C. § 61(a), which contains a general reference to gross income and a long list of included items. Cases of the fringes include such matters as the treatment of punitive damages, on which see Glenshaw Glass Co. v. Commissioner, 348 U.S. 426 (1955), covering exemplary damages in fraud cases and the punitive portion of recovery in an antitrust action. The doubts about recovery stemmed from the definition of income used previously by the court in Eisner v. Macomber, 252 U.S. 189 (1920): "'Income may be defined as the gain derived from capital, from labor, or from both combined,' provided it be understood to include profit gained through a sale or conversion of capital assets." Note, this definition excludes the gain received in *Glenshaw Glass* which is, however, taxable under the Haig–Simons definition.

[25] Once the point is grasped, it becomes clear that any attack on the Haig–Simons approach that is content to point out deviations from the system is not sufficient to condemn its usefulness. For an illustration of the error, see Bittker, *A "Comprehensive Tax Base" As A Goal Of Income Tax Reform*, 80 Harv. L. Rev. 925 (1967), effectively criticized in Musgrave, *In Defense of an Income Concept*, 81 Harv. L. Rev. 44 (1967), which, while it does not adopt the explicit framework here, takes much the same approach.

of their own labor. But tax neutrality has to yield something to administrative necessity, for it is simply impossible to value every pleasure or benefit that people routinely enjoy. The intangibles are overwhelming. Do persons with happy home lives get taxed at a higher level than persons who come from broken homes? Should government officials stand over the shoulders of all citizens in order to tax the value of home repairs? The opera fanatic who buys a box seat for $50 may in fact be willing to pay $75, but should $25 in consumer surplus be subject to taxes? Should the worker who loves his job be taxed more heavily than his companion who does not? Should the person who enjoys watching the sunrise or quiet contemplation be taxed for that as well?

It takes little theoretical insight to realize that the problems of monitoring and evaluation doom from the start the enterprise of taxing all imputed income. The conclusion follows a fortiori given that sound rules of taxation are designed to curb both individual and government abuse. Excluding imputed income is a flat violation of tax neutrality in that it biases the tradeoff between market and nonmarket transactions, and between work and leisure. The critical question is whether that violation can be justified. The relevant inquiries are two: first, will the total size of the pie be greater and, second, will the relative *individual* tax burdens remain unaltered?

The answer to the first question seems to be "yes." The administrative savings from excluding imputed income from the tax base are enormous. The need to value nonmarket goods is eliminated, while the discretion vested in the taxing authorities and the size of the government apparatus are both reduced. Revenue neutrality can be preserved, even if tax neutrality is not, by raising the rates on taxable income somewhat to offset the shortfall that might otherwise arise.

The answer to the second question is also "yes." At first blush, the exclusion of imputed income looks mischievous if one assumes, as does Nozick in *Anarchy, State and Utopia*, that one person enjoys going to the movies and the other watching the sunset, so that the first pays taxes on the income earned to pay for the movie ticket, while the other pays no taxes to watch the sunset. Yet the possibility of having the person with the greater total income paying the smaller taxes becomes far less likely given, as seems the case, that everyone has a large market basket of imputed income transactions that are kept out of the tax system. It matters little that the contents of each basket will differ so long as their total value is about the same. Every person has large amounts of imputed income, some from a good job and some from a good homelife. There is no group of individuals that has a monopoly on imputed income, as most people consume *both* some movies and some unpurchased leisure.

Excluding imputed income does not appear, therefore, to create any systematic bias across groups of individuals in the society at large, and is not obviously correlated with race, sex, age, religion, occupation, or even income levels. The rank ordering of individual utility tends to be preserved after the tax base is redefined. Those persons who would pay more in taxes with the comprehensive base continue to pay more even after imputed income is excluded. This diffusion of benefits and burdens also has important political ramifications, for it is hard to see the interest group that would make the inclusion or exclusion of imputed income the target of rent-seeking or factional politics. It is too hard for the players to identify those persons who would win and lose from the shift.

The recognition that imputed income falls outside the tax system thus appears to produce overall gains evenly shared by the population at large, at least with the approximate guesswork that must be made on matters of this scale. The loss of tax neutrality is a serious matter, but the best solution is simply not obtainable. The revenue needs of the state can be met by a higher tax on the smaller base, with no obvious redistributive consequences. To be sure, some items of imputed wealth are of sufficient magnitude that they might be brought back into the rate base – the rental values of private homes is an obvious candidate for the wrinkle upon the wrinkle. Yet suppose the trade-off between administrative costs and tax neutrality here is incorrectly drawn under the current system. Still the question seems close, so that the costs of error are relatively low. A society can easily flourish with such unresolved ambiguities.

C. When to tax: the realization and recognition of income. The second set of qualifications of the rate base have to do with the nature of the receipts and expenditures that trigger collection of the tax. As Simons himself repeatedly stressed, the proper definition of income does not depend upon any prior "receipt" or realization of gain. To illustrate his proposition, if I own 100 shares of IBM stock purchased at $100, but which are now worth $125, then $2,500 in gain is income whether I choose to hold or to sell the stock. Ignoring the transaction cost, holding the stock is no different from a sale and a repurchase of the same securities. The comprehensive definition of income thus includes $2,500 in gain (and would recognize a like amount in losses) whether or not the stock has been sold, and thus minimizes the ability of the strategic maneuvers of private parties to undermine the system.

Yet here, too, the concern with tax neutrality has generally not been strong enough to carry the day in all cases. Every modern tax system works off the concept of receipt of property that is immaterial under the Haig–Simons definition of income. Receipt of wages or the realization of gain, as from the sale of stock, has been generally regarded as a condition for the recognition of gain and for the levying of a tax. The effect in all instances is to delay the *time* for paying the tax until after the increment to wealth or consumption is obtained.

The justifications for the delay are practical in origin but theoretical in their significance. Taxation of unrealized appreciation, for example, can pose real questions of valuation given the absence of market transactions. These are themselves quite insuperable when dealing with real estate or with shares of a closed corporation, when there is no ready market. They are of some modest concern with the shares of public corporations. In both cases, there is also a nagging question of how some taxpayers will raise the cash to pay the tax, for it is quite possible to be cash poor and capital rich. Imposing the tax before realization of the gain can force a taxpayer to go to the market, to mortgage the shares or to sell them at an inopportune time. These transactions can be costly and inconvenient and could disrupt business objectives.

All this is not to say that there are no disadvantages in delaying taxation until the sale of shares or the receipt of cash. Where certain assets appreciate substantially, the clever taxpayer may be able to obtain cash today, without payment of the tax, by the use of a nonrecourse loan, secured by the shares of stock.[26] The system of delayed taxation also tends to discriminate against earned income and in favor of investment income. And it leads to genuine complications of income in periods of inflation or deflation as well. Nonetheless, the administrative burdens of the Haig–Simons definition are too great in a system that must collect taxes from millions of individuals. The deferment of taxation to a later period probably works a smaller shift in wealth between persons than it does between different kinds of income, and it spares everyone the enormous administrative costs that would otherwise be incurred. On balance, deferment looks wealth-enhancing and, hence, Pareto-superior, especially in light of the next feasible alternative. One might want to dispute that point,[27] especially as regards shares of publicly held corporations; but the debate here would not be on the soundness of the

[26] See Woodsam's Associate v. Commissioner, 198 F. 2d 357 (2d Cir. 1952). See, generally, Marvin Chirelstein, Federal Income Taxation §13.02 (1985).

[27] See, e.g., Slawson, *Taxing Ordinary Income the Appreciation of Publicly Held Stock*, 76 Yale L.J. 623 (1967). The opposite side of the coin is the immediate recognition of unrealized losses. Yet the parallel is not precise because even with the realization requirement a taxpayer could always choose to sell in order to recognize the loss. Note too that this strategic power has in more recent times been used by investors in various kinds of options. The basic principle is to invest in a portfolio of options to buy and sell at different prices and dates. As the portfolio is negatively correlated, some items will go up and others down. The losses can then be realized, while the gains are postponed. A forced accounting without realization at the end of the tax year defeats the strategic maneuvers of taxpayers. The problem does not exist in the same degree for stocks because their prices tend to be positively correlated and they have lower volatility.

general criteria, but on their application to a particular case – a second order problem.

The question of realization is at bottom a question of timing: *when* should certain forms of wealth be taxed. Often it is not sufficient to defer taxation until the receipt of wealth. Stated in standard tax language, the realization of gain or loss need not necessarily be the occasion for the "recognition" of the gain. Taxation can be deferred until some later point in the wealth production cycle, usually when the property received is reduced to cash or its equivalent. For example, a shareholder contributes property to his wholly owned corporation in exchange for an issue of its shares; the form of wealth has changed, and gain has been realized from the sale of the thing. But in general, the recognition of the gain for tax purposes will await the sale of the shares for cash by the shareholder, or the sale of the thing by the corporation.[28] Or two pieces of real estate are exchanged and both parties realize a profit, in that the property received is worth more to each party than the cost of the property surrendered. But, again, the deferred recognition of the gain seems appropriate.[29] The practical problems of taxation are evident, and there is a risk that the tax cost might well prevent what would otherwise be a beneficial economic exchange. The gains can still be taxed, either in the form of rental income or upon a subsequent cash sale.

The treatment of unrealized losses raises the same issues in reverse. Normally depreciation of property used in a trade or business precedes its sale; the refusal to make any allowance for depreciation before recognition could result in the bunching of losses in the year property is sold or abandoned. Yet taking these losses into account long after they are sustained produces serious economic distortions. In principle, the proper response is to value real estate at the beginning and end of the tax period, so that losses in depreciation can be combined with appreciation (or depreciation) in property value attributable to market forces to reach a net figure of taxable income or loss. This valuation process is cumbersome and unreliable. One could ignore depreciation over time, as one ignores appreciation (or depreciation) for changes in market value of stocks. But there is a difference: market forces can move value in either direction, while age and obsolescence exert a systematic downward pressure.

It seems, therefore, defensible (and probably correct) to use some simple taxation formula to capture that systematic downward shift in value in order to reduce the anticipated gap between economic and tax definitions of income, all at a tolerable administrative cost. Today, the tax system itself offers a bewildering array of options for depreciation not required by the

[28] See I.R.C. § 351.
[29] See I.R.C. § 1031.

basic theory.[30] The needless discretion they vest in taxpayers should be eliminated because of the strategic game playing (and consequent social losses) it invites. But some simple formula for depreciation over broad categories of property is surely appropriate,[31] even if the present menu of options is not.

The same logic applies to income received today for services to be performed tomorrow. Consider the receipt of the right to future payment from long-term service contracts. The associate who is made a partner at a law firm, the professor who receives tenure at his university, the federal judge appointed for life might be said to have received fair market value of the future income stream that attaches to his employment. Certainly there are chances that he will quit, be fired for cause, or die, but nonetheless the receipt of the contract right from the employer is not a matter of indifference to the taxpayer. There is a clear receipt of a thing of value (the contract right), and the net change in wealth is substantial, even if there can be genuine quarrels on the matter of valuation. But should the income stream, however valued or discounted, be taxed in the year the right is acquired? Here the problems of getting the money to pay taxes on a future and uncertain income stream are acute, for what bank will lend on the strength of the bare contract right that the government is so eager to tax. Nor is it possible at the moment that job rights vest to make an accurate assessment of the future income projection. Partnerships have good and bad years; universities have pay freezes; judges' salaries are tied up in politics. The receipt of the long-term contract right is a poor time to impose the tax. The reduction of the right to the cash is the appropriate instance, as the law now generally provides. Taxation of in-kind benefits (like the collection of taxes in-kind) is perilous and unnecessary business. A little waiting reduces uncertainty and administrative costs. The shift seems to meet the dual requirements of Pareto superiority and pro rata distribution of the gain.

D. Income or consumption taxes. The permutations for the recognition and deferment of gain can be extended one step further, since many people argue that the receipt of income should not be an occasion for taxation; instead, taxation should be further postponed until the moment of consumption. The shift to a consumption tax may appear revolutionary, but a few key structural changes in the tax laws could bring much of it about in a modest way. One change would be to forgive the gain on securities when the

[30] See I.R.C. §§ 167, 168.

[31] In a world without inflation, the proper formula for depreciation would reduce the value of a long term asset (which has uniform value in use) by the present discounted value of the last remaining year's use, not by straight line depreciation, which simply treats the value of each year's use equally. Again, the error, while large in principle, may not shift wealth between individuals, even if it could (by overencouraging investment) result in some allocative losses. See Marvin Chirelstein, Federal Income Taxation ¶6.07 (4th ed. 1985).

proceeds of sale are reinvested in other forms of investment property. Another would be to allow a deduction for savings. These changes would ignore the proper tax treatment of consumer durables,[32] and thus are not complete. Once the choice between the income and consumption tax is seen as one of the timing of gain, there is no obvious need to choose one pure type over another. An intermediate position may prove to be socially preferable. The question of whether the consumption tax is superior to the income tax is vexed indeed,[33] but here, as before, the structure of the inquiry is the same as in all other instances: is the change Pareto-superior with an anticipated pro rata division in the surplus? The proration requirement seems easily satisfied, so that the answer must rest on a detailed examination of the administrative and incentive effects of the two systems and the intermediate position, a task which is largely beyond the scope of this paper.

E. Pathological cases: tax subsidies. Many other deviations from the Haig–Simons definition are not consistent with the dual constraints of the general theory. The Lockean theory places a flat prohibition upon implicit transfers from the state that leave one group better off and another worse off. That prohibition reaches tax subsidies like all other transfers. Any argument that taxation is an efficient mode of implementing subsidies therefore misses the mark, because it presupposes that subsidies themselves are legitimate, a clear violation of the basic political norm.

Within this framework, a large number of special provisions of the Internal Revenue Code are simply improper. The rapid depreciation write-offs for low income housing represent one obvious subsidy that is indefensible on these grounds. The grant of percentage depletion allowances on natural resources in excess of original cost is also indefensible. The decision to keep municipal bond income outside the tax base is similarly suspect. The willingness to allow shareholders who make charitable gifts to deduct the full value of appreciated property without paying any tax on the interim gain is likewise inappropriate.[34] The free stepped-up basis at

[32] See Graetz, *Implementing a Progressive Consumption Tax*, 92 Harv. L. Rev. 1575, 1613–23 (1979). Note, there would be a real disincentive to purchase a home if the full purchase price was regarded as consumption in the year of acquisition. It is possible to defer the collection of the tax over a number of years to reflect the deferred receipt of the benefit. This delayed consumption tax on durables is best understood as the mirror image of the deferred deduction for depreciation now allowed under the income tax.

[33] See, e.g., Andrews, *A Consumption-Type or Cash Flow Personal Income Tax*, 87 Harv. L. Rev. 1113 (1974); Graetz, *Implementing a Progressive Consumption Tax*, 92 Harv. L. Rev. 1575 (1979); Kelman, *Time Preference and Tax Equity*, 35 Stan. L. Rev. 649 (1983). Note, throughout I have ignored the flat value-added tax, even though it is surely a plausible substitute for either income or consumption taxes.

[34] See I.R.C. § 170(e). In its simplest form, the taxpayer contributes shares that cost $100 but which are now worth $1000 to charity. The right calculation imputes the gain of $900 and then allows the deduction of the full $1000. The deduction appears to be $100, but is in reality more if the imputed gain is taxed at capital gains rates and the deduction is permitted against ordinary income.

the time of death is also a source of reproach.[35] Many of these gains are available only to a tiny segment of the population; many violate the principle of tax neutrality while creating additional administrative costs. The existence of a number of close cases should not blind us to the power of the theory in disposing of many easy cases, with enormous importance to the system as a whole.

F. Rate structures. The general theory has important implications for the rates of taxation. In traditional tax parlance, these rates can assume one of three forms. They can be regressive, progressive, or proportionate. All three systems share the basic belief that the amount of taxes owed should increase with the level of income earned. (I ignore here capitation taxes that call for all persons to pay a fixed amount of taxes, regardless of income.) All three systems assume that the rate base can be defined to exclude items of imputed income, and to respond to the demands for the deferred recognition of taxable income. They differ in the way they relate the increase of taxes to the increase in income. Regressive taxes increase more slowly than taxable income; proportionate taxes increase at the same rate; and progressive taxes, today the dominant form, increase more rapidly. From the Lockean perspective, a strong case can be made that the proportionate or flat tax is the only acceptable version, as Locke hints in his own brief account of taxation.

The first point in the argument is to note that within the Lockean world, the redistribution of income through the tax system is an unacceptable function of government, for no exchange can be Pareto-superior if it leaves some persons worse off.[36] Likewise, the requirement of the pro rata division

[35] See I.R.C. § 1014. To explain: if property was bought at $100 and is now worth $1000, the $900 in gain escapes taxation at death, creating the obvious incentive to postpone realization. One solution might be to allow the basis to carry over through death, so that the gain can be obtained on sale. That proves in essence to be quite unworkable if the property is held in trust, because there is no sane formula for the allocation of basis among the beneficial interests. The immediate income tax at death, coupled with the abolition of the estate tax, is the best solution.

[36] Here the learned can debate Locke's own position on the matter. The Second Treatise, his most influential work, contains no hint of any obligation to redistribute wealth that is enforceable by the state. In his criticism of Filmer, he has written passages that indicate the power of charitable obligations to the needy. Yet it is quite clear that even here he regards charity as a different domain from justice, and does not take into account the possibility that imperfect obligations of conscience are different both from legal obligations and pure consumption choices. The relevant passage is Chapter 4, ¶42, which reads as follows:

> 42. But we know God hath not left one man so to the mercy of another that he may starve him if he please. God, the Lord and Father of all, has given no one of His children such a property in his peculiar portion of the things of this world but that he has given his needy brother a right in the surplusage of his goods, so that it cannot justly be denied him when his pressing wants call for it; and, therefore, no man could ever have a just power over the life of another by right of property in land or possessions, since it would always be a sin in any man of estate to let his brother perish for want of affording him relief out of his plenty; for as justice gives every man a title to the product of his honest industry and the fair acquisitions of his ancestors descended to him, so 'charity' gives

of the gain entails that the just tax should not alter the rank ordering by wealth of individuals within the society. All of this is said with the understanding that *if* redistribution were an appropriate social goal, then taxation would be superior to ad hoc forms of direct regulation in bringing it about.[37]

If the questions of income redistribution are put aside, the concerns identified above are surely dominant. The progressive tax scores badly on the ground of tax incentives. One obvious point is that the higher marginal rates encourage individuals to conceal their revenue from the government, thereby increasing the portion of the tax burden that falls on others. Yet even if tax compliance were perfect, distortions would remain, for able high-income individuals will reduce the level of services they offer for sale because of the relatively low after tax return.

The progressive tax also scores very poorly on administration. The question is not one of computation. Instead, it involves the elaborate network of collateral rules that must be developed in order to protect the integrity of the progressive rate structure. Income splitting is of no consequence with the flat tax, for the total amount payable to the government is by definition independent of the number of persons to whom it is paid. But it becomes critical whenever any degree of progressivity is introduced into the system: then, to spread the wealth is to minimize the tax burden. Consider the rules that scrutinize the payment of salary to children, that regulate the taxation of income from family partnerships and multiple trusts and corporations, and that regulate the sale of appreciated property by donees. These, and many more, are all necessary government efforts to counter efforts by taxpayers to avoid taxes. Both private efforts to deflect the progressive tax and government efforts to maintain it are dead weight social losses that can be largely eliminated by the flat tax.

> every man a title to so much of another's plenty as will keep him from extreme want, where he has no means to subsist otherwise. And a man can no more justly make use of another's necessity to force him to become his vassal, by withholding that relief God requires him to afford to the wants of his brother, than he that has more strength can seize upon a weaker, master him to his obedience, and, with a dagger at his throat, offer him death or slavery.

It is far from clear how extensive a system of support for the poor this passage calls for. The duty to supply welfare is limited to cases of "extreme want" and not mere poverty. Locke, moreover, nowhere addresses the question of whether the money received has to be repaid should that become possible, and he does not ask whether "justice" and "charity" require the same modes of enforcement. It is quite possible that claims of justice are enforced through the legal system, and those of charity by a network of imperfect social obligations. I have ignored redistribution questions entirely here, but developed the case against redistributivist government policies in Epstein, *The Uncertain Quest for Welfare Rights* [1985] B.Y.U.L. Rev. 201 (1985).

[37] See A. Mitchell Polinsky, An Introduction to Law and Economics, 9–10, 105–113 (1983). The one great unanswered question is whether it is possible to have any effective scheme of income redistribution with a flat tax.

The progressive rate structure also introduces other complications. The constant, unhappy debate over joint returns for married couples arises because the progressive tax collides with the definition of the unit of taxation, be it individual, household, or family. With a flat tax, there is only one table, no matter what the taxable unit. There need be no question of a "marriage tax" when the income of husband and wife are treated as earned by a single person. Income averaging raises similar problems. The bulges in one year are not a reflection of permanent income. The taxpayer who earns $100,000 in each of two years is treated differently from one who earns $200,000 in one year and $0.00 in the other. A flat tax removes the need for further sets of costly provisions. At every point, the progressive structure of the taxes invites thrust and counterthrust. The effort to shift tax burdens is another illustration of the negative-sum games that a flat tax would largely forestall.

Last, there is the problem of rent-seeking through the tax system. Today, the requirement that all individuals in the same tax bracket pay the same tax provides an important brake against factional intrigue. It would be quite intolerable for the government to set individual tax rates for individual taxpayers: general tax brackets check that manifest form of abuse. But progressive taxation still leaves open a degree of freedom that can be exploited by political action. The flat tax gives the government only one degree of freedom: what is the level of the revenues and, hence, of taxation? That discretion it needs. The progressive tax leaves it a second degree of freedom: what is the level of the tilt for which there is no unique answer. It offers the government a discretion that has no social benefit, but the usual social costs. As persons know their anticipated income with some degree of reliability, they can seek to impose the costs of government upon others while keeping the benefits for themselves. Forestalling those struggles (while giving a tolerable match between the benefits and costs of government services) is one virtue of the flat tax. A rule that says you must pay a dollar for the dollar that you wish to exact from your neighbor is not a perfect safeguard against political intrigue, but it acts as an effective constraint. The flat tax has the necessary effect of reducing the total level of expenditures that are funneled through the government and, in consequence, reduces the tax gap between imputed and taxable income. It is an indispensable part of the Lockean program of taxation.

V. THE CONSTITUTIONAL DIMENSION

The last part of the inquiry is what set of institutions are needed in order to stabilize the power of the government to tax. Initially the question is, do we need any kind of constitutional constraint at all? The answer to that question depends (at least in part) on the dominant political mores of the time. A system (like England of the nineteenth century) may witness the simultaneous growth of two doctrines: the absolute sovereign power of Parliament and a strong social commitment to the principles of laissez-faire. But the question is whether that will endure or, as has been the case in England, whether the opportunities for gain through political markets will in the end undermine the position of voluntary markets. Here there is reason for pessimism: a political victory for voluntary markets does not preclude a future attack, as the opportunity for gains is still present. Yet a victory for government markets sets up entrenched groups whom it is very hard to root out after the fact. As rent-seeking and faction are the major sources of abuse, there is no obvious presumption that the form and objects of taxation should be left to legislative whim, and some strong reason to believe that in the long run the power to tax will be used to increase the size of government.

As a practical matter, however, it is not enough to identify a major source of abuse. The question is whether it is possible to construct at reasonable costs institutional arrangements that will control it. In this instance, constitutional restraints on the power to tax are the only available tool known to political theory. Whether these are obtainable politically or by judicial action is beyond the scope of this paper. What I do address briefly is the question of whether it is possible or desirable to frame constitutional limitations that address each of the six points raised in the proceeding section. The task is one that is undertaken only briefly, and with great trepidation. It seems clear that our own original constitutional structure did purport to impose explicit limitations upon the power to tax,[38] and contains other general provisions (such as the due process clauses and the eminent domain clause) that could be applied to the legislative power to tax.[39] Yet as noted earlier, where suspect classes and fundamental rights (as defined by the current jurisprudence) are not at issue, these limitations have all eroded with time; so today, over vast spheres of economic activity, the power to tax is plenary.[40]

But what kind of strategy could do better? Here it seems best to trace the possible constitutional responses to each of the six issues raised to see what could be done.

[38] See, e.g., Art. I, § 8, cl. 1: "The Congress shall have Power to lay and collect Taxes, Duties, Imposts and Excises, to pay the Debts and provide for the common Defense and general Welfare of the United States; but all Duties, Imposts and Excises shall be Uniform throughout the United States." The provision appears to limit the proper objects of taxation to the provision of various types of public goods, and was tied to the enumerated powers elsewhere in Art. I. Transfer payments, which consume an ever larger fraction of the government, were not part of the business of the federal government under the original scheme.

[39] I have discussed these issues at length in Richard A. Epstein, Takings: Private Property and the Power of Eminent Domain, Ch. 18 (1985).

[40] See, e.g., A. Magnano Co. v. Hamilton, 292 U.S. 40 (1934); Alaska Fish Salting & By-Products Co. v. Smith, 255 U.S. 44 (1921).

A. Cash or kind. In a fundamental sense, this limitation is already contained in the present constitution which, with its implicit distinction between the taxing and the eminent domain power, recognizes that far greater institutional safeguards are required when specific assets are taken from private individuals. One can quarrel with the present law for its inability to subject the full range of takings (e.g. through regulation) to the appropriate level of scrutiny, but those criticisms do not reach the fundamental decision to raise government resources by taxation.

B. The Comprehensive Tax Base. It seems very hard to define by constitutional means the appropriate base for taxation. In general, the federal statutes have taken the very broad base that the Lockean theory requires. Yet that theory is only the first approximation, given the administrative problems, for example, with imputed income. To draft a provision that speaks both to the original base and the permissible transformations of it seems a very hard task indeed. As the level of abuse from this quarter at least seems quite small, the current position is probably an acceptable one. Certainly the constitutionalization of the tax base would, even if on balance desirable, rate very low on the ladder of pressing constitutional reforms.

C. The realization and recognition of gain. There is no plausible reason to enshrine the timing of income in either direction. Thus, there are occasions in which recognition of gain and loss should proceed its realization, and others in which it should follow it. The key limitation is equal treatment across taxpayers, which is by and large observed in the major provisions concerned with the recognition of income and the allowance of deductions.

D. Income or consumption taxes. The choice between these two categories of taxes is simply a special case of the debate over realization and recognition. There is no reason for a constitutional provision to commit us to one form or the other.

E. Pathological cases. Here the case for some constitutional limitation seems more attractive, but nonetheless not clearly compelling. As noted above, there seems little reason for constitutional provisions that regulate the *timing* of income and deduction, above and apart from one that requires equal treatment across taxpayers. Yet there are many types of tax shelter which work not only to *defer* income from taxation, but to exclude it all together: percentage depletion beyond cost recovery, the exclusion of municipal bond income, and the tax free stepped-up basis at death. In principle, it should be possible to draft a provision that requires that each item of income be recognized at some point during the life of a transaction (i.e., from the time that all relevant players start and end with cash). Identifying a tax loophole is not all that difficult, at least in the easy cases.[41] But it is apt to be a fertile

[41] "While theorists may argue about what constitutes preferential treatment, sophisticated taxpayers have not experienced a similar difficulty." Blum, *The Effects of Special Provisions of the Income Tax on Taxpayer Morale*, 1955 Compendium 251.

source of litigation, and may not be an effective restraint upon the behavior of Congress, especially if there is some legislative power to exclude economic income from the tax base altogether. On balance, I think that the inquiry is at least worth pursuing further.

F. Rate structures. It is here that one sees the greatest opportunity for constitutional reform. At the general level, there is much to be said for a simple provision that says that "all income currently taxable shall be taxed at a uniform, flat rate," with no exclusions of any sort. Yet at the very least, it is problematic whether any system of welfare (or, indeed, any other) transfers could survive under this limitation, as the progressive tax is at least one important source of income redistribution. (How important it is depends at least in part on the way in which expenditures are skewed by government.) In any event, whatever the desirability of this provision as a general matter – and I believe it is great and consistent with the structure of the eminent domain clause – it would be a major revolution in taxation and political economy. Whatever doubts might exist about this provision, they do not carry over to the various special taxes (such as the windfall profits tax) which have begun to proliferate in recent years. Throughout the nineteenth century there was an active constitutional tradition that opposed special taxes for general revenues, and that position should be reaffirmed again today.[42] Special taxes offer greater opportunity for faction and present virtually no opportunity for Pareto-superior exchanges. Any income redistribution can be well done without them via the progressive tax. To enforce a constitutional prohibition against these taxes does not in my judgment require any new constitutional provisions, but only a renewed awareness of the importance of the uniformity and eminent domain provisions of the present constitution and the disproportionate impact tests that are explicit in the uniformity provisions and the "just compensation" requirement of the eminent domain clause.[43]

There is, I think, an important lesson that emerges from the foregoing analysis. In a world that operated without frictions of any sort, no individuals should be allowed to take property under the mantle of public authority. If transaction costs were zero, there would be no case for the state. Nozick would have made his case. But the existence of major frictions of all sorts calls for government. Within this environment, it becomes almost indefensible to argue that private property carries with it the absolute right under all circumstances to exclude others from its use. Yet as forced exchanges are allowed, someone must monitor their terms. As the direct measurements of

[42] See Diamond, *The Death and Transfiguration of Benefit Taxation: Special Assessments in Nineteenth-Century America*, 12 J. Legal Stud. 201 (1983).

[43] "The Fifth Amendment's guarantee that private property shall not be taken for a public use without just compensation was designed to bar Government from forcing some people alone to bear public burdens which, in all fairness and justice, should be borne by the public at large." Armstrong v. United States, 364 U.S. 40, 49 (1960).

benefits and costs are hard to make, a test of equal treatment across taxpayers becomes the next best alternative. In large measure, our current system of taxation, notwithstanding its impersonal and impenetrable character, provides much of the protection that is needed against government abuse. There are some changes, such as those which relate to flat and special taxes, that are important and obtainable. And there is a pressing need to get rid of the conscious subsidies built into the tax system. But most fine points of tax theory (on such matters as realization and recognition) are now construed in a way that is quite consistent with sensible Lockean principles. On these further constitutional control would be inadvisable.

CONCLUSION

In closing, it might be useful to summarize the article. Systems of taxation are needed to supply the public goods that are necessary to protect the lives, liberties, and estates of citizens from aggression by their fellow men. In principle, if one could measure perfectly the benefit that each person obtained from government, then the tax should be levied in proportion to the benefit so provided. Yet insuperable obstacles lay in the path of any system of direct measurement, not the least of which is the massive expansion of government that this scheme requires. To avoid these pitfalls, it is necessary to simplify the tax system to make it workable. Taxes are levied largely upon cash and cash equivalents, usually at the time of their receipt in monetizable form. Rates are kept flat and special exemptions and subsidies are rooted systematically from the tax system. The tax system is designed to minimize the inevitable distortions from the tax free world. These simple rules have some very durable properties, in that they guard against the abuses of faction and reduce the administrative power and discretion that is vested in the state. Controlling taxation is, of course, only one side of the problem. A comprehensive system of social control recognizes the need to impose parallel restrictions on the expenditure side of the budget and on the direct regulation of the economy. In one sense, it is easy to identify the most fundamental problem of all: too many resources today are channeled through government. Sensible constraints on the powers of taxation are not a conclusive remedy to all our ills. But they are a step in the right direction.

Law, University of Chicago

[2]

VOLUME 80 MARCH 1967 NUMBER 5

HARVARD LAW REVIEW

A "COMPREHENSIVE TAX BASE" AS A GOAL OF INCOME TAX REFORM

Boris I. Bittker *

Taking issue with those who contend that the income on which taxes are paid should be the same as what an economist would consider "net income," Professor Bittker urges that a neutral, scientific measure of taxable income is a mirage. In many of the vexed areas of income definition, the concept of economic income yields no help; in others, it implies results from which even its proponents would recoil. There is no touchstone for tax reform: proposals must be considered provision by provision and policy by policy, on their particular merits.

SINCE World War II, our ablest commentators on federal income taxation have repeatedly attacked the "exceptions," "preferences," "loopholes," and "leakages" in the income tax provisions of the Internal Revenue Code and have called upon Congress to reverse the "erosion of the income tax base" caused by these "special provisions." It is no exaggeration to say that a "comprehensive tax base" (hereafter CTB) has come to be the major organizing concept in most serious discussions of our federal income tax structure. This theme dominated the *Tax Revision Compendium* published in 1959 by the House Committee on Ways and Means and the hearings based on this collection of papers; it inspired the "optional simplified method" recently proposed by Senator Long; its exploration is a major task of the Special Committee on Substantive Tax Reform of the ABA's Tax Section; it was a major *Leitmotiv* in the responses of economists and others when the Joint Economic Committee in 1965 asked them to comment on the "fiscal policy issues of the coming decade"; and discussions of federal income taxation written for, or by, the nonexpert but interested citizen have brought it to the attention of a wider public.[1]

* Southmayd Professor of Law, Yale Law School. B.A., Cornell, 1938; LL.B., Yale, 1941.

I am very grateful for the comments and criticisms of Alan R. Bromberg, Marvin Chirelstein, and Joseph A. Pechman, who read a draft of this article.

[1] HOUSE COMMITTEE ON WAYS AND MEANS, 86TH CONG., 1ST SESS., TAX RE-

Some of this discontent with "preferences" and "leakages" has focused on the economic or social shortcomings of the particular provision under discussion; but increasingly a different line of argument has become popular. This approach accepts the rationale advanced in defense of the "preference," at least arguendo, but goes on to assert that equally persuasive arguments may be offered in support of virtually all other "preferences," including many that are still embryonic. Moreover, it is argued, a tax concession is a poor way to distribute a government bounty or to encourage activities that are in the public interest: the value of the concession varies with the beneficiary's tax status, the impact of the program may be erratic and unpredictable, its cost cannot be accurately estimated or budgeted in advance, and its operation is covert rather than open to public inspection and criticism.[2] The only road to a simplified and improved tax structure, it is contended, is to eliminate "preferences" ruthlessly, no matter how persuasive or seductive their individual appeals may be, and to impose the tax on the resulting CTB. The broader base will per-

VISION COMPENDIUM OF PAPERS ON BROADENING THE TAX BASE (Comm. Print 1959) [hereinafter cited as 1959 COMPENDIUM]; House Committee on Ways and Means, *Panel Discussions on Income Tax Revision*, 86th Cong., 1st Sess. (1960) [hereinafter cited as *1959 Panel Discussion*]; S. 3250, 88th Cong., 2d Sess. (1964) (Long proposal), *reprinted in* Bittker, *An Optional Simplified Income Tax?*, 21 TAX L. REV. 1, 37–51 (1965); *Report of the Section of Taxation on Substantive Tax Reform*, 90 ABA REP. 289 (1965); Galvin, *Progress in Substantive Tax Reform*, U. SO. CAL. 1965 TAX INST. 1; JOINT ECONOMIC COMMITTEE, 89TH CONG., 1ST SESS., FISCAL POLICY ISSUES OF THE COMING DECADE (Comm. Print 1965); D. BAZELON, THE PAPER ECONOMY 144–68 (1963); J. HELLERSTEIN, TAXES, LOOPHOLES, AND MORALS (1963); P. STERN, THE GREAT TREASURY RAID (1964).

[2] An offsetting advantage of tax concessions is that they leave taxpayers with greater freedom than some governmental programs; it was this, I take it, that led some advocates of a CTB in 1962 to favor the investment credit rather than a subsidy as a means of encouraging economic growth. Another premise that seems to be buried in the CTB approach is that "preferences" are not nullified by the market; a corollary is that the revenue gain to be achieved by eliminating preferences can be estimated without adjusting for changes in the pretax income to be received under the new tax structure.

It is odd that so many economists are advocating a "neutral" income tax base in the classroom at the same time that they are striving to persuade Congress that the income tax should be used as a flexible fiscal tool. This is not entirely a paradox; something can be said for the view that fiscal ends are best accomplished by changing the rate structure rather than the tax base. In the end, however, this effort to distinguish between legitimate and illegitimate fiscal uses of the tax system is likely to founder. Indeed, the 1962 depreciation guidelines and investment credit have been hailed as triumphs of a discretionary fiscal policy, though neither changed the rate structure. *See* Statement of Gardner Ackley, Chairman, Council of Economic Advisers, in *Hearings on Fiscal Policy Issues of the Coming Decade Before the Subcommittee on Fiscal Policy of the Joint Economic Committee*, 89th Cong., 1st Sess., at 3 (1965).

mit rates to be reduced, and with lower rates the benefit to be reaped by the restoration of any one "preference" will be lessened; this will let some of the steam out of efforts to renew the process of "eroding" the base. Alternatively, Congress could tax the augmented base at rates that will produce additional revenue, using the surplus to finance directly the programs that are now covertly financed by tax concessions. In either event, Congress will be willing and able (it is argued) to resist attempts to "erode" the new tax base since it will be armed with an argument — "one exception inevitably breeds another" — that now lacks persuasive force because today's Code is already riddled with "preferences" and "exceptions." [3] The aim, in short, is a reformed Internal Revenue Code with a "correct" tax base, to which all men of good will can and will rally when it is threatened by "exceptions," "special provisions," "preferences," "loopholes," and "leakages."

In trying to come to grips with the CTB approach to income taxation, I have encountered a distressing vagueness in the use of terms like "preference." Sometimes we are offered a goal no more precise than "an income-tax system which refuses special benefits to some taxpayers because their income comes from particular sources, and which taxes alike all dollars of income." [4] Of the more elaborate conceptual frameworks, the following are a fair sampling:

> "[S]pecial Tax Provisions" . . . means any and all provisions of tax law which are designed to afford significant preferential treatment within each of the normal basic taxpayer categories.
>
> . . . .
>
> Thus, this runs the whole gamut of taxpayer differentiation affected by type of entity, size of income, time and nature of receipts and

[3] *See* Blum, *Federal Income Tax Reform — Twenty Questions*, 41 TAXES 672, 679 (1963):

> There is nothing about the combination of rate reduction and base broadening which dictates that all preferential provisions be eliminated, but there are potent reasons for leaning over backwards before allowing any of them to remain . . . . [The] existence of any one special dispensation makes it easier to argue on behalf of others. . . . [T]he fewer gaps left in the base, the more rates can be cut without affecting revenue yields. . . . [A] Spartan attitude toward defending the integrity of the base will aid in creating the impression that the reform plan is intended to improve the system as a whole, with the chips falling as they may, and is not calculated to benefit certain identifiable groups possessing political strength.

[4] Paul, *Erosion of the Tax Base and Rate Structure*, in JOINT COMMITTEE ON THE ECONOMIC REPORT, 84TH CONG., 1ST SESS., FEDERAL TAX POLICY FOR ECONOMIC GROWTH AND STABILITY 297, 310 (Comm. Print 1956) [hereinafter cited as 1955 COMPENDIUM]; *see* note 10 *infra*.

expenses, geographical location, age, state of health, and family status.[5]

While theorists may argue about what constitutes preferential treatment, sophisticated taxpayers have not experienced a similar difficulty. Instead they have been guided by this single principle: It is more advantageous to accumulate wealth or enjoy personal consumption in ways calling for the payment of less total income tax than if the savings and consumption were financed only by money received in the form of ordinary income and if that money were spent on consumption or saved only in ways which did not give rise to deductions for tax purposes. There is no reason why we should depart from this realistic principle. Legislation is preferential to the extent it allows any taxpayer to accumulate wealth or enjoy personal consumption without paying the full tax. And the full tax is that which would be due if all of the taxpayer's economic enhancement were financed by cash received as ordinary income and if he did not qualify for any non-business deductions or extraordinary exemptions or credits in the course of saving or spending his income.

The wholly nonpreferred taxpayer thus is the man who receives everything in fully taxable forms, who satisfies his personal consumption and accomplishes his savings in nondeductible ways, and who does not otherwise qualify for special exemptions or credits. To the extent that any taxpayer fares better than this yardstick he is being preferred.[6]

Reference to a tax provision as "preferential" or "special" does not connote opposition to the social or economic objective which Congress has used the tax law to support. It does mean the provision deviates from a norm. Implicit in the reference is the idea that the income tax has an essential integrity; that there is a fundamental standard for determining the tax base and the applicable rates; that maintenance of the standard (restoration where it has been eroded) is important to society, high on its scale of values; that the proponent of a measure which deviates — which creates a preference — has a burden of proof which goes as much to the use of the tax system as the means of accomplishment as to the measure's specific social or economic objective.[7]

---

[5] Atkeson, *The Economic Cost of Administering Special Tax Provisions*, in 1955 COMPENDIUM 276, 279.

[6] Blum, *The Effects of Special Provisions in the Income Tax on Taxpayer Morale*, in *id.* at 251–52.

[7] Wolfman, *Federal Tax Policy and the Support of Science*, 114 U. PA. L. REV. 171, 173 (1965).

To determine the extent of erosion, we must first have some notion as to what the tax system ought to be. Since this is to a large extent a matter of equity, and since equity judgments are highly personal, no single standard will meet everybody's approval. Economists have defined the term "income" as consumption plus (or minus) the net increase (or decrease) in value of an individual's assets during the taxable period. I propose to use this definition with two modifications: First, capital gains will be included in income when realized or when transferred to others through gifts or bequests; second, gifts and inheritances are to be excluded from income. The first of these modifications is made because it is probably impractical to include capital gains in income until they are realized or transferred. The second accepts the present status of estate and gift taxation as separate from income taxation. As a working approximation, this concept of income is equivalent to gross receipts in cash and in kind (other than gifts and inheritances) received by the taxpayer during the taxable period less the expenses necessary for the production of such receipts, plus the net rental value of owner-occupied homes and net capital gains transferred at gift or death.[8]

Most provisions leading to erosion [of the corporate income tax base] . . . represent favorable treatment granted with the intention of promoting objectives deemed to be more important than revenue and equity considerations. The dominant consideration may be to provide an incentive to some highly desirable activity such as defense-plant expansion, to relieve a depressed area or industry such as coal, to help small business, or to remove existing discrimination by extending special tax treatment to comparable industries or types of income. . . .

. . . .

Two standards are used in this paper to identify preferential provisions. First, taxes should be neutral between different types of economic activity. Tax neutrality is used here in the sense that taxes be levied without discrimination and without favor between different forms of income, between different categories of expenditure, and between different industries. . . .

. . . .

Secondly, taxable income in most cases should correspond to commonly accepted business measures of net income consistently followed.[9]

---

[8] Pechman, *What Would a Comprehensive Individual Income Tax Yield?*, in 1 1959 COMPENDIUM 251, 259.

[9] Hellmuth, *The Corporate Income Tax Base*, in *id.* at 283, 284, 285, 286.

Some briefer statements are quoted below.[10]

When writers turn to the task of listing the sources of "erosion," the bill of particulars almost always begins with such exclusions as state and municipal bond interest, sick pay, foreign source income earned by citizens abroad, and social security payments. As the extracts set out above suggest, however, their authors are not exclusively concerned with items that are totally excluded from the tax base. Thus, the concept of "erosion" embraces deductions (percentage depletion), differential tax rates (the long-term capital gain rate),[11] rules relating to timing (postponement by qualified pension plans), and other provisions, regardless of the technical form in which they appear in the Code.

So far as I know, however, no one has attempted to list all the sources of "erosion" to be found in existing law,[12] although the

---

[10] Brazer, in *1959 Panel Discussion* 201: "[I]ncome is essentially equal to the value of rights exercised in consumption expenditure plus the change in one's capital position over the course of the year. Now, you have a loophole under this definition if you allow a deduction or an exclusion that is not justified under the terms of this definition." Sneed, in *id.* at 12: "[E]ach dollar of income to a taxpayer should be fully included in the tax base, irrespective of its source, except where administrative convenience requires otherwise. The Simons definition of income should be used as the ideal." For other statements see Surrey, *The Congress and the Tax Lobbyist — How Special Tax Provisions Get Enacted*, 70 HARV. L. REV. 1145, 1146–48 (1957); Blum, *Tax Policy and Preferential Provisions in the Income Tax Base*, in 1 1959 COMPENDIUM 77, 84; *see* Ture, *The Costs of Income Tax Mitigation*, 49 NAT'L TAX ASS'N PROCEEDINGS 51, 52 (1956); note 86 *infra*.

[11] The relationship of the CTB movement to differential rates is puzzling. Although the tax base might initially be regarded as independent of the rate structure, excluding an item is in effect interchangeable with putting a zero rate on it; and the capital gain provisions disclose a similar link between deductions and special rates. Percentage depletion can also be regarded as a device to moderate the tax rate applicable to a specified type of income. The advocates of a CTB regularly describe the capital gain provisions as a source of "erosion" that must be closed to achieve a CTB, and they sometimes apply the same label to the special rates applicable to joint returns. However, Pechman, *supra* note 8, at 276, calculates the yield of a comprehensive income tax both with and without income-splitting, asserting that this rate issue involves a value judgment that "cannot be resolved on a priori grounds." This may imply that some (but not all) special rates are inconsistent, on definitional grounds, with a CTB, for instance those that differentiate on the basis of the *source* of income, such as the capital gain provisions and the rate reduction applicable to Western Hemisphere Trade Corporations.

[12] The most extensive examination seems to be R. GOODE, THE INDIVIDUAL INCOME TAX 99–152 (1964). In my opinion, as will be seen, Goode's list is not exhaustive. In Pechman's estimates, the references to "all" eroding features were probably intended to refer only to those "leakages" that he was able to quantify. *Erosion of the Individual Income Tax*, 10 NAT'L TAX J. 1, 2 (1957); *What Would a Comprehensive Individual Income Tax Yield?*, in 1 1959 COMPENDIUM 251; *see* p. 929 *supra* for his definitions. Surrey has compiled a list of "principal income exclusions and preferences," but some of its inclusions are as surprising as some of its omissions, and I do not know how vigorously he would defend it. Thus, the ex-

philosophy of "treating all income alike" in order to achieve a CTB, with no seeds from which new "exceptions" can grow, is premised on our ability to identify the provisions to be eliminated. For this task we need more than a compilation of everyone's favorite complaints.[13]

From the rhetoric of the broad base approach to tax reform,[14] one might get the impression that its advocates (or at least the lawyers among them) would compute the taxpayer's gross income by using section 61(a) as a starting point, discarding as

---

clusion of the income of state and local governments is cited, but not the exclusion accorded to the income of tax-exempt institutions. Surrey, *The Federal Income Tax Base for Individuals*, in 1 1959 COMPENDIUM 1, 15. Heller acknowledges that "a consensus on a detailed definition may be difficult to achieve" and addresses himself only to provisions or omissions "which have received considerable attention as inroads on the equity of the income tax." He does not disclose whose blackballs were counted in this election, or how they were weighted; but I judge from his list that the criterion was not one-man, one-vote. Heller, *Limitations of the Federal Individual Income Tax*, 7 J. FINANCE 185, 192–93 & n.14 (1952).

Efforts to compute "effective" income tax rates, as distinguished from nominal rates, are necessarily premised on an "adjusted" taxable income figure, and thus require the author to offer his alternative to the Code's version of "taxable income." Here again, however, I know of no alternative definition that purports to eliminate all "preferences." *See, e.g.*, Musgrave, *The Incidence of the Tax Structure and Its Effects on Consumption*, in 1955 COMPENDIUM 96. For macroeconomic analysis, Musgrave's adjusted "broader income concept" may be adequate, but it would hardly qualify as a no-preference base for taxing purposes. *See also* Musgrave, *How Progressive is the Income Tax?*, in 3 1959 COMPENDIUM 2223; White & White, *Horizontal Inequality in the Federal Income Tax Treatment of Homeowners and Tenants*, 18 NAT'L TAX J. 225 (1965). Attempts by welfare economists to measure "income inequality" also require the scholar to devise an adjusted income base if he thinks that taxable income is a misleading or inadequate concept. *See* STAFF OF JOINT ECONOMIC COMMITTEE, 88TH CONG., 2D SESS., THE DISTRIBUTION OF PERSONAL INCOME 106 (Comm. Print 1964); J. MORGAN *et al.*, INCOME AND WELFARE IN THE UNITED STATES ch. 20 (1962); Lampman, *The American Tax System and Equalization of Income*, 49 NAT'L TAX ASS'N PROCEEDINGS 271, 277–78 (1956).

[13] *See* Blum, *Federal Income Tax Reform — Twenty Questions*, 41 TAXES 672, 691 (1963): "So long as comprehensive reform is only a slogan, referring generally to rate reduction and base broadening, and not a concrete program for action, an assessment of its chances is premature. . . . Until a specific program has been developed, we cannot expect that the merits of the idea will get an adequate airing."

[14] In the absence of an authoritative membership list, I have treated all who profess faith in a CTB as though they were full-fledged members of the club, although I recognize that they may not feel this way about each other. My concern is not to measure degrees of loyalty to the CTB rhetoric, but to see what it means and where it leads. The scholar whose professional work focuses on taxation may brush the rhetoric aside as a crude label for a program, the details of which he can consider on their individual merits. As the no-preference, comprehensive tax base concept moves into the larger world, however, it is bound to lose some of the qualifications that the experts tucked away in footnotes and appendices; and a fortiori it will lack those that were never made explicit.

a "preference" any provision which alters the result that would be reached if section 61(a) stood alone, whether it does so by excluding an item from gross income, by assigning it to a different year or to a different person, or otherwise. Having computed gross income by looking solely to section 61(a), we would then convert it into taxable income by deducting the expenses, losses, bad debts, and depreciation incurred in the taxpayer's business or profit-motivated transactions — but nothing else. A rigorous application of the "comprehensive base" approach, then, seems to imply that sections 61(a), 162, 165, 166, 167, and 212 are the only operative provisions needed for an ideal computation of taxable income.

Another answer to the same question — how can we arrive at a comprehensive base, devoid of all "preferences"? — that is suggested or implied by the commentators, especially the economists, is use of the Haig-Simons definition of income as the touchstone. Haig defined personal income as "the money value of the net accretion to one's economic power between two points of time," a formulation that was intended to include the taxpayer's consumption, and that was thought by Simons to be interchangeable with his own: "Personal income may be defined as the algebraic sum of (1) the market value of rights exercised in consumption and (2) the change in the value of the store of property rights between the beginning and end of the period in question."[15] At times, the "broad base" commentators seem to imply that a "true" or rigorous CTB would be achieved if Congress enacted the Haig-Simons formulation. It is always admitted, to be sure, that valuation difficulties or administrative problems require some departures from the ideal (for example, with respect to unrealized appreciation, imputed income from assets, and domestic services by the taxpayer or his wife); but I take it that these concessions assume that the departure *is* a preference, albeit an unavoidable one. Such concessions, in other words, are adjustments to practicality, rather than an integral part of the definition.[16]

---

[15] THE FEDERAL INCOME TAX 7 (R. Haig ed. 1921), *reprinted*, READINGS IN THE ECONOMICS OF TAXATION 54 (R. Musgrave & C. Shoup eds. 1959) (emphasis omitted); H. SIMONS, PERSONAL INCOME TAXATION 61–62, 206 (1938). When it came to a program for action, Simons was more latitudinarian than his definition; indeed, he said: "If one accepts our definition of income, one may be surprised that it has ever been proposed seriously as a basis for taxation." *Id.* at 103.

[16] If a concession to practicality is thought to be unavoidable, is it quibbling to call it a "preference" rather than a definitional criterion? I think not, for two reasons: (*1*) Whether practicality requires the concession is always a matter of

Still another criterion that has been tendered as the starting point in achieving a CTB, especially in the last few years, is the concept of personal income as employed by the National Income Division of the Department of Commerce in its national income statistics. Comparisons between the amount of taxable income as reported on tax returns and personal income as computed by the NID are sometimes efforts to estimate the amount of illicit underreporting of items that may be more accurately estimated by the NID than by taxpayers' admissions on tax returns. I detect, however, an incipient tendency to move beyond this use of the NID's conceptual framework, and to hold it up (with some modifications, primarily the inclusion of capital gains and losses and personal contributions for social insurance) as a normative model.[17]

I do not suggest that the advocates of the "broad base" approach have explicitly asserted that the way to extirpate all "preferences" and thus to "restore" the tax base is to repeal all substantive parts of existing law except section 61(a) and the business expense and loss provisions, or to enact the Haig-Simons or National Income Division definition. These seem to me the directions in which they point, however, and I have found in their writings no other standards by which "preferences" can be infallibly identified.

Against this background, I have set for myself the task of ex-

---

judgment; thus, to admit that the item is "income" within the Haig-Simons definition invites debate on the possibility of solving the practical problem — a debate which a whole-hearted supporter of a CTB ought to enter with an eagerness to be shown that inclusion *is* feasible. If the concession is buried in the definition, on the other hand, this debate is foreclosed. (*2*) As I will suggest later, one who thinks the item *ought* to be (but for practical reasons cannot be) included in income may want to make other adjustments in the tax base to counterbalance this unavoidable departure from principle.

[17] For the use of NID statistics as a test of underreporting see Holland & Kahn, *Comparison of Personal and Taxable Income*, in 1955 COMPENDIUM 313. For their normative use (explicitly or implicitly) see, *e.g.*, Surrey, *supra* note 12, at 16–17; Cohen, *Substantive Federal Tax Reform*, U. So. CAL. 1964 TAX INST. 711, 716; Galvin, *supra* note 1, at 3–4; *Resolutions on Substantive Tax Reform*, BULL. ABA SECTION OF TAXATION, July 1963 (Annual Report), at 4, 10 ("it may be that as a matter of equity the spread [between NID personal income and IRC taxable income] should be severely narrowed"); R. GOODE, THE INDIVIDUAL INCOME TAX 6 (1964) (supporters of income tax "are disturbed by special provisions allowing much income to escape taxation, the ingenuity of taxpayers in finding loopholes, the reluctance of Congress to repair the erosion of the tax base, and incomplete compliance with the law. In 1960, for example, the amount of income actually taxed equaled only about two-fifths of total personal income . . . .").

amining the major substantive areas of income tax law to see what changes would be required if our overriding legislative aim is to be a CTB without "preferences," "exceptions," or "special provisions." In some of these areas, CTB commentators have already specified a number of provisions that in their view constitute "preferences," and I have sought by extrapolation from these certified items to identify provisions that are equally deserving of the same label. In other areas, I have had to strike out largely on my own, since the possibility that "preferences" exist in these areas seems to have gone unnoticed.

For reasons that will be set out in more detail hereafter, I have concluded that a systematic and rigorous application of the "no preference" or CTB approach would require many more sweeping changes in the existing tax structure than have been acknowledged. I also believe that many of these changes would be quite unacceptable, despite their conformity to the Haig-Simons definition, to many of those who are attracted, in the abstract, by the idea of a CTB. At the same time, there are in my view many more ambiguities in the concept than have been acknowledged, and at these points it sheds less light than some of its supporters seem to claim. Some alleged "preferences," in other words, are as compatible with the Haig-Simons definition as their elimination would be. Finally, those who continue, in defiance of all experience, to hope for a simplified tax structure in a complex society are doubly deluded, in my view, if they believe that a CTB will make a significant contribution to simplification. Most of our troublesome complexities concern issues that are either independent of the definitional criteria or unavoidable once we accept the departures that even the most committed believers in a CTB accept as desirable or necessary.

I. Exclusions from Gross Income

Because tax differentials among taxpayers based on the *source* of their income are inconsistent with the Haig-Simons emphasis on consumption and net accretions to wealth as the proper measures of income, lists of "preferences" almost invariably begin with items that are now excluded from gross income, such as interest on tax-exempt bonds and social security payments. Indeed, although the concept of "erosion" takes in such tax concessions as deductions, credits, and differential rates, it has at its very core the idea that many items properly belonging in the income tax base have been excluded from it by statutory or administrative fiat. It is appropriate, therefore, to begin with the statutory and other exclusions from gross income in analyzing the implications of a CTB.

A. *Social Security, Welfare, and Other Public Transfer Payments*

An important theme in the literature of "erosion" is that social security payments are earned by the taxpayer's personal services and increase his wealth just as much as receipts from traditionally taxable sources. Since these payments are not geared to the taxpayer's financial needs, it is argued that their exclusion from gross income is a poor way to protect a minimum subsistence level and that direct public aid to the poor would insure that any given amount of governmental assistance would reach those who deserve it, rather than being wasted on less needy claimants. Including social security payments in gross income (with an adjustment to permit the taxpayer to recover his contributions [18]) along with analogous benefits like railroad retirement and veterans' pensions, therefore, has been a favorite way of "restoring" the tax base.

Social security, railroad retirement, and veterans' benefits are nominated for inclusion in the proposed CTB because they increase the taxpayer's net worth in the Haig-Simons sense and because if excluded they will have a differential value depending on his tax bracket and will not be openly reflected in the federal budget-making process. These characteristics are shared, however, by many other federal, state, and local government benefits, such as soil conservation and reforestation grants, subsidies to attract industrial plants, scholarships and fellowships, aid to the blind and other disabled persons, meals, clothing, and shelter supplied to patients and inmates of hospitals, prisons, and other public institutions, veterans' readjustment allowances, Medicare protection, and unemployment compensation. Some advocates of a CTB are prepared to tax these benefits (and those who eschew this responsibility impair their credentials as consistent enemies of "preferences"); but it must be noted that this route soon

[18] The employee's contributions — his tax payments — amount on the average to 10–20% of benefits, and a similar share comes from his employer's tax payments. *See* Deran, *Income Redistribution Under the Social Security System*, 19 NAT'L TAX J. 276, 281 (1966). The balance is often described as a gift from the Government. As suggested below, however, if gifts from private persons are to be excluded from the CTB, it is not clear why the exclusion of gifts from the public would be a "preference."

brings one face to face with the fact that every modern nation — even if it does not call itself a welfare state or a Great Society — provides its citizens with a variety of benefits through programs that involve no transfer of cash or identifiable "property."[19] This means that the "comprehensive tax base" must either measure the benefit derived by the taxpayer from *all* governmental services, or grant a "preference" to those who benefit from indirect government programs.

Thus, to tax the student who receives a federal or state scholarship, while exempting the one who can attend a public institution without charge, is a "preference" — as that term is used by the advocates of a CTB — to the latter; and the same can be said of an exemption for the businessman whose plant is made more accessible and valuable by public improvements while his competitor is taxed on a grant of land which was given him to induce a change of location; of an exemption for the farmer who benefits from a flood control project while his neighbor is taxed when a public agency plants trees on his land to check erosion; and of rental allowances vis-à-vis public or subsidized housing. Other troublesome areas are the services of welfare workers, county agricultural agents, and the like; the net deficit of the postal service; and government guarantees of loans to homeowners and businessmen. Even if we look only to public programs providing benefits that are susceptible to valuation and can be accepted or refused at the recipient's option, a policy of rigorously taxing direct grants would inevitably discriminate in favor of indirect benefits.

To be sure, a decision to tax all direct grants while exempting indirect benefits in order to avoid a valuation quagmire[20] is not

[19] Federal subsidy programs aggregating $8.5 billion (excluding veterans' benefits, public assistance, public health and school lunch grants, and aid to Indians) for fiscal 1967 are listed in U.S. BUREAU OF THE CENSUS, STATISTICAL ABSTRACT OF THE UNITED STATES 394 (1966), many of them providing indirect rather than direct benefits to individuals and business firms. *Cf.* R. TITMUSS, ESSAYS ON "THE WELFARE STATE" 44 (1959), arguing that state intervention in the economy in the interest of social policy did not commence in Britain with the "welfare state" of 1948, but with the introduction of progressive taxation in 1907.

[20] *See* MEASURING BENEFITS OF GOVERNMENT INVESTMENTS (R. Dorfman ed. 1965), which assesses the difficulties of measuring the *social* benefits from some public programs; to allocate these benefits, when measured, to individual taxpayers would compound the difficulties, to put the matter mildly. For an attempted allocation to various income classes see Gillespie, *Effect of Public Expenditures on the Distribution of Income*, in ESSAYS IN FISCAL FEDERALISM 122 (R. Musgrave ed. 1965); *see also* Conrad, *Redistribution Through Government Budgets in the United States, 1950*, in INCOME REDISTRIBUTION AND SOCIAL POLICY 178 (A. Peacock ed. 1954); Adler, *The Fiscal System, The Distribution of Income, and Public Welfare*, in FISCAL POLICIES AND THE AMERICAN ECONOMY 359 (K. Poole ed. 1951).

unreasonable; but it would require an admission that the aim of "taxing all income alike" and extirpating all "preferences" had been compromised. And once this is acknowledged, it is only a short step to the conclusion that public policy is not necessarily served by a single-minded effort to tax all grants that *can* be measured, and that it might be better to decide, program by program, which should be taxed and which should be exempt. To take just three examples, the exclusions granted by existing law to combat pay, unemployment compensation, and prizes for notable public achievement may reflect an intuitive sense of fairness or public pride. Assuming the irrationality of this feeling, what is gained by including these items in a tax base that will inevitably exclude a host of noncash benefits under public programs?

For a fully committed enemy of "preferences," governmental benefits belong in the CTB even if the recipient must pass a means test to qualify; thus, the exclusion allowed by existing law for public assistance is a hidden subsidy to local welfare programs, and it creates geographical disparities since it is worth more to the residents of a city that is generous in its welfare allowances or lenient in disregarding outside earnings than to those whose city is more strict in these respects. Pechman, for example, would include such payments in the tax base, relying on the personal exemptions (raised above the existing level, if necessary) and on increases in the welfare payments themselves to prevent the income tax from encroaching on the taxpayer's ability to feed, clothe, and house himself.[21] Even if every welfare recipient received a federal subvention precisely equal to the tax burden resulting from including his welfare payments in his gross income, I presume that this reform would be viewed as an improvement over existing law by a thoroughgoing enemy of "preferences" because it would bring the federal grant into the open and compel it to pass through the budgetary process. Some advocates of the CTB may falter at this point,[22] opening themselves to the charge of being "soft on preferences"; but even they, presumably, would favor including welfare payments in gross income if, as with social security payments, the recipient is not subjected to a means test. If so, they

[21] Pechman, *Erosion of the Individual Income Tax*, 10 NAT'L TAX J. 1, 12–14 (1957).

[22] L. Shere, Federal Tax Revision To Promote Economic Growth and Stability 10 (mimeo 1956), *reprinted*, *Hearings on 1957 Economic Report of the President Before the Joint Economic Committee*, 85th Cong., 1st Sess. 424 (1957), offers a list of objectionable exclusions that is identical with Pechman's, save for public assistance.

may reach the same practical result as Pechman (despite their rejection of his logical rigor) as the means test comes increasingly to be rejected as degrading and self-defeating in the administration of welfare programs.

In the foregoing discussion, I have accepted arguendo the theory that public assistance, veterans' benefits, scholarships and free tuition at public educational institutions, and the like are "subsidies" in their entirety and that social security payments are "subsidies" to the extent that they exceed the recipient's OASI payments. This premise is not unassailable, however; its validity depends upon the kind of cost accounting one chooses to use. If we take account of *all* taxes paid by the recipients of these public programs over their lifetime, it may be that they pay *in full* for what they get. Another possibility is that the price they pay cannot be estimated with reasonable accuracy; and that the case for excluding the benefits from income in order to make sure that the recipients are not taxed on a return of their contributions is as good as the case for treating the benefits as "subsidies." The CTB is to take no account of police, fire, and military protection, I assume, because there is no feasible way of comparing the taxpayer's benefits with his payments.[23] In the case of public assistance and social security, the cash receipts can be measured, but it takes an act of faith to come to a firm conclusion about the amount paid by the recipient for these benefits. Perhaps the exclusion of these items does not "erode" the base after all.

B. Charity and Other Private Transfer Payments

Government agencies were not the first to distribute welfare benefits, nor have they yet preempted the field. If grants from the public treasury to needy persons are to be included in gross income, is there any justification for permitting gifts by charitable institutions (which, in any case, are increasingly viewed as having a quasi-public status) to be excluded? If veterans are to be taxed on their G.I. benefits, can an exclusion be justified for scholarships

[23] Perhaps the rationale is that the "recipient" of police, fire, and military protection is society, not its individual members. In the case of public elementary and secondary school education, it might again be argued that the "recipients" of the expenditures are not the school children or their parents but society as a whole. (But Gillespie, *supra* note 20, at 146, allocates expenditures for education to school children.) Perhaps the same can be said of free college and university education. If so, what is the predicate for the conclusion that welfare, unemployment compensation, and social security programs provide individual, rather than social, benefits?

and fellowships awarded by Harvard or the Ford Foundation? If welfare checks are to be included in income, why not the amounts received by the *New York Times*'s Hundred Neediest Cases or the beggar on the streets? I presume that the CTB is to include charitable grants of all types in gross income, but I do not recall any explicit discussion of the issue; and I suspect that some who are attracted by the CTB concept will not be happy if it taxes private charity along with public transfer payments.

Workmen's compensation, military disability benefits, and sick pay, which are included in Pechman's list of unwarranted welfare-oriented exclusions, substitute for or supplement the taxpayer's wages when his earning capacity has been impaired by illness or accident; but these are not the only sources of such assistance. Existing law also excludes amounts received as damages for personal injuries in automobile and industrial accidents, payments under accident and health policies, and similar receipts. The ABA Committee on Substantive Tax Reform (in conjunction with its study of proposals to "broaden the tax base" by "including in gross income items not now included") recently asked the Treasury to estimate the revenue effect of including items of this type in gross income "to the extent that such amounts are in the nature of replacement of income rather than recovery of capital, with provision, however, for tax free recovery of cost of such items." [24] The terms of this inquiry imply that such receipts might continue to enjoy an exemption if they compensate the taxpayer for medical expenses, pain and suffering, and loss of limb or bodily function but not if they compensate him for loss of earnings or, perhaps, for a diminution in his earning capacity.

Aside from difficulties in administering this distinction, especially as respects lump-sum settlements of tort claims, it cannot be easily reconciled with a "no-preference" tax base. If the deduction for extraordinary medical expenses in existing law is a "preference," why is not the proposed tax-free recovery of medical expenses from a tortfeasor also a "preference"? In the same vein, if existing law is "eroded" by the extra 600 dollar exemption for the blind (and if, as argued, it would be preferable to bring assistance to the blind out into the open by direct government subsidies to those who need financial aid), is it not equally a "preference" to exempt the damages received by a blind taxpayer from the tortfeasor who caused his misfortune? If the pain

[24] *Report of the Section of Taxation on Substantive Tax Reform*, 90 ABA Rep. 289, 292–93 (1965).

of daily labor and the exhaustion of the taxpayer's body during his occupational career are not to be reflected in any tax concession, is it not a "preference" to exempt the compensation he may receive for pain and suffering or permanent injury caused by an automobile or industrial accident? The ABA Committee's request for a Treasury estimate does not mention the miscellaneous personal injury recoveries that are excluded by administrative practice or case law rather than by explicit statutory provisions (for instance, damages for libel of personal reputation); but a rigorous attack on "erosion" would, I presume, nullify these exclusions as well.

Here again, I suggest that a CTB devoid of "preferences" has ramifications that have seldom been explicitly acknowledged and that will be repellent to many persons who are attracted by the rhetoric of the broad base approach.

C. Personal and Dependency Exemptions

Although conditioned on the taxpayer's family status rather than on the source of his income, the personal and dependency exemptions "erode" the tax base on a grand scale. The 64 million individual income tax returns filed for 1963 claimed 183.5 million exemptions, removing 110 billion dollars from taxable income and thus reducing tax revenue by about 18.8 billion dollars.[25] If the purpose of the exemptions is to protect a minimum level of subsistence against income taxation, the unvarying allowance of 600 dollars for the taxpayer, his spouse, and each dependent is objectionable because much of the benefit goes to persons who are above the specified plateau. A "vanishing" exemption — diminishing rapidly for income above the subsistence level — or a credit of a fixed amount would be free of this defect; [26] but even a vanishing exemption or a credit would perpetuate another feature of the personal exemption: it is "inefficient" by welfare standards because it can be claimed by wealthy persons who are only temporarily in low brackets, as well as by the children and other dependents of high bracket taxpayers.[27]

[25] U.S. INTERNAL REVENUE SERVICE, STATISTICS OF INCOME — 1963: INDIVIDUAL INCOME TAX RETURNS 30 (1966).

[26] *See generally* M. LEVY, INCOME TAX EXEMPTIONS (1960); Note, *A Proposed Flexible Personal Exemption for the Federal Income Tax*, 18 STAN. L. REV. 1162 (1966).

[27] Perhaps an averaging system could be devised to prevent wealthy taxpayers with fluctuating incomes from getting "unnecessary" exemptions, but this would take some ingenuity. As to children and other dependents of high bracket

Since the advocates of a CTB argue that a direct government subsidy to the needy is preferable to the tax concessions of current law for taxpayers who are blind or over sixty-five, receive social security payments, or incur extraordinary medical expenses or casualty losses, one would expect them to ask that the personal and dependency exemptions also give way to federal public assistance to qualified persons. This expectation is borne out by their criticism of the extra exemptions allowed taxpayers who are over sixty-five or blind; [28] but they appear to accept the personal and dependency exemptions as an appropriate way of preserving a minimum level of income from encroachment by the tax. Yet if we convert the 183.5 million personal and dependency exemptions claimed for 1963 into a hypothetical federal subsidy of 18.8 billion dollars, it can hardly be disputed that the circle of persons to whom Congress would be prepared to allocate this subsidy would overlap only in part the circle of taxpayers claiming the exemptions.

For this reason, one might have expected the advocates of the CTB to argue that it is inconsistent with their approach to exempt entirely a family with three children having 3,699 dollars of income, if indigent families of this size are getting only (say) 2,500 dollars of public assistance. Why not tax the first family, and let Congress appropriate — as part of the open budgetary process — such "subsidies" as are appropriate to aid *all* needy families (including the 3,699 dollar family, if the imposition of an income tax pushes it below the subsistence level)? The arguments that

taxpayers, exemptions could be denied to them if we taxed family units as aggregates; but unless this (or the abolition of all personal exemptions) is a necessary concomitant of a CTB, it seems to follow that the CTB is thought by its supporters to be compatible with these "unnecessary" exemptions.

[28] *E.g.*, Shere, *supra* note 22, at 9, *Hearings*, *supra* note 22, at 429:

> Unfortunately the blind are only one of many disability groups that suffer from handicaps in life. Chronological age is not a satisfactory measure of fitness, and fitness is not an acceptable measure of taxable capacity under the income tax. . . . The benefits under . . . [the social security] system can be better adjusted to meet some rational standard than can the hidden benefits under the graduated income tax which are progressively scaled to income. The public would be in a better position to evaluate the sum total of benefits that are desirable for older and disabled persons if they were kept together in one place under the social security system . . . .

Pechman, *supra* note 21, at 19, adduces a different objection to these exemptions: "The aged and the blind would have a valid claim for an additional exemption if it could be shown that they are required to spend more out of a given income than other taxpayers. There are no data on the expenditures of the blind, but the available evidence indicates that a family headed by an individual over 65 years of age does not on the average spend more than other families in the same income group."

are adduced against the exclusion of public assistance from gross income seem to me equally applicable to the exemptions. Conversely, if the welfare function of the personal and dependency exemptions is compatible with a comprehensive tax base even though their benefits are "inefficiently" distributed, other welfare-motivated tax allowances (like the exclusion of unemployment compensation and social security benefits) can hardly be opposed on the ground that the tax law is the wrong forum for advancing social ends. Here again, I do not suggest that all preferences must be preserved if any are preserved, but only that we will not make much headway by unwarranted claims of logical rigor.

The exemptions are sometimes defended as devices for keeping unproductive tax returns off the administrative rolls, rather than for protecting a minimum subsistence level from taxation. This aim might account for the taxpayer's own exemption, but it does not explain those allowed for his wife and dependents; and it would suggest a "vanishing" exemption or credit rather than a constant amount that can be claimed even though the return is above the nuisance level and must be filed and audited in any event. Moreover, with the advent of the withholding system, administrative convenience became a less tenable ground for exemptions of any kind. Many taxpayers whose taxable income is completely offset by their exemptions must file returns to obtain refunds of withheld taxes; and these unproductive returns are thus part of the administrative load in any event. And now that we have automatic data processing, it may be less costly and troublesome to keep *all* potential taxpayers on the rolls at all times than to search annually for nonfilers to make sure that they are not subject to tax.

Another rationale for the exemptions is that they adjust the tax burden to the taxpayer's familial responsibilities. (They do this only at low levels of income, of course; for taxpayers in the middle or upper reaches, the 600 dollar exemption bears no sensible relationship to the cost of maintaining a wife, child, or other dependent.) But if the reduced rates applicable to taxpayers filing joint, head-of-household, and surviving spouse returns are objectionable because family expenses are costs of living that should be defrayed from after-tax income — as contended by some proponents of a CTB — the exemptions allowed for the taxpayer's spouse and dependents would seem objectionable for the same reason.

Finally, exemptions are the principal source of progressivity at low brackets and can be viewed as the equivalent of a zero rate of tax on the bottom bracket. So viewed, are exemptions consistent with a CTB? In one sense, yes; one might rationally argue for a CTB coupled with a rate schedule that (for example) imposed a zero rate on the first 25,000 dollars of income and a fifty percent rate on amounts above that level. But when a zero rate is imposed on amounts that vary with the size of the family and that are regularly discussed in terms of subsistence-protection (sometimes by advocates of the CTB themselves, in proposing an increase in exemptions to offset the burden resulting from taxing welfare and other transfer payments [29]), it seems to me that the "welfare" function of the exemptions is paramount. If so, the "nonbudgeted subsidy" argument of the CTB enthusiasts is not easily reconciled with preservation of the personal exemptions.

D. *Proceeds of Life Insurance*

If the war on preferences compels us to include in gross income the amounts received by a deceased wage-earner's family under the federal social security system, I suppose it also requires us to tax anything the family may receive from a tortfeasor for their decedent's wrongful death: in both cases, the payments increase the family's net worth and replace wages that would have been taxed as earned. At this point, however, consistency requires the advocates of a CTB to reconsider their apparent tolerance of section 101(a)(1), which excludes the proceeds of life insurance paid on the death of the insured. This is no doubt an unpalatable suggestion, but there is unfortunately no way to be comprehensive except by being comprehensive.

Death benefits of 4 to 5 billion dollars are received annually by the beneficiaries of life insurance policies, and almost all of this amount "leaks" from the income tax base through the exclusion of section 101(a)(1), although it comes within the Haig-Simons concept of income. To the extent of the policy's cash surrender value (if any), this "preference" bears a resemblance to the exclusion of gifts and bequests from gross income; but the theory that the income tax exclusion merely compensates for a federal

[29] *See* Pechman, *supra* note 8, at 267:

> The exemptions in effect provide a zero rate for that part of an individual's income which is below the minimum levels. Apart from the obvious humanitarian reasons, this zero rate is supported on the ground that taxation below the minimum levels will reduce the health and efficiency of the lowest income strata of the community and will eventually result in lower economic vitality, less production, and possibly higher Government expenditures for social welfare purposes.

gift or estate tax burden is flimsy. Decedents' estates filing taxable federal estate tax returns in 1963 included only about eighteen percent of the life insurance death benefits paid in 1962,[30] and the gift tax is even less of an obstacle to the tax-free transfer of life insurance. Moreover, some insurance proceeds are received in a business setting — for example, "key man" insurance — where the analogy to a bequest is not persuasive.

The inclusion of life insurance savings (imputed interest on the terminal reserve or increases in the cash surrender value) in gross income would be a palliative but not a corrective, since it would not affect pure term insurance, payments under double indemnity and other accidental death clauses, or mortality "gains" resulting from early death.[31] These payments (for instance, death benefits of 50,000 dollars under flight insurance purchased for a few dollars at an airport) are similar to gambling profits: without making the nation richer, they transfer wealth from long-lived insureds to the beneficiaries of short-lived insureds.

Let me make clear that I am not advocating the inclusion of life insurance proceeds in taxable income. I am simply recording my conviction that the exclusion of these receipts is a "preference" as that term is used by the advocates of a CTB, that it may promote the purchase of life insurance just as percentage depletion encourages the discovery and draining of oil wells, and that it invites the exclusion of other items that are functional substitutes for insurance. If I am wrong in thinking that the war on preferences requires repeal of section 101(a)(1), however, why do its com-

---

[30] Life insurance included in 1963 taxable returns totaled $680 million; death benefits paid in 1961 and 1962, the years of death for estate tax returns filed in 1963, were $3,581 and $3,878 million respectively. U.S. INTERNAL REVENUE SERVICE, STATISTICS OF INCOME — 1962: FIDUCIARY, GIFT, AND ESTATE TAX RETURNS 51 (1965); INSTITUTE OF LIFE INSURANCE, LIFE INSURANCE FACT BOOK 1966, at 37. Part of the amount included as "life insurance" in tax returns no doubt represents values other than death benefits (policy dividends, cash surrender values of insurance on persons other than the decedent, and so on); if these were taken into account, the proportion of death benefits included in taxable estates to aggregate benefits paid would be even smaller than 18%.

[31] A good deal of attention has been devoted to the "interest" component of life insurance, of course, but the beneficiary's tax-free receipt of the proceeds has elicited less criticism. *See, e.g.*, Irenas, *Life Insurance Interest Income Under the Federal Income Tax*, 21 TAX L. REV. 297, 314–18 (1966); Goode, *Policyholders' Interest Income from Life Insurance Under the Income Tax*, 16 VAND. L. REV. 33 (1962). Vickrey argues that it would be "theoretically correct" to require the beneficiary to report "that part of the benefit which consists of insurance proper, but not that part which is paid from the reserve," the latter being excluded, evidently, as a gift from the policyholder. W. VICKREY, AGENDA FOR PROGRESSIVE TAXATION 66 (1947).

manding generals have so much enthusiasm for repealing section 101(b) (the 5,000 dollar employee death benefit) and for taxing death benefits paid under the social security system?

E. Gifts and Bequests

Both Haig and Simons, who might be regarded as the spiritual forefathers of the CTB, believed that gifts and bequests constituted "income" as they defined the term. The theory that these items should be excluded from gross income because we have separate transfer taxes on gifts and bequests — which take no account of the recipient's other income — was characterized by Simons as "one of the most spurious and naïve types of argument in the literature." [32] To his rebuttal at the theoretical level one might add that only about one-eighth of inherited property finds its way into the taxable estates of decedents subject to the federal estate tax.[33] Most amounts received by bequest, in other words, bear no federal estate tax burden; and for those that do, the death tax burden is often less than the income tax that would be imposed on the recipient if this "leakage" were eliminated. As to gifts, the existence of a federal gift tax is an even weaker reason for excluding them from a CTB. The statistics on inter vivos transfers are fragmentary, but experience tells us that the donor who pays a gift tax is a *rara avis.*

Although advocates of a CTB sometimes call attention to this issue, the dominant mood is acquiescence in existing law. I do not know whether they have steered clear of section 102 (excluding gifts and bequests from gross income) because they think it is a "good" preference or out of political realism. Bunching of income would be a problem, of course, if section 102 were repealed; but the advocates of a CTB almost always favor income averaging rather than an exclusion as the appropriate remedy for this

---

[32] Simons, *supra* note 15, at 126–127.

[33] In the absence of a more authoritative estimate, I offer the following computation. R. LAMPMAN, THE SHARE OF TOP WEALTH-HOLDERS IN NATIONAL WEALTH 1922–56, at 23 (1962), estimates that about 30% of "personal sector wealth" was held in 1953 by "top wealth-holders" (persons with gross estates of $60,000 or more). Let us assume that the wealth owned by top wealth-holders who died in 1953 was 30% of the wealth owned by all 1953 decedents. Federal estate tax returns filed in 1954 reported net estates of $7 billion ($7.4 gross, less debts of $0.4). U.S. INTERNAL REVENUE SERVICE, STATISTICS OF INCOME — 1962: FIDUCIARY, GIFT, AND ESTATE TAX RETURNS 81 (1965). If these returns reflected 30% of the wealth owned by all 1953 decedents, the aggregate wealth transferred by death in 1953 was $23.3 billion (100/30 times $7 billion). Taxable estates aggregated $3 billion, or 13% of the aggregate amount transferred by death.

phenomenon, and sometimes they promise rates so low that timing will be unimportant. There are other reasons for excluding gifts and bequests from the income tax base, such as the distortions in family transfer patterns that would result from efforts to bypass as many generations or intermediate donees as possible, and the difficulties in taxing the beneficiaries of discretionary trusts. These, however, are no more self-evident or compelling — to me, at any rate — than the reasons that led Congress to enact many of the other "preferences" of existing law. Nor can gifts and bequests be excluded from gross income without inviting the exclusion of many other items that share some of their characteristics — scholarships and fellowships, prizes, some employee death benefits, life insurance proceeds, public assistance, social security payments, unemployment compensation, and so on.

F. Support, Dower, and Similar Rights

If a gold digger strikes it rich, would a CTB require the present value of her right to be supported by her wealthy husband to be included in her taxable income in the year of marriage, along with the estimated value of her dower rights? If this mode of improving one's economic status is to be granted a "preference" by being excluded from gross income because of valuation difficulties, should the amount actually spent by the husband on his wife's support be reported by her annually during the continuation of the marriage? As to wives, this refinement would be of little significance *if* the husband were allowed to deduct the amounts included in the wife's tax base (as with periodic alimony under existing law) and *if* the joint return of existing law were preserved in the reformed tax structure; but if support payments "belong" in a CTB, they ought to be accounted for by children as well as by the wife. Absent a "family" return aggregating the income of parents and children, however, the tax structure would be much altered by including support in the taxable base of children and other dependents. And even as to the wife, the advocates of a CTB ordinarily assert that family responsibilities are merely a form of personal consumption that are not legitimately reflected in a tax base — an approach implying that the husband should not be permitted to deduct the expense of maintaining his wife even if she is required to account for the support in *her* income.

A committee of the ABA Tax Section recently recommended that the Internal Revenue Code be amended to provide explicitly that the wife does not realize taxable income "from the acquisition of support rights or dower rights either on marriage, or annually thereafter."[34] Although this proposal merely codifies the administrative practice of the day, it implies that section 61(a) of existing law is broad enough, at least in theory, to require these items to be included in taxable income. Is the ABA proposal one of those "special exceptions" that would "erode" the tax law, to be resisted at all cost lest it serve as a precedent for more "preferences"? I put the question not entirely in a spirit of *Schadenfreude*, because genuine problems *do* arise if support is excluded from a CTB. Support is a next door neighbor of gifts and bequests; if wives and children are not taxed on the support they receive from the head of the family but are required to include gifts and bequests from him in their taxable income, some mighty fine distinctions will have to be drawn. This painful task may be avoided by excluding gifts and bequests, support payments, and life insurance death benefits from the proposed CTB. But the resulting disloyalty to the Haig-Simons definition will then be so monumental that I am baffled by professions of faith in that touchstone when the issue is the proper treatment of other types of transfer payments by individuals, private institutions, and public agencies.

G. Imputed Income from Taxpayer's Assets

The exclusion from gross income, as presently defined, of the net rental value of owner-occupied residences has been a common target of commentators, and some have also criticized the failure to tax imputed income from other assets, for example, the net rental value of household furnishings and the value of bank services provided in lieu of interest on idle balances in checking accounts.[35] Acknowledging that it would not be easy to value these

[34] BULL. ABA SECTION OF TAXATION, July 1965 (Annual Report), at 59. Thus far, the ABA Tax Section has not turned its attention to another danger that looms on the horizon if the tax base is broadened to take all economic enhancement into account. I mean the possibility that a wealthy bachelor may realize income on marriage equal to the present value of the tax savings resulting from filing joint returns until his death or divorce. For a calculation of this increase in his net worth see Hellborn, *Uncle Sam's Dowry*, 44 NAT'L TAX ASS'N PROCEEDINGS 310 (1951).

[35] It has been reported that a private bank proposes to provide its depositors with "a highly trained staff that will translate letters and documents, carry out personal secretarial assignments, get theater tickets and travel reservations and advise on investments," in the manner of "an exclusive private club where privileges and services will be extended only to properly sponsored and approved members." The bank would require minimum balances of $25,000 in personal checking accounts and $50,000 in business accounts. N.Y. Times, Aug. 12, 1965, at 29, col. 1.

economic advantages or to enforce compliance, most advocates of a CTB would evidently be satisfied with taxing the imputed rent of owner-occupied residences and willing to exempt imputed income from other assets. I presume that they would agree, however, that this tolerance, even if impelled by the pain and suffering that consistency would require, would "erode" the tax base.[36] I do not know the order of magnitude of the "special exception" that is thus to be granted to the owners of personal property, but it must be at least as substantial as many "preferences" that we are asked to nullify.

H. Income from Vicarious Enjoyment

Under existing law, the income from property transferred by gift is ordinarily taxable to the donee, not to the donor; but in some circumstances (as with so-called grantor or Clifford trusts), the income is imputed to the donor on the ground that he continues to enjoy it, though vicariously. It is often suggested that the tax base is "eroded" by excessive concessions to donors, and that the income thrown off by transferred property, family partnerships, and the like should be taxed to the donors whenever they vicariously enjoy it, not merely in the limited circumstances defined by existing law.[37] As the expression of an attitude, this is all very well; but it hardly constitutes a program for reform. Is it proposed that a taxpayer who makes a gift of stock to his ten year-old son be taxed on the dividends even if they are accumulated in a bank account rather than spent currently? — even if the parents are divorced and the mother rather than the taxpayer gets custody of the child? — even after the child reaches his majority? If the CTB requires inclusion in all these circumstances, what of the income generated by stock (or the reinvested proceeds thereof) that is donated by the taxpayer to adult children, friends, and charitable institutions?

The Haig-Simons definition seems to seize upon *legal* rights rather than vicarious enjoyment as the measure of income; but, as is true whenever we encounter an issue that is worth arguing about, it is sufficiently flexible, or ambiguous, to support either approach.

---

[36] *See* note 16 *supra.*

[37] Of course, the income generated by donated property, transfers in trust, and family partnerships is taxed to *someone*; it does not drop out of the income tax base entirely. Hence the claim that these income-splitting arrangements conflict with a CTB implies that the CTB concept dictates, or helps to determine, the taxpayer by whom a given item of income should be reported. This is, at best, a debatable theory. *See* pp. 974–77 *infra.*

If the CTB is to look solely to the taxpayer's legal rights, it will achieve consistency at the expense of realism, while if it accepts vicarious enjoyment as a determinant of income, it will plunge us into the same morass that the income-splitting practices of existing law create. Unless *all* donors are taxed on *all* income from property transferred by gift, distinctions will have to be based — just as under existing law — on the relationship between the donor and donee, the character of the property, the mode of transfer, and other factors thought to be relevant. No matter where these lines are drawn, they will grant "preferences" to those on the non-taxable side. Here again, there is no formula that will give us a tax base devoid of "exceptions," "loopholes," and "leakages."

I. Miscellaneous Exclusions

If the aim is to eliminate *all* exclusions of existing law so that *all* income is included in the CTB, what are we to do about such tax-exempt persons and institutions as the British ambassador, the Girl Scouts, the local Baptist church, the City of Boston, the Port of New York Authority, the Benevolent and Protective Order of Elks, the Teamsters, the Yale Club of New York City, and so on? There are occasional intimations that some of these exemptions are "preferences," [38] but I know of no authoritative list of those marked for extinction; and I suspect that even the most hardy advocates of a CTB will find reasons for keeping the list rather short. Still, as Blum says, one preference leads to another; [39] there is surely no magic in the line drawn by existing law between exempt and taxable institutions. Conversely, if we can have a CTB even though churches, universities, labor unions, and other socially useful institutions are tax-exempt, I do not see why the CTB is not also consistent with the partial tax-exemption, special deductions, or special rates that are available to cooperative societies, mutual savings banks, insurance companies, Western Hemisphere Trade Corporations, and other organizations. Once these provisions are accepted, in turn, it is but a small

[38] As pointed out in note 12 *supra*, Surrey's list of exclusions and preferences includes § 115, exempting the income of state and local governments. Hellmuth, *supra* note 9, at 312–13, says that "the possibility of including net income of Government-owned commercial enterprises, such as electric powerplants, could be raised." I do not know whether the question to be raised is whether the existing exclusion is a "preference," or whether the "preference" should be eliminated. If the exemption of governmental revenue is threatened by a CTB, I suppose that a fortiori § 501(c) is in jeopardy.

[39] *See* note 3 *supra*.

step to many other "preferences" that we are asked to eliminate in order to achieve a CTB. Thus, if Harvard's investment income is to be exempt from income tax because its activities are socially useful, is it persuasive to assert that a deduction must be denied to contributors to Harvard in order to keep the income tax structure "neutral"? Conversely, if the exemption of state and municipal bond interest is an illegitimate, because hidden, federal "subsidy," what is the proper label for section 115, exempting all income derived by a state or political subdivision from operating a public utility or exercising an essential governmental function? No doubt many if not most of our tax-exempt institutions operate at a loss, but some do not. For these, an exempt status can be predicated only on value judgments of the type that the CTB is supposed to avoid.

II. Personal Deductions

Advocates of a CTB are ordinarily hostile in theory to the personal deductions of existing law, arguing that the taxpayer's disposable income is the ideal tax base no matter how he may choose to spend it. But they do not cleave consistently to this theory. Thus, Pechman would preserve the deductibility of state income taxes to encourage use of these taxes at the state level [40] and to minimize interstate tax differentials, and he favors or would accept deductions for large charitable contributions, extraordinary medical expenses, and major casualty losses.[41] Senator Long's "optional simplified tax method" [42] is more hostile than Pechman's proposal to personal deductions, rejecting all of the "preferences" that Pechman favors or is willing to accept; but it makes its own "exceptions" to the tax base: alimony, bad debts, and section 212(3) expenses. Galvin would preserve the same personal deductions as Pechman (charitable contributions, medical expenses, and casualties) and would add the interest deduction to this list of acceptable "preferences," but only to the extent that these items amount in the aggregate to more than twenty percent of the taxpayer's adjusted gross income.[43] Some other enemies of "prefer-

[40] *Cf.* the suggestion that inclusion of interest from state and municipal bonds in the federal income tax base might cause the states to rely more heavily on regressive taxes, in Bronfenbrenner, *Economic Effects of the Taxation of Government Securities*, 35 Ill. L. Rev. 293, 305–07 (1940).

[41] Pechman, *supra* note 8, at 273–74.

[42] S. 3250, 88th Cong., 2d Sess. (1964).

[43] Galvin, *Tax Reform — What? Again?*, 17 Sw. L.J. 203, 219–20 (1963).

ences" find virtually all of the personal deductions acceptable, but want dollar or percentage floors to be established so only extraordinary amounts will qualify; in some cases, they also favor the imposition of ceilings to insure that extraordinary amounts will not qualify if they are *too* extraordinary.

I think it is fair to say of these proposals that they cannot be reconciled with the generalization ("no preferences") that we are often urged to accept as the prime criterion of a sound tax structure. They *can* be reconciled with other criteria, however, which might be verbalized as follows: The base to which the tax rates are to be applied should take account of costly catastrophes in the taxpayer's personal life and should offer him an incentive to make charitable contributions. It should also (some would say) allow him to deduct state income taxes in order to encourage, or refrain from discouraging, the levy of this type of tax by the states. Some other items such as interest and bad debts should be deductible to avoid the abrasive administrative burden of separating those that are business-oriented from those that serve only a personal purpose. Finally, the difficulty of verifying claims for personal expenditures and the fact that all taxpayers incur some items of this type as part of the normal cost of living, justify the imposition of a nondeductible floor on these expenses.

The principles that govern — as distinguished from those that are *said* to govern — the tax programs offered to us by their authors strike me as (*a*) sensible, and (*b*) familiar. I describe these principles as sensible because they involve an examination of each deduction to see what can be said for and against it, and as familiar because they do not depart in any significant sense from the principles embodied in every revenue act since 1913. Many of the proposed changes seem meritorious to me, but they stem from relatively minor differences in judgment; and they do not begin to resemble the dramatic leaning over backward against "exceptions" and "preferences" that is prescribed by Blum as the only posture capable of protecting the tax system against further "erosion." [44] In short, the proposals summarized above would invite — precisely as existing law invites — the proliferation of other personal deductions on the ground that they too deserve a boost from the tax structure or result from unexpected or catastrophic events in the taxpayer's personal life; and they also would invite the same process of refining, elaborating, and individualizing the concept of a "proper" deduction that has resulted in the

[44] *See* note 3 *supra*.

preposterous detail of the charitable contribution and medical expense provisions of existing law. On balance, however, I would prefer to amend or even to retain the personal deductions and face the troubles they inevitably spawn rather than abolish them. Evidently the enemies of "preferences" have come to the same conclusion.

III. The Personal-Business Borderline

Since the ideal of the advocates of a CTB is a tax on "net" income, they retain the distinction between the cost of living, which is not to be deductible, and the cost of *earning* a living. They cannot be blamed for the haziness of this distinction, of course, but they have blithely bestowed the pejorative terms "preference," "erosion," and "special exceptions" in the erroneous belief that the CTB concept is a useful tool of analysis in this area. In point of fact, however, it is of no assistance in separating personal from business expenditures, or in deciding whether or how to allocate the cost of items that inextricably confer personal benefits on the taxpayer at the same time that they serve his business purposes.

Thus: should taxpayers be allowed to deduct the expense of driving to and from work, of clothing or grooming themselves in the manner required by or suited to their jobs, of liberal or professional education,[45] of moving to new business locations, of curing or insuring against occupational diseases or job-related injuries, of entertaining customers and other business associates, or of maintaining themselves on business trips? The deduction of travel and entertainment expenses is so frequently denounced as a "preference" as to imply that the proposed CTB is not to make allowances for any borderline expenditures; but perhaps this hostility to "T & E" is an ad hoc or moral judgment that does not apply to moving expenses, work clothes, or accident insurance. Similarly, the ability of business executives and self-employed professionals to squeeze a variety of personal benefits out of their deductible expenditures — the lawyer who can use his secretary on personal errands; the physician who reads the *National Geographic* before putting it in his waiting room; the executive whose family occupies empty seats on a company plane — is often cited as a source of "erosion" in the tax base; but here again we are

[45] *See* Goode, *Tax Treatment of Individual Expenditures for Education and Research*, 56 Am. Econ. Rev. 208 (1966).

assailed by labels rather than offered an analysis.[46] Like it or not, our lives are not so compartmentalized that these borderline items can be readily classified.

The child care deduction of existing law, section 214, is a good example of this troubled area, and it nicely illustrates the irrelevance of the CTB concept to the problem of borderline expenditures. If the mother of small children takes a job outside the home, she may have to hire a nurse or baby-sitter; thus, section 214 is a plausible way to reflect the fact that the working mother's salary is not all gravy. But if section 214 is not a "preference" and does not "erode" the tax base, would it deserve these pejoratives if it were amended (*a*) to eliminate the family income limit of section 214 (b)(2)(B), thus permitting upper bracket families to qualify; (*b*) to permit all two-job families to deduct the increase in their living expenses resulting from the housewife's absence from the home (such as the extra cost of cleaning the house and of preparing meals or eating in restaurants); or (*c*) to permit bachelors to deduct the extra cost of living alone? Finally, what is the difference — so far as the concept of a CTB is concerned — between allowing the working mother to deduct her child care expenses and allowing the business executive to deduct the extra cost of custom-tailored clothing? If the answer is that the business man works in order to be able to live well, rather than the reverse, it is also true that some mothers do not hire a nursemaid in order to work, but work in order to hire a nursemaid.

A ground for eliminating provisions like section 214, and resisting the enactment of others, is that the business necessity of borderline expenditures is hard to prove or disprove, while their personal component is usually clear, with the result that deductions in this area cannot be adequately policed and will therefore breed exaggeration, fraud, and public discontent.[47] This is a plausible reason for restricting such deductions, but it is different from one-dimensional insistence on a CTB. Moreover, it leaves

[46] I have heard no clarion call for denying the academic community the right to deduct living expenses incurred while teaching away from home for the summer or traveling on sabbatical leave, or for taking into income such fringe benefits as free tuition for faculty children and personal use of university facilities; but perhaps these "preferences" are "desirable as means of carrying out supervening economic and social policy" rather than tainted by "mere submission to private interest groups and political expediency" (to use Heller's dichotomy, *supra* note 12, at 193).

[47] On the possibility of allocating such expenses see Klein, *The Deductibility of Transportation Expenses of a Combination Business and Pleasure Trip — A Conceptual Analysis*, 18 STAN. L. REV. 1099 (1966).

room for deciding that some borderline expenditures should qualify for deduction because their business function can be either established with reasonable certainty or properly assumed without proof, or because the personal benefit they confer is usually modest. In an analogous area — interest and bad debts — some advocates of a CTB, acknowledging that it may be difficult to say whether the taxpayer's payment or loss is personal or profit-oriented, have favored an unlimited deduction rather than an attempt to separate the business items from the personal ones or a Draconic denial of any deductions for interest and bad debts. This is a plausible approach (and it can with equal plausibility be applied to the business-personal expenditure area), but it is a judgment that derives no support from, because it is irrelevant to, the CTB concept.

IV. Business Deductions

If there is such a thing as a "classic" preference, percentage depletion heads so many lists that it surely qualifies for this accolade. In allowing the taxpayer to deduct more than his financial outlay in the interest of stimulating investment, however, percentage depletion has much in common with the investment credit. The former is more selective, to be sure, because limited to the mineral industries; but the investment credit is by no means "neutral" either. It is intended to prefer investment over consumption, and it distinguishes among competing investment opportunities: foreign investment, short-lived and nondepreciable assets, and most buildings do not qualify, and public utilities are treated less generously than other taxpayers.

I assume, therefore, that the investment credit has been less frequently described as a source of "erosion" only because it was unveiled too late to be included in most lists of "special provisions," not because it is consistent with a "no preference" tax system.[48] This impression is strengthened by the fact that percentage depletion and the investment credit were evidently bracketed by the ABA Committee on Substantive Tax Reform when it requested Treasury estimates of the impact on revenue of a variety of tax reforms, since one of its assumptions was that business and investment outlays would be capitalized and "the basis of such assets [would be recovered] over the useful life of

[48] Some proponents of a CTB no doubt regard the credit as a "good" preference because of the contribution it makes to economic growth.

the assets in accordance with any one of several methods of capital recovery used by the business and investor community."[49] This statement eschews explicit mention of percentage depletion, but it seems (and was understood) to be a roundabout way of asking the Treasury to assume that depletion deductions would be restricted to the taxpayer's cost; and it also seems to exclude the investment credit from the hypothetical tax structure whose revenue results were to be estimated by the Treasury.

In contemplating the depreciation or amortization of business assets by "any one of several methods of capital recovery used by the business and investor community," moreover, the ABA committee may also have been implying that a CTB is inconsistent with the recent statutory trend toward speeding up the write-off of a wide range of expenditures that under conventional accounting principles would either be written off more slowly or be held in abeyance and applied to reduce taxable income only on a sale or abandonment of the asset. These statutory provisions, some of them inspired by the allowance of accelerated amortization for wartime productive facilities, include: section 169 (grain storage facilities); section 173 (newspaper and magazine circulation expenditures); section 174 (research and experimental expenditures); sections 175, 180, and 182 (expenditures by farmers for soil and water conservation and for clearing and fertilizing land); section 177 (trademark and trade name expenditures); section 179 (additional first-year depreciation deduction for small business); section 248 (corporate organizational expenditures); and sections 263(c), 615, and 616 (expenditures for exploring, drilling, and developing mineral properties). To these statutory "preferences," we might add the administrative practice of allowing the taxpayer to deduct the cost of small tools and institutional advertising, when capitalizing these expenditures would be more appropriate,[50] as well as the 1962 depreciation guidelines, to the extent that they permit the taxpayer to assign shorter useful lives to his assets than an independent examination of his business practice would warrant.[51]

---

[49] *Report, supra* note 24, at 294.

[50] For 1964, it is estimated that $1.4 billion of "producers' durable equipment" (primarily tools) was charged to current expense. U.S. DEP'T OF COMMERCE, SURVEY OF CURRENT BUSINESS, Aug. 1965, at 12.

[51] Double declining balance depreciation was proposed as a practical substitute for "correctly-computed realistic depreciation" by G. TERBORGH, REALISTIC DEPRECIATION POLICY 149 (1954), but empirical evidence on loss of value through time (which should be controlling to those who hold to the Haig-Simons defini-

Such statutory and administrative provisions for the "expensing" or rapid amortization of capital outlays are usually proposed either as incentives to investment or as devices to avoid difficulties in allocating the expenditures in question to specific years; but voices are also sometimes raised in favor of allowing *all* capital outlays to be deducted in computing taxable income when incurred or over whatever period of time the businessman chooses to designate. One such proposal is based on the claim that existing practices sanction the current write-off of virtually all expenditures for intangible assets even though they have a protracted useful life, so that it is pointless to blow the whistle on outlays for tangible property. This suggestion might be regarded as a "no-preference" approach to the write-off of capital investments.[52]

It is also argued that technological developments in a dynamic economy "make any capital expenditure of certain benefit only for the present accounting period," so that expensing such outlays (with the exception, perhaps, of real estate improvements) would accurately reflect economic reality.[53] Though it may appeal to our vision of an America on the move, this theory cannot be reconciled with the fact that the average attained age of business equipment in use today is about ten years, a figure that has not varied more than a year or two in either direction for any year since 1920, and that is, of course, less than the anticipated *useful* life of the equipment. Moreover, equipment with an average attained life of five years or less accounted for about thirty-five percent of all business equipment in 1920 and for about the same percentage in 1965. As for business plant, as distinguished from equipment, its average attained age in our "dynamic" society is about twenty-four years, while it was only about twenty years in the period 1920–1930.[54] These macroeconomic estimates are confirmed by experience: few taxpayers have attempted to prove useful lives for their equipment shorter than those in the 1962

tion of income) is, by the author's own admission, totally inadequate. *Id.* at 39. Rapid depreciation may also be viewed as a rudimentary method of compensating for inflation; indeed, "expensing" of capital outlays would eliminate the complaint that depreciation does not provide an adequate replacement fund in an inflationary economy. The advocates of a comprehensive tax base, however, would presumably not find this a persuasive argument.

[52] Dean, *Four Ways To Write Off Capital Expenditures — Can We Let Management Choose?*, in 1955 COMPENDIUM 504, 509–11; Dean, *Capital Wastage Allowances*, in 2 1959 COMPENDIUM 813.

[53] Galvin, *supra* note 43, at 220. This argument implies that published financial statements overstate income on a monumental scale.

[54] *See* CAPITAL GOODS REV., Sept. 1964 (Machinery & Allied Prods. Inst.).

"guidelines"; and the vigorous complaints that we hear about the reserve ratio test stem from the fact that equipment is not being replaced at the rate implied by the 1962 guidelines, let alone at the rate that would be implied by a general expensing policy.

When all is said and done, then, statutory provisions and administrative practices that permit capital outlays to be deducted when incurred, or over periods shorter than their useful lives, are properly seen as "preferences" by the taxpayer who must depreciate his productive facilities over their useful economic lives and who cannot amortize any part of his investment in land, goodwill, and similar assets because their economic life is not reasonably predictable. Since they take no account of the taxpayer's net worth, such provisions are not easily reconciled with the Haig-Simons definition.

Indeed, one who is seeking to eliminate all "preferences" cannot avoid questioning the propriety — from the point of view of "treating all income alike" — of the rapid methods of depreciation that entered the Code in 1954 or that were approved earlier by administrative practice. The statutory methods are not permissible for used or short-lived assets; these limitations acknowledge an intent to stimulate investment rather than to "clearly reflect income," and this nonrevenue purpose would presumably require their ouster from a purified tax system.[55] Finally, one might go so far as to ask whether straight-line depreciation, though sanctioned by long usage, would be consistent with the CTB or would accurately reflect "the taxpayer's economic enhancement"[56] unless limited to the annual decline in the market value of the depreciable property. We are told, to be sure, that depreciation "is a process of allocation, not valuation,"[57] but if there is no decline in value, what is there to allocate?

It is obvious that these implications of a systematic program

---

[55] The debate among accountants and security analysts over the proper way — "flow-through" or "normalization" — to reflect the tax savings generated by the investment credit, the 1962 depreciation guidelines, and the 1954 accelerated depreciation methods springs from a candid acknowledgment that these write-offs are less "realistic" than the depreciation deducted for financial statement purposes.

[56] *See* p. 928 & note 6 *supra*.

[57] AMERICAN INSTITUTE OF CERTIFIED PUBLIC ACCOUNTANTS, ACCOUNTING TERMINOLOGY BULLETIN No. 43, at 76 (1961). *But see* Detroit Edison Co. v. Commissioner, 319 U.S. 98, 101 (1943): "The end and purpose of it all [depreciation accounting] is to approximate and reflect the financial consequences to the taxpayer of the subtle effects of time and use on the *value* of his capital assets" (emphasis added).

to "treat all income alike" would be highly unpalatable to many who profess to be attracted by the principle of eliminating "preferences" of every variety. In an effort to avoid these implications, they are likely to urge that tax "incentives" to invest in productive facilities will pay us dividends in increasing output, an improved growth rate, and less unemployment — forgetting that wholehearted devotion to a CTB leaves no room for such "special provisions." They may even argue that the CTB is compatible with the expensing or "fast" depreciation of capital outlays because these are mere matters of timing — forgetting that they have insisted on the importance of "mere timing" in criticizing other "preferences."

V. Problems of Timing

The Simons definition of income does not specify the period of time to which it is to be applied: that is left to the person who uses the definition, which refers only to "the beginning and end of the period in question." Similarly, Haig's definition refers to the accretion in the taxpayer's economic power "between two points of time." [58] Simons himself was not much concerned with the problems of the taxable period, or with the effect on the Treasury of moving income from one taxable period to another; and he had little patience for "those who persist in deploring long postponement of tax payment and the consequent interest cost to the Treasury," [59] referring to the issue as "this mosquito argu-

[58] *See* p. 932 *supra*.

[59] H. Simons, Federal Tax Reform 127 (1950); *see id.* at 155. Simons argued that the elimination of the special rate for capital gains, coupled with realization at death, would make the income tax virtually independent of time; taxpayers could then be allowed to depreciate assets at their discretion, to deduct losses on "wash sales," and so on. *Id.* at 44–52. But if time *really* does not matter, a carryover of basis generation after generation would be as satisfactory as realization at death, except for transfers to tax-exempt institutions. It would be interesting to know if Simons was so tolerant of postponement that he would have accepted "Yankee storekeeper" accounting: deduct inventory costs when incurred, but take sales into account only when the customer pays. For a proposal along this line see Carson, *An Investment-Recovery-First Concept of Taxable Profit*, 26 Accounting Rev. 456 (1951).

Simons's tolerance of tax postponement was not a peripheral aspect of his tax theory. The taxing system, he argued, "must not require or presuppose sharp allocations of income among short accounting periods . . . tax legislation calling for definitive annual determinations means awful complexity, difficult administration, expensive compliance, endless litigation, and bad taxpayer and Bureau morale," as well as — perhaps this was the worst of all — a "pestilential multiplication" of tax lawyers. "Income taxation has simply never faced squarely the axiom that an-

ment." His disciples, however, have not inherited his insouciance; they have condemned devices by which taxpayers can postpone the recognition of taxable income from one taxable year to another as "preferences" that are inconsistent with a CTB. Since these items do not drop out of the tax base entirely, the assertion that these "preferences" have the effect of "eroding" the tax base must mean that a CTB is a function of time, as well as of scope. Even if the tax base includes all appropriate items, then, it is not "comprehensive" if some of the items are included in the "wrong" period. As will be seen, however, this concern with timing is not pursued consistently; if it were, it would require changes in the existing structure of a far more sweeping character than has been acknowledged or, perhaps, recognized.

Before we proceed, however, a curious aspect of this area should be noted. The achievement of a CTB, it is often argued, is desirable because it will afford an opportunity to reduce the upper bracket rates and thereby mitigate the degree of progression. And one of the virtues claimed for a less progressive rate structure, in turn, is that it will reduce the importance of timing. The chain of reasoning seems to amount to this: postponement devices must be eliminated in order to create a CTB, which will in turn make possible a rate structure under which postponement devices will be innocuous. Notwithstanding this involuted way of returning to Simons's view that objections to the postponement of income are no more bothersome than mosquitoes, I intend in the discussion that follows to accept the contrary premise that timing *is* important.

The postponement of tax liabilities by the astute selection of an accounting method, contractual arrangement, or other device is often analogized to an interest free loan by the Government to the taxpayer. Translated into dollars, the value of postponing for five, ten, or twenty years the payment of a liability of 1,000 dollars is set out in the following table, depending upon whether the taxpayer discounts the future at five, ten, fifteen, or twenty percent:

Years	*5%*	*10%*	*15%*	*20%*
5	$216	$379	$503	$598
10	386	614	753	838
20	623	851	939	974

nual-income accounting is and should be tentative and provisional." H. SIMONS, *supra* at 58–60. The trouble with this line of argument is that no foreseeable income tax rate structure or general interest rate will make the timing of tax liabilities irrelevant or unimportant.

It is often argued that the same aggregate tax burden should be imposed over a period of time whether income is realized early or late in the period selected; and proposals have been made to neutralize the taxpayer's time preference by averaging income over the period and imputing interest on early tax payments.[60] This would reduce the importance of timing, but postponement would retain some of its charms if the interest rate were inadequate in the eyes of the individual taxpayer. A rate of five percent, for example, might seem satisfactory to a conservative fiduciary or to a public utility; but for many businessmen, a rate of ten or fifteen percent would be required to take the advantage out of postponement. And for taxpayers — there must be millions of them — who are perpetually in debt to personal finance companies, a rate of twenty-four or thirty percent might be necessary to achieve the desired result. On the other hand, a rate that is tailored to the needy or leverage-minded taxpayer would be so high that other taxpayers would be tempted to adopt devices to *accelerate* the realization of income.[61] And if an average rate were to be selected, the Government would be "borrowing" from some taxpayers (those who accelerate their liabilities) at too high a rate, at the same time that it was "lending" to others (those who postpone their liabilities) at too low a rate. I do not mean to suggest that averaging coupled with interest on early payments would not mitigate the importance of timing, but I do assert that the issue would continue to be of major importance. I see no possibility, with high income tax rates, of reducing the issue to the mosquito level to which Simons thought it belonged.

The continued importance of timing, even with averaging and imputed interest on early payments, is further assured because the "loan" that is obtained by postponing a tax liability has features that are overlooked by the academician but critical to the businessman. Loans from banks and other nongovernmental lenders can be procured only if the lender is satisfied with the debtor's financial ability, and are often accompanied by restrictions on the borrower's freedom; in the case of loans to corporations, for example, the salaries to be paid to shareholder-employees may be limited, dividends may be restricted beyond the limits imposed by state law, and the major shareholders may be required to

[60] *E.g.*, W. Vickrey, *supra* note 31, at 164–97.

[61] For some accounting ramifications of the phenomenon of "prepaid" federal income taxes see H.A. Black, Interperiod Allocation of Corporate Income Taxes 72–74 (1966).

endorse the corporation's notes. The loan that results from a postponement of tax liabilities, by contrast, is obtainable at the borrower's will, regardless of his financial condition, and entails no restrictions on his freedom. Moreover, it does not appear on his balance sheet as a liability, and hence does not reduce his power to get other loans. Finally, an ordinary loan carries a fixed maturity date, imposed by the lender, and is subject to extension only at his sufferance. Postponed tax liabilities, on the other hand, become "due" only if the taxpayer takes whatever step (sale of property, reduction of inventory, change of accounting method, withdrawal of funds, or liquidation) is required to realize the income in question. Thus, even if interest is imputed on early tax payments at the same rate that would be paid by the taxpayer for a commercial loan, he would be well advised to "borrow" from the Government by postponing his tax liability whenever possible rather than to borrow from a private lender.[62]

A. The Taxable Period

Income must be measured chronologically. The unit of time selected by the Internal Revenue Code is the twelve month taxable year, not the month, triennium, or decade; and this decision, though conforming to business custom, is by no means neutral in its impact, since tax rates are progressive and taxpayers have a variety of earning cycles. Although the twelve month taxable year is controlling for most purposes, it is modified by a variety of carryover provisions, which in turn specify their own chronological limits. These include section 170(b)(5) (five year carryforward of individual taxpayer's excess charitable contributions), section 172 (three year carryback and five year carryforward of net operating loss), and section 1212(b) (unlimited carryforward of individual's capital loss).[63]

[62] One can usefully compare the wide-open "loan" that is obtained by postponing the realization of income with the more conventional terms that will be imposed on a taxpayer by the Collection Division of the IRS if he has incurred a tax liability but wishes to pay it in installments or at a later time. It is also instructive to note the extent to which financially pressed businessmen are tempted to "borrow" government funds by failing to pay over taxes withheld from their employees' wages on the due date, despite the severe penalty on this practice. *See* Stutsman, *The Penalty for a "Withholding" of Withholding Taxes*, U. So. CAL. 1964 TAX INST. 657.

[63] Income averaging under §§ 1301–05 is another exception to the annual accounting principle. For the differential advantages to various categories of taxpayers resulting from averaging see Steger, *Averaging Income for Income Tax Purposes*, 1 1959 COMPENDIUM 589, 614–15.

I do not recall any suggestion that these modifications of the twelve month taxable year are "preferences," but I am not sure why they have escaped these labels. Can it be that existing law — so deficient, we are told, in so many other ways — has somehow succeeded in defining the taxable period in a way that is consistent in every respect with a CTB? Or are we to conclude that the concept of a CTB is independent of time, and that (as Simons argued) it requires only that all items of income be taken into account at some time or other, no matter when? If so, what are we to make of the assertion that the employee who recognizes income from a qualified pension plan at retirement rather than when his employer makes contributions is receiving a "preference"?

Perhaps the advocates of a CTB object to the delayed recognition of income from qualified pension plans only because it seems inconsistent with the twelve month taxable period that usually controls in computing taxable income. If the accretion in the taxpayer's economic power (Haig's criterion of income) is normally measured by comparing his wealth on December 31 with his wealth on January 1 of the same year, it may be asserted that the same two points in time ought to be used in measuring the economic growth resulting from his participation in a qualified pension plan. This is a persuasive, though perhaps not irrefutable, argument; but it would carry the advocates of a CTB into territory that they have hitherto not attempted to invade. Our network of statutory rules governing tax-free exchanges, as well as the statutory and nonstatutory rules of "tax accounting," will require agonizing reappraisal — as I will show in a moment — if consistency in applying the twelve month taxable period is a prerequisite to achieving a CTB. Moreover, the many carryovers and other exceptions to the twelve month taxable period that are to be found in existing law are not easily reconciled with the notion that the same two points in time must invariably be used in measuring the accretion in economic power that is to be the new measure of taxable income.

B. Averaging

The effect of the twelve month taxable period may be modified in the case of income that was earned or accrued over a longer period of time (as with back pay awards under section 1303 of pre-1964 law) or that substantially exceeds the taxpayer's average income during a specified base period (as with sections 1301–05 of existing law). If the averaging device applies only to a limited category of income, however, it is not easily squared with the demand, frequently voiced by advocates of a CTB, that income be taxed "without regard to its source." The "preference" accorded to capital gains is a rough and ready kind of averaging; neither the deduction allowed by section 1202 nor the alternative special tax rate takes account directly of the tax that would have been paid had the appreciation been measured and taxed in the earlier years, to be sure, but they are often defended as a simple way of mitigating the effect of bunching. This claim would be strengthened if the holding period were longer, as it was before 1942. By contrast, the income averaging provisions of current law do not even purport to deal with slowly maturing income, and they resemble the capital gain provisions in modifying the tax rate applicable to the computation year without regard to the tax that would have been payable if the averageable income had been received during the base period.

I have seen no analysis of the implications of the Haig-Simons definition for income averaging. In the case of income that is earned over a period of time, there may be a corresponding increase in the taxpayer's net worth to be accounted for annually under the definition; but if the accretion cannot be measured or is dependent upon successful completion of the project, the income would not be reflected in the taxpayer's net worth until the final year. Tempering the rate of tax in that year to take account of the income-maturing process seems consistent with the Haig-Simons formulation (indeed, it might be regarded as an optional retroactive adoption of accrual accounting), but only if all forms of slowly maturing income are entitled to this benefit. I am not sure, however, whether the averaging contemplated by some advocates of a CTB is to apply to all slowly maturing income regardless of its source, or only to capital gains.

Averaging that takes account of the income-maturing process does not necessarily do anything for the taxpayer with fluctuating income, since an "abnormal" amount of income in a given year may reflect nothing more than that year's activities. A reduction in the tax rate to mitigate this kind of "bunching" may be consistent with the Haig-Simons definition, but here again it would seem to be a "preference" — as that term is used by advocates of a CTB — if only a limited category of income qualifies for the rate reduction. The income averaging rules of the current Code (sections 1301–05) are not applicable to capital gains or to income from property received by gift or bequest during the computation year or base period. Perhaps these disqualifications can be excused as atoning in some measure for the "preferences" accorded to these types of income; otherwise, they would seem to be objectionable because they turn on the "source" of the taxpayer's income.

C. Accounting Methods

Aside from a few peripheral issues, the advocates of a comprehensive tax base have not directed their attention to accounting methods, possibly on the assumption that "exceptions" and "preferences" are not to be found in this area. In point of fact, however, accounting methods are composed of conventions, primarily governing the time when items are to be taken into account, that are often indistinguishable from "substantive" statutory provisions that are thought to deserve pejorative labels. The cash receipts and disbursements, accrual, installment, completed contract, and percentage of completion methods of reporting income can produce very different results in any given taxable period, and these divergencies may continue for many years — possibly for the full span of the taxpayer's natural or business life.

To illustrate the impact of accounting methods on the CTB concept, one example will suffice. The installment method of accounting (section 453) permits the taxpayer's gain on a sale of property to be spread out over the period of collection, even if the buyer is highly solvent and his obligation to pay is evidenced by promissory notes or other negotiable instruments. The rationale of this method of accounting, which an authoritative committee of the American Accounting Association considers too misleading for financial statement purposes,[64] was recently explained as follows by the Internal Revenue Service:[65]

> The method of reporting income on the installment basis was enacted by Congress as a relief measure, the idea being that it would enable merchants to actually receive in cash the profit arising out of each installment before the tax was paid. In other words, the tax could be paid from the proceeds collected rather than be

[64] Committee on Concepts and Standards Underlying Corporate Financial Statements, American Accounting Association, *Accounting Principles and Taxable Income*, 27 ACCOUNTING REV. 427, 429 (1952); *see* SEC Securities Act Release No. 4811, 3 CCH FED. SEC. L. REP. ¶ 72,124 (Dec. 7, 1965) (proper reporting of deferred income tax liability resulting from use of installment basis of computing income).

[65] Rev. Rul. 65-185, 1965-2 CUM. BULL. 153, 154.

advanced by the taxpayer. . . . It is this "ability to pay" concept which underlies the privilege of reporting income on the installment basis.

If the cash flow theory that underlies this method is acceptable to the proponents of a CTB, why is it a "preference" to permit employees to exclude from their gross income the contributions made by an employer to a qualified pension plan that will not pay any benefits in cash for many years? If all income is to be treated "alike," I see no escape from either repealing the installment method of accounting or extending it to all taxpayers.[66]

The installment method of section 453 is by no means the only accounting method that permits the taxpayer to reflect income in a later year than would be required by a consistent application of the Haig-Simons principle for measuring the taxpayer's economic gain, or that is available to some taxpayers but denied to others similarly situated. The completed contract and percentage of completion methods of reporting income can be used, under section 1.451–3(a) of the Regulations, only for building, installation, and construction contracts. Surely the systematic elimination of "preferences" would require either the abandonment of these accounting methods or their extension to all contracts taking more than one year to complete.

Even more basic is the fact that the cash receipts and disbursements method of accounting permits the taxpayer to control the timing of income by accelerating or postponing the receipt and payment of many items. Deferred compensation arrangements have been criticized by proponents of a CTB, who recommend that cash basis taxpayers be put on an accrual basis in this limited area; but a consistent application of this approach (which also underlies proposals to include the interest component of life insurance savings in the CTB as it accrues) would collide on a grand scale with the assumptions of cash basis accounting. Deferred compensation arrangements are a dramatic illustration of the "creative" use of cash basis accounting principles by the tax planner, but they do not begin to exhaust the possibilities.[67]

[66] For its limited applicability to income from personal services see W.W. Pope, 34 P-H Tax Ct. Mem. 1198 (1965) (carpenter-dealer allowed to use installment method for houses built and sold by him).

[67] *See* Goetz, *The Myth of Special Tax Concessions for Qualified Pension Plans*, 51 Iowa L. Rev. 561 (1966), arguing that the cash method of accounting, rather than "special" legislation, is responsible for the exclusion from the employee's current income of employer contributions to qualified pension plans and of the investment income thereon. Compare the right of cash basis taxpayers to exclude the

Indeed, a rigorous application of accrual accounting principles would require some items and transactions to be taken into account even earlier than the advocates of a CTB have proposed in their war on "preferences." For example, if social security benefits are to be stripped of their tax immunity, why wait until benefits are paid to the employee before requiring him to take them into account? If his employer bought an annuity for him, the contribution would be taxable when made under existing law, and we are asked to extend this rule to qualified pension plans as well. If this extension is required to achieve a "no preference" tax base, should not the employee be required to report, *when earned*, the present discounted value of social security benefits to be paid in the future? [68] If Medicare benefits are to lose their immunity, should not the taxpayer be required to report annually the value of the protection that is conferred on him, just as he would be taxed if his employer bought him an accident and health policy as compensation? There are, to be sure, reasons for not imposing the tax at this time, but they are not easily squared with the "no preference" approach.

Not even the pitiless suppression of all accounting methods other than accrual accounting, however, would give us a tax system devoid of "preferences" and "exceptions." In support of this dismal conclusion, let me simply remind the reader of the many variations of accrual accounting that are to be found in the Treasury Regulations, rulings, and judicial decisions.[69] Which ones are

interest component of U.S. savings bonds until redemption or maturity, despite the annual increase in redemption value.

[68] Of course, the scale of benefits might be revised later, but that can be taken into account when it occurs; surely few would contend that a *downward* adjustment of benefits is so likely that the fully insured employee has not experienced an accretion in net worth. The Tax Adjustment Act of 1966, § 302(a), 42 U.S.C.A. § 428 (Supp. July 1966), provides that persons previously outside the social security system are to receive monthly benefits of thirty-five dollars for life on reaching the age of seventy-two. Would a CTB require such a person to include in income the fair market value of a comparable annuity (about $5000) as soon as he qualifies? *See* United States v. Drescher, 179 F.2d 863 (2d Cir.), *cert. denied*, 340 U.S. 821 (1950) (employee must include in gross income the present value to him of a nonassignable annuity contract purchased and held for him by his employer).

[69] Consider, for instance, the pricing of inventories. LIFO was used in valuing 20% of total closing inventories on tax returns filed for fiscal 1963. 25 J. TAXATION 267 (1966). If it is a "preference" that ought to be purged from the comprehensive tax base (as Hellmuth, *The Corporate Income Tax Base*, in 1 1959 COMPENDIUM 283, 312, suggests), it would broaden the base far more than many targets that are frequently mentioned. Other ambiguities in the term "accrual accounting" are reflected by the recent debates regarding prepaid income, reserves for estimated expenses, accrual of vacation pay, dealers' reserves, and disputed liabilities.

"exceptions," and to what general rule, I leave to scholars more skilled than I in this type of taxonomy.

One final thought: if for some reason that escapes me we can achieve a tax base that is devoid of preferences without hacking away at accounting methods, it will be necessary to define just what it is that is to enjoy this immunity from reform. The difficulty, of course, is that many statutory provisions that bear on the timing of income could be dressed up as "accounting methods" and transferred to Subchapter E (Accounting Periods and Methods of Accounting). Among these are most if not all of the business deductions mentioned earlier (research and development expenses, depreciation, and so on), the nonrecognition provisions discussed below, and such more esoteric provisions as section 77 (commodity loans), section 165(h) (disaster losses), and section 165(e) (theft losses).[70]

D. Unrealized Appreciation

Appreciation in the value of the taxpayer's assets is not included in gross income under existing law until it has been "realized" by sale or other disposition. None of the proponents of a CTB, so far as I know, wants to substitute an annual net worth computation to take account each year of the taxpayer's increase or decrease in wealth.[71] I do not quarrel with this exemption of unrealized appreciation, but it unquestionably tolerates a "preference" and is inconsistent with the hope of achieving a tax base unsullied by human compromises. Although Henry Simons acknowledged that a yearly computation of the taxpayer's net worth was implied by his definition of income, and called the realization concept a "professional conspiracy against truth," [72] he thought that

[70] Compare the problem of distinguishing among "accounting method," "accounting practice," and "error" under sections 446 and 481. *See* Boughner, *Change in Accounting Method, Practice, or Correction of Error? The IRS Position*, 23 J. TAXATION 264 (1965).

[71] In 1937, however, an eminent committee that included the president of Equitable Life Assurance Society and a partner of Sullivan and Cromwell recommended an annual accrual of capital gains and losses; curiously, only the former chairman of the National Labor Relations Board objected to the taxation of "paper profits." TWENTIETH CENTURY FUND, INC., COMM. ON TAXATION, FACING THE TAX PROBLEM 476 n.15, 477, 490 (C. Shoup ed. 1937). Compare the stress on "realizable profits" and "realized cost savings" in E. EDWARDS & P. BELL, THE THEORY AND MEASUREMENT OF BUSINESS INCOME (1961).

[72] H. SIMONS, PERSONAL INCOME TAXATION 81 (1938). Referring to Seligman's insistence on realization as a condition to recognizing income while simultaneously favoring depreciation deductions (to which inventory write-downs and bad debt reserves might have been added), Simons said: "Surely no definition of income

no "workable scheme" could be devised to reach the theoretically correct result. He was not explicit about his reason for this conclusion, however, except for the statement that income taxation "simply must follow, in the main, the established procedures of accounting practice."[73]

Perhaps this source of "erosion" in the CTB is to be tolerated because of the difficulty of valuing the taxpayer's assets each year. In point of fact, of course, we somehow manage to value assets of almost every description in computing the gain or loss on taxable in-kind exchanges and in applying gift and death taxes; and Simons, like many other advocates of a CTB, wanted transfers by gift and at death to be treated as taxable realizations of gain, thus accepting the responsibility of valuing the assets at that

---

which admits 'mere value changes' only in one direction can well escape the fate of appearing ridiculous." *Id.* at 88. As to the phrase "inchoate income," coined by Seligman as a label for unrealized appreciation, Simons said that it "deserves prominent place among the curiosities of economic terminology." *Id.* at 87.

[73] *Id.* at 208. Thus, Simons in the end joined the "professional conspiracy against truth," or at least abdicated in favor of accounting procedures that he profoundly distrusted: "The reputable accountant never loses sight of the fact that his income statements are influential in matters of dividend policy. Income, for him, is perhaps only what may be reported safely to unsophisticated directors as income. He aims, it would seem, never to ascertain what income is, in any really definable sense, but rather to devise rules of calculation which will make the result a minimum or at least give large answers only in the future." *Id.* at 81. In point of fact, although some accountants may try to protect "unsophisticated directors" by refusing to count chickens before they are grandparents, others are told by their clients whether an optimistic or pessimistic income statement is wanted. *See* Briloff, *Needed: A Revolution in the Determination and Application of Accounting Principles*, 39 ACCOUNTING REV. 12 (1964); Cohen, *Accounting for Taxes, Finance, and Regulatory Purposes — Are Variances Necessary?*, 44 TAXES 780 (1966). Accounting principles often come in pairs or sets, from which management can select those that will yield the most useful financial statements. Consistency from year to year is about all that can be expected, and even this is not essential if the inconsistency is disclosed in a footnote.

As to the treatment of unrealized appreciation by accountants, it is interesting to compare the vigorous assertion that appreciation and depreciation in market values must be recognized in order to measure net revenue in W. PATON & R. STEVENSON, PRINCIPLES OF ACCOUNTING 238–43, 451–69 (1918), with Paton's equally firm assertion twenty years later that "appreciation in its various forms is not income." W. PATON & A. LITTLETON, AN INTRODUCTION TO CORPORATE ACCOUNTING STANDARDS 46, 62–63 (American Accounting Ass'n Monograph No. 3, 1940); *see Income Measurement in a Dynamic Economy*, in FIVE MONOGRAPHS ON BUSINESS INCOME 57 (S. Alexander ed. 1950) ("the accountant's use of realized rather than accrued gain is based principally on convenience"); Litherland, *Fixed Asset Replacement a Half Century Ago*, 26 ACCOUNTING REV. 475 (1951); AIA, STUDY GROUP ON BUSINESS INCOME, CHANGING CONCEPTS OF BUSINESS INCOME 23–24 (1952). For a contemporary proposal to take unrealized appreciation into account currently see E. EDWARDS & P. BELL, *supra* note 71, at 276–77.

time.[74] Moreover, once the giant step of taxing unrealized appreciation was taken for the first year, it would produce a grand list of values, and later changes in value might be satisfactorily approximated by index figures based on economic trends (subject to rebuttal evidence at the taxpayer's option). The first year, in other words, would be the hardest. At the very least, before accepting the "special exception" or "loophole" that is created by the exclusion of unrealized appreciation from gross income, the advocates of a CTB might be expected to examine the possibility of applying to this area the principle used elsewhere in the tax field: value those assets that *do* have an ascertainable market value, and hold the others in abeyance until valuation becomes feasible. This is what the proposed taxation of life insurance savings by requiring the annual increase in the policy's terminal reserve or cash surrender value to be reported would amount to.[75] If the exclusion of this type of unrealized appreciation erodes the tax base, what is the rationale for excluding other readily measurable appreciation?

Perhaps unrealized appreciation is to be excluded from the proposed CTB not because of anticipated difficulty in valuing assets but because "paper profits" produce no cash to pay the tax and may be wiped out in a later year. These are not untenable grounds for exempting unrealized appreciation, but they furnish equally persuasive support for other exclusions as well. One example: employees get no ready cash when their employer contributes on their behalf to a qualified pension or profit-sharing plan, and they will be involuntarily at the the risk of the market until the benefits are paid in cash. Why not, then, preserve the employee's right under existing law to exclude the employer's contribution from gross income; it is a "preference," to be sure, but so is the exclusion of unrealized appreciation. Indeed, if lack of cash and continued risk of the market are legitimate grounds for taking appreciation into income only when it is realized, why should we not amend existing law to allow employees to deduct or exclude from gross income their contributions to pension plans and their social security taxes? [76] The employee's claim is not properly answered by the assertion that he wants a "prefer-

[74] H. SIMONS, *supra* note 72, at 167.

[75] *See* Irenas, *Life Insurance Interest Income Under the Federal Income Tax*, 21 TAX L. REV. 297, 314 (1966).

[76] In computing "personal income," the National Income Division excludes *both* employee *and* employer contributions for social insurance. U.S. DEP'T OF COMMERCE, *supra* note 50, at 8.

ence" while the investor is getting only what natural law requires. The employee, in fact, is in the usual case asking only for postponement; under existing law, the investor's unrealized appreciation will be excluded from income permanently if he holds the property until death.

E. Realization of Gain or Loss on Transfer at Death or by Gift

Advocates of a CTB ordinarily propose to take account of unrealized appreciation and depreciation when property is transferred by gift or at death. In this way, they would convert the outright exemption enjoyed by such appreciation under existing law into a postponement provision. For a taxpayer who is fifty years old, a current increase in net worth would not be reported for twenty-four years if his life conforms to the 1958 Standard Ordinary Mortality Table; for thirty-five and sixty-five year-old taxpayers, the corresponding figures are thirty-seven and thirteen years. The value of postponing payment of a tax liability of 1,000 dollars for these periods of time, assuming various interest rates, is set out in the following table:

Years	*5%*	*10%*	*15%*	*20%*
13	$470	$710	$838	$906
24	690	898	965	988
37	836	971	994	999

If it is an unwarranted "preference" to allow employees to postpone the recognition of currently earned pensions and annuities until they start to receive payments on retiring from active service, realization at death also deserves the label "preference" even though it would constitute an important reform of existing law.

One need hardly add that the only version of realization at death that has been so far unveiled — the 1963 proposal of the Kennedy Administration — was a mere sieve when measured by the criterion of "treating all income alike." [77] Even this proposal,

[77] Some property was excluded entirely and granted a basis equal to its fair market value at death (personal residence and household effects); a carryover basis was provided for one-half the assets transferred to a surviving spouse; life insurance was not included; no provision was made for recapturing percentage depletion deductions in excess of the property's basis; and there was a minimum exemption (with a stepped-up basis) for $15,000 of unrealized appreciation. *Hearings on the President's 1963 Tax Message Before the House Committee on Ways and Means*, 88th Cong., 1st Sess., pt. 1, at 128–40 (1963). I do not quarrel with these ex-

however, encountered such heavy weather that it was replaced by a plan for a carryover of the decedent's basis, so that the gain would go untaxed until the taxpayer's heirs sold or exchanged the property in a market transaction. This modest suggestion — a "preference" proposed as a substitute for a "preference" that in turn would have only diluted a more formidable "preference"[78] — also failed to survive the House Ways and Means Committee's examination. Resistance to change in this area is so great that any reform, even a carryover of basis for inherited property, may be seen as a victory for the CTB ideal, justifying a ruthless elimination of "preferences" in other areas. A clear-eyed view of the landscape, however, would disclose that neither a carryover of basis nor realization at death would be more than a halfway house on the road to a truly comprehensive base.

F. Tax-Free Exchanges and Similar Transactions

In addition to exempting appreciation in the value of the taxpayer's property from his gross income if it is not realized by a sale or other disposition, existing law is riddled with provisions for the nonrecognition of the gain even if it is realized. These nonrecognition provisions, which may be regarded as "exceptions" in the sense that their repeal would result in taxability of the taxpayer's realized gain under section 61(a), are usually mandatory, but some are optional with the taxpayer. Among the most important are the following:

(*1*) section 351 (transfer of property to a controlled corporation);
(*2*) section 354 (exchange of stock or securities in a corporate reorganization, such as a merger or stock-for-stock acquisition);
(*3*) section 1031 (exchange of business or of investment property other than stock, securities, or inventory assets for other property "of a like kind," *e.g.*, an exchange of industrial equipment or of investment real estate);
(*4*) section 1033 (replacement of property lost by "involuntary conversion," such as condemnation or fire, with other property "similar or related in service or use"); and

---

emptions, but I should think they would be intolerable to anyone who worries about the erosion of the tax base resulting from the exclusion of welfare payments.

[78] Although it has been asserted that a carryover of basis "would accomplish the same result" as constructive realization at death, Somers, *The Case for a Capital Gain Tax at Death*, 52 A.B.A.J. 346, 347 (1966), they can be regarded as equivalents only if one assumes with Simons, *see* p. 958 & note 59 *supra*, that timing does not matter.

(5) section 1034 (sale of the taxpayer's principal residence at a gain if another residence is acquired within one year).

In addition to nonrecognition provisions, of which the foregoing are merely a sample, the Code contains a number of other provisions that operate similarly, though not under the same technical label. Examples are section 305, excluding stock dividends from gross income, and section 108, permitting the taxpayer to exclude income realized on the cancellation of his indebtedness for less than its face amount if he agrees to reduce the tax basis of his assets.

The policy underpinnings of these provisions are several in number, and they overlap in part. Some nonrecognition transactions are forced on the taxpayer, and some of these he may regard as misfortunes rather than profitable events. Whether the transaction is voluntary or not, he ordinarily either receives no cash or promptly uses any cash received to replace the assets that were disposed of, so that the imposition of a tax might compel him to sell other assets, to borrow, or to take some other inconvenient or uneconomic step. Often he does not wholly liquidate his economic interest in the assets given up, or he acquires an interest in similar property, so his profit is arguably a paper one. Another rationale for the nonrecognition provisions is a Congressional intent to encourage, or to eliminate barriers to, business adjustments, labor mobility, or other economic or personal behavior.

These all strike me as legitimate reasons for the nonrecognition provisions, and as to some transactions I find them persuasive or conclusive; but to those who envision a tax base without "preferences" or "exceptions," this attitude must seem fuzzy-minded if not downright pusillanimous. To be sure, the taxpayer's gain usually goes unrecognized only at the expense of a carryover of his basis, so that the unrecognized gain will be taken into account if he disposes of the property in a taxable transaction at a later date; but this postponement of income is itself a "preference." Moreover, nonrecognition in today's tax structure often leads to the exclusion of gain by reason of the stepped-up basis conferred on the property at death. Even if this "super-preference" were eliminated by a watertight requirement of realization of gain at death, however, the nonrecognition provisions would remain as an important source of "erosion."

Curiously, however, the nonrecognition provisions have been

little assailed by the advocates of a CTB. Criticism of details has been plentiful, but there has been no parallel in this area to the vigorous and nearly unanimous assault on such "preferences" as the exclusion of wage supplements or social security benefits. The economists, viewing the nonrecognition provisions from macroeconomic heights, may have thought them of minor importance; but it can be confidently predicted that their repeal would be as unpopular as restricting percentage depletion.[79] Even if the tax base were expanded by rules for realization of gain at death, the nonrecognition provisions would surely retain much of their appeal; indeed, given a choice, many individual taxpayers (as well as corporations and trusts) would undoubtedly prefer realization at death to a repeal of the nonrecognition provisions.

VI. The Taxable Unit

Before we can measure the "economic accretion" to which the "broad base" income tax is to be applied, we must specify the taxpaying unit whose economic betterment we want to measure. The "individual" income tax of existing law is not quite what its name implies; it is imposed on some income of trusts and estates, as well as on the income of individuals. Moreover, of the 64 million "individual" returns filed during 1965, 38 million were joint returns of married persons reporting their combined incomes.

For some purposes, the taxpayer is regarded by existing law as an isolated unit; thus, he must report gain realized on a sale of property even if the buyer is his wife or child. For other purposes, however, account is taken of the taxpayer's marital and family relationships: witness the separate rate structures for married couples, surviving spouses with dependent children, and heads of households; the dependency exemptions; the deductions allowed for medical expenses of the taxpayer's dependents and for alimony payments; the disallowance of losses on intrafamily transactions; and the effect of marriage on the numerous dollar and percentage limitations on deductions and other allowances. Our tax structure is similarly ambivalent as regards relations between the taxpayer and business or other economic entities in which he is financially interested. Sometimes the income of such entities is im-

[79] Since the average holding period for capital assets is probably longer for high bracket taxpayers, L. Seltzer, The Nature and Tax Treatment of Capital Gains and Losses 142–44 (1951) (1934–1937 statistics), the value of the realization concept, tax-free exchange provisions, and other postponement opportunities no doubt increases as we go up the economic ladder.

puted to the individual, sometimes his income and the entity's are computed as though they had nothing to do with each other, and sometimes there are separate computations that partially reflect an identity of economic interest. Although statutory provisions taking account of, or disregarding, family or economic relationships are sometimes said to "erode" the tax base, I think these claims stem from an inadequate analysis of the problem and that in reality the concept of a CTB is quite independent of the choice of taxpaying units.

A. *Family Relationships*

To begin with, I find nothing in the CTB concept that leads inexorably, or even points vaguely, to the conclusion that the income of individuals should be taxed, rather than the income of married couples, families, or households, or that tells us anything about the extent to which tax rates should take account of marriage bonds or family responsibilities. Since the tax base could be enlarged to include every item that constitutes "income" under the Haig-Simons definition even though the rate structure differentiated between single persons and married couples, why is the income-splitting joint return of existing law classified as a "leakage" or source of "erosion" by some advocates of a CTB? [80]

[80] *E.g.*, Pechman, *Erosion of the Individual Income Tax*, 10 NAT'L TAX J. 1, 21 (1957); Heller, *The Federal Income Tax and the Working Man*, in CIO CONFERENCE ON TAXATION 21, 23 (1953). Pechman, however, points out that the income-splitting issue "cannot be resolved on a priori grounds," and hence offers alternative calculations of the revenue yield obtainable by eliminating leakages, dependent on whether income-splitting is permitted or not. *What Would a Comprehensive Individual Income Tax Yield?*, in 1 1959 COMPENDIUM 251, 276. As pointed out in the text, however, an admission that the Haig-Simons definition is compatible with a structure that reduces the tax liability when a wealthy bachelor gets married is a dangerous concession for the advocates of a CTB. It clearly implies that the Haig-Simons definition is equally compatible with other adjustments of the tax liability to the taxpayer's marital or family status.

Simons himself was ambivalent on this issue. He asserted that "it would be hard to maintain that the raising of children is not a form of consumption on the part of parents" and that consequently no more should be allowed than "small, fixed credits" for minor children and other dependents who are incapable of self-support. H. SIMONS, *supra* note 72, at 140, 141. At the same time, however, he conceded, *id.* at 137–38, that:

> It seems reasonable enough that the credits for, at least, minor dependents should vary directly with the family income. This might be arranged — as indeed was done under the German *Reichseinkommensteuer* — by providing minimum and maximum credits per child, together with a credit expressed as a percentage of income between those limits. It may also seem reasonable that adult members of a taxpayer's household should be taxed with respect to that part of the joint consumption expenses attributable to them (less contributions by them), with deduction of the amounts so imputed in determining the taxable income of the householder. Consistency, of course, would

Although they are not as explicit on this point as one would wish, their objection to income-splitting evidently is that it violates their theory that the income tax should not take account of the way taxpayers choose to spend their income. In this view, I take it, a single man's tax should not be reduced by his acquisition of a wife any more than by his acquisition of a yacht.

This is one way of looking at life, of course, but it is surely not the only one, and others might conclude that tax distinctions based on marriage or other family responsibilities are of a different order from those based on the taxpayer's other expenditure choices. And if it be admitted that a CTB does not forbid taking account of family responsibilities by variations in the rate structure, I perceive no reason why a CTB is not equally consistent with the use of exclusions, deductions, or credits as the means of achieving the desired differentials.

In fact, even those who find it difficult or impossible to distinguish between the taxpayer's support of his wife and children and his other "personal" expenditures should not, in my opinion, move directly to the conclusion that all tax variations based on family responsibilities must be extirpated. An intervening question must be answered: *whose* income is being used for the "consumption" we are talking about? It is at least arguable that what we choose to call the husband's income is not "his" to the extent that he is required by law to use it for the support of his wife or children — that he is merely a conduit pro tanto, so that this portion of his earnings should be reported by, and taxed to, the wife or child. If married couples think of themselves as equally entitled to their combined income, how do the tax rates applicable to joint returns "erode" the tax base? If the husband's income is 25,000 dollars and the wife's zero, their tax on a joint return is less than a single person must pay on 25,000 dollars; but it is the same as the tax on two single persons with 12,500 dollars of income each.

Some commentators compare the husband with 25,000 dollars of income to the bachelor with the same income, saying that they have merely chosen to spend their money in different ways, and that their choices are irrelevant to a tax on *disposable* income. Others may find it more persuasive to compare the married couple to two unmarried persons with 12,500 dollars of income each; whether the couple resides in a community property state or not,

require the authorization of generous deductions with respect to amounts contributed to the support of persons outside the household.

marriage creates emotional, social, and legal claims so that the husband's salary is not "his" in the same sense that the salary of an unmarried taxpayer with no close relatives belongs to him. On this theory, if there are children, part of the husband's income "belongs" to them, not to him. Laymen are usually more legalistic than lawyers, and this bias may lead them to emphasize the husband's "right" to his salary and other income; but the insights of domestic life ought to dispel this preoccupation with legal concepts.

So far as I can tell, its advocates think that a CTB is consistent with allowing alimony to be deducted by the husband and reported by the ex-wife. If this is not a "leakage," would it be equally consistent with the Haig-Simons definition to allow a taxpayer to deduct amounts paid for the support of his wife and children, provided these amounts were reported by the recipient? Like alimony, these obligations stem from the fateful, but voluntary, decision to marry; and in both cases the taxpayer may have married in haste only to repent at leisure. Perhaps the tolerance shown toward alimony reflects the fact that the amount to be paid — the cost of support — has been fixed by an arm's-length agreement or by a court, while there is no such reliable basis for allocating a part of the husband's income to his wife or children during the pendency of the marriage; this ground would imply that some of the husband's income *ought* to be deductible by him and taxed to his wife or children, if only a satisfactory measure of the obligation of support were at hand. If so, it might be better to do what we can to allocate something (whether by a formal deduction coupled with inclusion in the recipient's income, as with alimony, or by some other means, such as a manipulation of the rate structure, exemption, or credit) rather than do nothing at all. In any event, tolerance of the alimony deduction suggests a sound, if unacknowledged, lack of assurance in the family-as-consumption theory — an implicit admission that support of one's family, though undertaken voluntarily,[81] should not be classed with the taxpayer's other consumption expenditures.

I do not mean to suggest that the joint return rate schedule, the dependency exemption, or any other structural provision of this area is immune to criticism or preferable to alternatives. What I do assert, however, is that the concept of a CTB is of no assistance in selecting the taxpaying unit. A decision to include every dollar

[81] It might also be noted here that a legal duty of support may devolve involuntarily on the taxpayer, for example in the case of indigent parents.

of economic betterment in someone's gross income does not help us to designate the appropriate someone. And a statutory provision can be an "exception" or a "preference" only if we have an agreed-upon standard.

B. Partnerships, Corporations, and Trusts

The ambiguity of the term "income" is encountered again when we ask if a taxpayer enjoys a "net accretion to" his "economic power" (Haig's formulation) when a partnership, trust, corporation, or other entity in which he is financially interested engages in profitable transactions. In the case of partnerships, the Internal Revenue Code requires each partner to report his share of the firm's profits, whether it is distributed to him or not. Ordinarily, of course, he has the legal right to compel a distribution, but an exercise of this right would often disrupt the business and his relations with his partners; and sometimes the partnership agreement permits a distribution of profits only by majority or unanimous vote of the partners. Since the Internal Revenue Code takes no account of practical or legal restrictions on the partner's right to withdraw his share of the firm's income, he is in effect taxed on "economic enhancement" rather than on the amount available to him for personal expenditures.

A shareholder of a corporation, however, is not taxed on its income until it is distributed to him, and this means no tax at all at the shareholder level if he holds the stock until death. (The corporation, of course, is taxed on its income as realized; but the aggregate burden of a corporate tax on the corporation's income and a personal tax on such gains as are distributed or otherwise realized by the shareholder may exceed or fall short of, but will almost certainly not correspond to, the tax that would have been paid if the same income had been realized by a partnership or individual proprietorship.) In contrast to the partnership, then, the corporation shields the shareholder against the individual income tax so long as the income is accumulated. And it does this even if the shareholder owns all of the stock and can withdraw the profits at will; spendable receipts are what count, not economic enhancement or even legal control over the profits. Natural law does not dictate this distinction between partnerships and corporations; in the case of two categories of corporations — foreign personal holding companies and foreign corporations realizing Subpart F income — the shareholder *is* taxed on his share of the corporation's undistributed income. Moreover, the existence of section

531 is a constant reminder of the intimate relationship between a corporation's profits and the tax status of its shareholders.

Trusts and estates fall between partnerships and corporations as respects the tax treatment of accumulated income: sometimes it is taxed to the beneficiaries even though not distributed to them (as with partners), but sometimes it is not taxed to them until distribution (as with shareholders). There are also circumstances in which trust income is taxed to the grantor of the trust, even though it cannot be distributed to him, because of the "non-economic" satisfactions he obtains by dedicating the income to the beneficiaries of the trust.[82]

In short, in its treatment of the taxpayer's financial interest in business and other entities, existing law wobbles between spendable receipts and economic enhancement as the criterion of income, and occasionally it fixes instead on vicarious enjoyment as controlling. We are sometimes told that some minor threads in this tangled web of rules are "preferences" that "erode" the tax base, the implicit premise being that the CTB concept implies a set of rules governing the attribution of entity income to the persons beneficially interested. Despite these fragmentary announcements, I know of no attempt to explain why a CTB is consistent with some attribution rules and not with others, nor any effort to spin out the implications that are thought to reside in this concept by systematically identifying the provisions in today's tax law that would have to be changed to achieve a CTB.

If corporate stock owned by the taxpayer were to be valued at the beginning and end of each taxable period in order to take the net accretion in unrealized gain or loss into account, as the Haig-Simons formulation seems to require, no other steps to reflect the taxpayer's interest in the corporation would be required. If unrealized appreciation or depreciation is to be disregarded, however, we might expect the advocates of a CTB to explore the milder measure of imputing the realized corporate income to the shareholders. There are obstacles in the way of doing so, of course, and the separate corporate tax may be viewed as rough compensation for failing to tax the shareholders; but this apology is just another way of saying that a CTB can be no more than a faintly flickering, far-off ideal. As to trusts, I presume (in the absence of an unequivocal statement by the CTB experts) that beneficiaries are to be taxed on income that is allocated to them, whether distributed or not. The status of the undistributed income of dis-

[82] *See* pp. 946–47 *supra* on the relationship of vicarious enjoyment to a CTB.

cretionary trusts, under the Haig-Simons formulation, is less clear. Perhaps it is income without a taxpayer, to be held in abeyance until the beneficiary who will receive it can be identified and taxed. There is little justification for taxing it to the fiduciary except as an interim measure, to be followed by an adjustment (additional tax or refund) when the real party in interest becomes identifiable. To the economists, this may seem obvious enough; but I suspect that the ABA Tax Section's Committee on Substantive Tax Reform will not be very comfortable with this application of the principle of "taxing all income equally."

Without claiming prescience, I venture to predict that many advocates of a CTB will draw back from the logical consequences of the idea that "economic enhancement" should be taxed wherever it can be identified, and will propose or acquiesce in an exception for the undistributed income of corporations and trusts. The justification that is likely to be offered for this exception is that the undistributed income of these entities is not presently available for expenditure by their shareholders or beneficiaries (except by selling or borrowing against their interests), and that it may never be distributed to them because it remains at the risk of the entity's activities. Fair enough. But cannot the same be said of the employer's contribution to a qualified pension plan, or even of the employee's own contribution if it is mandatory? And would the enemies of preferences be equally complacent if the personal holding company provisions were amended to permit the personal service income of movie stars — or of law professors and factory workers — to be accumulated in a corporation free of the individual income tax? My bones are not sensitive to the threat of rainy weather, but they tell me that *this* proposal would "erode" the tax base. But why would it, if an incorporated storekeeper is not taxed on *his* corporation's earnings until they are distributed to him?

Although the CTB concept thus implies a group of changes in the individual tax structure that are much more far-reaching than its advocates have acknowledged, it leaves us without guidance in a closely related area of the "taxable unit" problem, the separate corporation income tax. Just as the Haig-Simons formulation requires the taxable period to be specified without shedding any light on the criteria to be used in fixing a period, so it seems to require the taxable unit whose economic accretion is at stake to be prescribed by criteria that are not part of the definition of income. If the unit is selected on the basis of such "outside" criteria, however, it evidently follows that we can have a CTB whether corporations are taxed as separate entities or not. If so, the assertion that the dividends-received exclusion erodes the tax base [83] is puzzling: why is it not a partial nullification of a separate corporate tax that was not a necessary part of a CTB to begin with?

More important, is the tax base "eroded" if corporations are classified into categories (ordinary business corporations, personal holding companies, insurance companies, commercial banks, and so on) with the income of each category being computed and taxed in a manner — and at a rate — thought to be suited to its function in the nation's economy? If all incorporated taxpayers must be treated alike in order to achieve a CTB, today's rules will have to be drastically reformed at a variety of points that have not yet been identified for us by the CTB advocates. If, on the other hand, the aim of "taxing all income alike" is compatible with separate taxing systems or separate rate structures for insurance companies, personal holding companies, mutual savings banks, and commercial banks, I do not see why this aim is not equally consistent with taxing mining corporations differently from manufacturers, business executives differently from ministers, and married persons differently from bachelors.

VII. Conclusions

This attempt to work out the implications of the "no preference, comprehensive base" approach in a systematic way, and thus to ascertain where it would take us if it were converted from a slogan into a program for action, has led me to these conclusions:

(*1*) The systematic elimination of "preferences" in order to achieve a truly "comprehensive" base would require many more fundamental changes in existing law than are usually acknowledged. Among the areas that would be drastically affected by a whole-hearted use of the Haig-Simons definition are: mortality gains on life insurance; governmental benefits furnished in kind or in services; recoveries in suits for personal injury or death; charitable gifts to individuals; personal and dependency exemptions; tax-exempt organizations; the investment credit; deduction or rapid amortization of business assets; depreciation below

[83] *E.g.*, Pechman, *Erosion of the Individual Income Tax*, 10 Nat'l Tax J. 1, 12 (1957). I mean to imply not that the dividend exclusion is a desirable provision, but that the CTB concept sheds no light on the issue.

market values; inventory pricing; accounting methods; and tax-free exchanges. Some of these areas seem to have been disregarded by the proponents of the CTB, and others have not received the attention their importance deserves.

(2) At many points, the most enthusiastic proponents of a CTB have drawn back from its implications: they almost always advocate the exclusion from gross income of unrealized annual net worth increases, gifts and bequests, and imputed income from personal services, and support allowances for such personal expenditures as charitable contributions and medical care; and some also favor provisions to encourage investment, such as the investment credit or rapid depreciation. Their reasons for departing from the Haig-Simons definition are, in my opinion, no different from the reasons that are offered in support of all of the "preferences" of existing law: the necessity or desirability of avoiding difficulties in valuation or enforcement, of stimulating economic growth, of encouraging behavior thought to be socially useful, of alleviating economic hardship, of retaining the freedom of choice that results from use of tax concessions rather than some other governmental mechanism, or of pursuing other social policies. I dare say that they would give similar reasons for favoring perpetuation of many other preferences of existing law if they were required to express an opinion on all of those mentioned in this article.[84] In short, they harbor, in my opinion, the same attitude

[84] *See* L. Eisenstein, The Ideologies of Taxation 193, 197–98 (1961):

> Scholars who are hot for certainties . . . . must have answers if they are to be happy, and the answers must derive from some uniform standard which is objectively applied. Besides, the term "loophole" has become too charged with emotional overtones for the staid world of tax scholarship. . . . And so the scholars have turned to other words that are supposedly less partial and hence more informative.
>
> There are enough words to please everybody who wishes to appear impersonal and detached. Instead of loopholes the enlightened now speak of "erosions" of the tax base. Or they refer to special treatments and special provisions, special deductions and special exclusions, special exceptions and special accommodations, differentials and preferentials, discrepancies and discriminations, openings and leakages, tax shelters and tax havens, tax favors and tax advantages, tax mitigations and tax concessions. All these words, as well as others now in fashion, disclose a marked capacity for devising polite synonyms. They produce an air of impartial judgment. To call percentage depletion a loophole is to indulge in a personal prejudice. To call it an erosion is to make an objective appraisal . . . .
>
> My inquiry into loopholes confirms anew a familiar truth. Better answers require wiser questions. Ultimately dispensations for certain taxpayers are condemned, not because they conform to some definition of a loophole, but because they are considered undesirable for various reasons. . . . We cannot learn very much by asking what is a loophole. The only meaningful questions are those which focus on the precise purposes and effects of a dispensation. Of course, the answers will vary, for they will reflect different standards of good and evil . . . . No larger wisdom is discernible.

The following extract from *Report Supporting Resolutions on Substantive Tax*

toward the Haig-Simons definition of income that Congress is said to exhibit toward our progressive rate schedule: a declaration of faith, combined with advocacy or tolerance of numerous exceptions, each of which inures to the benefit of a "special" group of taxpayers.

(*3*) If I am right in asserting that most professed supporters of the CTB concept favor a host of important departures from the Haig-Simons standard, there ought to be an equally drastic revision of their rhetoric, including a renunciation of the claim that we can or should eliminate all, or even most, "preferences" and "special provisions" from the Internal Revenue Code. This means not that all provisions of existing law are equally good, but rather that we cannot avoid an examination of each one on its merits in a discouragingly inconclusive process that can derive no significant assistance from a "no preference" presumption that would at best be applied only on a wholly selective basis. Put another way, there are "preferences" and "preferences"; some are objectionable, some are tolerable, some are unavoidable, and some are indispensable. A truly "comprehensive" base, in short, would be a disaster.

It may be argued that the rhetoric of the CTB approach does not matter; we are used to political slogans and exhortations that contain a kernel of truth and do no harm even though they promise more than they can deliver. What concerns me is that the rhetoric

---

Reform, BULL. ABA SECTION OF TAXATION, July 1963 (Annual Report), at 5, 12–13, would have been admirable grist for Eisenstein's mill:

> There can be no wavering from a resolute determination that what is really income must be taxed without exception. Once there is a compromise with principle or a yielding to pressure to admit a special exception, the hole in the dike widens. All efforts at real reform go for nought. Having stated this broad proposition, however, one should note certain possible exceptions: for example, certain tax exempt organizations could continue their exempt status as under present rules; there could be a deferment of recognition of income in certain exchanges and corporate reorganizations; and such deferment might be extended to cover sales of property followed by reinvestment in comparable property.

I suspect that much of the enthusiasm for rigorous "broad base" reform among academicians would prove equally evanescent if subjected to cross-examination. Take, for example, these recommendations in JOINT ECONOMIC COMMITTEE, 89TH CONG., 1ST SESS., FISCAL POLICY ISSUES OF THE COMING DECADE (Comm. Print 1965): "broad-based, flat tax on all gross income" (Brown, in *id.* at 11, 14); "an adjusted gross income tax if possible" (Buchanan, in *id.* at 19, 21); "a general broadening of the tax base to include all forms of income" (Eisner, in *id.* at 42, 44); "[a tax] preferably on adjusted gross income with minor exemptions" (Groves, in *id.* at 61). I suggest that these shorthand expressions would, if expanded, translate into a somewhat broader tax base than we now have, but with a host of major and minor exclusions and deductions retained, rather than into a rigorous application of the Haig-Simons definition.

will foster changes in the tax structure not because they are desirable in themselves, but merely because they will broaden the base. Since I am convinced that a full-fledged CTB will, and should, remain miles away, I see no automatic advantage in moving a few feet in its direction. It is a truism that existing law bears more heavily on earned income than on income from investments, and I venture the judgment that the base-broadening provisions that are most likely to be enacted in the pursuit of a CTB would enlarge rather than narrow this disparity.

(*4*) To the extent that a departure from the Haig-Simons definition is compelled by administrative difficulties (valuation, enforcement, and the like) rather than by its contribution to a social or economic goal, the advocates of the CTB have given too little attention to the paradox of the "second best."[85] I take it that one of the virtues they see in the Haig-Simons definition is that its rigorous application would lead to an "ideal" distribution of the tax burden, by measuring the ability to pay that arises from "income" in the most accurate way.[86] If this is their view, it would be appropriate to quantify the tax burden distribution that would result from a rigorous application of the definition by taking into account, at the best estimates available, such difficult items as annual increases in net worth, imputed income from personal assets, housewives' services, and gifts and bequests. Even if the valuation problems are too formidable to justify inclusion of these items in the tax structure itself on a taxpayer-by-taxpayer basis, a rough and ready estimate would be better than nothing

[85] Lipsey & Lancaster, *The General Theory of Second Best*, 24 REV. ECON. STUDIES 11 (1956).

[86] *See* H. SIMONS, *supra* note 72, at 105–06: "Since the devices of accounting and tax legislation contemplate only very rough approximation to income, it is decisively important to see behind these methods of calculation an 'ideal income,' calculable by different and less practicable methods. Only on the basis of some broader conception is it possible to criticize and evaluate merely practicable procedures and to consider fruitfully the problem of bettering the system of presumptions." *Accord*, R. MUSGRAVE, THE THEORY OF PUBLIC FINANCE 165 (1959). (But Musgrave, *id.* at 165, refers to the "excellent analysis" of the income concept in N. KALDOR, AN EXPENDITURE TAX (1955), which concludes, at 70, that "the problem of *defining* individual income, quite apart from any problem of practical measurement, appears in principle insoluble.") *See* White, *Consistent Treatment of Items Excluded and Omitted from the Individual Income Tax Base*, in 1 1959 COMPENDIUM 317 ("Aside from practical difficulties in administration, the base of the individual income tax ought never, or hardly ever, to be determined on any criterion other than that of consistency with the economic [Simons] definition of personal income"); H. BRAZER, A PROGRAM FOR FEDERAL TAX REVISION 7 (1960); Blum, *Federal Income Tax Reform — Twenty Questions*, 41 TAXES 672, 680 (1963); authorities cited note 10 *supra*.

for the kind of macroeconomic model that I am suggesting. Having worked out in this way an approximation of the "ideal" distribution of the tax burden, it would be possible to test alternative reform programs to see which comes closest to the "ideal."[87] The "best" practical program, on this theory, would not be the one that eliminated the *most* "preferences," but the one whose tax burden distribution was closest to the ideal.

This method of judging the proximity of a proposal to the professed ideal would recognize that unavoidable preferences (those compelled by limitations in valuation techniques, anticipated problems in compliance, and similar factors) might be offset by deliberately preserving (or even creating) other preferences. It has often been pointed out that the elimination of an exclusion would serve no purpose if it is so equally distributed that the tax burden would be unaffected by the tidier system resulting from the change. I am suggesting nothing more than a generalized application of this well-known principle. If the tax base is to continue to exclude gifts and bequests, annual net worth increases, and imputed income from personal property, for example, the continued exclusion of unemployment compensation, social security payments, and similar items may distribute the tax burden more equitably (using the Haig-Simons definition as the touchstone) than a reform program that adds the latter category of items to the base.

---

[87] Such a study would employ the computer techniques pioneered by J. Pechman and described in his A NEW TAX MODEL FOR REVENUE ESTIMATING (1965), and applied in B. OKNER, INCOME DISTRIBUTION AND THE FEDERAL INCOME TAX (1966). The study proposed by the ABA Committee on Substantive Tax Reform of the Section of Taxation, 90 ABA REP. 289, 295 (1965), will be a step in the right direction if it is rigorous enough in its conception of a "broad income tax base." The proposed study ought to examine the effect of "preferences" on both "horizontal" and "vertical" equity (that is, within each income bracket and as among brackets, respectively). There may be "preferences" that, taken in combination, produce a distribution of tax liabilities within certain brackets comparable to the burden that would result from a more rigorous application of the Haig-Simons definition; and other combinations of "preferences" may have a similar effect as among income brackets. Finally, there may be more elaborate combinations that would perform the same function simultaneously for both the horizontal and vertical planes.

I do not wish to minimize the difficulties; to satisfy everyone, the study would have to offer a series of "ideal" distributions of the tax burden, each based on its own assumptions about the proper way to resolve the definitional issues in the concept of income. Moreover, since we lack information on the size and distribution of many items that are not now reflected on tax returns, a good deal of estimating ingenuity would be required. One of the dangers, of course, in the availability of *some* information in a form that permits easy computer use is that items that are not "machine-handleable" will be disregarded. *See* Spengler, *Machine-Made Justice: Some Implications*, 28 LAW & CONTEMP. PROB. 36, 44–45 (1963).

(5) There are many problem areas in which the search for "preferences" is doomed to fail because we cannot confidently say which provisions are "rules" and which are "exceptions." In these areas, we cannot comply with Blum's advice to "lean over backward" to avoid "preferences"[88] because, in the absence of a generally acceptable or scientifically determinable vertical, we cannot know whether we are leaning forward or backward. The central source of difficulty is the fact that the income tax structure cannot be discovered, but must be constructed; it is the final result of a multitude of debatable judgments.

If we were dealing not with an income tax but with a tax whose label described its reach with greater precision, an "exception" would be easier to identify. For example, in constructing a poll tax, we would have at the outset a consensus on what constitutes a natural person whose "head" is to be taxed. To be sure, even here there would be marginal cases — conceived but unborn children, persons who have been legally declared dead but who reappear, Siamese twins, and so on. These peripheral cases aside, a consensus on the base to which the tax is to be applied would be feasible, and it would warrant the use of terms like "exception" and "preference" to describe proposals to exempt from the tax such persons as children, foreign tourists and diplomats, or incompetents. And one could say of proposals to exempt soldiers on combat duty, Boy Scout leaders, or persons over the age of sixty-five or blind that, however meritorious such "preferences" might be when considered individually, there would be no satisfactory criteria for exempting one group of meritorious persons while refusing to exempt other persons such as Peace Corps workers, nurses, or the unemployed. Under these circumstances, it could be persuasively argued that a "pure" tax base would be a fortress that could be effectively defended against all comers, no matter how appealing their claims. When we turn to the field of income taxation, however, we do not begin with a consensus on the meaning of income, but with a myriad of arguments about what should be taxed, when, and to whom. The CTB concept is simply irrelevant to many of these issues — the taxable unit, the taxable period, the personal-business borderline, and others — and hence, notwithstanding the contrary assumption of some commentators, it can make no contribution to the elimination of "preferences" from these areas.

[88] *See* note 3 *supra*.

[3]

IN DEFENSE OF AN INCOME CONCEPT

R. A. Musgrave *

In reply to Professor Bittker's challenge to the advocates of a comprehensive tax base, Professor Musgrave rejects what he considers to be Professor Bittker's ad hoc approach. He argues that Professor Bittker's principal reason for denigrating the usefulness of the accretion concept as a basis of tax reform is that it is not 100 percent effective in solving all of the problems. Professor Musgrave insists that recognition of a basic income concept is prerequisite to the construction of an equitable income tax and believes that the accretion concept offers the best formulation. On most major issues this concept points to the proper solution, even though it may have to be qualified by considerations of administrative feasibility or, in some instances, may have to give way to other policy objectives.

IN his recent piece,[1] Professor Bittker launches a frontal attack on income tax reform aimed at realizing a closer approximation to the accretion concept. He feels that the accretion concept of income has little normative value, and gives little help in the practice of income definition. In fact, we are told that nothing is to be gained by trying to define a generalized income concept. Rather, treatment of particular income items should be considered provision by provision, with each item dealt with on its merits. The drive towards a comprehensive (*i.e.*, consumption plus accretion) base is rejected as leading to undesirable results, and should be replaced by an ad hoc approach.

Professor Bittker's discussion is helpful in examining technical issues and in noting that implementation of a normative income tax is not that simple. There is a place for the skeptic, but he greatly overstates his case. His counsel of despair is unjustified and damaging to income tax reform. While the accretion concept does not answer all problems (and what policy rule ever does?) it points to the solution of most specific issues of income definition; and though the concept has to be qualified in application by considerations of administrative feasibility, and equity must give way at times to other policy objectives, construction of a fair income tax is well-nigh impossible without the guidance of a basic income concept.

* Professor of Economics in the Faculty of Arts and Sciences and in the Law School, Harvard University. Diplom Volksw., Heidelberg, 1933; Ph.D., Harvard, 1937.

[1] Bittker, *A "Comprehensive Tax Base" as a Goal of Income Tax Reform*, 80 HARV. L. REV. 925 (1967) [hereinafter cited as Bittker].

I. Principles

While Professor Bittker's argument is largely in terms of specific points of income definition, the basic theme is that there is no need for a general income concept on which to build a rational income tax system. This, I believe, is an untenable position.

A. Income v. Consumption as an Index of Equality

Everyone will agree that taxation should not be used as a punitive device to damage one or another group of the population. Taxation should not be a tool of personal discrimination. This minimal condition for equitable taxation could be met by a random, lottery-type distribution of the tax burden, but no intelligent observer would be satisfied with this. An equitable distribution of the tax burden is more than a nonarbitrary one. It is necessary that the tax bill be allocated according to an equitable and positively defined pattern.

Two requirements follow. First, people in equal position should pay equal amounts of tax; second, people in unequal position should pay different amounts related in a meaningful fashion to difference in position. These two requirements are referred to respectively as "horizontal" and "vertical" equity. While vertical equity remains controversial,[2] few would disagree with the horizontal equity rule, and I assume that Professor Bittker as well accepts this norm. The question, however, is how the concept of equal position — the "index of equality" — is to be defined. This choice of index is not a purely objective matter. It depends on what society considers to be equitable, and how it wishes to pose the problem. At the same time, it does not follow that "anything goes." Certain criteria are more meaningful than others, and any one criterion must be interpreted consistently once it is chosen. In particular, two approaches must be distinguished.

The most obvious approach is to look for a general index of

[2] The more controversial problem of vertical equity is left aside in this discussion. Whether taxes should be regressive, proportional, or progressive (and how much so) depends essentially on society's view as to the desirable state of income distribution. Such at least is the case in the context of the "ability-to-pay" approach to taxation, which underlies this discussion. While we shall note that the definition of the tax base has important bearing on the vertical distribution of the tax burden (see pp. 51–52, *infra*), we need not consider here what the "proper" vertical distribution would be.

economic well-being which broadly measures a person's capacity to contribute or to "sacrifice" on behalf of government. This is the tradition of taxation according to ability to pay.[3] In colonial times, gross produce of land served as a more or less meaningful measure of well-being, and other simple proxies, such as the number of windows, are cited by tax historians. But today's economic society is too complex to permit so simple a solution. A more comprehensive criterion is needed, and income is the most appropriate choice.

Alternatively, one might argue, following Hobbes, that the taxpayer should contribute in line with what he "takes out of the pot," and not what he "contributes to society." The tax in effect becomes a fine on consumption (the sin of nonaccumulation) with equal taxes being paid by equal sinners. This view has considerable merit in the context of growth policy, provided that full employment is assured, but it seems less plausible as an equity rule. Certainly it is inferior to income if equality is to be defined in terms of general economic capacity.[4]

Nevertheless, there is no absolute standard by which the choice between the income or consumption index can be made. Reasonable men may differ on whether equal position should be defined in terms of capacity (income) or consumption. The choice is essentially one of value judgment. But whichever view is taken, the equitable tax should be a personal tax, assessed in global fashion on the taxpayer's total base. Thus, the proper counterpart to the personal income tax is not a sales, but a personal ex-

[3] This discussion, like the current debate over income tax reform and Professor Bittker's paper, is in terms of a "fair" distribution of the tax burden, as developed by the "ability-to-pay" school of thought. Thus the problem is dealt with independent of the expenditure side of budget policy. Alternatively, taxes could be considered as payment for public services rendered. This "benefit" approach has its advantages for purposes of economic analysis as it relates both sides of budget policy. *See generally* R. MUSGRAVE, THE THEORY OF PUBLIC FINANCE, pts. I & II (1959). However, the allocation function of tax policy (*i.e.*, allocating the opportunity cost of public services) must then be supplemented by the distribution function, which provides for corrections in the distribution of income. In the latter context the basic issue of ability to pay reemerges. If the "fair" tax distribution is disassociated from expenditure benefits, it becomes simply a matter of distribution.

[4] To tax consumption is to tax income while exempting saving. But why should saving be excluded from the measure of economic capacity? A person's choice between consumption and saving, after all, is his own decision. If *X* and *Y* both receive an income of $10,000, they may both choose between consuming or saving $10,000, as they wish. While their choices may differ, this does not void the equality of their prechoice position and hence their ability to pay taxes.

penditure tax, and quite parallel problems (*e.g.*, the need for a central concept) arise in its implementation.[5]

B. *Income as a Measure of Ability to Pay*

Fortunately, the choice between income and consumption is not at issue in this discussion. Historical development, if not logic, has made the choice in favor of income. I have no complaint about this, and Professor Bittker seems satisfied as well to proceed on this basis. Our ways part, however, when it comes to the question of how income should be defined and, indeed, whether it should be defined at all.

Whereas the choice between income and consumption as the appropriate tax base involves value judgment, there is a clear case for the Henry Simons income definition once the income alternative is chosen. It is this definition on which the case for a comprehensive income tax is based. Professor Bittker's impression[6] that the advocates of the comprehensive base waver between various income concepts — including aggregate gross income minus certain expenses, personal income as defined by the Department of Commerce, as well as the accretion concept — is mistaken. As the literature clearly shows, it is the accretion concept which people have in mind, and not the other two, which have no normative value.

According to this definition, income equals gain in net worth plus consumption during a given period.[7] What matters is *total* income thus defined. No distinction is to be made between either sources or uses of income. Gains may be factor earnings (*e.g.*, wages, interest, rent) in the economist's sense, or they may be mere transfers (*e.g.*, gifts or gambling gains); they may be expected or unexpected, irregular or regular, accrued or realized, from business or accident, and so on and so forth. All that matters is that there exists a gain which gives rise to consumption

[5] *See generally* N. KALDOR, AN EXPENDITURE TAX (1955).

[6] *See* Bittker 931–33.

[7] This concept was first proposed by Georg Schanz, in *Der Einkommensbegriff und die Einkommensteuergesetze*, 13 FINANZ ARCHIV 1 (1896), and introduced into American discussion in THE FEDERAL INCOME TAX (R. Haig ed. 1921). It was developed systematically by Henry Simons in PERSONAL INCOME TAXATION (1938), and FEDERAL TAX REFORM (1950). *See also* Pechman, *Erosion of the Individual Income Tax*, 10 NAT'L TAX J. 1 (1957), which laid the foundation for the subsequent discussion of a comprehensive tax base. Alternatively, income may be defined as potential consumption, *i.e.*, actual current consumption plus consumption foregone, as reflected in increased net worth. *See* H. SIMONS, PERSONAL INCOME TAXATION 55 (1938), where accumulation is deflated by consumer goods price increases.

or to increase in net worth. Similarly, it is left to the recipient whether he wishes to use his gain for one or another type of present consumption, or whether he wishes to postpone consumption and save.[8]

While income thus defined (accretion plus consumption) resembles the concept of income as used in economic analysis of capital theory, this is not what gives it legitimacy as an index of equality in the equity context. Indeed, the sum of individual incomes as defined under accretion exceeds national income in the economist's sense. National income excludes transfers, but gifts are accretion to the donee without reducing the income of the donor. The defense for the accretion plus consumption concept as an index of equality must rest on its superiority as an equity concept, not as a tool of economic theory. The most the economist can claim is that the meaning of accretion as an equity concept is appreciated more fully if the economic analysis of income is understood.

The merit of the concept may be demonstrated by considering two of the more popular arguments for discrimination. Traditionally a case has been made for taxing "unearned" (capital) income more heavily than "earned" (labor) income. Based initially on the labor theory of value, whereby labor only earns enough to sustain itself and hence cannot pay taxes, it was reformulated later with reference to the disutility of labor which presumably is absent in the earning of capital income. Taxpaying ability, in other words, was to be defined as income earned minus the value of sweat expended. This view was more convincing with an eighty than a thirty-five hour week, and would call for other adjustments as well, including differentiation between work incomes (miners v. professors) and an allowance for psychic income (work utility). Surely this would not be a workable concept or a very sensible one. Nor can much credence be given

[8] The equal treatment of income independent of source and use suggests that the income tax has the further advantage of being neutral in the sense of not distorting economic decisions. This is true to a degree, but the same can be claimed — and under certain assumptions, more persuasively — for a general consumption tax. The consumption tax is neutral between present and future consumption, while the income tax discriminates against future consumption. This fact has been used mistakenly by Irving Fisher in *Double Taxation of Savings*, 29 AM. ECON. REV. 16 (1939), to argue that the income tax is inequitable because it "double-taxes" savings. The point is that equity and neutrality are not the same thing. If income is chosen as the equity base, the consumption tax is inequitable because it undertaxes saving, and this is the case even though it may not be neutral. *See* R. MUSGRAVE, *supra* note 3, chs. 8 & 12.

to the proposition that capital income should pay more because it carries higher capacity to pay since it is joined with the presence of a capital reserve. This overlooks the fact that the choice between consumption and savings is open to recipients of both work and capital income, and that (under the proper accretion system) initial acquisition of capital through transfer is also subject to tax.

Next, it is frequently argued that unrealized capital gains do not constitute income. This position is untenable. Suppose I continue to hold an investment which has appreciated in value instead of realizing the gain. This is equivalent to my realizing the gain and reinvesting in the same asset. To tax gains only when realized is to make the tax contingent on the technicality of portfolio shifts rather than on the incidence of gain. Nor can it be argued that the unrealized gain should be exempt because it has not been withdrawn for consumption. If such were the position all income which is saved should be exempted and a consumption tax substituted for the income tax.[9] It is clear conceptually that unrealized gains constitute income, and a taxable income concept which in principle considers unrealized gains as nonincome is not a valid equity concept.[10] To be sure, administrative difficulties do not permit full implementation of this principle, but recognition of what should be done in principle — temporarily disregarding administrative difficulties — is crucial in choosing between alternative feasible solutions.

We conclude that the accretion plus consumption concept of income is the superior measure of taxpaying ability, once the income (as distinct from consumption) view has been chosen. Whereas the latter choice is a matter of value judgment, the accretion plus consumption concept of income follows as a matter of consistent thinking once the income approach has been decided upon.

C. *The Ad Hoc Approach*

Let us backtrack briefly and once more ask whether a generalized concept of tax base is needed to obtain an equitable solu-

[9] Still another, if less meaningful, criterion would be to define the tax base as consumption plus increase in liquid balances, in which case exemption should be given for investment from liquid balances, as well as for continued investment of unrealized gains.

[10] Of course such gains must be in real terms without reflections of change of price level. Similarly, the "good" income tax should allow for creditor losses and debtor gains due to inflation.

tion. Leaving aside the evident political fact that loophole pressures are difficult to meet without reference to a basic income concept, is it analytically possible to define an equitable solution in its absence? This, it seems to me, is the basic question which has to be faced in dealing with Professor Bittker's position.

To be sure, people with equal characteristics can be treated equally, and personal discrimination can be avoided, without resort to a generalized concept of tax base. Thus, all left-handed people may be asked to pay twice the head tax contributed by all right-handed people; all buyers of white bread may be taxed, while all buyers of dark bread are not, and so forth. But as noted before, absence of discrimination in this sense is not enough. Reasonable men will also demand that the taxable characteristics be chosen in a meaningful fashion. This means that the tax base should be chosen to give a "fair" result, which requires an explicit concept of fairness, such as asking for contributions in line with ability to pay, or in line with unwillingness to save and add one's earnings to the community's capital stock. Either concept, and perhaps still other criteria may be chosen, but I find it exceedingly difficult to visualize a standard of fairness which deals piecemeal with each specific characteristic of households (including various aspects of income, consumption, and other features), asking in each case whether it does or does not constitute a proper tax base, and doing so without the guidance of a general principle by which to relate specific decisions.

But even if the possibility of such an approach were granted, and I doubt whether it can be, it would surely lead to a broad bundle of taxes, and not to an income tax per se. If the problem of income taxation is discussed, and this is to what Professor Bittker addresses himself, the income components of the wide range of possible tax bases must be identified. And to do so, an income concept is needed.

We thus arrive at the conclusion that a pure ad hoc approach is not tenable on analytical grounds. A generalized concept of taxable capacity and taxable income is needed if there is to be a meaningful discussion of the equity aspects of tax reform. Short of this, one may discuss what treatment Congress intended to apply when present statutes were enacted and what interpretation the courts have given to the statutes, without asking whether Congress was correct in so intending in the first place. This, to be sure, is an essential step in the detailed implementation of tax policy, but it is not a basis for tax reform — the essence of which is consideration of change in existing statutes, including change of legislative intent — and, I gather, not the ground on which Professor Bittker's comments proceed.

D. Vertical Aspects of Base Imperfections

Defective definition of taxable income results in horizontal inequities because taxpayers in equal position (equal, that is, in terms of consumption plus accretion) do not pay equal tax. At the same time, it would be naive to overlook the fact that these "horizontal" inequalities are not random from a "vertical" point of view.

Some aspects of tax base definition are of primary concern to the lower and middle income groups. This includes such items as the treatment of imputed income from housing, of social insurance benefits, of interest paid on mortgages and consumer loans, and of various fringe benefits. Certain other omissions from the tax base, which should be included under a proper definition of income, relate to forms of income which are important primarily in the upper income brackets. These include interest received from tax-exempt securities, certain types of executive compensation, and — much the most important — capital gains.

As is well known, the income tax, though it has highly progressive bracket rates, ceases to be progressive above a certain level of income and in fact turns regressive. This is due very largely to the effects of taxing capital gains at a maximum rate of twenty-five percent.[11] The situation is thus one where steeply progressive rates apply to a limited group of high income taxpayers, while much of the income received in the high brackets is subject to a modest proportional rate. The result is not only horizontal inequity among high income recipients but also vertical inequity in that the progression expressed in statutory rates does not apply. Even if it is argued that these rates are too high, this is hardly the way of dealing with the matter. Obviously, equity would be served better if a more modest rate structure were applied uniformly over a more complete income base. This is precisely what the proponents of a comprehensive tax base have proposed.[12] The fact that various income omissions or prefer-

---

[11] *See* Pechman, *Individual Income Tax Provisions of the Revenue Act of 1964*, 20 J. FINANCE 260 (1965).

[12] A proposal of Senator Long would permit taxpayers to choose between a "broad base-low rates" and a "narrow base-high rates" package. S. 3250, 88th

ential treatments — and I have no hesitation in referring to them as tax loopholes — have such vertical implications adds to their distorting effects. At the same time, it serves to explain why they exist, and how political pressures in their favor come about.

E. Other Objectives

Before turning to cases, let us note that equity is not the only criterion of tax policy. While of great importance, it must give way on occasion to other objectives. For instance, it may be desirable to encourage investment via an investment credit, and even to limit such inducements to particular industries or types of assets. Or it may be desirable to encourage charitable donation by tax exemptions. Either measure is inequitable, but the cost in equity may be justified if the gain from the competing policy objective is the greater, and if other means of achieving the competing end are distinctly inferior.

It may be argued, of course, that any preferential treatment to achieve particular objectives is in fact a subsidy, and that it would be better to pay such subsidies on an explicit basis, without clouding their true nature by disguising them in the form of tax reductions. The problem here is essentially a political one. If the cash subsidy would be the same as the tax reduction, the result (in its economic and equity effects) is identical whichever technique is used. The tax relief is simpler, as it avoids the process of collection and payment. The situation differs, however, if the technique of tax relief leads to subsidies which Congress would not be willing to give in explicit form. In this case, faith in the democratic process suggests that the subsidy approach is superior.

However this may be, the proponent of a proper income definition (or opponent of loopholes) need not commit himself to an all-out opposition to tax remissions as an incentive device. Contrary to Professor Bittker's intimation,[13] acceptance of the investment credit does not require abandonment of a properly defined income base. All that need be recognized is that such incentives involve an equity cost, and that this cost must be taken into consideration when deciding on the incentive policy. The fact that equity considerations are not always controlling

Cong., 2d Sess. (1964). This seems to me a defeatist approach, which in the long run will make it even more difficult to secure a proper definition of the income base.

[13] Bittker 954.

does not imply, as Professor Bittker seems to suggest, that equity standards are a mirage.

F. Base Broadening v. Improvement

As Professor Bittker points out, much of the recent discussion has been in terms of "broadening" the tax base, with the promised reward that once the base is broadened, lower rates of tax will suffice to furnish the same yield.[14] I have never been happy with this emphasis on base *broadening* rather than *improvement*. Since the proper base (*i.e.*, the base corresponding to the accretion concept of income) is broader than the actual base, tax reform will involve base broadening; but this broadening is an incidental result, not the objective of the reform. If it were, a gross income tax using the entire GNP as base would surely be better than a net income tax; and a turnover tax would be better than a gross income tax. But equity is reduced if lower rates are traded against an undue expansion of the base to include items that are not components of accretion; and equity demands that the base be narrowed should there be instances where nonaccretion items are included. But having made this clear, the fact remains that existing departures from the proper concept are very largely in the form of omissions, and that the needed reform is, therefore, one of broadening rather than restricting the base.

II. Cases

I now turn to a brief consideration of some of the special problems of income definition which according to Professor Bittker demonstrate the uselessness of the basic income concept. I find, on the contrary, that the concept points a clear way to the proper answer in most instances; and if it must then be modified by considerations of administrative feasibility, this does not destroy the importance of recognizing the proper solution. Among feasible solutions, some are much closer to the proper measure than others, and the results — if second best[15] — will be far

[14] Bittker 926–27.

[15] Professor Bittker argues, in line with the second-best theorem in welfare economics, that where a number of imperfections exist, adjustment of any one partial defect towards the norm may only worsen matters. Rather, the optimal solution may be approached better by introducing offsetting imperfections. Thus, if industries *A*, *B*, and *C* are monopolistic while *D* and *E* are competitive, the competitive norm may be served better by making *D* monopolistic than by forcing *C* to become competitive.

better than what can be done without the guidance of a normative concept. While Professor Bittker's analysis of some of the technical difficulties is helpful, his all-or-nothing position is thoroughly unjustified.

A. Exclusions from Gross Income

1. Government Transfers and Public Services.—Advocates of the accretion concept have urged that transfers such as social security benefits and veterans' payments should be included in the tax base. Professor Bittker argues that if this is done, there logically should also be inclusion of all other benefits (in cash or kind) received from public services.[16] If fellowships are taxed, why not also tax income in kind received through free (or subsidized) education; in fact, why not impute income from all public services derived free of direct charge?

A distinction needs to be drawn between benefits from contributory insurance, cash subsidies, and income in kind from public services. Regarding insurance benefits, there should be tax free recovery of contributions, but taxation of interest earnings from the investment of insurance funds. Regarding cash subsidies, the choice between lower but tax exempt, or higher but taxable subsidies is essentially a political and administrative question. If the net result (in terms of after-tax income) is the same under both procedures, both policies are equivalent and, while tax reduction is simpler, either method is acceptable. But the results may not be the same. A more explicit, "out in the open" policy determination may be preferable, in which case transfers should be taxed.

Ideally, imputed benefits from public services would be con-

While instances might conceivably exist where the tax distribution under accretion could be approximated more closely by adding deletions so as to balance existing loopholes, I find it difficult to construct an illustration. Surely, undertaxation of capital gains is not "balanced" — in terms of *horizontal* equity — by exclusion of imputed rent, and depletion is not "balanced" by exclusion of fringe benefits.

Such balancing might occur after a rough fashion with regard to *vertical* equity, but this would surely be a poor solution. Vertical equity can be accomplished (in principle at least) by applying the desired rate structure to an income base defined so as to secure horizontal equity.

To be sure, the nature of fiscal politics may be such that certain vertical equity goals can be secured only by trading horizontal inequities. A choice may then have to be made, but to do so intelligently, the cost in terms of horizontal inequity must be known, and an income concept will again be needed.

[16] Bittker 935–38.

sidered in the same ways as transfers.[17] The accretion concept includes all gains, whether they be in cash or kind, obtained through market transactions, as gifts, or as imputed gains. The principle is clear, but as Professor Bittker points out, the difficulties of imputation would be insurmountable.[18] Feasibility suggests, therefore, that inclusion be limited to cash grants.

2. *Personal Exemptions.* — Professor Bittker suggests that the personal exemption is inconsistent with the idea of a comprehensive tax base. If the purpose is to protect minimum incomes, it would be better to combine full taxation with cash subsidies.[19] This again raises the question of how subsidies should be handled. But, more basically, I do not think that this properly interprets the role of exemptions.[20] The exemption, above all, should be looked upon as a matter of rate progression (vertical equity) rather than income definition. That is to say, the exemption merely sets a zero rate bracket and, under a negative income tax system, would be replaced by a set of negative (subsidy) rate brackets.

In addition, differential exemptions are a way of allowing for differences in the ability to pay of taxable units of unequal size. This adjustment, which also might be made through differential rates, is surely needed in any meaningful ability-to-pay concept. Leaving aside certain technical improvements which, as Professor Bittker notes, are in order (*e.g.*, replacing the exemption by a credit), I see no conflict between such an allowance and the case for a comprehensive tax base.

3. *Gifts and Bequests.* — Professor Bittker notes that the accretion concept of income requires inclusion of bequests and gifts in the recipient's income.[21] He is correct in so stating, as evidenced by the recent Carter Commission report which recommends inclusion of such transfers.[22] At the same time, inclusion

---

[17] The reader will recall (see note 3 *supra*) that this discussion is in ability-to-pay terms, disregarding benefit aspects. If benefits were to be imputed, only net benefits or burdens could properly be included in computing income.

[18] Bittker 936.

[19] Bittker 940.

[20] Proponents of the comprehensive tax base have invited the critique of exemptions by listing income loss due to exemptions in tables showing the various sources of base erosion. *See, e.g.*, Pechman, *supra* note 7, at 12.

[21] Bittker 945–46.

[22] *See* 3 REPORT OF THE ROYAL COMM'N ON TAXATION (Canada) 41, 70 (1966). Professor Bittker, however, does not favor this inclusion, partly because of the distortions in transfer patterns to which it would give rise. I find this ironical, given the degree of distortion now resulting from estate tax avoidance. A redefini-

of bequests and gifts in the income of the recipient leaves open the question whether society wishes to impose a prior tax on the donor or the decedent, a tax which would be outside the income tax system.

4. Imputed Rent. — Professor Bittker criticizes proponents of the comprehensive tax base for demanding inclusion of imputed rent in taxable income, without extending the same principle to imputed income from other assets.[23] The answer again is that in principle all imputed income (including even income from cash holding) should be taxed, but that it is not a feasible procedure. Taxation of imputed rent, on the other hand, is feasible. The inequity between owners and renters, which results from the present practice of deducting mortgage interest while not taxing imputed rent is unfair, especially at the lower end of the income scale, and could be improved even by a rough approximation to imputed rent.

B. Personal Deductions

Professor Bittker points to the allowance of personal deductions by the advocates of a comprehensive tax base as further evidence that the generalization of a comprehensive tax base cannot be accepted as the prime criterion.[24] Here a distinction should be drawn between (1) deductions which allow for disaster expenses, be they medical costs, disaster losses, or what not, and (2) deductions which are granted to induce certain uses of income such as charitable donations.

I see no conflict whatsoever between group (1) deductions and the concept of a comprehensive income base. The purpose is not to exclude specific income sources but to allow for situations where taxpayers with equal incomes and family size have strikingly different needs. The logic of the case points to combining such "disaster" items, and to rendering the joint deduction subject to a floor. By allowing for disaster situations, the equity goal, far from being offended, can be achieved more fully.

Deductions of type (2) are a different matter. Though they clearly offend against equity they may be in order if the rival policy objectives such as encouraging charity are worth the equity loss, and provided that tax deduction is a superior way of achiev-

tion of the taxable unit as proposed by the Carter Commission, together with inclusion of transfers, would reduce rather than increase such distortions.

[23] Bittker 947–48.

[24] *See* Bittker 950–52.

ing these objectives. In the case of charitable contributions in particular, the question arises whether Congress would be willing to adopt a system of subsidizing charitable gifts such that the subsidy rate (as is implied in the deduction system) rises with the taxpayer's income; and, indeed, whether Congress would be willing to appropriate amounts (corresponding to the revenue loss) for such purposes at all.

C. Personal-Business Borderline

Professor Bittker makes much of the difficulty of drawing a line between outlays which constitute business expenses and should be deducted to obtain net income, and others which bestow personal benefits and thus should not be allowed.[25] And he holds that the accretion concept does not help in drawing a line.

Again the case is presented as if all aspects of the problem were equally difficult and arbitrary. Thus insurance against occupational accidents is cited in the same sentence with entertainment expenses. As I see it, the former is clearly eligible as deduction, while the latter should be viewed with great suspicion. The reason is that such expenses can be used to bestow income so as to avoid personal income tax, and that this is in fact done to a substantial degree. This, above all, is an area where reference to an income concept is needed. Such reference is helpful because it tells us that consumption is part of accretion. Therefore, business costs undertaken to give consumption benefits constitute income to the recipients. Granted that there are situations in which consumption benefits are derived as a truly necessary part of doing business, the present rules (after some tightening in response to the administration proposal for more drastic revision in the Revenue Act of 1962) still leave the margin of error heavily in the direction of excessive allowance.

D. Business Deductions

Professor Bittker argues that if percentage depletion is to be classified as a preference, so should the investment credit or accelerated depreciation for wartime production facilities.[26] As noted before, he overlooks the fact that tax policy must balance

[25] Bittker 952.

[26] Bittker 954.

between various objectives. While both adjustments are inequitable, the investment credit serves the explicit purpose of encouraging general capital formation and economic growth. The depletion allowance, on the other hand, does not serve such an objective.

It has been defended traditionally on equity grounds, *i.e.*, as compensation for the "using up" of natural resources. This argument was proved fallacious because there is no case for permitting recovery (even if the loss of value were measured properly as a percentage of gross income) over and above the exploitation costs which are already expensed. The case for depletion then shifted to an argument based on national defense needs; and, more recently, the greater riskiness of such investment has been emphasized. Neither case is convincing, and even if there were a case for special aid, such aid is not granted effectively as a tax subsidy to gross income.

The cases of depletion and investment credit, therefore, are very different. While the investment credit offers a substantial policy advantage to be weighed against the equity loss, the depletion provision does not do so.[27]

E. *Problems of Timing*

Finally, let us consider various aspects of the timing problem. Here, as in other parts of the discussion, Professor Bittker makes the problem appear rather more complex and unwieldy than it really is.[28] There are three basic propositions to be made:

(1) Ideally, tax liability should become due when accretion occurs. This follows from the very approach to accretion as a measure of ability to pay. The present value of tax payments is reduced if tax payments are postponed. Therefore, horizontal inequities arise if different taxpayers are granted different periods of postponement.[29] While this difficulty is avoided if everyone pays, say, thirteen years after accretion occurs, it should not be too difficult to agree, on common

[27] Usually the choice is not between wholly abandoning equity and wholly foregoing desired economic effects, but a reasonable compromise may be worked out. *See* Musgrave, *Growth with Equity*, Papers and Proceedings, 75th Ann. Meeting, Am. Econ. Ass'n 323 (1963), in 53 AM. ECON. REV. (1963).

[28] *See* Bittker 958–73.

[29] Simons, as Bittker notes (958 n.59), deemphasized the importance of tax postponements. However, Simons failed to realize that the gains thus derived could be very substantial.

sense grounds, that concurrent incidence of the liability is to be preferred.[30]

(2) Obviously, it is not feasible to define concurrent on an "every minute" basis. While the choice of the accounting year is arbitrary, common sense suggests that use be made of an annual accounting period followed by business firms or the government.

(3) Most important is the fact that under a progressive income tax, liabilities differ depending on the time path of income. This distorts the intent of tax equity, thus calling for averaging of income. The same holds for the carryover of losses or unused credits under a flat rate tax.

Given these principles, which are wholly in line with the accretion approach, I do not follow Professor Bittker's complaint that provision for carryover of losses should have been criticized as an undue "preference." [31] On the contrary, income is to be defined in net terms, and failure to permit carryover would impose a penalty on taxpayers with irregular income, while favoring those with a steady income flow.

The case for income averaging is essentially the same. Professor Bittker comments that he has seen no analysis of the implications of the Haig-Simons definition for income averaging.[32] Again the principle of the matter seems quite clear. Ideally, all income would be taxed on an accrual basis. The tax would become due concurrent with the accretion of income. Thus gain from tax postponement, or penalties from tax anticipation would be avoided. At the same time, averaging would be applied to avoid the inequitable impact of rate progression upon irregular incomes. Ideally, averaging would apply annually and be over a lifetime period. For reasons of administrative feasibility, such averaging has to be applied from time to time and is limited to a period of, say, five years, but this does not change the principle involved.

Similarly, recognition must be made of the fact that income is not taxed on an accrual basis, but that (again for reasons of administrative feasibility) the tax becomes due at actual or (under the proper system) constructive realization. Such being the case, averaging involves the averaging of realized (actually or constructively) rather than of accrued income. The principle of the

---

[30] This is desirable also on fiscal policy grounds, as concurrent payments increase the effectiveness of the tax structure as an automatic economic stabilizer.

[31] Bittker 961–62.

[32] Bittker 963.

matter is clear, and there is no issue of preferences in the application of a general averaging rule.

F. *Unrealized Gains*

Finally, there is again the question of unrealized appreciation. Professor Bittker rightly notes that complete compliance with the accretion concept would call for annual taxation of accrued gains.[33] He recognizes the difficulty of annual valuation but wonders why advocates of the accretion concept have not favored annual valuation of at least those assets which permit the assessment. I see no objection to this, although I doubt whether it can be done readily over a wide range of assets. Moreover, advocates of the accretion concept, from Henry Simons on, have favored "constructive realization," *e.g.*, taxing of accrued gains at death or transfer. Thus, valuation would be needed at a much reduced scale only, and the administrative task would be greatly simplified. Professor Bittker is quick to point out that this is no perfect solution as it would leave capital gains income with the advantage of tax postponement.[34] This is correct, but the preference would be on a much reduced scale, and the remaining advantage could be approximately offset by applying an interest charge when the tax becomes due.[35] While stressing the difficulties of fully taxing capital gains, Professor Bittker leaves us uncertain whether he himself believes that unrealized gains are income, and hence should be taxed. Yet, this is the crucial issue, and one which cannot be solved without reference to a systematic income concept.

G. *Taxable Unit: Family Relations*

As Professor Bittker points out, the problem of formulating the taxable unit is not solved by the income concept.[36] Yet this task is not unrelated to what "index of equality" is chosen. In-

[33] Bittker 967.

[34] Bittker 970.

[35] Professor Bittker (958–60) notes correctly that the interest aspect was unduly minimized by Henry Simons, but that it has been emphasized by later writers. He then emphasizes distortions which may result if the wrong interest rate is chosen, and that borrowing rates for individual taxpayers will differ. Without entering into the question as to which is *the* proper interest rate (and a good case can be made for using the Treasury rate), the fact of the matter is that constructive realization with interest would leave us vastly closer to an accretion concept solution than does the present procedure. This is what matters, and not whether a completely perfect solution can be secured.

[36] Bittker 974.

deed, the definition of taxable unit has its logic — derived again from the underlying concept of ability to pay — and is not as arbitrary a matter as Professor Bittker suggests.

Clearly, the relative treatment of taxable units of different size should relate to the cost of maintaining households of different size, and clearly the present split-income system overtaxes single relative to married units, especially over the 25,000 to 70,000 dollar income ranges. Which technique is best to meet the problem (separate rate schedules for single and married with mandatory joint returns, etc.) is a different matter, but the present pattern can clearly be improved upon.

Also, the definition of the taxable unit needs to be designed to forestall tax avoidance through allocation of property income to minor children. Again the present law is far from satisfactory in this respect, giving substantial preference to capital as against wage income. While solutions of these problems do not follow directly from the income concept, reasonable standards can be developed which are in line with the basic rationale of the accretion approach. Surely the problem is not as wide open as Professor Bittker suggests.

H. Taxable Unit: Business

Professor Bittker notes correctly that the accretion concept requires the shareholder to be taxed on gains in the value of his shares, whether or not the underlying profits are distributed in the form of dividends.[87] Short thereof, he notes that retained earnings might be imputed to the shareholder. In fact, both should be done, allowing the share base to be written up for retention when computing capital gains. Having done so, the corporation tax (except as a withholding device) should be dropped.

So far so good. But instead of concluding that this avenue points to a reasonable and practicable solution of the problem, as developed in the Carter Commission Report,[88] Professor Bittker proceeds to ridicule the principle by asking what then should be done about discretionary trusts, or the employer's contribution to qualified pension plans. My answer is: (1) much would be gained if the taxation of corporate profits could be integrated in the individual income tax, even if these other and comparatively minor issues remained unsolved; and (2) appropriate answers

[87] Bittker 977–80.

[88] 4 ROYAL COMM'N REPORT, *supra* note 22, at 10–93.

to these other issues may be given as well. As to discretionary trusts, Professor Bittker himself notes the proper solution — interim taxation of fiduciary with subsequent adjustment when the party-in-interest becomes identifiable. As to employer contributions to qualified pension plans, such contributions and the earnings on them should be taxable to the recipient, with the tax (subject to interest for postponement) payable when benefits are received.

* * *

In concluding, I believe that Professor Bittker's message is wrong in both principle and application. His principle — that matters of income definition should be decided on an ad hoc basis — is mistaken. A generalized income concept is needed as an analytical tool if an equitable income tax base is to be defined. In application, his position — that the income concept is useless because it does not solve all problems and must be moderated by administrative feasibility — is also in error. In most situations, the concept points to the equitable solution, and administratively feasible measures can usually be found which approximate the proper result to a fair degree. We should, therefore, not heed his message, and get on with the task of tax reform, aimed at reforming the tax base in accord with the norm provided by the accretion concept. Considering the disappointing record of accomplishment after two decades of public (and congressional) discussion — especially the backsliding in the tax legislation of 1966, after modest progress in 1964 — everybody's, and surely Professor Bittker's, help is needed.

[4]

WHAT IS A COMPREHENSIVE TAX BASE ANYWAY?

HENRY AARON *

ECONOMISTS and lawyers have recently been treated to a lively, if inconclusive, debate over whether or not the concept of a comprehensive income taxe base can be given precise definition and whether or not it is useful in analysis of the tax system. The debate was sparked by a spirited article by Professor Boris Bittker [2] in which he argued that the concept is logically unclear and not very useful in practice and that some of the prescriptions which seem to flow from it are unacceptable to most people. This article drew published responses from one lawyer and two economists, all prominent tax experts,[1] who disputed Bittker's analysis and the conclusions he drew from it. The participants in the debate failed to convince one another, which is not unusual. It seems likely, however, that many other readers found themselves torn anew by issues presented in the exchange, which is regrettable. After the debate was over, the dust refused to settle.

This article will attempt to advance the discussion by bringing to the center of the argument a concept which lay behind certain of Bittker's objections to the Haig-Simons tax base, although it was not explicitly articulated, the concept of public goods. To anticipate my conclusion, I shall argue that the concept of a comprehensive tax base is subject to analytically precise definition, that this definition requires that we move far beyond the confines of the "tax base" to which we are all accustomed, that the definition cannot be applied *consistently* in practice, but that it is a useful *ad hoc* instrument for provoking the right questions, not for supplying the right answers.

One side comment on the method of analysis used in this paper is necessary. Tax experts, whether lawyers or economists, should recognize that legal and economic considerations are so interwoven in issues of tax policy that recommendations which ignore realistic institutional constraints, either legal or economic in nature, are likely to be constructive only by chance or if confined to narrowly technical matters. Nevertheless, clarity of thought is often served by resort to intellectual constructs which initially assume hypothetical conditions. Accordingly, Part I of this paper will discuss the necessary conditions for the existence of a comprehensive tax base. Part II will acknowledge that, in practice, these conditions are unlikely ever to be met. Consequently, practical obstacles preclude its full application, but Part II will suggest ways in which the concept of a comprehensive tax base can be usefully applied.

I

The comprehensive income tax base depends on an acceptable, comprehensive definition of income. The income definition used by Haig and Simons — net accretion of a spending unit's power to consume, over some period of time — generally has been interpreted to mean

* Senior Fellow, The Brookings Institution and Associate Professor of Economics, University of Maryland. The author wishes to thank Joseph Pechman, Boris Bittker, Oliver Oldman, and Stanley Surrey for helpful comments on an earlier draft.

[1] [4][8][9]. These comments and the original article [2], together with one brief additional comment by each author, where reprinted in [3].

net accretion to the power to consume *private* goods and services, *before* taxes are imposed.[2] That is, income has referred to the imaginary capacity of the household itself, before imposition of taxes, to consume marketed goods and services without outside constraint or limitation (other than laws prescribing anti-social behavior) without reducing its net assets. Unfortunately, the Haig-Simons definition of income comprehends only a part, and a decreasing part at that, of the list of decisions which affect the economic welfare of households. A long and growing list of goods and services which affect a household's welfare is supplied as a result of decisions over which each household has, at most, partial control. This list includes all goods and services provided by federal, state, and local governments, other than those which are voluntarily purchased in quantities determined by the purchaser. It includes also services other than direct cash transfers, of non-profit institutions, such as foundations or charities.[3] These commodities affect the household's welfare and, in some cases, directly add to the household's ability to pay (as, for example, with education in subsidized public colleges and universities which often replaces education in less subsidized private institutions). The chief obstacle to the extension of the income concept to include these other commodities is the difficulty of valuing them so that they can be added to the household's own income to produce a comprehensive measure of income. The way to overcome this obstacle is logically straightforward. The result, unfortunately, is completely impracticable.

During any period of time, each household consumes a set of marketed goods and services over the purchase of which the household has sole discretion. Included in this set are all tangible goods and services, all savings and any changes in the value of assets which the household could have realized but chose not to do so. The decision by the household to save, or not to realize an accrual, reveals that the household derives as much satisfaction, at the margin, from the increase in value of its financial portfolio as it would have derived from other goods and services not purchased because of saving or because of failure to realize an accrual. The income value of an accrual is the amount which the household would have realized if the accrual (positive or negative) had been realized.[4] In such a calculation, of course, decreases in assets represent negative income. As far as private good income is concerned, the correct measure of household consumption, therefore, is the market value of real goods and services which the household consumes including changes in assets.

By familiar accounting identities, such consumption of real goods and services, plus change in assets, is identically equal to a set of income flows. The sum of these flows measures private good in-

[2] The definition does not specify before the imposition of which taxes accretion is to be measured. As generally applied, accretion is defined gross of personal income taxes, but no effort is made to adjust for corporate income taxes, payroll taxes, or other taxes.

[3] The total welfare of each household depends, of course, on a host of other tangible and intangible factors, such as international and domestic political tensions, the weather, one's neighbors, chance occurences. A complete list of factors affecting household welfare would include such noneconomic events, as well as any changes in subjective attitudes within the household. The text argues that private good income excludes essential economic elements which affect the household's *economic* situation, as contrasted with its political contentment, psychological satisfaction, and so on.

[4] It should be acknowledged that the income value of an accrual, by this definition, is some amount less than the face value of the accrual, since realization of the accrual gives rise to tax liability. The income value is the face value less such tax liabilities. To the extent that taxes can be avoided through deferral of realization, income is generated over time in the amount by which the net of tax value of the accrual rises over time.

come, Y. This definition is the Haig-Simon definition of income, with one significant difference. *It excludes personal tax payments from income.* The reason for doing so is that gross income is not a quantity over which any household has discretion. Employers typically withhold personal income and payroll taxes, the self-employed typically must make estimated tax payments or face penalty. Market behavior by consumers reflects their disposable incomes, not some figure which would exist in an imaginary world where taxes were not imposed.[5] It is this net magnitude which measures real household income, the capacity of the household to purchase want-satisfying commodities measured at market prices.[6]

Private goods form only a subset of commodities which contribute to household welfare. A comprehensive income measure must also encompass benefits to a household generated by commodities about the purchase of which the household does not have sole discretion. But how should the *income* value of such commodities to the household be measured? Cost is not an acceptable measure, since the household has not revealed, through market behavior, that *it* places a valuation on the commodity equal to its cost. In the case of private goods, households willingly reveal, through market behavior, that their valuation of the commodity, *at the margin,* equals its price. There exists no institutional setting, however, which induces households truthfully to reveal the valuation placed on non-discretionary income. It is this valuation, by the household, which should be used in measuring the income value to the household of non-marketed goods. Let us proceed as if, contrary to fact, these subjective valuations or quasi-prices [7] were known. In that case, each household receives non-discretionary income which is definitionally equal to the product of the number of units of each good, concerning the purchase of which the household does *not* have sole discretion, multiplied by the quasi-price of that good.[8] Denote this non-discretionary income, Z. "Total" or "comprehensive" income, C, is the sum of discretionary and non-discretionary income, $Y + Z$.

This quantity, rather than pre-tax income as ordinarily defined, or even as defined by Haig and Simons, measures the value of goods and services received by each household. Rigorous application of the Haig-Simons income definition would produce inequities if what I have called non-discretionary income were excluded. For example, as noted by Bittker [2, p. 936], the Haig-Simons definition would require taxation of scholarships but would exclude the subsidy element in low tuition to public colleges and universities. But if this is an inequity, so

[5] If income taxes were *not* imposed, then the prices of many commodities would differ from those which now prevail, reflecting differences in demand for final goods between income tax recipients (i.e., governments) and income tax payers. Derived demand for factor inputs would also differ causing factor incomes to be different. For both reasons, the real goods and services consumed by households would differ, as would their value.

[6] There is at least one alternative measure of income, which includes consumers surplus. This alternative is not employed here for reasons set forth in the Appendix. Readers not familiar with the dual role of market prices as indices of relative valuation of commodities at the margin by households should read the Appendix before continuing.

[7] This term is taken from [11].

[8] The meaning of the word "non-discretionary" as employed here, has nothing in common with the concept of discretionary income as used by the Carter Commission in Canada. See [10, pp. 5-12]. The Carter Commission defines as discretionary income "the proportion of the [taxable] unit's total economic power that does not have to be exercised to maintain the members of the unit." In my opinion, this definition implies nothing precise regarding the income level at which discretion commences. I define as non-discretionary income any good or service which, in the opinion of the household, affects the household's welfare but over the purchase of which the household does not have sole discretion.

also is the similarity in treatment under the Haig-Simons definition that would be accorded to households with children in private schools (no income, if there is no scholarship) and to households with children in public schools (also no income, although there is in effect a full scholarship). And so on, through the full list of services received by a household which it has not purchased voluntarily in quantities of its own choosing.[9]

In summary, the correct definition of comprehensive income, C, is at once broader and narrower than the Haig-Simons definition – broader because it includes a large and growing number of commodities provided through some sort of collective decision, narrower because it excludes personal income taxes. It is the correct income measure because it alone measures the value to the household of all real goods and services which it receives.

II

Because of practical difficulties, tax experts unanimously despair of applying the Haig-Simons definition rigorously. They will be even more skeptical regarding the usefulness as a tax base of the comprehensive income definition presented here. Households do not reveal their valuations of non-discretionary income, and there is no practical way of making them do so. The income definition presented in Part I cannot under any imaginable circumstances be applied systematically in measuring income for tax purposes, since one of its elements, Z, is unknown. In addition, the definition of C is subject to many other practical problems[10] regarding the valuation of life interests in trusts, the gray area between personal and business expenses, and a host of other areas where hard and often sloppy distinctions must be drawn in practice. Nevertheless, as Pechman observed [3, p. 117], although we recognize some rules as only rough and ready instruments for dealing with complex situations, we have, in the back of our minds, an agreed upon idea of what constitutes income.[11]

The weakness of C as a practical instrument in tax administration is its strength as a guide to distributional questions of tax policy. The comprehensive income, C, of any household is likely to vary from the household income, X, that would prevail in the absence of government taxes or expenditures. Meaningful decisions regarding the equity of income distribution can focus only on C, however. Given present capabilities estimates of X would be little more than guesswork. Even if X could be known with certainty, however, it is not a comprehensive measure of income. For that reason, intelligent public policy can only

[9] The arbitrariness of the Haig-Simons definition, if non-discretionary income is excluded, may be illustrated with an example. Educators and analysts, representing a staggering range of political viewpoints, have recommended, as a solution to the malaise in some public schools, that free public education be replaced by a system under which parents are awarded scrip which can be applied against tuition, covering all costs of privately or publicly managed schools. Under the Haig-Simons definition, such scrip would be income, whereas the benefits of public schools are not income. The adoption of the scrip plan would change Haig-Simons income even if children remained in their present schools, but would leave C unaffected.

[10] See [2, *passim*].

[11] C cannot, in practice, be used as the base against which to levy income taxes for the practical reasons just presented. In addition, C, by definition, is net of taxes. To compute C gross of taxes might appear to entail awkward calculations, since, to do so, one must backtrack to pre-tax comprehensive income. As is obvious, a household's discretionary income would depend on the tax transfer system. In principle, however, the complexity would vanish if true valuation of non-discretionary income were revealed. To compute pre-tax comprehensive income, one would need only to solve a simple problem in elementary algebra. For example, if $V = C+T$ equals comprehensive income gross of taxes and taxes are a constant fraction, t, of V, then $V = C/(1-t)$, where C is observed comprehensive income. With nonproportional taxes, the computation might be lengthier.

be made by concentrating on *C* and on the impact which changes in policy will have on *C*. Any other measure such as pre-tax income, or disposable private income, or the difference between them, is incomplete and very likely to be misleading. The fact that an important element of *C*, namely *Z*, is not known, but must be estimated, highlights the subjective nature of *C*.[12] This lack of concreteness in the only truly comprehensive income measure, though regrettable, does not justify calculations of supposedly comprehensive estimates of income distribution or redistribution that ignore such important and unevenly distributed elements of income as Z. Because tax authorities cannot obtain truthful valuation of non-discretionary income, any feasible income tax must be levied on a decidedly "second best" base. This statement would be true even of a Haig-Simons base.

Given such a predicament, tax policy makers *should* confront proposed "reforms" in the tax system in the same way budget makers *should* confront proposed expenditures. In both cases, a desire to examine the proposal apart from its effect on aggregate demand requires that the proposal be paired with some offsetting change which cancels out the impact of the tax change on aggregate demand — for example, a new expenditure may be paired with an expenditure cut or a tax increase; a new tax proposal may be paired with another tax change with offsetting revenue effects.[13] The resulting package of proposals will generate benefits and costs — changes in real goods and services, C, available to households, and these changes should be evaluated on the basis of weights assigned to different households. In short, tax changes, like expenditure changes, should be subject to benefit-cost analysis. In any case, the decision to modify or to retain given tax provisions, like the decision to continue or modify expenditures, expresses results of a frequently implicit calculation in which benefits and costs are compared.

Tax reformers should not be unduly discouraged because they are unable legitimately to appeal to such simple litmus tests of tax proposals as whether or not the proposal causes taxable income to conform more closely to the Haig-Simons income definition. It seems extremely likely, to this writer at least, that most of the tax provisions now on the agenda for tax reform will fare just as badly under such empirical scrutiny as they fare when judged for conformity with some academic income definition.

For example, the exclusion of unemployment insurance from income taxation violates both the Haig-Simons income definition and the comprehensive income definition suggested here. These nonconformities, however, merely point the way to an examination of which taxable units save how much tax from this exclusion. Tax policy makers should then ask themselves whether the "costs" to the household that would be forced to pay more tax if this exclusion were repealed are worth more, in whatever value function the policy maker is using, that the benefits to various households that would flow from (a) lower general tax rates; (b) larger unemployment compensation payments; (c) more federally financed training for the unemployed; or (d) any other policy with the same impact on aggregate demand as the exclusion from income tax of unemployment compensation. If tax reformers who want unemployment compensation made subject to tax are unwilling to express a preference for and demonstrate the superiority of alternatives (a), (b), (c), or (d), on grounds of equity or impact on resource

[12] For a demonstration of the sensitivity of the estimates of the redistributional effects of public budgets to estimates of the relative value to households of public goods, see [1].

[13] For the classical treatment of these issues, see [7]. Musgrave omits changes in monetary policy from his list of possible offsetting policies.

allocation, then the appeal to some "true" income definition is empty scholasticism; if they are willing to express such a preference and support it, then the appeal to a "true" income definition is irrelevant.

Not every item on the reformer's agenda will survive the test. To tax scholarships, for example, may result in such serious horizontal inequities between families with children in private schools and families with children in public schools, the future survival and growth of private institutions may be so adversely affected, and taxing the subsidy element in publicly supported education may be so difficult, that sound tax policy may dictate continued exclusion of scholarship income from tax.

Whether or not unemployment compensation is included and scholarships are excluded from taxable income is not the major point of the preceding paragraphs, however. The crucial points are that (a) theory, in the guise of a normative income definition, can do no more than suggest the right policy questions, (b) the Haig-Simons tax base is not the right income definition to use for this purpose, and (c) the final decisions about the tax system should be made on the basis of hard facts concerning the impact of tax changes on resource allocation and explicit welfare judgments regarding the impact of tax changes on income distribution, in the same way that decisions on public expenditures should be made.

APPENDIX

There are at least two ways in which the benefits of household purchases can be measured. The one which has been employed most widely in compiling national income accounts and for most kinds of economic analysis evaluates *all* units of each commodity at its market price. The alternative approach goes back to the diamond-water paradox that so troubled Adam Smith and other classical economists. Noting that water was essential for life while diamonds (in the pre-industrial age) satisfied only vanity, they tried to distinguish between value-in-exchange and value-in-use.

The conflict was resolved in the late 19th century when it was noted that market prices reflect only the value which consumers placed upon commodities *at the margin*. The man who buys six shirts at \$7.50, for example, reveals through his market behavior that he is willing to surrender at least \$7.50 to acquire the sixth shirt, but that he is unwilling to surrender as much as \$7.50 for a seventh shirt. Quite possibly, the man would have purchased some, though fewer, shirts even if the price had been higher. Customarily, we value the six shirts at a total of \$45.00 in the national income accounts and use this figure to measure the income value to the purchaser.

Following the classical tradition, it may be argued that the value of the six shirts to the purchaser is not \$45.00, but rather some larger amount that shows the most that the man would have been willing to pay if confronted with the option of buying six shirts or none. For example, if the man would be willing to pay up to \$15.00 for one shirt, if he would raise his purchases to two shirts when the price was \$12.00, to three shirts at \$10.00, to four at \$9.00, to five at \$8.25, to six at \$7.75, and to seven at \$7.25, and if certain other conditions are satisfied,[14] the value-in-use of the six shirts would be \$(15+12+10+9+8.25+7.75) = \$62.00. In this situation the household has realized a subjective profit, called consumer surplus, of \$17.00. In one sense, \$62.00 is the value of the six shirts to the purchaser. But this approach is subject to a telling practical objection. Infra-marginal valuations are not known. Furthermore, the value-in-use of the commodity would exceed the costs of production including the producer's profit. Generalizing this fact to other commodities, national product, and national income would become impossible in practice to estimate. Furthermore, the conditions, discussed by Hicks, which accord the concept of consumer surplus even logical consistency probably do not exist. Thus, a household's private income is measured as a dollar total, which is identically equal to the sum of the

[14] For the most thorough discussion of the concept of consumer surplus, see [5], and earlier articles by the same author.

physical amounts of each commodity purchased (including assets) multiplied by its price. The household's market behavior reveals that, at the margin, the household values each commodity that it buys at (approximately) its price.[15] Market behavior also reveals that the household values any commodity it does not buy at less than its market price. Accordingly, if the household receives commodities gratis which, left undisturbed, it would not have purchased, then the value of these gifts *to the household* is the price the household would have paid at the margin for the gift. For example, assume a household wins a free trip to Las Vegas which could be purchased at $500, but that the household would have made the trip only if the cost to it were $300 or less. The value of the prize to the household is $300.[16] If commodities are provided at some price less than cost, the same principle applies. Thus, if the prize were instead the right to purchase a trip to Las Vegas at $200, the value of the privilege to the household would be $100. To put the same matter another way, *the value of the subsidy to the household* is $100.

This procedure of valuation applies not only to private goods and services, but also to collectively provided goods and services. Thus, the value to a household of "public goods" — that class of commodities which generates widely diffused externalities and which is typically provided by governments — is the amount which the household would be willing to pay for the commodity at the margin if its true preferences were known. This parallelism between private and public goods is well established and need not be presented here.[17]

[15] The word "approximately" is employed because households must buy discrete amounts of most commodities. In the example presented in the Appendix, for example, the man can buy only integral numbers of shirts, and the valuation he places on them is either greater than or less than $7.50, the market price, as we consider the last (sixth) shirt he bought or the first shirt he did *not* buy.

[16] Other benefits may accrue to others, such as to the person or business who provided the prize, in the form of advertizing or good will which are worth the difference between the value of the prize to its recipient ($300) and its cost ($500).

REFERENCES

1. H. Aaron and M. C. McGuire, "The Distribution of Benefits From Public Goods," *Econometrica* (forthcoming).
2. B. I. Bittker, "A 'Comprehensive Tax Base' as a Goal of Income Tax Reform," *Harvard Law Review*, Vol. 80, No. 5, March 1967, pp. 925-85.
3. B. I. Bittker, *et al., A Comprehensive Tax Base? A Debate*, Federal Tax Press, 1968.
4. C. O. Galvin, "More on Boris Bittker and the Comprehensive Tax Base: The Practicalities of Tax Reform and the ABA's CSTR," *Harvard Law Review*, Vol. 81, No. 5, March 1968, pp. 1016-43.
5. J. R. Hicks, "Generalized Theory of Consumer Surplus," *Review of Economics Studies*, Vol. 13, 1946, pp. 68-74.
6. M. C. McGuire and H. Aaron, "Efficiency and Equity in the Optimal Supply of a Public Good," *The Review of Economics and Statistics*, Vol. 51, No. 1, February 1969, pp. 31-9.
7. R. A. Musgrave, *The Theory of Public Finance*, McGraw-Hill, 1959.
8. ...., "In Defense of An Income Concept," *Harvard Law Review*, Vol. 81, No. 1, November 1967, pp. 44-62.
9. J. A. Pechman, "Comprehensive Income Taxation: A Comment," *Harvard Law Review*, Vol. 81, No. 1, November 1967, pp. 63-7.
10. Royal Commission of Taxation, *Report*, 6 Vols., Ottawa, 1966.
11. P. A. Samuelson, "Pure Theory of Public Expenditures and Taxation," in *Public Economics*, J. Margolis and H. Guitton, editors, St. Martins Press, 1969.

[17] See [6].

[5]

VOLUME 87 APRIL 1974 NUMBER 6

HARVARD LAW REVIEW

A CONSUMPTION-TYPE OR CASH FLOW PERSONAL INCOME TAX

William D. Andrews *

According to the prevailing ideal, taxable personal income should equal total accretion, which is the sum of personal consumption plus accumulation. Professor Andrews asserts that the worst inequity, distortion, and complexity in the present tax, and the most intractable difficulties in approaching the accretion ideal, have essentially to do with the accumulation component of accretion. He therefore urges that consideration be given to an alternative ideal in which personal taxable income would be computed on a simple cash flow basis to reflect only personal consumption, accumulation in the form of business and investment assets being comprehensively eliminated. Professor Andrews shows how pursuit of this goal would produce a substantial net simplification of the tax, as well as a fairer and more efficient distribution of tax burdens. He concludes by making several more particular recommendations, suggested by a study of the consumption ideal, for immediate improvements in the existing tax. These include cash flow accounting for loan proceeds to curb tax shelter abuses; nontaxation of reinvested capital gains, but taxation of net disinvestment at ordinary income rates; a zero basis for inherited business and investment property; and a supplemental cash flow tax for high-income taxpayers coupled with a sharp reduction of top rates on regular taxable income.

I. INTRODUCTION

SERIOUS thought about personal income tax policy has come to be dominated by an ideal in which taxable income is set equal to total personal gain or accretion, without distinctions as to source or use.[1] It will be convenient to call this ideal an accretion-type personal income tax.

---

* Professor of Law, Harvard Law School. A.B., Amherst College, 1952; LL.B., Harvard, 1955.

[1] H. SIMONS, PERSONAL INCOME TAXATION (1938), is the classic statement. For different views about the usefulness of any general prescriptive model, see B. BITTKER, C. GALVIN, R. MUSGRAVE & J. PECHMAN, A COMPREHENSIVE INCOME TAX BASE? A DEBATE (1968) (mostly reprinted from 80 HARV. L. REV. 925 (1967) and 81 HARV. L. REV. 44, 63, 1016, 1032 (1967–68)). For an argument that even the accretion ideal, properly understood, will admit some distinctions among current uses of funds but none among sources as such, see Andrews, *Personal Deductions in an Ideal Income Tax*, 86 HARV. L. REV. 309, 375 (1972). This Article is in some respects an extension of the argument there.

Accretion is the sum of personal consumption plus accumulation.[2] This relation is the real counterpart of the accounting identity by which income equals spending plus saving, income being the source of funds whose uses are spending and saving.[3] Computation of money income, however, does not require analysis of its spending and savings components, because income can be independently determined by reference to sources of funds, without regard to uses. Insofar as economic activity is adequately represented by monetary measures and transactions, therefore, it may seem that accretion need not be analyzed or measured in terms of its consumption and accumulation components.[4]

But economic activity is not wholly reflected in monetary transactions. Taxable income in a true accretion-type tax would include money income (as a proxy for purchased consumption and accumulation in the form of investment purchases and money savings) plus unpurchased consumption and unpurchased accumulation. Consumption and accumulation thus serve to identify two categories of adjustments that are needed to get from

---

[2] H. SIMONS, *supra* note 1, at 50. Arguably accretion should be defined to equal consumption plus accumulation plus the tax itself, since taxable income is computed without any deduction for the income tax itself. *See* Aaron, *What Is a Comprehensive Tax Base Anyway?*, 22 NAT'L TAX J. 543 (1969). But the failure to deduct the tax itself may be viewed as just a computational shortcut, since any particular rate of tax on taxable income is the equivalent of a tax at a higher rate on disposable income — that is, taxable income minus the tax. A tax of 40% on taxable income is the equivalent of a tax of 66⅔% on what is left for consumption and accumulation; a rate of 70% on taxable income is the equivalent of a rate of 233⅓% on what is left; and so on.

The original version of our modern income tax allowed a deduction for income taxes paid, thus making taxable income correspond to disposable income. *See* Act of October 3, 1913, ch. 16, § 2(B), 38 Stat. 167. The deduction has continued for state and local taxes but was dropped in 1917 for federal taxes, presumably because it was perceived to be an unnecessary computational complexity, at least in the case of the income tax itself. Senator Hollis said, "It is a pure matter of expediency. If you so arrange the income tax this year that you allow those who pay it to take back a third of it next year, you have simply got to put on a bigger tax . . . ." 55 CONG. REC. 6324 (1917); *see* C. KAHN, PERSONAL DEDUCTIONS IN THE FEDERAL INCOME TAX 67 (1960).

[3] Indeed Simons' definition specifies that *personal income* is the sum of consumption plus accumulation. *See* note 9 *infra*. We will try to keep separate names for real values and monetary measures. *See* p. 1120 *infra*.

[4] In an early formulation accretion was not analyzed into consumption and accumulation components. "Income is the *money value of the net accretion to one's economic power between two points of time.*" Haig, *The Concept of Income — Economic and Legal Aspects*, in THE FEDERAL INCOME TAX 1, 7 (R. Haig ed. 1921), *reprinted in* AMERICAN ECONOMIC ASS'N, READINGS IN THE ECONOMICS OF TAXATION 54, 59 (R. Musgrave & C. Shoup eds. 1959). Simons thought this formulation "does not go far to describe its content in relation to particular problems of income determination." H. SIMONS, *supra* note 1, at 61.

money income to total real accretion. The tax falls short of the ideal in relation to consumption insofar as it fails to reflect consumption income in kind, whether enjoyed as an incident of employment or as imputed income from services or property, or even the direct enjoyment of leisure time and activities.[5] Similarly, the tax falls short of the ideal in relation to accumulation insofar as it fails to reflect accumulation in kind in such forms as unrealized capital appreciation and the accrual of pension rights.[6] As we think about the tax in real terms, consumption and accumulation emerge as two distinct components of the underlying subject matter in terms of which the tax should ultimately be understood and evaluated.

Consumption and accumulation adjustments are analytically different in several ways. For one thing, failure to tax an item of unpurchased consumption is a matter of permanent exemption; if it is not taxed now it will not be picked up later on. Accumulation, on the other hand, is essentially a matter of timing; if pension rights are not taxed as they accrue, for example, pension income will be fully taxed if and when it is paid. Moreover, accumulation may be either positive or negative. Consumption, on the other hand, is always positive. Consumption is not always less than accretion; it will be more during any period of net disaccumulation. Indeed even accretion may be negative if disaccumulation exceeds consumption.

If we think about the personal income tax in real terms, as a tax on accretion, and of accretion as consumption plus accumulation (or minus disaccumulation), reflection will show that its worst inequity, distortion, and complexity arise out of inconsistency in the treatment of accumulation. Under existing law, as we shall see, the effect is often to impair the integrity of the tax in relation to consumption as well as accumulation, so that some taxpayers with high standards of living pay limited taxes. But the underlying source of difficulty is with the accumulation component of accretion. Savings out of ordinary income are fully taxed, while accumulation of wealth in kind through appreciation in value of property already owned is not reflected in current taxable income. Further complications arise from this disparity. Some gains, though realized, are unrecognized by reason of special statutory provisions like those governing corporate reorganizations. These are among the most complex provisions in the statute, and have a substantial effect upon the structuring of

[5] H. Simons, *supra* note 1, at 51–55, 110–24.

[6] *Id.* at 148–69. However, Simons did not believe that, as a practical matter, unrealized appreciation could be, or needed to be, taxed until the property was transferred by gift or at death. *Id.* at 100.

financial transactions. Recognized long-term capital gains are taxed at not more than half the regular rate. This discrepancy in rates means that realized capital gain income is partially permanently exempted from tax, even if and when devoted to consumption instead of accumulation. Wealth whose accumulation has already been taxed or permanently exempted is not to be taxed again, and so the statute has complex and imperfect provisions for computing and subtracting basis on sales, and for amortizing basis against ordinary income in the case of depreciable property. Distortions in the computation of depreciation and other items are sometimes grossly magnified by the way borrowing is treated in the case of leveraged investments, so that a limited passive investment may produce an artificial loss which shelters other income from tax even though that other income remains freely available for current consumption or other investments.

The way out of these difficulties, according to the accretion ideal, is to make taxable income provide a more comprehensive reflection of real accumulation, and therefore accretion, by including unrealized changes in the value of property in taxable income. Literal achievement of that goal would require that all assets be taken into account at current fair market value at the end of each accounting period. Although practical exigencies may prevent comprehensive inclusion of unrealized appreciation, improvement is thought to lie in that direction.

Another remedy for present difficulties lies in just the other direction. It involves putting the income tax treatment of business and investment transactions more completely on a simple cash flow basis. Investment expenditures would be deductible when made; on the other hand, all receipts from business and investment activities, including loan proceeds, would be immediately and fully includable in taxable income. This would have the effect of treating accumulation consistently by excluding it from taxable income even when it is represented by investment of realized gains or of ordinary income.

On its face this possibility may seem to be a step in the wrong direction, a step further away from fairness and equity as represented by the prevailing accretion ideal. But a cash flow income tax would correspond very closely to another ideal, that of a tax whose burdens are apportioned to current personal consumption expenditures rather than to total accretion. Net cash flow from business and investment activities is a simple and practical measure of cash flow devoted to consumption expenditure. It will be convenient to call this kind of tax a consumption-type personal income tax. Such a tax has been discussed and advocated in the economic literature,[7] and even tried, briefly, in Sri Lanka (formerly Ceylon) and India. But it has been discussed as an alternative or supplement to an income tax, not as an ideal implicit in or appropriate for the personal income tax itself.

Insofar as one thinks of economic activity as adequately represented by money transactions and historical costs, the existing personal income tax is largely an accretion-type tax. Money income is generally taxed whether spent or saved. But in real rather than monetary terms, the existing tax is a hybrid, closer in many respects to a consumption-type than an accretion-type tax. Unrealized capital appreciation and accruals under qualified pension and profit-sharing plans are a large portion of total real accumulation,[8] yet are not taxed. For many persons they repre-

---

[7] The best and most comprehensive discussion is N. KALDOR, AN EXPENDITURE TAX (1955). Earlier advocates include I. FISHER & H. FISHER, CONSTRUCTIVE INCOME TAXATION (1942); T. HOBBES, LEVIATHAN ch. 30 (1651); J. S. MILL, PRINCIPLES OF POLITICAL ECONOMY bk. V, ch. I, § 4 (Laughlin ed. 1884); A. PIGOU, A STUDY IN PUBLIC FINANCE, 102–133 (3d rev. ed. 1949); W. VICKERY, AGENDA FOR PROGRESSIVE TAXATION 329–66 (1947); Marshall, *The Equitable Distribution of Taxation* (1917), in MEMORIALS OF ALFRED MARSHALL 340, 350–51 (A. Pigou ed. 1925). Unfortunately Fisher, the first American writer in this list, put the matter as one of definition, defining income to mean yield, and his work has accordingly tended to be understood and criticized as a simple confusion in definition between income and consumption.

Keynes declined to discuss the desirability of a consumption-type tax, dismissing it as "perhaps theoretically sound . . . [but] practically impossible." *See* N. KALDOR, *supra*, at 12. For recent discussions of practical feasibility, see Kelley, *Is an Expenditure Tax Feasible?*, 23 NAT'L TAX J. 237 (1970), and Slitor, *Administrative Aspects of Expenditures Taxation*, in BROAD-BASED TAXES: NEW OPTIONS AND SOURCES 227 (R. Musgrave ed. 1973).

For contrary views favoring an accretion-type tax, see *e.g.*, H. SIMMONS, *supra* note 1, at 225–31; Seligman, *Income Tax*, in 7 ENCYCLOPEDIA OF THE SOCIAL SCIENCES 626 (1932).

It should be noted here that during World War II a consumption-type tax was proposed by the Treasury Department as a supplement to the existing income tax, but the proposal was rejected. *See* R. PAUL, TAXATION IN THE UNITED STATES 291–94 (1954).

[8] Capital gains are not included in personal income or personal saving as computed and reported by the Department of Commerce. One estimate of total accrued capital gains, realized and unrealized, for the period 1948–64 shows them to be more than twice the reported personal saving. The estimate is $682.5 billion for the period as compared with reported personal saving of $310.4 billion; accrued capital gains thus represent more than two-thirds of total personal saving including capital gains. Only $146.8 billion of the capital gains in this period were realized. Bhatia, *Accrued Capital Gains, Personal Income and Saving in the United States, 1948–1964*, 16 REV. OF INCOME AND WEALTH 363, 374–77 (1970). Thus unrealized capital gains ($536 billion) represent more than one-half of total capital gains and personal saving ($993 billion). For another discussion of the magnitude of unrealized capital gains, see Bailey, *Capital Gains and Income Taxation*, in THE TAXATION OF INCOME FROM CAPITAL 11 (A. Harberger & M. Bailey eds. 1969).

sent most real accumulation, and for such persons the existing tax may be well represented by the model of a consumption-type tax.

A person with a moderate amount of income-producing property, for example, may live on the yield without either drawing down or adding to principal. He may take care of the future by investing in securities that will show some appreciation in value as well as current yield. Money income for him provides a close measure of consumption expenditure. Real accretion, however, would also include unrealized changes in the value of his property.

Or an employee may spend his whole salary, without saving or dissaving, if his employer is making adequate provision for his retirement and other emergencies through pension plan contributions and the like. Again, current money income will provide a measure of current consumption expenditure, not of total real accretion which would also have to include the increase in value of accrued pension rights each year.

The question whether our existing personal income tax is better represented by the accretion model or by a consumption model can be restated by asking who to take as typical, an individual whose accumulation is represented by savings bank deposits and interest or one whose accumulation takes the form of unrealized capital appreciation or pension accruals. And the question of whether to prefer the consumption model or the accretion model as an ideal can be restated by asking whose tax treatment to take as a prototype. There is clearly a discrepancy in our present treatment, which ought to be removed, but there is no a priori reason to think the way to remove the discrepancy is by taxing unrealized appreciation and pension accruals. It may well be simpler, fairer, and more efficient to provide generally for tax deferral on savings accounts and other forms of saving out of realized income, while taxing eventual disinvestment from savings accounts and capital assets alike at full, ordinary income rates.

This conclusion may be resisted by one who looks to the income tax as a device for curtailing the accumulation of wealth as well as consumption. But the existing income tax has not been fair or effective in relation to accumulation of wealth, and it would not be easy to make it so. Even if it were practical, it is

---

Pension accruals are much smaller in amount. One estimate indicates that personal saving of $53 billion in 1970 included a $9.7 billion increase in private pension reserves. Also not included in personal income or saving was an increase of $9 billion in government insurance and pension reserves. U.S. BUREAU OF THE CENSUS, STATISTICAL ABSTRACT OF THE UNITED STATES: 1972, at 321.

not clear that we should want to tax the accumulation of fresh wealth without some corresponding imposition on existing stocks of wealth. If we are serious about reaching wealth, therefore, it would be better to strengthen and rely on estate and gift taxes for that purpose, focusing the income tax on the consumption component of accretion where it can be made to be most fair and effective.

Prevailing patterns of thought are reflected in common vocabulary. An accretion-type personal income tax is usually simply called an ideal or comprehensive income tax, personal income being defined to mean accretion.[9] No distinction is thus maintained between practical and ideal bases (money income and real accretion); or at least no name is saved for the former. A consumption-type personal income tax, on the other hand, has been called an expenditure tax, suggesting that it is something quite different from an income tax, indeed somehow its opposite, income and expenditure being contrary notions. This terminology obscures the fact that in practice such a tax would be based on a simple cash flow computation of net yield from business and investment activities, with no more effort to keep direct track of particular consumption expenditures than under the existing income tax.[10]

---

[9] The most familiar instance is in H. SIMONS, *supra* note 1, at 50:

> Personal income may be defined as the algebraic sum of (1) the market value of rights exercised in consumption and (2) the change in the value of the store of property rights between the beginning and the end of the period in question.

Haig proceeded the same way. *See* note 4 *supra*.

[10] There is some tendency to think an expenditure tax base would have to be defined net of tax, since whatever is paid in tax is unavailable for expenditure. Then, to get the equivalent of income tax rates over 50% one would have to have expenditure tax rates in excess of 100%. But there is no more to that point in relation to a consumption-type tax than an accretion-type tax; if tax payments are not part of consumption, they are not part of accretion either, since they are certainly not included in accumulation. Moreover, as a matter of computational convenience, it may well be better to define the practical base on a gross basis, as consumption expenditures plus the tax itself, since this corresponds to net cash flow from business and investment activities without any deduction for the tax. Statutory rates can then be kept on a scale of less than 100%, a scale with which we are familiar, though the effective rate in relation to what is left after tax will sometimes exceed 100% just as it does under present law. *See* note 2 *supra*.

It would make some real difference in timing of tax liability, beyond mere computational convenience, if taxable income were determined by deducting taxes on a cash basis, since each year's tax would then depend in part on what was paid in final settlement of the prior year's liability. *See* N. KALDOR, *supra* note 7, at 232–38.

Throughout this Article it is assumed that in both the accretion and consumption models, as under existing law, taxable income is determined without any deduction for the tax itself.

In this Article, *personal income tax* means any tax whose practical computation is based on personal income transactions. *Income* thus refers primarily to the money transactions that make such a tax a practical possibility. *Consumption*, *accumulation*, and *accretion* refer to real values, accretion being the sum of consumption plus accumulation. The monetary counterparts of consumption and accumulation, which add up to money income, are called *spending* and *saving*. The prevailing prescriptive model of a personal income tax is called an *accretion-type personal income tax*, and a model in which accumulation is comprehensively excluded is called a *consumption-type personal income tax*. The latter is also called a *cash flow personal income tax* because that describes its practical computation. For shorthand it will be convenient often to refer simply to the accretion model or ideal on the one hand, and the consumption or cash flow model on the other. The existing tax is a *hybrid personal income tax* since it conforms to the accretion ideal in some respects and the consumption ideal in others, but neither with any consistency.[11]

The difference between an accretion-type and a consumption-type personal income tax involves only accumulation, and it is in an important sense only a difference of timing. If an item of accumulation is not reflected in taxable income, the tax is not waived but only deferred. Under either kind of ideal, what is ultimately subject to tax is the same — funds or wealth available for private consumption.

This difference in timing corresponds to a difference in methods of accounting for business and investment activities. For a

---

[11] This terminology is parallel to common usage with respect to sales taxes. The term *sales tax* is understood to refer to any tax whose practical computation is based on sales transactions. Sales taxes are differentiated into several particular types according to what sales are taxed and with what refinements. A value-added tax is a species of sales tax in which a deduction or credit is given at each stage of production and distribution for taxes paid at prior stages. Value-added taxes may be of the consumption type, if an immediate deduction is given for capital investments, or of the income type, if capital goods investments are amortized over their useful life. The relation between a consumption-type and an accretion-type personal income tax, explored in this Article, is closely analogous to the relation between a consumption-type and an income-type value-added tax. *See* C. Shoup, Public Finance 250–57, 347 (1969).

The possibility of imposing graduated rates and granting personal exemptions arises from the use of personal income transactions as a practical base, not from the choice between consumption and accretion as a goal or ideal. Rate graduation and personal exemptions cannot be incorporated directly into a sales tax, whether it is of the consumption type or the income type, because the reporting of sales transactions by sellers gives no index of aggregate consumption or accretion of the individuals to whom sales are made.

consumption-type tax, accounting should be on a pure and simple cash flow basis.[12] For an accretion-type tax, accounting must be put on something approximating fair-market-value accounting for business and investment assets. Our existing hybrid tax can then be defined in relation to these ideals by reference to its method of accounting, in which the cost of business and investment assets is required to be capitalized but subsequent increases in value are not generally taken into account until realization.

The difference in timing between a consumption-type and an accretion-type tax is, however, immensely important in defining the real burden of the tax. Under the accretion ideal capital accumulation and its subsequent yield are both to be taxed as they occur, and such a tax would cast a heavier burden on some taxpayers than if the tax on capital accumulation is deferred until subsequent disinvestment. Consider a farmer who plants and grows 100 fruit trees. A 30% tax on his fruit, if and when it appears for harvest, with no tax on the growth of the trees unless and until they are disposed of, would leave him with the fruit of 70 trees. But if the Government took 30% of the trees themselves as they mature, and 30% of the fruit of the remaining 70 trees, the farmer would be left with the fruit of only 49. Or, similarly, consider an individual setting aside funds for retirement. A 30% tax deferred until retirement will leave him with 70% as much to spend as he would have had in the absence of tax. A 30% accretion-type tax imposed on the funds as earned and also on the yield from investing what is left, will leave substantially less.[13]

Nevertheless, the consumption and accretion ideals reinforce one another in important ways. Consumption is the major component of accretion for most taxpayers most of the time, and therefore under either ideal, the tax is in the long run mostly a tax on household consumption. The principal purpose of the tax, in terms of real goods and services, is to curtail private consumption so that resources will be released for public use. What makes

[12] Cash receipts and disbursements accounting as authorized under the existing income tax corresponds to cash flow accounting with respect to accounts receivable and payable. Cash receipts and disbursements accounting for farmers goes further since it results in immediate deductibility of various capital expenditures. *See* Treas. Reg. § 1.162–12 (1958); Treas. Reg. § 1.471–6 (1958); Davenport, *A Bountiful Tax Harvest*, 48 TEXAS L. REV. 1 (1969). There are also a number of special statutory provisions that authorize immediate deductions for a variety of things that, strictly speaking, represent capital expenditures. INT. REV. CODE OF 1954, §§ 174, 175, 180, 182, 263(c) [INT. REV. CODE OF 1954 hereinafter cited as CODE]. Pure cash flow accounting means immediate deductibility of all business and investment expenditures, and inclusion in current income of all cash receipts from business and investment.

[13] *See* pp. 1124–25 *infra*.

a personal income tax the fairest tax we have is that its burdens are generally cast in sensible relation to standards of living.

More particularly, the consumption ideal reinforces the main lesson of the accretion ideal: that distinctions should not be drawn, for personal income tax purposes, because items of income accrue from different sources. The municipal bond exemption is equally inconsistent with either ideal. On the other hand, both ideals face the same difficulties in reconciling real consumption with consumption expenditure, since, under either, money income only provides a measure of the latter. Problems of imputed income from services, consumer capital, and leisure are essentially the same under both ideals, as are problems of employee fringe benefits like travel and entertainment. The consumption ideal will do nothing, except indirectly in the case of consumer capital,[14] to eliminate or essentially alter any of these problems.

I believe, for reasons to be developed, that the consumption model offers better solutions to the question of how to treat accumulation than does the prevailing accretion model. But even if one is not prepared to abandon the accretion model as a goal, the consumption model can help achieve a better understanding of the existing tax by providing another frame of reference for critical evaluation. Indeed, the two models together may provide a kind of binocular or stereoscopic view that will give a better sense of depth and perspective than does either model alone. Studying the model of a consumption-type personal income tax will help us to be more analytic about accretion, separating the problems and implications of taxing its consumption component from those of also including accumulation. That may enable us to see better what can and must be done to preserve the integrity of the tax in relation to the consumption component of accretion, whatever one may further decide to do about accumulation.

The main purpose of this Article is to set forth the model of a consumption-type personal income tax as an alternative for understanding the practical potential of the existing tax. That is done in part V, and a reader who wants to do so can go directly to part V. Parts II, III, and IV are designed to pave the way by describing, respectively, the importance of deferral, the distortion, complexity, and inequity that arise from our existing hybrid treatment of accumulation, and the difficulties of resolving those problems by moving closer to a true accretion-type tax. Part VI addresses the questions of relative fairness and economic efficiency of the consumption and accretion ideals.

Part VII contains an attempt to show how the consumption ideal can be used to generate fair and practical solutions to par-

[14] *See* pp. 1155–60 *infra*.

ticular pressing problems under the existing personal income tax, that can be adopted and implemented in the immediate future even if one is not yet ready to abandon accretion in favor of consumption as an ultimate goal or ideal. Several recommendations are set forth. One is to deal with the tax shelter problem by making net cash flow a floor for the computation of taxable gain or loss. Another is to deal with various aspects of the capital gain problem along lines that would permit taxfree rollover while gains remain invested, but would require full taxation at ordinary income rates upon disinvestment. It is also suggested that investment property transferred by gift or at death be given a zero basis in the hands of the transferee, which, in conjunction with a rollover provision, would have the effect of taxing persons on a consumption basis to the extent that they use up such property to finance their standards of living. Finally, it is recommended that a cash flow, consumption-type tax should be adopted forthwith for persons with incomes over $20,000, with top rates under the existing tax to be reduced as the consumption-type tax is phased in. This arrangement would represent a superior way of achieving objectives now aimed at by both the minimum tax on tax preferences and the maximum rate for earned income.

This Article is only about personal taxes. It is almost entirely about the personal income tax, with some limited reference to estate and gift taxes. The simplification in the personal income tax that could be accomplished by adopting and pursuing the consumption ideal, as described here, would not be reflected automatically, therefore, in the corporate income tax. The argument may have implications with respect to the corporate income tax or a general sales or value-added tax, but these are not stated or explored.

II. The Value of Deferral

It has sometimes been thought that mere deferral of income taxes was not of great importance so long as every element of accretion was eventually accounted for.[15] Sophisticated taxpayers and their counsel, however, have realized that deferral is often of immense importance, and recent writing on matters of tax policy has come to reflect that realization.[16] Some appreciation of the value of deferral is essential for an understanding of the

[15] *See, e.g.*, H. Simons, *supra* note 1, at 208.

[16] *See, e.g.*, S. Surrey, Pathways to Tax Reform 108–11, 117–25, 317–19, 323–24 (1973); 3 Report of the Royal Commission on Taxation 344, 378–80 (Canada 1967); McKee, *The Real Estate Tax Shelter: A Computerized Exposé*, 57 Va. L. Rev. 521 (1971); Shoup, *The White Paper: Accrual Accounting for Capital Gains and Losses*, 18 Can. Tax J. 96 (1970).

argument in this Article because the difference between accretion and consumption ideals is essentially one of deferral, and because the defects in present law that make it an unacceptable hybrid arise from inconsistencies in matters of timing.

Deferral may be valuable under existing law partly because it leads to ultimate outright exemption or taxation at lower rates. Unrealized appreciation is completely exempted in the case of property held until death, because no income tax will have been imposed on such appreciation and the succeeding owner is given a stepped-up basis equal to value at or shortly after date of death.[17] Income whose recognition is deferred until after retirement is often taxed at lower rates then than if it had been taxed during higher-income, active employment years, and not infrequently the corollary of deferral is taxation at capital gain instead of ordinary income rates.[18]

But the important, underlying fact is that even if rates do not change and nothing is ever permanently exempted, mere deferral can be immensely important. Deferral reduces the burden of a tax because of the time value of money; it requires less than a dollar put aside today to meet a dollar of tax liability in the future. The magnitude of the effect, which is a function of interest rates, tax rates, and length of deferral, can be illustrated by several examples.

A. Productive Investment

The fruit farmer in the introduction is one example. A 30% tax on the growth of his 100 trees when they reach maturity would leave 70 trees, and an annual 30% tax on the fruit thereafter would leave the taxpayer each year with the fruit from 49.[19]

---

[17] CODE § 1014.

[18] For example, income offset by depreciation deductions may reappear as gain on disposition of the depreciated property; in the case of real estate a significant part of this may only be capital gain rather than ordinary income. *See* CODE § 1250. Similarly, income offset by the immediate deduction of capital expenditures may reappear as capital gain on disposition. If a stock dividend goes untaxed, the gain it represents will be deferred until the stock is disposed of, when it will probably be taxed as capital gain rather than ordinary income.

[19] Strictly speaking, of course, if the trees are depreciable, then the whole yield would not be taxed. On the other hand, under a true accretion-type tax the Government would take more than 30% of the trees themselves, since it would not wait for them to reach maturity. In any event a tax that takes capital appreciation into account (as a positive item) will ultimately cast a heavier burden than one at the same rates that applies only to yield. If capital depreciation is effectively taken into account as a net negative item, as under present practice in relation to leveraged tax shelter investments, then the burden will be less than if the tax were on cash flow. *See* notes 23–24 *infra*.

The example of the fruit farmer is from I. FISHER & H. FISHER, *supra* note 7, at 56–57.

On the other hand, if all tax on the trees could be deferred until the trees were disposed of, with a current tax being imposed only on the fruit harvested, the taxpayer would keep 70% of the fruit of 100 trees, which is 42.9% more than the fruit from 49.

If the rate of tax were 60% instead of 30%, then the difference would be between the fruit of 16 trees if both the growth of the trees and the fruit were taxed, and that of 40 trees if only the fruit were taxed. The value of deferral here is thus a 150% increase in after-tax yield.

B. Retirement Income

Consider a dollar of earnings put aside for retirement. Assume this sum is invested at 9% compound interest, and that it is to be utilized 24 years later. In the absence of tax the one dollar set aside would support eight dollars of retirement consumption 24 years later.[20]

Now consider the effect of a 33% accretion-type tax. This would take away one-third of the original dollar when earned, leaving only 67 cents to invest; and it would cut the rate of growth from 9% per annum to 6%. At 6% per annum for 24 years, 67 cents will produce a retirement fund of only $2.67, as compared with $8.00 in the absence of tax. On the other hand, if the tax were deferred until retirement, the taxpayer would pay only $2.67 tax out of $8.00, leaving $5.33 to spend. Deferral of the tax, without any change in rate, would double what the taxpayer has left to spend.

The effect is greater for higher interest rates, higher tax rates, and longer periods. A dollar held at 12% for 36 years, for example, would produce a fund of $64. A 70% true accretion-type tax would reduce the original dollar to 30 cents, and the rate of growth from 12% to 3.6%. At 3.6%, 30 cents will grow to about $1.07 in 36 years, which represents a reduction from $64.00 of about 98.3%. A 70% tax deferred until retirement would take only $44.80 out of $64.00, leaving $19.20 to spend. This is more than eighteen times the amount left by a 70% tax imposed on a true accretion basis.

C. Securities Yields

Consider a person who lives on the dividend income from securities that have doubled in value. Under existing law the

[20] There is a convenient rule of thumb that says money invested at x percent per annum compound interest will double in 72/x years. This rule is reasonably accurate for any period in excess of about three years — or even for shorter periods if interest is compounded more often than annually. Therefore, at 9% money will double three times in 24 years.

increase in value will not be taxed so long as he retains those securities; it will be taxed, however, if he sells, even though the proceeds are reinvested in similar securities. A 60% tax will leave 40 cents out of each dollar of pretax dividend income, so long as the tax on appreciation is deferred. If the appreciation were taxed currently, however, at 60%, it would take 30% of the taxpayer's capital to pay the tax. That would cut his annual dividends to 70% of their original pretax amount, and a further tax of 60% on the remaining dividend income would leave only 28 cents for each dollar of original yield prior to imposition of any tax. A 60% tax on a comprehensive accretion-type basis is therefore the equivalent, in this case, of a 72% tax on yield alone. The differential would be greater if unrealized appreciation were more than 50% of value.

D. *Deferral as the Equivalent of Exempting Yield*

A study of these examples will reveal a simple but accurate relation: where rates are constant, deferring the tax is the equivalent of imposing the tax initially, but exempting any subsequent profit due to continued investment of what is left after payment of the tax. For the fruit farmer, for example, in a 30% rate bracket, deferring tax until harvest left him with 70% of the fruit of 100 trees. This is exactly the same result as if the Government had taken 30 trees initially, but then exempted the fruit from the remaining 70. Or in the retirement income cases, for the taxpayer in a 33% bracket, deferral left 67% of what would have been available after retirement in the absence of tax. This is the same result as if the Government had taken 33% of the original dollar, but then let the remaining 67 cents grow to $5.33 without further tax.

In the case given of dividends on appreciated securities, the amount of gain on which tax is deferred is only part of the total value of the investment. Deferral of tax on the gain is the equivalent of exempting dividends on the gain which would have been left had the tax been imposed initially.[21]

E. *Deduction of a Capital Expenditure*

The relation can perhaps be seen more easily when deferral

[21] Using the securities example described in part C above, and assuming that the taxpayer owns 100 shares of stock which pay annual dividends of $5 per share, a deferred tax of 60% would reduce annual dividend income from $500 to $200. This is the same as if the tax were imposed initially on the capital appreciation, cutting the stock holdings to 70 shares, but then the dividend income on 20 of the remaining shares ($100) was exempted from tax, while that from the other 50 shares ($250) was taxed at 60%.

results from the immediate deduction of a capital expenditure.[22] Suppose a taxpayer invests $100 in a way that will increase his revenues (or decrease expenses) by $400 in some subsequent year. His anticipated, before-tax rate of profit over the period involved is 300%.

Now consider income taxes. If the expenditure is nondeductible, there will be a taxable gain of $300 in the later year. At 40% this would produce a tax of $120, which would reduce the proceeds in the later year from $400 to $280, and the rate of profit from 300% to 180%. Reducing the rate of profit from 300% to 180% is an unsurprising result for a 40% tax.

On the other hand, if the $100 expenditure is deductible when made, then the whole $400 return will be taxable in the subsequent year. At 40% the tax would be $160 and the net after-tax proceeds only $240. But the deduction reduced the after-tax cost of the expenditure itself from $100 to $60. An after-tax return of $240 from an after-tax investment of $60 represents a dollar profit of $180 just as if the original expenditure were nondeductible. But $180 profit on an after-tax investment of $60 is a 300% profit, just the same as if there had been no tax in effect.[23]

If only part of the original investment is deductible, the taxpayer's rate of return will be reduced by the tax but by less than

---

[22] Professor Shoup says

> The fact that completely accelerated depreciation, when coupled with complete loss offset, is equivalent to exemption of net return from the asset, under an income tax, was discovered by E. Cary Brown (see his "Business-Income Taxation and Investment Incentives," in *Income, Employment and Public Policy: Essays in Honor of Alvin H. Hansen* [New York: Norton, 1948], pp. 309–10), reprinted in Musgrave and Shoup, Readings in the Economics of Taxation.

C. SHOUP, PUBLIC FINANCE 302 n.20 (1969). Professor Surrey quotes Shoup, notes his use of the term "discovered," and observes:

> Perhaps a Congressman can be pardoned for not appreciating the benefit of deferral if its ramifications apparently eluded public finance specialists for 35 years of our income tax history.

S. SURREY, *supra* note 16, at 123.

[23] To summarize:

No Immediate Deduction

	Investment Cost	Return	Profit	
Before Tax	$100	$400	$300	300%
Tax	0	120	120	—
After Tax	$100	$280	$180	180%

Immediate Deduction

	Investment Cost	Return	Profit	
Before Tax	$100	$400	$300	300%
Tax	40 (saving)	160	120	—
After Tax	$ 60	$240	$180	300%

the nominal rate of tax. On the other hand, if the taxpayer is able to deduct more than the amount of his original investment, even though it is all taken back into taxable income on liquidation, the effect will be that his rate of return on net investment will be ***more*** than it is in the absence of tax.[24] This is essentially what is involved in leveraged tax shelter investments where a taxpayer is permitted to deduct capital expenditures paid for by lenders as well as himself.

III. The Existing Hybrid Treatment of Accumulation

The existing personal income tax is a hybrid of the consumption and accretion models in relation to accumulation. Annual savings represented by cash or the cost of purchased investment assets are effectively included in taxable income, but unrealized appreciation is not. Even realized gain on many particular exchanges goes unrecognized under special statutory provisions. Recognized gains are included in taxable income, but in the case of long-term capital gains are taxed at not more than half the rate applicable to other income. Moreover, employee retirement savings are often excluded from taxable income, and even retirement savings of the self-employed are excluded to a limited extent.

The prevailing notion appears to be that accumulation is included in taxable income, but that its inclusion is often deferred for a variety of reasons. Mainly, capital appreciation is not taken into account until realization because of the inconveniences and hardships of making the tax depend upon periodic general assessments of property value and of requiring premature liquidation of investments to raise funds with which to pay the tax. But waiting represents much more of a gap in the taxation of accumulation than is immediately obvious. Much accumulation ultimately escapes taxation altogether by reason of the step-up in

---

[24] Continuing the summary in note 23:

Immediate Deduction of 50%

	Investment Cost	Return	Profit	
Before Tax	$100	$400	$300	300%
Tax	20 (saving)	140	120	—
After Tax	$ 80	$260	$180	225%

(effective rate of tax reduced to 25%)

Immediate Deduction of 200%

	Investment Cost	Return	Profit	
Before Tax	$100	$400	$300	300%
Tax	80 (saving)	200	120	—
After Tax	$ 20	$200	$180	900%

(effective rate of tax reduced to ***minus*** *200%!*)

basis at death.[25] But even if that were changed, taxing accumulation as well as consumption is a matter of *not* waiting; any failure to tax accumulation as it occurs is thus a pro tanto omission from a true accretion base. Moreover, while waiting for realization may be convenient in relation to a single investment, the inconsistency between taxing realized gains and cash savings and not taxing unrealized and unrecognized gains, is the generating source of most of the worst complexity, inequity, and distortion in our existing tax.

A. Realization and Nonrecognition

The value of deferral makes it important, to taxpayers and Government alike, when gain is considered to be realized, because tax will be deferred until it is. In *Eisner v. Macomber*[26] the Supreme Court held that no gain was realized on the receipt of a simple stock dividend of common stock on the common stock of the same company, raising the matter, unfortunately, to the level of constitutional limitation. However doubtful its continuing constitutional authority,[27] the decision has been a kind of cornerstone around which subsequent legislation has been constructed. We do not tax mere appreciation in value; we do not tax undistributed corporate earnings to shareholders except in certain cases of foreign corporations controlled by United States shareholders,[28] or by consent;[29] and we still do not tax a stock dividend that effects no change in proportionate interests in the corporation.[30]

Indeed, subsequent legislation has often extended the idea by providing that gain (or loss) is not to be recognized even on

[25] CODE § 1014; *see* U.S. TREASURY DEP'T, TAX REFORM STUDIES AND PROPOSALS pt. 3, at 331–34 (Joint Publication of the House Comm. on Ways and Means and the Senate Comm. on Finance, 91st Cong., 1st Sess., 1969) (estimating that $12 to $15 billion of capital gains permanently escapes taxation each year as a result of § 1014).

[26] 252 U.S. 189 (1920).

[27] *See* Helvering v. Griffiths, 318 U.S. 371 (1943); Helvering v. Bruun, 309 U.S. 461 (1940); *Hearings Before the House Comm. on Ways and Means on the President's 1961 Tax Recommendations*, 87th Cong., 1st Sess. 313 (1961).

[28] *See* CODE §§ 551, 951.

[29] *E.g.*, CODE § 1373 (subchapter S corporations).

[30] CODE § 305. The treatment of stock dividends generally has had a tortuous history. At one point Congress provided that a stock dividend should be nontaxable "to the extent that it does not constitute income to the shareholder within the meaning of the Sixteenth Amendment to the Constitution." Int. Rev. Code of 1939, § 115(f)(1), 53 Stat. 47. The Government sought to tax a dividend of common on common under that provision, arguing that *Macomber* had no continuing constitutional validity; the Supreme Court held that the provision referred to the meaning of the sixteenth amendment as construed in *Macomber*, whether or not the constitutional provision would still be so construed. Helvering v. Griffiths, 318 U.S. 371 (1943).

certain exchanges and other transactions that come within the courts' concept of realization. Nonrecognition, like nonrealization, is generally a matter of further deferral of tax, since the basis of property received taxfree is determined in a manner that will preserve future taxability of the unrecognized gain.[31]

The nonrecognition provisions include the corporate reorganization provisions[32] under which investors may participate in a variety of mergers, spinoffs, recapitalizations, and other assorted transactions without recognition of gain or loss for income tax purposes if the requirements of the statute (and others supplied by courts) are met. The corporate reorganization provisions are sometimes described as intended to avoid tax when there has not been any genuine economic realization of gain,[33] whatever that may mean, but often their effect is to postpone tax on exchanges that represent much more a disposition than a mere modification of an old investment.[34] Property other than corporate securities may be able to be exchanged tax free for property "of a like kind," though essentially unrelated.[35] In certain circumstances even gain represented by cash proceeds may be unrecognized if the cash is reinvested in qualifying substitute property.[36]

There are contexts, unblessed by statutory nonrecognition provisions, in which the matter of what constitutes realization is still crucial and problematic. One involves the transfer of property in divorce (and premarital) settlements. A simple gift does not produce any realization of gain, but a transfer of property in exchange for a discharge of support obligations, or of marital property rights, does.[37] Yet a settlement that only secures obliga-

---

[31] Qualifying property received in a taxfree exchange takes the basis of the property surrendered. *E.g.*, CODE § 1031(d). When cash is also involved, or liabilities or nonqualifying property or partial recognition of gain, appropriate adjustments are made. *Id.* The use of "nonrecognition" to denote postponement is not entirely pure. There are instances of statutory nonrecognition at the corporate level that are not a mere matter of deferral because the corporate basis is not carried over anywhere after the transaction. CODE §§ 311, 336–37.

[32] CODE §§ 354–68.

[33] *See, e.g.*, Cortland Specialty Co. v. Commissioner, 60 F.2d 937, 940 (2d Cir. 1932), *cert. denied*, 288 U. S. 599 (1933) ("purpose [of reorganization provisions] was to relieve those interested in corporations from profits taxes in cases where there was only a change in the corporate form in which business was conducted without an actual realization of any gain from an exchange of properties").

[34] *See, e.g.*, Helvering v. Minnesota Tea Co., 296 U. S. 378 (1935) (transfer of assets was a reorganization even though transferors received only about 7½% of the outstanding stock of transferee). In a merger the shareholders of the smaller corporation will generally end up with less than a half interest in the business of their former corporation.

[35] *E.g.*, CODE § 1031.

[36] CODE §§ 1033 (involuntary conversions), 1034 (sale of principal residence).

[37] United States v. Davis, 370 U.S. 65 (1962); Rev. Rul. 57-507, 1957-2 CUM. BULL. 511.

tions without discharging them,[38] or that represents a division of property rather than a transfer,[39] may avoid realization. The urge to postpone tax liability in these cases distorts transactions and complicates behavior for the well-advised; failure to avoid realization presents a trap for the unwary.

The problems of defining realization and prescribing nonrecognition would obviously disappear under either a true accretion-type or a pure consumption-type tax. Changes in value are taxable under the former whether realized or not, while under the latter reinvested gains go untaxed in any event.

B. Long-Term Capital Gain Treatment

Even if realized and recognized, gain from the sale or exchange of a capital asset held for more than six months is taxed at not more than half the rate applicable to other income.[40] "Capital asset" is defined broadly to include corporate securities and investment real estate and most other kinds of property most individuals are likely to hold for accumulation, except property held primarily for sale in the ordinary course of business.[41]

As compared with the nonrecognition provisions, the capital gain provisions may only eliminate about half the current tax on a realized gain, but the elimination is permanent and outright, not a mere matter of deferral. Property received in exchange or on reinvestment of proceeds from a capital gain sale gets a full, current-cost basis; indeed there is no requirement that proceeds be reinvested at all, and capital gains may be spent forthwith for current consumption.

Still, the capital gain provisions can best be understood as an effort to deal with some very real problems in taxing accumulation. One common assumption about the purpose of the capital

---

[38] Rev. Rul. 59-47, 1959-1 CUM. BULL. 198; Rev. Rul. 57-506, 1957-2 CUM. BULL. 65. *See generally* Young, *Separation and Divorce and the Tax Laws: "Waltzes" and "Apache Dances"*, 22 TAX LAW. 551 (1969).

[39] *See, e.g.*, Wallace v. United States, 439 F.2d 757 (8th Cir. 1971); Collins v. Commissioner, 388 F.2d 353 (10th Cir.), *remanded for reconsideration*, 393 U.S. 215 (1968), *on remand*, 412 F.2d 211 (10th Cir. 1969).

[40] CODE § 1202 provides a deduction of half the excess of net long-term capital gain over net short-term capital loss. A deduction of half is tantamount to cutting the tax rate by half, or more because of rate graduation. CODE § 1201(b) sometimes reduces the effective rate further by providing a ceiling rate of 25% on the first $50,000 of net long-term capital gain in excess of net short-term capital loss. Sometimes capital gains are effectively untaxed at the margin since they offset otherwise nondeductible capital losses. *See* CODE § 1211(b). In any event, the reduced rate of tax on capital gains comes on top of the reduction in effective rates that results from the deferral itself and from the § 1014 step-up in basis at death.

[41] CODE § 1221. *See also* CODE § 1231 (prescribing capital gain treatment under certain circumstances for some property excluded from § 1221).

gain provisions is that they are to give relief from the hardship, under a graduated rate schedule, of having several years' appreciation (accumulation) taxed in a single year upon realization.[42] But this explanation is painfully inadequate. Most obviously, it is inconsistent with the statutory provision requiring only a six-month holding period for long-term capital gain treatment.[43] Moreover, while a single capital gain may represent realization of a gain that accrued over an extended period, there is no reason to think that capital gain income is generally a widely fluctuating item for many taxpayers. In many cases the timing of realization of capital gains is subject to more control than the timing of other income items. And capital gain treatment is not generally denied even when the gain from a single sale is spread out through several years, through use of installment sale reporting or other deferral provisions.[44] Finally, the explanation in terms of bunching fails utterly to provide any justification for relief in the case of taxpayers whose ordinary income puts them in high brackets year after year in any event. A very substantial amount of capital gains are reported by very high-bracket taxpayers for whom capital gain rates probably represent something far below the regular marginal rates that could be produced by any kind of spreading of their income among taxable periods.[45]

If the problem of capital gains were truly one of bunching, the sensible remedy would be one of spreading or averaging total income over a period of years.[46] Such a remedy would have no

---

[42] *See, e.g*, Commissioner v. Gillette Motor Transp., Inc., 364 U.S. 130, 134 (1960):

> This Court has long held that the term "capital asset" is to be construed narrowly in accordance with the purpose of Congress to afford capital-gains treatment only in situations typically involving the realization of appreciation in value accrued over a substantial period of time, and thus to ameliorate the hardship of taxation of the entire gain in one year.

[43] CODE § 1222.

[44] *See, e.g.*, Commissioner v. Brown, 380 U.S. 563 (1965).

[45] *See* Pechman & Okner, *Individual Tax Erosion by Income Classes*, in THE ECONOMICS OF FEDERAL SUBSIDY PROGRAMS, PART I — GENERAL STUDY PAPERS (Joint Economic Comm., 92nd Cong., 2d Sess., 1972) (capital gains as a percentage of adjusted gross income are less than 1% for taxpayers with returns less than $30,000, grow to 21% for returns over $100,000, and to 40% for returns above $500,000; therefore, as a percentage of gross income, before deduction of 50% of the capital gains, the percentages are about 2%, 35%, and 60%). Time series data would be helpful in assessing the effect of the capital gain rates, since realization of gains accrued over several years might push a taxpayer into a higher bracket for a single year. But a Treasury Department study indicates that many high-income taxpayers tend to show consistent income patterns from year to year. *See* U.S. TREASURY DEP'T, *supra* note 25, at 87.

[46] *See, e.g.*, Brazer, in Panel Discussion No. 2 on "Capital Gains and Losses," in PANEL DISCUSSIONS ON GENERAL TAX REFORM BEFORE THE HOUSE COMM. ON WAYS AND MEANS, 93D CONG., 1ST SESS. 262 (Comm. Print 1973) (suggesting an

value or effect for regular capital gain repeaters or for regular high-bracket taxpayers, who probably are the biggest beneficiaries of the present provisions.

Another popular justification for capital gain rates has to do with inflation.[47] If a person has invested a dollar of after-tax income in an asset that has grown in value, and later sells the asset, the proceeds should be regarded as taxpaid to the full extent of the real value of his original taxpaid investment, undiluted by inflation. In a very rough way, if capital gains were in fact about half due to inflation, the capital gain provisions would serve on average to accomplish this objective. At least, one might say, the capital gain provisions should not be repealed until something else is done about inflation.

This explanation is still, of course, much too rough, even though inflation is a very real problem. The capital gain provisions exempt half the realized gain from tax; the more one gains the more relief he will be granted. There is no very high correlation, however, between the amount of gain one enjoys and the burden of inflation he bears, except insofar as both are functions of wealth and time. For any two taxpayers with similar amounts of wealth held over the same period of time, the burden of inflation will be just as heavy for the one with no gains as for the one with large gains, and if relief is to be provided for the latter it should be provided for the former, too.[48] Justification of the existing capital gain provisions because *on average* they may compensate for inflation is essentially no justification at all, since the essence of justice in taxation is to treat individuals fairly in relation to one another, according to their relevant individual circumstances, without having one taxpayer bear another's share of the burden to make the average come out right.

The most nearly satisfactory explanation for the capital gain provisions is simply that capital gain rates serve to mitigate dis-

income averaging proposal coupled with reduction in the maximum tax on income from 70% to 50%); *cf.* CODE §§ 1301–05 (providing for income averaging over a 5-year period).

[47] *See, e.g.*, Wallich, in Panel Discussion No. 2, *supra* note 46, at 270–75; *cf.* Musgrave, in Panel Discussion No. 2, *supra* note 46, at 291–93 (agreeing that the inflation component of gain should not be taxed, but maintaining that this consideration does not legitimize present practice).

[48] This could be done by authorizing basis adjustments to reflect increases in general price levels for all assets held, say, for more than two years. A basis adjustment would be proportional to original investment, not gain, and would produce a loss for holders of fixed principal securities as well as reducing gains for equity holders. *See, e.g.*, Brinner, *Inflation, Deferral, and the Neutral Taxation of Capital Gains*, 26 NAT'L TAX J. 565 (1973). Under this approach some adjustment should also be made to reflect a taxpayer's gain from having debts of significant amount and duration outstanding during a period of inflation.

parity of treatment between unrealized gains and gains that are realized and recognized but reinvested. This explanation has both an efficiency and an equity aspect. It is economically inefficient to have a tax that gives people an incentive not to make otherwise desirable changes in investments.[49] Indeed it has been argued that the existing tax on capital gains is too high and that even the tax yield itself might be greater if the rate were reduced.[50] But whatever the incentive or inducement effects, it would be inequitable to impose a tax at ordinary rates on taxpayers with realized but reinvested gains while unrealized gains are allowed to accumulate taxfree. That is presumably why capital gain rates are made applicable to involuntary conversions as well as voluntary sales.[51]

This explanation, while it does not tie justification of capital gain treatment to a long prior period of accumulation, does presuppose reinvestment. It is true that the most typical kind of capital gain is gain from the sale of corporate securities. And it is also true that by tradition a prudent owner of wealth is supposed to try to live off dividends without dipping into capital, and that under this rule of behavior the whole proceeds from sales of securities, including any capital gain, would ordinarily be reinvested. Discussion of capital gains is sometimes seemingly conducted under the assumption that capital gains are in fact mostly reinvested. But there is nothing in the law confining capital gain treatment to reinvested gains, and under the influence of substantial tax rates on ordinary income it seems clear that some taxpayers, at least, will contrive ways of living off recurrent, spendable receipts that take the form and incur the tax of long-term capital gains.

Nontaxation of unrealized gains and special rates on realized capital gains are often defended by general reference to the need to encourage saving and capital formation. Full taxation of capital gains at ordinary rates, it is said, would represent an undesirable increase in the total tax burden on investment and savings.[52]

---

[49] *See* R. GOODE, THE INDIVIDUAL INCOME TAX 207–218 (1964); Brazer, in Panel Discussion No. 2, *supra* note 46, at 260; Wallich, in Panel Discussion No. 2, *supra* note 46, at 272–73.

[50] In 1963 it was proposed to reduce the includable portion from 50% to 40% in the case of gains from capital assets held for more than two years. The change was estimated to increase tax revenues in the short run but to reduce revenues in the long run. *See* H.R. REP. No. 749, 88th Cong., 1st Sess. 100 (1963). The proposal was rejected in the Senate, partly because of failure by the House to enact provisions for constructive realization of gain or for a carryover basis for property transferred at death. *See* S. REP. No. 830, 88th Cong., 2d Sess. 159–62 (1964).

[51] CODE § 1231.

[52] *See, e.g.*, Smith, in Panel Discussion No. 1 on "Objectives and Approaches to Tax Reform and Simplification," *supra* note 46, at 42–43; Ture, in Panel Discussion

This defense also depends on the assumption that capital gains are saved, and it provides no justification for distinguishing between capital gains and other forms of saving or investment return.

If we had a true accretion-type personal income tax in which appreciation in value was measured and taxed currently, there would be no occasion for special capital gain rates. If accumulation in a savings account, or by saving out of earnings, is taxable at ordinary rates, then accumulation by simple appreciation in value should be taxed as well. Similarly, there would also be no occasion for special capital gain rates if we had a pure consumption-type tax. Reinvested gains would be wholly exempt from current tax, and there would be no reason to tax consumption financed out of savings at any different rate than consumption financed out of current earnings. Savings would have borne no prior tax to take into account, and therefore questions involving inflation or overtaxation of savings would not arise.

The present capital gain provisions represent in effect an ill-conceived compromise between the nontaxation of unrealized appreciation and the full taxation of ordinary savings under existing law. Needless to say, the capital gain provisions are the immediate source of an immense amount of complexity, uncertainty, distortion of behavior, and inequity as between taxpayers to whom they are available and others to whom they are not.

C. Cost Recovery Provisions

Hybrid treatment of accumulation raises the problem of determining when receipts are to be considered a return or conversion of previously taxed accumulation. Thus we have problems, often quite intractable in practice, of determining when and at what rate the cost of an asset may be charged against income by way of amortization or depreciation;[53] of determining which cost to charge against sale proceeds when a sale is made out of a stock of fungible goods or securities acquired at different prices;[54] of determining when a particular receipt, like a corporate distribution in partial liquidation or in disproportionate redemption of shares, is to be treated as a return of capital;[55] and so forth. Because of the value of deferral, any provision for recovery of cost at a rate faster than actual decline in value reduces the effective

No. 1, *supra* note 46, at 168; Wallich, in Panel Discussion No. 2, *supra* note 46, at 276–78, 283, 313, 315–16.

[53] *E.g.*, CODE §§ 72 (recovery of basis in annuity contracts), 167 (ordinary depreciation), 169 (amortization of pollution control facilities), 179 (additional first-year depreciation), 453 (installment sale reporting).

[54] Treas. Reg. § 1.1012–1(c) (1957).

[55] CODE §§ 301–02, 316, 346.

rate of tax, computed on a true accretion basis, to something less than the nominal rate. Moreover, there is the immense practical problem of accurately ascertaining and auditing historical costs for personal investment assets. Some practitioners believe there is a substantial degree of unreported noncompliance with the individual income tax on capital gains resulting from the difficulty of ascertaining cost bases accurately, either for original reporting or on audit. Although the provision of a fair-market-value basis for property passing at death avoids a very real practical problem of ascertaining a decedent's cost as the basis for determining gain to another taxpayer on a subsequent sale, it does so only at the cost of permanently exempting gain accrued during the decedent's lifetime.[56]

These problems are inherent in any kind of accounting or computation of income based on historical costs, and therefore they may seem to be implicit in the notion of an income tax. Natural as they seem, however, importation of these problems into the income tax is the result of a policy choice to have the kind of hybrid tax we do. If we had a true accretion-type tax, all assets would be reinventoried at current value at the end of each period to determine gain or loss, and costs would become irrelevant after the period in which they were incurred. Depreciation would be determined by decline in value from year to year, not by reference to historical cost and estimated useful life. On the other hand, if we had a true consumption-type or cash flow tax, costs of investment assets would be deducted in the year incurred. In either case, current taxes would not depend on past costs, and there would be no need to match particular receipts to particular prior costs, or to determine cost recovery schedules, or anything else of that kind.

D. Borrowing, Leverage, and Tax Shelters

The distortions resulting from capital gain rates and from deferral are grossly magnified by the treatment of borrowed funds. People who borrow to finance the production of capital gains enjoy, within limits,[57] a full deduction for interest expense, while including in taxable income only one half of the investment gains. Thus one dollar of long-term capital gain income and fifty cents of interest expense will produce fifty cents of net gain without any

---

[56] CODE § 1014; *see* note 25 *supra*.

[57] CODE § 163(d) now limits the full deductibility of investment interest to the amount of ordinary investment income plus $25,000 per year. Investment interest in excess of this limit can in effect be set off dollar-for-dollar against capital gain income, or be half deducted and half carried over to future years in which the limit is not exceeded.

tax at all.[58] Moreover, individuals may borrow against unrealized appreciation without any immediate tax.[59] In such a case the tax is only postponed, but the postponement may be made to continue beyond the point when one's cash investment has been recovered and the funds either reinvested elsewhere or spent for consumption. In addition, depreciation is allowed on the whole cost of depreciable assets even when that cost is defrayed by borrowing, and even when there is no personal liability on the borrowing.[60] Thus a taxpayer may shelter other income through depreciation deductions based on an investment he himself has not made and is not even under any personal obligation ever to make.

The present treatment of borrowing is nearly pure accretion-type accounting.[61] Loan proceeds are received tax free because they are offset by the liability to repay; no accretion results from the loan itself. Of course no accretion results from a sale of property at fair market value since the proceeds of the sale only equal the value of the property disposed of. But the existing law, which does not tax unrealized appreciation, treats a sale as an appropriate occasion for recognizing previously unrealized gains. If appreciation were taxed as it occurs, in true accretion-type fashion, then neither loans nor sales at fair market value would need to be taken into account. But since we do not in fact take accretion into account as it occurs, we compute profit on sales. Arguably we ought to recognize loans, too, under the existing hybrid system, as a mode of realizing previously accrued gains.[62]

In a consumption-type tax, business and investment loans would be accounted for on a simple cash flow basis. Substantial loan proceeds would be includable in taxable income, and repayments would be deductible. Even under our existing tax the best way to limit the abuse of tax shelters might well be to adopt this form of accounting for loan proceeds, in certain circumstances at least, in an effort to achieve a hybrid treatment of loans that would match our hybrid treatment of the investment that the loan proceeds help finance.[63]

---

[58] *See generally* Halperin, *Capital Gains and Ordinary Deductions: Negative Income Tax for the Wealthy*, 12 B.C. IND. & COM. L. REV. 387 (1971).

[59] Woodsam Associates, Inc. v. Commissioner, 198 F.2d 357 (2d Cir. 1952).

[60] *See* Crane v. Commissioner, 331 U.S. 1 (1947).

[61] Cash receipts and disbursements accounting for interest expense would produce a deferral of tax relative to true accretion treatment if interest could be prepaid and deducted immediately. But the Internal Revenue Service has moved to curb abuse by disallowing deductions for any prepayment of interest if it would materially distort income or if it relates to a period more than twelve months beyond the end of the taxable year of payment. Rev. Rul. 68-643, 1968-2 CUM. BULL. 76.

[62] *See* S. SURREY, *supra* note 16, at 250-51, 394-96 nn.7, 8; pp. 1181-83 *infra*.

[63] *See* pp. 1153-55, 1181-83 *infra*.

As it is, taxpayers can set off the near perfect accretion-type treatment of the debt side of a transaction against the much less true accretion treatment of the investment side, and get a result with respect to net investment that cannot be justified by reference to any sensible standard or ideal. Tax can be deferred far beyond what would be allowed even by simple cash flow accounting. The result is that the effective rate of tax is not just reduced part way toward zero; it is pushed far below zero so that one finds investments that are suitable only for high bracket taxpayers since only they can make an adequate profit.[64]

The matter is one of leverage from two distinct viewpoints. First it is leverage in terms of the relation between deferral and investment. Without borrowing one can only defer recognition of an amount of gain not greater than his investment. But by borrowing he can make his gross investment exceed his net investment, and the amount he can defer, while limited to his gross investment, may exceed his net investment several times over. Thus it is that investors in tax shelters may not only deduct their whole investment, but actually get it back in the form of tax savings within a short period,[65] and still go on to shelter more income. The tax cost is a so-called phantom gain to be recognized some years hence, often after the cash flow from the investment has dried up.[66]

The matter can also be described as leverage in a second, more familiar sense, in terms of rates of return and effective interest costs. Because deferral reduces the effective rate of tax, the return on the investment side of a transaction will be reduced by less than the nominal tax rate. On the other hand, because borrowing is reflected on a true accretion basis and the interest expense is

---

[64] *See, e.g.*, 1 S. SURREY, W. WARREN, P. MCDANIEL & H. AULT, FEDERAL INCOME TAXATION 427–28 (1972) (projecting an after-tax annual rate of return of 20.2% for a 50% bracket taxpayer and 27.5% for a 60% taxpayer on a § 236 project on which cash distributions are limited to 6% of equity investment). For another example, see 2 *id.* at 99 (1973). *See also* McKee, *supra* note 16; pp. 1126–28 & notes 23–24 *supra*.

[65] In the illustration in 1 S. SURREY, W. WARREN, P. MCDANIEL & H. AULT, *supra* note 64, the rate of recovery of investment is projected at 12 months for the first of three equal installments, 15 months for the second installment, and 23 months for the third installment for a taxpayer with a 60% marginal rate. For a 50% taxpayer, recovery will be in 15, 22, and 33 months respectively.

[66] The phantom gain results from treating the unamortized mortgage balance as part of the amount realized on liquidation of the investment. *See* Crane v. Commissioner, 331 U.S. 1 (1947). Careful projections of rates of return will provide for accumulation of funds for several years prior to liquidation to provide for payment of tax on the phantom gain. *See* 1 S. SURREY, W. WARREN, P. MCDANIEL, & H. AULT, *supra* note 64, at 436 n.2. Should the property be held at death, the resulting step-up in basis might eliminate realization of even this phantom gain.

fully and currently deductible, the taxpayer's cost is reduced by the full amount of the nominal rate of tax. Thus the result is an increase in the difference between the expected investment return and its cost. Because of leverage, the modest decrease in the effective rate of tax on gross investment return that results from deferral may result in the effective elimination of tax, or better, on net equity return.

Consider, for example, a 60% taxpayer borrowing at 9% to finance a 10% pretax investment. If there were no deferral or capital gain effect so that the effective rate of tax was equal to the full nominal rate of 60%, then he would be borrowing at an after-tax cost of 3.6% to earn 4%, and his margin of profit on borrowed funds would be reduced by 60%, that is from 1% before tax to .4% after tax. If deferral reduces the effective rate of tax on gross investment from 60% to 40%, however, then he will find himself borrowing at an after-tax cost of 3.6%, to earn 6% after tax, and his profit margin on borrowed funds will have been *increased* from 1% before tax to 2.4% after. The effective rate of tax on this slice of net investment has moved from 60% to *minus* 140%. A negative income tax indeed! Leverage sometimes makes it profitable to borrow even at a higher pretax rate of interest than the pretax rate of return on the investment being financed.[67]

The interaction between true accretion treatment of borrowing and hybrid treatment of gain thus produces something much worse than either standing alone. The distortions and inequities of tax sheltering would be wholly eliminated under either a true accretion- or a pure consumption-type tax. Under a true accretion-type tax there would be no deductions except to the extent of real losses of funds personally invested or borrowed with an enforceable, personal obligation to repay. Under a consumption-type tax there would be no deduction against other income except for cash actually invested, and positive cash flow from the shelter investment would itself be subject to tax forthwith when received.

E. Summary

Not every problem under the existing personal income tax arises out of our treatment of accumulation. Some, like the matter of business entertainment, involve only consumption. A few have nothing to do with either consumption or accumulation but

[67] *See* McKee, *supra* note 16, for an extended analysis of the effect on after-tax rates of return and effective tax rates, of changes in different aspects of the treatment of real estate investments. He indicates that deferral and leverage would seriously impair effective tax rates on real estate investors even if conversion of ordinary income into capital gain were eliminated by full recapture of depreciation. *Id.* at 551–54.

arise out of simple source discrimination, as in the case of the municipal bond exemption. These problems are essentially unaffected by the choice between a consumption model and an accretion model as a critical frame of reference.

But many of the most intractable problems in the personal income tax arise directly out of the hybrid character of our treatment of accumulation. The complexities of corporate distributions and reorganizations, for example, at the individual taxpayer level, all have to do with matters discussed here: realization and nonrecognition, basis determination and recovery, capital gain or ordinary income treatment, and treatment of debt. Other seemingly simpler provisions, like that governing installment sales, have essentially to do with deferral or nonrecognition. The trust and partnership provisions involve complex problems of defining when gain will be recognized by individuals and whether it will be capital gain or ordinary income. The partnership provisions, in particular, have very complex provisions concerning the determination and recovery of basis, and the treatment of partnership borrowing. The whole matter of qualified pension and profit-sharing plans is primarily one of deferral, and other compensation schemes, like stock option plans, are designed to defer recognition of gain and to secure capital gain treatment when recognition occurs. Most of the problems that occupy most of the time of tax practitioners and administrators (not to speak of teachers, students, legislators, and taxpayers themselves) arise immediately out of our failure to take a consistent and comprehensive position with respect to inclusion or exclusion of real accumulation in taxable income.

It is time, therefore, to examine the practical possibilities for achieving more consistency in our treatment of accumulation, by conforming more closely to either the accretion ideal in which all real accumulation is included in taxable income or the consumption model in which accumulation is comprehensively excluded.

IV. True Accretion Treatment of Accumulation

According to prevailing doctrine, the way to deal with the problems described in part III is to move closer to a true accretion-type tax. Accordingly, we should impose a tax on unrealized gains, at least on transfer at death or by gift, if not currently as they accrue. In addition, we should eliminate special rates of tax on capital gains, allowing averaging to deal with any problem of bunching that may exist. Moreover, deductions for depreciation should be limited to real loss in value of net investment. If all this were done there would be no need for any general change in our treatment of borrowing proceeds, though in fact such a change may be the most practical way of curbing some of the worst abuses under existing law. We will now consider briefly whether these steps represent viable solutions to those problems.

A. Elimination of Existing Problems

If all accumulation were taxed currently as it occurred, even when it takes the form of unrealized appreciation in the value of property or contract rights, then indeed most of the difficulties in part III would be eliminated. Problems in the definition of realization and nonrecognition would disappear since gains and losses would be recognized in every case, whether realized or not. Insofar as special treatment of capital gains is to reduce the dichotomy in treatment between realized and unrealized gains, it would no longer be necessary. Cost recovery provisions would be simplified, since in effect cost would be constantly superseded by current value. Moreover, tax shelter possibilities arising out of the treatment of borrowed funds would be curtailed since both borrowing and the corresponding investment of funds would be consistently treated on a true accretion basis.

A few problems would remain. The need for cost-of-living adjustments to eliminate inflation from the tax base would be as great or greater than under present law. Moreover, while bunching would no longer result from the realization in one year of gain accrued over a span of years, there would still be bunching from the sudden recognition of previously unanticipated income streams from newly discovered resources or opportunities. Similarly, wealthy people would have large fluctuations in annual accretion from changes in general market outlook and discount rates. There would still be a need, therefore, for some kind of general averaging and carryback and carryover of investment losses.

B. Practical Problems

Comprehensive inclusion of unrealized appreciation in taxable income would entail enormous practical problems. These involve the necessity of valuing investment property in order to measure unrealized appreciation, and of raising funds with which to pay the tax.

1. Valuation. — Unrealized appreciation can only be measured by valuing property on hand at the end of each taxable period in order to see how much that value exceeds cost or prior value. Experience shows, however, that valuation of property is not a matter that can be handled adequately by taxpayers on unaudited returns. Except in the case of fungible property traded on a regular exchange, and even in that case when unusually large blocks are involved, valuation is a matter of reasonable ranges rather than discrete figures, and many taxpayers will naturally tend to pick figures in the favorable end of the range so far as their tax liability is concerned. Taxpayers will vary in the degree to which they will push their own interest in appraising property. Evenhanded application of the tax laws therefore cannot be obtained unless taxpayers' judgments on questions of valuation are subjected to rather regular examination by auditing authorities. Even then, however, there are not easily applicable criteria for arriving at uniformly fair figures. One has the sense that valuation questions take up a relatively large amount of time on audit, and that even so results are not very uniform as between different taxpayers.

The present income tax depends on property valuation in a relatively few isolated situations, principally when a taxpayer receives compensation in kind for services or for property given up in a barter exchange or claims a deduction for a charitable contribution of property. These situations represent sore points in the administration of the income tax as it is. The practical efficacy of the existing tax is heavily dependent upon the fact that it is mostly computed from cash transactions that do not raise questions of valuation. Any change that would make computation of tax liabilities depend generally on the valuation of investment assets would represent an enormous transformation in the tax from a practical operating viewpoint.

Some notion of the practical transformation that would result from making the income tax regularly depend on matters of property valuation can be gathered from considering experience under the estate tax. In certain respects, valuation under a true accretion-type tax would be less critical than under an estate tax since errors that produce an understatement of income for one year would produce an overstatement for the next year in which values are correctly reported.[68] On the other hand, the necessity of annual valuation would make the administrative burden of such an income tax greater. Furthermore, valuation during lifetimes would involve some kinds of wealth (annuities, conditional pension rights, employment contracts, human wealth generally) and elements of value that do not enter into estate taxation because they cease at death. Assessing changes in value also involves the problem of adjusting for inflation, which is not involved in fixing a value as of a single date. Furthermore, the administration of a decedent's estate typically involves collecting and listing assets

[68] Similarly, of course, an undervaluation for estate tax purposes may be partly offset by a corresponding increase in the gain recognized when an asset is subsequently sold, because the taxpayer will only have a basis in the asset corresponding to its valuation for estate tax purpose. *See* CODE § 1014.

and liquidating some of them in any event, which makes the process of overall valuation less of an added burden than it would be for a living taxpayer.

2. *Forced Liquidation.* — Taxes are payable in cash. Inclusion of unrealized appreciation in taxable income would create a tax liability without any corresponding immediate source of funds with which to pay the tax. In some cases this would not be a serious problem: part of the property could be sold, or the taxpayer could pay the tax with other funds. But in other cases — small farm owners, other owners of family businesses, elderly homeowners with small fixed incomes, and speculative investors heavily committed to a single project — the necessity of paying tax on unrealized appreciation might work a substantial hardship. It might compel the liquidation of part or all of an investment at a price below what it would otherwise be worth, because the sale is forced. Or, in any event, it might force a sale at a price below what the taxpayer himself thinks the property is worth. Moreover, a taxpayer may be discouraged from making vigorous selling efforts with respect to a small part of his investment, because of the adverse tax effect on the valuation of his remaining holdings if he secures a favorable price. Borrowing to avoid such a sale may be difficult or expensive, especially where the property is stock in a very speculative enterprise, and in any event would make the taxpayer's net investment even riskier than before. A tax on unrealized appreciation might therefore tend to discourage investment in illiquid and risky ventures.

C. *Theoretical Problems*

Fundamental difficulties with a true accretion-type tax can be put into a more conceptual framework by inquiring more closely into what is meant by value and by wealth.[69]

1. *Inflation.* — An increase in monetary values may not reflect any real accumulation or increase in value if the real value of money is going down. Changes in value that reflect only inflation are important, however, since the holder of property that goes up in money value is better off by that much than another who holds cash balances or fixed principal securities. The proper remedy, under an accretion model, if we wished to exclude inflation, would be a general adjustment that would not only offset any gain due to inflation for taxpayers holding assets that go up in value, but also produce a net loss for holders of fixed money amounts.[70]

2. *Interest Rate Changes.* — The value of an investment as-

[69] These notions are developed more comprehensively and rigorously in N. Kaldor, *supra* note 7, at 54–78.

[70] *See* Brinner, *supra* note 48.

set is the present discounted value of its estimated future yield. An increase in present value may result from an increase in the estimated future yield, an acceleration of the time at which that yield is expected to be received, or a decrease in the rate at which the estimated future yield is discounted.

Capital gains that result from decreases in general interest rates rather than increases in expected earnings present difficulties in an accretion-type system, because they represent an increase of potential spending power of a somewhat different kind than gains due to increased estimated earnings. Consider a bondholder or a holder of a fixed life annuity whose life expectancy remains constant. The estimated future yield of such an asset and its distribution over time are relatively invariable. But the present value will increase if the prevailing interest rate at which such investments are discounted goes down. Now if general interest rates go down, has the holder of such an asset had an increase in his welfare that deserves to be taxed? He has, of course, had an increase in the amount of current consumption he could purchase by liquidating his investment, and he should, as under present law, be taxed on this increase if that is what he does. But there has been no increase in the amount of consumption he can finance over the period of his investment. The present discounted cost of what he apparently wants — a fixed cash income — has gone up by just as much as the value of his investment. The holder of such an investment has in a sense only protected himself against a loss of income that he would have suffered if he had held only short-term notes or securities. We would not, of course, allow a holder of short-term or demand obligations or deposits any deduction for his loss of future income when interest rates go down; that loss will be adequately reflected by taxing him on only his reduced income as he receives it in the future. On the other hand, one may feel that the relative well-being of the holder of the long-term bond or fixed annuity will also be adequately reflected by taxing him on his unreduced income as he receives it in spite of the decline in general interest rates.[71]

Except in the case of quite safe fixed income securities, how-

[71] To impose a tax on the increase in value that results from a decline in general interest rates would partially defeat the purpose of the investor to secure a fixed disposable income on which to live, since it would represent a cash drain in anticipation of income not yet received. The taxpayer could sell bonds to pay the tax, and the resulting loss in future pretax income would be partly offset by the reduction in future taxes that would result from amortization of the premium whose accrual had already been taxed. But the offset will be only partial because the return of the tax on the premium, by way of amortization, will be without interest. As with most questions of timing the net burden is equivalent to that involved in making an interest-free loan.

An investor in bonds under a true accretion-type tax might try to protect himself against the risk of having to pay tax on a decrease in general interest rates by

ever, there is no way to measure the effect of general interest rate changes in isolation from price changes due to fluctuations in estimated future yield. The effect of a general interest rate change on the value of a particular investment depends on how the estimated future yield is distributed through time, and while that can be ascertained in the case of notes of varying maturities it cannot be known with any accuracy in the case of equity investments.[72]

3. Speculative Investments. — In any event, apart from the problem of discount rate, value depends on an estimate of future yield. If there is an established pattern of earnings then the future may be estimated by taking that pattern as a starting point. But where there is no established pattern, future yield may be highly conjectural, and in such a case, unless there is some kind of market or active selling effort, the concept of what a willing buyer would pay a willing seller may be highly abstract and quite hypothetical.

4. Human Wealth. — Should a person be taxed, under an accretion-type personal income tax, on the increase in the present discounted value of his estimated future earnings that results from being promoted in his job, or from taking a new job with higher pay or greater security or better prospects, or from matriculating at Princeton or marrying into a prominent family with good connections? Practical considerations would seem to require that we wait to see whether the improved prospects materialize in all these cases. A tax on unrealized future prospects would present virtually insuperable problems of valuation and of liquidity. But how are these essentially different from the problems of valuation and liquidity raised by any effort to be comprehensive in accounting currently for changes in value of material wealth, which also ultimately reflect changed evaluations of future prospects?

Again, what may seem to be only a theoretical problem becomes intensely practical when one faces the difficulty of trying to sort out changes in human wealth from changes in material wealth. A great many rights in the world of business represent mixtures of human and material wealth. Sophisticated employment contracts and deferred compensation arrangements give employees rights measured by reference to corporate securities, but conditioned in various ways on their continued performance of services. How would rights under such contracts be valued if

---

purchasing extra bonds on margin. If interest rates drop these could then be sold to raise the money to pay the tax. However, if interest rates rise, he might either end up paying higher interest on the loan than he receives on the margined bonds, or be forced to liquidate the bonds at a loss. It is not at all clear that we should want a tax system under which it is so difficult to secure a fixed income subject to a relatively stable burden of taxation.

[72] *See* N. KALDOR, *supra* note 7, at 44–45 n.1.

we sought to tax increases in value of material wealth but not of human wealth? An invention may be bought and sold, but its value may depend primarily on someone's skill in further developing it. Personal skills of key employees are a most important element in valuing most small businesses. Even in large publicly-held corporations it is often asserted that quality of management is one of the most important criteria for evaluation.

On the face of it, the key to separating changes in material from those in human wealth may seem to be salability: the increase in value to be currently reflected in an accretion-type tax would be that which a taxpayer could realize by making a sale of property without any continued obligation to perform services in connection with the property sold. But salability is not an easy line to draw, and it can be manipulated. The whole controversy about restricted property compensation plans has arisen from the imposition of restrictions on salability designed in part to defer tax on certain contingent, noncash bonuses.[73] On the other hand, even a public offering of securities is often a matter of selling interests in the profit potential of a business that will still depend heavily on continued performance of services by key personnel. Surely under a true accretion-type personal income tax we would tax a controlling stockholder on all his gain if he sells part of his own stock in a public offering; presumably we would also want to tax him on the gain on the stock he continues to hold, valued at something related to its public market price, although probably with a substantial discount in many cases.[74] Why, then, in theory at least, should we not tax an individual proprietor on the growth in value (including good will) of his business, including the money he could raise if he would incorporate his business and sell part of the stock to other investors?

Any attempt to isolate human wealth from material wealth in these contexts would require the drawing of difficult and arbitrary distinctions, and whatever lines are drawn would produce a considerable distortion of behavior by taxpayers seeking to get and keep themselves on the untaxed side of the line.

D. Partial Accretion-Type Solutions

In practice, few people advocate a true accretion-type personal income tax in which all changes in value would be currently and comprehensively reflected in taxable income; that ideal usu-

[73] CODE § 83 now takes some of the advantage out of deferral by requiring that the whole value of the property at the time the tax is imposed be treated in effect as compensation rather than as capital gain; the price of deferral is thus the loss of capital gain treatment on appreciation during the period of deferral.

[74] *Cf.* CODE § 83(a)(1), (b)(1)(A) (disallowing any discount for temporary restrictions on salability that do not create a substantial risk of forfeiture).

ally only inspires partial measures which approximate the true ideal in varying degrees.[75] The main compromise that has gained substantial support is a provision for recognition of previously unrealized gain (and loss) at death or on a transfer of property by gift. This proposal for constructive realization of gain has been advocated either with or without the elimination of special rates of tax for capital gains.[76]

Constructive realization would require valuation of property upon transfer, but this is typically already required for substantial transfers for federal gift and estate tax purposes, and thus would not raise anything like the practical problems that annual valuation would entail. Constructive realization would apparently involve problems of forced liquidation in some cases where an estate consists largely of a single, highly appreciated, indivisible asset, such as an interest in a family farm or other business. But most importantly, constructive realization would not completely eliminate the distortions that arise out of differences in tax deferral, as would a true accretion-type tax. Existing problems of defining realization and nonrecognition would persist, because deferral of tax, even if limited to a lifetime, would remain very important. Problems of cost recording and recovery would continue; in a sense they would be aggravated since constructive realization would require an executor to determine the decedent's basis for property, a determination that present law generally makes unnecessary. Constructive realization at death would impose a substantial posthumous cost on leveraged tax shelter inhabitants, but it would certainly not eliminate the shelter game.

Constructive realization at death or on gift would assure that all gains are ultimately taxed, and it has sometimes been suggested that the value of deferral could be offset by charging in-

[75] *See, e.g.*, Shoup, *supra* note 16 (commenting on proposal of Canadian Minister of Finance to tax unrealized capital gains and losses by Canadian residents in marketable shares of Canadian corporations on a 5-year accrual basis); Slawson, *Taxing as Ordinary Income the Appreciation of Publicly Held Stock*, 76 YALE L.J. 623, 624–26 (1967) (accounting for unrealized gains in marketable securities on an annual basis). Probably the most comprehensive accretion-type proposal would tax changes in value of interests in closely-held and unincorporated businesses and in real estate, as well as changes in the value of marketable shares of stock. *See* David & Miller, *A Proposal for Revision of Capital Gains Tax Provisions of the Federal Internal Revenue Code and Critique of Treasury Proposals in Related Areas*, in *Hearings on the Subject of Tax Reform Before the House Comm. on Ways and Means*, 91st Cong., 1st Sess., pt. 12, at 4275–303 (1969).

[76] *See, e.g.*, H. SIMONS, *supra* note 1, at 212; S. SURREY, *supra* note 16, at 195–97, 351–52 n.53; U.S. TREASURY DEP'T, *supra* note 25, at 329–51; Covey, Surrey & Westfall, *Perspectives on Suggested Revisions in Federal Estate & Gift Taxation*, 112 TRUSTS & ESTATES 102, 106–07 (1973) (discussing proposal for flat rate taxation of unrealized appreciation at death as an additional estate tax); Kurtz & Surrey, *Reform of Death and Gift Taxes: The 1969 Treasury Proposals, the Criticisms, and a Rebuttal*, 70 COLUM. L. REV. 1365 (1970).

terest when gains are finally realized and tax collected.[77] While interest could be computed on the assumption that gain accrued evenly during the holding period of a piece of property, an accurate imputation of interest would require a determination of when, during the period an asset was held, the appreciation in its value occurred. This would require periodic valuation of unsold property after all, retroactively arrived at several years after the dates in question. Moreover, taxing longer period gains at higher rates would also aggravate any continued failure to offset the effect of inflation.[78]

E. Summary

A true accretion-type personal income tax would be free of many of the complexities and inequities of the existing tax. But a true accretion-type tax is hardly attainable in practice. Even a rough approximation of an accretion-type tax would require an utter transformation of the practical administration and computation of the tax from one depending mostly on cash transactions to one in which current, comprehensive property valuation would play a central role. In practical operation the tax would become largely an incremental net wealth tax as well as a tax on income transactions.

Any partial step in the direction of fuller reflection of total accretion remains a compromise in which inconsistencies are inevitable. Some compromises are undoubtedly better than others, and some of our existing problems could probably be ameliorated by fuller reflection of real accretion, but no practical solution in this direction offers anything approaching the simple practicality of a consumption-type or cash flow personal income tax.

V. A Consumption-Type Personal Income Tax

A consumption-type personal income tax is often assumed to involve all the practical difficulties of the existing personal in-

[77] *See* Brinner, *supra* note 48 (suggesting that capital gains be computed on a real basis by adjusting purchase price for inflation, and then be included in income at more than 100%, the percentage increasing with length of holding period, to offset the value of deferral). By way of comparison, see Sanden, in Panel Discussion No. 2, *supra* note 46, at 248, 253, and Wallich, in Panel Discussion No. 2, *supra* note 46, at 279. Both suggest an extension of the minimum holding period necessary for capital gain treatment to one year, but propose inclusion of capital gains in income on a sliding scale, with the rate of inclusion *decreasing* the longer the assets have been held. Such a proposal attempts to adjust indirectly for the appreciation due to inflation, but again, the more one gains, the more one benefits from such a relief provision.

[78] Brinner, in his proposal, makes proper adjustments for inflation. *See* Brinner, *supra* note 48.

come tax plus whatever new ones are involved in getting from income to consumption expenditure.[79] The tax would, of course, be computed on personal income plus or minus net dissavings or savings, and discussion has focused on how much additional difficulty the adjustments for saving or dissaving would produce.[80]

This discussion overlooks the fact that a consumption-type tax would avoid all the difficulties that arise from the failure of money income to provide a satisfactory reflection of real accumulation. Income, to be sure, includes savings, and savings are a partial, imperfect, monetary measure of accumulation. A consumption-type tax requires deductions and additions to eliminate savings and dissavings. But these, being based solely on money transactions, are incomparably simpler than either making adjustments to include unrealized appreciation under a true accretion-type tax or living with the complexity and distortion that result from the existing hybrid treatment of accumulation.[81]

Under a consumption-type personal income tax, capital transactions are treated on a simple cash flow basis. Investments are simply deducted when made, and proceeds of sales and other capital transactions are added to income when received. All that is required is to separate business and investment activities on the one hand from personal consumption activities on the other, as under present law, and then to keep track of the former on a cash flow basis. Cash flow accounting for business and investment activities automatically provides a measure of cash spent on consumption activities, which is what we are after.

Precise measurement of current consumption spending would require exact accounting for cash and loan balances which might be something of a nuisance. But in practice there is no need for precision because only short term tax deferral or acceleration and relatively small amounts are involved. Ordinary cash bal-

---

[79] *See, e.g.*, R. GOODE, THE INDIVIDUAL INCOME TAX 33 (1964); J. PECHMAN, FEDERAL TAX POLICY 164–65 (1971).

[80] For recent evaluations of the feasibility of a consumption-type personal income tax, see Slitor, *supra* note 7; Kelley, *supra* note 7. Both authors conclude that a personal expenditure tax is feasible, though neither asserts, as I conclude, that such a tax would be vastly simpler in practice than either our existing hybrid tax or a true accretion-type personal income tax.

[81] A consumption-type tax is indeed more complicated than a simple tax on ordinary income alone that omits capital gains, since capital transactions can be ignored under the latter. It is against the background of such an income tax that some earlier English writers concluded a consumption-type tax would be impractical. This was essentially the comparison being made by Mill, Pigou, Keynes, and others in the English tradition when they said an expenditure tax would be difficult to implement as compared with an income tax, since the English income tax then made no provision for taxing capital gains. *See* N. KALDOR, *supra* note 7, at 12–13, 222 & n.1; J.S. MILL, *supra* note 7; A. PIGOU, *supra* note 7.

ances, including checking accounts and consumer loans, can therefore be left wholly out of account. In effect, both ordinary cash balances and consumer loans can be treated as falling in the consumption sector of an individual's activity rather than the business or investment sector, without any significant distortion of tax burdens.[82]

A precise measure of current consumption would also seem to require separation of consumption from the investment element in the purchase of consumer durables. Strictly speaking it is the current use value rather than the purchase price of an automobile, for example, that constitutes consumption. But again strict precision is unnecessary. The purchase price for a durable item represents the discounted value of its future usefulness, and the tax burden will tend to be the same in the end whether one is taxed or the other. Therefore, it would be acceptable to deal with the consumer durable problem on a simple cash flow basis, although it may be desirable in some cases to give taxpayers the option of deferring taxation on part of the purchase price with interest. Because purchase price can be taken as a proxy for use value, the consumer durable problem is much more manageable under a consumption-type tax than under a true accretion-type tax.[83] Under the latter, the money invested should be taxed when earned, and the imputed return received in the form of use value should also be taxed.

One of the general advantages of a consumption-type tax is that short-term deferral in the interest of simpler administration can be more readily tolerated than in the case of an accretion-type tax. Under a consumption-type tax the benefit of deferral is offset by a corresponding increase in the amount subject to tax at a rate equal to whatever interest rate the market charges the taxpayer for extensions of credit. No such offset occurs under an accretion-type tax where postponement has the effect of reducing the effective rate of taxation on income. Reverting to the example of the fruit farmer, it makes no difference whether we tax the growth of trees or the fruit under a consumption-type tax, because the ultimate burden is the same either way. Under an accretion-type tax it makes a substantial difference whether we tax the trees because we are supposed to tax the fruit, too, in any event, and a tax on both is substantially more burdensome.

These general observations are elaborated in the following discussion of how particular items would enter into the practical computation of a consumption-type personal income tax.

---

[82] *See* pp. 1154–55, 1160–62 *infra.*

[83] *See* pp. 1155–60 *infra.*

A. Ordinary Income

Ordinary income — wages, salaries, fees, dividends, interest, rent, and so on — would be treated exactly the same way under a consumption-type personal income tax as under any other personal income tax. They would be fully includable in taxable income for the period in which received and would continue to form the backbone of the tax. Withholding from salaries and wages could be continued as under the existing tax, and it could just as readily be extended to dividends and interest. Most people spend most of their ordinary income for current consumption,[84] and to that extent a consumption-type personal income tax would be no different from the existing tax. Deductions and additions to reflect savings and dissavings would for most taxpayers be in the nature of relatively minor adjustments that would not impair the general relationship between the tax and ordinary income as its chief determinant and as the source of funds with which to pay it.[85]

Similarly, ordinary, current deductions, business and personal, would be essentially unaffected by the shift to a pure consumption-type tax because they are addressed to the consumption rather than the accumulation component of accretion. Ordinary personal deductions for medical expenses, charitable contributions, and alimony, for example, would have the same justifications and problems as under existing law.[86] Furthermore, personal exemptions and a standard deduction could readily be continued under a consumption-type tax.

B. Ordinary Investments

The most obvious difference about a consumption-type income tax would be that ordinary investments would be accounted for on a pure cash flow basis. The cost of investment assets would be deductible in the year paid, while the proceeds of sale would be fully included in taxable income in the year received.[87] This

[84] *See* Bureau of Labor Statistics, Dep't of Labor, Handbook of Labor Statistics 1972, at 313, table 134 (1972); P. Samuelson, Economics 216 (9th ed. 1973).

[85] The consumption-type personal income tax as described here has no deduction for the tax itself. *See* notes 2, 10 *supra*.

[86] *See* Andrews, *supra* note 1.

[87] Kelley, *supra* note 7, at 238-41, presents a consumption-type tax return in which sales of investment assets are taken into account in computing taxable expenditure by adding *original acquisition cost* rather than sales proceeds. The result is correct because Kelley's return begins with taxable income, which includes any excess (or deficit) of sales proceeds over original cost. *Id.* at 240 n.5. Thus, original acquisition cost has no effect on taxable expenditure in Kelley's system, because its deduction in computing income is offset by its addition in getting to

does not necessarily mean there would be a large tax in a year when substantial sales are made, since it is likely that taxable proceeds would be largely offset by deductions for reinvestment in that year, or for extraordinary, yearend cash balances.

There is a tendency to think of this treatment of investment assets as involving at least some complication over and above the existing income tax treatment, because in a year when part of a taxpayer's income is invested a deduction must be claimed.[88] But this is viewing the matter in too narrow a time frame. Under the existing income tax the cost of an investment cannot be ignored; it must be recorded for future use as a basis either for amortization or in computing gain or loss on sale or other disposition. Surely it is simpler in the long run, for taxpayer and Government alike, to have deductions based on investment costs paid during the current year rather than on costs incurred in several past periods, some quite long ago. Deductions and profit computations based upon costs incurred long ago are often very difficult to determine or report accurately, and sometimes virtually impossible to audit satisfactorily. Thus, just as a matter of accurate accounting and reporting, cash flow treatment of ordinary investments would represent a vast simplification.[89]

Moreover, this treatment of ordinary investments would eliminate a whole host of complications in the existing income tax beyond the mere ascertainment of historical costs. Individual taxpayers would no longer compute depreciation or use other forms of cost amortization, since business and investment costs would be simply deducted forthwith. Furthermore, there would be no problems concerning realization and nonrecognition of gain or loss when an individual changes investments. If a taxpayer receives new investment property in exchange for old, or as an increment to old property in the case of a stock dividend or other dividend in kind, it would make no difference whether the transaction is one on which gain is realized and recognized under present law, since any gain recognized would in effect be offset by a deduction for the fresh investment. Thus, in the case of an exchange of securities there would be no need to determine whether it is pursuant to a plan of reorganization, since the deduction for reinvestment would offset any gain recognized. The whole law of corporate reorganizations as it bears on individual investors would be rendered obsolete.[90]

taxable expenditure. However, since we start with ordinary income instead of taxable income, and then add sales proceeds of investment assets, original cost does not enter even nominally into the computation.

[88] *See, e.g.*, Kelley, *id.* at 241 & n.6.

[89] Immediate deductibility of capital expenditures, partly for the sake of accounting simplification, is familiar under present law. *See* note 12 *supra*.

[90] *See* pp. 1129–31 *supra*.

Cash flow treatment of ordinary investments would also resolve present problems about when to account for compensation for services in the form of investment property such as stock bonuses or restricted property.[91] Again, cash compensation that the recipient invests would incur no tax; therefore no tax need be imposed on compensation paid in kind in investment property. Tax would properly await sale of the investment property and devotion of the proceeds to consumption expenditure in either case.

Finally, and above all, this treatment of ordinary investments would eliminate any need for special rates of tax on capital gains. The best justification for capital gain rates is to mitigate the disparity in treatment between unrealized gains and realized but reinvested gains.[92] A cash flow treatment of ordinary investments would eliminate that disparity entirely. Proceeds from the sale of investment property would be taxed only if devoted to personal consumption, in which event there would be no reason to distinguish them from ordinary earned income also directed to consumption.

Less persuasive justifications for capital gain rates would also be inapplicable. The argument based on inflation [93] would be met by the fact that no tax on the accumulation represented by the initial investment would have been paid in uninflated dollars, as it would have been under an accretion-type tax. Moreover, no profit would be miscomputed by subtracting old, low price-level costs from current, inflated sales prices. The level of current taxable proceeds may indeed be partly attributable to inflation, but the proceeds can be offset in the computation of taxable income by reinvestment of current dollars, and the tax on proceeds not reinvested would be wholly payable with current dollars. Even the notion that capital gain rates are justified to offset the hardship, given progressive tax rates, of realizing in one year a gain accrued over many would be met, since only proceeds devoted to current consumption would be subject to tax.[94]

C. *Business and Investment Loans*

Business and investment loans would be treated, just like ordinary investments, on a simple cash flow basis. Loan proceeds would be reported as income in the year received, and repayments of interest and principal would be deductible when paid. This

---

[91] *See* CODE § 83 (dealing with compensation in the form of property to which restrictions are attached).

[92] *See* pp. 1131–34 *supra*.

[93] *See* p. 1133 *supra*.

[94] Some provision for spreading the purchase price of large consumer durables and other extraordinary consumption expenditures would be appropriate, however. *See* p. 1157 *infra*.

treatment is unfamiliar, but would represent a clear net simplification for reasons similar to those favoring a cash flow accounting for ordinary investments.

Cash flow accounting for loans, as for investments, is only a matter of reporting currently events that would have to be recorded for future reference under the present tax or an accretion-type tax. While we do not tax loan proceeds as such under present law, we do tax forgiveness of indebtedness, or satisfaction of indebtedness by the conveyance of appreciated property, even when the result is a substantial tax liability in a year in which there are no cash receipts with which to pay the tax.[95] A record of money received and repaid on account of loans must be accurately kept in order to compute such gains. Cash flow accounting is only a matter of taking each receipt and payment into account in the year when it occurs.

Inclusion of loan proceeds in income would not ordinarily require large tax payments in the year of a loan, because normally such loans are to pay for capital investment that would be immediately deductible under a consumption-type tax. Cash flow accounting for loans and capital investments would assure, however, that deductions based on capital investment are limited to one's own net cash investment. This treatment of loans would thus end the tax shelter game that people play under present law, since the game depends heavily on letting high-bracket equity investors take tax credit for the investment of lenders' funds.[96]

D. Consumer Credit

A strict computation of current consumption would seem to require that consumer loans and credit, like business and investment loans, be treated as income when incurred and deductible when repaid. But it is much simpler and quite acceptable just to leave ordinary consumer loans and credit arrangements out of account. The effect of that is to treat payments on account of consumer loans, rather than the use of the loan proceeds, as taxable consumption expenditures. This might represent some deferral of tax in relation to consumption, but any general revenue loss or consumer benefit from such deferral would be offset by including the whole deferred price in taxable consumption expenditure without any deduction for interest charged by the

[95] *See* Crane v. Commissioner, 331 U.S. 1 (1947); United States v. Kirby Lumber Co., 284 U.S. 1 (1931); Parker v. Delaney, 186 F.2d 455 (1st Cir. 1950), *cert. denied*, 341 U.S. 926 (1951).

[96] Even if the tax treatment of investments generally is not put on a pure cash flow basis, a cash flow treatment of loans in excess of basis in related assets would probably represent the best and most comprehensive practical way to deal with tax shelter abuses under present law. *See* pp. 1181–83 *infra*.

financing party.[97] In cases of loans to finance purchase of consumer durables, this treatment would generally correspond more closely to real consumption than would inclusion of the loan proceeds immediately in income.[98]

A line would need to be drawn between consumer loans and business and investment loans, although there would not be much pressure on it because of the offsetting effect of allowing or disallowing a deduction for interest. In general, any loan incurred for business or investment purposes, or secured by business or investment property, and any unsecured loan of more than, say, one quarter of a year's income, as well as any other loan the taxpayer wishes to treat as a business or investment loan, would be presently includable in taxable income. On the other hand, large loans secured by consumer durables, including housing, could be treated as consumer loans, since the effect would be to cause net expenditure for consumer durables to be reflected in taxable income as it occurs.

E. Consumer Durables

Consumer durables theoretically have both an accumulation or investment aspect and a consumption aspect. A consumption-type tax may seem on its face to raise a question of separating the two that does not arise under an accretion-type tax since both consumption and accumulation are taxable under the latter. But closer examination will show that it is easier to approximate a correct treatment of consumer durables under a consumption-type tax than under an accretion-type tax. A theoretically correct treatment requires evaluation and imputation of rental or use value under either tax, but under a consumption-type tax purchase price can generally be included in taxable income as a proxy for use value. Purchase price will not serve as a proxy for use value under an accretion-type tax because there it already stands for the accumulation component of accretion, and subsequent return on that accumulation in the form of consumption use is supposed to be taxed as an additional element of accretion.

[97] Present law allows a deduction for interest paid even on consumer loans. CODE § 163. That deduction might be viewed as a departure from the general principle that personal expenses are nondeductible. But an accretion-type tax has the general effect of reducing the rate at which future consumption can be substituted for present consumption in the case of savers, and deductibility of interest on personal consumer loans simply produces the same effect in the case of borrowers. *See* Andrews, *supra* note 1, at 376 n.116; White, *Proper Income Tax Treatment of Deductions for Personal Expense*, in 1 HOUSE COMM. ON WAYS AND MEANS, 86TH CONG., 1ST SESS., TAX REVISION COMPENDIUM 365, 365–66 (Comm. Print 1959).

[98] *See* pp. 1155–57 *infra*.

Consider, for example, the purchase of an automobile for personal use. Theoretically, under a consumption-type tax, the purchase price should be deductible like any other investment, and rental value should be imputed to the owner over the useful life. But in practice imputed rental value is adequately reflected, on a discounted basis, by the purchase price. Indeed the best practical way to impute use or rental value would be on the basis of purchase price spread over some appropriate life with some appropriate interest return added on. If applicable rates do not change, a tax in the year of purchase on the purchase price will have the same discounted burden as a tax paid on the use value over time while use occurs. The practical thing to do, therefore, is to treat the purchase of a personal automobile like any other consumption expenditure, ignoring its investment aspect. This is accomplished by simply leaving such a purchase out of account in computing taxable income, thus making the expenditure subject to tax. Moreover, any proceeds from trading in or reselling used consumer durables can also be left out of account to the extent that they represent a recovery of taxpaid funds.[99] The most practical treatment of consumer durable purchases under a consumption-type tax would thus correspond with their treatment under the existing hybrid tax. It is not important to insist that the existing treatment of consumer durables shows implicit adoption of a consumption model for the tax. It is enough to assert that the consumption model offers a much more feasible goal to pursue in this connection, starting from where we are, than does the accretion model.

When an automobile is purchased on credit, the loan should be treated as a consumer loan. In practice, therefore, neither the purchase of the automobile nor the loan would enter into the computation of taxable income, and the result would be that consumption use of the automobile would be reflected in taxable income each year in the amount of payments of principal and interest made on the loan. This would correspond to present law except that the latter allows a deduction for interest.[100] A taxpayer might elect to treat the loan as an investment loan, paying tax on the whole loan proceeds in the year of purchase of the automobile and then deducting both principal repayments and interest in subsequent years. But if he had the funds with which to pay the increased tax presently due that would result from this election, he might achieve a better result by making a larger downpayment and borrowing less. This might enable him to get a lower interest rate on the smaller portion of the purchase price

[99] *See* pp. 1158–59 note 105 *infra*.

[100] CODE § 163.

that he would still borrow, and this lower interest rate would then automatically apply to his reduced tax deferral as well as the loan itself.

If consumer durable purchases in a particular year were substantial in amount, it might be appropriate to permit a taxpayer to defer them over a limited period, even if they were not financed by borrowing. The procedure would be to claim a deduction in the year of purchase but then to return the deducted amount to income with interest at a rate fixed by the Revenue Service over a limited period. This would in effect provide limited recognition of the accumulation aspect of such expenditures, though its main purpose would be to alleviate possible rate distortions in the case of large cash purchases. Perhaps, however, it would be better just to rely on a general averaging provision, similar to that under present law,[101] to avoid rate distortions.

F. Owner-Occupied Housing

Similar general conclusions apply to owner-occupied housing, which undoubtedly represents the most substantial item of consumer durable investment made by most taxpayers. Purchase price, however, is a less acceptable proxy for use value in the case of very longlife items like housing, because tax rates may change and property may go up or down in value for reasons not anticipated at the time of purchase. Nevertheless, it is still the case that the existing treatment of owner-occupied housing is more nearly consonant with a consumption-type model than with a true accretion-type model. Furthermore, whatever accommodations may be made to ease practical computation represent less of a distortion or departure from a consumption ideal than from a true accretion ideal.

A strictly correct treatment of housing would be to allow a deduction for purchase price and capital expenditures, but then to impute full rental value, with periodic changes in imputed rental to reflect market changes. This would involve the difficulties of real estate assessment and valuation on a national scale. It would also involve a duplication of the hardship that is now perceived by some to result from increasing real estate taxes in the case of elderly homeowners who do not have any corresponding increase in money income with which to pay those taxes. The fact is that home ownership during a period of rising real estate prices operates to allow older people to live in houses that are more expensive than they could afford to move into now, and that effect may be judged to be generally desirable. Furthermore, we may feel we do not want our income tax to impair that aspect of

[101] CODE §§ 1301–05.

homeownership by creating a tax liability that increases over time and that can only be met by having an increasing cash income. The economics of homeownership allow a person to buy a home for a lifetime out of the earnings of his relatively early productive years at price levels prevailing when he makes his initial purchase. It may well be enough for the income tax law to take this economic situation as it is and be satisfied with taxing a person on the cash expenditure it takes to provide lifetime housing, as the expenditure is made.[102]

The treatment of owner-occupied housing then would be virtually the same as under present law, except that there would be no deduction for mortgage interest, and there might be an option to deduct an initial downpayment, returning it to income over a short period of years with interest added annually to the deferred balance at a specified rate.

Proceeds on the sale of a house would present some new problems. The present rule permitting a homeowner to sell at a profit without tax if proceeds are reinvested in another principal residence should be continued.[103] This rule, for example, enables a person to move and purchase comparable housing in another location, without making the additional investment that would be required if he had to pay a tax on the heretofore unrealized appreciation on his first home. Profit on the sale of a house not reinvested in another residence would be included in taxable income, though no tax would be paid if proceeds were invested in any ordinary investment assets.[104] The new question would be whether that part of sale proceeds that represents a return of basis or cost and is not reinvested in housing should be able to be spent for other consumption on a taxfree basis on the ground that it represents a refund of money on which consumption tax has already been paid. The answer to that question should probably be yes, and again that answer is in accord with present law under which the sale proceeds from a house, to the extent they

---

[102] One fairly workable alternative treatment of housing under a consumption-type tax would allow an immediate deduction for purchase price and capital expenditures, but then impute income at a specified rate on the deducted amount. By itself this proposal would not require periodic valuations, and accordingly it would not correct for relative changes in property values after time of purchase. It would, however, make some continuing tax charge for continuing housing services and would thus subject housing services to changes in applicable tax rates, whether due to statutory changes or income level changes under a graduated rate schedule.

[103] CODE § 1034.

[104] This would avoid the problem that exists under present law of a recognized capital gain when people sell their home to move into rented quarters. It would largely obviate the need, therefore, for CODE § 121 (gain on sale of residence by a taxpayer aged 65 or older partly excluded from taxable income).

represent return of basis rather than profit, are freely available for consumption spending.[105]

Finally, it should be reemphasized that any practical solution to the problem of owner-occupied housing is more consonant with the consumption model than with the accretion model. The accretion ideal requires that the purchase price of a home come out of after-tax income because it is an item of accumulation, and then it requires that there be further additions to taxable income to reflect both imputed rental income and unrealized appreciation. The existing treatment of housing falls short of the accretion ideal immediately upon purchase and occupation of a home, without any change in value, by reason of failure to include imputed rental income. As a house increases in value, existing treatment falls doubly short by failing to include both an increase in imputed rental income and the appreciation in value as such. By contrast, existing treatment (except for deductibility of mortgage interest) is initially consistent with the consumption ideal since taxation of the purchase price serves as a proxy for taxing imputed rental value. Furthermore, the failure to impose additional taxes when value goes up is only a single-valued omission, since appreciation as such is not supposed to be taxed under the consumption model. That single-valued omission is much easier to rationalize than are the multiple shortcomings of present treatment of owner-occupied housing as tested against an accretion model.[106]

G. *Artworks and Unimproved Real Estate*

There would be a problem of classification under a consumption-type tax that does not often arise under the existing hybrid income tax. This involves assets held largely for financial gain though partly also for personal enjoyment. Consider, for example, the purchase of unimproved real estate which a person may at some future time use for a summer home. Or consider the purchase of a valuable painting, to be hung alternately in one's home and in a museum. The necessity of deciding whether such assets

---

[105] The law might provide that proceeds from the sale of a house, to the extent that they represent a return of cost or basis, would not be included in taxable income. In addition, if the funds representing a return of cost were invested, the taxpayer would get a deduction for the investment itself, but would be taxed on subsequent disinvestment and consumption. Alternatively, one could grant no deduction for the investment of such funds, but instead give the taxpayer a cost basis in the assets purchased. When the investments were then later liquidated and spent for consumption, the proceeds would be excluded from income to the extent of that basis.

[106] *See* H. Aaron, Shelter and Subsidies 53–73 (1972).

were purchased for profit or for pleasure will only arise under the existing tax if they are later sold at a loss,[107] since gain is taxable in any event, and we fail to impute income for pleasure use, whatever the purpose of purchase.

Under a consumption-type tax, a decision would have to be made forthwith whether a deduction would be allowed for investment in assets such as these, as for ordinary financial investments, or whether they should be treated as nondeductible consumer durables. This is, of course, exactly the same decision as would have to be made under a true accretion-type tax to determine whether to impute income from the enjoyment of such property. If for any reason the failure to impute income under present law would be acceptable under a true accretion-type tax, then the equivalent acceptable treatment under a consumption-type tax would be to treat the purchase of such assets as ordinary deductible investments. Moreover, compromises are conceivable which would subject the owner to some continuing taxation for his presumed enjoyment of the item. For example, it might be appropriate to allow a deduction for purchase of such assets but then to include in income imputed interest on the deducted amount at low compromise rates.[108] Alternatively, the purchase price might be included in taxable consumption over time, but without any interest charge on deferral of inclusion. Thus a deduction would be allowed initially for large purchases, but the deducted amount would be returned to income over some specified period or at some specified rate.

Again, the most important thing to recognize is that these problems are not peculiar to a consumption-type tax. They arise from the definition of consumption, which is a component of true accretion in any event. Moreover, a true accretion-type tax would have to face not only the question of imputing a consumption value to the holding of these assets, but also the problem of including unrealized appreciation in income as it occurs.

H. Cash Balances

It is often supposed that a consumption-type tax would require addition to income of cash balances at the beginning of each year, and deduction of balances left at the end. Money on hand at the end obviously was not spent during that year, and thus yearend cash balances should be treated like ordinary investments. A good counterargument can be made that household cash balances represent property devoted to household use and convenience. Bank balances produce imputed income in the form of checking services provided by the bank, and since the value

[107] CODE § 165(c)(1), (2).

[108] *See* N. KALDOR, *supra* note 7, at 198–201.

of those services is not separately accounted for in taxable income, the bank balances should be nondeductible, like the prices of consumer durables.

The most important thing about how to treat ordinary cash balances is that it makes little difference what the rule is. There is no need to include anything as an opening balance that was not deducted as a closing balance in the prior year, and therefore the inclusion side of the problem does not present any kind of auditing or underreporting problem. On the other hand, deduction at year end is only a matter of year-to-year deferral whose value will be limited. The distortions that could result from differences in reporting cash balances are only of the same order of magnitude as those that now arise in connection with cash accounting for items that may be paid or received at or around the end of the year.

If closing cash balances are permitted to be deducted and added to next year's income, there would be some inducement to defer payment of ordinary household expenses past the end of the year. A few days' deferral of payment would produce a year's deferral of the corresponding amount of tax, since the closing bank balance would be larger. On the other hand, if cash balances are simply left out of account there would be some tendency to push to make yearend investments, or to postpone disinvestments until the next year, or perhaps even to make temporary yearend investments just for the tax deduction they would generate. The choice of how to treat cash balances should depend primarily on a judgment about which of these inducements would be most bothersome or undesirable in its effects.

My hunch is that ordinarily yearend cash balances should be ignored. It seems simpler to treat ordinary cash balances as funds already devoted to household use. An exception should be made for unusually large closing cash balances, partly just to take care of temporary disinvestment. On the other hand, no deduction should be allowed for any investment made within thirty days of the end of the year which is liquidated the next year, but within thirty days of when it was made. The purpose of this rule would be, like that of the present wash sales provisions,[109] to take away the tax incentive for an artificial transaction that is unlikely to occur for any other reason. Any such temporary investment should be treated as if made just after the beginning of the new year. The amount of any such temporary investment would then be counted as a closing checking account balance, which would still be deductible if it was very substantial in amount.

Savings account deposits should be deductible as ordinary

[109] CODE § 1091 (disallowing deduction for loss on a sale of securities if substantially identical securities are purchased within 30 days before or after the sale).

investments, since they earn a return which will itself be subject to tax when spent. Like other investments, a savings bank deposit made in the last month of the year should not be deductible in the year made if there are withdrawals within thirty days.[110]

I. Gifts, Bequests, Inheritances, and Devises

As under present law, a transfer of property by gift, bequest, inheritance, or devise would not be a taxable event under a consumption-type personal income tax for either the transferor or the transferee.[111] Moreover, in general, the carryover basis rule applicable to inter vivos gifts under present law would be applied both to inter vivos gifts and to transfers at death under the consumption-type tax. With respect to investment property the carryover basis rule would not create any of the same practical difficulties as it does under present law, however, because basis for investment property under a consumption-type personal income tax would be zero.

For ordinary investment assets these rules would mean that making a gift is not regarded as consumption. Thus an individual would never be taxed on income that he saves and gives away, during life or at death, although there may be an estate or a gift tax on the transfer of investment property. Moreover, the recipient would not be taxed on receipt of such property unless and until he sells it without reinvesting the proceeds. Thus, under the consumption-type personal income tax itself, invested funds would not be taxed unless and until they are devoted to personal con-

---

[110] Even if cash balances are ignored once a consumption-type personal income tax is in effect, it is often thought that cash balances held on the effective date of such a tax would have to be taken into account since they are a source of funds available for consumption thereafter. But if the consumption-type tax is seen as a modification and continuation of the existing income tax, rather than as a new tax, cash balances can arguably be ignored because they presumably represent tax-paid funds. The hard transition problem is whether that argument can be extended to other kinds of property, and if not, how and where to draw a line. *See* note 140 *infra*.

[111] It is sometimes thought that gifts should be included in taxable income of the recipient under an accretion-type tax. *See* H. SIMONS, *supra* note 1, at 211–12. I believe that that thought is erroneous, and that the exclusion of gifts generally, when not made in a commercial or employment context, is essentially consistent with the accretion ideal. The exclusion simply operates to assure only one application of tax (on the donor) for one cycle of earning (by the donor) and spending or saving (by the donee). *See* Andrews, *supra* note 1, at 348–51. The same rationale for excluding gifts is equally applicable to the consumption model.

It is also widely thought that transfer by gift or at death should be the occasion for taxing donors and decedents on the unrealized appreciation in their assets. *See* pp. 1147–48 *supra*. Whatever the merits of this proposal for a quasi-accretion-type tax, it would be inappropriate and unnecessary in a consumption-type tax.

sumption, and they would then be taxed to the individual whose consumption they support.

In theory, cash gifts might also be made deductible by a donor and includable in income of the recipient, since such gifts have the same effect as if the donor had purchased an investment asset and transferred that. Indeed that should be the treatment of large cash transfers. As a practical matter, however, it is easier to leave small and moderate cash gifts out of account. Such gifts often go to support current consumption, and often consumption of items that the donee otherwise would have done without. Small cash gifts are like gifts of food or clothing or entertainment purchased by a donor for a donee and can be treated most practically as taxable consumption expenditure by the donor rather than the donee. This is accomplished simply by taking no account of such gifts on either the donor's or the donee's side.

Since donors are apt to be in higher income tax brackets than donees, allowing taxation to be shifted to the donee only when the gift is of investment property or large cash amounts will favor such gifts over gifts of consumption items. This bias can be conveniently offset by providing that only gifts of consumption items and small and moderate cash gifts are eligible for whatever annual exclusion is available under the gift tax. Substantial cash gifts not covered by that annual exclusion would be treated consistently with transfers of investment property — that is, by giving a deduction to the transferor and including them in income of the recipient.

Ordinary consumer durables should also be governed by the principle that lets the donee step into the donor's shoes. If an automobile, for example, has been paid for, its consumption value has already been taxed to the donor, and there is no reason to tax the donee on either its receipt or its use. Of course, if the donor had deferred tax on the purchase of the automobile, then either he or the donee should continue to be liable for the deferred tax.

Consumer durables with a longer useful life, such as housing, valuable jewelry, and works of art, present special problems. The idea that their consumption value is taxpaid by reason of the fact that their purchase was taxed as a consumption expenditure by the donor is perhaps more tenuous than in the case of shorter-lived assets.[112] In one way or another one might feel that there ought to be a fresh start with respect to such assets and that the recipients, at least, ought to be treated as if they had received cash and then purchased the consumer durable in question. How-

---

[112] This is because tax rates may have changed and because value may have increased for reasons not reflected in original purchase price. *Cf.* p. 1157 *supra.*

ever, it would be quite feasible to let the general rule prevail under which a successor steps into his predecessor's shoes for income tax purposes, relying on the transfer tax to impose some burden based on current values. Under existing law no new income tax burden is imposed on the passage of items like these by gift or at death, and concrete proposals for taxing unrealized appreciation at death have often contained generous exemptions for family residences.[113] Whatever reasons underlie such exemptions might support a lenient treatment under a consumption-type personal income tax as well.

J. Life Insurance Policies and Annuity Contracts

Life insurance policies and annuity contracts would be treated under a consumption-type personal income tax just like any other investment: premium payments would be deductible and proceeds would be fully taxable. In the case of annuity contracts this would be consistent with the treatment of qualified pension plans, and would have the effect of deferring tax on income devoted to purchase of the contract, together with interest return on the contract, until it is finally devoted to consumption. In the case of life insurance this treatment might seem to compound the tragedy of death by taxing policy proceeds. But the inclusion of proceeds would be offset by a deduction for investment, and the net effect would be that proceeds would be taxable only if and when devoted to consumption. Moreover, the deductibility of premiums would make it possible for taxpayers to carry larger policies in the first place. Because of graduated rates this will tend to outweigh taxation of the proceeds to the beneficiaries when spent, in any case in which beneficiaries enjoy a lower standard of living.

K. Summary

Not all problems under the existing personal income tax would be solved by adopting a consumption-type tax. Problems having to do solely with the consumption component of accretion, such as those involving business entertainment expenditures, would not be affected at all. Problems involving both the consumption and accumulation components of accretion, such as those of owner-occupied housing, would not be wholly solved. Moreover, there would be transition problems in converting the existing tax into

[113] For example, the Treasury Department's 1963 proposal to tax unrealized appreciation at death would have allowed personal residences to pass taxfree to spouses with a stepped-up basis. *See* HOUSE COMM. ON WAYS AND MEANS, 89TH CONG., 2D SESS., LEGISLATIVE HISTORY OF H.R. 8363, THE REVENUE ACT OF 1964, pt. 1, at 236–38 (Comm. Print 1966).

a pure consumption-type tax, which are touched on briefly in part VII.

But much of the law concerning business and investment transactions could be vastly simplified by a shift to a pure consumption-type personal income tax. Problems of realization of gain, computation of gain and determination of basis, capital gain treatment, deferral of tax under nonrecognition provisions including the installment sale provisions and those governing corporate organizations and reorganizations, amortization of investment, and treatment of discharge of indebtedness would all be simply swept away. And even problems like owner-occupied housing, that have both consumption and accumulation aspects, would be capable of much more satisfactory treatment. On balance, therefore, a consumption-type or cash flow personal income tax would represent an incomparably simpler tax to administer than either the present hybrid or a true accretion-type tax.

VI. Fairness and Efficiency

What must now be considered is whether a consumption-type personal income tax, even if easier to administer, would be as fair and as desirable from the standpoint of economic incentives as would an accretion-type tax. Interestingly, there is a considerable body of economic literature arguing that a consumption-type tax would be more desirable, but assuming it to be less capable of practical implementation.[114] We need now to consider both the arguments that have been made in favor of a consumption-type tax and the grounds on which one might prefer an accretion-type tax.

A. Accumulation as Consumption Foregone

The primary, intended, real effect of any general revenue-raising tax is to curtail some part of the private consumption of economic resources that would otherwise occur, in order to free those resources for public use, including redistribution to the poor.[115] If the purpose is to curtail consumption, then it is presumptively fair and efficient to distribute the burden of the tax proportionately or progressively in relation to levels of consump-

[114] *See generally* N. Kaldor, *supra* note 7, at 11–13 *and* authorities cited therein.

[115] A person may meet the burden of the tax by working harder to increase his income instead of curtailing consumption expenditure. But even such an increase is a curtailment of consumption, if consumption is understood to include the enjoyment of leisure by working less. While leisure is a component of consumption that may be reduced to pay the tax, however, it is unfortunately not one that is reflected in consumption expenditure or income, and therefore the income tax remains biased against other forms of consumption as compared with leisure.

tion prior to imposition of the tax. That way people who would enjoy the same standard of living in the absence of tax will live at the same level, albeit a lower one, after imposition of the tax. The tax may even reduce relative discrepancies in living standards if it is imposed on a graduated basis, although it will not alter rank order among consumers as such.

Accumulation, from this point of view, should not be taxed along with consumption because accumulation represents consumption already curtailed. Or it represents, in general, the market value of the excess of what one has contributed to production in a particular period, in labor or capital or both, over what he has withdrawn for private consumption during that period, and there is no reason to tax a person on that excess. "For," in Hobbes' words, "what reason is there, that he which laboureth much, and sparing the fruits of his labour, consumeth little, should be more charged then he that living idlely, getteth little, and spendeth all he gets; seeing the one hath no more protection from the Common-wealth, then the other?" [116]

It may be said that private investment is just as much a demand on output as is consumption, and that taxing accumulation will serve to release additional real resources for public use. But investment is not a final use of economic resources; it is an intermediate use by which more is ultimately to be produced for future consumption, private or public, or for further investment. A tax on investment as such means an additional burden on those products and processes that require substantial investment as compared with others that do not.[117] A general revenue tax ought to deal with final products, on an aggregate basis, without discrimination according to means of production. Moreover, changes in the rate of tax on consumption can themselves affect investment in facilities for the production of private consumption goods.

Some persons may bear the burden of an income tax without reducing current consumption, by reducing annual saving or by spending from previously accumulated wealth, even if the tax is measured solely by reference to consumption. Rational taxpayers will respond to any tax by reallocating their remaining resources

[116] T. Hobbes, *supra* note 7, at 181.

[117] In the case of the fruit grower described above, *see* pp. 1124–25 *supra*, a 30% accretion-type tax will leave him with 49% of the fruit he would have had if no tax at all had been imposed. On the other hand, farmers of annual crops such as potatoes can keep 70% of what they grow. This is inefficient since it will tend to induce farmers to produce more potatoes and less oranges than an optimal mix as determined by consumer preferences and factor costs operating in an undistorted market. Or, stated in another way, if the price of the oranges reflects the relatively higher tax cost to the grower, then consumer demand will be correspondingly reduced.

according to their own schedule of preferences, taking account of any price effects of the tax. A few people may even be so wealthy that their level of consumption is determined by taste alone without financial constraint. Nevertheless, a consumption-type tax will be fair because it will impose the same increase in the price for maintaining any particular level of consumption, however particular taxpayers may respond to the increase. An accretion-type tax, on the other hand, imposes a burden that may be quite out of line with levels of current consumption.

B. Accumulation as Consumption Deferred

It may nevertheless be objected that a saver is not to be viewed as a philanthropist contributing more to society than he withdraws. Accumulation is not consumption foregone; it is consumption deferred. Since a saver has not given up the claim against future output represented by his accumulated income, what reason can there be to exempt him from tax upon it?

But the issue as between an accretion-type and a consumption-type tax is not one of exemption; it, too, is only one of deferral. Under a consumption-type tax, deferred consumption is subject to deferred tax. Of course, deferral makes a difference, and in general the burden of a deferred tax is less than that of an immediate tax at the same rate, unless further appreciation and yield are to be exempted once the tax is imposed.[118] But to say the burden of a deferred tax is less does not indicate which kind of tax is fairer. The most sophisticated argument in favor of a consumption-type tax is that the lesser burden of a deferred tax is more appropriate because it ultimately imposes a more uniform burden on consumption, whenever it may occur, than does an accretion-type tax. Put the other way around, a consumption-type tax is preferable because an accretion-type tax imposes an excessive burden on deferred consumption.[119] Neutrality with

---

[118] *See* pp. 1123–28 *supra*.

[119] An accretion-type tax is sometimes defended by reference to neutrality, treating saving as just one more thing a person may do with his income. A consumption-type tax, it is said, would impose a penalty on spending as compared with saving. *See* Musgrave, *In Defense of an Income Concept*, 81 HARV. L. REV. 44, 46 (1967). Or, more elaborately, it is said that saving must involve some combination of satisfactions equal to what could have been derived from a little more spending at the margin; otherwise the person would have spent more and saved less. *See, e.g.*, Aaron, *supra* note 2, at 544.

But this line of reasoning is essentially like an argument against the deductibility of business expenses — one must get as much pleasure from a business expenditure as from a personal consumption expenditure, at the margin, or else he would make more of the latter and less of the former. What we recognize immediately, of course, with respect to a business expense is that satisfactions to be derived from it may be at least one step removed. The expenditure is instrumental

respect to consumption is important not only because it promotes efficiency in the allocation of income, but because it keeps the tax from bearing more heavily on one person than another on account of differences in need or taste for particular goods or services, now or in the future.

Consider again the case in Part II of a working person who puts $100 aside for retirement. At 9% compound interest, in 24 years it will grow to $800. A tax of 33% imposed on a consumption basis would take 33% of $800 leaving $533 to spend. A 33% accretion-type tax would cut the $100 to $67 at the outset, and cut its rate of growth from 9% per annum to 6%. At 6%, the $67 would double only twice making $267, or just half what is left under a consumption-type tax. The effective rate of tax in relation to consumption ultimately supported by the earnings in question is thus not 33% but 67%. All this is without even taking account of graduated rates, which are likely to make the relative burden of an accretion-type tax even heavier by subjecting earnings to high-income rates even when put aside to support consumption in low-income retirement years.

The logic of a consumption-type tax is that a 33% taxpayer who would have had $800 to spend in the absence of tax should have $533 after tax whatever combination of earnings and savings may have gone to produce the $800. An accretion-type tax is discriminatory because it will leave much less for the retiree whose potential $800 is the product of work and saving than for another taxpayer with $800 of current income.[120]

Mill called the discrimination of an accretion-type tax against deferred consumption a double tax on savings, once as they accumulate and again as they produce their own return.[121] Unfortunately, ensuing discussion has sometimes focused more on definitional than on substantive issues; the accumulation of savings and the earning of a return on the accumulation represent separate items of income or accretion, it is said, and therefore taxing both does not represent double taxation of a single item.[122] For all the argument, no careful writer seems to have denied that

---

in producing more income which in turn may be spent to purchase the ultimate satisfaction for which the original expenditure was made. Saving, similarly, can be viewed as an instrumental expenditure, made as a means of supporting future consumption. The way to achieve neutrality between ultimate ends — future and present consumption — is, as we have seen, to exempt savings, not to tax them.

[120] *See* pp. 1123–28 *supra*.

[121] J.S. MILL, *supra* note 7, at 545–46.

[122] *See generally* N. KALDOR, *supra* note 7, at 79–87 (focusing on the controversy over Mill's statement); R. MUSGRAVE, THE THEORY OF PUBLIC FINANCE 160–71 (1959); Musgrave, *A Further Note on the Double Taxation of Savings*, 29 AM. ECON. REV. 549–50 (1939).

an accretion-type tax imposes a heavier ultimate burden in relation to deferred consumption than to current consumption.

This discussion of neutrality has only to do with neutrality as to expenditures. A personal income tax is not neutral by any means, unfortunately, with respect to questions of productivity — how hard to work and how much, what risks to take with capital, and so on. Either a consumption-type or an accretion-type personal income tax will have substitution effects in favor of leisure over work, and, less clearly, in favor of conservative over risky investment. While both types of taxes are biased with respect to these things, a consumption-type tax is apparently less so.[123] This is an important advantage, though collateral, as it seems to me, to preserving expenditure neutrality between present and deferred consumption.

Insofar as accumulation is viewed as deferred consumption, a consumption-type tax seems fairer and economically more efficient than an accretion-type tax. If an accretion-type tax is to be preferred over a consumption-type tax it must be because accumulation somehow represents something more than deferred consumption, something that would not be adequately captured or reflected or burdened by the deferred imposition of a consumption-type tax if and when consumption ultimately occurs.

C. Accumulation and Wealth

The main reason for preferring an accretion-type tax to a consumption-type tax is the notion that it may help somehow to get at disparities in wealth as well as living standards. Wealth is something more than deferred consumption; it represents power and security and a source of funds with which to pay taxes whether it is spent or not. Exempting accumulation from the personal income tax would seem on its face to destroy any value the tax might otherwise have in dealing with differences in wealth as such, and to promote whatever tendency there is for the rich in our society to get richer while others continue to struggle. One may imagine that there are some people whose wealth produces such a flow of interest and dividends that they fail to spend even a major portion of it for current consumption, and wonder what equity there is in a change that would exempt that excess from the personal income tax.

It is true that wealth is a source of power. Indeed it is a source of power over and above what is represented by current income or accretion, since a wealthy man can spend all his current income and spend out of capital as well. But wealth is a stock, not a flow; it represents a different dimension along which to measure

[123] *See* N. KALDOR, *supra* note 7, at 102–14.

economic well-being, and there is no way that wealth and income can be added together in any single index of welfare.[124] If one is seriously concerned about disparities of wealth, therefore, what is needed is a tax on wealth as such, with its own set of exemptions and rates tailored to reflect our attitudes about the distribution of wealth. An income tax is at best only an indirect way of attacking the problem.

One way an accretion-type personal income tax may be thought to get at wealth, indirectly, is as a kind of proxy for a tax on the wealth from which the income flows.[125] Taxing dividends as income may be conceived as an indirect way of taxing the stock on which they are paid. Even this conception of the income tax, however, does not lead toward a true accretion-type tax, because income as a proxy for the value of the income-producing property includes only anticipated yield, not windfalls or gains resulting from changes in the rate of discount. Any attempt to elaborate the notion of income as a proxy for present value would lead, therefore, right back into the kinds of distinctions that plague our present tax.[126]

Taxing accretion, comprehensively defined, may alternatively be seen as an indirect way of getting at wealth since accumulation is the origin of wealth. If we had always had a true accretion-type tax, existing stocks of wealth would have borne a tax on their accumulation and the tax might be seen as mitigating the disparities that would otherwise have arisen.

It would be hard to make a convincing case, of course, for the notion that the existing tax has done much to mitigate disparities in wealth. The existing tax imposes a burden on the accumulation of wealth out of personal earnings, except in the case of qualified pension or profit-sharing plans, but on the whole the capital gain and capital recovery provisions operate to favor or even facilitate accumulation by way of growth in existing stocks of wealth. And

[124] *Id.* at 58–67. *See also* Samuelson, *The Evaluation of "Social Income": Capital Formation and Wealth*, in 1 THE COLLECTED SCIENTIFIC PAPERS OF PAUL SAMUELSON 299 (J. Stiglitz ed. 1966).

[125] Early income taxes with very high exemptions may have been conceived, to a degree, as indirectly measured taxes on the capital accumulation producing the income, earned income being assumed to be largely covered by personal exemptions. It is also this view of the matter that produced the strange interlude in our constitutional history during which Congress was barred from imposing individual income taxes. The main argument was that a tax on the income from property was a direct tax on the property itself, which could only be imposed if apportioned among the states according to population, a politically prohibitive requirement. *See* Pollock v. Farmers' Loan & Trust Co., 157 U.S. 429, *aff'd on rehearing*, 158 U.S. 601 (1895). This interlude ended in 1913 with the adoption of the sixteenth amendment which authorized taxation, without apportionment, of income from whatever source derived.

[126] *See* N. KALDOR, *supra* note 7, at 62–70.

even if the existing tax were now to be converted into a true accretion-type tax, it would still not deal with existing disparities in stocks of wealth. A true accretion-type tax might make it harder for the rich to get richer, but it would also make it harder for anyone new to join the ranks of the well-to-do, or, more generally, for one to save for years in which his income stream may be reduced. For many years to come, it would tend to preserve and protect existing disparities, not only by impeding the accumulation of wealth in new hands, but also by slowing the fall of the well-to-do who live beyond their current income, by enabling them to pay less than an adequate tax for their current standard of living. Which effect would be greater — making it harder for the rich to get richer or preserving existing disparities in wealth — depends on how accumulation is distributed in relation to wealth. It may be that on average accumulation represents an increasing fraction of income as income rises, though that is now much less clear than it was once assumed to be.[127] At any particular income level, however, it seems reasonable to assume that those with more wealth will feel free to spend more and save less.[128] At any particular income level, therefore, accumulation will tend to signify absence of wealth rather than its presence, and a tax on consumption would tend to be more progressive in relation to existing stocks of wealth than would a tax on accertion. On this assumption, it would be best to avoid any tax on accumulation, in the interest of those who most need to save, and to rely on steeper rate graduation and on other taxes aimed more directly at wealth to deal with the problem of excessive accumulation of wealth.[129]

Even if existing disparities could somehow be adequately dealt with, it is very unclear whether including accumulation in taxable income would be a desirable way to deal with the problem of wealth. Try to imagine that existing disparities in wealth are somehow eliminated and that all citizens can start afresh from a position of parity. Some people would then accumulate in order to provide for later consumption, and for them the effect of taxing accumulation would be to introduce an unjustifiable bias against deferred consumption as compared with immediate consumption.[130] There is no very good way of knowing to what extent

---

[127] *See* T. Mayer, Permanent Income, Wealth and Consumption 93–102 (1972); p. 1175 & notes 138–39 *infra*.

[128] *See* T. Mayer, *supra* note 127, *passim*.

[129] In general, when considerations of horizontal equity and vertical equity seem to conflict, decisions about the income tax base should rest primarily on horizontal considerations, because vertical considerations can be reflected in the rate structure while horizontal considerations cannot. *See* Andrews, *supra* note 1, at 337–41.

[130] *See* pp. 1167–69 *supra*.

accumulation should be regarded as deferred consumption, but to the extent it should be so regarded a consumption-type tax would be preferable.

Even to the extent, however, that accumulation exceeds deferred consumption wants, it is not clear it should be taxed, at least at the same rates as would be applicable to additional consumption. To the extent accumulation exceeds deferred consumption it is indeed consumption foregone, and the Hobbesian view of the purpose of the tax is of considerable validity in suggesting that accumulation should be exempted,[131] at least during the lifetime of the accumulator. Somewhat paradoxically, the desirability of an accretion-type tax to deal with disparities in wealth thus depends, after all, on the presence of unearned or undeserved or preexisting disparities, even though the tax will fail to deal directly with them.

One possibility would be to defer any tax on accumulation until death or until some earlier intergenerational transfer of property, and then subject it to estate or gift tax. In this way, to the extent accumulation turns out to represent deferred consumption by the accumulator, it will be taxed as such when consumption occurs, without any additional burden by reason of the deferral. On the other hand, to the extent of any excess of accretion over consumption during a particular taxpayer's lifetime, nothing will be taxed to him because his net lifetime accumulation represents an excess of contributions to the economy over withdrawals. But as this accumulation passes on it operates to create a kind of unearned original disparity in wealth in the hands of a new generation, which should be dealt with as such. Thus one comes to the conclusion that the way to make the tax system deal with disparities in wealth is by strengthening the gift and estate tax rather than through the income tax.[132]

In one sense, a consumption-type personal income tax plus a strengthened estate and gift tax might be looked at as a modified accretion-type personal income tax after all. One modification consists of deferring the tax on accumulation until subsequent consumption, death or earlier transfer as the case may be. But this modification is of crucial importance. It eliminates the discrimination against deferred consumption that would characterize a true accretion-type tax, at least when deferred consumption is by the same taxpayer. Another modification is the introduction

---

[131] *See* pp. 1165–67 *supra*.

[132] *See* Brannon, *Death Taxes in a Structure of Progressive Taxes*, 26 NAT'L TAX J. 451, 451–54 (1973); Kurtz & Surrey, *supra* note 76, at 1366–69; Westfall, *Revitalizing the Federal Estate and Gift Taxes*, 83 HARV. L. REV. 986, 988–89 (1970).

of separate and independent rate and exemption schedules for dealing with the problem of wealth. Estate and gift tax rates may be higher or lower than the income tax rates that would have applied to accumulation of the estate in question, but dealing with the problem through estate and gift taxation makes it possible to shape the rates appropriately for the level of wealth attained.[133]

In short, estate and gift taxes come much nearer to dealing directly with the problem of wealth than does inclusion of accumulation in the income tax base, and they are therefore to be preferred as a way of doing whatever it is we want to do to reduce disparities in wealth as such.

D. *Macroeconomic Effects*

It is not clear how a shift from an accretion-type to a consumption-type personal income tax would affect aggregate saving. The substitution or price effect would indeed be to increase the net interest return from saving and thereby to induce a shift from spending to saving. But for some persons at least there would be a contrary income effect. For one who is saving to meet some particular objective, exemption of savings from the personal income tax would make it easier to meet that goal and would therefore operate to let the individual spend a higher portion of his current income. There are no a priori grounds for predicting the relative impact of these effects, and there is no evidence by which to gauge their relative magnitude with any certainty, although it seems to be assumed that the net effect of the shift toward a consumption base would favor saving.[134]

---

[133] This is not to say the existing estate and gift taxes achieve this possibility. It would be more rational to have a unified transfer tax with a single rate schedule based on the aggregate of a person's inter vivos gifts and property left at death, *see* U.S. TREASURY DEP'T, *supra* note 25, at 351–87, or even an accessions tax under which rates would depend on the aggregate amount of gifts and property of decedents received by a particular recipient throughout his lifetime rather than the aggregate transferred by a particular transferor, *see* AMERICAN LAW INSTITUTE, FEDERAL ESTATE AND GIFT TAXATION 446–59 (1969).

[134] *See, e.g.*, N. KALDOR, supra note 7, at 91–96; R MUSGRAVE & P. MUSGRAVE, PUBLIC FINANCE IN THEORY AND PRACTICE 478–79; P. SAMUELSON, *supra* note 84, at 600 n.4. The effect of exempting savings from the income tax is analogous to the effect on work incentives of imposing an income tax in the first place. A personal income tax, whether of the consumption or accretion variety, operates to reduce the net return from gainful employment and thus is biased in favor of less work and more leisure. On the other hand, the income effect of an income tax is to require a person to work harder and earn more before taxes in order to support any particular standard of living. These two effects are contrary in their tendency, and there is no clear evidence to indicate that either one outweighs the other. *See* N. KALDOR, *supra* note 7, at 130–40; R. MUSGRAVE & P. MUSGRAVE, *supra*, at 467–69.

The possibility of an increase in aggregate saving raises two distinct issues. One is the question of maintaining full employment; the other is the issue of allocation of resources between consumption and investment, whether full employment is maintained or not.[135] The first issue involves stabilization; the second is concerned rather with growth. With respect to the former, it now seems clear that a shift toward consumption-type taxes need not have any depressing effect on the economy, because other measures can be taken, including adjustments in the general level of taxation, to avoid any such effect. Moreover, there does not now seem to be any tendency toward chronic oversaving to be concerned about. On the question of allocation the matter is not so clear. Some economists believe that present taxes are too heavily biased against investment and saving as compared with current consumption.[136] They are the ones who now believe, for example, that we should not increase the rate of tax on capital gains, realized or unrealized, because that would aggravate the bias against investment and saving. They also tend to believe that the corporate income tax might well be replaced, at least in part, by a value-added tax whose burden would fall more clearly on consumers rather than investors. If there is anything to their view, then a shift toward a consumption-type personal income tax should be favored since that would alleviate the burden on savings and investment without introducing the distinctions and discriminations involved in the capital gain provisions. Even if one has come to doubt the social utility of growth represented by an ever-increasing output of consumer goods, allocation of more to capital investment and less to current consumption may well be necessary to enable us to find the new ways to live that ecological considerations demand.

E. Redistribution Effects

There is some tendency to think that a consumption-type tax would be more regressive or less progressive than an accretion-type tax because consumption is a declining fraction of income as income increases. In part that notion reflects a habit of thought about general sales taxes; but a consumption-type personal income tax is a personal tax with graduated rates and personal exemptions that can be adjusted to whatever levels are thought to be appropriate. Indeed, the most general answer to the assertion that a consumption-type tax would be more regressive

---

[135] *See, e.g.*, N. KALDOR, *supra* note 7, at 173–88; R. MUSGRAVE & P. MUSGRAVE, *supra* note 134, at 465, 497–98.

[136] *See* pp. 1134–35 & note 52 supra.

than an accretion-type tax at any particular level of rates is that the rates could be adjusted to offset that effect.

In addition, almost all of the evidence supporting the notion that consumption is a declining fraction of income is single-year survey data.[137] That evidence is misleading because it classifies people according to their income for the survey year without regard to the level of their income over a longer period. As a result, low income people in the survey include people temporarily out of work, retired or otherwise in a low income bracket for the year in question, but whose long-range income, to which they look for support, is considerably higher and who may thus keep spending at their usual level despite the income drop. Conversely, people whose income is higher than usual in the survey year will show up as higher income persons, but may not increase their spending proportionately if they feel the increase is only temporary. Some economists have asserted that if people were classified according to their permanent income, consumption would turn out to be a nondeclining function of permanent income.[138] That assertion is hard to test conclusively, and many economists would doubt that it holds completely true, but most would agree that the degree to which consumption falls off as a fraction of income is less clear and probably less in magnitude than was once assumed.[139]

It may be, of course, that even though most people eventually spend a fairly comparable fraction of their permanent income, there are still a few very high-income taxpayers whose consumption does not represent a substantial part of their income even in the long run. But it is poor policy to unbalance the income tax in its impact on the vast majority of taxpayers in order to get at a very few for whom the relation between income, consumption, and wealth is somewhat out of the ordinary, especially since there are other ways of effectively taxing such persons.

F. Graduation and Rate Changes

Tax deferral may result in a taxpayer being in a different marginal rate bracket when he finally is taxed than he would have been at the earlier point in time. A lower marginal rate of tax in a subsequent period may result either from the operation of a graduated rate system producing lower marginal and average

---

[137] *See, e.g.*, P. SAMUELSON, *supra* note 84, at 210–18; Modigliani & Brumberg, *Utility Analysis and the Consumption Function: An Interpretation of Cross-Section Data*, in POST-KEYNESIAN ECONOMICS 388, 408–09 (K. Kurihara ed. 1954).

[138] *See, e.g.*, M. FRIEDMAN, A THEORY OF THE CONSUMPTION FUNCTION 220–24 (1957).

[139] *See, e.g.*, P. SAMUELSON, *supra* note 84, at 210–18. *See also* T. MAYER, *supra* note 127, at 93–102.

rates in a lower income period, such as retirement, or from changes in the statutory rate schedule between the earlier and the later point in time. When money is earned in one period and spent in another, the question arises whether it ought to be taxed at rates determined by reference to one period or the other.

With respect to rate graduation, the question invites an inquiry into the whole basis for progressivity in general taxes. Without accepting that invitation, it is still possible to indicate rather summarily what the major relations are. Insofar as progressivity rests upon either a policy of reducing discrepancies in standards of living or an assumption that persons with higher standards of living have more in the way of luxuries that can be dispensed with, the rate effects of a consumption-type tax seem more appropriate. Under a consumption-type tax, rates are determined according to the standard of living, as measured by the level of expenditure, which a taxpayer's income ultimately goes to support.

On the other hand, to the degree progression is justified by reference to an idea that very high incomes are essentially economic rents, one might conclude that an accretion-type tax is to be preferred. A person who earns a very high income within a particular period presumably enjoys the windfall of an advantageous economic opportunity to just as great a degree if he saves that income as if he spends it.

The idea that a progressive income tax might take away the part of a person's income that is attributable to accidents of economic opportunity is appealing, but hard to put into practice. There is no assurance that higher incomes are generally and consistently any more in the nature of rents than are lower incomes. More particularly, in the case of a high income for a short period, which is the case where the choice between an accretion-type and a consumption-type tax makes the biggest difference, there is no reason not to assume that the economic opportunity to charge a high rent was itself short-lived. Thus, even to the degree we think of progression as aimed at rents, that goal does not necessarily support an accretion-type tax, because the standard of living maintainable over a substantial period of time may be a better measure of economic opportunity for tax purposes than any single period's earnings.

With respect to rate changes there is an analogous dichotomy of possible views. Consider, for example, wartime tax rates. If higher rates are justified because of the special wartime need to curtail private consumption, then a consumption-type tax would seem to be called for, since it will increase the cost of wartime consumption whether financed out of current earnings or out of prewar savings. On the other hand, to the extent high rates are aimed at taking from people part of the higher wages and profits that wartime conditions enable them to earn, an accretion-type tax would seem to be indicated. Again the latter objective is appealing, but not easy to achieve. An excess profits tax may be a useful adjunct to wartime taxation, but there is very little warrant for treating a uniform fraction of everyone's wartime earnings as excess profits in this sense. The earnings of many people, in low and middle tax brackets particularly, would be effectively controlled during a period of high public need; to impose higher rates of tax on their earnings as such, whether spent or saved, because somebody else's current earnings may represent excess profits attributable to the emergency, would be very unjust.

G. Summary

The matter of choice between an accretion-type and a consumption-type tax, as a matter of fairness and efficiency, is hardly a simple one. But there are very substantial direct arguments in favor of a consumption-type tax. On the other hand most arguments in favor of an accretion-type tax seem to weaken under careful analysis. If, as indicated in parts IV and V, a consumption-type personal income tax represents a much more feasible goal than a true accretion-type tax, then considerations of fairness and efficiency certainly offer no reason to persist in pursuing accretion. Indeed they seem to add further reason for shifting our efforts in the direction of a cash flow or consumption-type tax.

VII. Recommendations

As indicated in Part V, a consumption-type personal income tax is quite realistic and practical as a long-range goal. It does not by itself represent an immediate solution, however, to our present problems, because people are adjusted to the existing income tax in too many ways. There would be substantial transition problems in moving to a pure consumption-type tax even if there were agreement on it as an ultimate goal.[140]

---

[140] The main problem is what to do about funds accumulated before the transition and spent for consumption thereafter. With respect to cash balances whose accumulation was recently taxed at ordinary income rates, another tax on expenditure would be unduly harsh. But giving full credit for the pretransition basis of investment assets generally would impair the integrity of the consumption-type tax too much and too long, and often with too little real justification. One might try to mediate between these poles by adopting a complex of rules dealing differently with different kinds of pretransition accumulation. Another general approach would be to adopt a consumption-type tax with very low rates and then phase it

Nevertheless, like the accretion model, the consumption model can be made to serve as a frame of reference for evaluating the existing tax and for generating more immediate proposals for improvement. One may use the consumption model this way even without abandoning the accretion model; the two together will give a better perspective on the existing tax than either taken alone. Faults that appear as such from the standpoint of both models are the most in need of correction. It seems appropriate, therefore, to close by summarizing some of the implications of the consumption model for more immediate reform of the existing tax.

A. *Source Distinctions and Rate Differentials*

The consumption ideal confirms the lesson of the accretion ideal that distinctions should not be made for personal income tax purposes among receipts from different sources. The exemption of interest on state and municipal bonds, therefore, is just as much of a departure from the consumption ideal as from the accretion ideal. Similarly, the deduction for percentage depletion in excess of cost and the bargain rate of tax for long-term capital gains, being based on the source of particular funds rather than any cost or expenditure required to derive them, are equally inconsistent with both ideals.

B. *Deferral with Respect to Net Accumulation*

The difference between the consumption and accretion models lies in their treatment of real accumulation. The accretion model requires that current income be taxed whether spent or saved, that unrealized appreciation be taken into income, and that deductions for amortization of capital expenditures be limited to real decline in value. Under the consumption model, however, unrealized appreciation is not taken into account, and current deductions are allowed for all business and investment expenditures, current or capital.

in by repeated, small rate increases, while phasing out the existing tax through a corresponding schedule of rate reductions. *See* pp. 1185–88 *infra*. A further step would be the adoption of a rule giving persons a zero basis in property transferred by gift or at death, coupled with a provision allowing taxfree rollover of investments. This would provide a cutoff point, after which credit would not be given for recovery of arguably taxpaid funds and any disinvestment would be taxed at ordinary rates. *See* pp. 1183–84 *infra*.

A converse transition problem exists with respect to taxpayers who have taken excess tax shelter deductions prior to transition. It would be too generous to forgive their potential tax on phantom gain, although meeting that liability may be more difficult after transition since the opportunity will be gone to offset it through new tax shelter deductions.

From either point of view, the existing inconsistency between full taxation of savings out of ordinary income and nontaxation of unrealized capital appreciation, plus the special tax rate for realized capital gains, is quite intolerable. Immediate proposals for change inspired by the accretion model involve limited steps toward more comprehensive inclusion.[141] On the other hand, the consumption model indicates that the way to deal with that inconsistency is by increasing opportunities for taxfree saving rather than seeking to impose taxes on unrealized gains and other untaxed sources of accumulation.

The consumption model provides support for proposals to deal with capital gains by instituting some system of rollover accounting whereby all taxes would be deferred on realized but reinvested capital gains.[142] As a corollary, capital gain income would be fully taxed at ordinary income rates when not reinvested. However, the allowance of rollover for realized capital gains, with the resulting increase in the deferral of tax on capital appreciation, would make it even more imperative that opportunities be increased for taxfree saving out of ordinary income, so that

---

[141] *See* pp. 1146–48 *supra.*

[142] *See* Clark, *The Paradox of Capital Gains: Taxable Income that Ought Not to be Currently Taxed*, in 2 HOUSE COMM. ON WAYS AND MEANS, 86TH CONG., 1ST SESS., TAX REVISION COMPENDIUM 1243, 1247–56 (Comm. Print 1959) (describing at length one method for managing a system of rollover accounting for capital gains). *See also* Smith, *Tax Treatment of Capital Gains*, in 2 HOUSE COMM. ON WAYS AND MEANS, *supra*, at 1233.

Most nonrecognition provisions in the existing personal income tax provide for deferred taxes by way of a substituted basis or basis adjustment for replacement property. If this technique were applied to a general rollover provision for capital gains it would require that particular replacement assets be identified somehow as replacements for those disposed of. Clark proposes to do it on an annual basis, making a pro-rata downward adjustment in basis of all investment assets acquired during any year equal to the net gain realized but deferred on assets disposed of during that year. As a result, the date of ultimate recognition of gains deferred in any particular year would depend upon when assets purchased during that year are sold.

A more general approach would be to credit deferred gains to a general deferred gain account, to be returned to income in any subsequent year in which aggregate disinvestments exceed aggregate investments (both computed on a cash flow basis, taking loan proceeds and repayments into account as well as asset sales and purchases). This test of net disinvestment might well be applied cumulatively from the date of adoption of the provision, rather than annually, so that a taxpayer who makes additional accumulations out of taxpaid income after the effective date would be able to withdraw these in a subsequent year before incurring liability for deferred capital gains. Certain complications and ambiguities of this kind are unavoidable so long as we continue to tax accumulation under some circumstances (savings out of ordinary income) while deferring it under others (capital gains), but a general provision of this kind would still be less complicated and less arbitrary than anything that depends on an identification of particular assets as replacements for others disposed of.

deferral would be available to all those who invest out of income from whatever source.

There are a number of ways in which the existing law permits taxfree saving out of ordinary income, which from the standpoint of the consumption ideal ought to be expanded. The most direct and obvious of these involves contributions to qualified pension or profit-sharing plans. The consumption model provides theoretical support for proposals to liberalize opportunities for taxfree retirement saving, particularly proposals to allow self-employed persons and uncovered employees to make tax deductible contributions to their own retirement plans.[143] It would also support a proposal to allow individuals to defer taxation on at least some portion of their savings, without restriction as to the time of withdrawal.[144]

Other provisions that have a similar effect for limited classes of taxpayers include the simplified accounting provisions applicable to farmers.[145] While these have been subject to abuse, which needs to be curbed, the fundamental idea of allowing an immediate deduction for cash expenditures in connection with a personal business is quite sound and completely consistent with the consumption ideal.[146]

---

[143] The House of Representatives recently passed a bill to increase the number of individual participants in taxfree retirement savings programs and to reduce the inequality in treatment of taxpayers in different employment situations. The bill would place a limit on contributions which could be made taxfree in the case of qualifying employee plans ($25,000 or 25% of one's compensation, whichever is less); it would increase the available deduction for self-employed individuals from 10% of compensation (not to exceed $2,500) to 15% (not to exceed $7,500); and it would allow individuals not covered by qualified or government pension plans to take a deduction of up to 20% of their earned income (not to exceed $1,500) for contributions to their own retirement fund. Money contributed under these plans after 1973 would be taxed at ordinary income rates when paid out at retirement, but the taxpayer would be able to average such payments forward over a 10-year period. *See* Employee Benefit Security Act of 1974, H.R. 2, 93d Cong., 2d Sess. (passed by the House, 120 CONG. REC. 1342 (Feb. 28, 1974)) (passed, after significant amendments, by the Senate, 120 CONG. REC. 2645 (Mar. 4, 1974)); HOUSE COMM. ON WAYS AND MEANS, PRIVATE PENSION TAX REFORM, H.R. REP. NO. 779, 93d Cong., 2d Sess. 1–39 (1974). The Senate bill is substantially the same as the House bill with respect to the above provisions, although even here there are significant differences of detail — such as allowing a 15- rather than a 10-year averaging period for lump sum payments.

[144] Under the present law a premature distribution to an owner-employee from a qualified plan results, roughly, in a tax of not less than 110% of the normal tax for the amount involved. CODE § 72(m)(5). Under the proposed Employee Benefit Security Act of 1974, passed by the House, *see* note 143 *supra*, this "penalty" tax would be strengthened, providing for a flat, nondeductible 10% tax on the amount of the distribution, in addition to any other income taxes payable on the distribution. *See* H.R. REP. NO. 779, *supra* note 143, at 116.

[145] *See* note 12 *supra*.

[146] Capital expenditures by a farmer are different in many ways from con-

C. *Tax Shelters, Borrowing, and Super-Deferral*

The consumption ideal confirms that something is acutely wrong with our present treatment of leveraged tax shelter investments insofar as they permit deductions in excess of a taxpayer's cash outlays. Indeed, it provides theoretical support for the most effective, practical way of dealing with tax shelter abuses which is currently advocated by a growing number of practitioners and analysts: that is to insist that investments financed through borrowing be accounted for on a net equity basis.[147] More particularly, aggregate deductions for depreciation would never be allowed to exceed a taxpayer's downpayment for the depreciable property plus principal payments on purchase money indebtedness.[148] Any borrowing subsequent to purchase would be applied against basis and any excess over basis would be included in income forthwith. This treatment of borrowing should not be confined to nonrecourse loans, nor even necessarily to loans secured by particular depreciable property. It should apply in the case of any borrowing incurred or continued to purchase or carry a particular investment. The matching of loans and investments would be similar to that undertaken to deny interest deductions for borrowing associated with an investment in tax-exempt securities.[149]

tributions to a retirement savings plan, but they do have this in common: both are instances where we may feel the act of saving or investment to be required rather than voluntary. They may seem to become voluntary, and deductibility may come to seem abusive, where contributions to a pension plan exceed reasonable retirement needs or where farming is conducted as a mere investment or secondary activity by a wealthy taxpayer whose primary activity is something else. It would not be feasible, of course, to make involuntariness a direct condition for deductibility, but it might be possible to take relative necessity or involuntariness as a general guideline for identifying categories of capital expenditures for which a deduction is most urgently necessary and most likely to be widely accepted as appropriate.

[147] *See* S. SURREY, *supra* note 16, at 250–51, 394–96 nn. 7, 8; DeWind, in Panel Discussion No. 4 on "Tax Treatment of Real Estate," *supra* note 46, at 520; Kurtz, in Panel Discussion No. 4, *supra* note 46, at 553.

[148] There are several variations for determining the rate of depreciation (straight line or accelerated) that would still be available to the taxpayer, and these in turn might be applied either to the net equity investment or to the total cost of the investment project. In the latter case, depreciation deductions in excess of current investment would be computed and accumulated for immediate deduction as subsequent repayments of principal on the loan occur.

[149] CODE § 265(2). The analogy to § 265(2) deserves to be explored further. As noted above, *see* p. 1126 *supra*, the effect of an immediate deduction for a capital expenditure is the same, if tax rates remain constant, as an exemption of return on the deducted investment. The effect of either an immediate deduction of capital cost or an exemption of return, as for municipal bonds, in the absence of debt financing, is thus to reduce the effective rate of tax to zero. Debt financing, if permitted without restriction, would in either case make it possible for the borrower to achieve a negative effective rate of tax on his net equity investment — that is,

Some of the practical advantages of this mode of dealing with tax shelter abuses are obvious. It does not depend upon property valuations or refined judgments as to actual economic depreciation; it depends rather on a simple cash flow computation like that involved in the consumption model. It also permits us to continue, for whatever reason, to allow taxpayers in particular lines of business, such as farming and real estate construction, to defer tax rather freely on funds that are in fact reinvested in the business. On the other hand, it requires taxpayers, even in these lines of business, to pay taxes on the portion of their revenues devoted to current personal consumption.[150]

---

to reduce the effective rate of tax *below* zero. Section 265(2) effectively prevents this, and puts a floor of zero on the effective rate of tax on tax-exempt interest. Limitation of deductions based on investment to net equity investment, if combined with full recapture provisions, would similarly put a floor of zero on the effective rate of tax on investments favored by the allowance of accelerated deductions of one sort or another.

[150] This limitation should be compared with the Limitation on Artificial Accounting Losses (LAL) proposed by the administration last year. U.S. TREASURY DEP'T, PROPOSALS FOR TAX CHANGE 14–18, 94–104 (1973) (Statement of Treasury Secretary George P. Schultz before the House Comm. on Ways and Means, April 30, 1973, and accompanying explanation). LAL would define certain losses due to accelerated deductions as artificial accounting losses and would prohibit their use to offset or shelter unrelated income of the taxpayer. Deductions would not be permanently disallowed, but rather deferred until there is related income or until the property in question is disposed of. Related income is sometimes defined as income from the property in question (nonresidential rental real estate), and sometimes as income from the same or similar properties (residential real estate, oil and gas properties, and farms in which the taxpayer is actively engaged as a trade or business, rather than as a passive investor).

LAL would limit deductions against unrelated income for the initial purchase of an investment, but it would not change the computation of taxable income from the property or related properties. Accelerated deductions, even those based on costs paid with borrowed funds, would be permitted against related income. As a result, "[t]axpayers may still purchase investments on which the income can be tax free for substantial periods . . . ." The reform would be that "the tax system will no longer pay them to buy such investments. They must buy with after tax dollars . . . ." *Id.* at 15–16.

The effect of LAL is to tolerate what may amount to a virtual exemption of income from a particular favored source if only the original net investment was made with after tax dollars, even if that original net investment is very small in relation to the gross investment and the amount of income exempted. On the other hand the limitation described in text makes no distinctions among items of income from different sources. It tolerates an accelerated deduction against income from any source, though only for a taxpayer's net investment of his own funds, but then requires that every penny of net cash return from the investment, in excess of previously unrecovered cost, be immediately included in taxable income.

A careful reader may recall the assertion that deferral of tax on an investment is equivalent to exemption of the yield therefrom, *see* p. 1126 *supra*, and wonder why a limitation that tolerates such deferral is any better than one that tolerates a virtual exemption of yield. The question deserves more extended consideration

Matching loans with particular investments would be a problem in some instances. In most cases, however, the matching would be rather obvious, and the provision would operate to curb the worst abuses even if it raises problems at the boundary. To deal with unsecured loans, one could put the burden on the taxpayer of associating such loans with one or more assets against whose basis the amount of the loan can be charged. Any excess of loan proceeds over the basis of such assets would be included in the taxpayer's income forthwith. The loan would thus be treated similarly to an open-transaction sale of the asset for tax purposes.[151]

The necessity of matching particular loans with particular investments is not an intrinsic characteristic of a pure consumption approach. If all investments were immediately deductible, as under the pure consumption model, then all business and investment loan proceeds would be immediately included in taxable income. It would be too harsh, however, to make business and investment loan proceeds fully and immediately taxable without an offsetting deduction for the investment of those proceeds in business or investment assets, or a corresponding credit for one's basis in existing investment assets, and the provision of such an offset is what requires the matching.

D. *Property Transferred at Death or by Gift*

Under existing law property transferred at death secures a new fair market value basis, with the result that appreciation in the hands of the decedent escapes income tax altogether. Since such property may be devoted to consumption expenditure by the recipient without the imposition of any income tax on anyone, this provision is inconsistent with the consumption ideal as well as the accretion ideal.

---

than can be given here, but some elements of an answer can be indicated. The equivalence between deferral on investment and exemption of yield holds only if applicable tax rates are constant and if what is exempted is strictly limited to yield from the investment of after-tax funds. In the case of a taxpayer with a growing income stream from favored investments both of these conditions are apt to be violated, and exemption of yield will be more valuable both because it applies to income otherwise taxable at higher rates and because the yield will contain elements of windfall profit and of compensation for personal effort as well as simple investment yield.

For another discussion of these two techniques for limiting tax shelter abuses, see S. SURREY, *supra* note 16, at 248–51, 392–96.

[151] Alternatively, the Code could provide that unsecured loans are to be first applied against certain assets — such as appreciated securities before other assets, securities before a residence, and the like. S. SURREY, *supra* note 16, at 395 n.8. The law might also provide that the loan, instead of being applied first against basis, be applied first against gain, or proportionately against basis and unrealized gain as in the case of an installment sale.

It has long been urged by accretionists, even those without a very acute understanding of the importance of deferral, that unrealized appreciation should be constructively realized and taxed to the decedent or his estate at the time of his death.[152] Opposition has been voiced largely on behalf of farmers and owners of other family businesses for whom the burden of forced partial liquidation to pay the tax might be particularly harsh. A less effective step would be a carryover basis for all assets transferred at death like that now applicable to inter vivos gifts. This would prevent permanent escape from tax, but would permit unlimited deferral and thus further extend the disincentive to change investments caused by deferral. Either constructive realization or carryover basis involves certain practical difficulties, since both require a fiduciary or a subsequent owner to determine the decedent's cost or other basis for assets that may have been purchased many years before.

A pure consumption-type personal income tax would avoid these problems. It would provide for a carryover basis, but in the case of business and investment assets that basis would always be zero since the decedent would have deducted his cost when he acquired the asset. Moreover, the zero basis would not operate to produce any tax if the asset were sold and proceeds reinvested since there would be an offsetting deduction for the reinvestment.

If we would adopt a rollover system of deferring tax on reinvested capital gains, then a zero basis rule for property acquired by gift or on the death of a prior owner deserves careful consideration. Rollover would assure that no tax is to be paid until the property is devoted to current consumption, and at that point it is not at all clear that any offset is required for taxes that may have been paid by prior owners.[153] A zero basis rule together with rollover would have the effect of transforming the tax into a pure consumption-type tax in relation to inherited wealth. It would also provide one mechanism by which a transition to a general consumption-type tax could be facilitated, since it could help reduce taxpayers' bases in investment assets to zero by making death or gift a cut-off point after which credit would no longer be given for the recovery of arguably taxpaid investment.

---

[152] *See* note 76 *supra*.

[153] An exception could readily be made for property passing to a widow or orphaned minor children of a decedent, allowing them to carry over the decedent's actual basis, on the ground that a single, nuclear family unit should not be required to pay tax twice, once on the accumulation and again on the consumption expenditure of the same funds. *Cf.* Andrews, *What's Fair About Death Taxes*, 26 NAT'L TAX J. 465 (1973).

E. *Special Problems of High-Income Taxpayers*

Many defects in the existing personal income tax have particularly to do with high-income taxpayers — taxpayers who are in high rate brackets or would be in high brackets if their whole income were effectively subject to tax. Many special problems result directly from the distorting effect of very high marginal rates. Only taxpayers in high marginal rate brackets, for instance, are driven into tax sheltered investments, or into artificial arrangements for disguising ordinary compensation as capital gain. Special problems also result to some degree from the fact that wealthy taxpayers are better able to arrange their affairs to take advantage of tax breaks. Capital gains, for example, are very highly concentrated among a comparatively few high-income taxpayers. It has been disclosed in recent years that some taxpayers with very high adjusted gross incomes have been able to arrange to pay no federal income taxes whatever.

Since 1969 there has been a limited resort to a new strategy for dealing with high-income taxpayers.[154] A minimum tax has been introduced which is supposed to have the effect, roughly, of imposing at least some tax on people whose tax preference items make their regular tax unduly low in relation to their total income.[155] On the other hand, there is a maximum rate of tax on earned ordinary income, whose purpose is to reduce incentives for converting compensation into capital gain.[156] The maximum tax also deals indirectly with preference items, but only for people with high earned incomes: the amount of compensation income eligible for the maximum tax is reduced dollar-for-dollar by the amount of certain preference items.

A consumption-type, cash flow computation could well be used as a base for dealing specially with high-income taxpayers even though the tax is not changed more generally to conform to the consumption model. A minimum tax could be imposed, for example, by taking some fraction of aggregate net cash flow from business and investment activities (*i.e.*, consumption expenditures) in excess of some specified minimum — say half of cash flow in excess of $20,000, for a conservative starter — and providing for a tax at scheduled rates on that amount if it exceeds taxable income. Some of the purposes of the present maximum tax might be served, on the other hand, by a provision that would put a ceiling on the rate of tax on any taxable income in excess of

[154] *See* S. SURREY, *supra* note 16, at 267–81.

[155] *See* CODE §§ 56–58.

[156] CODE § 1348.

aggregate net cash flow from business and investment activities.

Many of the purposes of both minimum and maximum taxes could best be accomplished, however, by introducing a supplemental tax on net cash flow from business and investment transactions (consumption expenditures) in excess of, say, $20,000, while making a corresponding reduction in rates on taxable income above that figure.[157] This would have the effect of establishing both a maximum rate on unspent income and a minimum tax on consumption financed otherwise than out of current taxable income. By making the income tax deductible in computing cash flow, it would be possible, for example, to cut the top rate of tax on unspent income to 40%, and then have a consumption-type, cash flow tax running up to 50%. The net effect in this case would be to preserve a top rate of 70% on ordinary income devoted to current consumption (40% plus 50% of the remaining 60%), as under the present tax, while in effect putting a minimum tax at graduated rates running up to 50% on consumption financed from other sources, and a top rate of 40% on income not devoted to current consumption. These figures are only illustrative. The cash flow tax could be initially introduced at much lower rates and increased from year to year in small steps to avoid sharp transition problems. It could ultimately be made to bear more or less of the total burden than that represented by top rates of 40 and 50%.

This change would have a number of advantages. For one, it would reduce the top rate of tax on taxable income as such, and thus reduce substantially the distorting effects of very high marginal tax rates on personal business and investment decisions and practices. It would accomplish this general result for investment income as well as compensation income, which is all that is now covered by the maximum tax. In addition, it would accomplish this result without the general sacrifice of progressivity that is involved in a simple reduction or ceiling on top income tax rates without the supplemental tax on cash flow. The total tax on households that receive and spend at high levels would be kept high, but it would be made to stand on two feet instead of one so that the marginal tax rate operating on changes in either base alone would be small in comparison with the total tax burden.

Consider, for example, a top-bracket taxpayer converting $100 of ordinary income into capital gain. Under existing law (ignoring existing minimum and maximum tax effects) the conversion would reduce his tax from $70 to $35, and increase what is left after tax from $30 to $65. Under the proposal here, if the

[157] Kaldor ended up making essentially the same practical recommendation for adoption in England. N. KALDOR, *supra* note 7, at 224–42.

taxpayer received all ordinary income, he would pay a regular income tax of \$40, and a supplemental tax of \$30 if the money is spent on consumption — the same total amount as under present law. If he is able to convert ordinary income to capital gain, assuming no change in the existing capital gain deduction, he would reduce his regular income tax from \$40 to \$20; but if the taxpayer spent whatever is left after tax, his supplemental tax would increase from \$30 to \$40. The total net effect would thus be only to decrease taxes from \$70 to \$60 and increase disposable income from \$30 to \$40.

Moreover, the supplemental tax on cash flow would perform the function of a minimum tax by assuring that people with high real incomes and standards of living pay some significant tax even if their incomes for some reason escape the regular income tax. This supplemental tax would not reach misers who live frugally while accumulating large incomes, but it seems likely that most of the taxfree millionaires who inspired the 1969 innovations live at standards that would be subject to this tax.

Furthermore, basing a minimum tax on a cash flow computation of consumption expenditures has certain definite advantages. Any attempt to base a minimum tax on accretion necessarily raises in an attenuated but direct way whatever objections stand in the way of simply eliminating those provisions that make taxable income fall short of that ideal. Whatever arguments about the content of taxable income underlie any particular exclusion or deduction will carry over to the definiton of total income for purposes of a minimum tax as well. Such a tax necessarily has the character of a compromise with respect to the issues involved in those provisions, and not a very logical one at that. Basing a supplemental or minimum tax on a cash flow computation of consumption expenditures, however, offers a way of changing the terms of discourse. Whatever the definition of regular, taxable income, it says, a person who spends more than \$20,000 a year on private, personal consumption ought to pay a minimum tax as prescribed in the rate schedule for the supplemental tax.

Finally, this supplemental tax would effect the introduction of a consumption-type, cash flow tax in a manner that would minimize transition problems. With a \$20,000 exemption and low initial rates the tax could be introduced without any special or elaborate transition provisions, since people living at that standard will not likely be living primarily on the liquidation of previously taxed accumulation. Even at low rates, the supplemental tax would produce information that we now lack about the relation between consumption expenditures and taxable income. Moreover, the supplemental tax would serve as a testing ground for a consumption-type tax to see if it would have the advantages in actual practice that it seems to offer in speculation. If it did live up to its promise, finally, the supplemental tax could be expanded in gradual steps to take over whatever greater portion of the burden of the whole tax might then seem desirable. Even without this last possibility, the supplemental consumption-type, cash flow tax offers the best general way of dealing with the special problems of high-income taxpayers.

F. Summary

Elimination of source distinctions and rate differentials, net equity accounting for debt-financed investments, a zero basis for inherited business and investment property, and a supplemental cash flow tax for high-income taxpayers are all directly aimed at strengthening the personal income tax in relation to personal consumption. Rollover treatment of realized capital gains and reduction in the top rate of tax for unspent income, on the other hand, would both reduce burdens on accumulation, as would the provision of increased opportunities for taxfree saving out of ordinary income. These changes are desirable in themselves from the standpoint of the consumption ideal, but they would also facilitate adoption of the others. Rollover for capital gains, for example, would make it more feasible to eliminate bargain rates and step-up of basis at death; and lower top marginal rates on income whether spent or saved would leave room to introduce the supplemental tax on cash flow. The main objective should be to repair and maintain the integrity of the personal income tax in relation to personal consumption, whatever may be done about accumulation.

[6]

COMMENTS

FAIRNESS AND A CONSUMPTION-TYPE OR CASH FLOW PERSONAL INCOME TAX

*Alvin C. Warren, Jr.**

In a recent article, Professor William Andrews proposed rejection of the accretion tax ideal in favor of a consumption-based tax scheme. One of his reasons for preferring the consumption-type tax model was its neutrality between persons who spend their income currently and those who save for future consumption. In this Comment, Professor Warren suggests that the neutrality of the consumption-type tax is obtained at the cost of allowing income from wealth to escape taxation. Finding the consumption-based tax to be analagous, if not identical, to a tax on wages alone, he rejects it as an insufficient compromise of the various legitimate objectives of a basic tax system.

WILLIAM Andrews has recently set forth a model of a consumption-type personal income tax as an alternative to the existing tax and the prevailing accretion ideal.[1] Under Andrews' approach, individuals would be taxed on the basis of their consumption, rather than the sum of consumption and accumulation. To accomplish that result, the personal income tax would be levied on a simple cash flow basis: business and investment expenditures (including capital outlays) would be deductible when made, while business and investment receipts (including returns of capital) would be immediately and fully includable in taxable income.[2] Professor Andrews argues that such a tax not only would be superior to the current income tax, but that it would even be preferable to a truly comprehensive accretion-type income tax.[3] Considerations of administrative simplicity, economic efficiency, and fairness all lead him to that conclusion. It is the last part of his argument — that a consumption-type income

* Associate Professor of Law, Duke Law School; Visiting Associate Professor of Law, University of Pennsylvania Law School (1974–75). B.A., Yale, 1966; J.D., University of Chicago, 1969. The author would like to thank his colleague, Daniel Halperin, for his comments.

[1] Andrews, *A Consumption-Type or Cash Flow Personal Income Tax*, 87 HARV. L. REV. 1113 (1974) [hereinafter cited as Andrews]. Expenditure taxation has a rich intellectual history among economists. *See id.* at 1117 n.7.

[2] *See id.* at 1149.

[3] The classic case for the accretion model is H. SIMONS, PERSONAL INCOME TAXATION (1938). *See also* sources cited in Andrews at 1113 n.1.

tax is fairer than a true accretion-type income tax — which is examined here.[4]

I. Accumulation as Consumption Foregone

Andrews begins his analysis of the fairness of a tax on income received but not consumed by characterizing accumulation as consumption foregone, and offers two reasons for its exclusion from the tax base given that characterization. First, we are told that the "primary, intended, real effect of any general revenue-raising tax is to curtail some part of the private consumption of economic resources that would otherwise occur, in order to free those resources for public use, including redistribution to the poor."[5] Since "the purpose is to curtail consumption," it is "presumptively fair" to distribute the burden of the tax "in relation to levels of consumption prior to the imposition of the tax."[6]

This argument confuses the effect of a tax with the base for measuring tax liability. Assuming a tax will be paid with resources the taxpayer would otherwise consume[7] does not indicate whether it would be fairer to levy the tax on the basis of accretion, consumption, wealth, or something else. If we thought a tax levied on the basis of waistlines were fair, it could still be collected in dollars (that is, resources that would otherwise be consumed) rather than pounds of flesh.[8] Later in his article, Andrews himself advocates, as a matter of fairness, a tax on the transfer of property between generations,[9] a base quite different from levels of consumption.

If, however, as Andrews suggests, the curtailment of consumption is not only the effect of any general revenue-raising tax, but also its purpose, then it might follow that the tax burden should be allocated in accordance with consumption levels. But why should it be assumed that the purpose of any general revenue-raising tax is to curtail consumption, as opposed to curtailing consumption and accumulation, redistributing wealth, or something else? Andrews does not indicate the premise on which his assump-

[4] As Andrews' equity and efficiency arguments are presented together, some of their common components will necessarily be discussed in the text, but no conclusion is intended regarding the merits of the efficiency analysis.

[5] *Id.* at 1165–66.

[6] *Id.*

[7] Andrews concedes that some persons may pay taxes without reducing current consumption, but maintains that a consumption-type tax will be fair "because it will impose the same increase in the price for maintaining any particular level of consumption . . . ." *Id.* at 1166–67.

[8] The waistline example is taken from E. Rolph & G. Break, Public Finance 179 (1961).

[9] Andrews at 1172.

tion rests, and without some acceptable explanation, assertions regarding the tax's purpose are not persuasive in weighing the relative fairness of alternative tax bases. And even if reduction of consumption were conceded to be the principal objective of taxation, it might still be possible to accomplish that goal by levies on bases other than consumption alone.[10] But, perhaps by stating that a consumption tax is "presumptively" fair, it is only meant that the postulated purpose and effect of the tax is a tentative measure of its fairness, subject to reevaluation when other equity goals, such as mitigation of disparities in wealth, are considered. In any event, the ultimate fairness of a basis for taxation simply cannot be derived from what is collected when the tax is imposed.

The second reason for not taxing accumulation when it is characterized as consumption foregone is that accumulation generally represents the market value of the "excess of what one has contributed to production in a particular period, in labor or capital or both, over what he has withdrawn for private consumption during that period, and there is no reason to tax a person on that excess." [11] The only explanation given by Andrews for not taxing it is to quote Hobbes' well-known question: [12]

> For what reason is there that he which laboureth much, and sparing the fruits of his labour, consumeth little, should be more charged than he that living idlely, getteth little, and spendeth all he gets; seeing the one has no more protection from the Common-wealth, than the other?

While Hobbes' question is certainly pertinent, it hardly demonstrates that there is no reason to tax accumulation. Nor is Hobbes' original rationale for taxation — "to defend private men in the exercise of their several trades, and callings" [13] — much help in deciding the fairest means of financing modern government. Since Hobbes' sovereign would use tax receipts to protect "the enjoyment of life, which is equally dear to poor and rich," the poor would be as indebted to the government for defense of their lives as the rich "saving that the rich, who have the service of the poor, may be debtors not only for their own persons but for many more." [14] Hobbes' argument not only contemplates a considerably narrower range of governmental functions than that prevailing in contemporary democracies, but it also assumes that taxes are to be levied in accordance with benefits received from the govern-

[10] *See* A. Prest, Public Finance 129 (1960).

[11] Andrews at 1166.

[12] T. Hobbes, Leviathan 298 (A. Lindsay ed. 1950).

[13] *Id.*

[14] *Id.*

ment — a standard long since replaced by ability to pay, whether that means accretion, consumption, wealth or whatever.[15]

More importantly for present purposes, the second reason for not taxing accumulation as consumption foregone suffers the fatal defect that in our society "the excess of what one has contributed to production" is not lost to the contributor. Rather, as Andrews puts it, a saver retains "the claim against future output represented by his accumulated income," [16] since savings remain available for the accumulator's future disposition. Thus accumulation is not really "consumption foregone" after all. It is consumption deferred, and we must turn to an examination of Andrews' argument for its exclusion from the tax base on that characterization.

II. Accumulation as Consumption Deferred

A. *Discrimination Against Future Consumption*

What Andrews calls "the most sophisticated argument" in favor of a consumption-type income tax is that such a tax is "more appropriate because it ultimately imposes a more uniform burden on consumption, whenever it may occur, than does an accretion-type tax." [17] Neutrality with respect to consumption is important for Andrews "not only because it promotes efficiency in the allocation of income, but because it keeps the tax from bearing more heavily on one person than another on account of differences in need or taste for particular goods or services, now or in the future." [18]

While Andrews is clearly right in asserting that an accretion-type tax creates a heavier ultimate burden in relation to future consumption than in relation to present consumption, his selection of taxpayers to illustrate the discrimination is somewhat puzzling. The example given is that of a taxpayer who puts aside $100 of current earnings for retirement. Invested at 9% compound interest, that sum will grow to $800 after 24 years. A consumption tax of 33% would leave the retiree with $533 to spend while an accretion tax of 33% imposed on the initial $100 and on the annual increase in value would leave only $267 after 24 years.[19] Andrews suggests that the "logic" of a consumption-type tax is that a 33% taxpayer who would have had $800 to spend in the

[15] The Hobbesian view also assumes it is better to contribute to the common pool than to withdraw from it, a judgment embraced in N. Kaldor, An Expenditure Tax 53 (1955) and, more cautiously, in Andrews at 1174.

[16] Andrews at 1167.

[17] *Id.*

[18] *Id.* at 1167–68.

[19] *Id.* at 1168.

absence of tax should have $533 after tax whatever combination of earnings and savings may have gone to produce the $800. An accretion tax is "discriminatory" because it will leave less for the retiree after 24 years than for another taxpayer with $800 of current income, presumably in year 25.

If Andrews' point is that otherwise similarly situated taxpayers are taxed differently solely because of differences in preferences "for particular goods or services, now or in the future," these taxpayers are neither otherwise similarly situated nor do they reveal different preferences in year 25. Relative to the taxpayer with current income, the retiree does not defer consumption: they both consume in year 25. Furthermore, the fact that the two taxpayers have different earning streams, and have not been presented with the same options before year 25, suggests their positions are not strictly comparable. The retiree may (or may not) pay for his consumption out of saved compensation while the taxpayer with current earnings may (or may not) pay for his consumption out of current income. But even if one pays with saved compensation while the other pays with current earnings, that does not establish discrimination since, as Andrews elsewhere indicates, fairness in taxation is to be measured between individuals, not funds.[20]

The two taxpayers are, of course, in identical positions with regard to consumption since they consume the same amount in year 25. If the appropriate index of equality for tax purposes is concluded to be consumption, then any tax, including an accretion-type tax, that treats equal consumers differently is discriminatory. However, that discrimination cannot be used to support the conclusion that the appropriate index of equality is consumption, as that conclusion was a necessary predicate for the finding of discrimination. To avoid circularity in the argument, a finding that the accretion-type tax discriminates among taxpayers on the basis of their preferences for present and future consumption must not depend on a prior assumption that consumption is the fairer tax base.

The discrimination of an accretion-type tax against taxpayers who have relatively greater preferences for future consumption can be clarified by comparing two workers, both of whom earn $100 in an initial year 1.[21] In a world without taxes, each has the

[20] *Id.* at 1133.

[21] To make comparisons easier, the examples in the text will follow as closely as possible those in Andrews. Accordingly, interest will be calculated by the rule of thumb used there, *see id.* at 1125 n.20, with the results rounded. Also following Andrews, the tax rate will be expressed as if the tax were part of the tax base, *see id.* at 1119 n.10, and the appropriate comparison will be assumed to be between equivalent rate taxes rather than between taxes yielding equivalent

choice of consuming $100 in that year or $800 after 24 years (with interest compounding at 9%). The price of consumption in the initial year relative to consumption after 24 years is 100/800, or 1/8. Imposition of a consumption-type income tax leaves the ratio at 67/533, or 1/8. If one taxpayer spends in year 1 and the other spends in year 25, both consume less after taxes, but their relative positions remain as they were in the non-tax world. Imposition of an accretion-type tax changes the ratio to 67/267, or 1/4, so the taxpayer with a greater relative preference for future consumption is taxed more heavily. Hence, although neither tax discriminates on the basis of "need or taste for *particular* goods or services, now or in the future,"[22] an accretion-type tax does discriminate against taxpayers with relatively greater preferences for future, as compared with present consumption.

This discrimination — which John Stuart Mill called a double tax on savings[23] — results from the fact that imposing a tax on accretion reduces the after-tax return on invested savings.[24] Despite the existence of a lengthy historical debate in rebuttal of Mills' position,[25] it seems to be beyond present doubt that relative positions of taxpayers are changed by an accretion-type, but not a consumption-type, tax. The traditional counterargument — that an accretion-type tax is discriminatory only if one embraces the consumption model[26] — is not persuasive because the accretion-type tax discriminates among taxpayers relative to the *no*-tax world, whereas the consumption-type tax does not.[27]

---

revenues. One practical problem with substituting a consumption-type tax for the present income tax is that the new tax would increase future revenues at the expense of current revenues. If the Treasury were unwilling to accept an immediate decline in tax receipts, rates under a consumption-type tax would have to be raised to maintain revenue yield. For calculation of comparable rates where the tax base is net of tax and where revenues are assumed to be equivalent, see N. KALDOR, *supra* note 15, at 232; A. PREST, *supra* note 10, at 48 n.1, 80–81; C. SHOUP, PUBLIC FINANCE 346 (1969).

Examples similar to that in the text can be found in R. GOODE. THE INDIVIDUAL INCOME TAX 25–28 (1964); A. PREST, *supra* note 10, at 80; W. VICKERY, AGENDA FOR PROGRESSIVE TAXATION 336 (1947).

[22] Andrews at 1167–68 (emphasis added). A selective excise tax, on the other hand, would discriminate among particular goods and services.

[23] J.S. MILL, PRINCIPLES OF POLITICAL ECONOMY, bk. V, ch. II, § 3 (9th ed. 1895).

[24] *Id.*

[25] *See* Andrews at 1168 n.122.

[26] *See, e.g.*, Musgrave, *A Further Note on the Double Taxation of Savings*, 29 AM. ECON. REV. 549 (1939).

[27] On the other hand, if saving were considered to offer imputed expenditures on such intangibles as prestige, power, and security, a consumption-type tax would discriminate in favor of that form of expenditure. *See* C. SHOUP, *supra* note 21, at 352; *cf.* pp. 941–42 *infra*.

Although the discrimination occasioned by an accretion-type tax seems real enough, it is probably overstated in the preceeding examples because of the implicit assumption that such a tax will not affect the gross rate of interest. Invested savings in all examples up to this point have earned a gross rate of return of 9% with or without a tax; only the net return fell, from 9% to 6%, when a 33% accretion-type tax was imposed. But if imposition of the tax also raises the gross rate of return, the discrimination is reduced or eliminated. Assume again that the pretax interest rate were 9%, so the retiree who saved and invested $100 in year 1 would have $800 after 24 years, and the ratio between the prices of present and future consumption would be 100/800, or 1/8 in a world without taxes. If imposition of an accretion-type tax caused the gross interest rate to rise to 13.5% (because savers continued to require a 9% net return while borrowers' demand for saved funds was relatively fixed), imposition of a 33% accretion-type tax would present our wage earners with the choice of consuming $67 in year 1 or $533 after 24 years, maintaining the ratio at 67/533 or 1/8. A consumption-type income tax would also leave the wage earners with the choice between $67 in year 1 or $533 after 24 years since the net rate of return, here 9%, would be the same as the gross rate of return when annual yield is not taxed. Finally, a retiree who saved and invested $100 in year 1 would have the same amount after taxes, $533, to consume 24 years later as would a taxpayer with $800 in current income. Thus, if the rise in gross interest rates fully offsets the tax imposed on income producing assets, an accretion-type tax would not discriminate against future consumption, whether equal earners or equal consumers are compared.

Unfortunately, there is no a priori method of determining what will be the actual effect of an accretion tax on rates of return. The impact of accretion-type taxation on the level of investment and rates of return will depend on the characteristics of the demand for, and supply of, investable funds.[28] Without knowing those characteristics it is impossible to identify the effects of an accretion-type tax on the interest rate and, accordingly, the amount of discrimination occasioned by the tax. One might nevertheless respond that elimination of an accretion-type tax is highly unlikely to cause interest rates to fall by the full amount of the tax, as in my extreme example, so some discrimination against future consumption is bound to remain.[29] Yet the quantum of discrimination is surely relevant for Andrews' fairness, as well as his efficiency, analysis if the discrimination is to be balanced

[28] *See* J. Due & A. Friedlaender, Government Finance — Economics of the Public Sector 301–03 (5th ed. 1973).

[29] *See* C. Shoup, *supra* note 21, at 346.

against equity arguments in favor of an accretion-type tax. Though some discrimination will occur as a result of an accretion-type tax, it may be considerably overstated by examples which assume no change in the gross rate of interest.

B. The Equivalence of a Consumption-Type Income Tax and a Tax on Wages Alone

Andrews carefully demonstrates that when tax rates are constant, deferral of a tax on an investment is equivalent to exemption of the investment's subsequent yield and appreciation.[30] He also asserts at several points that the difference between an accretion-type and a consumption-type tax is essentially one of deferral.[31] Considering those two statements together leads to the somewhat surprising conclusion that when tax rates are constant, a consumption-type personal income tax is the equivalent of a tax which permanently exempts all income from property, that is, a tax only on wages.

1. Assuming Constant Tax Rates. — That a consumption-type tax is equivalent to a tax on wages alone when tax rates remain constant can be seen by applying a wage tax of 33% to Andrews' retiree in the initial year, so he has only $67 left to spend or save in that year. If saved and invested at 9%, that amount will produce $533 to spend after 24 years since, by hypothesis, the wage tax does not reach income from property. That is exactly the result for the retiree in Andrew's example, where nothing would have been taxed in the initial year because there was no consumption, and the full $800 taxed when consumed 24 years later. Thus, if tax rates are constant, a wage tax, which does not reach income from property, will always leave taxpayers in the same positions as a consumption tax, which defers taxation when funds are saved.[32]

It may be objected that a consumption-type income tax is not equivalent to a wage tax because under the former even an idle taxpayer who has never earned wages and who lives entirely on interest receipts will have to pay taxes as the interest is spent.

[30] Andrews at 1123–28, 1167.

[31] *Id.* at 1115, 1120, 1124, 1167.

[32] Although the net of tax results will always be the same, it may be objected that there is a formal difference between the two taxes in that wage taxes are paid immediately, here in year 1, while the payment of consumption taxes is delayed, here until after 24 years. The difference in the date of payment of the two taxes can be eliminated by giving the wage earner the opportunity to defer his wage tax until consumption, with income earned on the deferred tax going to the government. In terms of our examples, the wage earner could either pay a $33 wage tax in year 1 or invest that $33 for 24 years at 9%, when $267 would be due the government as a deferred wage tax, again leaving $533 for consumption.

But if the interest-producing asset were purchased with wages earned after the imposition of the consumption-type tax, taxation of the idle taxpayer's consumption will again produce exactly the same result as would earlier wage taxation of the individual whose wages were invested to provide the idler with interest. Andrews' ideal consumption-type tax would provide that a transfer of property by gift or bequest would not be a taxable event, so deferral — the equivalent of exemption from taxation of income from property — can continue for generations, until consumption occurs.[33] If the interest-producing property had been purchased with wages saved under the current income tax, a transitional problem would arise in that taxation of the wage-earner, who would have received no deduction for saving under the existing tax, and taxation of the consumer would be double taxation to a supporter of the consumption model. As a partial solution, Andrews suggests exempting cash balances from the consumption tax if their accumulation was recently taxed at ordinary income rates.[34] The problem of what to do about consumption where accumulation has already been taxed is, in any event, a purely transitional one which does not undermine the basic equivalence of the wage and consumption-type taxes.

Finally, it may be asserted that the equivalence between deferral on investment and exemption of income or "yield" from property fails if the income contains elements of windfall investment profit. Andrews makes this point in distinguishing "windfall profit" from "simple investment yield."[35] Presumably the former means unanticipated appreciation while the latter includes only anticipated yield. Under that definition, all our examples thus far have been restricted to "simple investment yield."

Suppose that for some totally unanticipated external reason, the investment asset purchased by the retiree for $100 in the initial year doubled in value at once. The resulting $200 invested at 9% would yield $1600 after 24 years, and a consumption tax of 33% applied at that time would leave $1066 after taxes. A wage tax of 33% in the initial year would leave $67 after taxes

[33] Andrews at 1162.

[34] Andrews is, however, unwilling to apply this solution to all investment assets purchased before the transition to a consumption-type tax, explaining only that to do so "would impair the integrity of the consumption-type tax too much and too long, and often with too little real justification." *Id.* at 1177 n.140. Failure to give full credit for the pretransition basis of investment assets would, however, seem to involve the "double taxation of saving" and discrimination against deferred consumption found so objectionable in the accretion-type tax.

[35] *Id.* at 1182–83 n.150. At other points, however, Andrews indicates deferral is equivalent to exemption of investment income when both "yield and appreciation" (all "subsequent profit") are exempted, *id.* at 1126, 1167, a view which is consistent with the position taken in the text here.

to invest in that year, $133 after the unanticipated doubling, and $1066 after 24 years at 9%. Thus, the equivalence between a wage tax and a consumption tax holds even though the exempted "yield" contains elements of "windfall profit."

This equivalence compels reevaluation of Andrews' conclusion that source discrimination is no more appropriate under a consumption-type tax than under an accretion-type tax. Thus, exemption of interest on state and municipal bonds is said to be a departure from either ideal,[36] but as Andrews also indicates, a deduction for investment in municipal bonds reduces the effective rate of tax on that interest to zero no less certainly than does the exemption.[37] While it offers no justification for source discrimination among various kinds of wages or property income, the consumption ideal thus effectively exempts *all* property income from taxation while including *all* income from personal services. This result should not be too surprising once it is recalled that Andrews' proposal is designed to eliminate the tax on benefits that flow from deferring consumption. Since potential consumption increases over time only to the extent one invests in accretion-producing assets, those benefits are none other than income from property.

2. *When Tax Rates Are Not Constant.* — If different tax rates are applicable, a wage tax and a consumption-type tax are no longer precisely equivalent. The retiree who earns $100 and pays a 33% wage tax in year 1 will have $533 left after 24 years at 9%, but if the consumption tax rate after 24 years were only 20%, that tax would leave $640 for consumption. Such a disparity in rates between years may arise because the statutory schedules have been changed, because the taxpayer is subject to a different rate under a graduated tax, or because different taxpayers are involved.

The only relevant difference between a consumption-type personal income tax and a wage tax is thus the disparity that arises when tax rates are not constant.[38] But, identification of a

[36] *Id.* at 1178.

[37] *Id.* at 1181 n.149.

[38] The taxes will produce different results if (1) accumulation continues forever so there is never any consumption to tax; (2) consumption occurs without there ever having been prior earnings to tax; or (3) taxpayers irrationally ignore the effects of taxation and insist on saving a given fraction of pretax wages for future consumption. *See* R. MUSGRAVE, THE THEORY OF PUBLIC FINANCE 262, 266–67 (1959). If the exempted return on assets under a wage tax contains an element of compensation for personal services, *i.e.*, hidden wages, then the two taxes will be equivalent only if the wage tax can successfully identify wages, suggesting the administrative superiority of the consumption tax over the wage tax. *See* Andrews at 1183 n.150. Finally, the taxes may have different effects if their rates are adjusted to produce equivalent revenues. *See* note 21 *supra*.

consumption-type tax with a wage tax does not, by itself, indicate that either is less fair than an accretion-type tax. Indeed, to the extent discrimination against taxpayers with a relatively greater preference for accumulation is thought unfair, the former appear superior on equity grounds. Comprehending the identity between a wage and consumption tax does, however, make more apparent an important consequence of the latter tax base, which is that income from property escapes tax except to the extent that the applicable tax rate in the year of consumption is higher than the applicable rate in the year the invested wages were earned. Once that consequence is perceived, the question of the relative fairness of consumption-type and accretion-type taxes can be resolved only by balancing the equity argument for the former against equity considerations which call for taxation of all income from property. With the issue thus framed, we now turn to Andrews' discussion of the usual equity argument for including income from property in the tax base — the mitigation of disparities in wealth.

III. Accumulation and Wealth

A. *Disparities in Wealth*

As Andrews puts it, the main reason for preferring an accretion-type tax to a consumption-type tax is the notion that it may reduce disparities in wealth as well as living standards.[39] The current income tax is understandably rejected as ineffective in this regard. More importantly for our purposes, Andrews also argues that even if existing disparities in wealth could be adequately dealt with, taxation of accumulation as personal income might not be a desirable way to deal with the problem of wealth: to the extent accumulation represents deferred consumption, accretion-type taxation would be undesirable because of the resulting discrimination against future consumption; to the extent it exceeds deferred consumption wants, accumulation is consumption foregone, and such taxation would be undesirable for reasons which have been discussed above.[39] For Andrews the arguments against taxing accumulation which is foregone or deferred consumption outweigh any equity argument for taxing income from property in order to reduce disparities in wealth.

Andrews nevertheless concedes that "wealth is a source of power," which "represents a different dimension along which to measure economic well-being."[40] Given that conclusion, the

[39] Andrews at 1169.

[40] *Id.* at 1169–70.

reader may be surprised to find that not only is accumulation excluded from Andrews' personal income tax base, but also that he advances no proposal for a periodic tax on net wealth. On reflection, however, it should be clear that Andrews cannot support a periodic wealth tax to mitigate such disparities because that tax would discriminate against taxpayers with a relatively greater preference for future consumption, and is therefore inconsistent with the most sophisticated argument against the accretion-type income tax.[41] Indeed, *any* attempt to reduce discrepancies in wealth during an accumulator's lifetime is inconsistent with that argument since reduction of accumulation will necessarily raise the price of future consumption relative to present consumption.

Andrews attempts to avoid this difficulty, while adhering to the goal of reducing wealth discrepancies, by calling for stronger estate and gift taxes. However, these transfer taxes would raise the price of each taxpayer's future transfers as compared with his present consumption, which would result in discrimination against taxpayers who have a relatively greater preference to save in order to transfer wealth to their families. Andrews neither identifies that discrimination nor explains why it is acceptable when discrimination against taxpayers who have a relatively greater preference to save for their own consumption is not.[42] However, two answers might suggest themselves. First, the discrimination in favor of taxpayers with a relatively greater preference for present consumption caused by the estate and gift taxes may not be quantitatively as great as that caused by an accretion-type tax. Andrews does not, however, suggest or offer support for this rationale. Second, it may be that future transfers are thought to be qualitatively different from future consumption, so discrimination against the former, but not the latter, vis-à-vis present consumption is acceptable as a matter of equity. It is presumably this type of reasoning which leads Andrews to characterize transfers as creating "a kind of unearned original disparity in wealth in the hands of a new generation."[43] If so, the implied equity balance in Andrews' article is that elimination of wealth disparities between generations outweighs, as a matter of social justice, the resulting discrimination among taxpayers, while elimination of wealth disparities during the lifetime of accumulators is outweighed, as a matter of social justice, by the resulting discrimina-

[41] *See* N. KALDOR, *supra* note 15, at 90.

[42] The closest Andrews comes to suggesting the existence of this discrimination is by stating that deferral of the tax on accumulation until consumption or transfer "eliminates the discrimination against deferred consumption that would characterize a true accretion-type tax, *at least when deferred consumption is by the same taxpayer*." Andrews at 1172 (emphasis added).

[43] *Id.*

tion among taxpayers. Andrews does not argue for this balance as an original matter,[44] and this is not the place to examine it. Rather, what is crucial here is that the superiority, in terms of equity, of a consumption-type personal income tax over an accretion-type personal income tax depends on acceptance of that balance.

If one concluded, for instance, that taxpayers should not be able to accumulate an unlimited amount of wealth and the corresponding social power during their lifetimes without paying taxes on the accumulation, Andrews' argument would have to be rejected. That conclusion might be based either directly on a view of an equitable distribution of lifetime wealth, or on the pragmatic conclusion that taxing wealth once a generation would not sufficiently reduce disparities.[45] In either case, the appropriate response to Hobbes' question would be that taxing a man on what he has earned but not consumed is necessary to achieve a fairer distribution of wealth. Reduction of the after-tax return on invested savings — the discrimination against deferred consumption — could also be justified as necessary to mitigate lifetime wealth disparities. One might, of course, prefer a wealth tax over an accretion tax as the more effective method of mitigating such disparities,[46] but if the choice is limited to the consumption and accretion models for the personal income tax the latter would be preferable in terms of fairness.

In his discussion of existing wealth disparities, Andrews argues that a consumption-type tax would be preferable because it would be more progressive with regard to wealth than would an accre-

---

[44] Others have:

> It can also be argued that if an Expenditure Tax, as opposed to an income tax, enhances the opportunity for exceptional men to make fortunes through enterprise, there is a clear social gain in increased capital accumulation, which more than offsets any tangible loss in the guise of greater social or economic inequality. (This does not of course apply to inherited wealth . . . .)

N. KALDOR, *supra* note 15, at 50.

> [B]ut if all were done which it would be in the power of a good government to do . . . to diminish the inequality of opportunities, the difference of fortune arising from people's own earnings could not justly give umbrage.

J.S. MILL, *supra* note 23, bk. V, ch. 2, § 3 at 808.

[45] Thurow, *Net Worth Taxes*, 25 NAT'L TAX J. 417, 420 (1972), calculates that an inheritance tax of 100% on transfers over $50,000 would permit an individual who received $50,000 at age zero and lived until 70 to accumulate $1.1 million by age 35 and $39.5 million by age 70 if the inheritance were invested at 10% and absolutely nothing saved from earned income. If half the return on capital income were consumed annually instead of reinvested, there would still be $1.5 million of accumulation at age 70. Thurow concludes from such examples that even a very severe estate and gift tax would not place a very stringent constraint on the maximum amount of wealth an individual could possess. *Id.*

[46] *See generally id. passim.*

tion-type tax on the assumption that at any given income level, "those with more wealth will feel free to spend more and save less."[47] Even if this assumption were conceded, the conclusion that the consumption-type tax will be more progressive cannot be maintained if the comparison of taxpayers is not limited to a single year. Under a consumption tax, the high consumers are merely paying the deferred tax on their invested savings, while the high savers are simply deferring taxes until future consumption. Unless tax rates change, their burdens over time may be identical because, as Andrews demonstrates, the benefits of deferral achieved by the saver will be matched by a corresponding increase in future consumption tax liability.[48] The problem with a single-year comparison is even clearer when the consumption-type tax is viewed as the equivalent of a wage tax: if tax rates are constant, the high consumer and the high saver both pay what amounts to a deferred tax on prior wages; the amount of their current wealth is irrelevant. In fact, if the tax were structured as an equivalent wage tax, the low wealth taxpayer — who would have greater wages than the high wealth taxpayer with equivalent income because some of the latter's income would presumably come from property — would pay more in taxes in the single year in question, making the result regressive with regard to wealth.

B. *Redistribution and Graduated Rates*

Andrews also suggests that a consumption-type personal income tax can be as progressive as an accretion-type tax because graduated rates can be applied under either.[49] As long as attention is focused on the retiree and the taxpayer with $800 of current income in year 25, there is nothing inconsistent about introducing graduated rates into the consumption-type tax. Once attention is shifted to a comparison between two taxpayers who earn the same amount, but who have different relative preferences for present and future consumption, graduated rates under a consumption-type tax would result in discrimination against future consumption.[50]

Assuming a 33% tax rate on the first $100 and a 50% tax rate on everything above that, the worker who earns $100 in an initial year would have $67 in after-tax consumption in that year. The retiree who saves $100 in an initial year and invests it for 24 years at 9% would have only $417 in after-tax consumption.[51] It will

[47] Andrews at 1171.

[48] *Id.* at 1123–28, 1150.

[49] *Id.* at 1174–75.

[50] *See* C. SHOUP, *supra* note 21, at 352.

[51] This result can be seen from the following computation:

be recalled that the retiree must have $533 in after-tax consumption to maintain his position relative to the worker who has $67 in after-tax consumption in the initial year.[52] General averaging provisions would eliminate some, but not all, of this disparity.[53]

In a world without taxation, the relative positions of the taxpayer who earns $800 in year 25, the retiree who saves and invests $100 at 9% in the initial year, and the worker who spends $100 in the initial year are determined by the available rate of return: a dollar in the initial year is worth 8 dollars after 24 years. A proportional consumption tax maintains their relative positions: the retiree will be able to consume the same amount as the taxpayer with $800 of current earnings 24 years later, while they both will be able to consume eight times what the worker could consume in the initial year. Once graduated rates are introduced, however, the equality between the retiree and the taxpayer with income 24 years later can be maintained only by distorting the relative positions of the retiree and the worker who consumed in the initial year. Since the only difference between the retiree and that worker is their relative preference for present and future consumption, the resulting discrimination against the retiree — the taxpayer with the relatively greater preference for future consumption — is inconsistent with the best argument for adopting the consumption model to begin with. Thus the consumption-type personal income tax must either be limited to a proportional rate or suffer the defect Andrews finds so fatal in the accretion model.[54]

$$\begin{aligned}\text{After-tax income} &= 800 - [0.33 \times 100] - [0.50 \times (800 - 100)] \\ &= 800 - 33 - 350 \\ &= 417\end{aligned}$$

[52] *See* pp. 935–36 *supra*.

[53] Such provisions are suggested in Andrews at 1157. Without averaging, a graduated consumption-type tax could result in a greater tax burden for current consumers than for deferred consumers, depending on their spending patterns. For example, a consumer who earned and spent $10,000 in a single year might pay more in taxes than an otherwise comparable taxpayer who earned $10,000 in one year, but divided his spending evenly between two years. The differential in taxation, which favors the deferred consumer in this example, results from bunching of expenditures and would be eliminated by lifetime averaging.

But if consumption were averaged over a lifetime, a graduated consumption-type tax would discriminate against deferred consumption. A current consumer would have less total-dollar consumption than an equal wage earner who defers consumption since the latter increases the dollar amount available for consumption by the return on invested savings. Inclusion of that increment under a proportional consumption-type tax just offsets the benefits of deferral. Graduated brackets would subject the increment received by deferred consumers to higher rates, so future consumption would be made more expensive relative to present consumption.

[54] A graduated wage tax would not be subject to this objection, but Andrews concludes that the best argument for progressivity requires tax rates to be applied in the spending, rather than earning, period. *See id.* at 1176–77.

IV. Conclusion

That taxpayers may respond to a tax by reducing consumption in order to pay the government its due does not establish that the fairest index of taxability is consumption. Nor does the Hobbesian view of accumulation as the excess of what one has contributed to production over what one has withdrawn necessarily make taxation of the excess unfair, since the accumulator continues to control the excess for his own benefit.

Assuming the appropriate effect on interest rates, an accretion-type personal income tax will change the relative positions of taxpayers who have different preferences for present and future consumption by reducing the after-tax return on invested savings. To the extent that reduction is considered unfairly discriminatory, it must be weighed against the inability of a consumption-type personal income tax to mitigate lifetime disparities in wealth. That inability derives from the effective exclusion from the tax base of income from property, making a consumption-type tax the equivalent of a wage tax when rates are constant. If mitigation of lifetime wealth disparities were considered an important goal of a fair tax system, reducing the after-tax return on invested savings might be tolerated as a necessary cost of achieving that goal.

Introducing graduated rates into the consumption tax does not help to resolve the dilemma since their effect is inconsistent with the reason for rejecting an accretion-type tax to begin with. Instead, the choice between the consumption and accretion models for the personal income tax, as a matter of fairness, comes down to a choice between mitigation of lifetime wealth disparities and preservation of the pretax relative price of present and future consumption as the more important equity goal. One's ethical predilections rather than logic — at least legal or economic logic — have to provide the grounds for making that choice.

[7]

Would a Consumption Tax Be Fairer Than an Income Tax?

Alvin Warren†

The consensus that culminated in the adoption of the Sixteenth Amendment and the enactment of the federal income tax has been under attack in both academic and professional circles for several years. The view that consumption, not income, is the fairer basis on which to levy a progressive personal tax can be found in recent law reviews,[1] economic journals,[2] and Treasury Department study papers,[3] as well as the reports of commissions created to review the tax structures of the United Kingdom and Sweden.[4] And signifying the growing respectability of what is a very old idea among economists,[5] the Brookings Institution has recently sponsored a conference of experts to review the theoretical and practical considerations involved in a personal tax on

† Professor of Law, University of Pennsylvania Law School; Visiting Professor of Law, Harvard Law School, 1979-80.

1. The seminal work is Andrews, *A Consumption-Type or Cash Flow Personal Income Tax*, 87 HARV. L. REV. 1113 (1974) [hereinafter cited as *Consumption Tax*]; *see* Warren, *Fairness and a Consumption-Type or Cash Flow Personal Income Tax*, 88 HARV. L. REV. 931 (1975) (criticizing Andrews' argument); Andrews, *Fairness and the Choice Between a Consumption-Type and an Accretion-Type Personal Income Tax: A Reply to Professor Warren*, 88 HARV. L. REV. 947 (1975) [hereinafter cited as *Andrews' Reply*]; Klein, *Timing in Personal Taxation*, 6 J. LEGAL STUD. 461 (1977).

2. *See, e.g.*, Boskin, *Taxation, Saving, and the Rate of Interest*, 86 J. POLITICAL ECON. S3 (1978); Bradford & Toder, *Consumption vs. Income Base Taxes: The Argument on Grounds of Equity and Simplicity*, 69 NAT'L TAX A. PROC. 25 (1976); Feldstein, *The Welfare Cost of Capital Income Taxation*, 86 J. POLITICAL ECON. S29, S37-S39 (1978).

3. *See, e.g.*, U.S. DEP'T OF THE TREASURY, BLUEPRINTS FOR BASIC TAX REFORM 21-52, 113-44 (1977) [hereinafter cited as BLUEPRINTS]; P. MIESZKOWSKI, THE CASH FLOW VERSION OF AN EXPENDITURE TAX 3-4 (May 1977) (U.S. Dep't of Treasury, Office of Tax Analysis, OTA Paper 26).

4. *See, e.g.*, INSTITUTE FOR FISCAL STUDIES, THE STRUCTURE AND REFORM OF DIRECT TAXATION 33-34 (1978) (U.K.) [hereinafter cited as the MEADE REPORT]; S. LODIN, PROGRESSIVE EXPENDITURE TAX—AN ALTERNATIVE? (1978) (report of the 1972 [Swedish] Government Commission on Taxation) (translated into English in 1978).

5. In addition to the works cited in notes 1-4, *supra*, support for consumption taxation can be found in T. HOBBES, LEVIATHAN 226 (M. Oakeshott ed. 1960); J.S. MILL, PRINCIPLES OF POLITICAL ECONOMY bk. V, ch. I, § 4 (Laughlin ed. 1898). In more recent times, the most comprehensive treatment is found in N. KALDOR, AN EXPENDITURE TAX (1955). For further discussion, see I. FISHER & H. FISHER, CONSTRUCTIVE INCOME TAXATION 3-17 (1942); W. VICKREY, AGENDA FOR PROGRESSIVE TAXATION 329-61 (1947); Friedman, *The Spendings Tax as a Wartime Fiscal Measure*, 33 AM. ECON. REV. 50 (1943); Marshall, *The Equitable Distribution of Taxation* (1917) in MEMORIALS OF ALFRED MARSHALL 347, 350-51 (A. Pigou ed. 1925).

consumption.[6] The argument that the consumption tax is to be preferred as a matter of fairness has generally involved a comparison of the core ideas of the two taxes—income and consumption. Wealth—the third traditional candidate for taxation on the basis of economic resources—has typically been left out of the comparison on the ground that whatever considerations would support wealth taxation can best be taken into account by enacting a tax on wealth or transfers of wealth, and that those quite distinct considerations should not obscure the direct comparison of the income and consumption taxes on equity grounds. This Article examines the case for consumption-tax superiority in those terms. In keeping with the focus on the core ideas of income and consumption, practical compromises that are necessary to the implementation of the taxes and that can certainly raise questions of fairness are generally not discussed. Rather, this Article is meant to be directly responsive to arguments that the income tax is unfair in basic concept, quite apart from the difficulties that might arise in implementing that concept.[7]

Fairness in this context must mean, or at least involve, distributional equity—the question of how economic resources ought to be distributed in a fair society. But examining primarily that question would mean losing our subject to broader issues of political theory, such as the nature of entitlements and the appropriate relationship between the individual and the state. The subject of this Article, the core ideas of the two taxes, lies between the broader inquiry of political theory and the more particular delineation of compromises necessary for the implementation of either tax.

The income tax is undoubtedly familiar to the reader, but current consumption-tax proposals may not be. Although the case for income taxation has historically been linked with progression, while that for consumption taxation has not, the consumption tax proposed today is a personal levy that would be subject to graduated rates. In general, the goal of reaching personal consumption would be accomplished by taxing all expenditures on a cash-flow basis: all receipts, including borrowings, would be included in the tax base and all nonconsumption expenditures, including principal and interest payments on debts owed, would be deducted. Thus all savings would be treated as are certain retirement savings under present law: investments would be currently

6. *See* WHAT SHOULD BE TAXED—INCOME OR EXPENDITURE? (J. Pechman ed. 1980) (proceedings of conference) [hereinafter cited as BROOKINGS REPORT].

7. The relative superiority of consumption and income taxes in terms of administrative simplicity and economic efficiency are, accordingly, not discussed in this Article.

Consumption Tax

excluded or deducted, no tax would be imposed while the invested capital produced income so long as that income was not withdrawn for consumption, and all proceeds, whether capital or income, would be fully taxed when withdrawn for consumption.[8]

The result of such a cash-flow or expenditure tax, as it is called, is that only consumption would be taxed, but at rates that could be graduated on the basis of personal consumption. Personal progression is a crucial aspect of the case for such an expenditure tax, since a flat-rate tax on consumption could be more easily levied as a tax on value added, which would not involve the administrative burden of personal returns.[9] In accordance with current usage, the term "consumption tax" will be used here to indicate the cash-flow or expenditure tax as well as other arguably equivalent methods of reaching personal consumption.

The Article is divided into three parts. The first part elucidates the sometimes confused concept of income for tax purposes and identifies premises that would support that concept as a criterion of distributive fairness. The second part evaluates the arguments that have been advanced in favor of the consumption criterion as superior to the income criterion. It is concluded that while either tax can be justified as a means of implementing a plausible principle of distributional equity, the case for the superior fairness of the consumption tax is not persuasive on its own terms. A final part reasserts the relevance of wealth to the choice between the taxes on the grounds of fairness.

I. Income as a Criterion of Distributive Fairness

A. *The Concept of Income for Tax Purposes*

Although the theoretical tax literature is littered with multitudinous definitions of income,[10] Henry Simons's famous formulation has dominated policy analysis for more than forty years:

> Personal income may be defined as the algebraic sum of (1) the market value of rights exercised in consumption and (2) the change in the value of the store of property rights between the beginning and end of the period in question. In other words, it is merely the

8. *See* I.R.C. §§ 402-403, 408-409 (treatment of retirement savings).

9. The value-added tax has itself appeared in recent political discussions of tax policy options. *See The Tax Restructuring Act of 1979, Hearings Before the House Committee on Ways and Means*, 95th Cong. 1st Sess. (1979).

10. *See generally* H. Simons, Personal Income Taxation 59-102 (1938); Wueller, *Concepts of Taxable Income* (pts. 1-3), 53 Political Sci. Q. 83, 557 (1938); 54 Political Sci. Q. 555 (1939).

> result obtained by adding consumption during the period to "wealth" at the end of the period and then subtracting "wealth" at the beginning. The *sine qua non* of income is *gain*, as our courts have recognized in their more lucid moments—and gain *to* someone during a specified time interval. Moreover, this gain may be measured and defined most easily by positing a dual objective or purpose, consumption and accumulation, each of which may be estimated in a common unit by appeal to market prices.[11]

The obvious difference between this tax base and that specified by the expenditure tax is that only consumption remains in the latter, after accumulation has been removed.[12]

As used in this Article, "consumption" means the ultimate use or destruction of economic resources (as by the drinking of a glass of wine) and "accumulation," the retention or saving of such resources. "Economic resources" is not a self-defining term, for its scope depends on what is considered economic activity. It will be used here to mean goods and services, whether real or financial, that are generally the subject of market transactions in our society. This category can be defined in part in principle (excluding the pleasures of one's own psyche) and in part by custom (excluding the exchange of services typical of personal relationships). However far the penumbra of economic activity might be extended, it is the core that gives central meaning to the familiar measures of economic well-being—consumption, income, and wealth—that compete for use as tax bases. That familiar core will be our subject unless a particular argument directs attention elsewhere.

Simons's idea, which is usually referred to as the Haig-Simons or accretion concept of income,[13] is strictly personal in its application. As Simons himself put it, the concept is simply an arithmetical operation, designed to identify the change in a person's position over the course of an accounting period.[14] It does not provide a standard for deciding

11. H. Simons, *supra* note 10, at 50.

12. Personal consumption may, of course, exceed personal income in any given year through disaccumulation or borrowing, with the reconciliation accomplished by the algebraic summing of consumption and accumulation.

13. Professor Haig earlier introduced the accretion concept: "Income is the money value of the net accretion to one's economic power between two points of time." Haig, *The Concept of Income—Economic and Legal Aspects*, in The Federal Income Tax 1, 7 (R. Haig ed. 1921), *reprinted in* Readings in the Economics of Taxation 54, 75 (R. Musgrave & C. Shoup eds. 1959) (emphasis omitted). Both were apparently anticipated by Georg Schanz in Schanz, *Der Einkommensbegriff und die Einkommensteurgesetze*, 13 Finanz Archiv 1 (1896) (introducing accretion concept). *See* Musgrave, *In Defense of an Income Concept*, 81 Harv. L. Rev. 44, 47 n.7 (1967) (observing that Schanz was the first to propose the accretion concept).

14. H. Simons, *supra* note 10, at 51, 78.

Consumption Tax

whether a given receipt, transaction, event, or whatever is income in some abstract sense. Nor does the idea usefully illuminate the nature of the aggregate tax base, let alone the appropriate taxable unit or period, a limitation not always appreciated by either Simons's disciples[15] or the denigrators of his formulation.[16]

What then is the importance of the Haig-Simons definition? The view taken here is that the concept is an essential but incomplete perspective on the nature of the income tax base. Specifically, the concept permits the interpersonal allocation or attribution of income to individuals, an attribution that is necessary if the tax cannot be collected at the source or if progressive rates are to be applied on a personal basis. Consider an agrarian society in which all citizens toil with their own nondepreciating tools in a collective corn field, with the crop the only income produced by the economy during the year. No matter how the citizens divide the crop among themselves, the government can collect a ten percent income tax without the Haig-Simons definition; it need only take ten percent of the crop from the field, with the farmers dividing the rest in accordance with their claims, which we shall assume are based on the combined productivity of their labor and tools. Only if a personally progressive—or regressive—tax is levied, or if there is no convenient way of reaching the income at the source, or both, would it be necessary to determine how much of the society's income ended up in the hands of each individual. That is precisely the determination made by the Haig-Simons definition.

If the Haig-Simons formulation were not available, what would have permitted our hypothetical government to conclude that its ten percent tax was levied on income? Probably the most familiar and intuitive definition of income is that of product. As the Supreme Court once put it: "Income may be defined as the gain derived from capital, from labor, or from both combined."[17] This idea, which was espoused by early advocates of the income tax,[18] but which has been much denigrated by later theorists and abandoned by the Supreme Court,[19]

15. *See* Musgrave, *supra* note 13, at 53-62, *reprinted* in B. Bittker, C. Galvin, R. Musgrave, & J. Pechman, A Comprehensive Income Tax Base? A Debate 62, 72-80 (1968) [hereinafter cited as CTB Debate]; Musgrave, *Rejoinder*, in *id.*, at 114.

16. *See* Bittker, *A "Comprehensive Tax Base" as a Goal of Income Tax Reform*, 80 Harv. L. Rev. 925 (1967), *reprinted in* CTB Debate, *supra* note 15, at 1; Bittker, *Comprehensive Income Taxation: A Response*, 81 Harv. L. Rev. 1032 (1968), *reprinted in* CTB Debate, *supra* note 15, at 102; Bittker, *A Last Word, id.* at 125.

17. Eisner v. Macomber, 252 U.S. 189, 207 (1920).

18. *See, e.g.*, E. Seligman, The Income Tax 12-15 1911); *cf.* A. Smith, The Wealth of Nations bk. II, ch. ii, at 271 (Modern Library ed. 1937) (defining income in similar manner).

19. Commissioner v. Glenshaw Glass Co., 348 U.S. 426, 430-31 1955).

derives from the fundamental observation that labor as well as capital is productive, with the output of that productive activity constituting the tax base. Our agrarian tax plainly meets this definition of an income tax. Moreover, it is neither a consumption tax (the corn might not all be consumed), nor a wealth tax (some workers may have stores of corn from prior periods), nor a wage tax (it reduced the return to capital, *i.e.*, tools, as well as labor). It is, rather, a tax levied on social output or production for the period.

Unlike the Haig-Simons concept, the product formulation identifies a concept of the aggregate tax base: the product of the whole society's private capital and labor during the accounting period.[20] The product formulation can also be used to answer the question of whether a particular item constitutes income in some abstract sense; wages, for instance, do, while totally unexpected returns—windfalls—do not, if unrelated to an individual's labor or capital. Those two answers also illustrate the defect of the product view by itself, and the corresponding virtue of the Haig-Simons concept: arguably equivalent changes in personal economic position are treated differently depending on the origin of the change.

The Haig-Simons concept is necessary to identify personal income when a society wishes to implement a tax with personally graduated rates or is too complex to permit collection at the source. The arithmetical process of the Haig-Simons definition should not, however, obscure the nature of the aggregate tax base, which is the product of the society's private capital and labor for the accounting period. The Haig-Simons calculation simply identifies how much of that product has ended up in each taxable unit. What is involved here is not merely a quibble about whether an idealized "definition" of income for personal taxation should focus on the required interpersonal accounting or on the product that is accounted for. Rather, both perspectives are necessary to answer properly questions about income measurement in a complex society, with neither concept having primacy over the other.[21]

It is, of course, standard fare of tax analysis since at least Henry Simons that personal income does *not* sum to the total private social product of the accounting period.[22] Putting aside what is not central

20. The return on public capital, such as parks or dams, generally has not been included in specifications of the income tax base. *Cf.* Aaron, *What is a Comprehensive Tax Base Anyway?* 22 NAT'L TAX J. 543 (1969) (arguing that public goods and services would be included in an ideal tax base).

21. The equivalence of national product with income to a nation's factors of production is a familiar accounting identity in national income accounting. *See* R. STONE & G. STONE, NATIONAL INCOME AND EXPENDITURE 31-32 (10th ed. 1977).

22. *See, e.g.*, H. SIMONS, *supra* note 10, at 47.

for our purposes—institutional differences in the current measurement of individual and social income, as well as any conceptual problems in comparing aggregations of market prices[23]—it is difficult to see why Haig-Simons personal income would not aggregate to the total product of a society's privately owned capital and labor. To the extent that Haig-Simons income includes the product of all individuals' capital and labor, the sum of the individual amounts could differ from the social product only by the amount of transfers among individuals. Yet the Haig-Simons calculation takes all such transfers into account by offsetting entries, so the total should remain unchanged. A few examples will make this clear.

Suppose that a citizen of our agrarian society finds 100 ears of corn, which he is permitted to keep under local law. Although his Haig-Simons income has increased, while the society's product has not, the equivalence is maintained by the diminution in the Haig-Simons income of the loser of the corn. To be sure, the equivalence would not hold if the corn were literally manna from Heaven, but the income-as-product view admits of no free lunch (corn or otherwise), a view that seems perfectly sensible to me, since (alas) true manna has not been observed in recent times.

Now suppose that our citizen owns a certain amount of beach land, which vacationers have generally regarded as equal in desirability to a comparable amount of mountain land. If for some unanticipated reason the tastes of vacationers shift significantly in favor of the shore over the stream, our citizen will be the beneficiary of another gain. Once again, he would have Haig-Simons income—his land would trade for many more bushels of corn than it did before—while there would have been no addition to the society's product. Yet the equivalence holds because there would be a decline in the relative value of some assets other than the beach land, presumably including the mountain land.

To return to our own economic system, a capital gain due to a change in stock-market prices may likewise add nothing to the social product and yet provide Haig-Simons income to the recipient. Again, there would presumably be offsetting losses elsewhere in the economy, perhaps in the stock market, so that there is no incongruity in taxing capital gains (and permitting a deduction for capital losses) under an income tax where aggregate income is defined as the product of capital and labor.

23. Nor need we be concerned with such matters as whether national income is best expressed before or after taking into account depreciation of the capital stock and indirect taxes. *See* pp. 1117-20 *infra*.

Consider another category of transfers: gifts and bequests. Gratuitous receipts do, after all, increase either the consumption or wealth of the donee and should be counted as part of his Haig-Simons income. On the other hand, such receipts do not constitute an additional product of capital or labor, so they cannot be counted again if the donor has already included them as part of his income. Thus the equivalence holds only if the donor is permitted a deduction for the gift because his net worth has declined, a result which seems obvious under the Simons definition quoted above. As under current law, one might, of course, decide to tax the amount of the gift to the donor if the opportunities to shift tax liabilities by gift were thought too great under graduated rates.[24] And even if taxation to the donor rather than the donee were rejected for *inter vivos* transfers, it might be preferable with respect to bequests. What is not permissible under the Haig-Simons concept is inclusion of the receipt in both the donor's and the donee's income—the position erroneously taken by Henry Simons[25] and many other writers.[26] That position can be sustained only on a view of income quite different from the Haig-Simons concept, a matter to which we will return.[27]

The equivalence of aggregate Haig-Simons personal income and social product also holds in the case of technological advances that increase the society's production possibilities. Suppose in our agrarian society that a machine is invented that doubles the potential output of the field. If the machine is regarded as an output in the year of its production, social product is augmented by the same amount as the inventor's net worth. If a natural resource that, when used as a fuel, will double the output of the machine is then discovered under a citizen's privately owned home, inclusion of the resource in social production as a return to the homeowner's capital will accomplish the same result.

A final aspect of the equivalence between social product and total personal income is that there could be Haig-Simons income even in a society that had no social product. Survivors of a shipwreck who were marooned on a desert island, and who spent their time gambling their shares of the ship's food stores that washed ashore with them, would

24. Current law excludes gifts from the income tax base of the donee, *see* I.R.C. § 102, and effectively includes gifts in the income tax base of the donor by denying a deduction. The potential for such shifting can be thought of as a consequence of incorrectly defining the taxable unit as individuals or married couples, as opposed to the family.

25. H. SIMONS, *supra* note 10, at 134-40.

26. *See, e.g.*, BLUEPRINTS, *supra* note 3, at 36-38.

27. *See* pp. 1095-97 *infra*.

Consumption Tax

experience gains and losses among themselves as a result of the gambles, so some individuals might have positive income in the Haig-Simons sense.[28] There would not, of course, be any personal income in the aggregate since the gains would just offset the losses. Nor would there be any social product since neither capital nor labor would be employed in this society.

The equivalence argued for here does not seem confirmed in common experience in some instances because assets such as land and corporate securities appear to increase or decrease in value without any corresponding offset elsewhere in the economy. It is submitted that the equivalence exists, but is obscured by the complexities of our economy, especially when the general price level is not fixed. Imagine a simpler society in which there are only two assets of equal value—a parcel of land and a piece of machinery. If the land tripled in value relative to the machine, there would be no doubt that the landowner was better off relative to the machine owner (the machine could now be obtained in exchange for only a third of the land). Correspondingly, the machine owner would be worse off relative to the landowner (since the machine would now bring only a third of the land in exchange). The nature of relative prices is such that the landowner's gain is simply a different way of expressing the machine owner's loss.

Now consider the same transaction in a monetary economy in which the two assets are initially each valued at $100. It is conceivable that the land could increase in value to $300 without a corresponding decline in the dollar value of the machine if the society's monetary policy so permitted. Prior to the shift, the landowner and the machine owner each held one-half of the value of the society's real wealth. The shift increased the landowner's portion to 3/4 and diminished the machine owner's to 1/4, a gain of 1/4 to the former and a loss of 1/4 to the latter, even though there was no decline in the absolute dollar value of the machine. Whether that change in position should be reflected by a deductible loss of $100 to the machine owner and a $100 gain to the landowner instead of simply a $200 gain to the landowner depends on the proper accounting for changes in the monetary unit.[29] Whether

28. The example assumes that the gambles are entered into for profit and that there is no significant consumption in the act of gambling itself. One justification for the limitation on the deductibility of gambling losses under current law, *see* I.R.C. § 165(d) (gambling losses deductible only to extent of gambling gains), might be the presence of a significant consumption component in the gambling itself.

29. If the increase in the total value of both assets from $200 to $400 were considered general price inflation, it would be necessary under an income tax triggered by realization events to increase the basis of each asset by the rate of inflation (in the instant case, 100%) in order to compute income properly. Assuming the assets had been purchased

current law makes the correct accounting entries or not, the landowner's gain is matched by the machine owner's loss.

To recapitulate, it is the product of private capital and labor that provides the sum of taxable income for the period, and it is the Haig-Simons formulation that properly identifies that income with persons.[30] The first concept is inadequate without the second in a complex economy with progressive taxation; the second is a personal calculation that has no aggregate significance without the first.

B. *Why Tax Income?*

Using the Haig-Simons concept of income in order to compute each taxpayer's share of the annual social product, an income tax serves to deflect to the government a progressive portion of each citizen's share of the product otherwise allocated to him by transfers and the marketplace. Whether the tax proceeds are used for public goods and services or for redistribution to some persons, either in cash or in kind, those uses are funded by the output of labor and private capital during the current period. Levying the tax on income is on this view simply a logical concomitant of the proposition that society in general has a claim on its annual product that is prior to the claims of its individual citizens.

The existence of a collective claim on privately produced resources is so well-established as part of our polity that justification may seem superfluous. Nevertheless, economic theorists have formally shown that certain goods and services are best produced in the public sector,[31]

prior to the shift in market value for $100 each, the following gains and losses would result from sale after the shift:

	Landowner	*Machine owner*
Amount realized	$300	$100
Adjusted basis	− 200	− 200
Gain (loss)	100	(100)

For general discussions of the effects of inflation on income taxation, see INFLATION AND THE INCOME TAX (H. Aaron ed. 1976).

30. Viewing the Haig-Simons definition in this manner does not undermine the importance of its proper explication. Whether, for example, charitable contributions should be deductible can be thought of as raising the question of whose tax base—the donor's or the donee's—should include the consumption or accumulation that results from the transfer. *Cf.* Andrews, *Personal Deductions in an Ideal Income Tax*, 86 HARV. L. REV. 309, 344-75 (1972) (using Haig-Simons definition to determine propriety of charitable contribution deduction).

31. *See, e.g.*, Samuelson, *The Pure Theory of Public Expenditure*, 36 REV. ECON. & STATISTICS 387, 387-89 (1954); Samuelson, *Diagrammatic Exposition of a Theory of Public Expenditure*, 37 REV. ECON. & STATISTICS 350 (1955).

Consumption Tax

while political theorists have argued for centuries over the nature and extent of the collective claim for redistributive purposes, a subject that has commanded renewed attention in recent years.[32] But neither the theories of public goods nor those of distributive justice have depended on the source of revenues used for the two analytically distinct governmental purposes. Discussions of redistribution generally either have considered the appropriate distribution of economic resources without identifying the best measure of such resources or have assumed that it is income (as product) that is or is not subject to a collective claim. As a result, existing theories of distributive justice and public goods have little to add to the case for the income tax beyond establishing a social claim on private resources.

Specifying that claim as on social product can be justified on the theory that a producer does not have a controlling moral claim over the product of his capital and labor, given the role of fortuity in income distribution and the dependence of producers on consumers and other producers to create value in our society—factors that create a general moral claim on all private product on behalf of the entire society.[33] This rationale would apply *a fortiori* to other increments in Haig-Simons income, such as gifts and windfalls, which come to the recipient without even the claim due to production. Such a proposition is, of course, no more demonstrable than the proposition that society has a prior moral claim on wealth or consumption rather than on product. As Professor William Andrews has stated, the ultimate choice among these alternatives is not a matter of logical proof but of exposing the assumptions and identifying the consequences of each.[34]

Given that limitation, the case for taxing income can be stated by identifying as a plausible assumption the view that, for the reasons suggested above, the distribution of social product is a matter for collective decision. The collective decisionmaking apparatus of the society is conceived of as deciding both the amount and type of public goods to be produced and the distribution of that portion of private social product that remains after diversion of resources into the public sector to produce those public goods that are not financed by service charges. Whatever after-tax distribution is decided upon, that decision

32. The seminal work in rekindling interest in distributive justice is J. RAWLS, A THEORY OF JUSTICE (1971).

33. *See id.* at 72-74, 100-08, 310-15. For a recent argument that treatment of an individual's genetic endowment as an accident devoid of moral significance is inconsistent with basic concepts of individuality, see Posner, *Utilitarianism, Economics, and Legal Theory*, 8 J. LEGAL STUD. 103, 128 (1979).

34. *Andrews' Reply*, *supra* note 1, at 950.

is implemented by the income tax, which is levied on the amount of social product otherwise distributed to each taxable unit.[35]

As anticipated, this argument for the income tax does not appeal to some independently demonstrable principle but is tautological in the sense that it follows simply from the premise of the tax: given a legitimate social concern with the distribution of society's product, the income tax is justified as a means of effecting the desired after-tax distribution. The nature of the desired distribution goes to the content of the tax, rather than to its justification. Extreme egalitarianism would presumably argue for a tax characterized by progressivity, culminating in a confiscatory rate on positive income with corresponding provisions specifying a minimum after-tax income. A social decision to reduce inequality in the distribution of product, but not to the extent of eliminating incentives to work and invest, might lead to less progressivity with rates always under one hundred percent. It is a judgment of this latter type that seems to underlie much current discussion of distributive justice.[36]

Unlike the foregoing argument, the traditional case for the income tax in terms of fairness has appealed to some external standard to establish that income is an appropriate basis for taxation. Generally it has been argued that income is a superior index of an "ability to pay," and that the tax should be structured to result in "equal sacrifice" by taxpayers, the latter being especially relevant to the rate structure. Unfortunately, centuries of elucidation have failed to provide sufficient content to these concepts. For example, ability to pay has been defined as "the capacity of paying without undue hardship on the part of the person paying or an unacceptable degree of interference with objectives that are considered socially important by other members of the community."[37] Such definitions reduce to statements that society should appropriately tax what it should appropriately tax. This approach is no less tautological than the one taken here; it just appears so in that

35. This view includes the possibility of negative taxes and assumes that the desired after-tax distribution of income is a function of no personal characteristic other than pretax income. For example, if after-tax income were to be allocated on the basis of weight, intelligence, merit, or whatever, the Haig-Simons definition could be used for collection of revenue, but not for the simultaneous achievement of a given after-tax distribution.

36. *See, e.g.*, A. OKUN, EQUALITY AND EFFICIENCY—THE BIG TRADEOFF (1975); J. RAWLS, *supra* note 32, at 150-61.

37. R. GOODE, THE INDIVIDUAL INCOME TAX 18 (1964); *see* Gunn, *The Case for an Income Tax*, 46 U. CHI. L. REV. 370, 378-88 (1979). The theory of marginal sacrifice is discussed in W. BLUM & H. KALVEN, THE UNEASY CASE FOR PROGRESSIVE TAXATION 39-70 (1953).

Consumption Tax

apparently, but not really, independently verifiable grounds, such as ability to pay, are said to justify the tax.

To summarize, the personal income tax follows from, and is justified by, a societal judgment as to the appropriate distribution of social product or personal income. Society's interest in the distribution of income, in turn, depends on the view that the importance of fortuity and the interrelationships of contemporary society deprive producers of a controlling moral claim to what would be distributed to them in the absence of a tax system.

II. Consumption as a Criterion of Distributive Fairness

A. *Why Tax Consumption?*

It will be recalled that the consumption tax being proposed currently is a personal tax with graduated rates, falling on the consumption, but not the accumulation, branch of Haig-Simons income. In general, the tax would be administered on an expenditure or cash-flow basis: all receipts, including borrowings, would be included in the tax base and all nonconsumption expenditures, including principal and interest repayments, would be deducted.

The case for the resulting tax base as a matter of distributive fairness is that society's interest in a just distribution of economic resources goes to standards of living rather than to social product.[38] Under this view, the collective decisionmaking apparatus is conceived of as deciding both the amount and type of public goods to be made available for public consumption and the appropriate after-tax distribution of private consumption, which is effected by the consumption tax.

Specifying the social claim on private resources as a claim on consumed resources rather than on social product, as under an income tax, is justified on the view that the ultimate goal of productive activity is human consumption, so that unconsumed product is simply not relevant to a distributional calculus. In effect, unconsumed product is ignored until actually consumed, at which time it is subject to the social claim.

Under a consumption tax, a citizen's moral claim is for a fair share—however computed—of the goods and services consumed during the accounting period. Under an income tax, it is for a fair share of the goods and services produced during the period. An extreme egalitarian would seek equality among consumers (and nonconsumers) under the

38. *See Consumption Tax, supra* note 1, at 1167.

first, and equality among producers (and nonproducers) under the second. Either criterion of distributional equity seems plausible as an initial matter.

B. *Arguments that the Consumption Tax is Preferable as a Matter of Fairness*

Consumption tax advocates have advanced six grounds for regarding the income tax as inferior in terms of fairness: (1) the income tax unfairly takes into account resources left in the common pool; (2) consumption more closely approximates utility, the ideal measure of distributional justice; (3) income taxation discriminates against savers; (4) consumption taxation is preferable from a lifetime perspective; (5) the concept of income is inherently defective; and (6) consumption taxation would interfere less with individual liberty.

Each of these arguments, recited above in the rough order of their historical appearance, will be considered separately.

1. *The Common Pool*

From the perspective of the income tax, the consumption tax is deficient because it fails to take into account the fact that productive nonconsumers receive claims for future consumption in the form of property rights. Such producers have not only current consumption, but also an option for additional consumption that can be exercised at will. Why, from the point of view of distributional fairness, should the existence of such options be ignored?

The traditional answer, which derives from Hobbes, is that unconsumed resources are left in a common pool, so that it is inappropriate to tax a person until he withdraws his resources for personal consumption.[39] Indeed, leaving resources in the common pool can be characterized as socially desirable in that the capital so supplied will increase both future production and the future productivity of workers.[40]

The image of a common pool certainly fails to capture the reality of existing legal relationships in our society if it is meant to suggest that all members of the society have equal access to the pool, which is, after

39. T. Hobbes, *supra* note 5, at 226, makes the argument in the form of a question:

> For what reason is there, that he which laboureth much, and sparing the fruits of his labour, consumeth little, should be more charged, then he that living idly, getteth little, and spendeth all he gets; seeing the one has no more protection from the commonwealth, than the other?

The "common pool" language is used by other commentators. *See* C. Fried, Right and Wrong 147 (1978); N. Kaldor, *supra* note 5, at 53. The Hobbesian formulation is rejected in Warren, *supra* note 1, at 933.

40. *See* N. Kaldor, *supra* note 5, at 53; P. Mieszkowski, *supra* note 3, at 8-9; R. Musgrave & P. Musgrave, Public Finance in Theory and Practice 220-21 (2d ed. 1976).

all, merely the aggregate of society's current private wealth. That pool is not collectively owned, but held privately by shareholders whose shares are simply their claims on unconsumed product. The commonality of the common pool has only to do with the derivative benefit to society of saving and investment, not in any generality of ownership or control; nor is the aura of moral superiority that sometimes surrounds those who leave their goods in the pool justified. Accumulation of wealth in our society is not a matter of altruistically forgoing current consumption for the good of others. Rather, it is a matter of a saver choosing to defer until a later date either his own consumption or that of an object of his bounty.

As powerful an image as it is, the idea of a common pool simply does not add anything to the straightforward proposition that distributive justice should turn on standards of living. Like the Haig-Simons concept, the common pool idea can be cast in accounting terms: if product is not currently consumed, what happens to it? By definition, it remains in the pool of the productive resources, contributing to additional product and awaiting conversion into future consumption. The idea of such a pool may confirm the plausibility of consumption as a criterion of distributive justice, but it hardly shows the superiority of that criterion over the concept of income.

2. *Consumption Taxation and Utility*

It might be argued that distributive justice should be concerned not merely with income or other measures of economic well-being, but with all sources of an individual's utility, satisfaction, or welfare. Under this view, an ideal tax would be one that implemented society's view of the appropriate distribution of utility (to use the term still favored by economists) by taking into account not only income, but all other sources of satisfaction as well.[41] Although not perfect, a consumption tax would be the closest possible approximation to this ideal, because consumption is the closest observable phenomenon to utility.

This view focuses not on the individual's share of the social product, but rather on what he does with it: ultimately, product is desired, and presumably used, for the provision of satisfaction or utility:

> [F]undamentally income is a flow of satisfactions, of intangible psychological experiences. If one receives a dollar he receives something which he ordinarily can and does spend—perhaps for a dinner. Is his income the dollar, or is it the dinner which he buys

41. *See* Rosen, *An Approach to the Study of Income, Utility and Horizontal Equity*, 92 Q.J. Econ. 307 (1978) (using utility definition of horizontal equity to evaluate an existing tax structure).

> with the dollar, or is it, at bottom, the satisfaction of his wants which he derives from eating the dinner—the comfort and the sustenance it yields to him? If one spends his dollar for something more durable than a dinner—say a book or a pipe—is his true income the book or the pipe, or the series of satisfactions or "usances" arising from reading the book or smoking the pipe? There is no doubt as to the answer to these questions. A man strives for the satisfaction of his wants and desires and not for objects for their own sake.[42]

The argument that distributive justice would ideally comprehend all forms of utility should be rejected as a foundation for consumption taxation for three reasons. First, if consumption—or income—is ultimately a mental or psychological concept, the tax base no longer follows precisely from observable transactions. Rather, an accurate determination of tax liability on this theory would require knowledge of each person's capacity for pleasure, because identical objects purchased for identical prices would almost surely give rise to different amounts of psychic income in different psyches. There apparently could also be a kind of manna under this view, in that a pleasurable sensation arising without an increase in social product would presumably be income. The psychological nature of this concept plainly makes it unworkable as a touchstone for taxation, because it requires calculation of amounts that are totally unknowable. As stated at the outset, this Article generally avoids discussions of relative administrative practicality. But the impossibility of developing a workable consumption tax, founded on interpersonal utility comparisons that simply cannot be made, is a difficulty of a different order.

Second, even if the measurements were technically feasible and the underlying ideas could be made sufficiently intelligible, expansion of the concept of distributive justice in this manner would not be desirable as a matter of policy. Our society has never viewed taxation as a means of reducing all differences among individuals. The respect accorded noneconomic differences by our political system is based on

42. Haig, *supra* note 13, at 2. The language quoted in the text makes somewhat problematical Haig's connection with what is usually called the Haig-Simons concept. *But see* note 13 *supra*.

The most influential exponent of income as satisfaction was Irving Fisher, who thought the most fundamental concept of income was enjoyment or psychic income, consisting of agreeable sensations and experiences. *See* I. FISHER, THE NATURE OF CAPITAL AND INCOME 165-79 (1906). The goods or services that produced the satisfactions were important only as an approximation of the psychic flows, and the costs of those goods and services represented only a means of aggregating the approximate value of heterogeneous goods and services. Although he insisted on calling it an income tax, Fisher concluded that the closest achievable approximation of a tax on psychic flows was what today would be called a personal consumption tax.

Consumption Tax

more than the practical difficulties of moving beyond economic characteristics; arguably it derives from fundamental views about the primacy of persons over things, views that assume it is possible to treat people as distinct from their product, whether consumed or not,[43] a distinction that would not obtain under the broader utilitarian view of distributive justice.

Third, even if utilitarianism were accepted as an appropriate criterion for choosing among tax bases, it is not obvious that the best approximation of utility in terms of economic resources would be consumption alone. Individuals are certainly not indifferent to the holding of wealth, and it seems unlikely that the satisfaction derived from being wealthy is limited to any future consumption to be purchased with the wealth. Thus, wealth might be a suitable partial proxy for utility, and, in the absence of a wealth tax, so might income, which includes accumulation as well as consumption.

Thus the utilitarian formulation of distributive justice, along with the derivative concepts of consumption and income as psychic benefits, should be rejected even if workable, on the ground that psychological well-being is not an appropriate measure of distributive justice given our moral and political traditions.[44] Tax bases and the underlying concepts of distributive fairness should be limited to economic resources, and the choice among such bases is not made easier by taking consumption as a surrogate for utility.

3. *Discrimination Against Savers*

To demonstrate the unfairness of the income tax, Irving Fisher offered the example of three brothers who each inherit $10,000 in a tax-free world where the interest rate is five percent.[45] The first brother invests his inheritance in a perpetual annuity of $500 a year; the second puts his in a trust with income to accumulate for fourteen years, at which point the corpus will be worth $20,000 and will be used to purchase a perpetual annuity of $1,000 a year; the third purchases an annuity of $2,000 a year for about six years. In a world without taxation, the present value of each brother's asset is, at five percent, $10,000. The

43. *But see* R. Nozick, Anarchy, State, and Utopia 169-72 (1974) (equating taxation of income from labor or capital with forced labor and arguing that such taxation gives the state a property right in the individual); Posner. *supra* note 33, at 128 ("To treat the inventor and the idiot equally so far as their moral claim to command over valuable resources is concerned does not take the differences between persons seriously.") (footnote omitted).

44. An argument for the consumption tax on the basis of utilitarianism in the context of a life-cycle model is discussed in note 67 *infra*.

45. *See* I. Fisher, *supra* note 42, at 249-53.

present value of each brother's future tax liability would not, however, be the same under an income tax. If the tax rate were ten percent, those amounts would be, respectively, $1,000, $1,714, and $157.73.[46] Deferral of consumption results in additional interest and additional income taxes, from which Fisher concluded: "Such a system of taxation is clearly unjust and discourages the saver, while it encourages the spendthrift."[47]

One wonders not only why the tax is clearly unjust, but why the comparison is even relevant. Fisher's conclusion turns on the assumption that fairness is to be measured in terms of taxpayers' expectations (here expressed as a present capital value of $10,000), rather than outcomes. Fisherian capital theory takes expected income streams in future periods as given and discounts them to a current capital value that embodies the world's expectations about the asset's future. The Haig-Simons calculation, by contrast, takes market-determined capital values as given and identifies changes in their amounts to arrive at income for a past period. The Haig-Simons concept is retrospective, concerned with the change in each taxpayer's position during the period just ended, while the Fisherian analysis is essentially prospective: the brothers are said to be in the same position because they have the same prospect. Both views depend on capital values and so involve the market's evaluation of future income streams. The difference lies in the perspective from which interpersonal comparisons are made—the Fisherian comparison is forward-looking, while the Haig-Simons concept (and the standard-of-living view of the consumption tax) is backward-looking.

In a world characterized by uncertainty, expectations may not be what eventuates, so a choice must be made between comparing taxpayers on an *ex ante* or an *ex post* basis. Expectations are, of course, central to economic theory, which is in general concerned with the making of rational choices *ex ante*. But fairness in taxation should depend on outcomes, not expectations. If A and B have identical expectations about their financial futures, but A's hopes are dashed, while B's wildest dreams are realized, should not a fair tax system take into account the differences in outcome?[48]

46. *Id.*

47. *Id.* at 253.

48. For discussion of a similar issue in the theory of social choice—whether the mathematical expectation of welfare or the actual distribution of welfare should be considered in choosing among alternative social states—see A. SEN, COLLECTIVE CHOICE AND SOCIAL WELFARE 141-46 (1970); Diamond, *Cardinal Welfare, Individualistic Ethics, and Interpersonal Comparison of Utility: Comment*, 75 J. POLITICAL ECON. 765 (1967); Harsanyi, *Cardinal Welfare, Individualistic Ethics and Interpersonal Comparison of Utility*, 63 J. POLITICAL ECON. 309, 312-14 (1955).

Consumption Tax

Even if investment return is certain, as it is in the example of the three brothers, the discounting of future consumption to present value or the compounding of present to future value, which is the core of the Fisherian argument, cannot be carried over from *ex ante* to *ex post* perspectives. There is, to be sure, no difference between the perspectives in the purely hypothetical world of complete certainty in which an individual can see the future as clearly as the past. But that is not our world; nor is the ability to see into the future a necessary corollary of the existence of risk-free investments on which there is a guaranteed return.

Consider two taxpayers who each earn $200 in Year 1, and who accordingly have the same prospect. One (A) consumes all he can after taxes in Year 1, while the other (B) defers all his consumption—at ten percent interest—from Year 1 to Year 2, when they both die (as expected) without earning additional labor income. As the following table indicates, the rate of exchange between consumption in Years 1 and 2 is changed by an income tax, but not by a flat-rate consumption or wage tax.[49]

TABLE I

A	*No Tax*	*Income Tax*	*Consumption Tax*	*Wage Tax*
Pretax wage	$ 200	$ 200	$ 200	$ 200
Tax on wage (50%)	0	100	100	100
After-tax consumption (Year 1)	200	100	100	100
B				
Pretax wage	200	200	200	200
Tax on wage (50%)	0	100	0	100
After-tax investment	200	100	200	100
Pretax investment proceeds	220	110	220	110
Tax on investment proceeds (50%)	0	5	110	0
After-tax consumption (Year 2)	220	105	110	110
Ratio of Year 2 to Year 1 consumption	220/200	105/100	110/100	110/100

An income tax, unlike consumption or wage taxes of the same rate, reduces the value of future consumption relative to present consump-

49. Equivalent results under the consumption and wage taxes require the following assumptions in addition to fixed tax-rates: (1) accumulation does not continue forever, so there is never any consumption to tax; (2) consumption does not occur without there having been wages to tax; (3) taxpayers are rational and do not save a fixed fraction of their pretax wages; (4) wages can be distinguished from capital income; and (5) the pretax rate of return remains fixed. *See* R. MUSGRAVE, THE THEORY OF PUBLIC FINANCE 262, 266-67 (1959).

The fact that consumption and wage taxes of equal rates yield equal results is an aspect of the phenomenon that deferral of a constant-rate income tax is the equivalent of non-deferral coupled with exemption of the return on the invested proceeds of the taxed receipt. *See* MEADE REPORT, *supra* note 4, at 35-38; *Consumption Tax*, *supra* note 1, at 1123-28; Brown, *Business-Income Taxation and Investment Incentives*, in INCOME, EMPLOYMENT AND PUBLIC POLICY, ESSAYS IN HONOR OF ALVIN H. HANSEN 300, 309-10 (1948).

tion (from 110/100 to 105/100 in the example above)—a result that led John Stuart Mill to conclude that savings are "twice taxed."[50] *Ex ante*, the income tax arguably discriminates against B, because A and B start in the same pretax position in Year 1, but pay different taxes in terms of present value. While A's and B's consumption have the same pretax present value in Year 1, B's consumption has a lower Year 1 present value after payment of the income tax. The consumption tax can thus be said to be fairer *ex ante*, in that it does not discriminate against taxpayers with a relatively greater preference for future consumption.

The same argument cannot be made *ex post* without showing that A and B would be in equal positions in Year 2, but for the tax. B's consumption in Year 2 can be discounted to Year 1 to show *ex ante* equivalence, but can A's consumption in Year 1 be compounded to Year 2 to show *ex post* equivalence?[51] To do so would imply a capital return to all consumption expenditures over the remainder of the consumer's lifetime, meaning that, at any given moment, more recent consumption is worth less to consumers than an equivalent amount of earlier consumption—a result that is certainly not intuitively obvious.

Although rational consumers may discount the cost of future consumption to present value when choosing among allocations of consumption over their lifetimes *ex ante*, it does not necessarily follow that more recent consumption is worth less *ex post*. It is not at all obvious that consumption of a bottle of fine wine thirty years ago is, in any meaningful sense, equivalent to consumption of several cases today. It may well be that proximity in time is what matters, rather than priority. Because we go through time in only one direction during our lifetimes, we are never presented with an opportunity to prefer priority independently of proximity. Or it may be that a rational consumer would not discount consumption *qua* consumption, even *ex ante*, in that each period in his life would be given equal weight.[52] Marooned on a desert island with a lifetime store of goods, a consumer might well allocate an equivalent amount of goods to each of the remaining years of his life. From this perspective, the discount observed *ex ante* is due

50. J. S. Mill, *supra* note 5, at 54-55.

51. *See* White, *Proper Income Tax Treatment of Deductions for Personal Expense*, 1 House Committee on Ways and Means, Tax Revision Compendium 365 (Comm. Print 1959) (discussing an imputed return to consumption over time).

52. Rawls argues that individuals in the original position would have no time preference. *See* J. Rawls, *supra* note 32, at 293-98.

Consumption Tax

entirely to the productivity of capital, which permits the augmentation of consumption through deferral and investment.[53]

From either perspective, the discount observed in consumer decisions *ex ante* does not establish the propriety of compounding earlier consumption *ex post*. Yet that is the mandate of the Fisherian view, translated into *ex post* terms for the clearest comparison with the Haig-Simons concept: interest should not be taxed to B because it is not taxed to A, who had exactly the same amount of imputed return on his consumption. The Fisherian argument seems so strange in *ex post* terms precisely because, unlike the Haig-Simons concept, it is essentially an *ex ante* formulation. For myself, the discrimination argument is not convincing even when investment return is certain, as in the examples discussed so far. But even if the argument were accepted in those instances, its application to the more realistic case of uncertain investment return is more difficult—a matter addressed in the next section.

4. *The Consumption Tax From a Lifetime Perspective*

The Fisherian analysis has reappeared in recent years in arguments against the income tax based on life-cycle consumption models. The United States Treasury Department has presented the lifetime-consumption argument as a matter of "endowment": if the expected wage-stream for each individual is discounted to a comparable present value, and added to the value of property held at that point, then the sum represents an endowment that can be regarded as a good measure of ability to pay taxes.[54] Once endowment is accepted as the appropriate means of ranking taxpayers in terms of ability to pay, it follows that an income tax is inferior to a consumption or wage tax, since an income tax will tax equally endowed taxpayers differently, if their spending patterns differ. The Treasury Department concluded that a consumption tax is an "ideal [lifetime] wealth tax," as equivalent to a flat-rate tax levied on endowment.[55]

When investment return is certain, the endowment rationale is sim-

53. If the interest rate is thought to be determined ultimately by government policy, the reduction of the after-tax rate (from 10% to 5% in Table I) under the income tax suggests that the pretax interest rate might be commensurately raised to 20% if an income tax is imposed. Given such an increase, there would be no difference in result under the income and consumption taxes when rates and returns were certain, so neither tax could be said to be superior.

54. For taxpayers who leave no bequests and make no gifts, this endowment is also the present value of their expected lifetime consumption.

55. BLUEPRINTS, *supra* note 3, at 42; *see* Musgrave, *ET, OT and SBT*, 6 J. PUB. ECON. 3, 11-12 (1976) (describing endowment rationale in terms of equal options).

ply the Fisherian analysis extended over a taxpayer's lifetime. The Treasury's analysis made explicit the wage tax equivalence shown in Table I by permitting taxpayers to choose between the standard consumption tax treatment of deducting investments and including disinvestments (what is called the "qualified account" alternative) and simply excluding capital income from the tax base, which becomes to that extent a wage tax base (the "prepayment" alternative).[56]

a. *Risky Investments*

Assume that the two wage earners described above—each of whom earned $200 in Year 1—can invest and borrow at a riskless interest rate of ten percent and that there also exists a risky investment, such as a coin toss, that offers an investor the opportunity to triple his initial investment or lose it all after one year. Our two investors can vary the risk in their portfolios by varying the amount allocated to risky and riskless assets and by borrowing if they wish. In the interest of simplicity, imagine that each invests his entire after-tax wages of $100 in the risky asset under an income tax, so that each has a fifty percent chance of receiving $300 and a fifty percent chance of receiving zero in Year 2 before taxes.[57] The expected after-tax results are as follows:

	Winner	*Loser*
Amount realized	$300	$ 0
Basis	100	100
Gain (loss)	200	(100)
Tax (refund)	100	(50)
After-tax proceeds	200	50

Each has chosen an expected after-tax investment return with a mean of $125 and a standard deviation of $75.[58] Assume that one wins and the other loses, so that the amounts above are the actual results for the two investors.

What will be the result if a consumption tax is substituted for an

56. Some variant of this latter alternative is a feature of most comprehensive proposals for personal consumption taxation. *See, e.g.*, MEADE REPORT, *supra* note 4, at 175-83; *Consumption Tax, supra* note 1, at 1154-60. BLUEPRINTS refers to it as a "prepayment" option because the taxes due on disinvestment are, in effect, prepaid by the denial of a deduction for the amount of the investment at the time that the investment was made.

57. The conclusions that follow would not change if any other allocation were made between risky and riskless investments.

58. "Standard deviation" is the square root of the sum of the squared deviations from the mean, divided by the number of observations. *See* M. HAMBURG, STATISTICAL ANALYSIS FOR DECISION-MAKING 189 (1970). Because the after-tax win ($200) and loss ($50) positions both deviate from the mean by $75, the deviation in each case is also the standard deviation.

Consumption Tax

income tax? That will depend on whether taxpayers will change their investment behavior in response to the imposition of a different tax. We shall assume first that they do not, and then that they do. The second is the better assumption, but its implications are more easily understood after examining the results under the first. Under either assumption the asserted equality of treatment of equally endowed taxpayers will be shown to require acceptance of an *ex ante* perspective.

Assuming first that the wage earners will continue under the consumption tax their previous practice of investing their entire after-tax wages in the risky asset, the following table shows the results that will obtain and compares them with those under the income tax:

TABLE II

	Consumption Tax		
	Qualified Account Alternative	*Prepayment Alternative*	*Income Tax*
Investment			
Taxpayer A	\$200[a]	\$100[b]	\$100[b]
Taxpayer B	200[a]	100[b]	100[b]
Consumption			
A (Winner)			
Gross Return	600	300	300
Tax (50%)	300[c]	0	100[d]
Net Consumption	300	300	200
B (Loser)			
Gross Return	0	0	0
Tax (50%)	0	0	(50)[e]
Net Consumption	0	0	50

[a] \$200 of wages minus zero taxes due to \$200 investment.
[b] \$200 of wages reduced by 50% tax.
[c] 50% of \$600.
[d] 50% of \$200 (\$300-\$100)
[e] 50% of \$100 loss (\$0-\$100)

Under the prepayment (or wage tax) alternative, A and B pay taxes of equal present value, \$100. But how can it be said that their after-tax consumption (\$300 for A, zero for B) is of equal present value? The only perspective from which they are equally treated is *ex ante*, as of the instant before the gamble, with all differences between the winner and the loser ignored. That perspective is natural under the prepayment alternative: A does not pay more taxes than B even though A wins and B loses because no account is taken of changes in the positions of A and B subsequent to the receipt of wages.

At first glance, it might appear that the qualified account alternative—the usual consumption tax treatment of deducting investments and including disinvestments—does take the differences in their positions into account, because A pays $300 in taxes while B pays none. The apparent difference is illusory, however. The amounts gambled and won under this alternative are in pretax dollars, carrying with them an implicit tax liability, whereas under the prepayment alternative the amounts gambled and won are in after-tax dollars. When A wins $600 on qualified account, he receives only $300 in potential consumption, coupled with an unavoidable $300 tax liability. Likewise, B's $200 pretax loss involves the loss of only $100 in after-tax consumption. Thus the after-tax results under the qualified account alternative are the same as those under the prepayment alternative: $300 in consumption for A, and none for B. The *ex ante* infirmity that afflicts the latter is, upon reflection, equally damaging to the former.

The life-cycle analysis is necessarily *ex ante* and defective if outcomes are considered relevant, because the differences between gainers and losers on risky investments are ignored. As the table shows, the income tax taxes winners more heavily than losers. The differences between winners and losers are, after all, gains and losses, which is precisely what the Haig-Simons definition is designed to identify.

The foregoing analysis assumed that taxpayer pretax behavior—here, the investment of all available wages in the risky asset—remained unchanged under the various taxes. The theory of investor behavior under uncertainty is not one on which there is universal agreement, but it seems more reasonable to assume that taxpayers are motivated by the *after*-tax return on their assets. Investors will accordingly modify their portfolios to take into account the effects of applicable taxes. For purposes of simplicity, let us assume that taxpayers are motivated in investment decisions by the relationship between the mean and deviation of the possible after-tax outcomes.

On that assumption, substitution of a consumption tax for the income tax would not necessarily lead each of our wage earners to invest his entire wages in the risky asset, because that would increase the standard deviation and mean of expected after-tax returns to $150.[59] If each investor wanted to maintain an after-tax standard deviation of $75 under the consumption tax (as under the income tax), he would invest the tax savings from deducting investments in the riskless asset. In effect, such an investor could purchase all the risk he wanted with a

59. As indicated in Table II, the winner would receive $300 and the loser zero.

Consumption Tax

$100 after-tax investment; had a greater deviation been desired under the income tax, he could have borrowed at the riskless rate to purchase more of the risky asset. Given these assumptions, each investor would put $100 in the risky asset and $100 in the riskless asset on qualified account; each would also divide his portfolio evenly on prepayment account, $50 to the risky asset and $50 to the riskless asset, yielding the following results:

TABLE III

	Qualified Account		*Prepayment Account*	
	Winner	*Loser*	*Winner*	*Loser*
Amount realized on risky asset	$300	$ 0	$150	$ 0
Amount realized on riskless asset	110	110	55	55
Taxable consumption	410	110	205	55
Tax (50%)	205	55	0	0
After-tax proceeds	205	55	205	55

Once again, the supposed equality of treatment for equally endowed taxpayers requires adoption of an *ex ante* perspective. The winner and loser have identical taxes—$100 each on wages of $200—only under the prepayment alternative; only their *expected* consumption in Year 1 is equal under either alternative. The example is, of course, intended to illustrate, rather than demonstrate, the results of investment decisions under uncertainty.[60] The important conclusion for our purposes is that the endowment analysis requires an *ex ante* perspective, whether investors are thought to maintain or change their pretax investment behavior in response to changes in the tax base.

b. *The Consumption Tax and the Exclusion of Riskless Return*

The assumption that investment behavior depends on expected after-tax results suggests another argument for the consumption tax; it produces results that are essentially equivalent to those of an income tax that exempts the riskless return on all invested assets, regardless of the risk of the actual investment and the actual return. In the example discussed above, each investor has $100 to invest under the income tax

60. The mean in this case would be $130, rather than $125, as under the income tax. If the investors wished to maintain that mean under the consumption tax, they could invest $125 in the riskless asset and $75 in the risky asset, in which case the standard deviation would be $56.25. Relative to the income tax, the consumption tax would thus permit the investor to decrease the deviation while maintaining the mean, increase the mean while maintaining the deviation, or obtain some intermediate solution. No matter which of these alternatives was actually chosen under the consumption tax, the conclusion in the text—that equality of treatment requires an *ex ante* perspective—would apply.

in Year 1; if the riskless return were excluded on the amounts invested in all assets, the results would be as follows:

TABLE IV

	Winner	*Loser*
Amount realized	$300	$ 0
Basis	100	100
Gain (loss)	200	(100)
Exclusion of riskless return	(10)	(10)
Taxable income (loss)	190	(110)
Tax (refund)	95	(55)
After-tax proceeds	205	55

The expected investment return under this limited income tax continues to have a standard deviation of $75, but it now has a mean of $130. Thus the limited income tax results in an increased mean and an extra $5 received by both the winner and the loser, as compared with the results under a comprehensive income tax. This difference is due to the effective exclusion from the tax base of the riskless rate of return. The exclusion permits the taxpayer to invest in his preferred portfolio without the reduction of mean return that occurs under the standard income tax even if the riskless asset is chosen.

As a comparison of Table III and Table IV shows, the consumption tax reaches the same result as a limited income tax in this example.[61]

61. The equivalence can also be illustrated with simple algebra. Consider a two-period model in which wages (w) are earned in period 1. All after-tax wages are invested, a fraction (a) in a risky asset yielding x rate of return, the remainder ($1-a$) in a risk-free asset with rate of return r. Period 2 after-tax consumption under a flat rate (t) consumption tax (CT) is as follows:

$$(1-t)w \;+\; (1-t)wax \;+\; (1-t)w(1-a)r$$

The limited income tax (LIT) to be compared is a standard income tax (IT) with a deduction for the risk-free rate of return (r) on net invested assets [$(1-t)w$], which deduction is worth $(1-t)wrt$ to the taxpayer in period 2. Under the behavioral assumption that the investor will adjust his pretax investment behavior in order to obtain the same after-tax result under different taxes, the taxpayer will invest a larger portion of his net wages in the risky asset under the IT or LIT than he did under the CT. Since the investor is willing to invest aw in the risky asset under the CT, he can obtain the same after-tax results under the LIT, where he has only $(1-t)w$ to invest, by allocating $a/1-t$ to the risky asset, leaving $(1-(a/1-t))$ for the riskless asset. Period 2 consumption under the LIT is then:

$$(1-t)w \;+\; (1-t)^2wx\ a/1-t \;+\; (1-t)^2(1-(a/1-t))wr \;+\; (1-t)wrt$$

or

$$(1-t)w \;+\; (1-t)wax \;+\; (1-t)[(1-t) \;-\; a]wr \;+\; (1-t)wrt$$

or

$$(1-t)w \;+\; (1-t)wax \;+\; (1-t)w(1-a)r$$

Now suppose that all funds (w) are invested in the risky asset under the CT, so an investor under the LIT can reach the same result only by borrowing tw at an interest

Consumption Tax

The equivalence of a flat-rate consumption tax with a flat-rate limited income tax under these circumstances suggests that the difference between the income and consumption bases for personal taxation is not as great as is often suggested.[62] Indeed, the equivalence suggests that the case for the consumption tax could be stated as a case for exempting only the riskless return on invested assets from the income tax.[63]

What would be the justification for such an exemption? The Treasury Department has suggested that "much of what is generally labelled capital income is really a reward for postponing immediate consumption of past wages."[64] If this view were accepted, it might be argued that the riskless rate of return somehow compensates all investors for the pain of deferring their consumption—but that justification leads back to the realm of psychic benefits and detriments rejected above. One might as well argue for excluding wages as merely offsetting the pain of working.

An alternative argument for exempting the riskless rate of return from the income tax would be acceptance of the Fisherian analysis for certain, but not uncertain, investment return. That view, which was rejected above, would be entirely consistent with a consumption tax that differed in after-tax result from an income tax principally in the effective exemption of riskless investment return.

rate r. Period 2 consumption under the CT is:

$$(1-t)w(1+x)$$

Under the LIT, period 2 consumption would be:

$$(1-t)w \;+\; (1-t)^2wx \;+\; (1-t)twx \;-\; (1-t)rtw \;+\; (1-t)twr$$

or

$$(1-t)w[1 \;+\; (1-t)x \;+\; tx]$$

or

$$(1-t)w(1+x)$$

62. *See* Warren, *supra* note 1, at 938-41 (arguing that a consumption tax is equivalent to a tax only on wages under certain conditions).

63. On this view, the consumption tax and the limited income tax differ from a standard income tax in that only the latter reaches the return to riskless assets. All three taxes reach wages and returns not associated with risk-taking, such as pure windfalls from lucky opportunities that could not be expected. As to differences in the treatment of returns to risk-taking under the income and consumption taxes, see N. KALDOR, *supra* note 5, at 102-29 (suggesting that income and consumption taxes will have different effects on risk-taking); Brown, *Mr. Kaldor on Taxation and Risk Bearing,* 25 REV. ECON. STUD. 49, 52 (1957) (concluding that effects will be the same); Shoup, *Effects of Sales Taxation on Risk-Taking,* in FINANZ- UND GELDPOLITIK IN UMBRUCH 237 (H. Haller & H. Recktenwald eds. 1969) (suggesting that general sales tax has the same effect on risk-taking as an income tax, although it differs from income tax in that there may be different results in different industries).

64. BLUEPRINTS, *supra* note 3, at 136.

c. *Graduated Rates*

If all assets returned income at the same certain rate, equality of present value among equally endowed taxpayers consuming in different years could be maintained under a system of lifetime cumulative averaging even with graduated consumption tax rates.[65] Consumption from the current period would be added to that of prior periods, increased by the standard rate of return; graduated rates would be applied to the sum, and a tax credit given for tax paid in prior periods, again increased by the standard rate of return. Because there would be only a single rate of return, equivalent results would obtain under the prepayment and qualified account alternatives. If, therefore, the *ex ante* view were embraced, that view would be as applicable to graduated taxes as it was to flat-rate taxes, as long as investment return were certain.

However, once uncertainty is introduced, as it must be to reflect real investment results, cumulative averaging under the qualified account alternative with graduated rates will not accomplish equal treatment of equally endowed taxpayers, even given the *ex ante* perspective. There is simply no way each taxpayer's taxes could be increased at the individually appropriate rate. Taxpayers whose investments returned larger gains would have greater lifetime consumption and consequently pay higher lifetime taxes. Nor would there be equivalence of treatment between the prepayment and qualified account alternatives. The endowment rationale thus argues either for flat rates, so that no averaging is necessary, or for progressive taxation of wages, coupled with lifetime averaging. Only by completely excluding capital income from a graduated tax can the rank order of individuals achieved by discounting earnings be maintained when investment return is not certain. Instead of achieving equal treatment of equally endowed taxpayers, cumulative averaging of uncertain investment return under a qualified account consumption tax would simply extend the standard-of-living rationale from a single year to the taxpayer's entire lifetime. Like the income concept, which could also incorporate cumulative lifetime averaging,[66] that rationale requires an *ex post* perspective.

In summary, the life-cycle view is subject to the same objection as the Fisherian analysis—that it is necessarily *ex ante*, rather than *ex post*—whether certain or uncertain investment return is considered.

65. *See* W. Vickrey, *supra* note 5, at 172-97 (discussion of cumulative averaging, which is intended to make the income- or consumption-tax burden independent of the distribution of income or consumption over the taxpayer's lifetime).

66. *Id.* at 172-95.

Consumption Tax

Moreover, even if the *ex ante* perspective is accepted as appropriate, graduated rates make the equal treatment of equally endowed taxpayers impossible under standard, qualified account consumption tax treatment if investment return is not certain.[67]

5. *Income: An Inherently Defective Concept*

In addition to arguments that an income tax base is less fair than a consumption tax base, the case for consumption taxation has included the proposition that an income tax is necessarily inequitable because income is an inherently defective concept that cannot be rationally elaborated.

a. *Capital Gains*

The principal argument that income is impossible to define, even in theory, offered by Nicholas Kaldor in his influential book, *An Expenditure Tax*, is that the income concept cannot properly measure capital gains that are due to changes in the interest rate.[68] Kaldor com-

67. Professor Martin Feldstein has used the lifetime view in a somewhat different way to argue that the Haig-Simons principle conflicts with the notion of horizonal equity implied by economic theory. He concludes that if there is anything to be learned from utilitarianism about the equity of alternative tax bases, a tax on consumption or labor income is preferable to a tax on total income. Feldstein, *supra* note 2, at S37-38; *see* Feldstein, *On the Theory of Tax Reform*, 6 J. PUB. ECON. 77, 86-89 (1976).

The crux of Professor Feldstein's argument is that accretion reaches only income and not other possible sources of utility, such as effort, leisure, or prestige. Because these other items are left out of the accretion equity accounting, they may also be left out of the consumption equity accounting. But once they are removed, utility realistically depends on income only in a very short period; over a longer period it is dependent on consumption, so utilitarianism mandates taxation of consumption, not income.

This argument avoids the defects in the endowment argument pointed out in the text, *see* pp. 1101-05 *supra*, by reasoning to a conclusion in which the individuals under comparison have precisely the same consumption path, so that the difficulty of comparing equal earners who consume in different periods does not exist. The argument does not suggest that consumption taxation complies strictly with the utilitarian formulation of horizontal equity; rather, it simply indicates that if utility depends only on consumption, the consumption tax is superior. The conclusion of the argument also depends on the premise that the case for the income tax assumes equal tastes. Identical tastes might well be assumed for effort, leisure, and prestige under the Haig-Simons concept, with differences in tastes for present and future consumption permitted. In that case, individuals with the same present value of income may well have different consumption paths. If they, nevertheless, have the same utility level, then Professor Feldstein's argument for a flat-rate wage or consumption tax reduces to the argument presented in BLUEPRINTS, *supra* note 3: it depends on an equality of present value or endowment *ex ante*, and is subject to the same objections raised above. Progression, on that view, would again support a graduated wage tax rather than a graduated consumption tax on qualified account.

68. N. KALDOR, *supra* note 5, at 44-46, 69-70. Kaldor's other arguments on the grounds of theoretical inconsistency are, as he concedes, arguments against defects in the then existing system of taxation in the United Kingdom, not arguments against an income tax free of such defects. Thus, the proposition that wealth, as well as income, is a source of

pares increases in asset values that arise from increases in the expected income-stream produced by an asset with increases in asset values that arise solely from a change in the interest rate at which an unchanged income-stream is discounted. While the latter involves an increase in "spending power" due to the increased capital value, it is said to be inferior to a capital gain of the former type, which involves an increase in spending power even if the capital asset is not sold, because the annual income produced by the asset will be increased. Since there is no adjustment, even in theory, that could account for this difference in spending power, there is supposedly no way in which the concept of income can correctly treat these two very different kinds of capital appreciation.

Kaldor's argument may be illustrated as follows. If $10,000 is invested in a perpetual bond yielding ten percent, the bondholder will receive $1,000 annually in interest. If the interest rate subsequently falls to five percent, the capital value of the bond will increase, other things being equal, to $20,000; the bondholder will continue to receive $1,000 annually so long as he retains the bond. It is the fact that retention of the bond will not generate increased cash flow—and additional consumption possibilities—that supports the conclusion that the increase in current value cannot be considered taxable income. Yet the bondholder is certainly better off, even if he does not sell the bond, than a second bondholder who did not invest in this asset until after the decline in the interest rate. The first bondholder will receive twice as much each year as will the later bondholder, since the latter will receive only $500 annually from his $10,000 investment at five percent.

The conclusion that the Haig-Simons definition reaches the conceptually correct results in these cases is reinforced by considering another example. Suppose $10,000 is invested in a parking lot that produces $1,000 yearly in net income. Due to the unexpected construction of a nearby casino, the yearly income from parking doubles to $2,000, so that, other things being equal, the capital value of the parking lot also doubles to $20,000. The Haig-Simons definition would

"spending power," *id.* at 31-33, is an argument for enactment of a wealth tax, not for repeal of the income tax. And the concern that some receipts should be treated differently from others under a progressive tax because they are bunched into a single period—and may not be repeated—*id.* at 34-35, leads to the conclusion that some sort of averaging is appropriate under an income or consumption tax, not that the income concept is defective. The inconsistent exclusion of particular kinds of receipts, *id.* at 35-37, suggests that the income tax would be better if the tax base were comprehensive, not that a comprehensive income tax is undesirable. Finally, the need to adjust the taxation of capital income for inflation, *see id.* at 42-43, is in theory soluble by indexing the basis of assets and liabilities.

Consumption Tax

require inclusion of the $10,000 increment in income. When the parking lot owner receives $2,000 in income each year, he will be taxed on twice what the first of the foregoing bondholders receives ($1,000 in interest), leaving the taxpayers in their correct relative positions in terms of market value: the parking lot owner has a gain on his investment as well as additional annual cash flow; the first bondholder has a gain on his investment, but no more cash flow than he expected; and the second bondholder has no gain, and only his expected cash flow. To indicate that some market value—Kaldor's "spending power"—is more relevant than others is only to assert that spending—here cash flow—may be a better tax base than income, not that income is somehow a defective concept.

Notwithstanding the fact that a short-term investor (such as the later bond purchaser above) receives no deduction for the loss he suffers by holding cash when interest rates are falling, it has been argued that the investor who takes a long position should not be taxed on his gain, because his position relative to the short-term investor will be adequately reflected by the fact that his investment is earning interest at a greater rate than the short-term investor's.[69] This view would again seem to depend on a Fisherian view of.income as consumption; it does not, in any event, suggest that the accretion result is impossible to elaborate, even in theory. Imagine an investor who purchases a one-year bond for $10,000 at the end of Year 1, when the interest rate is ten percent, so that he will receive $1,000 in interest at the end of Year 2 as well as his $10,000 principal. If the interest rate falls immediately to five percent, the value of his bond will increase by $476.18 as shown in the following table:

TABLE V

Due in 1 year	*Present Value At 10 Percent*	*Present Value At 5 Percent*
$10,000 principal	$9090.91	$9523.80
$ 1,000 interest	909.09	952.38
Total	$10,000.00	$10,476.18

An investor who purchased the bond after the change in interest rates would have to pay $10,476.18 for the right to receive $11,000 in Year 2.

The Haig-Simons concept would tax the first investor on $476.18 in Year 1 and both investors on $523.82 in Year 2 ($11,000-$10,476.18).

69. *See Consumption Tax, supra* note 1, at 1144. Although Professor Andrews does not discuss losses, presumably he would also conclude that the loss incurred by a bondholder when interest rates increase should not be taken into account.

Taxing both investors only on their interest in Year 2 would achieve the same total tax, but in different years:

TABLE VI

	Haig-Simons Concept		*Tax on Interest Only*	
	Year 1	*Year 2*	*Year 1*	*Year 2*
1st Investor	$476.18	$523.82	0	$1,000.00
2nd Investor	0	523.82	0	523.82

The argument that taxing only the interest adequately accounts for the differences between the two investors depends on the consumption-tax premise that economic return should not be taken into account until consumed, whereas the result under the Haig-Simons concept reflects the fact that, in Year 1, the first investor has experienced a market gain relative to the second investor and that they are in identical positions thereafter. Relying only on the difference in interest received to reflect difference in position would require treatment that is just backwards in terms of market value, the touchstone for income taxation: the taxpayers would be treated identically when their positions differ in Year 1, and differently when their positions are the same in Year 2.[70]

70. As is traditional in accretion analysis, attention up to this point has been focused on assets, leaving liabilities totally out of account. But the bond transaction discussed above involves a borrower as well as a lender. If we assume that this loan functioned solely to permit the borrower to consume $10,000 in Year 1 instead of $11,000 in Year 2, no new social product would be created thereby, with the result that Haig-Simons income in Year 1 would appear to exceed social product by $476.18. There is, however, an offsetting loss in this case: the precisely equivalent diminution in value experienced by the borrower when the interest rate declined from 10% to 5%. Prior to that moment, the borrower could have discharged his liability by paying the lender $10,000; once the interest rate declined, however, the creditor would discharge the liability, by selling the bond to the issuer, only on receipt of $10,476.18, the market price of the bond.

Although liabilities have not been much discussed in the context of a comprehensive income tax, such a tax would necessarily take into account changes in what has been called the "anti-value" of liabilities, as well as changes in the value of the corresponding asset. W. Barnett, Note on Accounting for Transactions in Liabilities (unpublished manuscript on file with *Yale Law Journal*). The income tax now in effect, which is triggered by realization events, should require inclusion of the offsetting gain and permit deduction of the offsetting loss if realized. Transfer of $10,476.18 from the borrower to the lender in cancellation of the obligation should give rise to $476.18 in income to the lender as the excess of amount realized over basis and a $476.18 deduction to the borrower as the excess of amount paid over the amount received. *See, e.g.*, Commissioner v. Sisto Financial Corp., 139 F.2d 253, 255 (2d Cir. 1943); Elverson Corp. v. Helvering, 122 F.2d 295, 297 (2d Cir. 1941); Treas. Reg. § 1.163-3(c) (1979).

Thus far, only the effect of interest rate changes on debt instruments has been discussed, but the value of equity assets may also change with interest rates. Consider a taxpayer *A* who buys an asset—say, another parking lot—that will provide $100 in annual asset-services—in this case, parking spaces—in perpetuity. At a discount rate of 10%, *A* will pay $1000 for the asset, which will be worth $2000 if the discount rate at once falls to 5 percent, yielding an immediate gain of $1000 in Year 1. Again, where is the offsetting loss that is necessary if Haig-Simons income is to equal social product? The in-

Consumption Tax

b. *Human Capital*

A second theoretical defect that is said to inhere in the concept of income is its inability to deal with investments in "human capital."[71] An individual who invests part of his wages in the stock market or in real estate must invest after-tax dollars because wages are subject to the income tax. Similarly, a person who saves, that is, does not realize, the appreciation in value of corporate securities or real estate would have income under the Haig-Simons concept, although the realization criterion would preclude taxation under current law until the appreciated assets were sold or otherwise disposed of.

What then is the proper treatment of a taxpayer who forgoes several years of wages to attend professional school in order to increase his lifetime earnings? And what of the taxpayer who possesses a significant earning capacity due to some innate ability that is greatly valued in the marketplace? Finally, what of shifts in market valuations of an individual's ability, whether innate or developed?

Critics of the concept of income argue that all of these individuals possess human capital, which should in theory be treated by the Haig-Simons concept like all other capital investments. Thus the professional school student should be treated like the wage earner who invests in the stock market: forgone wages should be imputed to the student, as should a corresponding investment in educational capital.[72] To do otherwise, the argument runs, would be to permit investments in human capital to be made out of pretax dollars, while other investments must be made out of after-tax dollars. In realization terms, investment in human capital on this view is currently expensed (that is, deducted) in the year made if the investment involves forgoing wages, whereas other capital expenditures must, of course, be capitalized and recovered on sale or through depreciation or depletion deductions over the life of the asset. Similarly, the individual who has an innate ability to play basketball or to pick successful television shows has at some point in

crease in asset-value depends on a continuation of the previously expected return of $100 annually in asset-services; by hypothesis, there must be a taxpayer (or group of taxpayers) *B* who will continue to pay $100 annually for the asset-services. Although the fall in interest rates has not affected the annual rentals *B* must pay—$100 in perpetuity—the present value of that stream of future payments has grown from $1000 to $2000. Thus the anti-value of *B*'s implicit obligation has grown by precisely the same amount that the value of the asset (which depends on the existence of the implicit obligation) has risen, so *A*'s gain is just offset by *B*'s loss.

71. *See* MEADE REPORT, *supra* note 4, at 39-40; Klein, *supra* note 1; *Consumption Tax*, *supra* note 1, at 1145-46.

72. *A fortiori* out-of-pocket expenditures should be capitalized. *See* McNulty, *Tax Policy and Tuition Credit Legislation: Federal Income Tax Allowances for Personal Costs of Higher Education*, 61 CALIF. L. REV. 1, 14-36 (1973).

his life acquired significant human capital, which is an increment in wealth that should in theory be subject to taxation under the Haig-Simons concept. Finally, shifts in market valuation of various skills should presumably be recognized in the calculation of taxable income.

The logical implication of these results is that individuals would in theory be taxed on changes in the present value of what they could earn, quite apart from what they do earn. Yet the idea of any tax on earning capacity is inconsistent with widely accepted concepts of individual liberty because it would disregard such personal choices as which career to pursue, the amount of time to devote to work as opposed to leisure, and so on.[73] Consumption-tax advocates have thus concluded that the concept of income is not capable of rational elaboration in our society.[74] Apparently that conclusion would also apply to a comprehensive wealth tax applied during the taxpayer's lifetime, since human capital would presumably have to be included in such a tax base if logic required increments in such value to be reached by the income tax.

There are at least two possible responses to these concerns. The first is that the logical implication of the concept of income is indeed that human capital should be treated like other capital, so that in theory invested imputed income should be taken into the tax base, just as in theory imputed income that is consumed should arguably be taken into account.[75] Then, as in the case of consumed imputed income, the relevant issue becomes whether practical considerations preclude the taxation of such income. But even if this aspect of the concept of income were thought incapable of practical application, that would not establish that there was anything logically defective about the concept or the tax on incremental earning capacity that it would support. Rigorous as such a response might be, however, it is not very convincing, given the general institutional bias in our society against slavery and other means of permitting the realization of a market value for human capital.

The existence of that bias provides the ground for the second, and

73. Kelman suggests that, apart from this libertarian defect, a capacity tax "may be the ideal measure of ability to pay . . . might best achieve the tax system's goal of measuring the inequality of economic power . . . [and] might also best assess the sacrifices a particular taxpayer is making when he is asked to give a certain sum of money to the state." Kelman, *Personal Deductions Revisited: Why They Fit Poorly in an "Ideal" Income Tax and Why They Fit Worse in a Far From Ideal World*, 31 STAN. L. REV. 831, 841 (1979).

74. Klein, *supra* note 1, at 463-69.

75. For a discussion of imputed income that is consumed, see H. SIMONS, *supra* note 10, at 110-122.

preferable, response to this alleged defect in the concept of income. The bias reflects a view that persons cannot be forced to work against their will. Like other capital, human capital embodies a capacity for production, but for reasons of liberty we distinguish human capital with regard to forced production, reflecting the fundamental distinction between an individual and the fruits of his labor mentioned earlier.[76] Although the matter can be disputed, people may be thought of as distinct from things, even when the things are the product of human endeavor. The individual's personhood may be said to extend to his productive capacity, but not to his product.

The legal system has embraced the distinction between persons and things not only in the prohibition against slavery, but in statutes that prohibit long-term contracts for personal services[77] and commerce in infants,[78] as well as in the absence of specific performance as a remedy for breach of a contract to perform personal services.[79] The fact that the Haig-Simons calculation leaves changes in the value of human capital out of account is but another iteration of the same distinction.

Moreover, legal constraints deprive human productive capacity of significant marketable capital value in most cases. There is simply no way a medical school graduate can cash in on the high income potential of an M.D. without working as a physician. To be sure, a lending institution is likely to lend more to such a graduate than it would to a young artist with only a meager prospect. But no lender is very likely to extend credit even to an M.D. beyond the amount of a few years of salary, unless other security is provided. Indeed, the inability of a person in our society to become an indentured servant or to sell himself into slavery calls into question the very label of human "capital" in these cases. It is true that by discounting a stream of future earnings, the value of a prospective earnings pattern can be "capitalized," but if there is no way in which that capitalized value can be used currently to command economic resources, why should it be counted as part of the "store of property rights" in the Haig-Simons calculation?

76. *See* pp. 1096-97 *supra*.

77. *See, e.g.*, LA. CIV. CODE ANN. art. 167 (West Supp. 1978) ("Persons who have attained the age of majority cannot bind themselves for a longer term than ten years."). Even in the absence of statutory prohibition, the common law has been hostile to such contracts. *See* J. CALAMARI & J. PERILLO, CONTRACTS 47-48 (2d ed. 1977); 3A A. CORBIN, CONTRACTS § 684 (1960 & Supp. 1971).

78. *See, e.g.*, 18 PA. CONS. STAT. ANN. § 4305 (Purdon 1973) ("A person is guilty of a misdemeanor of the first degree if he deals in humanity, by trading, bartering, buying, selling, or dealing in infant children.")

79. *See* J. CALAMARI & J. PERILLO, *supra* note 77, at 585-87; 5A A. CORBIN, *supra* note 77, § 1204 (1964 & Supp. 1971).

For some individuals there is, of course, a significant market value to their services that can be realized in a guaranteed capital amount. An outstanding professional athlete may be able to trade his production for future years for a large sum of money, which he will receive even if he is injured and cannot perform. In fact, if the relevant period is short enough, most taxpayers can anticipate the return on their future labor by sale or hypothecation. But even when a value can be so obtained, the rights of the purchaser or lender are not the same as those obtained when goods are involved. If the professional athlete fails to perform, he cannot be forced so to do, even though the delivery of goods sold under a contract might be required. If an individual has borrowed against future earnings, which he fails to receive because he declines to work, the lender cannot foreclose on the borrower's productive capacity and operate it to regain his loan proceeds. The legal rules reflect a physical as well as philosophical difference between goods and personal services: goods can be forcefully separated from their owner with relatively little effort, as compared with forcing an individual to work against his will.

A different way of putting the legal point is that unlike the marketing of goods, the sale or hypothecation of future services does not really involve the transfer of services, but only of the right to claim damages if they are not later transferred and, in some cases, the right to prevent transfer to another buyer. In terms of the distinction between persons and things, a legal education is inherently a part of the lawyer's person, unlike his possessions or product. Whether income from personal services can be anticipated or not, human capital thus has a legal status fundamentally different from that of other capital, so that the different treatment accorded it by the income tax is not at all illogical.

Stating the point yet another way, the concept of human capital is not helpful in defining the income tax base, because the concept is entirely an *ex ante* formulation when there is no market mechanism for realizing the value of the capital. While the human capital amount that is arrived at by summing the present value of future income streams has had a great impact on economic theory[80] and is undoubtedly useful for some purposes—such as deciding whether to go to professional school in order to increase lifetime earnings—that amount is not germane to the interpersonal calculation of the income tax base, which

80. *See* Sahota, *Theories of Personal Income Distribution: A Survey*, 16 J. ECON. LITERATURE 1, 11-19 (1978).

Consumption Tax

concerns changes in power to command goods and services in the marketplace.[81]

c. *Conceptual Incoherence*

Whatever the particular treatment of capital gains and human capital, income also has been rejected as a generally incoherent concept for purposes other than taxation. These well-known objections to the idea of income do not, however, undermine its appropriateness as a tax base. Three different versions of conceptual incoherence can be identified.

First, income has been rejected in economic and accounting analysis because the concept includes not only gains that were, or should have been, anticipated to some extent, but also totally unexpected windfalls.[82] Such unanticipated changes in position are irrelevant to the economist, who seeks to explain behavior based on what individuals know about the future. An accountant reporting on the stewardship of management in order to provide a sound basis for investment decisions, and a financial analyst seeking to maximize future wealth, would also find such unanticipated changes irrelevant. Accordingly, economists and accountants have attempted, without great success, to develop concepts of income that omit such windfall gains and losses.[83] In addition,

81. As in the case of changes in the rate of interest, it should be inquired whether the view taken here of human capital is consistent with the idea of income as product that the Haig-Simons definition allocates among taxpayers. If production of a new machine is regarded as income to be allocated to its owner, why is not the same true of a medical school education? One might respond that the medical-school education is necessarily not a completed asset, because it is not clear that the graduate will work as a physician. But that response leads to the conclusion that a society with more doctors (or lawyers) is no better off than the identical society, save the professional education. The preferable answer seems to me that there is indeed social product, but a product that is not subject to the same market transactions under existing legal rules. Hence the Haig-Simons definition appropriately leaves it out of account when computing personal income.

82. *See* J. HICKS, VALUE AND CAPITAL 171-81 (2d ed. 1946); N. KALDOR, *supra* note 5, at 67-69; Solomons, *Economic and Accounting Concepts of Income*, 36 ACCOUNTING REV. 374, 374-83 (1961).

83. *See* J. HICKS, *supra* note 82, at 172-73 (defining income as "the maximum amount which can be spent during a period if there is to be an expectation of maintaining intact the capital value of prospective receipts . . ."). When applied *ex post* to the actual values of capital at the beginning and end of an accounting period, the result is simply the Haig-Simons formulation. When applied *ex ante* at the beginning of the accounting period, the definition requires a hypothetical minuend: that is, the value that the capital is *expected* to have at the end of the period, from which the (known) capital value at the beginning can be subtracted in order to yield the period's income. If applied *ex post*, but adjusted to eliminate changes in expectations, the definition requires a hypothetical subtrahend: that is, a revised initial value—as estimated at the close of the period—which may be subtracted from the known value of the capital at the end of the period, in order to yield the period's income. *See* N. KALDOR, *supra* note 5, at 62-63; MEADE REPORT, *supra* note 4, at 31-33 (suggesting and rejecting following definition of taxable income as

modern financial analysis has emphasized cash flows and fund accounting more than the distinction between income and capital.[84] For our purposes, however, these concerns and modifications are simply not germane. Economic, accounting, and financial analyses are necessarily concerned with the future. Their orientation is, by hypothesis, *ex ante*. But for tax purposes, income *ex post* is what matters, and that concept should include all gains and losses, whether anticipated or not. As argued earlier, distribution of tax burdens should be concerned with what has happened, not with what can be expected.

A second version of the incoherence argument appears as a problem in national-income accounting, which is itself an *ex post* measure. A nation's production may be defined as the aggregate of the goods and services produced during the accounting period, but disparate physical quantities cannot be meaningfully summed. Accordingly, the national product is computed by summing each good's and service's total market value, the result of multiplying the physical quantity of that good or service by the market price per unit.[85] But a problem arises when aggregations made at different times (or in different places) are to be compared: since prices and quantities may have changed, how can the sum of quantities with different multiplicands be compared in any meaningful sense? In terms of the Haig-Simons definition, this objection might be framed as follows: how can wealth at the beginning of the period be compared with wealth at the end, when the prices and quantities that are multiplied and summed may be different?[86]

In general, the incomparability of national income aggregates can be resolved by the use of index numbers—the second-period quantities can, for example, be multiplied by the first-period prices, so that comparison in those prices is possible. Alternatively, the comparison can be made with first-period quantities at second-period prices. Such index numbers necessarily yield only approximate (and sometimes dif-

alternative to Haig-Simons concept: amount that individual "could consume in any one year and yet be left with the resources and expectations at the end of that year which would enable him to maintain the same level of consumption indefinitely in the future"); Alexander, *Income Measurement in a Dynamic Economy*, in STUDY GROUP ON BUSINESS INCOME, AMERICAN INSTITUTE OF ACCOUNTANTS, FIVE MONOGRAPHS ON BUSINESS INCOME 1, 62-73 (1950), *reprinted in* STUDIES IN ACCOUNTING THEORY 126, 177-88 (W. Baxter & S. Davidson eds., rev'd by D. Solomons 1962) (suggesting use of concept of "variable income" to eliminate such changes in expectation).

84. *See, e.g.*, E. FAMA & M. MILLER, THE THEORY OF FINANCE 58-340 (1972).

85. *See* R. STONE & G. STONE, *supra* note 21, at 11-30. Duplication must be avoided by counting only the value added by each industry, since some products may be used in the production of others.

86. *See* Samuelson, *The Evaluation of "Social Income": Capital Formation and Wealth*, in F. LUTZ, THE THEORY OF CAPITAL 32, 56 (D. Hague ed. 1961).

ferent) solutions, so an average of their results may be considered the most accurate comparison.[87]

Whether or not this response to the charge of incommensurability is acceptable for national-income accounting purposes, the charge is irrelevant for tax purposes. The need for index numbers that arises from the national-income accountant's desire to eliminate changes in relative prices does not exist in defining the tax base, which should take into account gains and losses due to changes in relative prices, as well as gains and losses due to changes in quantities.[88] The comparison under the Haig-Simons concept is of wealth, not product, at two different times. Thus the aggregate value assigned by the market to a particular bundle of rights is the ultimate goal of the inquiry, and not a mere intermediate step leading toward a final calculation of changes in quantity of output. In short, the intertemporal comparison called for by the income tax is quite intelligible, given the use of index numbers in periods of inflation, a modification that is widely understood today.[89]

The last objection to income on the grounds of incoherence, which is also found in the literature of national-income accounting, accepts the *ex post* approach and the index-number solution to the problem of comparing consumer commodities in two different periods, but argues that aggregation of consumption and accumulation in any single period cannot result in an intelligible amount.[90] The argument can be stated in conceptual terms, or as following from the purpose of the income measurement. Focusing first on the concepts to be aggregated, consumption and accumulation can be said to be dissimilar, indeed opposite, quantities—the former relating to resources that have been used up (final goods), the latter pertaining to resources that have not (intermediate goods)—so that their sum is not meaningful.[91] Under the view of the Haig-Simons definition taken here, that argument is not convincing unless production and product are also to be regarded as incoherent concepts. If those concepts are conceded meaning, then there

87. *See* R. STONE & G. STONE, *supra* note 21, at 95-97; I. FISHER, THE MAKING OF INDEX NUMBERS (3d ed. 1927).

88. *See* Hicks, *Maintaining Capital Intact: A Further Suggestion*, 9 ECONOMICA 174, 178 (1942) (suggesting that "depreciation" of assets be distinguished from "capital losses" on such assets due to unexpected obsolescence). The Haig-Simons concept would make no such distinction among diminutions in market value. For additional discussion of this issue, see Pigou, *Maintaining Capital Intact*, 8 ECONOMICA 271 (1941); Hayek, *Maintaining Capital Intact: A Reply*, 8 ECONOMICA 276 (1941).

89. *See* H. Aaron, *supra* note 29.

90. *See* Samuelson, *supra* note 86, at 44-51.

91. *See Consumption Tax*, *supra* note 1, at 1115 (arguing that consumption and accumulation adjustments to tax-paying capacity differ in a number of ways).

is nothing incoherent about regarding admittedly different *uses* of income (or product) as summing to total income (or product).

The alternative version of this argument suggests that the purpose of national-income accounting is the measurement of a society's welfare, and that while consumption and accumulation are valuable indices of such welfare, their sum does not represent a single preferable index because it fails to capture the future welfare that comes from owning capital.[92] For our purposes, it is enough that consumption is equally defective as a measure of welfare on this view; only a wealth-like magnitude can provide a meaningful single index of such welfare, because only such a magnitude is sufficiently future-oriented.[93]

To summarize, our brief review of the non-tax objections to the concept of income indicates that for many purposes the concept may indeed be an inadequate, and, in some cases, an incoherent idea. But none of those objections leads to the conclusion that the concept of income should be rejected as a tax base because it is inherently defective.

6. *The Consumption Tax and Liberty*

As compared with a tax on personal earning capacity, both the consumption and income taxes are concerned with what an individual chooses to do, rather than with what he might do. Accordingly, it can be argued that both are preferable to a tax levied on capacity because they interfere less with personal choice and liberty. It has been further argued that if taxation of capacity is to be avoided in the interests of liberty, only consumed products should enter the tax base, so the consumption tax is to be preferred to the income tax because the former is levied only when a person chooses to consume.[94]

This argument fails to accept the distinction between persons and things that was given as the reason for not taxing capacity in the case of human capital.[95] It would seem perfectly plausible to exclude leisure and talents from the tax base on the grounds of personal liberty and at the same time to include economic capacity in the form of unconsumed income; forcing a person to share his income from working is simply not the same as forcing him to work in the first place.[96]

There is, moreover, a sense in which consumption taxation is less consistent with individual freedom than is income taxation. The dis-

92. *See* Samuelson, *supra* note 86, at 51-56.

93. *Id.*

94. C. FRIED, *supra* note 39, at 147-50.

95. *See* pp. 1113-17 *supra*.

96. *But see* R. NOZICK, *supra* note 43, at 169 (viewing income taxation as "on a par with forced labor").

tributive premise of the consumption tax is that quantitative consumption decisions are for collective, not individual, judgment. It certainly does not seem obvious that this premise shows more respect for individual liberty than does the income tax view that distribution of product is for collective decision. A person's collective responsibilities are concluded at the time of production under the income tax; by contrast, under the consumption tax those responsibilities are not discharged until a person consumes his last resource. It is precisely this inability to escape collective responsibilities by consuming existing resources that has attracted some supporters to the consumption tax in the United Kingdom.[97]

III. Conclusions and the Relevance of Wealth

The arguments for the superiority of the consumption tax over the income tax are not convincing even on the terms in which the case has been made—a direct comparison of income and consumption taxes, with the question of wealth taxation put aside for another day.

The Haig-Simons definition of income is best understood as an interpersonal perspective on the measurement of each taxable unit's share of the product of the society's private capital and labor during the accounting period. The equity case for income taxation thus can be premised on society's claim on a portion of that product for redistribution or for the production of public goods. Consumption can also be justified as a criterion of distributional equity, by relating society's claim to standards of living rather than to product. Essentially *ex post* constructs, either conclusion requires agreement that outcomes rather than expectations are what matter for fairness in taxation.

Much of the recent case for substituting a consumption tax for the income tax depends on the diametrically opposed premise—that expectations alone are relevant. The *ex ante* view of Fisherian capital theory, while appropriate to economic analysis in general, is not suitable for interpersonal measurement of tax equity, which should be evaluated on an *ex post* basis. The life-cycle hypothesis, the human capital construct, and the discounting of future consumption to present value in general are therefore not helpful in comparing the two taxes. Nor does the consumption tax appear superior in terms of conceptual coherence or its effect on personal liberty. Nor, finally, do appeals to metaphors such as a common pool or to unknowable levels of psycho-

97. *See, e.g.*, N. KALDOR, *supra* note 5, at 31-34; MEADE REPORT, *supra* note 4, at 33.

logical satisfaction help to choose between taxes that must realistically be levied on economic resources.

In short, either levy can be justified as fair tax policy in the abstract, with the choice depending on whether the social-product or standards-of-living version of distributive justice can be said to be superior as a matter of political or moral philosophy. In the absence of a clear showing as to that superiority, no choice can sensibly be made between the two taxes—at least as long as wealth is excluded from the comparison.

This indeterminacy suggests that wealth should not be ignored in discussions of the choice of a tax base.[98] Indeed, the strongest argument in favor of income taxation as opposed to consumption taxation as a matter of fairness is that only income taxation reaches wealth or the return to wealth.[99] The income tax includes wealth in the tax base from two different perspectives.[100] On the sources side of the personal income account, income from capital as well as labor is taxed. If all income from all capital were reached, as advocates of a comprehensive income tax base urge, the levy on such income could be considered a proxy for the taxation of the capital itself. On the uses side of the personal income account, inclusion of accumulation means that additions to wealth are taxed each year. The income tax can accordingly be thought of as an incremental tax that reaches the capital amount of all wealth, but only once with respect to each increment to wealth.

Two objections to these reasons for preferring the income tax are at once apparent. First, it is not obvious that wealth should be subject to taxation. Second, if wealth is to be taxed, the base of the consumption tax may be a better proxy than the base of the income tax, especially when existing wealth taxes are taken into account. As to the first point, the argument for wealth taxation on fairness grounds must be that no citizen is entitled to a disproportionate share (however determined) of the benefits of holding wealth. Accumulation itself and not merely its supposed goal of consumption would be made subject to collective decisionmaking on the theory that wealth not only embodies capacity

98. For a recent attempt to introduce the wealth tax into discussions of United States tax policy, see Cooper, *Taking Wealth Taxation Seriously*, 34 RECORD OF THE ASS'N OF THE BAR OF THE CITY OF NEW YORK 24, 24-57 (Jan.-Feb. 1979). For a general discussion of the wealth tax, see C. SANDFORD, J. WILLIS & D. IRONSIDE, AN ANNUAL WEALTH TAX (1975).

99. *See Consumption Tax*, *supra* note 1, at 1169; *Andrews' Reply*, *supra* note 1, at 957.

100. The precise character of the inclusion of wealth under the income tax appears more elusive when our discussion of risky and riskless assets is recalled. Under certain assumptions, it could be argued that the only difference between the consumption and income tax bases is the treatment of riskless return on invested assets. Even under those assumptions, however, the income tax is arguably preferable to the consumption tax if it is thought that the distributive claim extends beyond wages and windfalls. *See* pp. 1105-07 *supra*.

Consumption Tax

for future consumption, but also yields current benefits such as security and independence, which are no more subject to a controlling moral claim by the wealth-holder than are income or consumption. Indeed, such benefits can be conceived of as imputed and consumed income.

One response to this sort of argument for wealth taxation might be that there is no greater reason for collectivizing wealth than there is for collectivizing other forms of security, independence, and power.[101] If the wealthy investor must share his wealth with less wealthy, should not the talented professional whose wealth is in the form of human capital have to do the same? This argument, like that in favor of measuring and taxing income invested in human capital, ignores the fundamental distinction between persons and things.[102] If that distinction is accepted, it does not seem inconsistent to set social limits on differences in marketable wealth, and not to set similar limits on other sorts of differences that might be substitutes for such wealth.

Even assuming that wealth provides a plausible basis for a collective claim, there are several shortcomings with the income tax as a proxy wealth tax.[103] First, previously accumulated wealth would not be taxed currently (although it would have been taxed when accumulated, and current income therefrom would be included in the tax base). Second, tax rates arguably should be graduated on the basis of wealth, rather than on the basis of income or increments to wealth. Finally, at any given level of income, the rich may save less, so a graduated consumption tax might be more progressive with respect to wealth than would be a graduated income tax. Even if the empirical premise in the last argument is rejected, the first two points identify undeniable differences between wealth and income tax bases.

Related to the efficacy of the income tax as a proxy wealth tax is the effect of other taxes reaching capital, such as the estate and gift taxes, state and local property taxes, and the corporate income tax. It might be that given the existence of these other levies, income taxation is not the best means of accomplishing the desired result, particularly if other policies—such as including bequests in a donor's consumption tax base—are considered.[104]

101. This argument would proceed as follows: If wealth is to be taxed because it affords to its holders a substantial measure of security, independence, and power, then other personal holdings—such as a prominent family name, innate physical or mental talents, or personal charisma—that can just as surely provide security, independence, and power should be taxed as well; if we cannot or will not reach the latter, then we should not single out the former for taxation. *See* Klein, *supra* note 1, at 467-69.

102. *See* pp. 1114-15 *supra*.

103. *See Consumption Tax, supra* note 1, at 1118-19, 1170-72.

104. *See* Graetz, *Implementing a Progressive Consumption Tax*, 92 HARV. L. REV. 1575, 1624-25 (1979).

In short, considerations of wealth raise many issues that cannot be decided by an abstract comparison of the income and consumption bases. Only polar conclusions are possible. If the argument for wealth taxation were completely rejected—perhaps because capacity of any sort were concluded to be too inchoate to support a collective claim, or because the current benefits of holding wealth were rejected as trivial—then the choice for a consumption tax would presumably be clear, since only that tax wholly excludes wealth from the tax base. On the other hand, if wealth were thought to be an appropriate subject for a distributive claim, and if consumption were deemed an inadequate proxy for wealth, then it would be inappropriate to substitute a consumption tax for the income tax without simultaneous enactment of an appropriate wealth tax, whatever that might be.

If the choice to be made were between a consumption tax with some form of wealth or transfer tax and an income tax with or without such taxes, then a decision would not be possible in the abstract. Rather, the choice would depend on the exact components of the two alternative tax packages. The way the issue has been formed by most recent consumption tax proponents—income versus consumption taxation, with the question of wealth taxation put aside for another day—is thus inadequate unless wealth is rejected entirely as a basis for taxation.

[8]

Time Preference and Tax Equity

Mark Kelman*

One might prefer a progressive tax on consumption[1] to a tax on income[2] for many reasons. Perhaps most significantly, a tax levied

---

* A.B. 1972, J.D. 1976, Harvard University. Professor of Law, Stanford University. I wish to thank Tom Heller, Mitch Polinsky, and Roberta Romano for their valuable comments on an earlier draft. Errors remain mine. This research was supported by the Stanford Legal Research Fund, made possible by a bequest from the Estate of Ira S. Lillick and by gifts from Roderick E. and Carla A. Hills and other friends of the Stanford Law School.

1. Under standard accounts of a consumption or expenditure tax, individuals would be taxed on their consumption only. Business and investment expenditures, as well as loan repayments, would be deducted when made; all receipts, including borrowings and returns of capital, would be immediately included except where reinvested. Savings would be treated as qualified retirement savings are currently treated under I.R.C. §§ 402–403, 408–409 (1976): Current savings and income earned from those savings would be excluded from income until the funds were withdrawn for consumption, at which time both the initial investment and the return would be taxable. *See* N. KALDOR, AN EXPENDITURE TAX (1955); UNITED STATES DEP'T OF THE TREASURY, BLUEPRINTS FOR BASIC TAX REFORM 113–44 (1977) [hereinafter cited as BLUEPRINTS]; WHAT SHOULD BE TAXED—INCOME OR EXPENDITURE? (J. Pechman ed. 1980) [hereinafter cited as WHAT SHOULD BE TAXED]; Andrews, *A Consumption-Type or Cash Flow Personal Income Tax,* 87 HARV. L. REV. 1113 (1974) [hereinafter cited as Andrews, *Consumption Tax*]; Graetz, *Implementing a Progressive Consumption Tax,* 92 HARV. L. REV. 1575 (1979).

Although defining consumption is generally unproblematic, several troublesome areas do exist. For example, commentators disagree about whether or not medical care expenditures constitute consumption: If they do, they should be taxed, but if such expenditures simply restore the taxpayer to his baseline (pre-disease) psychic position, they should not be taxed. For another example, some commentators believe that gifts (including charitable ones) do not constitute consumption because the donor does not appropriate any resources for his exclusive use. Others believe that gifts do constitute consumption either because they presumptively increase the donor's utility at least as much as an alternative expenditure or because the tax ought to be levied on the donor's actual total receipts as well as the donee's without regard to their use (because the sum of windfall and earnings capacity, constrained only by the state's desire not to force people to exercise their capacity, is the ideal base). *Compare* Andrews, *Personal Deductions in an Ideal Income Tax,* 86 HARV. L. REV. 309, 350–75 (1972) (arguing that neither medical care expenditures nor charitable gifts constitutes consumption) [hereinafter cited as Andrews, *Personal Deductions*] *with* H. SIMONS, PERSONAL INCOME TAXATION: THE DEFINITION OF INCOME AS A PROBLEM OF FISCAL POLICY (1938) *and* S. SURREY, PATHWAYS TO TAX REFORM 12–14, 20–22 (1973) (both arguing that gifts should be taxed to the donor because they give him psychic benefits) *and* Kelman, *Personal Deductions Revisited: Why They Fit Poorly in an "Ideal" Income Tax and Why They Fit Worse in a Far from Ideal World,* 31 STAN. L. REV. 831 (1979) (proper base is net receipts).

2. From a use perspective, income is seen as the sum of certain carefully defined uses that we call consumption plus accumulation. *See* H. SIMONS, *supra* note 1, at 50 (income

solely on consumption would raise the effective after-tax rate of return on investment relative to the rate of return that would prevail in a world with an income tax.[3] To the extent that one believes both that increasing private investment is important[4] and that the level of investment increases significantly as the after-tax rate of return rises,[5]

---

defined as "the algebraic sum of (1) the market value of rights exercised in consumption and (2) the change in the value of the store of property rights between the beginning and end of the period in question"); Andrews, *Personal Deductions, supra* note 1, at 375–80, 382–85. Income may alternatively be seen, from a source perspective, as the sum of the market value of all net receipts, i.e., the excess of windfalls, market earnings, and nonmarket entitlements over the costs of their acquisition. Under this second view, consumption tautologically equals income minus savings. *See* Kelman, *supra* note 1, at 834, 841; Warren, *Would a Consumption Tax Be Fairer Than an Income Tax?*, 89 YALE L.J. 1081, 1084 (1980). The fact that with the source approach one may *define* income in terms of sources does not imply that income from any of the sources is entitled to privileged treatment. The fact that something is a windfall or a government transfer puts it *in* the tax base rather than providing a grounds for pushing it out. *See* Commissioner v. Glenshaw Glass Co., 348 U.S. 426 (1955) (punitive damages award taxable though a windfall). Though Andrews seems to worry that those who define income in terms of source rather than use will be tempted to make arbitrary source distinctions by including or excluding certain items from the tax base, *see* Andrews, *Personal Deductions, supra* note 1, at 375–77, the fact is that those who *define* income in terms of source never actually mention it again in reaching substantive tax policy decisions regarding the scope of the base.

3. For example, assume a taxpayer in the 50% bracket earns $1,000 in year one that he can invest in an asset earning 10%. In a world with an income tax, he would have $525 [($1000 × .5) + ($50 × .5)] available for consumption in year two, while in a world with a consumption tax, he would have $550 [$1100 × .5]. If, instead of investing, he chose to spend his income immediately, he would have $500 under either tax. Thus, if there are people who would prefer $550 next year to $500 now but not $525 next year to $500 now, more investment will occur under a consumption tax than an income tax. *See* R. GOODE, THE INDIVIDUAL INCOME TAX 40–41 (1964). But the net effect of a consumption tax on private savings is ambiguous: While the consumption tax would encourage saving by causing a drop in the implicit price of future spending relative to current spending, the fact that one could save less and have more available at retirement (a quasi-income effect) might discourage private savings. *See* Andrews, *Consumption Tax, supra* note 1, at 1173; Feldstein, *The Welfare Cost of Capital Income Taxation,* 86 J. POL. ECON. S29, S30–31 (1978); *see also* R. GOODE, *supra,* at 40–46.

4. *See, e.g.,* N. TURE, TAX POLICY, CAPITAL FORMATION AND PRODUCTIVITY (1973); Feldstein, *Does the United States Save Too Little?*, 67 AM. ECON. REV. 116 (1977); Jones, *The Need for Capital,* 28 NAT'L TAX J. 265 (1975). *But see* Kuttner, *Tax Policy and Capital Formation in the U.S. and Europe: Reconciling Growth with Equity,* 15 TAX NOTES 163 (1982) (advocating increased reliance on centralized capital formation plans); Pechman, *Tax Policies for the 1980's,* 11 TAX NOTES 1195, 1195–97 (1980) (claiming that the potential productivity gains from increased private investment would not be great and disputing the proposition that private investment in the United States lagged in the 1970's).

5. *Compare* Boskin, *Taxation, Saving, and the Rate of Interest,* 86 J. POL. ECON. S3 (1978) (savings rate highly sensitive to changes in the rate of return) *with* David & Scadding, *Private Saving: Ultrarationality, Aggregation, and "Denison's Law",* 82 J. POL. ECON. 225 (1974) *and* Howrey & Hyman, *The Measurement and Determination of Loanable-Funds Saving,* in WHAT SHOULD BE TAXED, *supra* note 1, at 1–31 (savings rate insensitive to the rate of return). *But see* R. BIRD, TAX INCENTIVES FOR INVESTMENT: THE STATE OF THE ART 46–57 (1980) (arguing that current evidence is generally inconclusive on the issue of savings elasticity); note 3 *supra* (effects of a consumption tax on savings are ambiguous).

a consumption tax may make good macroeconomic sense.[6] A consumption tax might also be simpler to administer than an income tax, especially in avoiding the thorny problems of depreciation measurement and inflation adjustment.[7] Furthermore, a consumption tax might avoid certain obvious horizontal inequities and inefficiencies, especially the "discrimination" in favor of human capital over other capital investments[8] and in favor of unrealized over realized gains,[9] that we see under an actual, as opposed to a theoretical, wealth accretion tax.

One might also favor a consumption tax if one believes that it is unfair to tax people on their income, which measures what they have produced rather than what they have consumed or "used up." This belief is justified in two different ways when used to support arguments in favor of a consumption tax. Often, the justification is that a tax is essentially punitive and that only a citizen's consumption—not his saving—is sufficiently antagonistic to the interests of other citi-

6. A consumption tax—the exemption of all savings from taxation—will be desirable only if this more neutral but less targeted exemption is more efficient than trying to channel foregone government revenues into specific investments. For examples of the more targeted approach, see I.R.C. §§ 38, 46–48 (1976) (tax credits for particular investments); *id.* § 103 (exempting interest from certain bonds). For a typical argument in favor of targeting, see HOUSE COMM. ON WAYS AND MEANS, 1 TAX REVISION COMPENDIUM 181, 182–83, 186–89 (Comm. Print 1959) (Walter Heller, "Some Observations on the Role and Reform of the Federal Income Tax") ("In casting about for ways to promote growth, Congress might also . . . offer taxpayers special deductions for increasing their savings or for making specified forms of investment, as West Germany did in the postwar recovery period") (footnote omitted). Typical arguments against increased government targeting of investment decisions are summarized in Sneed, *The Criteria of Federal Income Tax Policy,* 17 STAN. L. REV. 567, 587 (1965) (From a free market perspective, "the aim of fiscal policy is to make the presence of government as unobtrusive as possible so that the optimum allocation of resources may be approached as closely as possible.") (footnote omitted); *see also* Andrews, *A Supplemental Personal Expenditure Tax,* in WHAT SHOULD BE TAXED, *supra* note 1, at 127, 128.

7. *See, e.g.,* BLUEPRINTS, *supra* note 1, at 44–45; Andrews, *Consumption Tax, supra* note 1, at 1133–39, 1143. But Graetz points out a number of serious implementation problems with a consumption tax: The most serious are the treatment of appreciating consumer durables, Graetz, *supra* note 1, at 1613–23, and of taxpayers investing in immediate deduction accounts while directing future appreciation into yield-exempt accounts, assuming both forms of consumption tax treatment are available, *id.* at 1605–11, as the Treasury suggests they should be, *see* BLUEPRINTS, *supra* note 1, at 119–31. Furthermore, as Goode notes, the problem of measuring on-hand assets at the time of transition to a consumption tax could be crippling. Goode, *The Superiority of the Income Tax,* in WHAT SHOULD BE TAXED, *supra* note 1, at 49, 57–68; *see also* Graetz, *supra* note 1, at 1658–59; Gunn, *The Case for an Income Tax,* 46 U. CHI. L. REV. 370, 388–92 (1979).

8. *See, e.g.,* Klein, *Timing in Personal Taxation,* 6 J. LEGAL STUD. 461 (1977); Boskin, Notes on the Tax Treatment of Human Capital, Dep't of the Treasury Conference on Tax Policy (1976). *But see* Warren, *supra* note 2, at 1113–17.

9. *See* BLUEPRINTS, *supra* note 1, at 46–48; Andrews, *Consumption Tax, supra* note 1, at 1129–31, 1141–43.

zens to merit "punishment."[10] Sometimes, the justification takes the form of an essentially illogical syllogism: When the government *uses* the tax money it raises, it consumes what would otherwise be consumed by private citizens; it therefore must tax citizens in proportion to the *consumption* that the tax has diverted from the private to the public sphere.[11]

Rather than dealing with any of these arguments, I intend to focus on one aspect of the debate between a leading income tax proponent, Professor Warren,[12] and recent consumption tax advocates, particularly the United States Treasury Department[13] and Professor Andrews:[14] the comparison of the utility positions of persons who consume in the present versus those of persons who save and thereby defer consumption into the future.

---

10. *Compare, e.g.,* T. HOBBES, LEVIATHAN 226 (M. Oakeshott ed. 1960) *and* N. KALDOR, *supra* note 1, at 53 (both advocating the consumption tax because savers have not yet cashed in their claims on social product) *with* Warren, *supra* note 2, at 1094–95 *and* Warren, *Fairness and a Consumption-Type or Cash Flow Personal Income Tax,* 88 HARV. L. REV. 931, 933–34 (1975) (rejecting the Hobbesian argument).

11. Andrews has made this argument several times. *See, e.g.,* Andrews, *Fairness and the Personal Income Tax: A Reply to Professor Warren,* 88 HARV. L. REV. 947, 951–52 (1975); Andrews, *Consumption Tax, supra* note 1, at 1165–67. It seems to me that Andrews' argument is confusing and/or misleading in two distinct ways. First, it incorrectly assumes that the government consumes the tax revenue it receives. It might be true that the government invariably consumes under one possible contrast between consumption and non consumption: the distinction between exclusive and nonexclusive use of resources. The government may invariably "use up" or preclude others from using resources when it spends: Even redistributed funds ultimately claim resources, and the government gains no pleasure from the act of giving comparable to that experienced by private spenders who derive pleasure in giving money away. *See* Andrews, *Personal Deductions, supra* note 1. For a critique of this contrast between consumption and nonconsumption, see Kelman, *supra* note 1, at 844–49. But the more germane contrast between consumption and nonconsumption in the context of choosing either consumption taxation or income taxation is whether to consume resources which give rise only to current benefits (current consumption) or to consume those which will generate benefits over a longer period (saving); obviously, under this distinction, the government saves as well as consumes. Second, even if one grants that the government only consumes the revenue it raises, the choice of the appropriate tax base bears no logical relation to its spending pattern; if the government bought only cake or only bombers, no plausible account of fairness demands that it levy a tax in proportion to pre-tax consumption of cake or bombers. Even if the government only consumes, it may still tax those who save. *Id.* at 853–55; Warren, *supra* note 10, at 932–33.

12. The argument for an income tax is made most explicitly in Warren, *supra* note 2, at 1097–1109.

13. *See* BLUEPRINTS, *supra* note 1, at 38–42.

14. *See* Andrews, *supra* note 11, at 947–53; Andrews, *Consumption Tax*, *supra* note 1, at 1167–69. For an earlier version of the same sort of argument, see I. FISHER, THE NATURE OF CAPITAL AND INCOME 249–53 (1906).

I. The Debate

Advocates of a consumption tax frequently highlight the following sort of example: T1 and T2 each have $10,000 of net noninvestment receipts (earnings plus windfalls) in year one and $0 in year two. T1 spends all his receipts in year one; his consumption stream in a nontax world is $10,000 in year one and $0 in year two. T2 saves all his income in year one, earns a 10% rate of return, and then dissaves both principal and interest the second year. His consumption stream in a nontax world is $0 in year one and $11,000 in year two. With a consumption tax, the discounted present value of the taxes T1 and T2 owe will be the same, assuming that T1 and T2 pay taxes at the same rate and that T2's tax rate does not change in year two. If the tax rate were 20%, T1 would owe $2,000 in year one, while T2 would owe $2,200 in year two; because we have assumed a 10% rate of return/discount rate, these tax payments have the same present value. This equality extends to the present value of T1 and T2's posttax consumption streams. The present value of T1's $8,000 consumption in year one equals the present value of T2's $8,800 consumption in year two. With an income tax, however, the present value of T1's tax payment will not equal the present value of T2's tax payment. T1 would pay $2000 in taxes in year one and $0 in year two, but T2 would owe $2,000 in year one and $160 in year two (20% of the $800 return on the $8,000 he would have left to invest after paying the first year's tax). Thus, the present value of T2's tax is higher than the present value of T1's tax. Correspondingly, the present value of T2's deferred $8640 consumption in year two is less than the present value of T1's $8000 nondeferred consumption stream.

Consumption tax advocates argue that this result is unfair in two related but distinct ways. First, they claim that in a nontax world, T1 and T2 have the same discounted consumption stream. The value of $1.10 of consumption one year away, *if we decide to discount future consumption back to present value,* is only $1. We "know" that T2 has not consumed more, in utility terms, than T1 (though his nominal income appears to be higher) because T1 could have been T2; he could have chosen to postpone $10,000 of current consumption for $11,000 of future consumption.[15] While T2 has a higher *explicit* positive consumption stream due to the fact that he consumes goods with

15. Andrews emphasizes in particular the fact that the two hypothetical taxpayers could have the same consumption stream, *see* Andrews, *supra* note 11, at 947-53, but the point is also made sharply by the Treasury Department, *see* BLUEPRINTS, *supra* note 1, at 39-40; note 63 *infra*.

a higher market value, his total utility is no greater than T1's because of the *implicit* negative cost of deferring consumption. Consumption tax advocates argue that this nontax equivalency of consumption streams mandates taxes (and after-tax consumption streams) with equivalent present values.

Second, consumption tax advocates assert that T1 and T2 have the same earnings potential ex ante, that is, that they have equal endowments.[16] One plausible account of taxpaying ability focuses on the taxpayer's *ex ante capacity*—his power to appropriate resources as discerned from a before-the-fact-of-earning vantage point. Of course, the tax system often focuses on *ex post outcomes*—what the taxpayer has actually appropriated. For instance, a graduate of a residency program in orthopedics may have the ex ante capacity to earn $2 million in his lifetime, but if he *actually* voluntarily chooses to earn only $100,000 as a dishwasher, we certainly would not tax him on his capacity. But the decision to focus on ex post outcomes in the doctor's case may not negate the general significance of ex ante capacity as a relevant measure of taxability; it may simply mean that there is a libertarian *constraint* on the tax system that prohibits the government from forcing people to work or to maximize income simply to meet their tax obligations.[17] If the proper tax base is ex ante capacity, then the tax and the after-tax consumption streams ought not to vary simply because of a taxpayer's decisions about the timing of consumption,[18] nor should the tax vary for taxpayers who have identical discounted income streams *and* who plan identical consumption paths but whose receipts arrive at different times.[19]

One could grant that T1 and T2 are equal consumers or have equal endowments and simply deny the importance of such equality in fashioning a tax,[20] but this is not Warren's predominant strategy.

16. *See* BLUEPRINTS, *supra* note 1, at 38-40.

17. *See* Kelman, *supra* note 1, at 841-44.

18. The example in the text, where only T2 deferred his spending until the second year, is one where intertemporal allocation decisions affect the taxpayer's liability under an income tax but not under a consumption tax.

19. Assume that T1 and T2 each plan to spend $10,000 in both years one and two. T1 earns $19,524 in year one and sets aside $9,524 of his income at 5% interest to finance his planned spending in year two; he then earns nothing in the second year. T2 earns and spends $10,000 in each year. Once more, T1 and T2's lifetime incomes, discounted back to present value, are the same ($19,524 is the discounted value of $10,000 now plus $10,000 a year from now, using the 5% discount rate); the difference in their tax liability under an income tax results solely from the timing of their receipts.

20. The fact that two taxpayers have equal endowments and presumptively equal "total" consumption streams seems to be of no moment to either consumption or income tax advocates when we compare two taxpayers who choose different trade-offs between work and

Instead, Warren argues that while the two taxpayers appear ex ante to have equal endowments and consumption *opportunities,* the ex post reality is that their endowments and consumption realizations do in fact differ. T1 could have been T2, just as the orthopedist-turned-dishwasher could have been rich, but only T2 and an actual orthopedist ended up appropriating more resources. Furthermore, Warren claims that the ex post perspective is clearly preferable because it focuses on actual outcomes. To substantiate his intuition that the tax system ought to focus on outcomes, Warren notes that taxing investors on their expected returns rather than on their actual returns would be clearly inappropriate. For example, suppose that T1 invests $1,000 with a certain return of $50 beyond principal while T2 invests $1000 with a 50% chance of returning $100 beyond principal and a 50% chance of returning only principal. In each case, the expected return, ex ante, is $50, but it would seem odd to tax T2 on only $50 even if he had $100 or to tax him on $50 if he earned nothing.[21]

According to Warren, even if Y has to be promised $1.10 in the future for him to agree to defer $1.00 of consumption in the present, once he receives the $1.10 he is better off by $.10 than a person who did not save.[22] Accordingly, Warren would deny that those who defer current consumption in order to consume more later have con-

leisure. For example, suppose that T1 and T2 could each make $20,000 if they worked a 40-hour week (equal endowment); T2, though, chooses to work only 30 hours and earns but $15,000 in money income. (Presumably, the "consumption" value of T2's extra leisure time is at least equal to the consumption value of the goods he could have obtained with the extra money. Otherwise, he would have chosen to work the full 40 hours.) Yet, T1 will clearly and uncontroversially be taxed more. In efficiency terms, neither an income nor a consumption tax is neutral between work and leisure; in horizontal equity terms, neither treats taxpayers with equal endowments and equal total consumption equally. The general point that taxpayers with equal consumption and endowments need not be taxed equally is made forcefully by Harold Groves:

> A and B each earn $2,000 in 1970 and A saves the money while B spends. In 1971 each again earns $2,000, but A has an increment of $100 in interest; B also has an increment of $100 from extra labor (working overtime). . . . Has A any reason to complain? Each pays on $4,100, which is what he received and spent. The choice of timing in expenditures is the taxpayer's. One sacrifices in the postponement of consumption, the other in extra effort. Society gains capital in one case, labor in the other. Is there more to this than the simple fact that anyone who chooses to enlarge his income and makes an extra sacrifice to this end must share his reward with the government?

H. GROVES, TAX PHILOSOPHERS: TWO HUNDRED YEARS OF THOUGHT IN GREAT BRITAIN AND THE UNITED STATES 109 (D. Curran ed. 1974); *see also* R. GOODE, *supra* note 3, at 55-56; Gunn, *supra* note 7, at 378.

21. *See* Warren, *supra* note 2, at 1102-05.

22. *Id.* at 1099-1101.

sumption equal to those who consume the lesser amount now. Thus, discounting future receipts back to present value is inappropriate because the discount rate is nothing more than an expression of ex ante time preference, which disappears ex post. Full taxation of deferred receipts is therefore appropriate at the time of receipt.

It strikes me that different conceptions of the *origin* of interest make Warren's claim that the saving taxpayer is in fact better off ex post than the spending taxpayer more or less plausible. In addition, different accounts of the origin of interest may influence our position on whether ex post or ex ante treatment of income is "appropriate." I will divide explanations of interest into three "psychological" (time preference or supply side) accounts and one "physical/external" (demand side) account.

Under the "supply side" accounts, the demand-for-loanable-funds curve intersects the supply-of-loanable-funds curve at a point where the supply curve is price elastic, that is, where the amount of loanable funds made available by savers is sensitive to the rate of return they can earn on their savings. In this situation, psychological factors that would alter a person's willingness to supply funds at different interest rates and thus alter the location of the supply curve would have a significant effect on the equilibrium rate of interest and savings. "Time preference"—the phenomenon that people demand more than $1.00 in the future to give up consuming $1.00 now— has three psychologically grounded explanations: Deferring consumption (1) requires sustaining the pains of pure impatience; (2) poses some risk of death, which means that one might *never* get to consume; and (3) entails consuming after one's preference structures are likely to have changed, which means that the same bundle of goods might produce less enjoyment for a "future" self than for the "current" self. While income tax advocates could plausibly adopt certain of the supply side theories, on balance these theories are probably more consistent with advocacy of a consumption tax.

Under a "demand side" theory, the possible demand curves intersect the supply-of-loanable-funds curve at points where the supply curve is inelastic or price insensitive; thus, the psychological factors that might alter the propensity to save at different interest rates will be of no moment. Instead, the equilibrium rate of interest and savings is affected only by a shift in the location of the demand-for-loanable-funds curve, which is determined by the demand of would-be investors for whom capital is physically productive. The physical/external or demand side theory of interest questions the existence, or more realistically the significance, of psychological time preference. According to the demand side view, people generally would be indifferent between $1.00 now and $1.00 next year *except for the vital fact* that anyone given $1.00 now can transform it into $1.10 next year. This transformation is possible because invested capital, as a matter of physical/economic reality, is productive. This demand side theory of interest requires that the supply of savings be limited to an amount less than the quantity of capital projects that can earn a rate of return greater than the return required to induce taxpayers to save; thus, the return that *each* saver, even a marginal saver, earns is best characterized as rent.[23]

My view is that adopting one or the other of these accounts of interest might lead one to different conclusions about the appropriateness of a consumption tax. It seems to me that the consumption tax is hard to justify on fairness grounds if the demand side theory of interest is a reasonably accurate account of the origin of interest. It is not surprising that many income tax advocates more or less consciously adopt the demand side theory.

I must immediately disclaim any intention to argue for one the-

23. When there is a fixed supply of a good, the price of that good will equal the demand price to the purchaser of the marginal good rather than the cost to the supplier. Thus, assuming that there are ten and only ten widgets in the world, even though they cost but $1/widget to make, if ten consumers are willing to pay $10/widget, $10 will be the price, and $9 of pure rent (return to a scarce factor above its production cost) will accrue to the widget-maker. *See* R. LIPSEY & P. STEINER, ECONOMICS 338, 914 (5th ed. 1978); P. SAMUELSON, ECONOMICS: AN INTRODUCTORY ANALYSIS 538-40 (6th ed. 1964). Even under the supply side theories of interest, *some* people would be willing to save at rates of interest below the market rate. These people are called inframarginal savers. Thus, assume that X would trade $1.00 now for $1.05 next year, but the prevailing 10% interest rate permits him to earn $1.10. X is *subjectively* better off, both ex post and ex ante, if he saves $1.00 now, which turns into a $1.10 next year, than if he consumes the $1.00 now, even though under the equal endowment and discounted equal consumption views, he is not. But he is better off in ways that do not generally matter in tax policy terms: He seems just like any consumer who enjoys consumer surplus, i.e., he would but does not have to pay more than the prevailing market price for something he consumes. The tax system has never paid attention to the sort of psychic benefit that consumer surplus represents. Only if all, or nearly all, X's are earning more on savings than they would require to save does a real problem exist.

Klein notes that the problem of differential saver surplus, *see* Klein, *supra* note 8, at 470, like that of differential consumer surplus, ought not to worry us much, though Gunn is bothered by the inframarginal saver, *see* Gunn, *supra* note 7, at 377. Of course, *consumer* surplus may not ordinarily be an issue because it does not appear to be distributed unevenly across classes; thus, it poses no vertical equity problems. But *saver* surplus may be troublesome if we believe that the *rich* are generally the inframarginal savers, that middle class taxpayers are the marginal savers, *and* that Congress will not adjust tax rates to account for this hypothesized difference. If this is the case, then the inclusion of interest in the tax base would protect tax progressivity even assuming that "utility," not income, is the appropriate base. *See* notes 61, 69-71 *infra* and accompanying texts.

ory of interest over another or to suggest that these accounts of interest are mutually exclusive, jointly exhaustive, or in any sense "right." I simply hope to clarify an area of discourse by pointing to its possible conceptual underpinnings, yet at the same time I hope to muddy it by demonstrating the complexity of relevant concerns.

II. Supply Side Accounts of the Origin of Interest

A. *Interest as Compensation for Forbearance: A Discussion of Impatience and Regret*

A common account of the origin of interest, generally associated with Irving Fisher, is that people are simply impatient to consume as a psychological matter.[24] Thus, even if they were certain that they would be around a year from now and that they would have the same capacity to enjoy goods that they currently have, people would still prefer current consumption. The ambivalent attitude people generally have about their personal identity supports this notion of pure impatience: While future selves are doubtless "me" in some significant sense (people certainly do not treat saving for the future as giving a gift to a different person), they are less clearly "me" than the immediate, sentient self. Even if the future self is absolutely certain to enjoy a good as much as the present self, that future self is distinct enough from the present self for the utility it (the future self) derives from consuming that good to be at least partially discounted.[25]

If people demand more than a dollar of consumption in the future to give up a dollar of present consumption solely as compensation for squelching their impatience, it is unclear whether a consumption or an income tax is "fairer." At least two views are possible. According to one view, this theory of interest erases any distinction between the ex post and ex ante views of the taxpayer, implying that saver and consumer are equally well off from either perspective. There are pleasures in the world that come from consuming and displeasures in the world that come from enduring the impatience that accompanies waiting. The consumer consumes $1.00 in year one and bears, ex ante or ex post, no pain from waiting; the

24. *See, e.g.,* I. Fisher, The Theory of Interest as Determined by Impatience to Spend Income and Opportunity to Invest It (1930); Koopmans, *Stationary Ordina! Utility and Impatience,* 28 Econometrica 287 (1960). Fisher's views are reflected in Blueprints, *supra* note 1, at 136.

25. For a discussion of temporally divided selves, see Kelman, *Choice and Utility,* 1979 Wis. L. Rev. 769, 778-87; *see also* J. Elster, Ulysses and the Sirens: Studies in Rationality and Irrationality 36-86 (1979).

saver consumes $1.10 in year two, but he has borne the $.10 displeasure of waiting and thus has netted the same $1.00 of satisfaction. The fact that the saver ultimately gets to consume does not cancel out the pain of waiting. Thus, because the saver and the spender are equally well off, regardless of one's time perspective, it seems fair to exempt the interest received by the saver—a consumption tax feature—as compensation for the disutility of squelching his impatience, assuming one perceives this disutility to be a reasonably universal correlative of the market activity of saving.[26]

According to another view, however, the impatience that a person feels ex ante when he is deciding whether or not to save is due to a misperceived attachment to his *current* sentient self. That is, before the fact he thinks he would prefer the person who now has the money to spend it. But if he spends instead of saving, he may well end up regretting that "someone" in his past—someone no longer sentient and therefore not quite fully him anymore—spent the money rather than saving it for his now-sentient self. In other words, perhaps there is a psychological mirror-cost to the cost of impatience: the cost of regretting that an old self was the one who consumed, a cost that is *first* perceived ex post.[27] If this cost of regret does exist, then the future sentient self would prefer having perhaps only $.90 currently to having consumed $1.00 a year earlier because he is more concerned with his contemporary self. This focus on the future self might sound a bit bizarre, but the implication for the present is that if the future self could come alive for a moment to decide whether to save or to consume, he would choose to save, even at a *negative* interest rate, because the to-be-sentient self's interests are more powerful for him than the once-sentient self's interests. But current decisionmakers in actuality will ignore the interests of the future self.[28]

26. For a discussion of the "near-universality" requirement, see notes 44-48 *infra* and accompanying text.

27. Although Warren is not explicit about this point, I think he makes a similar argument:

> Although rational consumers may discount the cost of future consumption to present value . . . *ex ante*, it does not necessarily follow that more recent consumption is worth less *ex post*. It is not at all obvious that consumption of a bottle of fine wine thirty years ago is, in any meaningful sense, equivalent to consumption of several cases today. It may well be that proximity in time is what matters, rather than priority. Because we go through time in only one direction . . . we are never presented with an opportunity to prefer priority independently of proximity.

Warren, *supra* note 2, at 1100.

28. The reason for this behavior is unclear. Perhaps they continue to be overly attached to their current selves, even when they are in a sense "angry" at later selves who showed that same attachment; they deal with the "anger" by another round of indulgent short-sighted-

Conceivably, the implicit psychic cost of waiting could be perfectly counterbalanced by the psychic cost of regret. If so, we are back in a situation in which the saver who has more explicit goods, seems to be better off ex post than the spender, even though saving did not appear ex ante to be a better choice because of the ex ante self's disregard of the ex post self's potential cost of regret. This ex post difference would indicate that interest income should be taxed. Of course, there is no reason to believe that the psychic cost of regret is the same as the cost of waiting: It could well be higher or lower.[29] If impatience outweighs regret, the saver will be somewhat less well off than the consumer, either ex post or ex ante, in the absence of a compensatory interest payment, though not by as much as one would believe if one focused solely on the costs of bearing impatience.

If there is impatience but no regret, the consumption tax looks fairer, whether one looks ex post or ex ante; if regret counterbalances impatience, though, and one takes the typical ex post view, the saver is better off and ought to be taxed, as income tax advocates suggest, even though ex ante, when the taxpayer focuses only on impatience, a promise of higher future receipts seems only to compensate for the pain of postponement.

B. *Interest as Compensation for the Risk of Death*

Let us now assume that the reason a taxpayer demands $1.10 next year to give up $1.00 now is that he fears that, if he defers consumption for a year, he will die during that year and therefore consume nothing. He may be indifferent between $1.00 today and a *certain* $1.00 in a year, but since future consumption is inherently uncertain, he demands interest.

The rate of interest that a person focused solely on the uncertainty of future consumption would demand is determined by two factors, one relatively "objective," the other subjective. First, if the would-be saver desires simply to equalize his expected consumption,

ness. Perhaps the failure to learn how to avoid regret reduces cognitive dissonance: The current self wants to consume and can avoid feeling troubled by that consumption only if it fails to perceive that it is jeopardizing a future self. Thus, one first fails to save because one discounts the future self; when the future self becomes current, one is prone not to save because that now-current self not only has the initial self's attachment to the present but also has a sense of regret and deprivation that can only be overcome by a guiltless, blind, current-regarding spending spree.

29. We observe only positive interest rates in the real world, which might, at least at first blush, suggest that regret does not *equal* or *outweigh* impatience. But positive interest rates may occur simply because people *experience* regret but never learn to adjust their behavior to avoid it.

whether he saves or consumes, the interest rate will be determined entirely by the *objective* mortality rate.[30] Thus, assuming that the mortality rate is 50% and that dying cuts off all consumption, that is, that parties receive no benefit at all from directing their unspent bequests to beneficiaries,[31] then the objective mortality-rate-determined interest rate must be 100%. If all persons are given $1000 initially, savers must then receive $1000 in interest (and thus have $2000 available to consume in year two) in order to equalize consumers' consumption from spending $1000 immediately because only 50% of those savers will get to enjoy the consumption stream. Second, if savers are risk averse, they might have to be compensated *more* than is needed to equalize the expected consumption of savers and consumers: There might be a *subjective* pain parallel to the pain of bearing impatience that arises from worrying about never consuming, and parties may demand additional compensation to bear that pain. Since the portion of interest determined by the risk of death that is attributable to subjective risk aversion, rather than the objective mortality rate, is precisely like impatience,[32] we will generally focus in this section, except where explicitly noted, on the portion of interest that is mortality-rate-determined. As to that portion of interest attributable to risk *aversity,* there should be no ex post/ex ante split, just as in the simple impatience case.[33]

1. *The distinction between the ex post and ex ante perspectives and the straightforward argument for the ex post view.*

Accounting for interest as dependent upon the objective mortality rate, there appears to be quite a pronounced split between the ex ante and ex post perspectives. Before the fact, the taxpayer will decide to save until the return on the last dollar saved makes him no better off than he would be if he consumed $1.00 currently. (The bundle with "X% chance of zero utility plus 100 - X% chance of $1.10," where X equals the probability of dying during the coming year, must be at least marginally preferable to the bundle with

30. The interest rate (i) will be determined by the mortality rate (m) according to this formula: i = [1/1-m]-1 if people receive *no* benefit at all from bequests so that death eliminates consumption utility entirely.

31. I will relax that assumption later. *See* notes 43-48 *infra* and accompanying text.

32. For a discussion of the similarity between subjective risk aversion and impatience, see note 36 *infra* and accompanying text.

33. The pain of waiting cancels out the ultimate gains from incremental consumption of a good where there is only impatience and no regret. So too, bearing the anxiety of never being able to consume partly cancels out the ultimate ability to consume more by surviving the year.

"100% chance of $1.00" for the person to save). As compared to another taxpayer with the same ex ante assessment of the risk of death who consumes immediately, this saving taxpayer will appear to be equally well off before the fact: Both taxpayers are using their $1.00 to maximize utility, given that both have the opportunity to either consume a given amount immediately or to consume more later if they survive. *But once both have survived the year,* the one who earned the $.10 return has "won" his bet and clearly seems, ex post, better off than the taxpayer who did not save. The risk of death, which called forth the positive rate of return, has simply disappeared ex post. Even if the expected value of saving and spending were once identical, the saver's lot has improved relative to the consumer's. Thus, Warren's arguments for the income tax appear quite sound if the rate of interest is objectively mortality-determined.

2. *Arguments that the ex ante view might be preferable although there is an ex post/ex ante split.*

Group versus individual rationality: Does the annuity analogy justify an ex ante view? The predominant argument for the ex post perspective here is that we cannot say that the interest earned by the saving taxpayer—an explicit receipt—is counterbalanced by any implicit cost that went into producing that receipt. If the reason we discount future consumption back to present value is that it somehow gives less utility—that the increase in the *number* of baubles the taxpayer can appropriate is offset by the fact that these baubles are consumed *later*—this compensation-for-the-risk-of-death accounting of interest dictates that we not discount that future consumption. An income tax would thus be appropriate.

We might be somewhat more prone to adopt the consumption tax feature of exempting interest from taxation for individual savers—to adopt the ex ante perspective—if savers *as a group,* if not as individuals, were in the same position ex post as spenders *as a group.* While we generally view taxation as requiring comparisons between *individuals,* at times we fall back on a second-best *group* rationality. For instance, individual mortality gains and losses are not accounted for in taxing annuities:[34] For the *group* of annuitants, capital is

34. *See* I.R.C. § 72 (1976). Throughout this discussion, however, remember that the group treatment of annuitants is by no means a fundamental principle of our income tax. The first post-16th amendment income tax allowed annuitants to defer taxation until their investment in the annuity was fully recovered, but all receipts thereafter were denominated as income. *See* Tariff Act of 1913, ch. 16, 38 Stat. 114, 167 (repealed 1916).

neither under- nor overrecovered, though an individual annuitant who dies prematurely (in actuarial terms) will be taxed as having income before he has fully recovered his capital investment, and a long-lived annuitant's income will be understated.[35] Ex ante, each annuitant can expect to recover a fixed sum; those who live longer than life expectancy will in fact have recovered more ex post, but we do not tax them to the full extent of their relative ex post enrichment because those who have done worse have recovered less.

A similar approach may be applied to savers and consumers as groups. Looking only at the interest determined by the objective mortality rate and assuming no utility from bequests, the following would be true: If there were a group of 100 savers with a 10% mortality rate saving $10 each, the group as a whole would ultimately consume $1,000; that is, the 90 people surviving would consume $[10 + ([1/(1 - .1)] - 1)10]$ dollars apiece while the ten dying people would consume nothing since we have hypothesized no utility from their knowledge that they have made bequests. A similar group of 100 consumers also would have had $1,000 of consumption ex post had each person spent the $10 instead of saving it. If we decide not to make adjustments *among* savers for winners and losers in the mortality sweepstakes, just as we made no adjustments *among* annuitants, then equalizing savers as a group with consumers as a group ex post may be a reasonable policy. This group ex post equalization could then at least arguably justify treating individuals who are equal ex ante with equality, that is, exempting interest from income.

In the case of annuities, the ex ante *dollar* value—which is, by definition, the anticipated ex post value—is indeed equal for all annuitants with the same life expectancy, and unless life expectancies have been inaccurately predicted, *dollar* losses will balance dollar gains precisely ex post. Utility gains and losses will simply track dollar gains and losses. But the "expected dollar value" for consumers and savers as groups will be the same only if the interest rate is objectively determined by the mortality rate, as hypothesized above. If,

35. Thus, assume that each of three annuitants, A, B, and C, has a life expectancy of 25 years and purchases a $100,000 annuity which returns $5,000 a year. Under I.R.C. § 72 (1976), each annuitant will exclude from taxation as a return on capital 100,000/125,000 of the $5,000 annual receipts. If A lives 20 years, B the expected 25 years, and C 30 years, the *group* will receive $100,000 + $125,000 + $150,000, a total of $375,000 in annual payments, and the *group* will exclude $80,000 + $100,000 + $120,000, a total of $300,000 from taxation. Thus, for the group as a whole, the appropriate amount of income beyond capital recovery will be taxed, even though C excludes more receipts from income than that figure which actually represents a return of invested capital and A never fully recovers her actual investment.

however, savers are risk averse, they may appear overcompensated in *dollar* terms though they will be equivalent in *utility* terms: They have borne a subjective disutility—their psychological risk aversion—that has not disappeared ex post.[36]

On the whole, the annuities analogy is not an especially powerful argument for the ex ante consumption tax view. First, it requires us to decide, rather atypically, that individual taxpayers in different positions ought to be taxed the same because they are each part of groups that are, as groups, in the same ex post position. Then, we must depart from the strict dollar equivalency treatment that prevails in the annuities area where the group of annuitants that is in an equivalent condition ex ante recovers, as a group, the same ex post dollar sum. In the context of group savings, the group of savers that was equal to the group of consumers ex ante may be better off in dollar terms ex post though no better off ex post in utility terms due to the additional component of interest attributable to compensation for risk aversion. The anomalousness of both these suppositions may only sustain the initially plausible argument that income taxation is basically more reasonable if interest compensates for the risk of death.

The ex ante perspective and individual rationality: the absence of a loss deduction. The annuitant and the saving taxpayer seem most similar in that both "win" their "bets" simply by surviving. Where the only ex post "victory" is survival, ex ante treatment may seem marginally more appropriate for the reasons described below. Individualized ex post treatment would not be administratively untenable in such cases: It would mandate that those whose investment pay-offs exceeded expected value, including interest-earning survivors and annuitants who outlived their life expectancy, recognize income on their "victories." At the same time, those whose investments fared worse than expected, including those who died before consuming savings and annuitants who died "prematurely," would recognize corresponding losses. Thus, investment losers would deduct returns

36. To continue the numerical example from the text, suppose people get more disturbed about the prospect of never consuming their income and demand $.20, instead of roughly $.11, to defer consumption of a dollar for a year when there is a 10% risk of dying. The group of savers would then be considerably better off ex post in *dollar* terms than the group of consumers: 90 savers would be left consuming a total of $1080 ($12 each) whereas the immediate consumers would have consumed only $1000. But these savers have borne a *utility* cost ex post as well as ex ante for which the last $.09 of interest payments compensated them. The risk of consuming nothing may disappear once one has survived the year, but the psychic displeasure at bearing that risk is not cancelled out.

below expected value,[37] including lost principal;[38] dead savers would deduct all unconsumed principal and accrued interest, and prematurely dying annuitants would deduct unrecovered capital. In the case of lottery losses, we might decide that mere *participation* in the lottery is an item of consumption worth the entry fee;[39] if so, lottery losses would obviously be nondeductible while gains would still be taxable.[40]

But this individualized ex post treatment would require treating death as a loss event and survival as a gain event for tax purposes. Both results seem a bit peculiar, though not irrational. Trying to explore why may be a quixotic quest, but I will suggest three explanations.

First, when someone wins a lottery or his investment does better than expected, he has gained an entitlement that he did not have at the beginning of the accounting period. The survivor, though, has explicitly *gained* nothing from surviving. He simply remains at a significant baseline position: alive. But our ordinary accounting of in-

37. As a practical matter, we do not include expected return in gross income and then give a deduction for the gap between expected and actual return; instead, we simply tax actual return. Of course, the effect is the same: Expected return - [expected return - actual return] = actual return.

38. Presumably the reason we do not allow long-term capital losses to be fully deducted currently, *see* I.R.C. § 1211 (1976), is that the taxpayer would then invariably choose to realize losses on those assets that had declined in value during the taxable year, while postponing payment of taxes on the unrealized gains on other assets he holds. Thus, taxpayers' Haig-Simons income, *see* note 2 *supra,* could be even more distorted by the realization requirement than it is currently. *See* J. PECHMAN, FEDERAL TAX POLICY 109 (3d ed. 1977).

39. Gambling losses are deductible only to the extent of gambling gains. *See* I.R.C. § 165(d) (1976). Presumably, net gambling losses represent consumption. Perhaps, however, § 165(d) is a tax "disexpenditure"—the nonrecognition of a deduction or loss that would ordinarily be recognized to properly measure income in order to discourage undesirable behavior. *Cf.* I.R.C. § 162(c), (f) (1976) (disallowing deductions for bribes, kickbacks, and fines even when these payments are indubitably helpful in producing income).

40. If, for instance, a taxpayer buys an apple for a dime and sells it for a quarter, he will have fifteen cents of income. But if he eats it he will not recognize a loss of a dime: The expenditure will be accounted for as consumption. In essence, then, we can think of a lottery as having no losing participants: For example, in a ten-person lottery, we can think of the nine people as not "losing" but "consuming" $1 though the tenth person will "win" $10. The expected ex ante return is not $1 but $2—$1 of expected return on the "investment" plus $1 of "lottery" consumption per person. The only significant tax decision is whether to tax all the lottery participants on the *expected* $1 per person nonconsumption gain or only the winner on the full $10 receipt ex post. The winner's gain, of course, seemingly should be only $9 were it not for the consumption thought to be inherent in participation. In the life insurance area, though, the taxpayer initially receives no deduction for premiums, presumably because there is consumption value in "being protected," but all of the proceeds of insurance are exempt if the insured actually dies (in a perverse sense "winning" the lottery); thus, the consumption component is counted only if one survives, or "loses" the lottery. *See* I.R.C. § 101 (1976).

come is associated with acquisition, with change, with a concrete event that occurs at a specific point in time. Of course, if one concentrates on the monetary rather than the survival criterion and contrasts the saver/survivor (SS) with the nonsaver/survivor (NSS) rather than with the saver/nonsurvivor (SNS), one sees that the SS has indeed gained command of resources at an explicit point during the accounting period in a way that the NSS has not. But that is an atypical focus for comparison. In the core cases in which Warren highlights an ex ante/ex post split, for example, he compares lottery winners or successful investors with lottery losers or unsuccessful investors, not winners with nonparticipants.[41]

Second, the lottery winner or successful investor may be differentiated from other taxpayers because of his concrete receipt of money. Differentiation is a critical factor in making judgments as to taxability.[42] But if we focus on survival as the critical event for the "successful" saver, then the would-be taxpayer is not differentiable from the typical taxpayer. Again, of course, one could focus instead on the comparison between the SS and the NSS, but this atypical focus seems peculiar in this context as well.

Finally, and most significantly, were we to allow loss deductions for the nonconsumption inherent in dying, as we must if we are to run an *individualized* as opposed to a *group* ex post system, we would be accounting for nonuniversalized psychic events to an unsound, perhaps intolerable degree. Of course, it is not that anyone likes death. But a loss deduction for death assumes that savers who die universally experience death as a total loss of dominion over resources, similar to the loss experienced by a losing investor. Given the existence of directed bequests, this belief would be very hard to maintain. It is well worth noting, too, that we do *not* currently allow a loss deduction at death. This fact may provide a reason, which Warren ignores, for exempting interest from taxation: Because we do *not* take an ex post perspective on the loss side, perhaps we ought not to on the gain side either. Thus, given the current administrative practice of disallowing loss deductions at death, Warren's analogy to risky investments is misplaced: "Losers" *do* get to deduct their capi-

41. *See, e.g.,* Warren, *supra* note 2, at 1102–07.

42. Given a stable revenue target, a uniform proportional increase in each taxpayer's base will simply be accompanied by a decline in rates; thus, we can ignore events known to have a universal, nondifferentiating effect on the sorts of concerns we generally account for in determining the tax base (e.g., if we taxed consumption, and thought that leisure had a consumption value, but that everyone enjoyed the same amount of leisure, there would be little point in adding the "money" value of leisure onto everyone's tax return).

tal losses when risky investments fail.[43]

At this point, I think it is important to describe more carefully this problem of individualized versus universal events and more generally the role of "psychic income" or utility in tax design because these issues are fundamental to determining whether or not a deduction for the nonconsumption inherent in death is appropriate. I think Professor Warren is fundamentally wrong when he argues that preferences about the tax base can be successfully divorced from beliefs about the utility of income.[44] I agree that the tax base can and must be defined without regard to *interpersonal variations in subjective reactions to uniform events*. But *generalized* judgments that certain events typically affect the "well-offness" we derive from market activities must, somewhere down the line, underlie the distributional preferences that animate tax design.

For example, we can and should design the tax system to ignore the fact that one of two people earning $100,000 loves his job while the other does not or that one purchaser of $100,000 worth of goods enjoys a great deal of consumer surplus while the other does not; these are highly variable individualized psychic reactions. But the tax system *must* make certain general conclusions about the utility we derive from certain events, such as "Those with higher incomes are virtually always better off than those with lower incomes and therefore we should tax them more." Our acceptance of this general conclusion regarding the relationship between utility and income is obvious if the aim of the taxation and spending system is to redistribute wealth from richer to poorer citizens.[45] To further illustrate this

43. I find the third explanation far and away the most cogent of these three.

44. "[I]t might be argued that the riskless rate of return somehow compensates *all* investors for the pain of deferring their consumption—but that justification leads back to the realm of psychic benefits and detriments rejected above." Warren, *supra* note 2, at 1107 (emphasis added); *see also* Gunn, *supra* note 7, at 382-86.

45. Warren seems to believe that the case for an income tax depends in large part on the fact that a society uses its tax and transfer systems to *distribute* the social product which in the first instance falls into private hands. *See* Warren, *supra* note 2, at 1091-92. But I take it that no one would care about distribution except for its presumed general impact on welfare or utility positions; thus, the backdrop impetus for the tax still seems utility oriented, even for Warren, though he thinks he is eliminating *any* utility focus.

Our acceptance of the general utility/income relationship also seems likely, though less clearly so, if the aim of taxation is instead simply to fund the purchase of collective goods because an "equal sacrifice" perspective on the financing of public goods would probably prevail over an "equal benefit" view. Under an equal benefit view, richer taxpayers are taxed more because they presumably benefit more from the provision of collective goods, such as defense. But it seems strained, to put it mildly, to argue the benefit one derives from defense against foreign invasion varies proportionately with the worldly goods one has that need protection from the invaders. Equal sacrifice principles, on the other hand, mandate that each

point, consider Andrews' argument that payments made to purchase medical care ought not to be part of the tax base.[46] His argument takes the universal form: Good health is, in essence, a nondifferentiated psychic benefit. It has a roughly equal presumptive value for all persons, as do involuntary departures from this baseline.[47] Likewise, the main argument *against* the medical care deduction is that health care purchases do in fact involve highly differentiated reactions to similar external events.[48]

Given this theoretical distinction, the problem now is to distinguish subjective utility variations from general utility judgments. One possible solution is to be extremely skeptical about assuming sufficiently uniform psychic reactions to essentially nonmarket events. I see little harm in designing a tax system that presumes (perhaps

---

taxpayer "feel" the tax pinch equally. Depending on whether or not one accepts the traditional utilitarian assumptions about the declining marginal utility of money, one would attempt to equalize sacrifice by levying either flat sum, proportional, or progressive taxes. *See, e.g.*, W. BLUM & H. KALVEN, THE UNEASY CASE FOR PROGRESSIVE TAXATION 56-64 (1953).

Gunn suggests a third alternative, far more divorced from presumptions about the well-offness derived from higher income. He argues, in essence, that government *ought* to finance public goods out of taxpayer contributions that seek to equalize the *time* that each taxpayer must work to finance the goods. *See* Gunn, *supra* note 7, at 385. While such a view is in some ways appealing, it is hard to square with the prevailing acceptance of the dogma of tax progressivity: I have difficulty imagining anything but a proportional, non-progressive tax—one that equalizes time devoted to government service—if time, rather than utility, is accepted as the ultimate contribution base. Even worse, the sharp rejection of a consumption/utility perspective utterly divorces taxation policy from ultimate distribution policy, forcing each of them to be defended completely separately.

46. *See* Andrews, *Personal Deductions, supra* note 1, at 335-37.

47. Thus, Andrews implicitly compares two taxpayers, A and B, each of whom has $50,000 to spend on traditional consumption items. A is in perfect health, but B has a broken leg. We could thus add, say, $10,000 for perfect health to A's nominal income but only $7,000, the presumed value of being in generally good health except for the broken bone, to B's nominal income. Alternatively, we could deduct $3,000 from B's income because of the broken leg, on the assumption that being free from the injury is worth $3,000. Essentially, Andrews' approval of I.R.C. § 213 (1976)—which allows B to deduct the $3,000 he spends fixing his broken leg—is grounded on the assumption that B's spending to remedy his departure from perfect health roughly measures the uniform, nondifferentiated psychic loss that accompanies this sort of injury: Broken legs are events that are generally considered bad (just as the receipt of money is generally considered good) rather than events that are susceptible to differential subjective valuation.

48. The critique of Andrews focuses on the fact that taxpayer spending on "disease" is not at all uniform, both because of discretion in defining disease and because of variations in treatments for uniformly acknowledged illnesses. *See* Kelman, *supra* note 1, at 858-79. Thus, even if there are some core diseases to which we might presume people respond in similarly negative ways, when we allow deductions to turn on the actual variations in medical care spending, we have no reason to believe we are correctly measuring variations in the actual severity of disease rather than individualized reactions to the same degree of disease.

counter to the facts) that people have reasonably uniform reactions to their income receipts or to their consumption purchases at market prices. Once we launch inquiries, however, into psychic reactions to nonmarket events—inquiries into such matters as how taxpayers react to disease, to divorce, to the death of a loved one, to their favorite baseball team winning the pennant, or *to their own death as a consumption-destroying event*—our ability to pick a fair base that seems nonarbitrary dwindles, measurement problems increase, and the tax system's congruence with our dominant conceptions of a separated private and public life declines. I think it would be hard to explain to a taxpayer why his neighbor gets a psychic-income-based deduction for a treated backache when the taxpayer does not get one for his divorce. I also suspect that aches and pains, ungrateful kids, and the pleasure one derives from testamentary dispositions are all "events" the value of which is difficult to measure. Moreover, these events seem to occur in "private" and to reflect peculiarities of individual temperament, whereas taking a job with a certain wage seems "public" in locus and readily measurable in value.

If death diminishes (or totally eliminates) consumption for some, but not all, and if the reaction to death as a consumption-destroying event seems to occur in private, then we cannot really press for the loss deduction at death that the individualized ex post view of savings requires. If we fail to take an individualized ex post view on the loss side, though, it is not clear that we can comfortably take one on the gain side either. The ex ante consumption tax view, which would exempt interest from taxation but allow no deduction at death, might then be thought to prevail.

C. *Interest as Compensation for a Changed Personality*

Another account of the origin of interest is that a person demands more than a dollar in the future to defer a dollar of present consumption not because of impatience or fear of intervening death but because he believes that in the future he will not have as much capacity to enjoy consuming as he has now. To give a concrete illustration, imagine young people deciding to spend money on a trip now, rather than when they are retired, because they fear they will be unable to enjoy a trip of equal cost as much when they are less physically fit. If they decide to save, they may find that a number of different things have occurred by the time the saving period has ended, and they are ready to receive their principal plus their return.

First, they may find that, while they are in fact less able to enjoy the same goods than they would have been when they originally saved, the rate of return has exactly compensated them for the loss of psychic capacity. Thus, they enjoy the $1.10 they receive after a year exactly as much as they would have enjoyed $1.00 a year earlier. If this is the case, then the consumer and the saver are equally well off, whether we take an ex post or ex ante view; the taxpayer both expects to receive the same utility in life whether he receives it now or later and does in fact receive the same utility. This result parallels the case where interest is a return for impatience, and there is no corresponding psychic cost of regret. In this situation, the consumption tax feature of exempting interest from taxation seems fairer.[49]

Second, they may enjoy the $1.10 more than they would have enjoyed the $1.00 originally. They are then in much the same position as the person who demanded compensation for the risk of death but ended up not dying. The same observations we made about that phenomenon could be repeated here: These savers feared a kind of partial death (the inability to enjoy goods as much as they did ex ante), but they did not in fact end up "partially dying." The same arguments about the validity of the ex post (income tax) and ex ante (consumption tax) perspectives would thus apply.[50]

Third, they may receive the $1.10 but have changed so much for the worse that they enjoy it less than they would have enjoyed the $1.00 originally. Our young people are thus analogous to the saver who in fact dies, whose gamble did not pay off. The problems and policies we mentioned in the discussion of death are again relevant. While a loss deduction might at first seem justified, the "loss" might not be universal enough to account for in the tax system.[51]

III. Demand Side Accounts of the Origin of Interest

A. *Demand Side Theories of Interest and Their Supply Side Correlates*

All of the accounts of interest discussed thus far have assumed that people have a significant psychological "time preference" in their consumption patterns—that people demand $1.10 next year to give up $1.00 now because they prefer current to future consumption. If the *only* market for saved funds were a market between those who borrowed funds to finance current consumption and those who lent funds at interest to finance future consumption, one could be certain

49. *See* notes 24-26 *supra* and accompanying text.

50. This is discussed in Part IIB. *See* notes 30-48 *supra* and accompanying text.

51. *See* notes 43-48 *supra* and accompanying text.

that the origin of interest was psychological because such a market would not reflect interest stemming from productive investment.[52] But the bulk of borrowed funds is invested rather than used for personal consumption. Without making a far more complicated argument than I have made thus far, we cannot assume that *anyone at all* is willing to pay $1.10 a year from now to get $1.00 to consume now or that anyone would require $1.10 next year to give up consuming $1.00 now just because the interest rate is 10% per year. And it is perfectly plausible that the only reason people prefer $1.00 now to $1.00 next year is that invested funds are, as a matter of physical fact, productive.[53] In other words, people *might be* indifferent if given a choice between receiving $1.00 now *which they had to consume* and receiving the same $1.00 to consume next year.

Economists have developed a number of accounts of why "capital" might be productive. The traditional Böhm-Bawerkian view was that the "roundabout" processes that waiting permits are intrinsically superior to processes in which the entire product is immediately consumed and that, in fact, longer-lasting "periods of production" are intrinsically superior to shorter ones.[54] One can eas-

52. For a discussion of such a market, see Samuelson, *An Exact Consumption-Loan Model With or Without the Social Contrivance of Money,* 66 J. POL. ECON. 467 (1958). Note that if the purpose of all consumption borrowing and saving were simply to average out lifetime income, *see* note 59 *infra* and accompanying text (discussing Friedman's permanent income hypothesis), borrowers (those with transitory income below permanent income) would not to have to pay interest to lenders (those with transitory income above permanent income), assuming the market were competitive: The lenders would suffer no opportunity costs because they would have set money aside even if there were no borrowers. Assuming (heroically) that all people would correctly perceive their permanent income, there would always be sufficient money available to meet borrowing demand.

53. "Time-preference is a subordinate factor compared with the productivity of investment in determining the rate of interest. . . . In the short run, it merely adapts itself to the given marginal productivity of investment." F. HAYEK, THE PURE THEORY OF CAPITAL 413 (1941).

The fact that people consume anything at all proves that future consumption, at least across generations, is discounted, i.e., that some positive time preference exists. For a reasonably convincing proof of the existence of time preference, at least with regard to consumption by descendants, see Olson & Bailey, *Positive Time Preference,* 89 J. POL. ECON. 1 (1981). Olson and Bailey do not, however, refute Hayek's point that interest is basically nonpsychological.

Moreover, even if some positive time preference does exist, the interest rate need not be related to it: If the demand curve for loanable funds intersects the supply curve at a point where the supply curve is inelastic, psychological time preference will not affect the interest rate, even though it might if the intersection were at a point where the supply curve was elastic.

54. 2 E. BÖHM-BAWERK, CAPITAL AND INTEREST 79–88 (G. Huncke trans. 1959); *see also* L. LACHMANN, CAPITAL AND ITS STRUCTURE 81–83 (1956) (trying to explain why Böhm-Bawerk's undefended assertion that roundabout production means are superior is in fact correct.)

ily be more skeptical than Böhm-Bawerk about "roundaboutness" and still assume first that there are *some* processes that involve intermediate goods that are more efficient than those processes that do not and second that these processes, which rational entrepreneurs will adopt, require that the whole product of the primary processes not be consumed. The standard, if somewhat inane, illustrations of this theory of the productivity of capital are that one might maximize the crop that could be consumed over a lifetime by using some of the first harvest as seed or fertilizer for the next crop rather than for food or maximize herd size in the long run by letting some of the cattle breed rather than consuming them in the first period.

Other accounts of the productivity of capital focus on its connection with constant technological flux.[55] Whenever a capital asset generates resources in excess of those needed for its reproduction, the investor in that asset receives a positive return: The goods produced by the asset have greater value than the cost of maintaining a capital stock sufficient to generate the production flow. In a world of technological progress, the substitution of more productive techniques for existing ones raises available income.[56] The additional income resulting from technological progress can itself be consumed or invested, but only if there is some investment in the creation and utilization of new knowledge will technological progress continue.

For our purposes, the accuracy of these theories of the origins of capital productivity is immaterial. As long as private borrowers actually demand capital to invest (for whatever purpose) rather than simply to spend, the interest rate will be positive even if no significant psychological time preference exists.[57]

55. *See* D. DEWEY, MODERN CAPITAL THEORY 7-11, 24-50 (1965).

56. Technological progress will render some capital assets obsolete. These assets will remain in use for a time (until total receipts no longer cover variable costs), but they will not be replaced by the same obsolete asset. Instead, the resources generated by the initial asset (that could simply be used to replace it and thus generate the same flow of resources) will be used to build a newer and better asset that produces the same flow of resources at a lower real construction cost (that is, less consumption must be foregone to build it).

57. Another significant source of demand for funds is the central government, which needs to finance its deficits. *See, e.g.,* Garguly, *The Effect of Government Debt on Interest Rates,* AM. ECONOMIST, Spring 1980, at 52. But the dominant basis of this demand is obviously not the productivity of its investments. Rather, government borrowing would seem to be grounded in a collective time preference that is closer to the consumption/loan model than to the investment/borrowing model. *See* notes 24-29 *supra* and accompanying text. Presumably, however, contrary to the case of personal consumption, some political constraints exist on the degree to which future taxpayers can be sacrificed for current taxpayers. But this conclusion assumes a political process model that is highly debatable: The government deficit that must be financed by borrowing is very likely determined in ways that focus only indirectly, if at all,

The troublesome aspect of a capital productivity account of the origin of interest is that it explains only the location of the demand-for-loanable-funds curve but does not explain why the amount of capital supplied does not shift with changes in an interest rate that initially may be determined by the marginal productivity of capital. One explanation is that the supply-of-loanable-funds curve is inelastic where the demand curve intersects it; thus, most of the rate of return represents economic rent to a factor—capital—in basically fixed supply. Of course, the supply of capital need not be absolutely fixed; it need only be limited to less than the amount demanded by those who can earn a rate of return exceeding whatever (even if tiny) compensation those limited suppliers of capital demand to satisfy their time preference. If the supply of capital is lower than the demand for capital at interest rates above those determined by the suppliers' time preference, the demand price, which is set by the inherent physical productivity of the marginal capital available, will determine the interest rate.[58] For example, assume that $1 billion will be saved if the interest rate is anywhere between 0% and 20% and that $2 billion will be saved if it rises above 20%. Assume further that the rate of return is 50% on the first $100 million invested, 15% on the next $900 million, and 10% on the next $1 billion. Given these assumptions, the interest rate will remain at 15% and the savings/investment level at $1 billion; the return to savers represents rent even though at some levels of interest the supply of loanable funds is elastic.

Three of the traditional accounts of household savings decisions predict this minimal price sensitivity in the quantity of savings supplied. Obviously, these theories are neither complete nor mutually exclusive. They are merely consistent in their prediction of the price insensitivity of saving. First, according to Friedman's permanent income hypothesis, people save when their transitory income (the in-

on the trade-off between future and present consumption. Instead, the deficit determination is likely to be arrived at by treating the revenue potential as relatively fixed by past decisions on politically acceptable taxes and setting outlays by some combination of inertia and bargaining among politically powerful subgroups. Still, from the vantage point of *savers*, the government borrowers are another source of demand for loanable funds that is essentially unconstrained by time preference. *See* note 58 *infra*.

58. Moreover, if both the government capital demand (GD) and the supply of savings (s) are assumed to be fixed, then the interest rate will be determined by the marginal productivity of the (s–GD)th dollar saved. The government is then an interest-price taker, though, of course, interest rates will rise (assuming the marginal productivity of capital is generally declining) as GD rises and government borrowing squeezes out less productive capital investments.

come they actually receive in a particular year) is above their permanent income (their expected average annual income over their lifetime).[59] Thus, if a taxpayer's projected annual income stream for three years were $40,000, $10,000, and $40,000, he would save $10,000 in year one, borrow $10,000 in year two, and repay his $10,000 of loans (a form of savings) in year three. His saving would be aimed at maintaining a constant annual consumption stream and would not vary with fluctuations in the interest rate.

We would also expect little price sensitivity if savings behavior were accurately described by Marglin's disequilibrium hypothesis that people save only when they have not yet learned to spend growing income.[60] Thus, if her actual income stream were $10,000, $10,000, $30,000, $30,000, a taxpayer would tend to save only in the third year, when she had not yet learned to spend her growing income. Often, observed savings behavior is consistent with both the Friedman and Marglin theories. For instance, a law student may choose to borrow both because his transitory income is below his permanent income and because he has developed tastes as an adolescent to which he has become habituated. But if a first-year associate in a ritzy law firm saves, he is almost certainly engaging in disequilibrium savings (he has yet to shed the spending habits of his student days

---

59. *See* M. FRIEDMAN, A THEORY OF THE CONSUMPTION FUNCTION (1957); Ando & Modigliani, *The "Life Cycle" Hypothesis of Saving: Aggregate Implications and Tests,* 53 AM. ECON. REV. 55 (1963). Friedman's work was directed predominantly at demonstrating the folly of Keynesian macroeconomic meddling: He felt the attempt to increase aggregate demand by counter-cyclical devices such as tax cuts would be futile because the spurt in transitory income the taxpayer derives from a tax cut would not be spent. Nonetheless, Friedman's work can be seen as a general theory of the origin of savings.

60. *See* Marglin, *What Do Bosses Do? The Origins and Functions of Hierarchy in Capitalist Production,* 6 REV. RADICAL POL. ECON. 60 (1974); *see also* Brown, *Habit Persistence and Lags in Consumer Behavior,* 20 ECONOMETRICA 355 (1952) (transitory spending associated with spending in highest previous spending year, a pattern consistent with disequilibrium views but inconsistent with permanent income hypotheses). Marglin's predominant purpose was to demonstrate that very little saving would go on if income were put in private hands because, contrary to both Friedman and Duesenberry, *see* note 59 *supra* and accompanying text; note 61 *infra* and accompanying text, Marglin believed that people quickly learn to spend everything they make and will save only until they adjust. His underlying theme was that corporate hierarchies exist to avoid dispersion of funds into private hands; if funds were dispersed, practically no saving would occur. Again, as is the case with Friedman, *see* note 59 *supra*, the *aim* of the work does not preclude using Marglin's arguments as the basis for a theory of when and why saving occurs. I will not pursue the additional point that nondisequilibrium saving in Marglin's world—the retention of corporate earnings—may also be price insensitive: While he is not specific on this point, I understand him to believe that corporate shareholders tolerate corporate retentions, even where they would not save the earnings stream if it were distributed, out of apathy or inability to control expansionary managers who save to expand, regardless of the rate of return to their investment.

and learn those of his new class) rather than permanent income savings (his transitory income as a first-year associate, though above student income, is still almost certainly below projected permanent income).

Finally, the saving decision would be price-insensitive if one accepts Duesenberry's relative income hypothesis that people save only the residual amount above that sum needed to maintain a maximum status position in the community.[61] Under this theory, only the rich or relatively rich save, and the amount they save is simply what is left over after they have spent enough to appear to be as rich as anyone else around.

Of course, if we see little price sensitivity—that is, paying people more to save does not induce them to do so—then we have no reason to believe that saving is a painful decision with an implicit cost that can be counterbalanced by a higher explicit return.

B. *Implications for the Consumption/Income Tax Debate*

Without question, if this demand side account of interest is correct, the saver is better off than the consumer both ex post and ex ante.[62] Under this account, interest is simply rent; there is no cost involved in deferring consumption and no need to discount future consumption back to present value to establish psychic equivalence. Being paid for the use of the scarce savings one happens to have is just plain good fortune. One would have chosen to save anyway, regardless of the interest rate, because one happened to be in one of the positions in which people tend to save. Basically, the *capacity to save* is simply another aspect of economic power. This capacity may arise from a favorably timed earnings cycle: Under Friedman's view, one will be in a position to save if one happens to earn more than

61. *See* J. DUESENBERRY, INCOME, SAVING, AND THE THEORY OF CONSUMER BEHAVIOR (1949). Duesenberry's formulation is a bit imprecise; for instance, it is not clear what the relevant community reference group is. Thus, an insular group of extremely rich people, emulating one another's consumption practices, conceivably would save less than a poorer person who is the only *relatively* rich person in town.

62. I sense that many income tax proponents more or less self-consciously adopt the theory of interest as rent: They disclaim the idea that interest compensates for disutility voluntarily borne by the saver. For example, Warren writes as follows:

> Marooned on a desert island with a lifetime store of goods, a consumer might well allocate an equivalent amount of goods to each of the remaining years of his life. From this perspective, the discount observed ex ante is due entirely to the productivity of capital, which permits the augmentation of consumption through deferral and investment.

Warren, *supra* note 2, at 1100–01; *see also* Gunn, *supra* note 7, at 375–76.

one's expected average annual income early on, thus enabling one to save and dissave rather than to borrow and repay. Under Marglin's view, one will save if one has a sudden spurt of income. Alternatively, under Duesenberry's view, the capacity to save is related not to the timing but to the relative size of one's receipts: If one is relatively well-off, one is prone to earn interest.

To illustrate more concretely, let us first consider taxpayers who have different time paths of earning and/or consumption. Three taxpayers, T1, T2, and T3, all have $10,000 of income and $10,000 of consumption in year one, but in years two and three, their paths diverge. T1 receives and consumes $10,000 in both years two and three. T2 receives $19,524 in year two, invests $9,524 of it in a 5% investment, and then receives nothing beyond returned principal and interest in year three; he consumes $10,000 in years two and three. T3 receives $10,000 in both years two and three, but chooses to consume nothing in year two and $20,500 in year three (his $10,000 from year three and $10,500 from his 5% investment purchased with his $10,000 income from year two).

Comparison of T1, T2, and T3

	Constant Consumption	Deferred Consumption
Accelerated Earnings	T2	
Constant Earnings	T1	T3

The Treasury Department *Blueprints* report, defending the intuitive appeal of the consumption tax, focuses on the equivalence of T1 (the consumer) and T3[63] (the purely psychological saver) and on the equivalence of T1 and T2[64] (the prototypical Friedman or Marglin

63. Consider first two individuals with no initial financial or physical wealth, no bequest, the same pattern of labor earnings, and different patterns of consumption. Intuition suggests that, unless these individuals differ in some respect other than how they choose to use their available resources . . . they should bear the same tax burden measured by the present value of lifetime taxes. The tax system should not bear more heavily on the individual who chooses to purchase better food than on the one who chooses to buy higher quality clothing. Nor should it bear more heavily on the individual who chooses to apply his endowment of labor abilities to purchase of consumption late in life (by saving early in life) than it does on the one who consumes early in life.

BLUEPRINTS, *supra* note 1, at 39-40.

T3 is a prominent figure in Andrews' work as well. *See* Andrews, *supra* note 11, at 947-48; Andrews, *Consumption Tax, supra* note 1, at 1167-69 (characterizing the saver as a deferring consumer).

64. Now, suppose that the two individuals have different time paths of labor earn-

saver).[65] From the interest-as-rent perspective, the argument in *Blueprints* seems confused and ideological. T3 is, from that perspective, a trivial, perhaps nonexistent, phenomenon: He is not in one of those positions where people save regardless of interest, but saves in order to enjoy more goods later while he "devalues" these future goods. There may be a handful of savers who are rationally and intentionally *choosing* between current consumption and devalued future consumption, but most savers do not actually compare the value of future and present goods. They merely find themselves in a position where they are *not spending* everything now, which leaves them little choice but to save.[66] And the Treasury Department report simply muffs the example of T2 to make the equivalence claims sound appealing: The statement that T2 works *twice* the hours of T1 in the earlier year[67] is just plain wrong. The whole point is that T2 can work *fewer* than twice the hours if he is able to work more hours early. The favorable time path of his earnings is precisely his economic advantage over T1. One can work fewer total hours over the course of two years if one can work more of them in the first year (or,

---

> ings but that the two paths have the same present discounted value. For example, individual A may earn $10,000 per year in a given 2-year period, while individual B works for twice as many hours [sic] and earns $19,524 in the first of the 2 years but earns nothing in the second. . . . Each individual prefers to consume the same amount in both periods, and in the absence of tax, each would consume the same amount . . . . An income tax imposes a higher burden on the individual who receives labor income earlier . . . .

BLUEPRINTS, *supra* note 1, at 40.

65. In Friedman's view, T2 would save because his transitory income, $19,524, is well above his $10,000 expected average annual income; in Marglin's view, T2 would save because he has not yet learned to spend more than $10,000 per year.

66. The argument need not be that savers have absolutely no choice but to save—that their activity is *fully determined*; rather, it might be that the savings decision does not focus on what we see as being *significant choice*—the taxpayer's balancing of the costs and benefits of saving. For a fuller discussion of intentionalist and deterministic discourses, see Heller, *Is The Charitable Exemption From Property Taxation an Easy Case? General Concerns About Legal Economics and Jurisprudence,* in ESSAYS ON THE LAW AND ECONOMICS OF LOCAL GOVERNMENTS 183 (D. Rubinfeld ed. 1979); Kelman, *Interpretive Construction in the Substantive Criminal Law*, 33 STAN. L. REV. 591, 597-98, 642-52 (1981).

If saving is pictured as fundamentally a voluntary act of particular wills (the intentionalistic view), we are more likely to regard the return to saving (interest) as merited (just as the criminal is punished for his *chosen* misconduct) and, in the more tax-relevant utility terms, as compensation for the marginal actor. Freely chosen decisions may give windfalls to the inframarginal, but for the key figure, the marginal actor, they are always a virtual toss-up. On the other hand, if saving is pictured as fundamentally involuntary and accidental (the deterministic view) and the interest rate is seen as reflecting factors that have little to do with the savings rate, there is no meaningful connection between interest and sacrifice and no reason to discount the presumed utility of interest income as compared to income from other sources.

67. *See* note 64 *supra*.

more realistically, if unusually high returns to one's skills are available in the first year), assuming that one will save for one of the three price-insensitive reasons described above.

Thus, while T1 and T2 have the same consumption stream, they have the same endowment *only* if we decide to discount all receipts, including interest, back to present value. But discounting is the *question,* not the basis for an answer. If T2 is better off than T1 because of the favorable time path of his earnings, his taxes should reflect his higher level of utility. If interest rates rose dramatically so that a T2′ need earn only $11,000 in year one to fund the same consumption stream as T1, T1 and T2′ would still have the same total discounted streams; the advantage of being a T2, someone who could work less earlier and save, would be more obvious. T2′ would clearly be better off than T2, insofar as he could finance the same consumption stream with about half the labor; yet assessing each one's endowments in terms of the prevailing interest rate in his world makes them both look equal to the T1 in his world and therefore equal to each other.

Moreover, if saving is generally determined by a favorable time path of earnings, rather than by (or in addition to) high relative income, then even a periodic wealth tax (which would supplement a consumption tax), for example, a tax levied at death, would not adequately tax the benefit of being able to save.[68] Both the life-cycle and the disequilibrium savers typically dissave all their savings before death, unlike the Duesenberry saver who perpetually spends only enough to maintain status; thus, a wealth tax would not reach the capacity to earn interest that the life-cycle and the disequilibrium savers enjoyed because of the favorable time path of their earnings.

Let us now contrast our consumer, T1, with a Duesenberry saver, T4, who sets aside some portion of his receipts because they exceed the amount he must spend to keep up his status. Andrews seems aware that some people might consider T4 to be better off than nonsavers because of his capacity to save and earn interest.[69] But I take it that Andrews would argue that if a significant relative privilege is vertically rather than horizontally variable, it can best be accommo-

68. Andrews advocates the use of a periodic wealth tax to supplement a consumption tax, believing that the failure to tax the rich on their capacity to save in a system with only a consumption tax would be unfair. Andrews, *Consumption Tax, supra* note 1, at 1172-73; *see also* text accompanying note 69 *infra*.

69. *See* Andrews, *Consumption Tax, supra* note 1, at 1175 ("It may be, of course, that even though most people eventually spend a fairly comparable fraction of their permanent income, there are still a few very high-income taxpayers whose consumption does not represent a substantial part of their income . . . .").

dated through rate adjustment.[70] Thus, according to my view of Andrews's position, if we were, for example, to conclude that the deference of the masses is a benefit that ought to be taxed and that it is earned only by those with high income, we still might choose not to measure the value of deference separately and then add it to each individual's base. Instead, we might levy a tax on those with high income that takes into account the fact that they all receive deference. Similarly, if interest-earning capacity is a benefit that only those with high consumption have, we need not explicitly include interest in the tax base; instead, we may choose to account for that benefit by setting higher scheduled rates for high levels of consumption.

My disagreement with Andrews is simply a political process judgment.[71] I suspect that Congress, faced with the inevitable presence of some nonsaving, high-level consumers, would be reluctant to raise the tax rate on the consumption of rich taxpayers just to prevent interest from escaping the tax base. Individuals could readily claim that they were being taxed on a counterfactual assumption: The mere fact that *most* people who spend a lot save (and, under this demand side account of interest, earn rent) cannot possibly mean that *all* such people save.[72]

IV. Conclusion

If savers were consumers who had to be paid to defer consumption, a consumption tax would, at first glance, appear more equitable than an income tax, even though many savers would be inframarginal:[73] Savers' surplus might be no more pressing a concern

70. "There is some tendency to think that a consumption-type tax would be more regressive or less progressive than an accretion-type tax because consumption is a declining fraction of income as income increases. . . . [T]he most general answer to [that view] . . . is that the *rates* could be adjusted to offset that effect." *Id.* at 1174–75 (emphasis added). Andrews makes a parallel argument with regard to the medical care deduction. Andrews, *Personal Deductions, supra* note 1, at 337–39. Richer taxpayers are likely to have better access to health care so that a deduction for medical care spending will not be vertically equitable, but Andrews views this disparity in treatment as unimportant. Vertical differences can be accounted for in the rate structure so long as persons in the same economic class have equal access to health care.

71. I previously expressed this disagreement in my criticism of Andrews' position on the medical care deduction. *See* Kelman, *supra* note 1, at 873–74.

72. Moreover, consumption tax rates might have to become excessively high, perhaps even well in excess of 100%, to tax the rich as highly as they are (at least nominally) taxed now. Such taxes might be politically infeasible. *See* Minarik, *Conference Discussions,* in What Should Be Taxed, *supra* note 1, at 297, 305–07.

73. For a definition of "inframarginal saver," see note 23 *supra*.

in tax design than is consumer surplus.[74] If, however, the reason that taxpayers had to be paid ex ante to defer consumption was their fear of death, we might, again at first, prefer the ex post treatment of taxing interest because an interest-earner would win his "bet" ex post by merely surviving. On the other hand, ex ante treatment might be more compelling because the lucky outcome is not an easily quantifiable financial return above expected value but survival, an event with a highly variable and individualized value. Similarly, if there were a mirror-image psychological phenomenon that counterbalanced impatience—a regret at having consumed in the past—then the ex ante psychic equivalence of current consumption and the *promise* of consuming principal *plus* interest would be dissolved ex post. The existence of regret would make the taxation of interest seem more justified than if there were only impatience.

If savers are rentiers, earning a rate of return independent of time preference, the capacity to save gives rise to an ability to command equal resources with less work that is not counterbalanced by any reasonably universal psychic detriment. Under this view, exempting interest-earning capacity from the tax base would seem inconsistent with our general policy of redistributing wealth from those who have exercised their exceptional capacities (scarce skills) to those who, because they have less valued marketable capacities, are generally presumed to be getting less out of (public, market, or economic) life. This view of interest as rent best coincides politically with opposition to the abolition of some variant of a tax on income: An annual income tax is more desirable than a combined consumption and wealth tax if a significant root of savings capacity is not just abnormally high earnings but also a time-pattern of receipts that produces *intra vivos* savings but no lifetime wealth accumulation.

74. *But cf.* note 23 *supra* (raising the possibility that saver surplus might be of greater concern than consumer surplus because it might not be equally distributed across economic classes).

[9]

Fairness and the Consumption Tax

Barbara H. Fried*

I Introduction

For over a century, tax scholars and economists have debated the merits of replacing the existing income tax with a tax on consumption. While a traditional accretion-type, or Haig-Simons, income tax taxes annual increases in an individual's wealth from labor and capital, whether saved or consumed,[1] a consumption tax taxes annual consumption only, whether financed out of current earnings, accumulated savings, or funds borrowed against future earnings. Proposals for a consumption tax have taken two basic forms. The first, a cash-flow tax, taxes annual consumption directly, through an income tax on current earnings (both wages and income from capital), with a deduction for savings. The effect of a cash-flow tax is thus to tax all earnings, but to defer taxation until they are spent on personal consumption. The second basic form, the yield-exempt version, taxes wage income in full as earned, whether saved or consumed, but exempts all income from capital. Under a plausible set of assumptions, the two forms of consumption tax—a tax on consumption only and a tax on wages only—impose an equivalent tax burden in present value terms.[2]

Over the years, proponents have pointed to a number of advantages of a consumption tax. These benefits include efficiency gains that result from

---

* Associate Professor, Stanford Law School. I am grateful to David Anderson, Ian Ayres, Guyora Binder, Richard Craswell, Dan Farber, Mark Kelman, Bill Klein, Ed McCaffrey, Peggy Radin, Bill Simon, and most especially Joe Bankman and Jeff Strnad, for their helpful comments on earlier drafts. An earlier version of this article was presented at faculty workshops at U.S.C. and Stanford law schools, and profited from the comments of participants at both schools. This research was supported by a bequest from the Claire and Michael Brown Estate.

1. More formally, following the formulation given by Henry Simons, annual taxable income under an accretion tax is defined as the "algebraic sum of (1) the market value of rights exercised in consumption and (2) the change in the value of the store of property rights between the beginning and end of the period in question." Henry C. Simons, Personal Income Taxation 50 (1938).

2. The equivalence can be illustrated by the following example. A taxpayer earns $100 in wages in year 1, intending to defer consumption of the earnings until year 2, and earning 10% interest on the savings. At a 40% tax rate, under the yield-exempt version of the tax, the taxpayer will pay $40 in year 1, leaving him with $60 after-tax to save. At a 10% interest rate, the $60 will grow to $66 by year 2, and all of this sum will then be available for consumption. Under a cash-flow version, the taxpayer will pay no tax in year 1, investing the full $100. This investment will yield $110 in year 2, of which the government will take $44, leaving the taxpayer with $66 to spend. For a discussion of the conditions that must obtain for the equivalence to hold, see Michael J. Graetz, *Implementing a Progressive Income Tax*, 92 Harv. L. Rev. 1575, 1600-11 (1979). The most significant conditions are: first, that tax rates remain constant across time and across income levels, so that (in the above example) $100 today is taxed at the same nominal rate as $100 plus accrued interest in the year of consumption; and second, that consumption not be deferred indefinitely (for example, through a series of bequests that go unspent).

eliminating the deadweight loss from a tax on savings;[3] a boost in national productivity from increasing the national savings rate;[4] the impossibility of ever administering a conceptually pure income tax, contrasted with the administrative simplicity of a pure consumption tax;[5] and the greater fairness of a consumption tax to savers. This article will deal only with the last of these supposed advantages—the question of fairness.

Two general arguments have been made on behalf of the greater fairness of a consumption tax. Each of these arguments mimics in structure one of the two basic forms of the proposed consumption tax schemes. The first, mimicking the structure of the cash-flow tax, is the so-called "foundational" argument. This argument, which is usually traced back to Hobbes, asserts that wealth ought not to be regarded as appropriated for private purposes until withdrawn for personal use from the "common pool" of national savings.[6] Under the Hobbesian view, a "fair tax" is defined simply as a tax that applies only to personal consumption. As critics have noted, the argument is open to attack for ignoring the psychic benefits in the form of power, influence, security, and the like that come from the mere possession of wealth.[7]

3. A brief but useful summary of the recent economic literature on welfare gains from a consumption tax can be found in John Whalley, *Lessons from General Equilibrium Models, in* UNEASY COMPROMISE: PROBLEMS OF A HYBRID INCOME-CONSUMPTION TAX 15, 36-37 (Henry J. Aaron, Harvey Galper & Joseph A. Pechman eds., 1988). For more detailed discussions in the economic literature, see Alan J. Auerbach, Laurence J. Kotlikoff & Jonathan Skinner, *The Efficiency Gains from Dynamic Tax Reform*, 24 INT'L ECON. REV. 81 (1983); Martin Feldstein, *The Welfare Cost of Capital Income Taxation*, 86 J. POL. ECON. S29 (1978); Lawrence H. Summers, *Capital Taxation and Accumulation in a Life Cycle Growth Model*, 71 AM. ECON. REV. 533 (1981). Efficiency gains from reducing the distortion in intertemporal choices will obviously be offset at least in part by efficiency losses from whatever tax makes up the revenue shortfall—in all likelihood an increase in the wage tax. Estimates of the net efficiency gains from a consumption tax, taking into account the effects of substitute taxation, have varied widely. Summers has estimated the welfare loss from an income tax to be as much as 10% of GNP. Summers, *supra*, at 543. Most other scholars have put the figure considerably lower. *See, e.g.*, E. Philip Howrey & Saul H. Hymans, *The Measurement and Determination of Loanable-Funds Saving, in* WHAT SHOULD BE TAXED: INCOME OR EXPENDITURE? 1 (Joseph A. Pechman ed., 1980); Auerbach et al., *supra*, at 94.

4. *See* Michael J. Boskin, *Taxation, Saving, and the Rate of Interest*, 86 J. POL. ECON. S3 (1978); Martin Feldstein, *Does the United States Save Too Little?*, 67 AMER. ECON. REV. 116 (1977). For earlier expressions of this view, see IRVING FISHER & HERBERT W. FISHER, CONSTRUCTIVE INCOME TAXATION: A PROPOSAL FOR REFORM 61-91 (1942); A.C. PIGOU, A STUDY IN PUBLIC FINANCE 96-99, 121 (3d ed. 1962).

5. For strong endorsements of a consumption tax as preferable to an inevitably imperfect income tax, see, for example, David F. Bradford, *The Case for a Personal Consumption Tax, in* WHAT SHOULD BE TAXED: INCOME OR EXPENDITURE?, *supra* note 3, at 75, 102-09; NICHOLAS KALDOR, AN EXPENDITURE TAX 44-46, 74-75 (1955); U.S. DEP'T OF TREASURY, BLUEPRINTS FOR BASIC TAX REFORM 44-45 (1977) [hereinafter BLUEPRINTS]; William D. Andrews, *A Consumption-Type or Cash Flow Personal Income Tax*, 87 HARV. L. REV. 1113, 1133-39, 1143 (1974).

6. *See* THOMAS HOBBES, LEVIATHAN 266-67 (Clarendon Press 1958) (1651). Hobbes's version of the argument runs as follows:

> [T]he Equality of Imposition consisteth rather in the Equality of that which is consumed, than of the riches of the persons that consume the same. For what reason is there, that he which laboureth much, and sparing the fruits of his labour, consumeth little, should be more charged, than he that living idlely, getteth little, and spendeth all he gets; seeing the one hath no more protection from the Common-wealth, than the other?

Id. at 267. For modern endorsements of the foundational argument, see CHARLES FRIED, RIGHT AND WRONG 147-50 (1978); N. KALDOR, *supra* note 5, at 53; Andrews, *supra* note 5, at 1164-67.

7. *See, e.g.*, HAROLD M. GROVES, TAX PHILOSOPHERS 109 (Donald J. Curran ed., 1974) (sug-

It is also open to attack on the ground that the power to direct investment of one's savings as one sees fit to further private, as opposed to public, ends is a form of private appropriation.[8] The foundational argument raises a number of other problems as well, and an adequate treatment of it has yet to be undertaken.

For present purposes, however, I intend to set the foundational argument aside, and focus only on the second argument, the object of scholarly debate for the past century. Mimicking the structure of the yield-exempt tax, the second argument seizes instead on the unfairness of taxing returns to capital per se. The article will suggest that this argument is not one but three, resting implicitly on three radically different and mutually inconsistent notions of fairness: (1) that returns to capital should be exempted as a means of perfecting the income tax; (2) that they should be exempted as a means of implementing an endowments tax; and (3) that they should be exempted to preserve the relative pre-tax welfare of savers and spenders. When the three arguments are disentangled and the implications of each examined, it will be suggested that none presents a persuasive case for the greater fairness of a consumption tax.

All three versions of the argument against taxing the income from capital per se ultimately rest on the same claim: that an income tax is likely to disadvantage savers relative to consumers, as compared to the respective positions of such parties in a no-tax world. This claim is generally illustrated with some variant of the following example. Two taxpayers, Profligate and Thrifty, each earn $100 in wage income in a world without taxes. Profligate spends the entire $100 in the year it is earned. Thrifty sets it aside for consumption upon retirement fourteen years later. At 5 percent compound interest, Thrifty's initial $100 will double in value to approximately $200 at the end of that period.

Assume now the adoption of a 40 percent cash-flow consumption tax. Profligate earns $100 in year 1, and receives no deduction for savings. He thus pays a tax of 40 percent of $100, or $40, leaving him with $60 for consumption. Thrifty saves his entire earnings in year 1, and so pays no tax until year 14. In that year, Thrifty pays a tax of $80 (40 percent of the $200

gesting that the "*power* of disposition (the availability of choice) is the essence of income"); RICHARD A. MUSGRAVE & PEGGY B. MUSGRAVE, PUBLIC FINANCE IN THEORY AND PRACTICE 227 (5th ed. 1989); H. SIMONS, *supra* note 1, at 96-97 (noting the variety of motives for savings beyond postponed consumption, and concluding that "there is something sadly inadequate about the idea of saving as postponed consumption"); C.W. Guillebaud, *Income Tax and the 'Double Taxation' of Saving*, 45 ECON. J. 484, 489-90 (1935); Alvin Warren, *Would a Consumption Tax Be Fairer Than an Income Tax?*, 89 YALE L.J. 1081, 1094-95 (1980).

8. *See* RICHARD GOODE, THE INDIVIDUAL INCOME TAX 22 (1964); Richard Goode, *The Superiority of the Income Tax*, *in* WHAT SHOULD BE TAXED: INCOME OR EXPENDITURE?, *supra* note 3, at 43, 52-53. As Goode put it:

> Investment, no less than consumption, is a withdrawal from the common pool in the sense that it is an exercise of a claim on the use of resources. . . . Taxes are levied because it is necessary to compel people to relinquish their claims on resources and thus to allow the government to use them. Whether consumption claims or investment claims should give way is a question of policy.

R. GOODE, THE INDIVIDUAL INCOME TAX, *supra*, at 22.

he dissaves) and is left with $120 for consumption. Thus, Thrifty will again enjoy twice as much consumption as Profligate—that is to say, the ratio of the two taxpayers' funds available for consumption (1:2) remains unchanged under a consumption tax from the no-tax world. Moreover, Thrifty and Profligate will pay an identical tax in present value terms: Although Thrifty will pay a tax of $80 as compared to Profligate's tax of $40, Thrifty's tax is not due until the end of fourteen years, and the present value of that liability (at 5 percent interest) is only $40.

Under a 40 percent income or accretion-type tax, however, the tax liabilities of Profligate and Thrifty diverge. Profligate will still pay $40 in tax in year 1, leaving $60 for consumption. But Thrifty will pay a tax on wages in year 1 and also a tax on interest as it accrues in years 1 through 14, leaving only $91 for consumption in year 14.[9] Thus, rather than having twice as much ultimate consumption as Profligate as a result of saving, Thrifty ends up with only about 50 percent more. The present value of Thrifty's tax liability likewise increases relative to Profligate's as the amount Thrifty has available for consumption decreases.

For present purposes, the most important moral drawn from the above tale is that an income tax discriminates against savers by leaving them in a worse position relative to spenders than they would be in the no-tax world. The charge has been put two ways: that an income tax alters the relative present values of the explicit after-tax consumption streams of savers and spenders; and that it imposes different present value tax liabilities on saving and spending.[10] The two claims—which are merely two sides of the same coin[11]—are, in one form or another, at the root of most defenses of a consumption tax. Such claims have gained quite widespread acceptance, leading even strong proponents of an income tax to concede its unfairness, although concluding that the unfairness is outweighed by other considerations.[12]

9. That is, the $60 after-tax wages set aside in year 1, compounding at a 3% after-tax interest rate. For a similar example illustrating the supposed discriminatory effect of an income tax, see Andrews, *supra* note 5, at 1121. The example is a simplified version of Irving Fisher's famous example of three brothers. *See* IRVING FISHER, THE INCOME CONCEPT IN THE LIGHT OF EXPERIENCE 12-13 (1906). A later, essentially unchanged version can be found in IRVING FISHER, THE NATURE OF CAPITAL AND INCOME 249-53 (1927).

10. For the former version, see ANTHONY B. ATKINSON & JOSEPH E. STIGLITZ, LECTURES ON PUBLIC ECONOMICS 71 (1980) (noting the widespread intuition that a consumption tax is horizontally equitable, because it affects "individuals with the same present value of receipts . . . identically, regardless of the timing of their wage income"); Andrews, *supra* note 5, at 1167. For the latter version, see DAVID F. BRADFORD, UNTANGLING THE INCOME TAX 162 (1986); *see also* JAMES E. MEADE, THE INTELLIGENT RADICAL'S GUIDE TO ECONOMIC POLICY 93-94 (1975).

11. That is, a saver is relatively worse off than a spender in an income-tax world by the present value amount of his greater tax liability. For a presentation of both sides of the coin, see I. FISHER, THE NATURE OF CAPITAL AND INCOME, *supra* note 9, at 249-53; N. KALDOR, *supra* note 5, at 84-86.

12. *See, e.g.*, Alvin C. Warren Jr., *Fairness and a Consumption-Type or Cash Flow Personal Income Tax*, 88 HARV. L. REV. 931, 946 (1975) ("[T]he choice between the consumption and accretion models for the personal income tax, as a matter of fairness, comes down to a choice between mitigation of lifetime wealth disparities and preservation of the pretax relative price of present and future consumption as the more important equity goal."); *see also* Richard Abel Musgrave, *A Fur-*

As a factual matter, the charge may be correct (although, contrary to the general assumption, not necessarily so). Under one plausible set of assumptions, an income tax, unlike a consumption tax, will indeed alter the relative values of savings and consumption, disadvantaging savers as compared to at least some consumers.[13] It is easy enough to show that such distortion exists, or might exist; the problem lies in explaining why it is unfair.

It is inadequate simply to assert that an income tax is unfair because it places a heavier burden on those who choose to defer their consumption than on those who do not. That response—arguably all that some of its most enthusiastic proponents have alleged on behalf of the fairness of a consumption tax[14]—obviously depends on the assumption that equal spenders (and not equal earners or equal owners, for example) *ought* to bear equal tax burdens. It depends, in short, on the *prior choice* of consumption over accretion as a "fair" measure of taxable income, a choice made on other, still-to-be-explained, grounds.

A number of other claims have been offered that purport to explain that choice, rather than simply rest on it. As suggested above, the answers fall into three different groups. The first, originating with Nassau Senior's theory of "Abstinence" in the early nineteenth century, argues that savers and spenders ought to bear equivalent tax burdens because they have equivalent wealth ex post, once the costs of deferring consumption are properly accounted for.[15] The second, suggested at least in passing by David Bradford, argues that savers and spenders ought to bear equivalent tax burdens, whether or not they are in equivalent positions ex post, because they face equivalent choices ex ante.[16] The third, put forth by Andrews, Bradford, Fisher, and others, suggests that savers and spenders ought to bear equivalent tax burdens because they are entitled to preserve the relative ex post advantages, whether equivalent or not, that they enjoy in a no-tax world.[17] Despite their frequent conflation in the consumption tax debate, the three arguments have little in common. The first (focusing on ex post wealth) is an argument for a consumption tax as a perfected income tax—that is, one that, accounting properly for the costs for which interest com-

ther Note on the Double Taxation of Savings, 29 AMER. ECON. REV. 549 (1939); Warren, *supra* note 7, at 1099-1100.

13. For further discussion of the conditions that must hold in order for savers to be relatively disadvantaged by an income tax, see Part IV *infra*.

14. *See, e.g.*, Andrews, *supra* note 5, at 1167 ("The most sophisticated argument in favor of a consumption-type tax is that the lesser burden of a deferred tax is more appropriate because it ultimately imposes a more uniform burden on consumption, whenever it may occur, than does an accretion-type tax."); *see also* BLUEPRINTS, *supra* note 5, at 42 (arguing that an income tax is unfair because it alters the present value of a tax on labor earnings, based on the timing of earning and consumption decisions, "discriminat[ing] against people who earn early in life or prefer to consume late in life"); Peter Mieszkowski, *The Choice of Tax Base: Consumption versus Income Taxation*, *in* FEDERAL TAX REFORM: MYTHS AND REALITIES 27, 29-33 (Michael J. Boskin ed., 1978); William D. Andrews, *Fairness and the Personal Income Tax: A Reply to Professor Warren*, 88 HARV. L. REV. 947, 949 (1975).

15. *See* Part II *infra*.

16. *See* Part III *infra*.

17. *See* Part IV *infra*.

pensates, would exclude interest from an income tax base on the ground that it does not represent an accretion to wealth at all. The second (focusing on ex ante choice) argues for a consumption tax as a form of endowments tax—that is, a tax levied on the ex ante expected value of a taxpayer's earning capacity, irrespective of the actual uses to which this capacity is put. Only the third is an argument for a consumption tax in its own right, rather than as a means of implementing another theoretical tax base, although precisely what theory of fairness underlies this last argument remains something of a mystery.

The balance of the article explores each of the three arguments in turn, concluding that all three offer surprisingly weak cases for a consumption tax on fairness grounds. The article proceeds in a somewhat different fashion with respect to the three arguments. In assessing the first two arguments (discussed in Parts II and III respectively), the article generally takes as given the fairness of income (in the first case) and endowments (in the second) as tax bases. It concludes, however, that if consumption tax proponents' ultimate objective is to implement either tax base, a consumption tax is a poor means to do it. In assessing the third argument (discussed in Part IV), the article considers directly the merits of the underlying claim that a fair tax base is one that preserves the relative positions of taxpayers in a no-tax world.[18] Preliminary to that inquiry, the article notes that, contrary to common wisdom, savers may in fact *not* be disadvantaged relative to spenders under an income tax. The answer depends on which groups of spenders and savers one compares, as well as what one deems to be the appropriate tax treatment of consumer interest on the borrowers' side. Assuming that savers *are* disadvantaged relative to spenders, the article then turns to the central question of why that result is unfair. Although commentators on both sides have presumed without discussion that such an outcome is in fact unfair, it is far from obvious what theory of distributive justice underlies that presumption. After laying out the possible alternative theories, the article concludes that, on reflection, few commentators on either side are likely to subscribe to any of them.

The critique offered here does not foreclose the possibility that the

18. There are two reasons for addressing the merits of the theory of fairness underlying the third argument, but not those underlying the first and second. First, the first two arguments for a consumption tax can be disposed of on the narrow ground that a consumption tax fails to implement either a perfected accretion-type income tax or an endowments tax. Thus, one need not reach the more controversial question of whether either income or endowments is itself a fair measure of taxable income. The same cannot be said of the third argument. For at least some groups of savers and spenders, under one plausible set of assumptions about the effects of a tax on savings, a consumption tax is in fact the best means to preserve the relative pre-tax values of saving and consumption. *See* notes 117-123 *infra* and accompanying text. Thus, it is necessary to reach the ultimate question of why that result is thought to be fair.

Second, the theories of fairness underlying the choice of income or endowments as a tax base have been developed and critiqued—extensively, in the case of income—in the tax literature. Again, the same cannot be said of the fairness arguments for preserving the relative pre-tax positions of savers and spenders. As a result, it is impossible to assess the case for adopting a consumption tax on that ground without first exploring the normative theory of fairness that might underlie it.

greater fairness of the consumption tax could be defended on other grounds. Some possibilities are discussed briefly in the conclusion. It does, however, suggest that the fairness arguments for a consumption tax that have dominated the tax literature do not withstand scrutiny.

II. A Consumption Tax as a Perfected Income Tax

The basic argument for a consumption tax as a perfected income tax is usually put along the following lines. Assume that two equal earners in a no-tax world, Saver and Spender, have $100 each of current income left over after paying for their basic subsistence needs. Each of them has two choices: either to spend the $100 this year on discretionary consumption, or to save it to finance consumption the following year, earning a 10 percent riskless rate of return on savings in the interim.[19] The two options can be thought of as an immediate choice between two commodities—"consumption today" and "consumption next year."[20] Like any other choice between competing commodities (between say, "food today" or "clothing today"), a well-designed tax system should assume that whichever choice is made at the margin, it will not alter the relative wealth of the choosers. When the income tax treats one of the benefits of "consumption next year"—an explicit interest payment of $10—as an accretion to Saver's wealth, while treating Spender (who has chosen "consumption now") as realizing no accretion to wealth, it overtaxes the former relative to the latter, thereby violating the fundamental principle of horizontal equity that identically situated taxpayers should be subject to an identical tax.[21] Hence, the argument goes, in order to be fair, the accretion-type income tax should impose equal tax burdens on Spender and Saver,

19. For simplicity's sake the example assumes a two-period world in which taxpayers face only two choices: to consume in year 1 or year 2. Obviously, in the real world taxpayers have the option to shift consumption between a multitude of time periods extending over their lifespans (or, if one takes account of bequests to heirs, beyond that). Although taking account of those multiperiod choices would complicate the examples used throughout this article, doing so would not fundamentally alter the analysis.

20. For an explicit description of the choice between present and deferred consumption as a choice among alternative commodities (such as "food today" versus "food next year") that is based on personal tastes, see D. Bradford, *supra* note 10, at 163; *see also* Mieszkowski, *supra* note 14, at 33-34; Joseph E. Stiglitz, Economics of the Public Sector 441 (2d ed. 1988); William Vickrey, Agenda for Progressive Taxation 336 (1947). For a critique of this description as ignoring significant differences between intertemporal consumption choices and the choice among different commodities for current consumption, see Stephen A. Marglin, *What Do Bosses Do?: Part II*, 7 Rev. Radical Pol. Econ. 20, 35-36 (1975).

21. The argument assumes that a "fair" income tax is one that would be neutral as between all forms of accretions to wealth, taxing all equally. Needless to say, our current income tax base falls short of the goal in numerous respects, many of them far less debatable than the one considered here. Moreover, in many people's minds the goal of neutrality is neither desirable nor achievable. For an early, formative attack on a so-called "comprehensive tax base," see Boris I. Bittker, *A 'Comprehensive Tax Base' as a Goal of Income Tax Reform*, 80 Harv. L. Rev. 925 (1967). For related attacks on the goal of "horizontal equity," see note 133 *infra* and accompanying text. However, to make the "perfected income tax" argument of any interest, one need not accept the premise that the ultimate goal of our tax system should be neutrality. There may be some value to understanding what constitutes a real accretion to wealth, if only as a means of recognizing when the tax system is creating subsidies or incentives for one set of choices over another (here, for spending over saving, by overestimating savers' accretions to wealth).

because even though Saver earns interest while Spender earns nothing, the two taxpayers are actually in equivalent positions ex post.

Over the years, two explanations have been suggested for the ex post equivalence between Spender's bundle of goods (present consumption of $100) and Saver's bundle of goods (future consumption of $110). The first, originating with Nassau Senior's "Abstinence" theory of interest,[22] implicitly assumes that the $110 of goods consumed by Saver next year will generate more utility than the $100 of goods consumed by Spender today, but argues that Saver's additional utility is offset by an equal psychic cost incurred by having to wait for the future consumption. Thus, the bundle of goods that Saver receives in year 2 is $110 worth of consumption, minus the $10 in psychic pain, yielding $100 in total utility.

A second, more peculiar, explanation for the equivalence ignores the possibility of psychic costs from the act of deferral, but argues that the utility of constant-dollar consumption declines over a taxpayer's life by precisely the amount of the discount rate. Thus, assuming a 10 percent discount rate, $110 of consumption by Saver in year 2 will generate the same utility in year 2 as $100 of consumption would have generated in year 1.

In either case, the argument amounts to the claim that the $10 interest payment merely leaves Saver in year 2 in the identical position as Spender was in year 1—with a bundle of goods worth (in future value terms) only $100, the value of Spender's present consumption. In the first case, Saver's "bundle" is made up of $110 in utility from $110 of explicit consumption in year 2, and $10 in disutility from the pain of abstinence in year 1. In the second case, it is made up of $100 worth of utility from $110 of explicit consumption in year 2. To put the argument another way, in the first case it is assumed that hidden psychic costs offset the extra benefits of increased consumption to Saver; in the second, it is assumed that there are no extra benefits to begin with.[23]

Thus, a perfected income tax ought to impose the same tax burden on spenders and savers, so that a taxpayer's ex post accretion to wealth will be equal at the margin, whichever consumption choice she makes. Equality can be achieved either by taxing *both* savings and consumption (that is, taxing Saver on the $10 explicit interest payment and Spender on the psychic income from current consumption, in an amount equal to the interest forgone) or by taxing *neither*. The two methods amount to the same thing, since a tax on both savings and consumption would, in effect, impose a flat rate surtax

22. NASSAU WILLIAM SENIOR, OUTLINE OF POLITICAL ECONOMY 58 (George Allen & Unwin Ltd., 6th ed. 1938) (1836).

23. It should be noted that while both arguments generally assume that the sole benefit derived from wealth is the explicit consumption stream it finances, neither argument depends on that assumption. Even if a would-be saver values wealth only for the security, influence, prestige, and power that its mere possession brings, she will still opt to save only if the aggregate benefits of saving (including the psychic benefits of possessing greater wealth) outweigh the pain of deferring consumption or the loss due to the declining utility of deferred consumption. In this respect, neither argument is susceptible to the attack made against the Hobbesian foundational argument for resting on an impoverished notion of personal wealth. *See* notes 6-7 *supra* and accompanying text.

on wage income, the same result that would be obtained by taxing neither and raising nominal tax rates on wages. But by opting instead to tax only savings and not current consumption, the current income tax system overtaxes Saver relative to Spender.

As a preliminary matter, it is important to note the relatively limited scope of the claim made for a consumption tax under these two versions of the perfected income tax argument. The argument by its terms deals only with that portion of the actual return to the marginal saver[24] that she demanded ex ante as the price of deferral—that is, the real return on riskless investments. It ignores the portions of the return to the marginal saver that represent compensation for inflation, or reflect positive and negative returns to risk. It ignores as well the surplus (over individual reservation price) paid to the inframarginal saver. The significance of those omissions will be considered in more detail in Section E below, after the traditional arguments for exempting the pure interest component of investment return are dealt with on their own terms.

A. *The Problem of Unstable Preferences*

Both versions of the perfected income tax argument assume that the interest payment demanded ex ante (equal to the anticipated disutility of deferral) merely compensates the marginal saver for the actual, ex post disutility of deferral. It should be emphasized that both versions of the perfected income tax argument—unlike the endowments tax argument discussed in Part III below—adopt an ex post and not an ex ante measure of wealth. Saver is assumed to have a right *not* to the expected return itself, but rather to compensation for her ex post costs. Because of the difficulty of measuring those costs directly, however, we instead measure them indirectly by the price demanded ex ante for bearing them (that is, the expected return on the investment).

Translating the ex ante reservation price demanded for deferral into a measure of the ex post cost of deferral entails a number of conceptual difficulties. Chief among them is that for the identity between price and cost to hold, time preferences, whatever their source, must remain stable over the deferral period. If Saver and Spender systematically overestimate the ex

24. For a given rate of return, a marginal saver is one who will save instead of spend only if the rate of return falls no lower than it is at present. In comparison, an inframarginal saver would willingly save instead of spend at a rate of return lower than the present one. The amount by which the actual interest rate exceeds the minimum return an inframarginal saver would demand in order to save is referred to as "inframarginal surplus."

For ease of exposition, the discussion here and in Part IV focuses on marginal and inframarginal *savers* rather than on marginal or inframarginal units of *savings*. Under a conventional marginalist analysis of savings behavior, however, every saver is by definition a marginal saver with respect to the last dollar she opts to save under prevailing interest rates. Furthermore, virtually all savers will be inframarginal with respect to a substantial portion of other dollars saved (that is to say, they would have opted to save at least some portion of dollars actually saved even under lower interest rates). The analysis throughout the article can accommodate this correction simply by substituting "marginal dollars saved" for "marginal savers" and "inframarginal dollars saved" for "inframarginal savers."

post disutility of deferred consumption (relative to current consumption) in making their savings decisions, the interest payment demanded by Saver will in fact leave her better off ex post than Spender.[25] Although economists have long assumed that such irrationality accounts for some portion of the preference for present over future consumption,[26] its prevalence is a matter of some dispute.[27] To the extent irrationality does exist, however, it clearly undercuts the "perfected income tax" argument for exempting interest on fairness grounds (although it may well strengthen the case for preferential treatment on purely paternalistic grounds). I would like to set the problem of irrationality aside, however, and assume that savers do incur some form of disutility from their choice to defer consumption that is not matched by any (unanticipated) disutility to spenders. The question is, what significance should that fact have in constructing a perfected income tax base?

B. *Interest as Payment for Abstinence*

The essence of the "cost of abstinence" argument is that interest merely compensates the marginal saver for the psychological discomfort of forgoing current consumption (measured by the discount rate demanded ex ante for enduring it). The argument, first put by Nassau Senior in the 1830s, was widely adopted throughout the late nineteenth and early twentieth centuries.

25. In the case of abstinence theory, for example, as Professor Kelman has suggested, the pain of abstinence for savers may be counterbalanced by an unanticipated ex post cost to spenders, in the form of regret for past consumption decisions that failed to take adequate account of future needs. If so, the saver with greater explicit wealth will in fact be better off ex post than the spender, "even though saving did not appear ex ante to be a better choice because of the ex ante self's disregard of the ex post self's potential cost of regret." Mark Kelman, *Time Preference and Tax Equity*, 35 STAN. L. REV. 649, 660 (1983). If time preference is instead hypothesized to arise from the declining utility of consumption over time, irrationality could result from spenders' systematically underestimating the utility their future selves will derive from consumption. *See* text accompanying notes 49-50 *infra*. Similarly, for the suggestion that the instability in preferences in intertemporal choices is one of the chief factors that defeats the analogy between savings decisions and other decisions involving a choice between two commodities, see Marglin, *supra* note 20, at 35-36.

26. *See* EUGEN V. BÖHM-BAWERK, THE POSITIVE THEORY OF CAPITAL 253-59 (William Smart trans., London, Macmillan & Co. 1891) (1889); *see also* IRVING FISHER, THE THEORY OF INTEREST 81-83 (1930) (attributing such a preference in part to the absence of foresight and in part to a lack of self-control (a related irrationality)); JOHN RAE, THE SOCIOLOGICAL THEORY OF CAPITAL 54 (Charles Whitney Mixter ed., 1905).

27. *See* Joseph Bankman, *Tax Policy and Retirement Income: Are Pension Plan Anti-Discrimination Provisions Desirable?*, 55 U. CHI. L. REV. 790, 816-21 (1988); Deborah M. Weiss, *Paternalistic Pension Policy: Psychological Evidence and Economic Theory*, 58 U. CHI. L. REV. 1275, 1300-11 (1991). It is difficult if not impossible to measure irrationality in time preference directly. Some have inferred that such irrationality is widespread, from the finding that a significant portion of the population saves amounts inadequate to fund post-retirement consumption at the level of average lifetime consumption. *See* Alan S. Blinder, Roger H. Gordon & Donald E. Wise, *Social Security, Bequests and the Life Cycle Theory of Saving: Cross Sectional Tests*, *in* THE DETERMINANTS OF NATIONAL SAVING AND WEALTH 89 (Franco Modigliani & Richard Hemming eds., 1983); Laurence J. Kotlikoff, Avia Spivak & Lawrence Summers, *The Adequacy of Savings*, 72 AM. ECON. REV. 1056, 1067 (1982) (concluding that for the poorly educated, post-retirement consumption is significantly below average lifetime consumption). However, that finding itself has been contested, and even if accurate, does not necessarily support an inference of irrationality. Others have inferred irrationality from radical changes in prospective discount rates over different time horizons that seem difficult to attribute to anything but irrationality in the initial time preference. *See* Weiss, *supra*, at 1300-03.

In recent debates, it has been embraced explicitly relatively infrequently.[28]

The argument raises two serious problems. First, taking account of the discomfort of deferral requires us in effect to give savers a basis in their psychic disutility—or, more precisely, a basis in the psychic pleasure they could derive from current consumption, which creates an entitlement to the marginal payment they demand to forgo it. Such a step represents a radical departure from customary tax policy, a point highlighted by comparing the proposed solicitude for savers' psychic discomforts with our customary treatment of workers. The marginal worker is, by definition, indifferent ex ante between working at the market wage and not working. That is to say, the equilibrium wage rate (reflecting the marginal supply price of labor) exactly compensates for the disutility of forgoing leisure. But if the marginal worker chooses to work, she will be taxed in full on her explicit wages, without any offset for the psychic disutility of work.[29] The anomaly of giving savers a basis in the disutility of forgone consumption when we refuse to give workers a basis in the disutility of forgone leisure is exacerbated when one recognizes that a consumption tax will shift the current income tax burden

---

28. John Stuart Mill provided influential, early support for Senior's abstinence theory. 1 JOHN STUART MILL, PRINCIPLES OF POLITICAL ECONOMY 278-79, 495-500, 568 (New York, D. Appleton & Co., 5th ed. 1896). Most political economists through the mid-1920s, progressives and conservatives alike, followed suit, conceding that the pain of abstinence created a moral entitlement to whatever minimal payment was demanded in return for bearing it. There were however a few strong dissenting voices on the left, including the early Socialists, the Fabian Socialists, and a few progressives like Edwin Cannan and Herbert Davenport. *See* EDWIN CANNAN, HISTORY OF THEORIES OF PRODUCTION AND DISTRIBUTION 197, 213-14 (2d ed. 1903); HERBERT JOSEPH DAVENPORT, ECONOMICS OF ENTERPRISE 363 (1913); HERBERT JOSEPH DAVENPORT, VALUE AND DISTRIBUTION 45 (1908). For an overview of the late nineteenth and early twentieth century debate surrounding Seniorian abstinence theory, see Barbara H. Fried, Robert Hale and Progressive Legal Economics ch. 4, at 18-22, 51-55 (Mar. 1992) (unpublished manuscript, on file with the *Stanford Law Review*).

For recent discussions of abstinence theory, see Kelman, *supra* note 25, at 658-60; Warren, *supra* note 7, at 1107 (noting the argument but dismissing it on the ground that it requires one to account for psychic benefits and detriments).

29. *See* H. GROVES, *supra* note 7, at 109 (discussing the inconsistency of allowing for the psychic costs of saving while ignoring (inter alia) the psychic cost of labor); Alan Gunn, *The Case for An Income Tax,* 46 U. CHI. L. REV. 370, 378 (1979); Joseph Bankman & Thomas Griffith, *Is the Debate Between an Income Tax and a Consumption Tax a Debate about Risk?,* 47 TAX L. REV. (forthcoming 1992-1993) (manuscript at 7, on file with the *Stanford Law Review*); *see also* JOSIAH STAMP, THE FUNDAMENTAL PRINCIPLES OF TAXATION 58 (1921) (arguing that while interest may be compensation for "abstinence," there is no reason why interest income earned in that form should not be taxed like any other income). For an acknowledgment by proponents of a consumption tax that both an income and a consumption tax are biased in favor of leisure over work, see N. KALDOR, *supra* note 5, at 130-40; Andrews, *supra* note 5, at 1169.

It has been suggested that labor is in fact taxed on a consumption tax model, due to our failure to tax human capital (in the form of wage-earning capacity) as it is accumulated, deferring taxation until such capacity is exercised by generating an explicit wage stream. In other words, labor is taxed on a cash-flow version of a consumption tax. *See* William A. Klein, *Timing in Personal Taxation,* 6 J. LEGAL STUD. 461, 470-73 (1977). For reasons that are too lengthy to explore here, I believe that it is inaccurate to characterize the current treatment of human capital as adhering to any simple consumption tax model, and that it is far from clear that financial capital *is* disadvantaged relative to human capital. If one concluded otherwise, however, it would obviously undercut the suggestion that extending consumption tax treatment to financial capital alone under a "perfected income tax" argument would put such capital on preferential footing as compared to human capital, as the argument here in effect asserts that human capital already enjoys that advantage, albeit through a cash-flow rather than yield-exempt version of a consumption tax.

entirely onto labor. At least in the short run, the effect will be to increase the relative tax burden of labor as compared to leisure.[30] Thus, to have any credibility at all, the "cost of abstinence" justification for a consumption tax would have to take account of the *relative* inequities caused by ignoring the psychic disutility of abstinence and labor.

Second, it is unclear what the supposed nature of the disutility is, and what moral significance is being claimed for it. Senior's original abstinence thesis was developed against a backdrop of rising socialist attacks on interest as an unearned surplus stolen by capital from labor's rightful product. Its relationship to those attacks is unmistakable.[31] The availability of capital in the productive process, argued Senior, depended on the willingness of capitalists to abstain from current consumption of their wealth. Thus, abstinence, like labor and nature, was a distinct factor of production, which—like labor—exacted from its agents an absolute sacrifice: "To abstain from the enjoyment which is within our power, or to seek distant rather than immediate results, are [sic] among the most painful exertions of the human will."[32] It followed that the remuneration demanded and paid for that exertion was no less deserved than the wages paid to workers for the disutility of labor. In Senior's famous phrase, "Abstinence . . . stands in the same relation to Profit

30. This need not be the case. The revenue shortfall could instead be made up by a lump-sum tax. Moreover, in the medium or long run, if the elasticity of the savings rate relative to the after-tax rate of return is high enough, it is conceivable that the resulting increase in savings rates under a consumption tax could trigger sufficiently rapid economic growth to avoid any revenue shortfall, and indeed even permit a *lower* rate structure on wages. For such a suggestion, see DAN FULLERTON, JOHN B. SHOVEN & JOHN WHALLEY, REPLACING THE U.S. INCOME TAX WITH A PROGRESSIVE CONSUMPTION TAX: A SEQUENCED GENERAL EQUILIBRIUM APPROACH 24-25 (National Bureau of Economic Research Working Paper No. 892, 1982) (demonstrating that with savings elasticity of 2.0 the wage tax rates could be lowered within a short period of time); Summers, *supra* note 3, at 541-42; *see also* Boskin, *supra* note 4, at 57 (arguing for a savings elasticity of 2.0). While many economists believe that the higher savings rate under a consumption tax will in the long run permit a lower wage rate, they also believe that the long run will be sufficiently long that on a present value basis the benefits will be outweighed by transition costs. *See, e.g.*, ALAN J. AUERBACH & LAURENCE J. KOTLIKOFF, DYNAMIC FISCAL POLICY 127-34 (1987). Even disregarding the possible gains from a higher savings rate, if (as most economists believe) the labor supply is less sensitive to tax rates than is savings, a shift to a pure wage tax might well reduce efficiency losses by minimizing tax-induced distortions in aggregate consumer preferences. If one takes the supply price of labor (deduced from its elasticity) as measuring the psychic disutility of labor that *ought* to be counted as a cost in a perfected income tax—a move that entails some of the same difficulties suggested below with respect to savings—then a shift to a pure wage tax may also reduce the inequities of our current imperfect income tax, by shifting the tax burden onto the sector with lower unaccounted-for costs. But all of this seems strained at best, and takes us far beyond any analysis consumption tax advocates have offered.

31. For a survey of early socialist exploitation theories emerging contemporaneously with the development and popularization of Senior's thesis, and a discussion of the connection between the two, see EUGEN V. BÖHM-BAWERK, CAPITAL AND INTEREST: A CRITICAL HISTORY OF ECONOMICAL THEORY [sic] 286, 315-27 (William Smart trans., 1890; Augustus M. Kelly 1970) (1884); *see also* H.J. DAVENPORT, ECONOMICS OF ENTERPRISE, *supra* note 28, at 370-76; Walton H. Hamilton, *Property—According to Locke*, 41 YALE L.J. 864, 870 (1932) (discussing abstinence theory as a self-conscious extension of the labor theory of value).

32. N.W. SENIOR, *supra* note 22, at 59. As Herbert Davenport noted, to the same argumentative end Courcelle-Seneuil used the term *travail de l'épargne* (the labor of saving) to describe the act of saving. H.J. DAVENPORT, VALUE AND DISTRIBUTION, *supra* note 28, at 46 n.4.

as Labour does to Wages."[33]

The spectre of all savers—the Rothschilds of the world included—suffering under the enormous weight of self-denial provoked (not surprisingly) a contemptuous response from the socialist camp. Lassalle's diatribe against Senior is probably the most famous example:

> The profit of capital is the 'wage of abstinence.' Happy, even priceless expression! The ascetic millionaires of Europe! Like Indian penitents or pillar saints they stand: on one leg, each on his column, with straining arm and pendulous body and pallid looks, holding a plate towards the people to collect the wages of their Abstinence. In their midst, towering up above all his fellows, as head penitent and ascetic, the Baron Rothschild! This is the condition of society! How could I ever so much misunderstand it![34]

It is conceivable that attacks like Lassalle's were meant to suggest (albeit in inchoate premarginalist form) the possibility that a significant amount of savings particularly among the wealthy was inframarginal. The implications of that possibility are explored below. But the skepticism it reflects about the sacrifice entailed in deferring consumption can be applied to marginal savers as well. The price demanded at the margin for forgoing current consumption reflects the relative preferences attached to current and future consumption given present and expected future wealth. This price says nothing about the absolute hedonic content of either choice. Herbert Davenport, one of the few progressive economists to embrace the early socialists' skepticism and translate it into marginalist terms, argued that that fact robbed abstinence theory of any ethical significance in justifying a "right" to interest. To the extent that the pain of abstinence is taken merely to denote the fact that interest must embody attractions sufficient at the margin to displace the attractions of present consumption, Davenport noted, the existence of such "pain" is axiomatic. In that limited sense of an opportunity cost, equal to the margin of displacement between present and future uses of wealth, abstinence reflects a cost as much for Mr. Rockefeller as for a pauper.[35] But the existence of such a margin of displacement says nothing about the measure of pain undergone or the resistance overcome:

> The marginal postponement of consumption, like any other case of margins, is a ratio relation; any particular item of saving is marginal, not because of the high significance of the abstinence protest, but merely because the forces making for present consumption, representative, it may be, of very great or of very limited present need, are at an approximate equilibrium against the estimates of the advantages promised by postponement.[36]

---

33. N.W. SENIOR, *supra* note 22, at 58-59.

34. FERDINAND LASSALLE, KAPITAL UND ARBEIT 110 (Berlin 1864), *quoted in* E. V. BÖHM-BAWERK, *supra* note 31, at 276.

35. H.J. DAVENPORT, THE ECONOMICS OF ENTERPRISE, *supra* note 28, at 361-66.

36. H.J. DAVENPORT, VALUE AND DISTRIBUTION, *supra* note 28, at 259-60. Fisher's "impatience" theory, explaining the positive supply price for savings, is indistinguishable from Davenport's theory of marginal displacement. Both are merely labels for the relative preference for present over future consumption. Fisher, like Davenport, rejected the notion that one can deduce from opportunity costs the existence of a real cost analogous to labor. Thus, Fisher expressly repudiates the Seniorian argument that "abstinence or waiting exists as an independent item in the cost of produc-

Two points embedded in Davenport's critique are worth some thought in assessing the validity of the abstinence claim. The first is that there is no ground for assuming that the pain incurred by savers is homogeneous, and hence that the interest payments that savers demand for saving are proportionate to the pain that saving entails for them.[37] Taxpayer *A*, eking out a subsistence income now but fearing even greater impoverishment in future years, is willing to set aside $100 of current income for as little as 1 percent interest. Taxpayer *B*, well off now but expecting even greater wealth in the future, will not set aside $100 for less than 10 percent interest. Everything (besides wealth) being equal, the most plausible explanation for this disparity in reservation prices is surely not that *A* suffers a pain of deferral significantly less in absolute terms than *B*, but that he values a marginal dollar of future consumption significantly more. That is, for *A* the expected disutility of future want (or to put it another way, the high utility of money in warding off future want) will dominate the reservation price; for *B*, for whom the marginal utility of an additional dollar in the future is very low, the disutility of forgoing present consumption will dominate the reservation price.

If the sole aim were either to maximize efficiency in the choice between savings and consumption or to create incentives to save, then in both cases, given the existing distribution of wealth, the reason for the disparity in reservation prices would be irrelevant. But from the perspective of fairness, the disparity seems at first blush troubling, as it suggests that by comparing only *A* and *B*'s respective reservation prices, we understate *A*'s sacrifice relative to *B*'s. Davenport, not surprisingly, concluded that focusing on reservation prices would therefore systematically discount the sacrifice of the poor.[38] One need not embrace that conclusion or its implicit assumptions both as to the declining marginal utility of money and the interpersonal comparability of utility to accept Davenport's essential point. If abstinence justifies interest only to the extent it entails real pain—the "grief and groan of saving," in Davenport's words[39]—one cannot deduce the extent of that pain from the price demanded for bearing it.

The same objection, however, could be raised with respect to any purchase, where consumers are given a basis in goods equal to their nominal cost, irrespective of the (differing) subjective utility of the relinquished purchase price in their hands. For instance, *A* scrapes together $1000 out of her meager earnings to buy a beat-up jalopy to enable her to get to and from work. *B*, fabulously wealthy and the owner of six other cars, on a whim purchases an identical jalopy for $1000, for occasional use at his country

tion," concluding that one who lives off income from capital is "a 'rentier.'" I. FISHER, *supra* note 26, at 486-87; *see also* I. FISHER, THE NATURE OF CAPITAL AND INCOME *supra* note 9, at 171-72.

37. H.J. DAVENPORT, VALUE AND DISTRIBUTION, *supra* note 28, at 45.

38. "To the rich marginal purchaser, the utility obtained and the utility foregone are of approximately equal, but of slight, subjective value; to the poor purchaser the same equality between obtaining and foregoing holds, but the terms in the equality ratio are of very considerable subjective value." H.J. Davenport, *Doctrinal Tendencies—Fetter, Flux, Seager, Carver*, 14 YALE L. REV. 300, 316 (1905).

39. H.J. DAVENPORT, VALUE AND DISTRIBUTION, *supra* note 28, at 49.

house. Most people (despite the official skepticism among economists about interpersonal utility comparisons) would assume that relinquishing the $1000 was relatively more painful for *A* than for *B*. Notwithstanding that fact, *A* and *B* are both treated as having an equal basis in their cars, equal to the nominal price paid. The answer to a charge of unfairness seems to be that if the money sacrificed has greater utility in *A*'s hands, so also does the jalopy gotten in return. The same answer seems dispositive with regard to savers *A* and *B*, *assuming* we are willing to give savers a basis in their psychic disutility to begin with. In other words, if $100 of present consumption has a greater value to *A* than *B*, then the minimum compensation *A* will demand for deferring it for one year ($1, compared to $10 for *B*) must have a greater absolute subjective value as well.

Second, Davenport argued, there is no reason to assume that abstinence inflicts pain at all, in any normal hedonic calculus. The choice between present and future consumption may be merely a choice between "positive gratifications."[40] If so, "it would be a waste of sympathy to grieve with one who has to choose between two pleasures, and to call either pleasure a pain because it is conditioned on going without the other pleasure."[41] Moreover, if there is any pain involved in saving, Davenport argued, it lies in the fact that a present pressing want remains unappeased, *not* in the fact that a saver possesses income he could have used to alleviate it had he not concluded that his future wants were even more pressing.[42]

It is conceivable that Davenport was wrong here—that the existence of a

40. *Id.* at 46-47.

41. *Id.* at 47.

42.

> [W]here the individual is in possession of sufficient money to buy him a meal, but decides to save his money and to lend it, . . . the *abstinence* [is not] a pain. It is only the *hunger* that is pain. A man having the hunger but no money has unquestionably one pain and no more, that of hunger. So much is clear. If now we take this man to have both the hunger and the money, he has not now two pains, one of hunger and one of abstinence, but only the one original pain of hunger. His is, indeed, the fortunate case of one who need have no pain at all if only he would let go of his money. Perhaps to lose his money would be painful, but only in the sense that it would involve the continuance of the pain of hunger. But to lend the money is not a pain, and the only pain in the case is that gnawing at his vitals that he has declined to still. . . . Were this not the truth, the case of one having both the hunger and the money would be the especially grievous case; . . . the rich who could spend, but do not, would be the unfortunates of the world . . . .
>
> . . . There is nothing especially touching, then, in the fact that [a man] has the dollar, and that, in spending it now or later, he has to forego an alternative spending. It appears, then, that not only the necessity of a choice between pleasures is not a pain, but also, and with equal certainty, that the necessity of a choice between pains is not a pain.

H.J. DAVENPORT, ECONOMICS OF ENTERPRISE, *supra* note 28, at 361-62. For a similar critique of "abstinence" as not reflecting a real cost, see I. FISHER, *supra* note 26, at 486-87, 539. Davenport is ambiguous as to whether abstinence differs from labor in this respect, but one can make the case that it does. Labor, it is true, could be described as the choice to forgo leisure for money, just as abstinence is the choice to forgo present consumption for future consumption. But unlike abstinence, labor clearly involves an affirmative act that for many people imposes a disutility of its own beyond the absence of leisure. Fisher, for one, unambiguously embraced the view that labor (at least when "disagreeable") reflects the only true cost in production, although he distanced himself on other grounds from the socialist conclusion that interest was therefore morally unjustifiable. *See id.* at 20, 22-24, 540; I. FISHER, THE NATURE OF CAPITAL AND INCOME, *supra* note 9, at 171-75.

choice (forgone) to alleviate want could itself inflict a psychological pain that would not exist in the absence of any choice at all. Indeed, Senior's own description of the "pain" of abstinence as lying in burdensome exertions of the will is not inconsistent with that characterization.[43] But that rejoinder seems strained at best. A more promising response for consumption tax advocates would be to concede that Davenport was right as a descriptive matter that the "pain" of abstinence may amount to no more than an opportunity cost, but to argue that this cost is sufficient to create an entitlement to interest. *A* and *B*'s ownership of their respective $100 gives them the right to consume their money currently, retaining the full value of whatever pleasure that afforded them, and hence, the lesser-included right to whatever price they demand for forgoing that opportunity in favor of another, less attractive one. That response, however, gives up any distinct claim on behalf of abstinence theory in favor of the broader claim that any right (here, the right to consume one's own wealth currently) necessarily carries with it a subsidiary right to one's reservation price for relinquishing it, *whatever the reason for demanding that price*. This claim—in effect equating efficiency with equity concerns—subsumes the abstinence argument, along with any other explanation for a positive supply price for interest, for the claim remains true irrespective of the ground for preferring present to future consumption. That economy of explanation, however, is achieved at the cost of whatever moral weight the Seniorian rhetoric of sacrifice lends the cause.[44]

C. *Lower Value of Deferred Consumption*

Alternatively, it has been argued that interest should be exempted under a perfected income tax because it exactly compensates for the fact that the utility of constant-dollar consumption declines over a taxpayer's lifetime. Thus, where the abstinence argument assumes that savers are paid more to compensate for the pain of deferring consumption, this argument assumes that the commodity they receive—consumption in the future rather than today—is worth less, by the amount of the discount rate. The argument closely parallels the argument for indexing inflation gains under an income tax; nominal increases in wealth over time overstate real wealth, not (as with inflation) because it takes more dollars to buy the same goods but because the subjective value of the purchased goods declines.

43. "To abstain from the enjoyment which is in our power, or to seek distant rather than immediate results, are [sic] among the most painful exertions of the human will." N.W. SENIOR, *supra* note 22, at 60.

44. In addition, the response is not self-evident. There are many situations in which a right to *X* does not carry with it a right to retain the full reservation price demanded for relinquishing *X*. Again, leisure is one notable example, and any satisfactory defense of exempting interest would have to take account of the anomaly of simultaneously taxing the marginal wages of forgone leisure. The argument that the right to present consumption *should* carry with it the right to the payment exacted for forgoing it is weakened considerably if the reason we fail to tax consumption is because it is administratively difficult to tax consumer surplus in nontangible forms, rather than because we believe that spenders have an entitlement to that surplus.

The argument has never been put forth explicitly in the pro-consumption tax literature, leaving some reason to doubt how seriously any advocate would take it. But since a number of critics have suggested that it underlies at least some proponents' support of a consumption tax,[45] it is worth noting briefly the obvious difficulties it entails.

As Professor Warren notes, one cannot deduce the declining value of consumption merely from the existence of a positive time preference—that is, from the mere fact that people apparently prefer present to future consumption. The fact that we go through time only in one direction precludes us from separating the value of proximity from that of priority.[46] Fisher, perhaps inadvertently, highlighted the same problem when he defined time preference (or "impatience") as "the (percentage) excess of the present marginal want for one more unit of *present* goods over the *present* marginal want for one more unit of *future* goods," but then elided the two in concluding that "all time preference resolves itself in the end into the preference for comparatively early *income* over comparatively remote, or deferred, *income*."[47] As Warren's remarks suggest, the two concepts—remote and deferred income—are hardly the same thing.

One also cannot deduce the declining value of consumption by analogy to the time value of money itself. That value would exist due to the explicit productivity of capital, irrespective of the uses to which the income from capital is put.[48] But as Professor Warren notes, for an analogous argument to hold true with respect to consumption, the value of early consumption would have to compound into the future.[49] Not only does the value of consumption not compound over time; it is, by definition, exhausted at the time of consumption, except perhaps for pleasant memories, acquired wisdom, or other residual human capital we may carry with us into later life as a result of our consumption experiences.

Thus, one can justify discounting the utility of future consumption only by hypothesizing one of two things. Either (1) our pleasure at nominally equal amounts of consumption systematically declines as we age, at a rate exactly equal to the discount rate throughout our lifetimes, or (2) we sys-

45. Henry Simons apparently understood Fisher's conclusion that equal present value consumption streams ought to bear equal present value taxes to rest, at least in part, on the assumption that the value of consumption declined over time. *See* H. SIMONS, *supra* note 1, at 90 (arguing that this assumption was based on a faulty analogy between values realized in consumption and yield to capital in the productivity sense); *see also* Stanley A. Koppelman, *Personal Deductions Under an Ideal Income Tax*, 43 TAX L. REV. 679, 701 (1988) (citing to Fisher and Andrews as arguing that "consumption has a time value—present consumption is more valuable than an equal nominal amount of future consumption"). While this understanding is a conceivable moral of Fisher's tale of the three brothers, it seems an unlikely one, and is not one Fisher himself ever offered directly. For other rejoinders to the argument, not targeting any particular proponents, see Gunn, *supra* note 29, at 374-78; Warren, *supra* note 7, at 1099-1101.

46. Warren, *supra* note 7, at 1100.

47. I. FISHER, *supra* note 26, at 62-63.

48. *See* H. SIMONS, *supra* note 1, at 90 ("What is discounted in the valuation of property is future yield . . . which may or may not be consumed. What are discounted are yields, not 'consumptions.' ").

49. *See* Warren, *supra* note 7, at 1100.

tematically prefer our younger selves to our older selves, and thereby weight the subjective utility derived from later consumption at a rate that declines apace with the discount rate for money. Just to state both hypotheses is, one suspects, to refute them in most people's minds. Assuming that the first hypothesis is false, the second hypothesis would require the belief that a 55 year-old, while deriving the same pleasure from equal amounts of consumption as she remembers deriving when she was age 8, would—*if she could go back in time*—nonetheless give preference to the pleasures of her 8 year-old self, to the extent of voluntarily transferring (at a 5 percent discount rate) $1000 of consumption today for $100 of consumption then. Why one should imagine such a heroic attachment to our younger selves—and imagine that the attachment to one's current self grows weaker for each year of passing youth by precisely the amount of the discount rate—is somewhat perplexing. As suggested above, if there is any stable time preference for consumption, it is most likely for proximity over priority. That is, our 8 year-old would enormously prefer $1000 of consumption at age 8 to $1000 of consumption at age 55; likewise, our 55 year-old (were she permitted to go back and correct history) would enormously prefer $1000 of consumption at age 55 to $1000 of consumption at age 8. This suggests that savers and consumers alike routinely underestimate the utility that future consumption will have to their future selves. In other words, they are *not* rational in predicting future utility. It is difficult to see what moral one should derive from that fact with regard to a fair tax on explicit consumption at either age, except perhaps that we should disregard such preferences entirely.

Finally, even if it is true that we consistently prefer earlier to later consumption, the implication that the tax system ought to take account of that fact is radical indeed. Like the abstinence argument, once it is reduced by Davenport's critique to a mere opportunity cost argument, it suggests that taxes should be levied not on the market value of income or consumption (the conventional view in both an accretion and consumption tax base), but rather on the subjective utility that income or consumption provides. The customary pragmatic objection to a tax based on subjective utility, that it is unmeasurable and hence unadministrable,[50] is somewhat alleviated here, as the argument assumes that the utility of money to each individual declines annually throughout her life by the discount rate in effect as she makes the annual decision not to dissave.[51] But other objections remain. The "declin-

50. *See, e.g.*, N. KALDOR, *supra* note 5, at 51 (arguing that "tax systems are not, and never could be, so constructed as to take into account the peculiarities of individual temperaments").

51. The assumption that the utility of consumption declines with age implies that the disutility of the nominal *tax* levied on interest will also decline over the taxpayer's life by the amount of the discount rate. This fact does not, however, necessarily dispose of the "declining utility of consumption" argument against taxing interest. The claim is that there is no increment in real value to begin with on which to levy a tax (whether or not the tax becomes less painful over time). Note, however, that the assumption that tax payments will become less painful over time, as consumption becomes less pleasurable, does explain why—if one subscribes to the "declining utility of consumption" hypothesis—one would *not* have to index tax rates on *wages* to decline over a taxpayer's lifetime. Although an 8 year-old who earns and spends $1000 currently has had an accretion to wealth (measured by the utility of the consumption it commands) that is by hypothesis some 10 times greater

ing utility of consumption" hypothesis extends only to *intra*personal utility comparisons over a lifetime; it says nothing about the *inter*personal comparisons necessary to conclude that rates not only ought to decline at the same annual rate for all taxpayers over their lifetimes, but ought to start at the same absolute level as well. While the latter, unprovable assumption might be an acceptable (indeed, essential) premise underlying tax policy generally, it seems odd to indulge it here, while at the same time insisting that the tax system account punctiliously for intrapersonal changes in utility over time. More importantly, even if a utility-based system were administrable, it is doubtful we would choose to abandon the advantages that an objective, market-based measure of wealth provides. These include liquidity, as well as taxpayer support resting on a widely-shared perception that what ought to count in measuring ability to pay is explicit wealth or consumption, rather than the subjective pleasure either provides.[52]

D. *Other Hypotheses About Savings Behavior*

The "cost of abstinence" and "declining utility of consumption" arguments both assume that the equilibrium interest rate is set to compensate for the reduced value of future consumption to the marginal saver. Other explanations for savings behavior, however, have been offered. The one that has dominated economic literature for the past thirty years is the life cycle hypothesis, which postulates that an individual's savings rate is driven by the desire to spread consumption equally over her lifetime.[53] How well does the argument for exempting interest under a "perfected" income tax fare under the life cycle hypothesis?

At first cut, it may appear that if savings is solely a means to smooth out consumption streams, any interest received is pure surplus to the saver. Consider, for example, a saver, *Q*, in a two-period world with no time preference (that is, where a dollar of consumption today, all other things being

than that which the same $1000 will yield her when she is 55 years old, the disutility of a 30% tax on that $1000 will also be 10 times greater when she is 8 than when she is 55. Thus, a uniform tax rate on wages across time will automatically impose an equal tax burden on taxpayers throughout their lifetime, even assuming that the value of wages declines. The difference between interest and wages in this respect follows simply from the fact that we give taxpayers no basis in their disutility, thus treating wages as an increment to wealth.

52. On the latter point, see Jeff Strnad, *Taxation of Income from Capital: A Theoretical Reappraisal*, 37 STAN. L. REV. 1023, 1094 n.159 (1985) ("People's concern may focus more on *what* other people have in the way of available consumption or available power to consume than on how deeply people enjoy that consumption."); Warren, *supra* note 7, at 1096-97 (arguing that ignoring utility is preferable on both philosophical and practical grounds).

53. For early presentations, see MILTON FRIEDMAN, A THEORY OF THE CONSUMPTION FUNCTION (1957); Alberto Ando & Franco Modigliani, *The "Life Cycle" Hypothesis of Saving: Aggregate Implications and Tests*, 53 AM. ECON. REV. 55 (1963). A number of earlier accounts relied implicitly on a life cycle model in describing the likely direction of time preference. *See, e.g.*, E. v. BÖHM-BAWERK, *supra* note 26, at 249-52; I. FISHER, *supra* note 26, at 66-67, 73-75, 383-84 (referring to the "time shape" of income). For more recent developments of the hypothesis, see A. ATKINSON & J. STIGLITZ, *supra* note 10, at 73-77; Summers, *supra* note 3. For a summary of recent critiques of the life cycle hypothesis as unsupported by empirical data on savings behavior, see Laurence J. Kotlikoff, *Intergenerational Transfers and Savings*, J. ECON. PERSP., Spring 1988, at 41.

equal, is worth the same thing as a dollar of consumption in the next period), with a concave utility function (such that aggregate lifetime utility will be maximized if consumption in each time period is equalized), and with an expected earnings pattern of $50,000 in period 1 and $10,000 in period 2. At a zero interest rate, *Q* will save $20,000 in period 1, so as to equalize consumption in both periods at $30,000. Given the existence of a positive interest rate, *r*, *Q* will save slightly less, to reflect the increase in consumption in period 2 resulting from the interest paid on any amount saved.[54] But given that *Q* would have saved a greater amount at a zero interest rate, whatever interest is paid appears to be pure surplus.[55]

The above analysis, however, focuses solely on the income effect of positive interest payments, ignoring any possible offsetting substitution effect. At a high enough interest rate, the substitution effect will dominate the income effect—that is to say, the utility gain to *Q* from increasing nominal consumption in period 2 by the amount of interest earned will outweigh the utility loss from an unequal consumption stream. At that point, *Q* will save *more*, not *less*, as interest rates increase. For the incremental dollars saved, interest will not be pure surplus to *Q*. Instead, it represents compensation for the utility loss from enduring a more unequal consumption stream. In short, in the first case posed above, *Q* is a rentier, but only because he is inframarginal with respect to life cycle savings decisions. When he becomes marginal, interest represents the minimum payment demanded for deferring consumption.

The point may be made clearer by focusing on a saver with *lower* earnings in period 1 than period 2. Consider, for example, taxpayer *X*, who earns $10,000 in period 1 and $50,000 in period 2. One would normally expect *X* not to be a saver. In a no-interest world, *X* would borrow $20,000 in period 1, and in a world with interest rate *r*, *X* would borrow slightly less, to reflect the fact that her consumption in period 2 will be reduced by the $20,000 repayment of principal *plus* interest accruing on the $20,000. But at a sufficiently high interest rate, *X* will stop borrowing and become a saver. For *X* turned saver, like *Q* turned greater saver, interest is *not* pure surplus; it represents compensation for the utility loss from enduring an even more unequal consumption stream.

Once again, the question is what significance this observation should have in determining the fair treatment of *Q* or *X* under an income tax. In a sense, the problem posed is merely a variant of the "declining utility of deferred consumption" argument above. In both cases, interest compensates for the decreasing utility of explicit consumption over time. Here, the decrease results from greater inequality in intertemporal consumption, rather than from the lower value of future consumption per se. Despite this difference, however, the same responses apply. The measurement problems that

54. To be precise, *Q* will save an amount x such that at interest rate r, $\$50{,}000 - x = \$10{,}000 + x(1 + r)^n$, where n equals the number of years from period 1 to period 2.

55. *See* Kelman, *supra* note 25, at 673-76.

would usually weigh against taking account of the subjective utility of wealth for tax purposes would again be somewhat less troubling here, as the portion of the discount rate attributable to *X*'s having to endure an uneven consumption stream would by definition exactly compensate for the disutility this burden entails. But again, it seems hard to justify taking subjective utility into account in the case of savings, given our refusal to consider it elsewhere in the tax system.[56]

56. A number of other hypotheses of savings behavior have been offered, including the suggestion that savers save in order to make bequests and other intergenerational transfers ("bequest savers"); that they save to protect against disease and other hardships of old age ("precautionary savers"); that they demand interest as compensation for the risk they will die before future period consumption ("risk of death savers"); that they save a fixed percentage of their income irrespective of interest rates ("rule of thumb savers"); that they save only when their income is increasing at a faster rate than their taste for consumption ("disequilibrium savers"); and that they save only the residual amount above what is required to maintain their relative status positions in the community (a Veblenesque view of savings behavior, updated in JAMES S. DUESENBERRY, INCOME, SAVING AND THE THEORY OF CONSUMER BEHAVIOR (1949)). On bequest and precautionary savers, see LAURENCE J. KOTLIKOFF, WHAT DETERMINES SAVINGS? 39-162 (1989); Kotlikoff, *supra* note 53, at 41-58. On risk of death, disequilibrium, and Veblenesque (or Duesenberry) savers, see Kelman, *supra* note 25, at 660-75. On rule of thumb savers, see Lawrence H. Summers, *The After-Tax Rate of Return Affects Private Savings*, 74 AM. ECON. REV., May 1984 (papers & proceedings), at 249, 250.

Most of these hypotheses fit comfortably within the analysis already offered in the text, and readers who have already had their fill can probably skip the balance of this footnote in good conscience. For those few hardy souls who have not, what follows is a brief sketch of how the "perfected income tax" argument would play out with respect to each of them.

The first three hypotheses (concerning bequest, precautionary, and risk of death savers) all fit within a conventional marginal analysis, in that they assume that the price demanded ex ante by the marginal saver exactly compensates for the expected decline in the value of future consumption. For risk of death savers, like "abstinence" savers, "lower value of deferred consumption" savers, and life cycle savers whose earnings are lower in early years, interest compensates for attributes of deferred consumption that make it less attractive at the start than present consumption. For bequest and precautionary savers, on the other hand, like life cycle savers whose earnings are higher in early years, deferring consumption is initially an attractive tradeoff—that is to say, these savers would save some amounts of money at low or even negative interest rates in order to provide for desired bequests or protect against calamities in old age. However, for the *marginal* units saved by such savers, the benefits of present consumption outweigh the benefits of saving for bequests or precautionary purposes by the amount of the interest rate. That is to say, the prevailing interest rate is the minimum payment demanded for the utility loss endured by trading off one more unit of present consumption for future wealth. Thus, the arguments for and against not taxing interest to bequest, precautionary, and risk of death savers are identical to those for the other savers discussed in the text: Interest compensates for the expected disutility at the margin from trading off present consumption for future wealth.

There is, however, one important difference in the case of precautionary and risk of death savers. For these savers, unlike the other savers considered, the expected (ex ante) decline in the value of future consumption for which interest is demanded reflects the weighted probabilities of divergent ex post results. In the case of risk of death savers, the divergent possibilities are survival to enjoy future consumption, where such consumption has a utility equal to that of present consumption, versus death, which destroys all utility from future consumption (assuming that no utility is derived from bequests). In the case of precautionary savers, the possibilities are a financially disastrous old age, for which increased savings are even more valuable than anticipated, versus a relatively carefree one, for which they are far less valuable than the earlier consumption forgone. As a result, in both cases, unlike the other hypotheses for savings behavior considered above, the actual ex post positions of most savers in each group will diverge from their expected ex ante positions: One portion of each group will be better off than expected as a result of the marginal decision to save, and another will be worse off than expected. For an exploration of the equity issues raised by that ex ante/ex post split

E. *Inframarginal Savers and Returns to Risk*

As noted above, the argument for a consumption tax as a perfected income tax has implicitly focused on the case for exempting the real riskless rate of return to the marginal saver, ignoring the problems of inframarginal surplus and positive and negative returns to risk. Given the significant disparities in ex post wealth thereby disregarded, it is not self-evident that a consumption tax would move us closer to a perfected income tax than our current, admittedly imperfect scheme, even if we grant the arguments above for exempting the pure interest component of the marginal saver's return.

1. *The inframarginal saver.*

Consistent with classical (premarginalist) price theories, the original Seniorian version of abstinence theory assumed that forbearance from current consumption imposed on all savers a psychic cost equal to the market price of interest. To translate it to modern terms, the argument assumed that the supply price demanded for loaning capital was perfectly elastic across its entire range, equal at each point to the market rate of interest. By definition, then, whatever persuasiveness the Seniorian argument had extended to all savings.

That assumption was undone by the marginal revolution, which made clear that the cost of deferring consumption (measured by the reservation price of the saver) equals the market rate of interest only for the marginal saver, the implicit hero of all of the arguments above. For inframarginal savers, whose reservation price is by definition less than the market rate of interest, a portion of the interest payment represents pure surplus.[57] Thus,

in the context of risk of death savers, see Kelman, *supra* note 25, at 660-69. For a discussion of similar problems raised by the premia demanded ex ante for risky investments, see Part II.E *infra*.

The last three hypotheses (concerning rule of thumb, disequilibrium, and Veblenesque savers), unlike all the other hypotheses previously discussed, assume savings behavior that is *non*marginal with respect to interest rates. In other words, each assumes that the class of savers described will save the identical amount at lower, or even zero, interest rates. As a result, the entire return to savers is arguably surplus. If so, the case for exempting interest to those groups under a "perfected" income tax seems far weaker than with respect to savers whose motivations conform to any of the previously discussed theories. For a thoughtful discussion of this point with respect to disequilibrium and Veblenesque savers, see Kelman, *supra* note 25, at 675-79. Obviously, none of these three hypotheses alone could account for the existence of a positive interest rate. That would require the presence of other savers, whose decisions are influenced by interest rates, and whose supply price at the margin (in conjunction with demand) sets the marginal interest rate.

57. If the price of capital is purely demand-driven at the margin (that is, if the demand for loanable funds intersects the supply curve at a point where supply is inelastic), a portion of interest payments would represent a surplus over cost even for the marginal saver. On the historical development of Böhm-Bawerkian demand-side theories of interest, see MARK BLAUG, ECONOMIC THEORY IN RETROSPECT 527-34 (1978). For a contemporary treatment, see Kelman, *supra* note 25, at 670-79. Most economists have rejected a pure demand-side explanation of interest rates. *See, e.g.*, Summers, *supra* note 56. Consistent with that view, the discussion in Parts II.B and II.C above assumed that the marginal saver received no surplus over reservation price. If that assumption is incorrect, this would further undermine the arguments for adopting a consumption tax as a perfected income tax, as it would mean that, even granting the premises of abstinence theory or the declining utility of deferred consumption, a consumption tax would undertax the ex post wealth of even the marginal riskless saver, as compared to the marginal spender.

building on the original example of Saver and Spender, assume we have another saver, Infrasaver, who has $100 to save, has a personal discount rate of 6 percent, and faces a market rate of interest (set by Saver's discount rate) of 10 percent. In year 2, Infrasaver will end up with a bundle of goods worth $104, as compared to $100 for Saver or Spender.[58] A perfected income tax—if one were to take the notion seriously—should tax the $4 surplus as a clear accretion to wealth to Infrasaver.

The problem, obviously, is how to isolate that surplus in practice. An earlier generation of progressive economists, sympathetic in principle to a tax targeting inframarginal savers' surplus, ultimately concluded that the problem was intractable, and that a choice had to be made either to treat *all* interest or *none* as unearned.[59] Whether for practical reasons, or from a general sense that the tax system ought not to take account of inframarginal taxpayers, most contemporary commentators have likewise assumed that the "cost of deferral" argument for a consumption tax must disregard inframarginal savers, and stand or fall on its applicability to the marginal case.[60]

The readiness of commentators, past and present, to ignore the problem of inframarginal surplus is somewhat perplexing. First, the customary arguments for ignoring *consumers'* surplus do not necessarily carry over to savers' surplus, given that in the former case, the surplus is psychological and the costs are financial, and in the latter case, the surplus is financial and the costs are psychological.[61] Second, depending on the identity of the taxpay-

58. If we assume that Infrasaver's personal discount rate reflects the pain of abstinence, in year 2 Infrasaver will have $110 worth of future consumption, minus $6 in pain from forbearing from present consumption. If we assume the discount rate reflects the lower utility of later consumption, in year 2 Infrasaver will have $104 worth of utility from $110 in explicit consumption.

59. For support in principle of taxing the inframarginal savers' surplus on fairness grounds, see ROBERT LEE HALE, *Economic Theory and the Statesman, in* THE TREND OF ECONOMICS 191, 203 (Rexford G. Tugwell ed., 1924); L.T. HOBHOUSE, THE LABOUR MOVEMENT 59-62, 74-78 (2d ed. 1906); JOHN A. HOBSON, THE ECONOMICS OF DISTRIBUTION 309-35 (1916); JOHN A. HOBSON, THE INDUSTRIAL SYSTEM: AN INQUIRY INTO EARNED AND UNEARNED INCOME 227-32 (2d ed. 1910); J.A. HOBSON, TAXATION IN THE NEW STATE 77 (1919); ALFRED MARSHALL, PRINCIPLES OF ECONOMICS app. K at 830-31 (8th ed. 1920); 2 F.W. TAUSSIG, PRINCIPLES OF ECONOMICS 516-17 (1911). The attack on inframarginal savers' surplus in the early part of the century was part of a broader Progressive attack on "unearned" incomes in any form, whether accruing to land, labor, or capital. For a discussion of the Progressive rent theory movement and its influence on tax legislation in England and the United States, see Fried, *supra* note 28, ch. 4.

In England, the difficulty of isolating inframarginal savers' surplus was resolved in the 1907 and 1909 Labor budgets by treating all interest income as "unearned" and subject to a higher rate of tax than wage income. *See* F. SHEHAB, PROGRESSIVE TAXATION: A STUDY IN THE DEVELOPMENT OF THE PROGRESSIVE PRINCIPLE IN THE BRITISH INCOME TAX 246-52 (1953). In the United States, the "earned income" credit in effect from 1924-1931 and 1934-1941, ranging from 10% to 25% of the tax due on the first $10,000 to $30,000 of "earned" (generally, wage) incomes, was a gesture in the same direction. However, as certain amounts of unearned income were presumed to be earned income for these purposes, the differential effects of the credit were relatively modest. *See* U.S. DEPARTMENT OF TREASURY, THE TAX TREATMENT OF EARNED INCOME (1947).

60. *See, e.g.*, Klein, *supra* note 29, at 470; Warren, *supra* note 12, at 937; *cf.* Kelman, *supra* note 25, at 657 n.23 (arguing that deviation from the general rule would be justified only if all or nearly all savers were inframarginal, or if there were a distributional bias in inframarginal savings that could not be counteracted by adjustments to the general rate structure).

61. To the extent that objections to taxing surplus rest on its illiquidity, surplus in the form of

ers holding marginal and inframarginal investments, it is conceivable that a rate structure *could* be devised that isolated inframarginal surplus. If, for example, inframarginal investments are disproportionately held by wealthy taxpayers and marginal savings by the less well-off,[62] an income tax with an exemption for the first x dollars earned (with x set high enough to cover the bulk of annual interest income to lower- and middle-income taxpayers) could effectively exempt the bulk of marginal and near-marginal savings from taxation, while taxing the bulk of inframarginal savings.[63]

Third, even if it is impossible to isolate inframarginal savings, that still leaves two choices. We can undertax the aggregate class of savers under a consumption tax, or we can overtax them under an income tax. Given that both choices equally depart in principle from a perfected income tax, it is difficult to see any a priori fairness argument for preferring the former to the latter.[64] Empirical evidence regarding the shape of the supply curve (and

---

a cash payment in excess of psychological costs obviously does not pose the same problems as surplus in the form of psychological benefits. To the extent the concern is with measurement problems, even though the psychological cost to savers and the psychological benefit to consumers might be equally difficulf to measure, we might more happily tolerate the possibility of overtaxing in the latter case, where the effect would be, at worst, to undercount psychological costs rather than overestimate psychological benefits. Both of the foregoing points, however, may simply express in another form doubt as to whether psychological costs and benefits should be counted at all.

62. The argument here is not that the class of marginal *savers* is disproportionately made up of the less well-off. Under conventional marginalist analyses of savings behavior, every taxpayer is assumed to be a marginal saver with respect to the last dollar she opts to save under prevailing interest rates. *See* note 24 *supra* and accompanying text. The argument is rather that marginal or near-marginal *savings* are disproportionately held by the less wealthy, and inframarginal *savings* by the wealthy. The intuition behind the argument is that the value of current consumption (and hence the disutility of deferring it) declines as the level of consumption rises, until—having run out of enticing consumption ideas entirely—the Rothschilds of the world would save at a negative interest rate, if necessary. For typical expressions of this view, see J. STAMP, *supra* note 29, at 56-57 ("If a man is so rich that he finds it hard work to spend his money and it accumulates almost without effort on his part, is it any reason why his taxation should be restricted [to expenditure]?"); *see also* I. FISHER, *supra* note 26, at 72-76; JOHN MAYNARD KEYNES, THE GENERAL THEORY OF EMPLOYMENT, INTEREST AND MONEY 96 (1958). As savings represent consumption deferred to the future, not consumption forgone, for both rich and poor the intuition depends on the assumption that the current income effect dominates the future income effect—that is, that savings levels will correlate positively with current income (with the poor dedicating most of their income to meet current needs) and not with future anticipated income level (leading the poor to set aside a relatively greater proportion of their income to provide for future needs). That assumption is obviously open to dispute. For the contrary view, concluding that rich savers are more sensitive to interest rates than poor savers, see N. KALDOR, *supra* note 5, at 92; 2 F.W. TAUSSIG, *supra* note 59, at 517.

63. From 1954 until 1986, such an exclusion existed for dividends received. *See* Internal Revenue Code of 1954, Pub. Law 591, ch. 736, § 116(a), 68A Stat. 3, 37 (exempting the first $50 of dividends received), *amended by* Revenue Act of 1964, Pub. Law 88-272, § 201(c), 78 Stat. 19, 32 (increasing the amount exempted to $100), *repealed by* Tax Reform Act of 1986, Pub. Law 99-514, § 612(a), 100 Stat. 2085, 2250. The apparent purpose of the exclusion, however, was to alleviate the double taxation of dividends, not to respond to the considerations suggested in the text. For legislative history of the 1954 and 1964 acts, see H.R. REP. NO. 1337, 83rd Cong., 2nd Sess. 5-7 (1954), *reprinted in* 1954 U.S.C.C.A.N. 4025, 4030-32; H.R. REP. NO. 749, 88th Cong., 2nd Sess. 1 (1964), *reprinted in* 1964 U.S.C.C.A.N. 1313, 1340-42. For related proposals for an income or wealth tax that would exempt only that portion of savings that reflects deferred consumption (rather than, say, future bequests), see Andrews, *Fairness and the Personal Income Tax: a Reply to Professor Warren*, *supra* note 14, at 957-58.

64. There is conceivably an argument on horizontal equity grounds, if we fail to tax the inframarginal surplus of spenders. *See* notes 132-137 *infra* and accompanying text.

hence the extent of inframarginal surplus) might well tip the balance in one direction or another. If, for example, the bulk of savings were marginal, so that the bulk of interest paid were compensation for the costs of deferral, the case for a consumption tax as a perfected income tax would surely be strengthened. But no evidence supports that conclusion, and proponents of a consumption tax have in any event shown little interest in the empirical data one way or the other.

2. *Returns to risk.*

More troublesome than the problem of the inframarginal saver is the fact that a consumption tax disregards ex post disparities in wealth for winners and losers in risky investments.

Investment returns include three components: an inflation premium, the real, riskless rate of interest, and positive or negative returns to risk. As suggested above, the fairness argument for exempting the return to Saver in the original example deals only with the second component: Saver is presumed entitled to exclude that portion of her actual (ex post) return that compensates for the cost of deferring consumption. By hypothesis, this cost is equal to the price demanded ex ante for bearing it, or the riskless interest rate.

Debates on the relative merits of a consumption tax and an income tax largely ignore the effects of the first component, inflation, treating the positive return to capital as a real return in constant dollars. Proponents of the perfected income tax defense of a consumption tax are no exception. The omission is understandable, and not troubling as a theoretical matter. Given the universal agreement among serious tax scholars that a properly designed income tax would exempt inflation returns,[65] consideration of the fairness of a consumption tax per se has properly focused on the real return to capital in excess of inflation. Moreover, for precisely the reasons it is universally agreed that an income tax should exempt inflation returns, a perfected income tax version of a consumption tax should exempt them as well. They do not represent a real accretion to wealth, but merely compensate for the decreased real value of the principal.[66] The failure to deal with inflation explicitly does, however, obscure a central practical difficulty with the argument for a consumption tax as a perfected income tax: the argument is about almost nothing. The most recent reliable study of interest rates has found that the real, riskless rate of return over the past 65 years has averaged

65. *See, e.g.*, Daniel Halperin & Eugene Steuerle, *Indexing the Tax System for Inflation, in* UNEASY COMPROMISE: PROBLEMS OF A HYBRID INCOME-CONSUMPTION TAX, *supra* note 3, at 347, 348-53; INFLATION AND THE INCOME TAX (Henry J. Aaron ed., 1976); U.S. DEPARTMENT OF TREASURY, TAX REFORM FOR FAIRNESS, SIMPLICITY AND ECONOMIC GROWTH 17, 77, 111, 160 (1984); Warren, *supra* note 7, at 1089 n.29.

66. The argument for exempting inflation returns is just a more persuasive variant of the "decreased value of future consumption" argument described above. In the latter case, the decreased value of future consumption is assumed to come from a decline in the utility of identical acts of consumption over time. In the former case, it comes from a decline in the purchasing power of the dollar over time.

just one-half of one percent.[67] At that rate of return, an income tax—even one at relatively high rates—will have a negligible effect on savers, measured by the percentage decline in their aggregate wealth from a no-tax world.[68] But over the same period, the annual risk premium for an investment in common stock averaged 6.4 percent.[69] Assuming that historical experience holds true roughly in the future, any fairness concerns posed by a tax on the real, riskless return are surely dwarfed by concerns as to the appropriate treatment of returns to risk.

In that respect, it has generally been assumed that an income tax comes much closer to a true measure of ex post accretions to wealth than a consumption tax.[70] The assumption rests on the simple fact that an income tax takes account of the different ex post positions of individual winners and losers who (ex ante) faced the same investment choices, while a consumption tax levies an equal tax (explicitly or implicitly) on both.[71]

At the same time, it is at least arguable that on an *aggregate* basis a

---

67. IBBOTSON ASSOCIATES, STOCKS, BONDS, BILLS AND INFLATION: 1991 YEARBOOK 140-41 (1991). The riskless rate of return is calculated by comparing the return on short-term treasury bills with the inflation rate over the same period, and averaging the results over a number of years. The real, riskless rate of return has been at a historic high for the past five years, possibly reflecting a lagged response to the negative real rate of return during the historically high inflation of the late 1970s. Without the last five years factored in, real interest rates from 1940-1985 averaged only 0.3%. IBBOTSON ASSOCIATES, STOCKS, BONDS, BILLS AND INFLATION: 1986 YEARBOOK 62 (1986). For a discussion of the methodology used in the Ibbotson studies and the design problems in earlier studies that found somewhat higher real rates, see Bankman and Griffith, *supra* note 29 (manuscript at 21-22).

68. As Bankman and Griffith note, $100 invested at 0.5% will grow to $105 at the end of 10 years. If the annual return is reduced to 0.25% as the result of a 50% income tax on earnings, the amount available at the end of 10 years will be $102.50, reflecting only about a 2% decline in terminal wealth from a no-tax world. Bankman & Griffith, *supra* note 29 (manuscript at 22).

69. IBBOTSON ASSOCIATES, STOCKS, BONDS, BILLS AND INFLATION: 1986 YEARBOOK, *supra* note 67, at 55.

70. *See, e.g.*, Michael J. Graetz, *Expenditure Tax Design*, *in* WHAT SHOULD BE TAXED: INCOME OR EXPENDITURE?, *supra* note 3, at 161, 170-72; Warren, *supra* note 7, at 1101-03.

71. In the case of a yield-exempt version of a consumption tax, demonstrating the different results under an income and consumption tax is fairly straightforward. Assume a 50% income tax and a 50% (yield-exempt) consumption tax, and two taxpayers, Lucky and Unlucky, each of whom earns $200 in wages, reduced to $100 after-tax. Each invests her $100 in after-tax wages in a risky investment with a 50% chance of winning $100 (that is, doubling in value) and a 50% chance of losing $50 within the same taxable period. Lucky's investment pays off, yielding $200 total end wealth; Unlucky's does not, yielding $50 total end wealth. The results under a consumption tax and an income tax are as follows:

	Yield-exempt Consumption Tax	Income Tax
Lucky		
After-tax proceeds to invest	$100	$100
Gross yield on investment	200	200
Tax (50% of gain)	0	50
After-tax yield	200	150
Unlucky		
After-tax proceeds to invest	$100	$100
Gross yield on investment	50	50
Tax (reimbursement of 50% of loss)	0	(25)
After-tax yield	50	75

consumption tax is a more accurate measure of the return from risky investments than an income tax, even if the income tax provides for full deductibility of losses. If the risk premium demanded by the market reflects an incremental cost of bearing risk that survives ex post, the class of marginal investors in risky assets is arguably no better off ex post than the class of marginal investors in riskless assets, notwithstanding the higher explicit wealth of the former.[72] An income tax levied on explicit wealth will therefore overtax the aggregate well-being of high-risk investors relative to low-risk investors (as well as to current marginal spenders) by the amount of the risk premium. A consumption tax, by exempting the entire return to risk, will accurately measure aggregate wealth ex post to the extent that the market performs as anticipated.[73]

This raises at least three questions: (1) whether the risk premium reflects an ex post cost that *ought* to be accounted for in a perfected income tax; (2) whether it is possible to account for this cost on an individual basis under an income tax by modifying the measure of ex post income; and (3) if not, whether the aggregate fairness achieved by a consumption tax is preferable to the (admittedly imperfect) results under an income tax. All three questions raise complicated issues, and a full exploration of them is beyond the scope of this paper. A few preliminary observations, however, may be helpful.

The argument for exempting the portion of the return to risk equal to the risk premium has obvious parallels to the "abstinence" and "cost of deferral" arguments for exempting the riskless interest rate. In each of these cases, the compensation demanded ex ante to bear an incremental cost is treated as leaving the marginal saver no better off ex post, because her increase in explicit wealth is offset by an equal implicit cost. But precisely how persuasive this argument is with regard to risk premia depends in large part

---

As the above numbers indicate, under a consumption tax Lucky and Unlucky bear the same present value tax burden of $100, notwithstanding the disparities in their ex post wealth ($200 versus $50). That follows necessarily from the fact that a yield-exempt version of a consumption tax explicitly ignores the ex post results of investments. Under an income tax with full loss offsets, Lucky pays a (present value) tax of $150 and Unlucky pays $75. Even with partial or no deductibility of losses, an income tax, by taxing winners more heavily than losers, will reflect more accurately ex post disparities in wealth than will a consumption tax.

In the case of a cash-flow consumption tax, the result is the same but the demonstration somewhat more complicated, since any illustration depends on recognizing that the explicit tax levied on the full amount of ex post winnings under a cash-flow tax merely substitutes for the tax forgone on the original wages invested, leaving Lucky and Unlucky with the same end wealth as under a yield-exempt tax. *See* Warren, *supra* note 7, at 1102-04.

72. For comments in passing that seem to point to this conclusion, see N. KALDOR, *supra* note 5, at 59 (arguing that a fair tax should take into account the psychic income savers derive from returns, based on their own valuation of risk factors); Erik Lindahl, *The Concept of Income, in* ECONOMIC ESSAYS IN HONOUR OF GUSTAV CASSEL 399, 402 n.* (Augustus M. Kelly 1967) (1933).

73. It should be noted there is no reason to expect that the market *will* perform as anticipated. Like any diversified portfolio, the diversification of the market will offset the risk characteristics of individual investments, but not the systematic risk inherent in the market as a whole. Thus, one would expect actual results over any given period for the aggregate class of investors to diverge from anticipated results.

on the nature of the cost for which they are compensating—that is, on the source of the risk aversion.

Before examining that question, however, it should be noted that there is a crucial difference between the effects of a tax on risky returns and a tax on riskless returns that undercuts the argument for exempting returns to risk from taxation no matter how we characterize the source of risk aversion. An income tax decreases the after-tax return to risk, but at the same time it also decreases risk (measured by the standard deviation of potential outcomes from the mean expected return) by shifting a portion of it onto the government. Viewed from that perspective, the portion of the positive and negative returns claimed by the government might more properly be thought of not as a tax at all, but merely as the aliquot share of winnings and losses to which the government is entitled as an involuntary coinvestor.

An example will clarify the point. Assume a marginal investor in a no-tax world has invested $100 in a risky asset which has a 50 percent chance of paying $200 and a 50 percent chance of paying $50. The investment has an expected yield of $125,[74] with a standard deviation of $75. Assume further (for simplicity's sake) that the riskless interest rate is zero, so that the entire expected return on capital of $25 represents the risk premium demanded by the marginal investor. If a 20 percent income tax is imposed with full loss offsets (so that the government will take 20 percent of the earnings and reimburse 20 percent of the losses), the investment will have a 50 percent chance of paying $180 *after-tax*[75] and a 50 percent chance of paying $60 *after-tax*[76] for an expected after-tax yield of $120.[77] The expected return on the taxpayer's investment has declined 20 percent (from $25 to $20). But the standard deviation has declined 20 percent as well (from $75 to $60), reflecting the portion of upside and downside risk shifted onto the government. In short, an income tax will reduce the *riskiness* of the taxpayer's investment proportionate to the reduction in the investment's expected return.

Two conclusions follow from that observation. First, in an income tax with full loss offsets where the borrowing and lending rate for capital is equal and the cost of risky investments remains constant, it is possible for the marginal investor to put herself back in the same position she held in a no-tax world—in other words, to achieve the same expected return *with the same*

74. That is, (0.5 x $200) plus (0.5 x $50).

75. That is, $200 pre-tax yield minus (0.2 x $100) tax on gain.

76. That is, $50 pre-tax yield plus a reimbursement of (0.2 x $50) loss.

77. This assumes that the imposition of an income tax will not change the pre-tax price of risky investments. The assumption is not a trivial one, however. As noted below, the likely effect of a tax on risk is to increase the demand for risky assets. *See* text accompanying notes 78-79 *infra*. The increased demand will (all other things remaining constant) drive up the price of risky assets, and hence drive down their expected return. This result could be avoided only if the supply of risky assets were simultaneously increased as well. This could be accomplished only if the government dumped back onto the capital market the slice of risk it assumed in imposing the tax, by, in effect, short-selling its future expected tax revenues. *See* LOUIS KAPLOW, TAXATION AND RISK TAKING: A GENERAL EQUILIBRIUM PERSPECTIVE 3-4 (National Bureau of Economic Research Working Paper No. 3709, 1991); Jeremy I. Bulow & Lawrence H. Summers, *The Taxation of Risky Assets*, 92 J. POL. ECON. 20 (1984).

level of risk—simply by increasing the riskiness of her portfolio of assets.[78] Where that possibility exists, it is difficult to see any argument for the unfairness of a tax on risk premia, since the effects of the tax can be eliminated entirely.

Second, even where an investor cannot adjust her portfolio to counteract fully the effects of a tax, her anticipated costs of bearing risk will be lowered by the tax itself. This is in obvious contrast to the pure time preference argument, where a tax lowers the *return* to deferred consumption but not the cost. Assume, for example, that the marginal investor above held a portfolio of $100 investments, all with a 50 percent chance of yielding $200 and a 50 percent chance of yielding $50. Assume further that the portfolio as a whole performs as expected, with winners equalling losers, for an average (pre-tax) return on investment of $25. In a no-tax world, the entire return (equal to the ex ante risk premium) merely compensates the investor for her risk aversion. After imposition of a 20 percent income tax, the return is reduced to $20. But the imposition of the income tax has simultaneously reduced the level of risk to one that the new marginal investor would price at $20—the after-tax premium the market offers for bearing it—shifting the remaining risk to the government. Whether *this* investor would price it at $20 depends on her individual risk preferences. If (in the most likely case) her risk aversion increases nonlinearly with the level of risk, so that a 20 percent increase in the riskiness of an investment would increase the investment's disutility by more than 20 percent, she would price the risk *below* $20. That is to say, the formerly marginal investor would now be inframarginal with respect to risk. The tax reduces the investor's overall wealth, by reducing her risk-taking below its optimal (marginal) level.[79] As suggested above, the formerly optimizing investor's rational response in such a situation would be to increase the pre-tax level of risk until she is again marginal. But from the narrow perspective of a perfected income tax, which looks to whether an increase in explicit wealth exceeds the marginal costs of generating it, the investor has no complaint even if she does not adjust the riskiness of her portfolio. As the tax has reduced the cost of risk more than it has reduced the return, the $20 after-tax premium will generate a surplus over the marginal costs of bearing the risk.

In either case—that is, with or without portfolio adjustments—the effect of an income tax will be to leave the marginal investor in a no-tax world in at least as good a position after-tax, when measured by the difference between expected return and anticipated costs.

But does this dispose entirely of any argument that an income tax un-

78. *See* L. KAPLOW, *supra* note 77, at 12-14; Roger H. Gordon, *Taxation of Corporate Capital Income: Tax Revenues Versus Tax Distortions*, 100 Q.J. ECON. 1 (1985); Warren, *supra* note 7, at 1104-05; Bankman & Griffith, *supra* note 29 (manuscript at 31).

79. This assumes that the marginal risky investor in a no-tax world would be able to select an optimal level of risk to begin with. If, however, the marginal investor cannot *adjust* the level of risk to compensate for the effects of the tax, perhaps because of the lumpiness of investment opportunities, there is no reason to assume that she would have been able to assemble an initial portfolio in the no-tax world that optimized her risk preferences.

fairly overtaxes the true marginal return to risk? Perhaps not, for two reasons. First, to describe a tax on risky investments as no tax at all, but rather as the division of profits and losses among involuntary coinvestors, arguably puts the cart before the horse. It is true that an income tax with full loss offsets effectively makes the government a full partner in taxpayers' risky investments, thereby leaving the marginal investor in no worse an expected position than in a no-tax world. Nevertheless, it might be argued that this effect cannot justify the decision to impose the tax in the first place. Such a decision must rest on a prior determination that explicit returns to risk in a no-tax world are a genuine accretion to wealth. Thus, to take the case of the risky investor whose ex post return equals the ex ante risk premium, while an income tax may not worsen her position, if the premium does not leave her better off than those who invest in riskless assets or consume their wealth currently, we have no justification for imposing the tax to begin with.

Second, the argument proves only that the marginal investor's *expected* position in a no-tax world may be unchanged by imposition of an income tax. It does not necessarily mean that an income tax accurately measures the actual ex post positions of risky investors, compared either to investors in riskless assets or to current consumers. For both of the foregoing reasons, it is worth considering how returns to risk ought to be treated under a perfected income tax.

By definition, the premium that investors demand for investing in risky assets over and above the riskless return reflects compensation for the expected costs of bearing risk—that is, for risk aversion. The appropriate treatment of risk premia under a perfected income tax, therefore, depends in the first instance on the source of that aversion to risk.

At least three possibilities suggest themselves. First, risk aversion may reflect the psychological discomfort of enduring uncertainty while awaiting the outcome of an investment.[80] If so, the argument for exempting a portion of the ex post return to all investors equal to the risk premium closely parallels the "pain of abstinence" argument for exempting the riskless rate of return, and raises some of the same questions: Does the psychological cost of bearing uncertainty survive ex post in any meaningful sense, and is it the sort of cost the tax system ought to take account of?[81]

But it seems unlikely that risk aversion reflects the psychological pain of uncertainty. If it did, a gamble with an instantaneous payoff would carry no risk premium at all. Two other explanations seem far more plausible: that risk aversion reflects the declining marginal utility of wealth, so that from

80. For a similar suggestion with respect to the compensation demanded for enduring the risk of death, see Kelman, *supra* note 25, at 661-62.

81. An additional note of skepticism might be in order here as to whether (as the theory assumes) winners as a class end up incurring the same psychological costs from risk-taking as losers. Even assuming that both bear the same cost from uncertainty during the bet, one suspects that for losers that cost is likely to be exacerbated by lingering ex post regret for risk-taking, while for winners it is likely to be substantially offset by ex post elation at having beaten the odds. But this is perhaps merely to express doubt that the pain of uncertainty could ever be the sole psychological significance of risk.

any given initial wealth the disutility of losing $*x* will outweigh the utility of gaining $*x*;[82] or that it reflects the higher psychological cost attached to losing what one already has than to failing to gain an additional advantage.[83] While either of these two hypotheses will result in investors' weighting losses more heavily than equal gains, starting from any initial position, the two are not the same. The first hypothesis assumes that the marginal utility of wealth to any individual declines monotonically over the entire range of wealth. As a result, starting from any given point of initial wealth a loss of $*x* will fall on a higher part of the utility curve than a gain of $*x*. Therefore, the disutility caused by the loss will exceed the utility created by the (equal) gain. The second hypothesis (what one might call the "endowment effect" hypothesis) assumes no generalizable utility curve for money for any individual—indeed, it at least implicitly refutes that such a thing exists. Instead, it argues that people attach a psychological cost to the very act of losing something they already have that is unrelated to the utility its possession generates and disproportionate to the pleasure that gaining an equal amount might generate. Thus, although intrapersonal comparisons rarely present themselves in this form in real life, it would be entirely consistent with the endowment effect hypothesis to find that while an individual might in general value the 10,000th dollar she receives far more highly than the 100,000th dollar, she might nevertheless attach a greater disutility to losing the 100,000th dollar once she had it than to gaining the 10,000th dollar for the first time.

Under both hypotheses, the argument for exempting risk premia would be that risky investors, although they receive a rate of return nominally greater than the riskless rate, actually derive no additional utility from it. The argument is obviously analogous to the "lower value of deferred consumption" argument above: Risky investors as a group are no better off ex post than riskless investors, not because the higher aggregate return is offset by an implicit cost of bearing risk, but because the higher return has no greater aggregate utility to begin with. As with the "lower value of deferred compensation" argument, however, treating riskless and risky investors as

82. For an endorsement of the declining marginal utility of money as the source of risk aversion, see N. KALDOR, *supra* note 5, at 104. The argument is usually traced back to Bernoulli, who formulated it to explain the so-called St. Petersburg Paradox, which posed one variant of the puzzle as to why people would refuse a mathematically fair bet. The answer, Bernoulli argued, lay in the fact that the utility loss from an expected loss of the wagered amount would outweigh the utility gain from an equal expected gain, due to the diminishing marginal utility of money. Thus, people would rationally refuse to pay $1 million for a 50% chance of winning $2 million and a 50% chance of winning nothing. For an explanation of the Bernoulli hypothesis and subsequent modifications to take account of the fact that within certain income ranges people do in fact take fair and even losing gambles, see M. BLAUG, *supra* note 57, at 332-36.

83. This phenomenon, sometimes called "loss aversion," has been well documented in the experimental work in cognitive psychology of Kahneman, Tversky, and others. *See, e.g.*, Daniel Kahneman & Amos Tversky, *Choices, Values and Frames*, 39 AM. PSYCHOLOGIST 341 (1984); Daniel Kahneman & Amos Tversky, *Prospect Theory: An Analysis of Decision Under Risk*, 47 ECONOMETRICA 263 (1979). For a recent survey of the literature, see Daniel Kahneman, Jack L. Knetsch & Richard H. Thaler, *The Endowment Effect, Loss Aversion, and Status Quo Bias*, 5 J. ECON. PERSP. 193 (1991).

therefore alike for tax purposes would require that we tax wealth according to the subjective utility each taxpayer receives—something we have, as noted above, generally declined to do.

Assuming that a perfected income tax *ought* to take into account the psychological cost of risk under any of the three hypotheses, the question remains whether that is best done through a consumption tax. A consumption tax would accurately account for such cost on an aggregate basis, but would ignore the individual variations from the mean expected return for winners and losers. If the goal is a perfected income base, it would clearly be preferable to reflect the cost through modifications to a conventional income tax, thereby providing an accurate measure of individual as well as aggregate income from risk. Are such modifications possible?

Under the first hypothesis, the answer is, in theory, yes. If risk aversion reflects the pain of bearing uncertainty, the cost is by definition borne equally by all marginal investors, winners and losers alike. A conventional income tax could be adjusted to account for that cost both individually and in the aggregate, simply by adding an amount equal to the risk premium to the basis of all risky assets.[84] As a practical matter, however, one would have to know what the risk premium is for any given asset—a task that may present insurmountable administrative problems.

Under the second and third hypotheses, however, it may be impossible even in theory to extrapolate any useful information about the positions of individual winners and losers from information about investors' *aggregate* ex post well-being. That is clearly the case with the "declining marginal utility" hypothesis. The risk premium, under this hypothesis, reflects the *average* utility of all possible independent outcomes (winning everything, losing everything, and all positions in between), as compared to investing current wealth risklessly. But ex post, a given investor faces only one outcome—the aggregate return on her investments. The utilities assigned to all other possible outcomes ex ante, reflected in the composite risk premium demanded, are now irrelevant. The only figure that remains relevant, the utility assigned to the actual outcome, is impossible to deduce from the composite risk premium.[85]

84. Thus, in the case of a $100 investment with an expected return of $125 in a no-tax world, an ex post payment of $130 would in the first instance generate a $5 taxable gain; a return of $120 would generate a $5 deductible loss. The foregoing analysis, however, is incomplete. A tax on gains and a deduction of losses (both measured against the $125 basis) will shift a portion of the upside and downside risk of investment onto the government, thereby reducing the variance of this risk. A reduction in variance will in turn drive down the premium demanded by the market for bearing risk (that is, the investment's expected return), and hence (assuming that the psychological cost of uncertainty varies with the amount of uncertainty) the psychological "cost" of risk itself to be added to the basis of the asset. Depending on tax rates and risk functions, the risk premium will presumably equilibrate somewhere between the riskless rate of return and the risk premium demanded in the no-tax world. It is this equilibrium premium that would be added to the basis of all assets.

85. An example may make this clearer. Assume a $50 investment with a 50% chance of yielding $100 and a 50% chance of yielding $25, and a riskless interest rate of zero. Assume a marginal investor makes two such investments, one of which wins and one of which loses. The investor ends up with a $25 profit from the two investments, exactly equal to the aggregate premium she demanded ex ante for making them rather than investing in a riskless asset that would guarantee a

Whether it is also impossible to identify the positions of individual winners and losers under a "loss aversion" theory depends on what one hypothesizes to be the nature of the aversion. If it reflects a disutility associated with losing ground from one's current position that does not vary with the amount lost, then the cost is borne ex post only by losers, and equally by all losers.[86] A perfected income tax could therefore reflect that cost accurately on an individual basis by taxing any return in excess of basis in full, and treating any loss of principal as generating a tax loss equal to the sum of (1) the risk premium divided by the probability of losing, and (2) the explicit loss.[87] It seems likely, however, that the aversion to loss does vary with the amount lost. If it does, we face the same difficulty as above in translating aggregate into individual experience. Under a perfected income tax, winners would still be taxed in full on their accretion to explicit wealth and losers given some deduction in excess of explicit losses, but the precise deduction appropriate for any given level of loss would be indeterminate.

Given the impossibility of determining the source of risk aversion and reflecting its cost accurately in a perfected income tax, is the aggregate accuracy achievable through a consumption tax preferable to a conventional income tax?[88] It is hard to see the argument for group fairness per se. Although our tax system has on rare occasion relied on aggregate (group) fairness as a justification for ignoring offsetting intragroup differences among taxpayers,[89] it is difficult to reconcile that notion of fairness with the predominantly individualistic premises of the tax system. Why should a taxpayer who suffers extraordinary losses for which a tax deduction is denied

combined yield of $100. Yet it is clear that, however steeply the marginal utility of money declines for this investor, she is better off ex post with $125 than she would have been with $100. The apparent paradox is resolved by realizing that the $25 premium reflects the combined utilities of four possible outcomes (lose and lose, lose and win, win and lose, win and win) and not the utility of any one certain outcome (in this case, win and lose). While the existence of a risk premium reflecting the declining marginal utility of money tells us that the investor values winning $100 less than she disvalues losing the same amount, it tells us little more about the absolute or relative utility placed on winning that amount.

86. That is, a loss of any amount carries with it an additional disutility, above and beyond the explicit dollar loss from the mere act of losing, equal to the risk premium divided by the probability of losing.

87. Thus, in the case of a $100 investment with a 50% chance of returning some amount less than $100 and an expected return of $125, a return of $101 would yield a $1 taxable gain; and a return of $99 would yield a $51 deductible loss (that is, a $1 explicit loss; plus a $50 loss from the disutility of losing, equal to the risk premium ($25) divided by the probability of losing (0.5)). A return of $100 would yield no gain and no loss.

88. Again, as noted above, a consumption tax would be accurate in the aggregate only to the extent that the market performs as expected over the relevant period. *See* note 73 *supra*.

89. For an exploration of this issue as it pertains to the fairness of exempting interest as a compensation for the risk of death prior to the time of consumption, see Kelman, *supra* note 25, at 662-69. The example Professor Kelman discusses—treatment of annuitants under former I.R.C. § 72—is no longer the law. Under the 1986 Act, annuitants or their estates are now required to adjust ex post for any under- or overrecovery of capital under the prospective exclusion ratio provided in § 72(b). *See* I.R.C. § 72(b)(1)-(3) (1988). However, group rationality is at least one of the explanations still offered for the continuing failure under I.R.C. § 101 to tax ex post mortality gains and losses generated by the pure "insurance" component of life insurance. *See* I.R.C. § 101(a)(1) (1988); WILLIAM A. KLEIN, JOSEPH BANKMAN, BORIS I. BITTKER & LAWRENCE M. STONE, FEDERAL INCOME TAXATION 173-74 (8th ed. 1990).

take solace from the fact that another taxpayer with extraordinary winnings arising from a similar transaction escapes taxation altogether? Nevertheless, group fairness might be defensible as a reasonable approximation of individual fairness. If, over investors' lifetimes, risky investments generally take the form of repeat, independent gambles (such as lifetime stock purchases), the majority of investors should end up over time with an aggregate return on all risky investments converging toward the mean, with a minority (the tails of the distribution) ending up very big winners and losers. For the majority, a consumption tax would thus reasonably approximate individual fairness, at least on a lifetime basis.[90] To the extent one focuses on the minority outliers, however, a consumption tax will achieve greater aggregate fairness for risky investors, but only at the cost of far greater individual unfairness than under a conventional income tax. For that tradeoff to seem attractive, one would have to have more confidence that risk aversion ought to be counted as a cost for tax purposes than, one suspects, most people could muster.

Finally, the discussion until now has assumed an income tax with full loss offsets. In fact, of course, taxpayers' ability to use capital losses is curtailed by a number of provisions in the Code, including sections 1211 and 1212, which limit current deductions to capital gains income (plus $3000 of ordinary income in the case of individuals), with the unused balance carried over.[91] It is unclear how serious a limitation this poses in practice.[92] But any discussion of the appropriate treatment of risk under a perfected income tax must account for Congress's decision in principle to limit deductibility of losses while taxing gains in full. That decision raises two questions as to the consumption tax solution to risk. First, given that the limitations on loss deductions constitute a clear and deliberate departure from any conceptually defensible version of a perfected income tax, is it pointless to try to "perfect" the treatment of risk in other, more debatable respects? Second, would a consumption tax (by exempting all gains and losses from taxation) undo whatever we hoped to accomplish by the current asymmetrical treatment of gains and losses? The answer to both questions depends on the purpose of the loss limitations. If they are intended simply to raise additional revenue by overtaxing aggregate investment returns, a consumption tax would hardly

---

90. For these investors, at least, there is a far stronger case for aggregate treatment of returns to risk than for investors in annuities or life insurance. Since in the latter cases the event (death) that triggers wins or losses is a singular event in all taxpayers' lives, each taxpayer will over her lifetime either win or lose the mortality gamble. There is no possibility of converging toward the mean by repeat, independent bets.

91. Corporations may in general carry unused capital losses back three years and forward five years. I.R.C. § 1212(a) (1988). Individuals may not carry unused capital loses back, but may carry them forward indefinitely. *Id.* § 1212(b). In addition, the "at risk" rules, *see id.* § 465, the limitations on utilization of passive losses, *see id.* § 469 (1988 & Supp. 1989), and the limitations on interest deductions, *see id.* § 163(d) (1988), all have the effect of limiting directly or indirectly the value of capital loss deductions.

92. *See* Rosanne Altshuler & Alan J. Auerbach, *The Significance of Tax Law Asymmetries: An Empirical Investigation*, 105 Q.J. ECON. 61 (1990); Joseph Bankman, The Effect of the Net Operating Loss Rules on Investment in the Venture Capital Industry (May 26, 1992) (unpublished manuscript, on file with the *Stanford Law Review*).

be more palatable than an income tax with full loss offsets. Indeed, assuming that the returns to risk over time are positive, a consumption tax would be far less palatable, since it would ignore all losses only at the cost of ignoring greater gains. On the other hand, if the loss limitations are intended instead to avoid asymmetric realizations of gains and losses, to avoid shifting market risk onto the government, or to prevent the use of passive (investment) losses to shelter wage income, a consumption tax may well be more palatable than an income tax with full loss offsets.

F. *Summary of the Perfected Income Tax Arguments*

For both the riskless interest rate and returns to risk, the case for a consumption tax as a means of implementing a perfected income tax—whatever the origin of the positive reservation price for deferral and risk—turns on the validity of using subjective utility as a measure of taxable wealth. For two of the explanations offered (traditional abstinence theory as an explanation of risk-free interest and the discomfort of bearing uncertainty as an explanation of risk premia), the claim is that, while the interest paid to savers is an admittedly valuable increment in explicit wealth, that increment is offset by the psychological costs of producing it. For the other explanations discussed, the claim is that savers' greater explicit wealth had no greater utility to begin with. That is to say, payment is demanded as compensation not for an actual psychological cost, but for an opportunity cost. In the case of interest, the opportunity cost is the cost of forgoing the pleasure of current consumption for the slightly lesser pleasure of future consumption. In the case of risk premia, the opportunity cost is the cost of forgoing a certain future return for an equal expected, but less certain, one.

It is obvious why such costs—actual or opportunity—should be counted for *efficiency* purposes. They (tautologically) measure the relative subjective values placed on present versus future consumption, or safe versus risky investments, thereby providing a measure of the deadweight utility loss from distorting taxpayers' choices between them through a tax on capital income. But the case for counting such costs on equity grounds is far less clear. It flies in the face of the almost universal acceptance by income and consumption tax advocates alike of explicit wealth rather than utility as the appropriate measure of taxable capacity. For income tax advocates, such acceptance is reflected in the definition of the tax base as the annual increments in the *market value* of one's wealth. For consumption tax advocates, it is reflected in the definition of the tax base as the *market value* of rights exercised annually in consumption.[93] It also flies in the face of consumption tax propo-

93. *See* I. FISHER, THE NATURE OF CAPITAL AND INCOME, *supra* note 9, at 165-79; I. FISHER, *supra* note 26, at 3-6; N. KALDOR, *supra* note 5, at 27-29; H. SIMONS, *supra* note 1, at 50. At least some economists have embraced explicit wealth (whether measured by accretion or consumption) as a tax base *only* as a proxy for utility. Irving Fisher, for example, stated that the psychic pleasure of things is measured by placing "a valuation in terms of money . . . on them," and offered this description of the process:

To accomplish this appraisement it is only necessary for the individual to answer the ques-

nents' willingness to ignore the psychic costs of producing other forms of income, most notably the psychic cost of labor. Given the persistent resistance to anything but an objective measure of wealth in other contexts in constructing a tax base, it is somewhat puzzling why the argument for a utility measure here has been accorded as much respect as it has over the past 100 years. One suspects that for at least some proponents of a consumption tax, the answer may lie in an unexamined reliance on the implicit logic of an efficiency analysis to sustain an equity argument.

With respect to the riskless interest rate, the usual measurement problems that argue against a utility measure of wealth are less vexing. One can assume that the ex post disutility to the marginal saver—whatever its psychological origin—is by definition always equal to the explicit benefit derived. But the same could be said of the marginal return to labor. Moreover, objections to a utility-based tax system have not been solely administrative. While some proponents of explicit wealth as a tax base have endorsed it only insofar as it provides a workable proxy for utility,[94] their view is by no means universal. The Hobbesian foundational argument for a consumption tax, for example, regards explicit levels of consumption as the ultimate object of taxation.[95] Other grounds have been offered as well for rejecting utility as an appropriate measure of taxable capacity, including the belief that people ought to be treated as distinct from their product, and the belief that people care most about the resources others have available for consumption, rather than the pleasure they derive from that consumption.[96] None of this precludes the possibility that one could defend a utility-based measure of taxable wealth in general, or even defend it solely with respect to the marginal decision to save, reverting to an objective measure for all other purposes.[97] Both arguments, however, have yet to be made by consumption tax proponents.

> tion what money is he willing to pay for any enjoyment brought about by means of external wealth, such as a box of sweets or a cigar. If the event is one which cannot be connected with purchasable commodities, it is necessary to imagine an exchange, even when actual exchange is impossible.

I. FISHER, THE NATURE OF CAPITAL AND INCOME, *supra* note 9, at 177; *see also* Robert Murray Haig, *The Concept of Income—Economic and Legal Aspects, in* THE FEDERAL INCOME TAX 2 (Robert Murray Haig ed., 1921); RICHARD W. TRESCH, PUBLIC FINANCE: A NORMATIVE THEORY 265-71 (1981). But even in these cases, if economists are willing to commit to wage income as a proxy for utility (thereby ignoring at least directly the psychic disutility of labor), the same commitment would seem to be in order with respect to income from capital. While some economists have supported in principle the use of utility as a tax base, none has seriously suggested putting the proposal into practice. *See* note 134 *infra*.

94. *See* note 93 *supra*.

95. *See* note 6 *supra* and accompanying text.

96. Strnad, *supra* note 52, at 1094 n.159; Warren, *supra* note 7, at 1096-97.

97. For discussions assuming utility to be the appropriate tax base, see the sources cited at note 134 *infra*. As to the possibility of defending a utility-based measure only with respect to interest, one could argue that the very fact that the market has put an objective price on the decreased utility of future relative to present consumption differentiates this claim from most other claims for utility-based measures, where the tax system would have to account for the differing individual valuations placed on identical commodities. But again, that fact does not differentiate this claim from the claim that we should account for the subjective disutility of labor.

Although fairness arguments have focused almost exclusively on the real riskless interest rate, historically this rate has accounted for a relatively small portion of the total real return to capital, the balance of the return being attributable to premia paid on risky investments. With respect to risk premia, the case for a consumption tax as a perfected income tax seems far weaker than with respect to the riskless rate of interest. As with interest, there is reason to doubt whether a perfected income tax ought to take account of the disutility associated with risk. But there are additional problems as well. First, assuming full deductibility of losses, a tax on risk reduces the riskiness of an investment to the individual holder, and thus reduces the investment's disutility along with its expected return. As noted above, that effect has two consequences. Assuming a constant price for risky assets,[98] investors who are able to adjust their portfolios to increase the level of risk can return themselves to their pre-tax level of risk and expected return. Investors who cannot adjust their portfolio positions will still have the marginal cost of bearing risk reduced along with the marginal return. In both cases, from a purely consequentialist perspective it is hard to see the argument that an income tax unfairly overtaxes risky investors by ignoring the costs associated with risk-taking. Second, a consumption tax would at best account for the disutility of risk-bearing only on an aggregate basis, at the cost of ignoring the significant disparities in ex post well-being among individual winners and losers. Even if one believes the psychic disutility of risk should be accounted for, it is doubtful that the resulting tax burden would come closer to a perfected income tax than our admittedly imperfect income tax.

III. A Consumption Tax as an Endowments Tax

A consumption tax has also been defended as fair on the ground that it levies an equal tax burden on taxpayers who have equal wealth ex ante. The defense amounts to an argument for a consumption tax as a form of endowments tax—that is, a tax levied on people in accordance with their *capacity* to generate wealth, as measured by their initial endowments at "the beginning of [their] working years."[99] Such endowments are generally defined to include not only the monetary value of financial and physical assets on hand, but also human capital in the form of skills and time that can be devoted to market pursuits.[100]

The customary defense of an endowments tax is that it embraces the fairest notion of ability to pay, making no distinctions among taxpayers who begin their working years with equal abilities to generate income through a combination of work and savings, but who make different voluntary choices

98. *See* note 77 *supra.*

99. BLUEPRINTS, *supra* note 5, at 39; *see also* Bradford, *supra* note 5, at 108. For a more explicit statement that the "strong" equity case for a consumption tax rests on its being a method of implementing an endowments tax, see D. BRADFORD, *supra* note 10, at 315; *see also* Mieszkowski, *supra* note 14, at 30-31.

100. *See* BLUEPRINTS, *supra* note 5, at 39; D. BRADFORD, *supra* note 10, at 315.

as to the level and timing of work and savings throughout their lifetimes.[101] As between two current earners, one of whom saves and the other of whom spends, the principle implies that the two, facing the same opportunity to generate income from capital, ought to bear the same tax, regardless of the choices they make. This argument has an obvious kinship to the argument for a consumption tax as a perfected income tax, but is getting at something quite different: not to show that Saver and Spender *are* equally well off ex post, but to show that they *could have been*.[102] As with the perfected income tax argument, there are two ways to equalize the tax burden: either by taxing both the potential imputed income (equal to the forgone interest) to Spender and the potential explicit income to Saver, or by exempting both. If the aim of taxation is to tax ability to pay as measured by ability to generate an explicit income stream, the former would seem preferable as a matter of theory. But in practice, there is no difference between the two, as the former in effect merely imposes a surtax on wages.

A number of objections have been raised to an endowments tax: It ignores unforeseeable shifts in actual (ex post) earnings that generate windfall gains and losses for savers;[103] it assumes without defense its fundamental premise that fairness *ought* to turn on expectations rather than outcomes;[104] and its underlying rationale is impossible to reconcile with the progressive rate structure advocated by at least some of its proponents.[105] Whatever the ultimate merits of an endowments tax, however, the problem with using an endowments rationale for a consumption tax is that a consumption tax does not effect it. A consumption tax is not a tax on ex ante wage-earning potential; it is a tax on actual (ex post) wages.[106] As has frequently been re-

101. *See, e.g.*, BLUEPRINTS, *supra* note 5, at 39 (suggesting that to the extent we believe taxes ought to be levied on the basis of 'ability to pay,' initial endowment is a "good measure of ability to pay over a lifetime"); D. BRADFORD, *supra* note 10, at 315 ("Ideally, I think of the object of a good tax system as placing a relatively heavy burden not on those who make certain choices from their opportunities, but on those who have relatively good options for choice, that is, good endowments."); Richard A. Musgrave, *ET, OT and SBT*, 6 J. PUB. ECON. 3, 11-12 (1976).

102. The two arguments converge if one assumes that all failures to maximize explicit income streams from work and savings reflect deliberate (rational) choices to trade off work for leisure and interest for current consumption. For by definition, individuals rationally choosing leisure or consumption are as well off (measured by total psychic satisfaction) as they would have been had they opted to maximize explicit wealth. *See* D. BRADFORD, *supra* note 10, at 163. But the argument for an endowments tax per se is animated by a concern that people be taxed in accordance with their potential to generate income. *See, e.g., id.* As such, the argument does not depend upon the vitality of the (heroic) assumption that people who face the same choices ex ante will always end up with the same overall wealth ex post, realized in different forms.

103. *See* E. Cary Brown, *Comments, in* WHAT SHOULD BE TAXED: INCOME OR EXPENDITURE?, *supra* note 3, at 114.

104. Alvin C. Warren Jr., *Comments, in* WHAT SHOULD BE TAXED: INCOME OR EXPENDITURE?, *supra* note 3, at 121.

105. *See id.* at 121-22.

106. *See, e.g.*, BLUEPRINTS, *supra* note 5, at 38-40; Mieszkowski, *supra* note 14, at 30 (defining "a person's endowment, or basic wealth, as the present value or discounted stream of future wage payments"); Andrews, *Fairness and the Personal Income Tax: A Reply to Professor Warren, supra* note 14, at 955-56 (describing a "consumption tax with flat, fixed rates [as] the mathematical equivalent of a one-time, lump-sum tax on wealth, wealth being defined to include the present discounted value of all future [actual] earnings as well as material wealth"). For a redefinition of an

marked, there are powerful and ultimately conclusive reasons *not* to tax earnings potential, including the difficulty of measuring it and our collective (libertarian) distaste for indirectly compelling individuals to use their talents in the most lucrative fashion available to them by taxing them as if they had.[107] But given that a consumption tax (like an income tax) abandons an endowment measure of taxable wealth entirely with respect to *human* capital, it is far from obvious what justification there is for reverting to such a measure only with respect to income from financial capital. Indeed, it is hard to see any fairness rationale at all for the hybrid approach that results—taxing ex post (actual) wage income and ex ante (potential) income from savings.

IV. A Consumption Tax as a Way to Preserve the Relative Positions of Savers and Spenders in a No-Tax World

Finally, a consumption tax has been defended as fairer than an income tax on the ground that a consumption tax does not alter the relative values of present and future consumption, and hence the relative well-being of spenders and savers, in a no-tax world. The argument is the most obvious lesson to be drawn from the tale of two taxpayers (Profligate and Thrifty) that opened this article—indeed, it merely restates the mathematical conclusion of that tale.[108] It is also the one most frequently offered in defense of a consumption tax.[109] At the same time, the argument is the most difficult to interpret, as it is usually treated as self-evident by its proponents, and hence offered up without any elaboration. As a result, one can only surmise what theory of fairness underlies this assertion.

The argument that savers and spenders are entitled to preserve their relative positions in a no-tax world is obviously closely linked to the argument in Part II for a consumption tax as a perfected income tax. For at least some of its proponents, it may be simply a different way of putting the same point. That is, the *reason* it is wrong to distort the relative positions of savers and spenders in the no-tax world is that the positions were *identical* in terms of

"endowments" tax explicitly to measure the "capacity of each person to *spend* over his or her lifetime"—that is, as a consumption tax, with gifts and bequests included in the tax base—see Henry J. Aaron & Harvey Galper, *Reforming the Tax System*, *in* ECONOMIC CHOICES 1984, at 87, 102 n.13 (Alice M. Rivlin ed., 1984) (emphasis added). By disavowing any intention to account for earning capacity, such a redefinition obviously avoids the charge that the resulting tax base fails to do so. But this reformulation clearly changes the meaning of endowments in the process, from earning capacity to spending capacity *given* explicit wage earnings, gifts, and bequests.

107. *E.g.*, Kelman, *supra* note 25, at 654 n.20; Warren, *supra* note 7, at 1114-15.

108. *See* note 9 *supra* and accompanying text.

109. *See, e.g.*, I. FISHER, THE NATURE OF CAPITAL AND INCOME, *supra* note 9, at 253 (noting that a Fisherian "income tax"—which is to say, a consumption tax—"would not disturb the comparative merits of [the] different income streams" resulting from different savings patterns); N. KALDOR, *supra* note 5, at 81-87; *id.* at 87 (arguing that the real problem with an income tax is that it reduces the " 'economic reward for waiting' " relative to present consumption, by "disturb[ing] the relationship of prices between present goods and future goods, in favour of present goods"); A.C. PIGOU, THE ECONOMICS OF WELFARE 671-72 (2d ed. 1924); Andrews, *supra* note 5, at 1167-69; *see also* Warren, *supra* note 12, at 946 (lauding this feature of a consumption tax, although ultimately concluding it may be outweighed by the equity arguments for mitigating lifetime wealth disparities).

well-being. But the argument by its terms applies whether or not savers and spenders as a class are in equivalent ex post positions in the no-tax world. Moreover, it appears to be getting at something quite different. The perfected income tax argument is concerned with the theoretical justification for imposing an income tax in the first place. Focusing on the paradigm case of the marginal saver in a no-tax world, it concludes that it is unfair to tax her as if interest payments had left her wealthier than the marginal spender when, in fact, they merely compensate for her equal, offsetting costs. The argument here, on the other hand, seems to be concerned with the *effects* of an income tax on the relative positions of savers and spenders. As I will suggest, the argument, although not explicit on this point, must therefore have in mind the case of everyone *but* the marginal saver—the one person who by definition will not be disadvantaged by the tax—asserting that the effect of a tax on interest is to reduce unfairly the aggregate and individual welfare of inframarginal savers relative to spenders.

The argument raises two sets of questions: whether savers are in fact disadvantaged relative to spenders; and if so, why that should be thought unfair. Each will be considered in turn.

A. *Are Savers Disadvantaged Relative to Spenders by an Income Tax?*

As discussed above, the claim that savers are disadvantaged by an income tax is at best debatable with respect to a tax on risk. Under a plausible set of assumptions, any investor in risky assets—marginal or otherwise—can restore the same level of surplus she enjoyed in the no-tax world simply by increasing the level of pre-tax risk in her portfolio of investments.[110]

With respect to a tax on the real, riskless rate of interest, the claim is also more problematic than generally thought. The common intuition that savers *are* disadvantaged by an income tax can be illustrated by the following example. Consider four taxpayers (*A*, *B*, *C*, and *D*), who have personal discount rates for saving of 3 percent, 8 percent, 9 percent, and 10 percent, respectively.[111] Assume a zero rate of inflation, and an equilibrium interest rate of 10 percent in a no-tax world. Assume further that after imposition of a 33 percent tax on interest, the nominal equilibrium interest rate shifts to 12 percent, yielding an 8 percent after-tax return.[112] In the no-tax world, *A*, *B*,

110. *See* notes 74-78 *supra* and accompanying text.

111. As in Part II, for ease of exposition, the example focuses on inframarginal *savers* rather than inframarginal *savings*. However, under most hypotheses of savings behavior, every saver will continue to save until the cost of the last dollar saved exactly equals the marginal return—that is, until they are marginal savers. *See* note 24 *supra*. Thus, it should be understood throughout the discussion that *A*, *B*, *C*, and *D* represent a unit of savings rather than a particular saver, and that the surplus at issue accrues to "inframarginal dollars saved" rather than "inframarginal savers."

112. The precise rise in the nominal interest rate after the imposition of a tax on interest will depend upon the elasticity of the savings supply at the old equilibrium interest rate. The more price-inelastic the supply, the greater will be the portion of the tax borne by savers, rather than passed through to borrowers in the form of an increase in the nominal (pre-tax) interest rate. Unless supply is completely price-inelastic over the relevant quantity range, some portion of the tax will be passed through to borrowers. Although *which* of the above savers in a no-tax world (*A*, *B*, *C*, or *D*) will become spenders once a tax is imposed obviously depends on the real after-tax rate of interest, the

C, and *D* will all choose to save. In the after-tax world, *A* and *B* remain savers, but *C* and *D* will choose to spend currently. Represented graphically in Figure 1 below, the before- and after-tax positions are as follows:

Figure 1

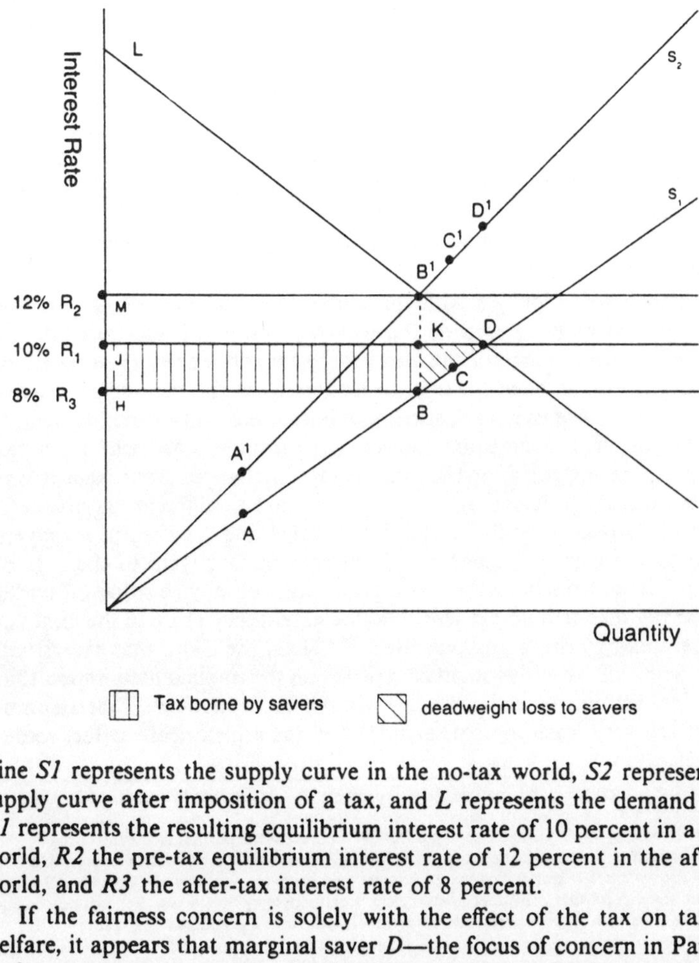

Line *S1* represents the supply curve in the no-tax world, *S2* represents the supply curve after imposition of a tax, and *L* represents the demand curve. *R1* represents the resulting equilibrium interest rate of 10 percent in a no-tax world, *R2* the pre-tax equilibrium interest rate of 12 percent in the after-tax world, and *R3* the after-tax interest rate of 8 percent.

If the fairness concern is solely with the effect of the tax on taxpayer welfare, it appears that marginal saver *D*—the focus of concern in Part II—is the one saver in a no-tax world who will *not* be disadvantaged in any respect by the imposition of an income tax on savings, as *D* is by definition indifferent between saving at a 10 percent interest rate (her choice in a no-tax world) and currently consuming (the choice to which she is pushed by the

analysis that follows does not fundamentally change whatever degree of elasticity is assumed. The analysis may, however, be fundamentally changed if one assumes that interest paid on consumer debt should be deductible to borrowers. *See* notes 114-116 *infra* and accompanying text.

imposition of a tax). The fairness problem, if any, lies with the effect of the tax on *A*, *B*, and *C*.

With respect to *A* and *B*—savers before and after imposition of the tax—the argument that a tax on savings decreases welfare is straightforward. In a no-tax world, *A* and *B* enjoyed a suppliers' surplus equal to $7 and $2, respectively, for every $100 saved. After imposition of a tax, *A*'s surplus is reduced to $5 (after-tax interest of $8, minus a discount rate of $3) and *B*'s surplus is reduced to zero (after-tax interest of $8 minus a personal discount rate of $8). In the case of *C*—an inframarginal saver before imposition of the tax, who becomes an inframarginal spender after the tax is imposed—the effect of the tax is to deprive him of an opportunity to derive the 1 percent surplus he enjoyed from saving rather than spending in a no-tax world. The total surplus lost by savers is represented by the area bounded by *H*, *J*, *B*, and *D*.[113] This lost surplus is, presumably, the focus of concern for consumption tax proponents.

There are two difficulties with the above analysis. First, it ignores the treatment of consumer interest on the borrowers' side. If consumer interest is deductible under an income tax and borrowers and lenders (savers) are in the same tax bracket, then the cost to lenders from the tax will be exactly offset by the benefit of the tax deduction to borrowers. As a result, the entire tax will be passed through to borrowers in the form of a grossed-up pre-tax interest rate, leaving the after-tax interest rate unchanged from what it was in a no-tax world.[114] If borrowers and lenders are in different tax brackets, the most likely reason would be that low-bracket and tax-exempt taxpayers gravitate to the role of lenders and high-bracket taxpayers to the role of borrowers. If so, lenders (savers) as a group will actually be *better* off under an income tax than in a no-tax world, to the extent they share in the joint tax gain generated by arbitraging tax rates.[115] Thus, the claim that savers will be made worse off by an income tax depends on the implicit assumption that interest paid for consumer borrowing will *not* be deductible. That assumption is at the very least controversial,[116] and (as a historical matter) some-

113. Of that total area, the triangle *BDK* represents the deadweight loss imposed by the tax, and rectangle *HJKB*, the portion of the tax revenues generated by a tax on savings that is borne by savers. The remaining tax revenues (rectangle *JKMB'*) represent the portion of the tax borne by the borrowers through an increase in the cost of borrowing. Note that the resulting rectangle *MB'BH* shows only the revenue generated by a tax on interest paid to savers, ignoring any possible offsetting revenue loss in the event that consumer interest paid is deductible by borrowers. For further consideration of the treatment of borrowers, see notes 114-116 *infra* and accompanying text.

114. Thus, in the above example, one would expect a flat tax rate of 33% to result in a pre-tax interest rate of 15%, yielding an effective after-tax rate of 10% to both borrowers and lenders (that is, the same as in a no-tax world).

115. Thus, in the above example, if one assumed interest was effectively deductible at the 50% tax bracket and taxed at the 33% bracket, then borrowers who would pay 10% in a no-tax world would pay up to 20% (pre-tax) in the tax world; savers who would lend at 10% would demand 15% (pre-tax) to lend the same amounts. One would expect the pre-tax equilibrium interest rate to settle between 15% and 20%, leaving both savers and borrowers better off after-tax than they were in a no-tax world, and the government correspondingly worse off.

116. The customary argument *against* allowing a deduction for personal interest is that the decision to accelerate consumption by borrowing is itself a consumption decision that (like other acts

what surprising given that prior to the Tax Reform Act of 1986 all consumer interest was in fact deductible.

Second, assuming that some portion of the tax on interest *is* ultimately borne by savers, the example proves only that savers are absolutely worse off under an income tax than in the no-tax world. But the charge by consumption tax proponents is not that savers are made absolutely worse off by an income tax. It is that they are made worse off relative to nonsavers. Whether that claim is true depends upon which group of nonsavers the inframarginal savers are compared to. For reasons that are not entirely clear, debate has generally focused on the comparison of savers to nonborrowing spenders, that is, those individuals who in a no-tax world finance current consumption out of past or current earnings. That limitation would make sense if the sole fairness concern with an income tax were that it alters the relative value of the choices to save or spend a *current* endowment. But most consumption tax advocates have argued more generally that a tax ought not to alter the relative values of intertemporal consumption decisions, whenever endowments are actually earned. That is to say, an ideal tax should distort neither the choice to defer consumption nor the choice to accelerate it.[117] If one accepts that premise, then there are *four* groups of taxpayers, not two, whose welfare is relevant in assessing the fairness of a tax on savings: early earners who defer consumption by saving (group 1); early earners who consume currently (group 2); late earners who accelerate con-

---

of consumption) ought not to be deductible. While the argument has a surface plausibility, it is difficult to reconcile with our decision under an income tax to tax interest paid to savers for deferring consumption. As suggested at length in Part II, the decision to tax savers rests on the determination that for tax purposes consumption will be treated as not having a time value—that is, that deferred consumption generates no less utility for savers than equivalent nominal amounts of present consumption. Hence, the interest they receive for trading present for future consumption reflects a real increase in wealth. But if so, it should be equally true that *accelerated* consumption generates no greater utility to borrowers than would deferred consumption financed out of later earnings, and hence in decreasing their nominal consumption by the amount of interest paid on consumer loans, borrowers are reducing their real wealth as well. To be consistent, therefore, consumer interest should be deductible under the income tax. For arguments to that effect, see William D. Andrews, *Personal Deductions in an Ideal Income Tax*, 86 HARV. L. REV. 309, 376 n.116 (1972); Alan Gunn, *The Income Tax, the Consumption Tax and the Deductibility of Interest on Personal Debt*, *in* THE QUEST FOR TAX REFORM 167 (W. Neil Brooks ed., 1988).

117. *See, e.g.*, BLUEPRINTS, *supra* note 5, at 42; N. KALDOR, *supra* note 5, at 84-86; Andrews, *supra* note 5, at 1167-68; Andrews, *Fairness and the Personal Income Tax: A Reply to Professor Warren*, *supra* note 14, at 947-53. Andrews argues that a fair tax would not alter the relative positions of "equal consumers" in a no-tax world—that is, individuals who consume the same amounts at the same time, irrespective of the pattern of wage earnings and savings that go to finance that consumption. Andrews illustrates his argument by reference to *late* consumption, financed by deferred or current earnings. He posits two taxpayers who consume $800 in year 25. One finances that consumption by investing $100 of current earnings in year 1, which at 9% interest by year 25 has compounded to $800; the other finances it by $800 of current earnings in year 25. Andrews, *Fairness and the Personal Income Tax: A Reply to Professor Warren*, *supra* note 14, at 948 n.3. A fair tax, Andrews argues, would leave both taxpayers in the same relative after-tax position irrespective of their earnings patterns. *Id.* at 949. Presumably the same logic would apply to taxpayers with equal *early* consumption, financed for one by current earnings and for the other by a loan against future earnings. This logic would require, however, that an income tax not affect the relative values of financing present consumption either out of present earnings or by borrowing against future earnings.

sumption by borrowing (group 3); and late earners who defer consumption until earnings are received (group 4).[118]

As with savers, the effect of an income tax on the above-described groups is less clear cut than generally thought. For spenders who are forced to finance current consumption by borrowing against future earnings (group 3), a tax on interest will change the utility of current consumption if it changes the cost of borrowing from what it was in a no-tax world. As noted above, whether it *would* change the cost of borrowing, and in what direction, depends on the elasticity of supply and demand, and, more importantly, on whether consumer interest is deductible. If it is deductible, borrowers will be at worst in the same position under an income tax as in the no-tax world, and they may well be better off. If consumer interest is not deductible (the general treatment in our current tax structure),[119] borrowers will be worse off than they were in a no-tax world, assuming some portion of the tax is passed through to them in the form of a higher pre-tax borrowing rate. Consider, for example, taxpayer *F*, with a private discount rate for borrowing of 14 percent. *F*, who could have borrowed funds to finance current consumption at 10 percent interest in the no-tax world, will pay 12 percent after imposition of a tax if interest is nondeductible, and 8 percent if it is deductible. *F* will borrow before and after imposition of a tax on savings, whether interest is deductible or not. But, if interest is nondeductible, *F*'s surplus from borrowing will be reduced from 4 percent to 2 percent by imposition of a tax; if interest is deductible, *F*'s surplus will be increased from 4 percent to 6 percent.

For nonborrowing spenders (group 2), a tax on savings should have no effect on welfare.[120] Consider taxpayer *E*, with discretionary income to consume or save, and with a private discount rate for saving of 15 percent. Since *E*'s discount rate exceeds the effective interest rate before and after imposition of a tax, *E* will spend the same amount of money on the same

118. If individuals' discount rates for lending and borrowing are identical, and lending and borrowing rates are identical, virtually everyone will be either a lender or a borrower—that is, everyone will fall within group 1 or 3. For example, in a world with a lending and borrowing rate of 10%, an individual with an initial private discount rate of 15% (that is, one who demands 15% interest to save $1 of current earnings) would consume all current income as per group 2, generating inframarginal surplus from consumption, until her discount rate for an additional dollar of consumption dropped below 10%, and then would save the balance (as per group 1); or, if her discount rate was still above 10% at the last dollar of current income consumed, would then borrow additional funds (as per group 3) until her marginal discount rate fell to 10%. Only if the last dollar of current earnings brought her marginal time preference exactly to 10% would she neither borrow nor lend. For a description assuming that all individuals are in fact either lenders (if their initial private discount rate is lower than the market rate) *or* borrowers (if it is higher), with members of each group lending or borrowing until their marginal rates of time preference are equal to the market rate of interest, see I. FISHER, *supra* note 26, at 104-06, 117-19. Of course, if individuals had a higher discount rate for saving than for borrowing (as seems likely to be the case), they could be inframarginal with respect to the decision to consume their entire current earnings, and yet choose *not* to borrow at all.

119. The only exception is home mortgage interest, which is deductible under I.R.C. § 163(h) (1988).

120. This assumes that under a general equilibrium analysis a tax on savings will not alter the cost of consumption goods.

amount of consumption goods in both a no-tax and a tax world, deriving whatever pleasure their consumption affords. It is true that a change in the effective interest rate paid to lenders or charged to borrowers in some sense alters *E*'s opportunity sets. Using the above numbers, for example, the effect of the tax on interest is to lower *E*'s opportunity cost of not saving from 10 percent to 8 percent. If the tax also changes the effective cost of borrowing, it will by definition also change the cost *E* avoids by not borrowing to finance current spending. But as *E* would not have opted to save or borrow under either rate, it is hard to see how the change in costs or benefits associated with those counterfactual choices affects *E*'s actual welfare.

Finally, for future earners who opt not to accelerate consumption by borrowing (group 4), as for current earners who opt not to save (group 2), a tax on savings should have no effect on welfare. Consider a taxpayer, *G*, with expected future earnings he could borrow against, and a personal discount rate for borrowing of 6 percent. Since *G*'s discount rate is lower than the interest rate for borrowing both before and after imposition of a tax (whether interest is deductible or not), both in a no-tax and a tax world *G* will defer consumption of earnings until they are actually earned. While *G*'s opportunity sets are (like *E*'s) in some sense altered by the change in interest rates in the tax world, since *G* would not opt to borrow or lend in either world, that change will not affect *G*'s actual welfare.

Given the above, if the asserted unfairness of a tax on savings rests on the more general claim that such a tax distorts the values of intertemporal choices, then the claim is obviously true, assuming consumer interest is not deductible. For current earners deciding whether to defer consumption (groups 1 and 2), if any portion of a tax on interest is borne by savers, then savers' welfare will be reduced, while nonborrowing spenders' welfare remains unchanged. For future earners deciding whether to accelerate consumption (groups 3 and 4), if any portion of the tax is passed through to borrowers in the form of a higher pre-tax interest rate, then borrowers' welfare will be reduced, while nonborrowers' welfare remains unchanged.

If the charge of unfairness of a tax on savings focuses instead on the relative disadvantage suffered by savers per se, then the accuracy of the charge depends on which group savers are compared to. If they are compared to current earners/current spenders (group 2) or late earners/late spenders (group 4), the claim is obviously correct. Savers' welfare is reduced by the tax, while the other two groups' welfare remains unchanged. If, on the other hand, savers are compared to borrowers (group 3), then under a plausible set of empirical and legal assumptions (that is, that at least a portion of the tax is passed through to borrowers through an increase in interest rates, and that interest is nondeductible), borrowers could be disadvantaged as much as or even more than savers. If so, the fairness argument would seem to collapse entirely.

Which of these comparisons is relevant depends on what consumption tax advocates take to be ethically significant about savers as a class, a question commentators have failed to address thus far. Assume, for example, that what is ethically significant about savers is that they are compelled to enter a market transaction to shift consumption to a different time period than earnings to reach the desired consumption stream. If consumption tax advocates are chiefly concerned that savers not be disadvantaged relative to *other* groups who are compelled to shift consumption, the relevant comparison might be to group 3 (borrowers). As noted above, savers are not necessarily disadvantaged relative to that group.[121] If instead consumption tax advocates are chiefly concerned that savers not be disadvantaged relative to groups whose desired consumption patterns in a no-tax world coincide with their earnings stream, the relevant comparison is to group 2 (current earners who do not save) and group 4 (future earners who do not borrow).[122] Savers are disadvantaged relative to both of these groups. If, on the other hand, what is ethically significant about savers as a class is that they are willing to shift consumption to a *later* period than earnings, thereby adding to the national savings rate, the relevant comparison would be to groups 2, 3, and 4, none of which defers consumption past earnings, and most particularly to group 3, whose members dissave.[123]

The larger point of the above discussion, obviously, is that the premise on which this argument for a consumption tax rests—that savers *are* disadvantaged relative to spenders by an income tax—is in doubt. It depends on unarticulated assumptions, both factual and normative, that may not be true or widely shared.

B. *Why Are Savers Entitled to Maintain Their Relative Pre-tax Position?*

Assuming that consumption tax advocates intend a comparison for which it *is* true that a tax on savings disproportionately hurts inframarginal savers, the question is, so what? A tax that reduces the welfare of inframarginal savers relative to nonsavers is unfair only if savers and nonsavers have an entitlement to the relative levels of well-being they would have enjoyed in a no-tax world. Consumption tax advocates have never explained the rationale behind such an entitlement, and it is unclear on what theory of distributive justice it would be based. One can deduce such an entitlement from the premise that the appropriate measure of ability to pay is consumption and not income.[124] But this tautology just returns us to the

121. *Blueprints* implicitly adopts as relevant the comparison of savers to borrowing spenders (group 3), but concludes erroneously, or at the very least too hastily, that an income tax disadvantages the former relative to the latter. *See* BLUEPRINTS, *supra* note 5, at 42 (noting that "the income tax makes early earners and later consumers worse off than late earners and early consumers," and that "[a] consumption tax is neutral between these two patterns").

122. Andrews, for example, argues that the most significant comparison is to group 4. *See* Andrews, *Fairness and the Personal Income Tax: A Reply to Professor Warren*, *supra* note 14, at 949-50.

123. *See, e.g.*, N. KALDOR, *supra* note 5, at 86 (noting, on the assumption that interest is deductible to borrowers, that an income tax "affords a special incentive to ante-date consumption in time").

124. *See* Edwin Cannan, Book Review, 31 ECON. J. 206, 213 (1921) (reviewing A.C. PIGOU,

Hobbesian foundational argument. The question is, is there some independent normative defense of the entitlement? Two general possibilities suggest themselves, tracking the contemporary debate on distributive justice: The entitlement to one's no-tax level of well-being either is grounded in a notion of historical entitlement, or is derived from some end-state theory of distributive justice. While a full consideration of either claim is beyond the scope of this article, a few preliminary observations may suggest the difficulties each entails, and may caution against any facile assumption that such an entitlement should be presumed to exist here. For simplicity's sake, the discussion that follows will focus on the claims of savers relative to current earners/current spenders, that is, on groups 1 and 2. Analogous arguments, however, could be made with respcct to the other possible comparisons, and would raise similar difficulties.

1. *Do inframarginal savers have a historical entitlement to surplus value?*

First, the argument might be based on what would be described in the contemporary debate about distributive justice as a historical theory of entitlement—that is, on the principle that the distribution of wealth is justified by the justice of the process that brings it about.[125] The strongest version of historical entitlement theory, which would claim for inframarginal savers an entitlement to retain the absolute level of benefits that the market rate of interest in a no-tax world provides them, faces several serious difficulties. First, the government already influences the level of welfare associated with virtually every choice through a variety of nontax policies, and interest rates are no exception.[126] When the government acts to increase the money supply, for example, thereby driving down pre-tax interest rates, or when it acts

---

THE ECONOMICS OF WELFARE (1920)) (sharply criticizing Pigou for resting on precisely this circularity in charging that the income tax discriminates against saving relative to spending).

125. For a discussion of historical theories of entitlement, contrasting them with end-state theories, see ROBERT NOZICK, ANARCHY, STATE, AND UTOPIA 150-60 (1974). Nozick's principle of "justice in holdings" is the most notable recent example of an historical theory of entitlement. *See id.* In contrast, classical utilitarianism, the Rawlsian difference principle, and radical egalitarianism all represent different forms of end-state, or patterned, theories of just distribution, in which the distribution of assets is justified by its correspondence with some structural principle of distributive justice.

126. *See* Bankman & Griffith, *supra* note 29 (manuscript at 11) (noting, inter alia, that funds for interstate highways rather than mass transit increase the consumer surplus of rural taxpayers who rely on automobile travel relative to urban taxpayers who rely on mass transit). C.W. Guillebaud made a related observation with respect to interest:

> [T]he State, through the exercise of its general function as a co-operating factor in the productive organisation of the community, and through the expenditure of the revenue which it receives from the taxpayers, will increase the productivity of the capital accumulated by the action of savers above what it would have been in the absence of the State. The State is accordingly entitled to a share in this additional income.

Guillebaud, *supra* note 7, at 489. For a more general critique along the same lines, see Louis Kaplow, *Horizontal Equity: Measures in Search of a Principle*, 42 NAT'L TAX J. 139, 146 (1989) (noting that those who construe horizontal equity to require that we judge tax reform by the degree to which it modifies pre-reform distribution of income have the obligation to show "why the status quo is to be intrinsically valued, thus supporting a preference against all changes in position, when the status quo was itself the product of countless changes throughout history").

to stimulate demand for loanable funds, thereby driving these rates up, it alters the welfare of inframarginal savers. Strict libertarians, who acknowledge the essential similarity between taxation and other forms of government regulation, have concluded that the government ought not to interfere with market-based distribution in *either* form. But for those who stop short of that radical laissez-faire conclusion, the obvious moral to be drawn is the opposite one: If one form of government intervention in the workings of the market does not violate private entitlements, why should the other?

Moreover, even if it were possible to isolate a 'natural' equilibrium rate of interest in a no-tax world, it is unclear on what theory of distributive justice inframarginal savers would have a right to whatever absolute benefit that rate may yield. Such a right cannot be reconciled with the principles of an income tax. Under a conventional income tax, which measures accretions to wealth by the changes in the *market value* of a taxpayer's net wealth, ignoring the psychic cost of deferral entirely, a tax levied on the full amount of real interest is entirely appropriate. Even under a perfected income tax that gives savers a tax basis in the psychological cost of deferral, the surplus hypothetically enjoyed by inframarginal savers over their marginal counterparts (resulting from the relatively lower psychological cost that inframarginal savers incur) ought, on fairness grounds, to be treated as a taxable gain.[127] While it is true that a tax on interest is levied not on the inframarginal surplus per se, but instead on the entire return, the fact that the *effect* of the tax on savers is simply to reduce or eliminate inframarginal surplus makes it possible to defend an income tax as a plausible, though imperfect, means of taxing the surplus itself.[128]

It is equally hard to deduce the right to a saver's surplus from any more fundamental notion of historical entitlement that would call into question the fairness of the income tax altogether. Traditional (Lockean) liberal political theory, which grounds private ownership of property on the sacrifice entailed in its creation,[129] might be construed to entitle savers to the portion of the return that compensates them for the pain of abstinence.[130] But it is hard to see how this entitlement would extend to the surplus that inframarginal savers enjoy over their marginal counterparts, a surplus which

127. *See* notes 57-58 *supra* and accompanying text.

128. An income tax is imperfect because the amount of the tax is invariant with the level of surplus. Thus, in the above example, *C*, who ceases to be a saver at all, and *B*, who becomes the new marginal saver, are effectively deprived of 100% of their surplus. *A*, who remains inframarginal, is deprived of only two-sevenths of her surplus. It might also seem somewhat peculiar to describe an income tax as a *tax* on surplus, at least with respect to *C*, as the effect of the tax is not to transfer *C*'s surplus value to the state, but rather to eliminate it entirely in the form of a deadweight loss, as *C* shifts from saver to spender.

129. By "Lockean" I mean to denote views generally ascribed to Locke in political debate in the nineteenth and twentieth centuries, not views that Locke himself necessarily would have subscribed to. For the argument that Locke would *not* have endorsed the individualistic view of property rights to which his name is now indelibly attached, see JAMES TULLY, A DISCOURSE ON PROPERTY 98-99 (1980).

130. This assumes (*contra* Davenport) that such pain is regarded as a relevant sacrifice for these purposes. For a discussion of Davenport's criticism of abstinence theory, see notes 35-44 *supra* and accompanying text.

owes itself to the mere fortuity of different preference structures, not to individual effort. While recent libertarian reinterpretations of Lockeanism offered by Robert Nozick and others would extend an absolute entitlement to all surplus value generated by a market exchange, the logic of such an extension is dubious.[131] More to the point, it is not a view any proponent of a consumption tax can subscribe to, given that it would preclude most taxes, including a consumption tax, as a form of theft.

More plausibly, the argument for an historical entitlement may rest on the more modest demands of horizontal equity within an income tax. That is, conceding that the surplus enjoyed by inframarginal *savers* represents an accretion to wealth that the government may justly appropriate, it could nonetheless be argued that horizontal equity requires that we appropriate an equal portion of the surplus of inframarginal *spenders* (resulting from their greater than marginal taste for current consumption) through a tax on the pleasure derived from consumption.[132] Hence, as we are unable or unwilling to do the latter, we should refrain from the former as well.

But there are a number of problems with that argument. First, it is hard to see the normative appeal of maintaining the relative rank ordering of taxpayer wealth—the aim of horizontal equity—absent some belief that the initial rank ordering was itself just.[133] In the case of inframarginal surplus accruing to savers and spenders as a result of differing tastes, it is hard to see the argument that the initial ordering *is* just, for the reasons discussed above.

131. As applied to interest, Nozick's historical entitlement theory would argue that the inframarginal saver deserves whatever surplus his inframarginal tastes produce, because this surplus is generated by the exchange of something the saver rightly owned (the right to currently consume one's own capital that was acquired by just means) for a price the borrower voluntarily paid. *Cf.* R. NOZICK, *supra* note 125, at 151. For a similar, less developed argument for an entitlement to market-generated surplus, see RICHARD A. EPSTEIN, TAKINGS: PRIVATE PROPERTY AND THE POWER OF EMINENT DOMAIN 162-66, 334-38 (1985). The difficulty with Nozick's argument is that it assumes the very thing that must be proved: that the right to whatever is produced by one's efforts ought to carry with it the right to any surplus value *above* the sacrifice entailed in producing it.

132. For an explicit argument to that effect, see Martin Feldstein, *On the Theory of Tax Reform*, 6 J. PUB. ECON. 77, 82-83 (1976).

133. It has been suggested that horizontal equity has a rationale distinct from entitlement theory, occupying a middle ground between entitlement and end-state theories like utilitarianism. *See* Mervyn A. King, *An Index of Inequality: With Applications to Horizontal Equity and Social Mobility*, 51 ECONOMETRICA 99, 99-100 (1983). That may be true when horizontal equity is invoked in the specialized sense of proscribing differential treatment of taxpayers on invidious grounds such as race or sex. *See, e.g.*, RICHARD A. MUSGRAVE, THE THEORY OF PUBLIC FINANCE: A STUDY IN PUBLIC ECONOMY 160 (1959); *cf.* Anthony B. Atkinson, *Horizontal Equity and the Distribution of the Tax Burden*, *in* THE ECONOMICS OF TAXATION 3, 18 (Henry J. Aaron & Michael J. Boskin eds., 1980) (summarizing the views of commentators who consider principles of horizontal equity to be buffers against discrimination). But if one views horizontal equity in the more general and common sense of requiring the preservation of pre-tax rankings among all taxpayers, it is hard to see how an entitlement to maintain those relative rankings could be derived from anything but an initial entitlement to the rankings themselves. This point has been made by a number of economists in the past decade, who argue, in response to the view espoused by Feldstein and others that preservation of the initial (pre-tax) ranking of wealth is per se desirable, that unless the initial ranking is taken to be fair, the principle of horizontal equity has no normative force. *See* Atkinson, *supra*, at 17-18; David M. Gordon, *Taxation of the Poor and the Normative Theory of Tax Incidence*, 62 AM. ECON. REV. 319, 321 (1972); Kaplow, *supra* note 126, at 146-47; King, *supra*, at 100; Robert Plotnick, *The Concept and Measurement of Horizontal Equity*, 17 J. PUB. ECON. 373, 375-76 (1982).

Second, like the horizontal equity argument with respect to *marginal* savers and spenders in Part II above, the argument assumes the matter to be resolved. Horizontal equity requires only that like taxpayers be taxed in like fashion. It leaves open (begs) the question of who is "like" for these purposes. If—as at least some economists have assumed—the relevant measure of likeness is utility,[134] an income tax will obviously discriminate against those with a higher taste for future rather than present consumption, just as an income *or* consumption tax will discriminate against those with a higher taste for consumption than leisure.[135] If instead the relevant measure is assumed to be explicit wealth—the conventional view—then taxing inframarginal savers' surplus (in the form of cash) while ignoring inframarginal spenders' surplus (in the form of greater pleasure derived from current consumption) does not violate horizontal equity. The foregoing is underscored by noting that *any* tax except a head tax reduces the relative consumer surplus associated with the particular activity or attribute being taxed. Thus, as has been noted, a tax on labor will tend to decrease the consumer surplus of work as compared to leisure; a tariff on imported cars tends to reduce the consumer surplus of those who prefer imports to domestic cars.[136] If we believe that this differential effect does not violate horizontal equity, it is because for a variety of practical or philosophical reasons we view workers and nonworkers, Ford owners and Audi owners, as not "similarly situated" for these purposes. That is to say, for all taxes we implicitly accept a tax base considerably narrower than taxpayer welfare. That observation does not preclude the possibility that the utility derived from inframarginal saving and spending decisions ought to be treated as "like." But as suggested in Part II above, it does shift onto consumption tax advocates the burden of explaining why they should be.[137]

Third, even assuming that utility were deemed the appropriate tax base, it is unclear one can compare the utility derived by the class of inframarginal savers to that derived by the class of inframarginal spenders, or by any one saver to any one spender, from their respective decisions whether or not to

134. *See* Feldstein, *supra* note 132, at 83; Harvey S. Rosen, *An Approach to the Study of Income, Utility, and Horizontal Equity*, 92 Q.J. ECON. 307, 307-08 (1978) (adopting Feldstein's "utility" definition of horizontal equity in preference to the traditional definition "in terms of some observable index of ability to pay such as income, expenditure or wealth"); *see also* King, *supra* note 133, at 101 (arguing that "[h]orizontal equity implies that a tax should leave unchanged the rankings of utility levels"). King leaves open, however, the question of how to define utility, noting that it could be a "function only of income and prices." King, *supra* note 133, at 101.

135. *See* Feldstein, *supra* note 132, at 82-83, 88-89.

136. Bankman & Griffith, *supra* note 29 (manuscript at 11).

137. Guillebaud suggests that savers and spenders might be unlike in their debts to the state, as well as in the form of utility that these individuals derive from their actions:

> [T]he State incurs additional costs and renders additional services to the property-owners, which it does not incur or render in respect of the citizen who is expending his income on consumable goods. It is therefore right that the State should receive a contribution from the property-owner, whose income is safeguarded by the State, to cover these costs and services.

Guillebaud, *supra* note 7, at 488.

defer consumption—a matter to be returned to shortly. If such comparisons are not possible, then devising a horizontally equitable tax is not possible.

2. *Does the distribution of surplus between savers and spenders in a no-tax world correspond to some end-state theory of fairness?*

Alternatively, it could be argued that inframarginal savers and spenders have an entitlement to the relative distribution of welfare they would enjoy in a no-tax world, because the distribution itself, whether earned or not, corresponds to some end-state notion of distributive justice. Like the historical entitlement argument, no end-state defense has been offered explicitly in the consumption tax literature. But it is possible that in some inchoate form it underlies at least some people's view that a tax on savings is unfair—for example, in a general sense that the distribution of welfare between savers and spenders in a no-tax world is roughly equal, and that a tax on savings moves it (undesirably) in the direction of inequality.

Any end-state defense of a consumption tax poses a number of difficulties—indeed, so many difficulties that it may not be worth taking the defense seriously enough to work them through. The first problem is defining what universe of decisions we are comparing. It makes no sense to compare the aggregate utility derived from all savings to that derived from all current consumption. The vast majority of earnings even for high savers are consumed currently rather than saved. Therefore, aggregate utility derived from consumption will be much higher than that derived from savings. Instead, one would have to compare the utility of savings only to that portion of current consumption that realistically represents savings forgone—that is, the portion of discretionary income that could have been saved but was not. How precisely that portion would be defined for each taxpayer, however, is not obvious.

The second difficulty lies in agreeing on a definition of fairness. If we are concerned solely with the fairness of the end-state distribution of welfare, it is hard to see the rationale for considering the utility generated by the act of saving or spending in isolation, rather than as one component of the overall welfare of savers and spenders as a class. In the latter case, the fair distribution of surplus from decisions concerning the timing of consumption would presumably be dictated by one's more general notions of distributive justice. Proponents of an egalitarian redistribution of wealth on utilitarian or Rawlsian grounds, for example, would presumably regard a tax on interest that reduces savers' welfare as a step in the right direction if inframarginal savings are held disproportionately by the wealthy, and as a step in the wrong direction if they are held disproportionately by the poor. The point, obviously, is that whatever one's vision of distributive justice, one cannot assess the merits of any given distribution of surplus from saving and spending decisions except in the larger context of savers' and spenders' aggregate endowments. Moreover, even if one chose to treat the welfare effects of intertemporal consumption decisions in isolation, it is unclear what would constitute a fair division of the surplus. If one regards the surplus as an unearned windfall to its recipients created by the fortuity of inframarginal tastes, it seems hard to defend as fair any particular distribution of the surplus as between spenders and savers other than equality.

Third, whatever definition of fairness one adopts, whether imposition of a tax represents a move away from, or toward, that ideal is almost certainly unanswerable. There are two problems here: an analytical one and an empirical one. The analytical problem is whether one can devise a common measure for the welfare of spenders and savers that permits one to compare the two. The answer is yes, but only if one assumes interpersonal comparability of utility—more particularly, if one assumes that each individual's reservation price for a commodity provides a uniform measure of the commodity's utility. In that case, the relative levels of welfare enjoyed by savers and spenders will be equal to their relative levels of inframarginal surplus, measured by the difference between their personal discount rates and the market rate of interest. The following logic underlies that assertion. If one starts with the axiomatic assumption that the marginal spender turned marginal saver will derive identical utility from the choice to spend or save, and if one assumes further that *all* marginal savers and spenders derive the same utility from their respective decisions to save or spend (that is, if one presumes the interpersonal comparability of utility as measured by reservation prices), the utility derived by inframarginal savers and spenders will equal the utility of their marginal counterparts *plus* whatever surplus they enjoy by virtue of the lower (in the case of savers) or higher (in the case of spenders) price they put on deferring consumption. Since the first component will be equal for both inframarginal groups, their relative well-being will be determined by the second—that is, by their inframarginal surplus.

But how is inframarginal surplus to be defined for these purposes? Surplus (whether consumers' or savers') does not measure the absolute welfare associated with a given choice. It measures the increase in welfare generated by that choice over other competing choices (or, in more conventional economic terms, the gains from trade from any given starting position). For inframarginal *savers*, the definition of surplus—equal to the interest rate they were paid minus their personal discount rate—thus reflects the increase in welfare generated by the choice to trade off current for future (increased) consumption.[138] This suggests that the surplus enjoyed by inframarginal *spenders* should be defined as the converse: that is, as the increase in welfare generated by trading off future (increased) consumption for current consumption. For nonborrowing spenders (group 2), who must choose between consuming existing wealth currently or saving it for future consumption, each decision to consume rather than save generates surplus, in an amount equal to the consumer's personal discount rate for saving (reflecting the psy-

138. To draw upon an example given above, recall taxpayer *A*, who has a personal discount rate for savings of 3%, and who faces an interest rate to lenders of 10% in the no-tax world and 8% (after-tax) in the tax world. If *A* decides to save rather than spend he acquires a surplus of 7% in the no-tax world and 5% in the tax world.

chological cost of deferring consumption) minus the actual interest rate paid to lenders (reflecting the benefits of savings forgone). Thus, for taxpayer *E* above, assuming a personal discount rate of 15 percent, and interest rates of 10 percent in a no-tax world and 8 percent (after-tax) in a tax world, the decision to consume currently generates a surplus of 5 percent in the no-tax world and 7 percent in the tax world.[139]

Given the above analysis, the claim that the distribution of welfare between savers (group 1) and spenders (group 2) in a no-tax world is fairer than what results from a tax on savings translates to the claim that the pre-tax inframarginal surplus of savers and spenders, represented in Figure 2 by triangles *ODJ* and *MDN*, respectively, reflects a fairer division of welfare than the after-tax surplus of each group, represented by triangles *OBH* and *KBN*, respectively. This claim depends, however, on the validity of the underlying assumption that the reservation prices attached to commodities *do* provide a common measure of the utility such commodities provide. Economists routinely indulge that assumption in assessing the relative welfare gains and losses of various subsidies and taxes.[140] Fisher and others have likewise indulged it, in assuming that nominal consumption is an acceptable tax base only because it provides a reasonably good proxy for what they took to be the ideal tax base: "real income" in the form of actual pleasure derived from consumption.[141] But the assumption that the utility of a commodity for all purchasers is measured by the price they would pay for it is obviously open to doubt. One would expect the utility of a nominal amount of consumption to vary not only with the wealth of the consumer (the premise behind the conventional assumption of the declining marginal utility of wealth), but also with her absolute capacity to derive pleasure from consumption, whether now or in the future. Clearly, this is simply Davenport's point all over again: Any would-be saver's reservation price for saving (whether marginal or not) merely reflects her relative preference for present versus future consumption. It says nothing about the absolute hedonic content of either choice. In the context of a perfected income tax, it was suggested above, there is a rejoinder to Davenport: that the trade will still be an even one, since the value of what the marginal saver/spender gets is by defi-

139. While a tax on savings increases spenders' *surplus*, it has no effect on spenders' welfare. *See* note 120 *supra* and accompanying text. That apparent inconsistency is explained by the fact that surplus measures the *relative* advantage gained by one choice over another, not the absolute utility such a choice generates. Thus, when saving is made absolutely less attractive by a tax, the *relative* advantage of spending rather than saving increases, although the absolute pleasure derived from spending remains unchanged.

140. For a conventional analysis equating welfare gain (or loss) with changes in consumer surplus, see J. STIGLITZ, *supra* note 20, at 259-61, 446-49; R. TRESCH, *supra* note 93, at 64-65. For an application of that analysis to savings decisions, see Strnad, *supra* note 52, at 1092-98. For a defense of the interpersonal comparability of the utility of money that underlies such analyses, see Arnold C. Harberger, *Three Basic Postulates for Applied Welfare Economics: An Interpretive Essay*, 9 J. ECON. LITERATURE 785 (1971).

141. *See* note 93 *supra*. *But cf.* I. FISHER, THE NATURE OF CAPITAL AND INCOME, *supra* note 9, at 39-40 (noting the common error of believing that "wealth consists of utility," which would make the law of diminishing marginal utility of wealth a contradiction in terms).

Figure 2

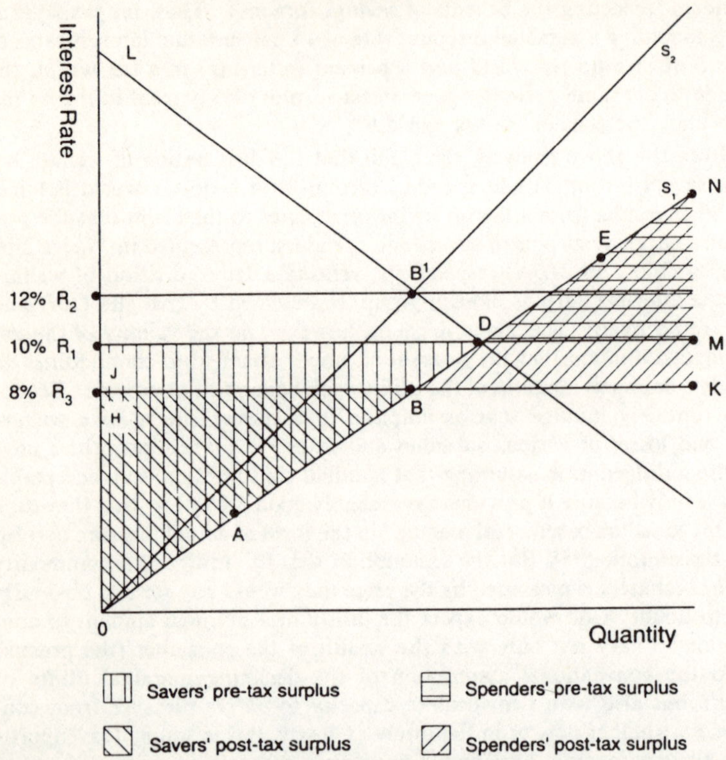

nition equal to value of what she gave up, even if the absolute utility of either choice is unmeasurable. But that rejoinder is of no help here. For what we care about in this context is precisely whether we can measure the absolute utility generated by saving and consumption decisions.

Even if one takes the *aggregate* surplus of each group, as measured by the supply curve for savings, as a reasonably good approximation of the groups' aggregate relative utilities in the no-tax and tax worlds, there remains an empirical problem in determining whether imposition of a tax reflects a move toward or away from a "fair" distribution. The answer depends on the shape of the supply curve, an empirical question that may be impossible to resolve. If one's goal were equality between the two groups, for example, it is not hard to imagine configurations for a supply curve that would leave the class of savers far better off than the class of spenders in the no-tax world, with a tax on savings therefore possibly representing a move *towards* greater equality.[142]

142. That would be true if, as is certainly the case, some inframarginal savers actually had a

Finally, the entire analysis above goes only to a fair distribution of utility between the aggregate classes of savers and spenders. The analysis ignores the discrepancies that exist in the utility derived by individual members of each class (for example, as between individuals *A*, *B*, and *C* above). As suggested in Part II, the choice to focus on group rather than individual fairness is unusual in tax law, and seems to require some defense.

3. *Summary.*

Thus, it is unclear what underlies the widespread assumption that inframarginal savers and spenders have a right to maintain their relative pre-tax levels of surplus. Grounding that right in historical theories of entitlement runs into several problems. The goal of maintaining savers' and spenders' relative levels of pre-tax wealth has appeal only if such rankings are themselves just. It is hard to see the argument that they *are* just, given that the pre-tax surplus enjoyed by inframarginal savers and spenders owes nothing to savers' and spenders' own efforts. Instead, that surplus results from the fortuities of the market rate of interest—itself produced in part by government nontax policies—and from savers' and spenders' inframarginal tastes. In addition, savers' surplus is in the form of explicit wealth, while spenders' surplus is in the form of psychic income. Under a conventional income tax, where the tax base is explicit wealth rather than utility, it is entirely appropriate to tax the former surplus and not the latter. Finally, even if the tax base were utility rather than wealth, we can levy an equal tax on equal levels of utility derived by inframarginal savers and spenders only if we can compare their respective levels of utility. Such a comparison may not be possible.

Grounding savers' and spenders' rights to their relative pre-tax well-being in end-state theories of entitlement is even less promising. It is not obvious why the utility generated by surplus from inframarginal saving and spending decisions should be considered in isolation, rather than as merely one component of overall well-being. If such surplus is considered in isolation, it is unclear what distribution would be fair, given that inframarginal surplus is an unearned windfall to its recipients. Finally, determining whether a tax on savings moves savers and spenders closer to the ideal distribution or further away again requires that we be able to compare the utility levels of inframarginal savers and spenders. As noted above, that comparison may not be possible.

In sum, it is difficult to explain the right of inframarginal savers and spenders to maintain their relative pre-tax positions by any conventional theories of distributive justice. Even if such a right can be defended, as argued in part IV.A above, there are significant empirical and normative difficulties in showing that a consumption tax *would* preserve the relative pre-tax posi-

negative discount rate, most other inframarginal savers had a low discount rate, and the supply curve sloped steeply right below equilibrium price and then flattened out. In such a case, the aggregate surplus of savers as a class could well exceed that of spenders as a class.

tions of savers and spenders. Given both problems, it is perplexing why this argument for the greater fairness of a consumption tax has received widespread deference from commentators on both sides.

V. Conclusion

Of the three theories of fairness implicit in the arguments for exempting the return to capital, none makes out a persuasive case for a consumption tax over an income tax. The first, the argument for a consumption tax as a perfected income tax, has a number of serious problems. It requires selective use of a utility-based rather than wealth-based measure of income; it depends on the assumption of rationality in saving and spending decisions; and it ignores inframarginal surplus. Framed with an eye only to the riskless interest rate, it ill fits the equity considerations that are raised by risk premia, the predominant component of capital income. The second fairness claim, the argument for a consumption tax as an endowments tax, embraces a view of a fair tax base, measuring capacity to earn rather than earnings themselves, that is not widely shared by tax theorists. More importantly, it implements that view only with respect to financial capital, reverting to an ex post income tax for wealth generated by human capital. It is hard to defend the resulting hybrid tax system on any ground.

The third fairness claim, the argument that a consumption tax is fair in itself because it preserves the relative status of savers and spenders, although the one most clearly and frequently endorsed by consumption tax proponents, seems the least persuasive, at least in its current underdeveloped state. It is not clear that a tax on income from capital does disadvantage savers relative to spenders. The answer depends in part on the deductibility of consumer interest on the borrowers' side, and in part on the group of spenders to which savers are compared. More importantly, assuming that savers *are* disadvantaged relative to some group of spenders deemed relevant for these purposes, commentators who have supported a consumption tax on this ground have failed to articulate a theory of entitlement that explains why that differential effect is unfair. As suggested above, it is difficult to deduce that entitlement from traditional historical or end-state theories of distributive justice. If proponents have some other explanation for the normative basis of savers' entitlement, it remains to be offered.

This hardly disposes of the case for a consumption tax on fairness grounds. A serious consideration of the (Hobbesian) foundational argument has yet to be undertaken. Moreover, both the Hobbesian argument and the arguments considered above for exempting the returns to capital, whatever their other differences, all share certain fundamental premises about fairness. In particular, all assume that the definition of a fair tax base should be determined independent of other government welfare policies, and all appear to assume that it should be derived from notions of horizontal equity—that is, from the government's obligation to preserve the relative pre-tax rankings of individual wealth, however wealth may be defined for these purposes.

While that individualistic, entitlement-based view of fairness has dominated tax debate at least among noneconomists for the past century, other views of fairness obviously are possible. One could, for example, support a consumption tax on utilitarian (welfarist) grounds, if it could be shown that exempting the return to capital, with redistributive transfers by the government, would maximize aggregate well-being. Under that view, efficiency and incentive considerations would themselves constitute key elements of an equity argument.[143] Alternatively, one could support a consumption tax as a reward for the pure virtue of thrift. More than a hint of such a view is detectable in Hobbes's attack on an income tax as rewarding the "luxurious waste of private men," and punishing those who "laboureth much, and sparing the fruits of [their] labour, consumeth little."[144] One suspects that the retributive view of justice implicit in Hobbes's attack, although rarely articulated in the academic literature, has a fairly strong hold on the popular imagination.[145]

Finally, in this, as many other matters, the ultimate resolution of the fairness debate may depend on which side—income tax or consumption tax proponents—bears the burden of proof. But the evident weakness of fairness arguments that have dominated the tax literature over the past century indicates that consumption tax proponents have not met whatever burden they bear.

143. While receiving scant attention in the legal tax literature, welfarist arguments for a consumption tax have been prominent in the economics literature. For a summary of the economic literature dealing with the optimal tradeoff between wage and capital taxes, see Bradford, *supra* note 5, at 103-04; A.B. Atkinson & A. Sandmo, *Welfare Implications of the Taxation of Savings*, 90 ECON. J. 529 (1980).

144. T. HOBBES, *supra* note 6, at 267; *see also* R.A. Musgrave, *In Defense of an Income Concept*, 81 HARV. L. REV. 44, 46 (1967) (describing the Hobbesian expenditure tax as "in effect . . . a fine on consumption (the sin of nonaccumulation) with equal taxes being paid by equal sinners").

145. Although closely allied to the argument that a consumption tax creates greater incentives for savings, the retributive justice argument is conceptually distinct. One could obviously support rewarding the virtuous and punishing the sinful as a matter of moral dessert, even if one believed it would have no effect on the choices of future would-be sinners.

[10]

Revisiting the Uneasy Case For Progressive Taxation

By WALTER J. BLUM

The writer (a co-author of "The Uneasy Case for Progressive Taxation") believes that recent trends in U. S. society, including a decline in economic progress, a high rate of inflation, an increase in welfare payments, and the expansion of the government's role in our society, make the case for highly progressive taxation less easy to support. Walter J. Blum is the Wilson-Dickinson Professor of Law at the University of Chicago.

Has the strength of the case for the progressive taxation of income changed since the early 1950s when "The Uneasy Case for Progressive Taxation"[1] was written? One way of addressing this question is to note four developments that have occurred in our society since then and comment on the bearing they possibly might have on the central progression issue.

Preliminary Considerations

Several preliminary observations are in order. The enquiry will focus on the personal income tax, although the much more significant relationship is that between the distribution of income among persons (or perhaps families) and our whole basket of taxes. The more narrow perspective seems appropriate for this review. Historically, the arguments over progressive taxation have generally revolved about the income tax; and it has been a tax on income that has supplied the main element of progression for our overall system. We will find it easier, moreover, to think about the consequences of a progressive tax levied on income than to talk about the effects of a bundle of taxes whose aggregate burden can be plotted alongside the distribution of personal income.

---

[1] Walter J. Blum and Harry Kalven, "The Uneasy Case for Progressive Taxation," 19 *University of Chicago Law Review* 417 (1952).

The progessivity of a tax could be measured not only against income but against wealth or consumption. Perhaps the relationship between tax burden and personal consumption, now that there is an increased interest in replacing the tax on income with a tax on expenditures, should be considered. But at the moment there is no widespread enthusiasm for an expenditure tax outside some academic circles; and the difficulty encountered in understanding this generally unfamiliar levy would tend to complicate further the discussion of the progression issue. Very likely there will be more heard on the topic of progressive expenditure taxation a decade from now.

It is also helpful to simplify the discussion by finessing all problems of describing what is meant by greater and lesser degrees of progression. This can be done by comparing two alternative types of rate patterns. One consists of any set of marginal rates graduated so that a higher rate applies to additional increments of income. *Steep* progression can be achieved by this pattern. The other consists of a flat marginal rate applied against all taxable income in excess of a specified excluded amount. The excluded amount is, in effect, subject to a zero rate of tax while the balance of taxable income is taxed at the flat rate. Under this pattern—technically called "degression"—the degree of progressivity in effective rate can be altered mainly by changing the size of the zero rate bracket. This pattern results in *mild* progression. For convenience in making the comparison, it will be assumed that the set of graduated marginal rates which one has in mind includes a zero rate bracket equal in width to that found in the alternative degressive tax. To sharpen the comparison between mild and steep progression, these alternative rate structures will be assumed to produce equal amounts of revenue for the government.

We will be dealing with the progression issue in the context of our own society. The matter likely would appear quite different in a totalitarian society highly controlled from the center. The issue for us is tightly connected with the features of our society, including the fact that most economic enterprise is conducted outside of government, people are generally free to spend or save their after-tax dollars, and individuals usually have considerable latitude in choosing their work patterns.

Finally, for most of the hundred-plus years of controversy over progressive taxation, the debate dealt with tax policy as something apart from policy concerning redistribution of income through the tax system. Among scholars, the prevailing view for a long time was that the progression question could be examined on various tax criteria, such as "fairness" or "ability-to-pay," while assuming that the redistributive impact of alternative tax schemes was a neutral factor—one not to be advanced as a reason for or against adopting a particular tax policy. There are still traces of this separation between taxation and redistribution; but, for the most part, those who speak about "fairness" or "ability-to-pay" are simply using the language of public political controversy. Most serious commentators now recognize that such a separation is artificial and obscures analysis of the progression issue.

Let us turn now to changes that have taken place in our society that may bear upon the question at hand.

Slower Pace of Economic Progress

First, our economy is not as lively as it was a quarter of a century ago. The gross national product, the output per hour of labor and the rate of capital formation are improving at a very slow pace, if at all. The record in the past decade has been poor compared to our own earlier performance and to that of most other developed countries.

While the causes of this decline are uncertain and no doubt diverse, several parts of the puzzle seem to be related to our question. All other things being equal, the economic situation would improve if saving increased relative to consumption, if more ventures were undertaken, if greater investments were made in capital goods, and if people on the whole gave up some leisure and worked more. Let us consider how progressive taxation bears on these matters.

As to saving in the private sector of the economy, steep progression is a depressant. The well-to-do on average save a greater fraction of their income than the less affluent. By imposing relatively higher taxes on the affluent and relatively lower taxes on the others, steep progression will result in a lesser aggregate of private savings. It is, in theory, possible to compensate for this difference by having the government do the saving through running a budgetary surplus year by year. Experience should tell us that this corrective is not likely to be adopted even when there are strong declarations of good intentions.

As to enterpreneurship (which can be thought of as taking business risks), the recent stagnation of the economy again points away from steep progression. An enterpriser is more likely to get a venture off the ground if there is no need to count on others for 100 percent of the capital required. In theory, a good proposition will attract sufficient funds from others; but practical experience suggests that the financiers will be more ready to do business if the enterpriser shares in making the investment. A steep progressive tax that dampens personal savings by those in the potential pool of enterprisers might reduce the total of new ventures.

a steep progressive tax that dampens personal savings by those in the potential pool of enterprisers might reduce the total of new ventures

More important is the bearing of marginal rates on risk-taking itself. Steep progression, as compared to a mild degressive form, results in imposing sharply higher marginal rates on relatively few taxpayers and slightly lower marginal rates on a relatively large number of taxpayers. Under a structure of sharply graduated rates, gains generally will count more heavily than losses in the computation of taxes. Big net gains will push the taxpayer into higher rate brackets, while big net losses will be deductible against income taxed in lower rate brackets inasmuch as the taxpayer's total taxable income will be smaller. This effect, which is likely to dampen enthusiasm for taking risks, becomes more pronounced when the marginal rates are more steeply graduated.

As to capital formation, the basic relationship between progression and total investment in plant and equipment can be captured in crude terms. A combination of greater savings and more risk-taking by enterprisers will bring about a higher level of capital formation. Businessmen who are seeking profits will find numerous opportunities to improve the "bottom line" by buying or modifying capital goods capable of making their operations more efficient. By retarding savings and risk-taking, steep progression acts to slow down capital formation.

As to inducing people to trade their leisure for working more, a tax on income penalizes work but not the enjoyment of leisure. Steep progression, as we noted, puts relatively heavy penalties on a small number of taxpayers and relatively light penalties on a larger number of taxpayers. Standing alone, such a distribution of penalties plausibly might encourage a broader shift away from work to indulgence in leisure. But we cannot ignore an offsetting consideration: some taxpayers who are highly penalized under steep progression might elect not to give up work for leisure but rather to swap leisure for more work in order to reach a level of after-tax income they regard as desirable. We therefore cannot be confident that steep graduation of rates leads to less total work (and more total leisure) than does mild progression. Likewise, there is no reason to believe that the opposite result will ensue.

On this quick analysis of incentives and penalties, the low economic performance of our society would appear to strengthen the case against a steeply progressive income tax. Yet the contrary has been vigorously urged on political or social grounds.

The core contention is that economic stagnation is now a permanent condition and, as a consequence, our society can be analogized to a zero-sum game. In such a society, new or additional demands on government can only be met by taking resources away from others; no longer can they be satisfied out of the increase in resources that is made available through economic growth. This zero-sum limitation produces greater tensions in society, making it more difficult to achieve the political compromises needed for adjusting to changed conditions or threats to the social fabric. Stalemate, the argument goes, might be avoided if the distribution of income is so altered that it is widely perceived as "fair." A steeply progressive tax has a special role to play: it is an important, if not indispensable, factor in generating a strong consensus that the after-tax distribution is "fair" under the prevailing circumstances.

some argue that a steeply progressive tax has a special role to play: it is an important, if not indispensable, factor in generating a strong consensus that the after-tax distribution is "fair" under the prevailing circumstances

There may well be a kind of self-fulfilling prophecy in this reasoning. The highly redistributive taxes might themselves contribute significantly to bringing about the economic conditions associated with the zero-sum society idea. Even apart from that prospect, however, the argument runs into a major dilemma.

The dilemma lies in translating the prescription into a schedule of tax rates. As between steep and mild progression, there is no obvious way of deciding which is fairer in the abstract. Surely people will differ on this issue in the future as they have in the past. Some will accent economic considerations, while others will more or less ignore them. Some will take a short-run view, while others will think about a longer term. Some will feel deeply about a particular position they take, while others will not be so certain of theirs. The question itself is intrinsically political in nature. In a representative democracy such an issue is best resolved by the legislature, the only institution that is in a position to read and weigh the views of the populace on fairness and then reach a decision that takes account of the spectrum. If tax policy is to be predicated on public perceptions of fairness, the tax voted by the legislature, I suggest, must qualify as being the fairest of the fair.

But let us suppose for the moment that in a zero-sum society a steeply progressive tax is more widely perceived as fairer than a mildly progressive levy. Would adopting the more redistributive tax achieve the stated goal of reducing political tensions and easing stalemates? On my reading of human nature, the underlying confluence of forces is not likely to move the political process in that direction. Persons subject to sharply higher marginal rates hardly would become more agreeable to government spending programs that resulted in allocating more resources to others in society; and in turn the others, whose taxes have been slightly reduced by adopting steep progression, cannot reasonably be expected to moderate their demands for government funding of their preferred programs. It is even conceivable that high progression could serve to exacerbate political tensions and prolong political stalemates. In short, we need to be reminded that all such projections concerning political responses are merely conjectures.

Stagnation in the economy, I submit, weakens the case for steeply progressive taxes.

Increase in Inflation Rate

Second, our society has experienced a significant degree of inflation during the past decade. We have been unable to stabilize the price level or confine inflation to the much lower rate enjoyed during the prior two decades.

In examining how this change bears upon the progression question, an adjustment in perspective is in order. No knowledgeable person has argued that steeply progressive taxes are at the root of our inflation. Nor has it been argued that inflation can be effectively curbed by doing away with graduated rates. The enquiry at hand is more modest: is a steeply progressive or a mildly progressive tax more compatable with a soundly conceived program to reduce the rate of inflation?

In an analysis of inflation, concededly a complex subject, the most durable and instructive relationship is that between the amount of money and the supply of goods. Roughly put, the general level of prices will increase if the amount of money increases faster than the supply of goods. Conversely, the general level of prices will fall if the amount of money decreases faster than the supply of goods. This unrefined formulation is adequate to approach our question, bearing in mind that we are comparing alternative tax patterns set to yield the same total revenues. Because of this equal-yield assumption, the choice between high and low progression ought not to influence the amount of money in the economy. That amount ultimately rests on the monetary policy pursued by the Federal Reserve—our central bank. There is no reason to believe that the Reserve's decision regarding the "proper" amount of money should be affected by the legislative decision to rely on a highly or a mildly progressive tax for obtaining a given amount of government revenue. This tax choice, however, might impact on inflation through its effect on the supply of goods.

Recall the point that, as compared to mild progression, steep progression would tend to be more of a depressant on the economy because it leads to relatively lower levels of savings, risk-taking and capital formation. Higher levels would result, over time, in a greater total supply of goods. And if the improved levels of savings, risk-taking and capital formation do not cause the Federal Reserve to deviate from its policy for determining the amount of money it otherwise would allow in the economy, the larger supply of goods should tend to hold down prices.

There might be another connection between progression policy and inflation. It is apparent to all that inflation brings about innumerable unintended changes in the relative burdens imposed on individuals or the benefits enjoyed by them. One significant set of such changes concerns the distribution of burdens under an income tax. Inflation creates nominal but not real gains for owners of assets other than money; it creates real losses for moneyowners and creditors and it creates real gains for debtors. Only through the use of fantastically complicated tax rules could the tax base deal generally with gains and losses that are real rather than nominal. As a practical matter, we must live with rules under which the effect of inflation on taxes will impact unevenly on different individuals. These unintended and often undesirable consequences are magnified when the tax is steeply progressive.

Thus, in a society that seeks to reduce a persistently high level of inflation, the case for a steeply progressive tax is weaker than in a society not faced with that challenge.

Increase in Government Welfare Payments

Third, government welfare payments have increased dramatically since the early fifties, both in absolute terms and in relation to total government expenditures. The welfare system has been expanded to provide virtually all our needy people with the necessities of life, although there continues to be much disagreement as to what constitutes an adequate minimum standard of living.

This welfare system does redistribute income from the nonpoor to the poor. There is, moreover, fairly wide agreement in our society that under existing conditions such a reallocation is sound policy. Controversy regarding the welfare system is mainly over its structure and magnitude but not over the principle that the needy are to be protected through welfare measures.

At first impression this development might seem to bolster the case for steep progression in an income tax. The welfare system does reallocate income in favor of the poor. Some commentators contend that it is only logical to finance such a reallocation through redistributive taxes. On closer inspection this notion turns out to be groundless.

Under a soundly constructed income tax, the zero-rate bracket (in conjunction with the definition of taxable income) would be set to shield the poor altogether from payment of tax. To collect a tax on those below the poverty level, as defined for purposes of welfare benefits, would be to incur costly administrative burdens that are a dead loss. If the prescribed support level is to be preserved, then the dollars taken from the poor by the tax would have to be replaced through increasing net welfare benefits by like amounts. So it is reasonable to assume that the poor will not be called upon to pay an income tax whatever degree of progressivity is built into the levy.

The relevant inquiry for us concerns not the poor minority but those above the welfare poverty level who do pay an income tax. Does the case for imposing a relatively greater share of the total income tax burden on the affluent among this majority grow weaker or stronger as the total size of welfare payments to the poor are increased?

If one views the welfare system as designed primarily to provide fall-back support for the needy, welfare expenditures are like all other government expenditures. The case for steep progression is no better or worse merely because the government is spending funds for welfare instead of, say, defense. Increased welfare payments from this perspective are a neutral development in thinking about progression policy.

The matter is not much different if one views the welfare system as designed primarily to be a mechanism for redistributing income to those at the bottom of the range. The fact that society generally agrees on redistributing income to the bottom tier does not carry any necessary implication about how the concomitant burden is to be shared by taxpayers. There are two distinct redistribution issues involved. So long as they are kept separate, the case for steep progression among those who do pay taxes is not advanced.

Cynics or perhaps political realists have contended that the larger the transfer payments, the weaker the case for steep progression. Welfare programs not infrequently come to be treated in some quarters as creating welfare rights which give rise to entitlements. The expansion of entitlements, it has been asserted, might lead to perpetuation of an underclass in our society. The thesis is that the development of an entitlements psychology will undercut efforts to inculcate stronger work motivations and build higher skills among the welfare beneficiaries. The crux of the cynic's concern is that steep progression might facilitate an expansion of entitlements; fewer voters will strongly resist the enlargement if they think the well-to-do alone are bearing the cost.

I leave this argument without comment.

Expansion of the Government's Role in Our Economy

Fourth, the role of government in our society has grown markedly since the early fifties. The public sector of the economy has expanded more rapidly than the private; the welfare program has spread out; government controls, especially over business affairs, have proliferated; and the size of the bureaucracy has increased. On a variety of measurements, the relative power of the government over the lives of individuals has mushroomed. Recent events, moreover, remind us again how difficult it is to cut back on government programs once they are entrenched. Government personnel and their constituents often can be politically potent.

How might these observations enter into consideration of the progression question? It seems futile to speculate whether government on the whole would tend to be less prone to growth under a milder version of progression. Perhaps the public willingness to endorse larger government appropriations might be diminished if more persons felt the heavier weight of a tax burden which they associated with the programs being funded. This is a more general version of the point that the acceptable level of welfare spending might turn out to be loosely linked to the distribution of the tax burden. Put as a general proposition, however, it does not seem persuasive.

Another line of thought seeks to relate government power with progression policy. Many of the values that have been important in our society will be impaired, it is said, if the balance of power shifts too much in favor of the public domain at the expense of the private or quasi-private area. At some point on the scale, dominance by the government saps the vitality of other organizations and inhibits the formation of new institutions that can check its exercise of power.

This concern often is offered in support of plans to confine government power by putting a limit on expenditures or curtailing the amount of revenue to be raised through taxes. It might possibly have special relevance to progression policy. The existence of large pools of private wealth seems to be important in restraining the continual encroachment of government. Steeply progressive taxation inhibits the growth of these pools.

All this is part of an old controversy over the place of sizeable private wealth in a societal system that embraces representative democracy and enterprises whose owners and managers are outside of government. I am not about to rehash that fundamental argument, but wish only to make a limited comment based on the increase in government power that has already occurred. As that power has grown in the past quarter of a century, the case for steeply progressive taxation might seem less attractive to those who place a high value on privately controlled universities, hospitals, research centers and the like; on privately controlled newspapers, periodicals, broadcasting stations and the like; and on new high-risk enterprises, new modes of art, new styles and the like. The necessary financial support for these things conceivably might be obtained by assembling small sums from many interested parties. In the actual event, however, the existence of large pools of private wealth often turns out to be the crucial source of support or the catalyst.

Progressive Taxation in the Present

"The Uneasy Case for Progressive Taxation" was concluded with an observation: "But in the end it is the implications about economic inequality which impart significance and permanence to the issue and institution of progression. Ultimately a serious interest in progression stems from the fact that a progessive tax is perhaps the cardinal instance of the democratic community struggling with its hardest problem." In the early 1950s the case for progressive taxation was not easy. Subsequent developments in our society have made it no less, and perhaps even more, uneasy. ●

[11]

California Law Review

VOL. 75 | DECEMBER 1987 | NO. 6

Social Welfare and the Rate Structure: A New Look At Progressive Taxation

Joseph Bankman†
Thomas Griffith‡

The progressive rate structure of the federal income tax has always been controversial. In this Article, Professors Bankman and Griffith explore the moral underpinnings and economic effects of the progressive income tax. Observing that all rate structures must be premised upon, and measured by, a theory of distributive justice, they first consider possible normative bases for a tax structure. They select as the normative basis for their analysis welfarist theories of distributive justice, which judge the tax structure on the basis of its effect on societal welfare. They next reexamine the traditional economic arguments against progressive taxation. They critically analyze both the labor-related efficiency costs of progressive taxation and the traditional arguments that progressivity imposes significant administrative costs, promotes the misallocation of capital, and increases tax evasion. Finally, they describe an optimal tax model for calculating the most desirable tax rate, balancing the costs of progressivity against possible gains from redistribution. The model proposed by Bankman and Griffith produces two results of particular importance. First, under most welfarist theories, the optimal tax rate is progressive, but not confiscatory. Second, a progressive tax is best implemented not by graduated or rising marginal

† Associate Professor of Law, University of Southern California. A.B. 1977, University of California, Berkeley; J.D. 1980, Yale University.

‡ Associate Professor of Law, University of Southern California. A.B. 1971, Brown University; M.A.T. 1972, Harvard University; J.D. 1982, Harvard University.

Early drafts of this Article were presented at the University of Southern California Faculty Workshop Series and to the Southern California Tax Policy Group, and benefited from comments made by members of those groups. In addition, we would like to thank Linda Beres, Richard Craswell, Catherine Hantzis, Lori Hasencamp, William Klein, Norman Lane, Michael Levine, Laura Lin, Grace Mueller, Alan Schwartz, and, especially, Jeff Strnad.

rates, but rather through a combination of cash grants and constant or even declining marginal rates.

INTRODUCTION

The federal income tax rate structure is progressive: High income individuals pay a greater percentage of their income to the government than do low income individuals.[1] A progressive rate structure has been part of the federal income tax system since its inception in 1913.[2] Notwithstanding its lineage, the progressive rate structure has always been controversial, and the degree of progressivity has been subject to constant, and occasionally radical, change. Congress has adopted well over a dozen progressive rate structures since the income tax was first enacted, and change continues today.

The importance and persistence of the tax rate controversy might be expected to have generated a rich legal literature. In fact, although tax lawyers and academics have at various times spoken out in favor of or in opposition to the progressive tax,[3] serious legal scholarship in the field is scarce. The complex issues raised by the progressive rate structure are comprehensively analyzed in only one article, *The Uneasy Case for Progressive Taxation,* written by Professors Walter J. Blum and Harry Kalven, Jr. in 1952.[4] Blum and Kalven's analysis is erudite and thoughtful and has shaped the opinions of two generations of tax scholars. However, Blum and Kalven did not and could not discuss the implications of recent developments in economics and moral theory for the structure of the progressive income tax.

This Article explores the moral, economic, and administrative effects of a progressive rate structure with reference to the insights of

1. I.R.C. § 1 (West Supp. 1987).

2. Income Tax (Revenue) Act of 1913, ch. 16, 38 Stat. 114, 166-67 (current version at I.R.C. § 1 (West Supp. 1987)). This act imposed a "normal" tax of 1% and a "surtax" ranging from 1% on net incomes between $20,000 and $50,000 to 6% on net incomes exceeding $500,000.

3. *See, e.g.,* C. GALVIN & B. BITTKER, THE INCOME TAX: HOW PROGRESSIVE SHOULD IT BE? (1969); W. KLEIN, POLICY ANALYSIS OF THE FEDERAL INCOME TAX 8-45 (1976); REPORT OF THE ROYAL COMMISSION ON TAXATION (Canada 1966); Blum, *Progressive Taxation Reconsidered—North of the Border,* 45 TAXES 718 (1967); Blum, *Revisiting the Uneasy Case for Progressive Taxation,* 60 TAXES 16 (1982); Blum & Kalven, *The Uneasy Case for Progressive Taxation,* 19 U. CHI. L. REV. 417 (1952); Cohen, *Reflections on the U.S. Progressive Income Tax: Its Past and Present,* 62 VA. L. REV. 1317 (1976); Doernberg, *A Workable Flat Rate Consumption Tax,* 70 IOWA L. REV. 425 (1985); Feld, *Fairness in Rate Cuts in the Individual Income Tax,* 68 CORNELL L. REV. 429 (1983); Graetz, *The 1982 Minimum Tax Amendments as a First Step in the Transition to a "Flat-Rate" Tax,* 56 S. CAL. L. REV. 527 (1983); Groves, *Toward a Social Theory of Progressive Taxation,* 9 NAT'L TAX J. 27 (1956); O'Kelley, *Tax Policy for Post-Liberal Society: A Flat-Tax-Inspired Redefinition of the Purpose and Ideal Structure of a Progressive Income Tax,* 58 S. CAL. L. REV. 727 (1985); Smith, *High Progressive Tax Rates: Inequity and Immorality?,* 20 U. FLA. L. REV. 451 (1968); Vickrey, *The Problem of Progression,* 20 U. FLA. L. REV. 437 (1968).

4. Blum & Kalven, *supra* note 3. The article was published in book form in 1953. W. BLUM & H. KALVEN, THE UNEASY CASE FOR PROGRESSIVE TAXATION (1953).

modern political theory and economics. Part I discusses the normative underpinnings of a tax rate structure. Popular and scholarly literature is often premised on the assumption that a proportionate tax is somehow "natural" but that progressive or regressive taxes require justificatory theories. In fact, all rate structures must be premised upon, and measured by, a theory of distributive justice. This Article examines "welfarist" theories of distributive justice, which judge a society's tax structure by its impact on the welfare of the members of that society.

Part II examines the case against a progressive tax. It first addresses the impact of the progressive tax on the supply and the allocation of labor. A progressive tax produces higher marginal rates than an equal revenue proportional tax; these rates discourage work effort and reduce welfare. However, the magnitude of the welfare loss is less clear cut than is generally asserted, and much of the loss appears to be borne by discrete socioeconomic groups. Tax relief targeted at these groups is likely to be more effective in reducing the efficiency costs of taxation than a reduction in the level of progressivity.

Part II then explores the administrative costs imposed by a progressive rate structure. We conclude that only a small portion of administrative costs associated with the income tax is attributable to a progressive rate structure. Finally, Part II critically examines the asserted links between progressivity and the misallocation of capital, and between progressivity and tax evasion. We conclude that these asserted costs of progressivity are less serious than opponents of progressive taxation have argued.

In Part III, we evaluate the costs and benefits of progressivity under various welfarist ethics. To make that evaluation, we rely on models developed in a branch of public economics known as optimal taxation. Optimal tax models calculate the most desirable tax rate under a variety of empirical assumptions and theories of distributive justice. Two conclusions are emphasized. First, the optimal tax under most normative theories and empirical assumptions is progressive, but not confiscatory. Second, the optimal progressive tax is not characterized by graduated or rising marginal rates. Instead, it is implemented through a combination of cash payments and constant, or even declining, marginal rates.

Definitions and Assumptions

The progressivity of a tax rate structure is defined by the effective tax burden on differing income classes. Under a progressive tax, the percentage of income paid to the government, or average tax rate, rises as income rises.

A progressive tax may be implemented through graduated marginal rates: The first $10,000 of income might be taxed at 10%, while all subsequent income might be taxed at 30%. A progressive tax may also be implemented by a combination of constant or declining marginal rates and cash transfers or "demogrants."[5] For example, all income might be taxed at a 30% rate, and all taxpayers might receive a $2,000 demogrant from the government. Under either approach, an individual with an income of $10,000 would pay a net tax of $1,000 for an average tax of 10%; an individual with an income of $20,000 would pay a net tax of $4,000 for an average tax rate of 20%. Each tax structure would be progressive because the percentage of income paid to the government would increase with income.

Under a regressive tax, the percentage of income paid to the government falls as income rises, although the absolute amount paid to the government may rise, fall, or remain constant. Proportionate and regressive taxes, like progressive taxes, may be implemented solely through the marginal rate structure, or through a combination of the marginal rate structure and cash payments.

Under a proportionate, or "flat," tax, the percentage of income paid to the government remains constant as income rises.[6] High income individuals pay a greater absolute amount of tax to the government than low income individuals, but the ratio of tax to income is identical.

It is important to distinguish a "flat" tax from a "broad-based" tax.[7] A flat tax collects a constant percentage of the income of individuals. A broad-based tax reduces the number of tax preferences and establishes a more uniform treatment of different items of income and expense. There is no necessary connection between a broad-based tax and a flat tax. It is possible to imagine a progressive tax structure with no tax preferences and a proportionate tax structure with many tax preferences.

The current nominal rate structure is progressive and is implemented through a series of graduated marginal rates. The 1988 rate

5. The idea of a demogrant as a replacement for the personal and dependency deductions was suggested (and later abandoned) by George McGovern in his unsuccessful 1972 presidential campaign. *See* McGovern, *On Taxing and Redistributing Income*, N.Y. REV. BOOKS, May 4, 1972, at 7 (proposing a "Minimum Income Grant"). The idea had been developed earlier by Earl Rolph and James Tobin. E. ROLPH, THE THEORY OF FISCAL ECONOMICS (1954); Tobin, *Raising the Incomes of the Poor*, in AGENDA FOR THE NATION 77, 105-14 (K. Gordon ed. 1968); Rolph, *The Case for a Negative Income Tax Device*, 6 INDUS. REL. 155, 160-63 (1967); *see also* A. KRAGEN & J. MCNULTY, CASES AND MATERIALS ON FEDERAL INCOME TAXATION 760-62 (4th ed. 1984).

6. The term "flat tax" is sometimes used to describe a tax that is proportionate above an exempted amount of income. Such a tax is really a progressive tax with two rates—a zero rate up to the exemption amount and a constant positive rate above that amount. The average rate of such a tax increases with income because the exempted amount is a decreasing percentage of the taxpayer's total income. The progressivity of such a tax increases as the size of the exemption increases. A shift to a proportionate tax with a small exemption would reduce the level of progressivity in much the same manner as a shift to a truly proportional tax.

7. *See* Pechman, *Introduction*, in A CITIZEN'S GUIDE TO THE NEW TAX REFORMS 1, 2-8 (J. Pechman ed. 1985).

structure has four separate brackets for individual taxpayers. Under that structure, a married couple with no children filing a joint return pays a nominal or statutory rate of tax of 15% on taxable income below $29,751; 28% on additional income up to $71,900; 33% on additional income up to about $220,000; and 28% on all additional income.[8]

In practice, of course, there are a number of reasons why nominal rate structures may not reflect the actual distribution of the tax burden. First, Congress may define taxable income to exclude many items included in most economic definitions of income.[9] For example, taxable income currently does not include certain medical benefits, the rental value of owner-occupied housing, or unrealized capital gains.[10] In addition, taxable income is reduced by personal exemptions and other deductions.[11]

Second, taxes may affect behavior and therefore shift the incidence of the tax burden. Individuals facing high marginal rates may switch to more pleasant jobs at lower pay, replacing taxable salary with untaxed psychic benefits, or they may reduce their taxable hours worked and increase the amount of untaxed domestic labor they perform.[12] Employers also may find it necessary to raise the pre-tax wages of highly taxed employees in order to retain them. The actual impact and even the direction of the changes in behavior caused by an income tax are extremely difficult to determine.

Finally, the nominal rate structure does not incorporate the conse-

8. I.R.C. § 1 (West Supp. 1987). The 33% rate is used to phase out the benefits of the personal exemption and the 15% rate on the first $29,750—leaving the high income taxpayer with an average, as well as a marginal, tax rate of 28%. Without the phaseout, the average tax rate would never quite reach 28%, since the taxpayer would pay only a 15% rate on the first $29,750.

9. Most tax scholars have adopted the "Haig-Simons" definition of income. Goode, *The Economic Definition of Income*, in COMPREHENSIVE INCOME TAXATION 1, 7-8 (J. Pechman ed. 1977). Under the Haig-Simons formulation, economic income is defined as the amount a person might have consumed during a time period without altering his wealth. H. SIMONS, PERSONAL INCOME TAXATION 49-50 (1938); Haig, *The Concept of Income—Economic and Legal Aspects*, in THE FEDERAL INCOME TAX 1, 7 (R. Haig ed. 1921). For a discussion of some conceptual problems relating to the definition of income, see A. ATKINSON, THE ECONOMICS OF INEQUALITY 35-60 (2d ed. 1983).

10. The exclusion of medical benefits is statutory. *See* I.R.C. §§ 105, 106. The nontaxation of imputed rental income is without specific statutory or case authority but is nonetheless a fundamental feature of the present tax law. *See* 1 B. BITTKER, FEDERAL TAXATION OF INCOME, ESTATES AND GIFTS ¶ 5.3.3 (1981). The nontaxation of appreciated property is generally attributed to the Supreme Court's decision in Eisner v. Macomber, 252 U.S. 189 (1920).

11. *See, e.g.*, I.R.C. § 63 (West Supp. 1987) (standard deduction in lieu of itemized deductions); *id.* § 151 (personal exemptions); *id.* § 163 (deductions for certain interest expenses); *id.* § 164 (deductions for certain taxes); *id.* § 170 (deduction for charitable contributions); *id.* § 213 (deduction for medical expenses).

12. A classic discussion of the problems posed by imputed income may be found in H. SIMONS, *supra* note 9, at 110-24. A survey of the economic literature on the effects of the tax system's treatment of imputed income may be found in A. ATKINSON & J. STIGLITZ, LECTURES ON PUBLIC ECONOMICS 23-61 (1980).

quences of government expenditures on the wealth of individuals.[13] The amount of benefit that individuals of different income classes derive from many public services—national defense, interstate highways, the judiciary—is extremely difficult to determine.[14] It is generally assumed, however, that the combined tax-transfer system of the federal government is much more progressive than the tax system alone.[15]

Determination of the effective tax rate raises difficult empirical, theoretical, and normative issues. Most analysts, however, believe the effective federal income tax rate structure is progressive, although not as progressive as the nominal rate structure.[16]

I
A Normative Framework

A. Past Literature: The Default Assumption in Favor of a Proportionate Tax

There are countless attributes and consequences of any rate structure. A tax structure may affect aggregate production of goods and services in one way, disadvantaged groups in another way, and education and family structure in still another. To determine the desirability of a tax structure, it is necessary to have a theory of distributive justice that determines whether, and how much, to weigh the particular consequences of that structure.

A number of legal scholars have discussed the consequences and desirability of progressivity.[17] Very few, however, have identified the normative theory that supports and drives their conclusions. Key assumptions upon which those conclusions are based are left unstated or unexamined.

Perhaps the most significant and pervasive assumption is that the burden of proof lies on supporters of progressivity. A proportionate tax is often seen as "natural" or "neutral," and therefore is thought to require no justificatory theory.[18] In contrast, arguments in favor of a

13. For a comprehensive analysis of redistributive government transfer payments, see R. Boadway & D. Wildasin, Public Sector Economics 445-96 (2d ed. 1984).

14. If one considers the impact of the more easily allocated public services such as education, transportation, and health services, the progressivity of the federal tax-transfer system is substantially increased. R. Musgrave & P. Musgrave, Public Finance in Theory and Practice 261-65 (4th ed. 1984). The distributive effect of public services such as national defense or the court system is obviously much more problematic.

15. A. Atkinson & J. Stiglitz, *supra* note 12, at 283-84; R. Musgrave & P. Musgrave, *supra* note 14, at 256-65.

16. *See, e.g.*, A. Atkinson & J. Stiglitz, *supra* note 12, at 29-30; R. Boadway & D. Wildasin, *supra* note 13, at 419; J. Pechman, Who Paid the Taxes, 1966-85? 42-62 (1985) (federal tax structure progressive except at the bottom of the income scale).

17. *See* sources cited *supra* note 3.

18. *See, e.g.*, Kiesling, *Violations of Scientific Impartiality in Tax Analysis*, 40 Pub. Fin. 157

progressive tax are considered successful only if accompanied by a convincing theory of distributive justice. The theoretical case for a regressive tax, such as one that requires equal contributions from each taxpayer, is thought so weak that it is rarely discussed.[19] The belief that progressive and regressive taxes must meet affirmative burdens operates as a default assumption in favor of a proportionate tax.

The assumption that a progressive tax must meet an affirmative burden while a proportionate tax need not is perhaps the core premise of Blum and Kalven's influential article, *The Uneasy Case for Progressive Taxation*.[20] Although first published in 1952, *The Uneasy Case* is still uniformly cited as the best analysis of progressivity in the legal literature; both its conclusions and method of argument have been widely copied by supporters of a proportionate tax.[21] Indeed, the viewpoint expressed in *The Uneasy Case* and the mode of analysis upon which it is premised are probably more widely accepted today than at the time the work was first published.[22]

In *The Uneasy Case,* Blum and Kalven define the rate structure debate as follows: "On what grounds is a progressive tax on income to be preferred to a proportionate tax on income?"[23] Blum and Kalven begin the article with a brief and "admittedly not conclusive" discussion of the costs of progressivity.[24] They assert, however, that this brief analysis is sufficient to establish a prima facie case against progressive taxation.[25]

Blum and Kalven then discuss and reject various ethical theories said to support a progressive tax structure. In particular, they reject the

(1985) (arguing that "ethics free" tax analysis requires an indifference to distribution of utility and a benchmark assumption of constant marginal utility of money).

19. *See* Shannon, *The Tax Expenditure Concept in the United States and Germany: A Comparison,* 33 TAX NOTES 201, 209-10 (1986) (arguing that a regressive tax, while supportable on other grounds, would be inconsistent with the principles underlying the income tax).

20. Blum & Kalven, *supra* note 3. Blum repeated his view that the case for progressive taxation is uneasy in Blum, *Revisiting The Uneasy Case for Progressive Taxation, supra* note 3, at 16-21, and Blum, *The Uneasy Case for Progressive Taxation in 1976,* in INCOME REDISTRIBUTION 147-56 (C. Campbell ed. 1977)

21. Almost all articles that discuss the issue of progressivity refer to Blum and Kalven. *See, e.g.,* W. KLEIN, *supra* note 3, at 12; Doernberg, *supra* note 3, at 427; Gwartney & Long, *Is the Flat Tax a Radical Idea?,* 5 CATO J. 407, 411 (1985); Lane, *A Theory of the Tax Base: The Exchange Model,* 3 AM. J. TAX POL'Y 1, 29 n.46 (1984); O'Kelley, *supra* note 3, at 728 n.3, 729 n.9; Shannon, *supra* note 19.

22. At the time *The Uneasy Case* was published there was a tradition in the economics literature in favor of progressive taxation. *See, e.g.,* A. PIGOU, THE ECONOMICS OF WELFARE, 710-36 (4th ed. 1932); H. SIMONS, *supra* note 9, at 1-40; W. VICKREY, AGENDA FOR PROGRESSIVE TAXATION (1947); Vickrey, *An Exchange of Questions between Economics and Philosophy,* in ECONOMIC JUSTICE 35-62 (E. Phelps ed. 1973) (originally published as *The Goals of Economic Life,* in GOALS OF ECONOMIC LIFE (A. Ward ed. 1953)).

23. Blum & Kalven, *supra* note 3, at 419.

24. *Id.* at 430.

25. *Id.* at 430-44.

argument that welfare would be improved by redistributing wealth from rich to poor. The connection between wealth and welfare, Blum and Kalven state, is too tenuous to serve as the cornerstone of tax policy.[26]

Blum and Kalven's critique of the progressive tax, although in our opinion unconvincing, is detailed and considered. Its impact is dulled, however, by the authors' failure to subject the proportionate tax structure to an equally rigorous critique.[27] While Blum and Kalven closely examine and reject certain theories of distributive justice that might justify progressive taxation, they fail even to articulate what a normative basis of a proportionate tax might look like.

Since the publication of *The Uneasy Case*, academic and popular support for a flat tax has grown.[28] But few scholars have identified a theory of distributive justice upon which that tax could be predicated.[29] In fact, while there are a number of plausible theories of distributive justice that support a progressive tax or even certain regressive taxes,[30] it is surprisingly difficult to derive a theory of distributive justice that supports a proportionate tax. The few theories implied or suggested by flat-tax proponents are inchoate, inconsistent, or unsatisfactory.

Many commentators appear to support a proportionate tax on efficiency grounds. Richard Doernberg, for example, argues that progressivity operates as "an excise levy on increasing productivity."[31] Further,

---

26. *Id.* at 472-79. Blum and Kalven recognize, however, that welfare considerations are valid when comparing the tax burden on two individuals, one with an income below subsistence and one with an income above. *Id.* at 473.

27. *See*, H. GROVES, TAX PHILOSOPHERS 59 (1974) (noting failure of Blum and Kalven to defend proportional taxation).

28. Of the few articles in the legal literature published since 1952 that have taken a position on the rate structure, most have been critical of progressivity. *See, e.g.*, Blum, *Revisiting the Uneasy Case for Progressive Taxation*, *supra* note 3; Doernberg, *supra* note 3; O'Kelley, *supra* note 3. *But see* W. KLEIN, *supra* note 3.

29. Two writers who based their support of a flat tax on a theory of distributive justice are F.A. Hayek and Charles O'Kelley. *See* Hayek, *Progressive Taxation Reconsidered*, in ON FREEDOM AND FREE ENTERPRISE 265 (M. Sennholz ed. 1956) (arguing that high marginal rates on the wealthiest taxpayers reduce upward mobility without significantly redistributing economic advantages to the poor); O'Kelley, *supra* note 3 (making a Rawlsian argument for a proportional tax structure); *see also* J. RAWLS, A THEORY OF JUSTICE 277-80 (1971) (discussing tax implications of his theory of justice).

30. A regressive lump-sum tax might be justified on "efficiency" grounds. *See infra* text accompanying notes 61-62. A regressive tax might also be justified by a benefits-received theory of taxation, provided that it could be empirically demonstrated that the benefits of government to an individual rise less rapidly than his income. A proportionate or progressive tax might also be justified on benefits-received grounds, provided that government benefits to an individual were believed to rise as fast or faster than income. Most benefits-received notions of taxation rest, however, on a consent theory of government, which generally does not permit compulsory taxation. *See* K. WICKSELL, A NEW PRINCIPLE OF JUST TAXATION (1896), *translated and reprinted in part in* CLASSICS IN THE THEORY OF PUBLIC FINANCE 72 (R. Musgrave & A. Peacock eds. 1958); Wagner, *Normative and Positive Foundations of Tax Reform*, 5 CATO J. 385 (1985).

31. Doernberg, *supra* note 3, at 428.

he says, "High marginal rates have spawned a cottage industry of tax planners who have dreamed up an impressive array of income-shifting devices."[32] In *The Uneasy Case,* Blum and Kalven claim that a graduated rate structure "greatly complicates the positive law of taxation" and "dampens incentives."[33]

Efficiency fails to justify a proportionate tax for two reasons. First, as noted below, the same efficiency-based reasoning that rejects a progressive tax in favor of a proportionate tax would, if applied consistently, reject a proportionate tax in favor of a lump-sum head tax.[34] A head tax is "efficient" because it is unavoidable and does not change the behavior of any taxpayer.[35] Since a poor taxpayer pays a greater portion of her income under a head tax than does a rich person, an exclusive concern for economic efficiency implies a regressive, rather than proportional, tax. Second, the concept of economic efficiency carries normative force only when tied to the welfare of individuals. But scholars who support a proportionate tax on efficiency grounds do not articulate the link between efficiency and welfare. Indeed, some scholars, such as Blum and Kalven, who believe a proportionate tax is superior to a progressive tax on efficiency grounds reject the notion that any meaningful connection can be drawn between income and individual welfare.[36]

A proportionate tax might be supported more plausibly as a compromise between the perceived efficiency costs of a progressive tax and the perceived inequities of a lump sum tax. Such a "compromise" choice of a proportionate tax is suggested by Blum and Kalven's discussion of the effect of progressivity on savings. They argue that the switch to a proportionate rate structure would increase savings,[37] but go on to state:

> A regressive tax system would be even more efficacious in promoting savings, but surely in our society the proposal to have such a system would give way before considerations of justice among taxpayers. This is sufficient evidence that the drawbacks of progression in terms of productivity must be weighed against its possible merits in allocating the tax burden fairly.[38]

The difficulty with this position is that it does not explain what conceptions of fairness and justice are strong enough to rule out a regressive tax

32. *Id.*

33. Blum & Kalven, *supra* note 3, at 444.

34. *See infra* text accompanying notes 61-65.

35. In a simple partial equilibrium analysis, any tax that changes taxpayer behavior is generally assumed to be inefficient. Such a tax will tend to decrease societal wealth. R. BOADWAY & D. WILDASIN, *supra* note 13, at 174-75. The reduction in societal wealth caused by an income tax, as opposed to a lump-sum head tax, under both partial and general equilibrium analyses, is discussed *infra* text accompanying notes 57-101.

36. Blum & Kalven, *supra* note 3, at 472-79; *see also supra* note 26.

37. *Id.* at 441-42.

38. *Id.* at 443-44 (footnote omitted).

but are not strong enough to justify a progressive tax. It would appear mere chance that the opposing goals of efficiency and justice should reach equipoise at a proportionate tax.

Other possible arguments in support of a proportionate tax lack even surface plausibility. For example, a proportionate tax can be shown to leave unchanged the level of inequality as determined by measures that consider only the relative amount of income held by each income task, such as the Gini coefficient[39] or the variance of the logarithms of incomes. It is not clear, however, that leaving such measures unchanged is desirable,[40] and there are other statistical measures of inequality that are not left unchanged under a proportionate tax.[41]

Perhaps the most realistic, but least satisfying, explanation for the appeal of a proportionate tax lies in the concept of "prominence."[42] This concept is grounded in the tendency of individuals seeking to solve a problem in concert with others to settle on the most prominent, or conspicuous, solution.[43] Because it is so simple, a tax structure that imposes the same rate on all individuals is more "prominent" than any of the countless rate structures that impose different rates on individuals of different rate classes. Faced with a requirement to select a tax structure, an individual might choose a proportionate rate structure simply because no other rate structure comes immediately to mind. It is as if, in choosing a tax structure, the polity were a lost traveller faced with a selection of equally well trodden paths. Lacking any convincing rationale to turn right or left, the traveller continues on the path that leads straight ahead.[44]

Perhaps we can do no better than the lost traveller and are con-

39. The Gini coefficient is one-half the expected difference between the incomes of two randomly selected individuals as a proportion of mean income. A Gini coefficient of zero indicates complete equality. A. ATKINSON, *supra* note 9, at 53-54; J. MEADE, THE JUST ECONOMY 116-17 (1976).

40. A measure of inequality explicitly incorporating normative judgments is considered in A. ATKINSON, *supra* note 40; *see also* A. SEN, CHOICE, WELFARE AND MEASUREMENT 416-20 (1982).

41. One such measure is the variance of incomes, which indicates a reduction in inequality upon the application of a proportionate tax. A. ATKINSON, *On the Measurement of Inequality*, in SOCIAL JUSTICE AND PUBLIC POLICY 15, 22-23 (1983). For discussions of the characteristics of various measures of inequality, see A. ATKINSON, *supra* note 9, at 53-59; J. MEADE, *supra* note 39, at 112-35.

42. *See* T. SCHELLING, THE STRATEGY OF CONFLICT 53-80 (1960). One test of the prominence concept involved a game played by isolated individuals, who were asked to respond to the following question: "Name 'head' or 'tails.' If you and your partner name the same, you both win a prize." Respondents overwhelmingly answered "heads." *Id.* at 55 n.1.

43. *Id.* at 57-58.

44. Blum and Kalven use a similar metaphor to argue against a progressive rate structure, quoting with approval a nineteenth-century economist: " 'The moment . . . you abandon . . . the cardinal principle of exacting from all individuals the same proportion of their income or their property, you are at sea without rudder or compass, and there is no amount of injustice or folly you may not commit.' " Blum & Kalven, *supra* note 3, at 461 (quoting J. MCCULLOCH, TAXATION AND

demned to raise and redistribute a substantial portion of the world's wealth on a formula selected through intuition. But before resigning ourselves to that fate, it would be worthwhile to examine theories of distributive justice that might shape the tax structure.

B. *Entitlement and Welfarist Theories of Distributive Justice*

There are many theories of distributive justice. A detailed discussion of all such theories is beyond the scope of this Article; for our purposes, it is sufficient to explore the differences between entitlement and welfarist theories of distributive justice.[45]

Under entitlement theories, a person deserves goods because of some action the person has taken or some trait the person possesses. One entitlement theory is the notion, sometimes associated with John Locke, that a person has a right to what he produces.[46] A modern variant, offered by Robert Nozick in *Anarchy, State and Utopia,* states that a person is entitled to those goods acquired in uncoerced exchanges with others.[47]

Welfarist theories of distributive justice, on the other hand, judge the goodness of social states solely by the welfare or utility enjoyed by the individuals in those states.[48] Perhaps the two best known welfarist theories are utilitarianism, which judges the welfare of a society according to the unweighted sum of the utilities of its individual members,[49] and the

---

THE FUNDING SYSTEM 142 (London 1842)). The difficulty with the metaphor is, of course, its assumption that a proportionate tax offers some sort of safe harbor.

45. Theories of distributive justice are summarized in R. MUSGRAVE & P. MUSGRAVE, *supra* note 14, at 82-101; A. SEN, RESOURCES, VALUES AND DEVELOPMENT 277-92, 300-02 (1984). Recent and classical writings on distributive justice in taxation are collected in ECONOMIC JUSTICE (E. Phelps ed. 1973).

46. For Locke's elaboration of his theory of property, see chapter 5 of J. LOCKE, THE SECOND TREATISE OF GOVERNMENT, 18-30 (C.B. MacPherson ed. 1980) (1690).

47. R. NOZICK, ANARCHY, STATE, AND UTOPIA (1974). Nozick adopts a theory of property rights under which a person has a right to property if he acquired it in accordance with the principle of "justice in acquisition" or in accordance with the principle of "justice in transfer" from someone else who was entitled to it. *Id.* at 149-294. Nozick attempts to distinguish his theory from desert theories that judge the goodness of the world according to whether the distribution of goods is consistent with a person's endowment with some quality. Instead, Nozick evaluates the justice of a person's property holdings solely according to the method by which such holdings were acquired. Thus Nozick rejects theories of distribution of the form "To each according to his *X*" as consequentialist and ahistorical rather than process-based. *Id.* at 198-204.

The tax system most consistent with Nozick's views is, perhaps, consent-basis taxation along the lines suggested by Wicksell. *See* K. WICKSELL, *supra* note 30. For recent applications of a consent-based normative theory to tax reform, see Dorn, *Introduction: The Principles and Politics of Tax Reform,* 5 CATO J. 361 (1985); Wagner, *supra* note 30. For critiques of entitlement theories of taxation, see Okun, *Further Thoughts on Equality and Efficiency,* in INCOME REDISTRIBUTION 13, 27-28 (C. Campbell ed. 1977); Vickrey, *supra* note 22.

48. Formal definitions of welfarist and other theories of distributive justice may be found in A. SEN, *supra* note 45.

49. The classic work is J.S. MILL, UTILITARIANISM (London 1863). The utilitarian ethic is still widely debated. *See, e.g.,* UTILITARIANISM AND BEYOND (A. Sen & B. Williams eds. 1982); J.

"leximin," based loosely upon the philosophy of John Rawls, which judges the welfare of a society according to the well-being of its least well off member.[50] Lying between utilitarianism and the leximin with respect to preference for equality are weighted utility theories that, like utilitarianism, consider the welfare of each individual in determining social welfare, but that give greater weight to the well-being of the less well-off members of society.[51]

Although concern for incentive and demoralization effects may lead some welfarist theories to consider how individuals acquired goods in determining distribution, the fundamental focus of welfarist theories is often thought to be at odds with that of entitlement theories. Under entitlement theories and certain other nonwelfarist theories, an individual has a *right* to a good regardless of whether her ownership of the good is consistent with the welfare of others or even with her own welfare. For example, according to Nozick, a person who acquires a good in a just manner would have a right to the good even if it were of little or no value to her and of enormous value to others.[52]

In contrast, welfarist theories consider the fact that a person has created a good only to the extent that allocating goods to their creators improves social welfare by encouraging production or stability. The creator would not, however, have a claim to the good derived solely from the act of creation. Thus, welfarist theories of distributive justice permit taxation either to finance public goods or to redistribute income, if the well-being of individuals in the society is thereby improved.

C. *A Welfarist Theory of Distributive Justice*

In the following sections we discuss the implications of welfarist theories of distributive justice for the tax structure. We focus on welfarist

---

SMART & B. WILLIAMS, UTILITARIANISM: FOR AND AGAINST (1973). For an axiomatic derivation of utilitarianism, see Harsanyi, *Cardinal Welfare, Individualistic Ethics, and Interpersonal Comparisons of Utility*, 63 J. POL. ECON. 309 (1955).

50. J. RAWLS, *supra* note 29. The leximin is derived from the second of Rawls' two principles of justice, which maintains that society should be structured so as to maximize the amount of primary goods held by the least well off class. *Id.* at 60-61, 101. This principle is to guide societal structure only after society has implemented Rawls' first principle of justice, which calls for the maximization of the liberty of each individual, consistent with the preservation of a like amount of liberty for others. *Id.* at 60. The welfarist leximin, unlike Rawls' theory, maximizes the welfare, not the primary goods, enjoyed by the worst off individual and considers the distribution of liberty only as it affects the level of welfare. *See* A. ATKINSON & J. STIGLITZ, *supra* note 12, at 339-40.

Under a leximin, if the least well off individuals in two societies are equally well off, the societies are judged by the welfare of the second least well off individual and so on. If only the welfare of the least well off individuals are considered, then the term "maximin" is used rather than leximin. *Id.*

51. Welfarist theories that weight the welfare of the better off members of society more heavily than the welfare of the less well-off are logically possible but appear to have no adherents. The least egalitarian of the plausible welfarist theories is utilitarianism.

52. R. NOZICK, *supra* note 47, at 30.

rather than entitlement theories, in part because we believe that such ethics, while not without problems, have more to commend them. It seems plausible, at least, to judge government policies by the impact those policies have on the welfare of the individuals in the society.

One particularly attractive feature of a welfarist analysis of taxation is its responsiveness to the efficiency effects of various tax structures—effects that nearly everyone finds relevant. Another virtue of welfarist theories is their consistency with the Pareto principle: They view as desirable any change that makes some member of society better off without making any other member worse off.[53] Entitlement theories, on the other hand, may not endorse a tax that increases the welfare of an "undeserving" individual even if that change does not reduce the welfare of any other person. While it may be possible to formulate a coherent ethical theory that rejects the Pareto principle, acceptance of this principle is frequently considered a prerequisite of any acceptable social decision-making rule.[54]

A final reason for our focus on welfarist theories is that entitlement theories do not clearly justify any rate structure. *Any* tax imposed on an unwilling taxpayer may be inconsistent with a system based on the view that a person has a right to what he produces. Under such an entitlement theory, a state might be permitted only to levy taxes that lead to Pareto improvements—making every member of the society as well off or better off than she was before the tax. For example, compulsory taxation might be justified to maintain a government strong enough to protect the rights of the individuals living under it. Even if this notion is accepted, however, it provides little guidance as to the appropriate rate structure.

The tax implications of welfarist ethics have been explored in the important economics literature on "optimal taxation."[55] Mathematical models derived from that literature can be used to determine the optimal rate structure under a wide variety of economic assumptions and welfarist ethics.

Welfarist ethics are not without their own difficulties, however. Many reject such theories because they do not value rights except to the extent that they improve the welfare of individuals. Others find the inter-

53. *See* A. ATKINSON & J. STIGLITZ, *supra* note 12, at 339-40. This is true even under the leximin, which, generally speaking, judges social states by the well-being of the worst off member of the state since, if the level of welfare of the worst off individual is the same in two social states, one looks to the well-being of successively better off individuals to order the states. A. SEN, *supra* note 40, at 24-25.

54. *See* Y. NG, WELFARE ECONOMICS: INTRODUCTION AND DEVELOPMENT OF BASIC CONCEPTS 30-32 (1980); Michelman, *Property, Utility, and Fairness: Comments on the Ethical Foundations of "Just Compensation" Law*, 80 HARV. L. REV 1165, 1176 (1967). The Pareto principle is shown to be inconsistent with absolute individual rights in Sen, *The Impossibility of a Paretian Liberal*, 78 J. POL. ECON. 152 (1970).

55. *See infra* text accompanying notes 178-241.

personal comparisons of utility required by welfarist theories to be not only difficult to make, as most supporters of welfarism would admit, but also meaningless.[56]

The rejection of an exclusively welfarist ethic does not necessarily imply acceptance of an ethic that is exclusively entitlement-based. Conceivably, a just society could consider both the welfare of individuals and entitlements in determining a fair system of distribution. Optimal taxation analysis should be of interest to those who believe in a mixed ethic, since it provides insight into the tax structure inspired by any theory of distributive justice that is at least partly concerned with individual welfare.

In Part II, we discuss the efficiency costs of a progressive rate structure. We then use the methods of optimal taxation to explore how the efficiency costs and redistributive features of various progressive rate structures comport with a wide variety of welfarist ethics, ranging from utilitarianism to the Rawlsian leximin.

II
An Analysis of the Prima Facie Case Against Progressivity

The prima facie case against progressivity argues that the progressive rate structure is undesirable because it reduces labor efficiency and output, increases the cost and complexity of tax administration, promotes the misdeployment of capital, and reduces tax compliance. In this Part, we critically analyze each of these criticisms and find that each is overstated.

56. The seminal attack on interpersonal comparisons of utility is contained in L. Robbins, An Essay on the Nature and Significance of Economic Science 136-43 (2d ed. 1935). Robbins argued that there was no way of "scientifically" comparing the utility levels of different people. *Id.* at 139-40. Robbins' views were accepted by most economists and public choice theorists; by 1952 Blum and Kalven reflected the conventional wisdom in their rejection of interpersonal utility comparisons. *See* Blum & Kalven, *supra* note 3, at 472-79; Scitovsky, *The State of Welfare Economics*, 41 Am. Econ. Rev. 303 (1951) (noting and deploring the widespread rejection of interpersonal utility comparisons).

In recent years, some economists have argued that noncomparable ordinal utility measures provide insufficient information for social decisionmaking and thus interpersonal comparisons may be necessary. *See, e.g.*, Y. Ng, *supra* note 54, at 12-15; A. Sen, *supra* note 40, at 264-68; J. Meade, *supra* note 39, at 20-29.

Lerner has demonstrated that even if we cannot determine how additional consumption increases the welfare of any particular individual, we can still determine that expected utility is maximized by the equalization of incomes as long as we know that for each person additional units of consumption increase utility at a diminishing rate. A. Lerner, The Economics of Control 29-32 (1944). Sen has shown that this result generalizes to all welfarist social welfare functions. Sen, *On Ignorance and Equal Distribution*, 63 Am. Econ. Rev. 1022 (1973).

A. *Effects of Progressivity on the Labor Supply*

1. *Purported Decline in Efficiency and Output*

The progressive rate structure is often criticized as inefficient. This criticism centers around two arguments. First, progressivity is claimed to reduce work effort. Second, progressivity is said to increase the complexity of the tax law and thereby increase the costs associated with tax planning and compliance.

The progressive rate structure's reduction of the labor supply has often been considered a strong argument for a proportionate tax.[57] Blum and Kalven, for example, cite reduced work effort, together with the increased costs of tax planning, as establishing "a sort of *prima facie* case" in favor of a proportionate tax structure.[58] More recently, an increase in work effort has been predicted by sponsors of legislation designed to reduce the progressivity of the tax structure.[59] Most supporters of a progressive tax structure accept the notion that progressivity entails a "trade-off" between equity and efficiency.[60]

Individuals who believe that progressivity adversely affects labor output are unlikely to believe that the tax system is the sole determinant of work effort. But it is generally assumed that the net effect of a progressive rate structure is to reduce significantly labor output and efficiency. One scholar concludes:

> By progressively reducing the net return from any given increment of gross income or gain, progressive taxation discourages additional efforts or activities, or a change in the direction of efforts or activities, which might be prompted by greater material rewards.[61]

The intuition behind the view that an income tax reduces work effort is not difficult to apprehend. Individuals value both consumption and leisure, so that an individual will work only if the value of the additional consumption she will enjoy by doing so is at least as great as the value of the leisure she gives up. Imposing an income tax reduces the amount of additional consumption an individual will be able to enjoy by working an extra hour. If all else is equal, an individual will be less will-

---

57. *See, e.g.*, R. HALL & A. RABUSHKA, THE FLAT TAX 23, 70-72 (1985); Blum & Kalven, *supra* note 3, at 444; Johnson, *President Reagan's Modified Flat Tax: Analysis and Comparison*, 5 CATO J. 499, 502-03 (1985); O'Kelley, *supra* note 3, at 743; Smith, *supra* note 3, at 456; Vickrey, *supra* note 3, at 447.

58. Blum and Kalven, *supra* note 3, at 430.

59. *See Major Tax Reform Options: Hearings Before the Senate Comm. on Finance*, 98th Cong., 2d Sess. pt. 1, at 58, 61 (1984) (statement of Senator Kasten that "the steep and graduated tax schedule provides an incentive to avoid activities that are subject to high taxes—activities such as work"); *id.* at 285, 287 (statement of Senator Quayle, Sponsor of the SELF Tax Plan Act of 1985). *See generally 1985 Tax Reform: Hearing on S.409, S.411 and S.1006 Before the Senate Comm. on Finance*, 99th Cong., 1st Sess (1985).

60. *See, e.g.*, A. OKUN, EQUALITY AND EFFICIENCY: THE BIG TRADEOFF (1975).

61. Smith, *supra* note 3, at 456; *see also* Doernberg, *supra* note 3, at 445-46.

ing give up leisure because the additional consumption earned will be reduced.

Consider, for example, an individual with a pre-tax wage of $10 per hour who would be willing to sacrifice an hour of the leisure she currently enjoys in return for $9 of consumption. In the absence of a tax, the individual will work that hour and will receive a net benefit of $1 because she receives consumption worth $10 for the sacrificed leisure worth $9. On the other hand, if an income tax of 20% is imposed, the individual will not work the additional hour, because the sacrifice of $9 of leisure will yield only $8 of consumption. This change in the willingness of individuals to sacrifice leisure for consumption is the "substitution effect" of the tax.

The tax-induced distortion of the trade-off between leisure and consumption is inefficient. Indeed, in this case the tax has benefitted no one. The individual is worse off because she is denied the gain she would have made by exchanging leisure for consumption; the employer is worse off because he loses the benefit of the labor; and the fisc is not enriched, because no tax revenues are raised. This tax-induced distortion could be avoided by a head or lump-sum tax, which would be due regardless of income and therefore would not influence the work-leisure decision.

The above example is simplistic, of course. An income tax seldom causes an individual to stop working entirely. Moreover, any tax based on income will have an "income effect" as well as a substitution effect. The income effect reflects the fact that a poorer individual will value a given amount of income more than a richer individual. For a poorer taxpayer, therefore, a tax that reduces net wealth tends to increase the value of additional income and the willingness to work. The increase in work effort due to the reduction in income by a tax may more than offset the decrease in work effort due to the substitution effect.

It is nonetheless true that an income tax, unlike a lump-sum tax, drives a wedge between the value of an individual's labor and the amount an individual receives for that labor. This wedge, rather than the aggregate effect on work effort, creates the efficiency loss. An increase in the marginal rates increases this wedge between the value of an individual's labor and the amount she receives for it. Very high marginal rates are quite inefficient; the efficiency costs of a tax system vary with the square of the marginal tax rate.[62] An increase in the marginal tax rate from 70% to 80%, for example, causes more than twice as great an efficiency loss as an increase from 30% to 40%.[63] It is high marginal rates, and not

62. R. BOADWAY & D. WILDASIN, *supra* note 13, at 387-89.

63. This measure of welfare loss is derived from a partial equilibrium analysis. *Id.* at 391. However, a rate increase has also been found to generate a more than proportionate welfare loss under general equilibrium analysis. *See* Fullerton, Shoven & Whalley, *Replacing the U.S. Income*

progressivity, that produce large efficiency losses.

A progressive tax does not necessarily require steep marginal rates. The effective tax burden on each income class under current tax law, for example, is about the same as the burden under the law prior to the enactment of the Tax Reform Act of 1986, yet marginal rates on almost all taxpayers are lower because the tax base is broader. As discussed below, a combination of cash grants and constant marginal rates can produce a fairly high degree of progressivity with relatively modest marginal rates.[64]

Moreover, a switch from a progressive to a proportional tax that raised equal revenue would not eliminate efficiency costs, nor would it reduce efficiency costs for all taxpayers. Instead, a proportionate tax would produce higher marginal rates for lower-income taxpayers and lower marginal rates for higher-income taxpayers. Although the mean marginal rate, as adjusted to reflect the fact that high-income individuals would have more dollars subject to tax than low-income individuals, would be somewhat lower under a proportionate tax than under a regressive or progressive tax that raised equal revenue,[65] the precise impact of the elimination of progressivity would depend on the distribution of income in the society and the particular rate structure chosen.

Progressivity, then, is responsible for only a fraction of the efficiency costs associated with the income tax. Nevertheless, if the efficiency costs of the income tax are extremely high, even a modest portion of those costs might be unacceptable. Therefore, it is important to examine the total labor-related costs associated with the tax.

2. *Empirical Approaches and Estimation*

The responsiveness of individuals to changes in their wage rates (with total wealth held constant) is measured by the compensated elasticity of the labor supply.[66] A high compensated elasticity indicates that the wage rate has a substantial effect on work effort so that individuals will work fewer hours if their effective wage rate is reduced by an income tax. A low compensated elasticity indicates that work effort is only

---

Tax with a Progressive Consumption Tax: A Sequenced General Equilibrium Approach, 20 J. PUB. ECON. 3 (1983).

64. *See infra* text accompanying notes 177-241.

65. The reduction in the adjusted or weighted mean marginal rate may be illustrated by imagining a two-taxpayer society in which one taxpayer earns an hourly wage of $30 and the other taxpayer earns an hourly wage of $10. Assume the replacement of a two-level 30% and 10% progressive tax with a proportionate tax of 20%. Under the progressive tax, a $30 wage was taxed at a 30% rate and a $10 wage was taxed at a 10% rate, for a weighted mean of 25%. The proportionate tax produces a weighted mean of 20%. The nonweighted mean would be 20% in either case.

66. For a discussion and formal definition of compensated elasticity, see R. BOADWAY & D. WILDASIN, *supra* note 13, at 248-55, 297-301.

slightly affected by changes in the wage rate so that a reduction in the effective wage rate will not cause a significant reduction in hours of labor. If the compensated elasticity is low, the efficiency costs of an income tax will be small and the costs associated with progressivity smaller still.

At least four different approaches have been used to estimate compensated elasticity: cross-section studies,[67] controlled experiments,[68] time-series studies,[69] and direct interviews.[70] Each approach raises both recurrent and unique sets of methodological issues, and a given study may attack those issues in a manner different from other studies.[71] Notwithstanding the great diversity in methodology, however, estimates

67. Cross-section studies examine the relationship across society between labor supply, wage rate, and nonwage income. A finding that, among individuals with equal combined wage and nonwage income, low wage rates are associated with short workweeks suggests that wages have a large effect on the marginal tradeoff between work and leisure. If, in such circumstances, low wages reduce work effort, taxes would also reduce work effort, since taxes reduce effective wages. The main drawback of cross-section studies is that the approach shows only correlation, not causation. A positive relationship between wage rate and work effort may suggest that high wages increase labor supply, but it may also suggest that the willingness to work longer hours leads to higher wages.

Examples of recent cross-section studies include: Cain & Dooley, *Estimation of a Model of Labor Supply, Fertility, and Wages of Married Women*, 84 J. PUB. ECON. 179 (1976); Cogan, *Fixed Costs and Labor Supply*, 49 ECONOMETRICA 945 (1981); Hausman, *Stochastic Problems in the Simulation of Labor Supply*, in BEHAVIORAL SIMULATION METHODS IN TAX POLICY ANALYSIS 47 (M. Feldstein ed. 1983); Ippolito, *Income Tax Policy and Lifetime Labor Supply*, 26 J. PUB. ECON. 327 (1985). Leading cross-section studies are collected in INCOME MAINTENANCE AND LABOR SUPPLY: ECONOMETRIC STUDIES (G. Cain & H. Watts eds. 1973) [hereinafter INCOME MAINTENANCE] and TAXATION AND LABOUR SUPPLY (C. Brown ed. 1981). An excellent summary of cross-section literature is found in M. KILLINGSWORTH, LABOR SUPPLY (1983).

68. *See, e.g.*, A GUARANTEED ANNUAL INCOME: EVIDENCE FROM A SOCIAL EXPERIMENT (P. Robins, R. Spiegelman, S. Weiner & J. Bell eds. 1980); THE NEW JERSEY INCOME-MAINTENANCE EXPERIMENT, VOL. II: LABOR-SUPPLY RESPONSES (H. Watts & A. Rees eds. 1976); WELFARE IN RURAL AREAS: THE NORTH CAROLINA-IOWA INCOME MAINTENANCE EXPERIMENT (J. Palmer & J. Pechman eds. 1978). In theory, the correlation-causation problem described in relation to cross-section studies could be circumvented through controlled experiments in which individuals in similar economic circumstances are subject to varying tax rates and are given varying amounts of nonemployment income. Costs and political controversy have limited this approach to short-term experiments with individuals below or near the poverty level. The results of such experiments are obviously biased by the sample group and period. Moreover, the controlled experiments have suffered from design defects and the inability to maintain "laboratory" conditions.

69. Time-series studies measure the relationship between wages and work effort over time, and are extremely sensitive to exogenous influences on the economy. For example, increased work force participation by members of certain minority groups may be caused more by a lessening of discrimination than an increase in wage rates. *See, e.g.*, Abbott & Ashenfelter, *Labour Supply, Commodity Demand and the Allocation of Time*, 43 REV. ECON. STUD. 389 (1976); Jones, *New Estimates of Hours of Work per Week and Hourly Earnings, 1900-1957*, 45 REV. ECON. & STATISTICS 374 (1963).

70. Direct interviews simply ask taxpayers how they would respond to a change in the tax rate. This approach requires taxpayers to predict a reaction to a counterfactual situation. *See, e.g.*, Break, *Income Taxes and Incentives to Work: An Empirical Study*, 57 AM. ECON. REV. 529 (1957); Brown & Levin, *The Effects of Income Taxation on Overtime: The Results of a National Survey*, 84 ECON. J. 833 (1974).

71. *See supra* notes 67-70. All approaches raise certain recurring issues such as the selection of data sets and the choice of statistical methods.

of compensated elasticity cluster around a reasonably narrow range. A majority of studies have found the compensated elasticity with respect to labor for males (the dominant wage-earner group) of all income classes to be low, ranging from 0.1 to 0.3.[72] With total income held constant, a tax cut that increases after-tax wages by 10% would be expected to increase labor supply by less than 3%.[73]

The effect on work effort of a compensated elasticity of 0.3 may be illustrated by hypothesizing a graduated progressive tax structure with

72. The authors reviewed the conclusions of 21 studies published in the last 15 years. Thirteen reported compensated elasticity for males (or, where reported figures are disaggregated by race or income and no aggregate figures are given, for white males or males with incomes above the poverty line) of less than 0.2; three reported compensated elasticity of above 0.2; and five reported compensated elasticities that ranged above and below 0.2. The studies reviewed are: A. TELLA, D. TELLA & C. GREEN, THE HOURS OF WORK AND FAMILY INCOME RESPONSE TO NEGATIVE INCOME TAX PLANS: THE IMPACT ON THE WORKING POOR (1971); Ashenfelter & Heckman, *Estimating Labor-Supply Functions*, in INCOME MAINTENANCE, *supra* note 67, at 265; Ashworth & Ulph, *Endogeneity I: Estimating Labour Supply with Piecewise Linear Budget Constraints*, in TAXATION AND LABOUR SUPPLY, *supra* note 67, at 53; Ashworth & Ulph, *Household Models: On the Structure of Family Labor Supply Decisions*, in TAXATION AND THE LABOUR SUPPLY, *supra* note 67, at 117; Atkinson & Stern, *On the Switch from Direct to Indirect Taxation*, 14 J. PUB. ECON. 195 (1980); Atkinson & Stern, *On Labour Supply and Commodity Demands*, in ESSAYS IN THE THEORY AND MEASUREMENT OF CONSUMER BEHAVIOR 265 (A. Deaton ed. 1981); Atrostic, *The Demand for Leisure and Nonpecuniary Job Characteristics*, 72 AM. ECON. REV. 428 (1982); Blundell & Walker, *Modelling the Joint Determination of Household Labour Supplies and Commodity Demands*, 92 ECON. J. 351 (1982); Boskin, *The Economics of Labor Supply*, in INCOME MAINTENANCE, *supra* note 67, at 163; Brown, Levin & Ulph, *Estimates of Labour Hours Supplied by Married Male Workers in Great Britain*, 23 SCOT. J. POL. ECON. 261 (1976); Fleisher, Parsons & Porter, *Asset Adjustments and Labor Supply of Older Workers*, in INCOME MAINTENANCE, *supra* note 67, at 279; Garfinkel, *On Estimating the Labor-Supply Effects of a Negative Income Tax*, in INCOME MAINTENANCE, *supra* note 67, at 205; Hall, *Wages, Income, and Hours of Work in the U.S. Labor Force*, in INCOME MAINTENANCE, *supra* note 67, at 102; Ham, *Estimation of a Labour Supply Model with Censoring Due to Unemployment and Underemployment*, 49 REV. ECON. STUD. 335 (1982); Hausman, *Labor Supply*, in HOW TAXES AFFECT ECONOMIC BEHAVIOR 27 (H. Aaron & J. Pechman eds. 1981); Hausman & Wise, *Social Experimentation, Truncated Distributions, and Efficient Estimation*, 45 ECONOMETRICA 919 (1977); Kniesner, *An Indirect Test of Complementarity in a Family Labor Supply Model*, 44 ECONOMETRICA 651 (1976); Ruffell, *Endogeneity II: Direct Estimation of Labour Supply Functions with Piecewise Linear Budget Constraints*, in TAXATION AND LABOUR SUPPLY, *supra* note 67, at 101; Wales & Woodland, *Labour Supply and Progressive Taxes*, 46 REV. ECON. STUD. 83 (1979); J. Dickinson, Revealed Preferences, Functional Forms and Labor Supply (Discussion Paper No. 546-79, Institute for Research on Poverty, University of Wisconsin) (1979); R. Ransom, Estimating Family Labor Supply Models Under Quantity Constraints (Working Paper No. 150, Industrial Relations Section, Princeton University) (1982). Many of these studies are summarized in INCOME MAINTENANCE, *supra* note 67, at 332-33, and M. KILLINGSWORTH, *supra* note 67, at 119-21, 193-94.

73. A few recent studies have challenged the methodology used in traditional studies and have found the compensated elasticity to be greater than 0.3. *See, e.g.*, Hausman, *supra* note 67; Hausman, *supra* note 72. The methodology and data base of these studies, however, are problematic. *See* Browning, *A Critical Appraisal of Hausman's Welfare Cost Estimates*, 93 J. POL. ECON. 1025 (1985); Heckman, *Comment*, in BEHAVIORAL SIMULATION METHODS IN TAX POLICY ANALYSIS 70-82 (M. Feldstein ed. 1983). Moreover, these studies have produced implausible compensated elasticity estimates. The leading revisionist study, for example, predicts that a male currently working 40 hours per week in a high wage job would choose to work over 67 hours per week if he were offered overtime at time-and-a-half wage rate. Browning, *supra*, at 1031.

marginal rates of 33% and 20% that is replaced by a proportionate tax of 25% without altering the amount of revenue collected. The reduction in the top marginal tax rate would increase the after-tax wage rate of the high-bracket taxpayers by about 13%.[74] Assuming a compensated elasticity of 0.3, this reduction would trigger a 3.9% increase in the labor supplied by those taxpayers.[75] On the other hand, the increase in the bottom marginal rate would decrease the after-tax wage rate of the lower-bracket taxpayers by about 6%.[76] This would trigger a 1.8% decrease in the labor supplied by those taxpayers.[77] Thus, the net effect of the change will be less than a 3.9% increase in the labor supply (with the precise result dependent on the distribution of taxpayers and income levels).

The relatively modest estimates of how responsive most individuals are to changes in the wage rate suggest that work is conditioned more by social forces and mores than by wages.[78] Work plays a central role in determining an individual's social standing and self-esteem.[79] Moreover, even individuals who view work primarily as a source of wages may not have the freedom to vary their work week.[80]

Estimates of aggregate labor-related efficiency costs vary. One recent study estimated that the total efficiency costs of the 1984 federal tax system ranged from 7.5% to 28.5% of tax revenue.[81] The tax rate

74. The 33% progressive bracket would reduce a before-tax wage of $10 per hour to an after-tax wage of $6.67 per hour. The 25% proportionate tax would reduce a before-tax wage of $10 to an after-tax wage of $7.50 per hour. The $7.50 per hour after-tax wage rate under the proportionate tax is approximately 13% greater than the $6.67 per hour after-tax wage rate under the progressive tax.

75. A compensated elasticity of 0.3 times a 13% wage increase equals a 3.9% increase in labor output.

76. The 20% progressive tax would reduce a before-tax wage of $10 per hour to an after-tax wage of $8 per hour. The 25% proportionate tax would reduce a before-tax wage of $10 to an after-tax wage of $7.50 per hour. The $7.50 per hour after-tax wage rate under the proportionate tax is approximately 6% less than the $8 per hour after-tax wage rate under the progressive tax.

77. A compensated elasticity of 0.3 times a 6% wage reduction equals a 1.8% decrease in labor output. The 1.8% figure measures only the substitution effect. This is appropriate since it is the substitution effect that results in efficiency loss. As noted in the text accompanying notes 61-62, the imposition of a tax also will cause an income effect, which will increase work effort. The combined impact of the income and substitution effects is measured by the uncompensated elasticity of labor. Most estimates of uncompensated elasticity for males are either negative or close to zero, indicating that an income tax either increases work effort or leaves work effort unaffected. *See* M. KILLINGSWORTH, *supra* note 67, at 119-22, 185.

78. A. ATKINSON, *supra* note 9, at 44-45; *see also* Break, *supra* note 70 (survey of taxpayers found taxes played little role in the decision to work); Brown & Levin, *supra* note 70 (same results).

79. Gramm, *Labor, Work, and Leisure: Human Well-Being and the Optimal Allocation of Time*, 21 J. ECON. ISSUES 167, 175 (1987).

80. The long-run elasticity of the labor supply is likely to be somewhat greater than the short-run elasticity because individuals will be able to modify their educational investment and career choice in light of the expected after-tax wage. *See* Diamond, *Negative Taxes and the Poverty Problem—A Review Article*, 21 NAT'L TAX J. 288, 291 (1968).

81. Browning, *On the Marginal Welfare Cost of Taxation*, 77 AM. ECON. REV. 11 (1987).

used to determine such costs included social security taxes, sales and excise taxes borne by labor, and other income-related taxes; efficiency gains from replacing only the income tax with a lump-sum tax would be a smaller percentage of tax revenue.[82] Another study estimated that the 1973 United States income tax produced an efficiency loss of somewhat more than 20% of tax revenue.[83] This estimate included gains attributable to the elimination of certain tax preferences, such as the favorable treatment of owner-occupied housing. A study of the 1973 United Kingdom income tax structure estimated its efficiency costs to be about 4% of tax revenue.[84]

Replacing the studied tax structures with a proportionate tax would generate less labor-related efficiency gains than these estimates. This is because the switch to a proportionate tax, unlike the switch to a lump-sum tax, would reduce rather than eliminate the efficiency losses by high-income taxpayers and would tend to increase the efficiency costs borne by low-income taxpayers.

On the other hand, for some policymaking purposes, aggregate efficiency costs may be less important than marginal costs. The marginal cost of a tax is the cost of raising an additional dollar of tax revenue. Such costs are difficult to measure, but they are likely to be substantial. Recent estimates of the marginal cost of the United States tax structure, for example, range from under 10% to over 100%.[85]

In sum, although the claim that progressivity substantially reduces work effort must be viewed with skepticism, significant efficiency costs may be incurred if progressivity leads to high marginal rates. Appropriate policymaking requires an explicit weighing of these costs against the benefit of redistribution.

3. *A Targeted Approach to Labor-Supply Efficiency*

An analysis of the impact of taxation on the aggregate labor supply may provide insufficient information for policymaking if different segments of the labor market vary in their responsiveness to the tax rate. Disaggregated labor supply studies suggest that two socioeconomic groups are particularly influenced by high marginal rates. The largest and most significant of these groups for policy purposes is married women. Nearly all studies of the labor supply find that married women in general, and married women with young children in particular, are

---

82. *Id.* at 14-15.

83. Fullerton, Shoven & Whalley, *supra*, note 63, at 7.

84. J. PIGGOTT & J. WHALLEY, U.K. TAX POLICY AND APPLIED GENERAL EQUILIBRIUM ANALYSIS (1985).

85. Ballard, Shoven & Whalley, *General Equilibrium Computations of the Marginal Welfare Costs of Taxes in the United States*, 75 AM. ECON. REV. 75 (1985) (marginal costs range from 15% to 50%); Browning, *supra* note 81, at 11 (marginal costs range from under 10% to well over 100%).

much more responsive to changes in the tax rate than are men or single women. Estimates place the compensated elasticity of labor for married women close to 1.0;[86] the substitution effect of a tax-induced 20% decrease in the after-tax wage rate would be expected to cause a 20% decline in work effort.

The responsiveness of married women to changes in the effective wage rate may be explained in part by the fact that although men who enter the paid work force receive strong social approval, women who enter the paid work force may face social indifference or disapproval.[87] Therefore, men may work for social reasons while married women may work only if the economic return or job satisfaction outweighs the social pressure to remain home.

The responsiveness of married women to wage rates may also be explained by social and economic factors that often require women to take low-paying service jobs such as sales clerks or waitresses.[88] These jobs, while in many respects undesirable, generally permit easy exit from and entrance to the labor force, plus some flexibility of hours while employed.[89]

Factors that are less directly related to gender also may account for the responsiveness of married women to the wage rate. Married women are usually members of two-income households. In any two-income household, the ability of one earner to leave the work force is enhanced because there will be income even without the foregone wages. In such circumstances, the spouse whose labor decision is most marginal (generally, the lower paid spouse) will not participate in the formal marketplace unless his or her after-tax wages rise above the untaxed imputed value of the household services otherwise performed. Current estimates of labor supply elasticity focus on the responsiveness of married women; a more

86. Five out of the 14 "second generation" studies discussed in M. KILLINGSWORTH, *supra* note 67, at 193-99, 202, estimated the compensated elasticity of the supply of labor by married women at greater than 1.0, and two estimated compensated elasticity at ranges both above and below 1.0. Only two studies estimated compensated elasticity at less than 0.4. *Id.* Earlier studies, with somewhat lower compensated elasticities, are cited in *id.* at 122-23 and in Cain & Watts, *Toward a Summary and Synthesis of the Evidence*, in INCOME MAINTENANCE, *supra* note 67, at 328, 336-37. Estimation of the compensated elasticity for married women raises the methodological problems discussed *supra* at note 67.

87. *See* Harris, *Careers, Conflict, and Children: The Legacy of the Cult of Domesticity*, in CAREER AND MOTHERHOOD 55 (A. Roland & B. Harris eds. 1979); Brown, *Sex Typing in Occupational Preferences of High School Boys and Girls*, in SEX ROLE ATTITUDES AND CULTURAL CHANGE 81 (I. Gross, J. Downing & A. D'Heurle eds. 1982); Rodman & Safilios-Rothschild, *Weak Links in Men's Worker-Earner Roles: A Descriptive Model*, in FAMILY AND WORK 55, 57 (M. Brinkerhoff ed. 1984).

88. Holden & Hansen, *Part-Time Work, Full-Time Work, and Occupational Segregation*, in GENDER AND THE WORKPLACE 217 (C. Brown & J. Pechman eds. 1987).

89. Carey & Hazelbaker, *Employment Growth in the Temporary Help Industry*, MONTHLY LAB. REV., April 1986, at 37, 38.

precise analysis would be likely to find *all* second earners to be highly responsive to changes in the wage rate.

Current tax policy increases the welfare losses resulting from the high responsiveness of second earners to the wage rate by levying high marginal rates on their income. Even second earners drawing a modest wage may be taxed at a high marginal rate because their tax rate is determined by the level of combined family income rather than by their own earnings. Many commentators have criticized the steep marginal rates on second earners as inefficient and unfair.[90]

A second group that appears responsive to the wage rate is comprised of elderly persons.[91] Middle-class and upper-class elderly may have sufficient funds that they need no longer work. Other elderly individuals may be reluctant to work because of ill health or a desire to enjoy deferred leisure activities.[92] Moreover, the elderly may perform part-time labor that may easily be varied, such as consulting and clerking.[93] Finally, the decision not to work may entail no social stigma since older individuals are often not expected to work.[94]

Current tax policy strongly discourages work by elderly individuals. At certain income levels, individuals between the ages of 65 and 70 lose 50¢ of social security benefits for every dollar they earn, up to a loss of half of their benefits.[95] Moreover, elderly individuals must include in taxable income up to half of otherwise-excluded social security benefits at a rate of 50¢ for each dollar of income they receive in excess of $25,000.[96] These reductions in benefits cause many elderly individuals to face a marginal rate of over 70% and a few elderly individuals to face rates greater than 100%.[97]

The responsiveness of second wage earners and the elderly to effec-

90. *See, e.g.*, Bittker, *Federal Income Taxation and the Family*, 27 STAN. L. REV. 1389 (1975); Blumberg, *Sexism in the Code: A Comparative Study of Income Taxation of Working Wives and Mothers*, 21 BUFFALO L. REV. 49 (1971); Gann, *Abandoning Marital Status as a Factor in Allocating Income Tax Burdens*, 59 TEX. L. REV. 1 (1980); Note, *The Case for Mandatory Separate Filing by Married Persons*, 91 YALE L.J. 363 (1981).

91. Most studies of labor-supply responsiveness focus on individuals under age 65. There is evidence, however, that changes in the wage rate may have a significant impact on work effort of the elderly. *See* W. BOWEN & T.A. FINEGAN, THE ECONOMICS OF LABOR FORCE PARTICIPATION 284-86 (1969).

92. *See* L. COPPERMAN & F. KEAST, ADJUSTING TO AN OLDER WORK FORCE 42-43 (1983).

93. *See id.* at 34-48; Parnes & Nestel, *The Retirement Experience*, in WORK AND RETIREMENT 155, 168 (H.S. Parnes ed. 1981).

94. *See* M. DOERING, S. RHODES & M. SCHUSTER, THE AGING WORKER 85-89 (1983) (older individuals considered less suitable for employment than younger individuals); Fine, *Older Workers in Pursuit of New Careers*, in TOWARD AN INDUSTRIAL GERONTOLOGY 39 (H.L. Sheppard ed. 1970).

95. *See* 42 U.S.C. § 403(b) (1986).

96. I.R.C. § 86 (West Supp. 1987). For joint returns, the phaseout of the exclusion begins when the taxpayers' income exceeds $32,000 rather than $25,000. *Id.*

97. Kemp, *A Fair, Simple, and Pro-Growth Tax Reform*, 5 CATO J. 481, 493-94 (1985).

tive wage rates suggests that high marginal rates on the income of these groups impose substantial efficiency costs. The reduction in overall progressivity urged by proponents of a flat tax would reduce these costs. Reducing overall tax rates to a level that would be optimal for members of these groups, however, would probably also seriously diminish total revenues. Moreover, a reduction in overall progressivity would be a terribly expensive and imprecise way to address the needs of discrete socioeconomic groups.

A more effective way to reduce the efficiency costs of the income tax would be to target reductions of the marginal tax burden to these highly responsive groups. For example, the marginal tax burden on married women—or more generally, working spouses in two-earner families—might be reduced by treating each spouse as a separate individual for tax purposes. Alternatively, the two-earner deduction, which was eliminated by the Tax Reform Act of 1986,[98] might be restored. A deduction for work-related child care expenses also might alleviate the inefficiency caused by the nontaxation of self-provided child care.[99] Eliminating the phaseout of social security benefits would reduce the marginal tax on the elderly. Tax burdens on the elderly and on second wage earners also could be reduced by adopting a separate rate schedule for these groups.

Adoption of any of these proposals might, of course, be undesirable for other reasons. Separate filing status is inconsistent with the treatment of the family as a single unit; child care expenses contain elements of personal consumption; the phaseout of social security benefits reflects a conscious societal judgment as to the nature and purpose of those payments; and a special tax rate for one group might seem unfair.[100] Compared to the case for a proportionate tax structure, however, the case for reducing marginal rates on the elderly and second wage earners appears extremely strong. Both sets of reforms involve difficult noneconomic issues. But the efficiency gains (per dollar of tax revenue) from a reduction in overall progressivity appear modest in comparison to the efficiency gains from selective reduction of rates on the elderly and second wage earners.[101]

These cursory suggestions regarding the tax treatment of working spouses and the elderly are not intended as complete solutions to com-

---

98. Pub. L. No. 99-514, § 131(a), 100 Stat. 2085, 2113 (1986) (repealing I.R.C. § 221).

99. Blumberg, *supra* note 90, at 59-80; Schaffer & Berman, *Two Cheers for the Child Care Deduction*, 28 TAX L. REV. 535 (1973).

100. W. KLEIN, *supra*, note 3, at 289; Feld, *Another Word on Child Care*, 28 TAX L. REV. 546 (1973); McIntyre, *Individual Filing in the Personal Income Tax: Prolegomena to Future Discussion*, 58 N.C.L. REV. 469, 470 (1980).

101. *See* Boskin & Sheshinski, *Optimal Tax Treatment of the Family: Married Couples*, 20 J. PUB. ECON. 281-87 (1983) (deadweight loss of income tax reduced by lowering marginal rate of tax on "secondary earners").

plex problems. Rather, they illustrate a variety of possible forms of targeted relief. The basic point remains: Targeted relief is a more efficient means to combat disincentives to labor than is the reduction of overall progressivity.

B. *Administrative Costs of a Progressive Rate Structure*

Progressivity is widely believed to be responsible for much of the complexity of the tax system.[102] According to Blum and Kalven, progressivity "produces a tax law of almost impenetrable complexity. It invites a distorting attention to the tax aspects of any economic transaction. It affords an excessive stimulus to tax avoidance with perhaps incalculable consequences for taxpayer morale and the general respect for the law."[103] Charles Galvin writes that "[f]or the principle of progressivity we pay a high price in the extraordinary complexity of our present system,"[104] and he attributes most problems of administration to the graduated rate structure.[105]

The amount of tax levied on a particular sum under a graduated rate structure depends on the marginal rate of the taxpayer. A wealthy taxpayer in the 28% bracket will pay $28 tax on an additional $100 of income; a poor taxpayer in the zero bracket will pay no tax on the same amount. Determining the proper taxpayer is therefore important under a graduated tax. Under a proportionate tax, the identity of the taxpayer generally is irrelevant since all income is taxed at the same rate.[106] The taxpayer's identity will affect tax liability under a proportionate tax only if one taxpayer has an otherwise unusable net loss (in which case some additional income may still leave him in the zero tax bracket) or if the proportionate tax has an exemption amount and one taxpayer has income below the exemption level.

In most cases, of course, determining the proper taxpayer is easy. Single individuals are taxed on the salary they earn; there can be no serious argument that the wage earner is not the proper person to pay taxes on her own wages.[107] When wealth is transferred among members of the

---

102. *See, e.g.*, C. GALVIN & B. BITTKER, *supra* note 3, at 16-19; Blum & Kalven, *supra* note 3, at 434-35; Wallis, *The Case for Progressive Taxation: Easy or Uneasy?*, in INCOME REDISTRIBUTION 135 (C. Campbell ed. 1976); *see also* Doernberg, *supra* note 3, at 428 (arguing that progressivity promotes economic inefficiency and high economic costs).

103. Blum & Kalven, *supra* note 3, at 434-35.

104. C. GALVIN & B. BITTKER, *supra* note 3, at 16.

105. *Id.* at 16-17. Galvin blames progressivity for "the abstruseness and complexity of the income tax [that] will cause the self-assessment system to collapse." *Id.* at 16.

106. The determination of the proper taxpayer may still be important for reasons unrelated to progressivity. For example, the government may wish to reassess the tax liability of a taxpayer on whom the statute of limitations has not yet run, as opposed to a related taxpayer whose misfeasance is protected by the statute.

107. The principle that wage income is taxed to the wage earner applies to both married and

same family, however, determining the proper taxpayer may be quite difficult. For example, it is not obvious whether interest on a wage earner's invested capital that is spent on a child's education should be taxed to the wage earner, to the wage earner and spouse, or to the child.[108]

The treatment of property transfers among family members or unrelated individuals who share family-like ties is the source of much of the complexity associated with a graduated rate structure. The specific provisions governing gifts, trusts, family partnerships, loans at below-market rates of interest, unearned income of minor children, and divorce or separation agreements can be attributed largely to the progressive rate structure. All of these provisions could be simplified or eliminated by switching to a proportionate tax.[109]

Complexity is also generated by attempts of unrelated parties to

---

single taxpayers. *See* Helvering v. Eubank, 311 U.S. 122 (1940) (assignment of income attributable to past services held invalid); Lucas v. Earl, 281 U.S. 111 (1930) (assignment of future income held invalid); 3 B. BITTKER, *supra* note 10, ¶ 75. The application of that principle to married taxpayers, however, is somewhat clouded by the treatment of married individuals as a single taxpaying unit that may file a joint return. *See* I.R.C. § 1 (West Supp. 1987).

108. Under current law, determining the proper taxpayer in such circumstances depends primarily upon the legal ownership of the invested capital, the child's age, and the child's total unearned income. I.R.C. § 1 (West Supp. 1987) (net unearned income of children under age 14 to be taxed at parents' rate); 3 B. BITTKER, *supra* note 10, ¶¶ 75.3, 80 (income taxed to owner of capital or trust beneficiary).

109. I.R.C. § 1015 (1982 & Supp. III 1985) limits the basis of property acquired through gift to the lesser of the donor's basis or the fair market value of the property at the time of the gift. Absent such a limitation, a low-bracket family member could donate property that has declined in value to a high-bracket family member, and the loss on the sale of the property would be recognized by the high-bracket donee. Curiously, the tax law does not directly prevent the similar income shifting possible through the donation of appreciated property from a high-bracket to a low-bracket family member.

The so-called grantor trust rules treat the grantor of certain trusts as the owner of the trust corpus and the recipient of trust income. I.R.C. §§ 671-679 (West Supp. 1987). These rules prevent a high-bracket family member from placing income-producing property in a family-controlled trust, naming a low-bracket family member as the trust beneficiary, and thereby shifting property income to the low-bracket family member.

The family partnership provisions prevent a high-bracket family member from using a partnership to shift personal service income to a low-bracket family member. I.R.C. § 704(e) (1982).

The rules governing below-market interest rate loans limit the use of such loans to shift interest income to low-bracket taxpayers. I.R.C. § 7872 (West Supp. 1987). Prior to the enactment of such rules, high-bracket family members with excess cash often made no-interest loans to low-bracket family members; the low-bracket family members would invest the cash and recognize the interest income. Section 7872 limits the tax advantages of such loans by imputing a market rate of interest income to the high-bracket creditor.

The rules governing unearned income of minor children are designed to limit minimization of family tax burden through donation of income-producing property to (generally low-bracket) children. Under newly adopted I.R.C. § 1(i) (West Supp. 1987), net unearned income of children under age 14 is taxed at the parents' rate.

The divorce and separation agreement provisions characterize certain payments as nondeductible to the payor and excludable from the income of the payee; other payments are deductible to the payor and included as income to the payee. I.R.C. §§ 71, 1041 (West Supp. 1987). The complexity of those provisions is, in part, attributable to the progressive rate structure: If the

shift items of income or loss. Members of a partnership, for example, might agree to allocate tax-exempt income to a high-bracket partner and ordinary income to a low-bracket partner.[110] The mismatching of items of income and expense through prepayments may also achieve a kind of tax-rate arbitrage.[111] Tax provisions governing the allocation and recognition of items of income and loss among parties with common business relationships can be attributed in part to the graduated rate structure.[112]

A third and less significant source of progressivity-related complexity is the interaction between the graduated rate structure and the annual accounting period. A given sum earned during a period of high income will be taxed at a greater rate than will an equal amount earned during a period of low income. A taxpayer may be in the 28% bracket one year, and the 15% bracket the next year. Progressivity-related questions may therefore arise as to the year in which income should be recognized. Such questions have contributed to the development of complex accounting provisions.[113]

---

ex-spouses are in different marginal tax brackets, the combination of deduction/inclusion may be more advantageous than the combination of no deduction/no inclusion.

Differing interpretations of the above statutory provisions have generated a large number of cases and administrative rulings; still more complexity has been added by judicial and administrative efforts to limit intra-family income shifting.

110. The general rule of I.R.C. § 704(a) permits any agreed-upon allocation of partnership income and loss. However, section 704(a) is constrained by section 704(b), which strikes down allocations that lack "substantial economic effect." I.R.C. § 704 (1982). Section 704(b) and Treas. Reg. § 1.704-1(b) (as amended in 1987) limit but do not prevent the use of partnerships to achieve rate arbitrage.

111. Such a mismatching might occur, for example, when a high-bracket taxpayer prepays an expense to a low-bracket taxpayer. The prepayment may reduce the amount of expense by the amount of after-tax interest earned on the prepayment by the low-bracket taxpayer. In effect, the high-bracket taxpayer has used the low bracket taxpayer to earn interest at the low-bracket taxpayer's marginal rate. Similar results may be realized by deferring payments from a low-bracket taxpayer to a high-bracket taxpayer. *See* Gunn, *Matching of Costs and Revenues as a Goal of Tax Accounting*, 4 VA. TAX REV. 1 (1984).

112. *See supra* note 109 and accompanying text; I.R.C. § 267 (West Supp. 1987) (sales among related parties); *id.* § 482 (transfers among related business organizations); *id.* § 707(b) (sales between partnerships and partners); *id.* § 1239 (sale of depreciable property among related parties).

113. *See* I.R.C. §§ 446-483 (West Supp. 1987). These and other accounting provisions concern the timing of items of income and expense—an important issue under any rate structure. *See infra* notes 125-36 and accompanying text. Although most accounting provisions would retain their present form even under a proportionate tax, a few could be eliminated or simplified under a proportionate tax. For example, a taxpayer who takes an item into income in year one, only to find that she must return the item in year two, may take advantage of I.R.C. § 1341. Under that section, the taxpayer is allowed either (1) to treat the return of the item as an expense in year two, or (2) to recompute her taxes in year one without taking the item into income. I.R.C. § 1341 (1982). The two alternatives differ only to the extent that the taxpayer is in different marginal rates during the two years.

The progressive tax has had a somewhat greater influence on the development of case law. Certain accounting-related judicial doctrines and a substantial number of cases can be attributed to the graduated rate structure. *See, e.g.*, North Am. Oil Consol. v. Burnet, 286 U.S. 417 (1932) (disputed funds taxable at high marginal rates that prevailed in year funds were received, rather than

Complexity associated with progressive rates therefore centers around three major areas: intra-family transfers, tax arbitrage among unrelated parties, and, to a lesser degree, determination of the appropriate accounting period in which to recognize items of income or expense.

More accurately, these complexities are due to the implementation of progressivity through a graduated rate structure, rather than to the principle of progressivity itself. A progressive tax does not require a graduated rate structure. For instance, the progressive tax discussed in Part III of this Article consists of generally constant or proportionate marginal rates combined with a cash transfer or demogrant. This tax, like a proportionate tax, makes the identity of the taxpayer irrelevant.[114]

In practice, of course, the progressive tax is and has always been implemented through a graduated marginal rate structure. It is useful, therefore, to examine the complexity-related costs of such a rate structure. We consider here two possible social costs arising out of such complexity: taxpayer time spent in tax planning and return preparation, and the expense of purchasing professional tax preparation and planning.

1. *Individual Tax Planning and Return Preparation Costs*

Most taxpayers devote significant amounts of time to the tax law only when preparing and filing their annual returns. In preparing their tax returns, individuals may encounter difficulties in three areas: determining the definition and amount of business or other deductible expenses; accounting for various sources of income; and computing separately items of capital loss.[115] These accounting problems undoubtedly frustrate taxpayers, lengthen the filing process and encourage some taxpayers to seek professional assistance. These determinations do not, however, bear any necessary relationship to the progressive rate structure.

Most taxpayers will encounter the progressive rate structure only once when filing their returns—while using the tax table to compute the amount of tax due after taxable income is determined. Few taxpayers are apt to be confused by the tax table; and, in any event, confusion on this matter would be unrelated to progressivity. Even under a proportionate tax such as a state sales tax, most taxpayers elect to use a tax table, rather

at lower marginal rates that prevailed in year in which claim to funds originated or the year in which litigation over funds ceased); Alice Phelan Sullivan Corp. v. United States, 381 F.2d 399 (Ct. Cl. 1967) (recovery of previously deducted item taxed at marginal rates that prevailed in year of recovery). *See generally* 1 B. BITTKER, *supra* note 10, ¶ 5; 4 B. BITTKER, *supra* note 10, ¶ 105.

114. Under both a proportionate tax and the tax discussed *infra*, the determination of the proper accounting period may affect the present value of tax liability and therefore be of considerable importance to the taxpayer. For a discussion of deferral, see *infra* text accompanying notes 135-45.

115. *See* I.R.S. Form 1040, lines 7-21, 25 (1986); *id.*, Schedule A, lines 20-23; *id.*, Schedule D.

than a calculator or mathematical algorithm, to determine their tax liability.

The relative insignificance of progressivity-related determinations in taxpayer planning and return preparation is demonstrated by the results of tax compliance surveys. This literature also suggests that taxpayer record keeping and return preparation, as opposed to professional tax advice, constitutes by far the largest segment of the economic tax compliance costs.

In a recent comprehensive study, 2000 randomly selected Minnesota residents were surveyed immediately after the deadline for tax returns for the 1982 tax year.[116] Respondents were asked to provide a detailed breakdown of the total time spent in tax planning and return preparation. The reported hours were multiplied by the respondent's after-tax wage rate and added to the costs of professional tax planning and return preparation to determine individual compliance-related costs. The individual responses were then weighted to reflect national demographics. The authors of the survey, economists Slemrod and Sorum, concluded that annual taxpayer compliance costs of the federal and state income taxes were between $17 and $27 billion, over 85% of which was attributable to the costs of individual, as opposed to professional, tax planning and return preparation.[117]

The survey did not attempt to isolate the portion of individual time spent on, and therefore attributable to, progressivity-related determinations. The survey did, however, provide a rough breakdown of individual time expenditure. Over three-fifths of all time was spent on record keeping.[118] Presumably, this consisted of time spent collecting statements of wage and interest income, and business expenses—activities wholly unrelated to the rate structure. Approximately one-half the remaining time was spent filling out the return.[119] Tax research and time spent with tax advisors—the only activities likely to have any relation to progressivity—accounted for only about fifteen percent of the total time.[120]

Unfortunately, this survey suffers from a number of methodological problems. First, the percentage of respondents was rather low, and there was no check on nonrespondents to search for response bias.[121] Second,

116. Slemrod & Sorum, *The Compliance Cost of the U.S. Individual Income Tax System*, 37 NAT'L TAX J. 461 (1984).

117. The amount spent on professional tax assistance was estimated at $3 to $3.4 billion. *Id.*

118. The weighted average number of hours spent was 21.7 hours, 13.8 of which was devoted to record keeping. *Id.* at 467.

119. Return preparation occupied 4.4 of the 8.1 hours devoted to non-record-keeping tax preparation. *Id.*

120. *Id.*

121. The overall response rate was 32.6%. *Id.* at 463. The impact of the response bias is

the survey lacked a straightforward way of valuing the time spent on tax preparation and filing.[122] Finally, the survey, by its nature, measured taxpayer recollection rather than observed behavior. The respondents may not have been able to provide an accurate breakdown of past expenditures of time. These and other methodological flaws cast doubt on the actual dollar figures derived.[123] Nevertheless, these results are roughly consistent with other studies.[124]

We believe the broad results of these studies—that compliance costs result primarily from individual taxpayers' attempts to cope with record-keeping and return-preparation requirements—are accurate. The empirical literature confirms our impression that tax lawyers who claim progressivity is a major cause of complexity have projected their vision of the tax laws onto the average taxpayer. Reforming certain deductions that require record keeping, or simplifying tax returns and instructions, would do far more to reduce compliance costs than would changing to a flat tax rate.

---

difficult to estimate. The survey was conducted through a written four-page questionnaire. It is possible that only individuals who found filing their tax return difficult and time consuming would bother to fill out the questionnaire. On the other hand, it is possible that only individuals who found filing relatively simple would have the patience to complete the questionnaire.

122. The survey treated time spent completing a tax return as identical to time spent at work. Respondents were asked to provide their marginal wage rate and the rate at which they would agree to work additional hours. The value of each taxpayer's time was set at the larger of those two figures, less income taxes. Taxes were estimated on the basis of demographic data. Unfortunately, slightly over half of the respondents failed to provide accurate information on their wage rate. Responses to the wage-rate question included "time-and-a-half," "retired," or "variable." The wage rate of such respondents was estimated through regression analysis. *Id.* at 465.

123. One additional methodological problem is that the survey was sent only to Minnesota residents, whose compliance costs may differ from costs incurred by residents of other states. Another problem is that for certain classes, the number of absolute respondents, as well as the response rate, was quite low. The survey received less than 50 responses from households with gross incomes of less than $10,000 a year. *Id.* at 464. The authors concluded that their figures were more likely to overestimate than underestimate actual return preparation costs. *Id.* at 473.

124. A number of compliance studies have documented the surprisingly large amount of time that taxpayers spend on record keeping, as well as the time requirements and relative difficulty of reading tax return instructions and completing tax return forms. In one survey, the most difficult tax problem was described as "getting data together so as to itemize deductions"; completing the return and figuring the tax due was described as the second most difficult problem. TAXATION: A REPORT OF THE COMMISSION ON FEDERAL PAPERWORK 10 (1977) (citing UNIVERSITY OF MICHIGAN, A STUDY OF PUBLIC ATTITUDES TOWARD A SIMPLIFICATION OF THE INCOME TAX FORM (1966)). Another study found that a college-level reading ability was required for comprehension of 90% of the instructions for the 1975 Federal Income Tax Short Form 1040A. *Id.* at 20 (citing A. GAETJEN, READABILITY STUDY OF THE EMPLOYERS' TAX GUIDE, 1975 REVISION, AND THE 1975 FEDERAL INCOME TAX SHORT FORM 1040A (COMM'N ON FED. PAPERWORK 1976)). The estimate by Slemrod and Sorum that aggregate taxpayer compliance costs comprise between 5% and 7% of revenue raised falls in the middle of the other studies, which, depending on the methodology used and the definition of compliance costs adopted, estimate such costs at between 2.4% and 11.5% of revenue collected. Slemrod & Sorum, *supra* note 116, at 462-63 (citing and discussing other studies).

2. Costs of Professional Advice

Criticism of the complex nature of the progressive tax structure may stem from a belief that such complexity greatly increases the need for professional tax advice and planning. The survey evidence indicates that such professional services represent a relatively small portion of total tax compliance costs. They nevertheless amount to billions of dollars per year.[125] Professional services are thus a significant, though indirect, cost of the tax system.

Blum and Kalven seem to believe that progressivity is responsible for much of the cost of these services: "It is remarkable how much of the day to day work of the lawyer in the income tax field derives from the simple fact that the tax is progressive. Perhaps the majority of his problems are either caused or aggravated by that fact."[126] This assertion might be tested through a carefully designed cross-section study of lawyers' and accountants' time. Such a study, however, apparently has never been attempted or even suggested.

Absent empirical data, comments on the relative cost of progressivity-related tax planning are necessarily sketchy. However, the assertion that tax lawyers spend most of their day on progressivity-related issues is inconsistent with our experience and intuition that such issues occupy only a small portion of a tax lawyer's time.

Blum and Kalven's assertion is also controverted by a careful analysis of the current tax structure. We noted above that a graduated rate structure fosters complexity primarily in three areas: intrafamily transfers, accounting periods, and some enterprise taxation.[127] A much more significant source of complexity, however, is the montage of situation-specific definitional, preferential, and timing-related provisions in the tax law.

Income usually is defined as wealth accrued during an accounting period.[128] Often, however, wealth is accrued in noncash form; employer-provided meals are one example. Taxation of such noncash compensa-

125. *See supra* note 117 and accompanying text.

126. Blum & Kalven, *supra* note 3, at 431.

127. *See supra* notes 102-13 and accompanying text.

128. H. SIMONS, *supra* note 9, at 49-50; Haig, *supra* note 9, at 1, 7. A number of scholars have urged that the tax base should be—and to some extent is—limited to personal consumption. *See* Bradford, *The Case for a Personal Consumption Tax*, in WHAT SHOULD BE TAXED: INCOME OR EXPENDITURE? 75 (J. Pechman ed. 1980); Andrews, *A Consumption-Type or Cash Flow Personal Income Tax*, 87 HARV. L. REV. 1113 (1974). James Strnad has argued that, under certain circumstances, the income tax base and the consumption tax base are one and the same. Strnad, *Taxation of Income from Capital: A Theoretical Reappraisal*, 37 STAN. L. REV. 1023 (1985). *But see* Kaplow & Warren, *An Income Tax by Any Other Name—A Reply to Professor Strnad*, 38 STAN. L. REV. 399 (1986); Warren, *Would a Consumption Tax Be Fairer Than an Income Tax?*, 89 YALE L.J. 1081 (1980). The analysis of progressivity in this Article, while primarily directed at an income tax base, should apply as well to a consumption tax base.

tion raises difficult conceptual and administrative issues, which are resolved through specific and elaborate provisions governing the taxation of fringe benefits.[129] Similar conceptual and definitional issues are raised not only by the distinctions drawn between nondeductible personal expenses and deductible business expenses,[130] and between capital and ordinary gain and loss,[131] but also by the regime governing foreign taxpayers operating in the United States and U.S. taxpayers operating in foreign jurisdictions.[132]

Further complexity is generated by the use of the tax code to address various social concerns.[133] There are literally hundreds of preferences in the tax laws, ranging from provisions exempting ministers from taxation on housing subsidies to those that permit the purchase of farmland through the issuance of tax-exempt bonds.[134]

Finally, the number of progressivity-related issues appears small by

---

129. Taxation of non-cash compensation is now almost entirely statutory. *See* I.R.C. § 83(a) (West Supp. 1987) (property transferred in connection with performance of services); *id.* § 101 (life insurance proceeds and employee death benefits); *id.* § 105 (amounts received pursuant to accident and health plans); *id.* § 106 (employer's contributions to accident and health plans); *id.* § 119 (meals and lodging provided for convenience of employer); *id.* § 132 (exclusion of fringe benefits that qualify as a no-additional-cost service, qualified employee discount, working condition fringe, or de minimis fringe; also special rules pertaining to other fringe benefits).

130. *See id.* § 183 (characterization of activities as for-profit or not-for-profit; tax treatment of losses incurred in not-for-profit activities); *id.* § 280A (deductibility of expenses incurred in connection with homes held for personal and business use). The distinction between business and personal expenses is difficult to articulate and has produced an enormous body of case law. *See* 1 B. BITTKER, *supra* note 10, ¶¶ 20-26; M. CHIRELSTEIN, FEDERAL INCOME TAXATION 87-102 (4th ed. 1985).

131. I.R.C. §§ 1201-1256 (West Supp. 1987). Some portion of the rules governing partnerships and corporations may be attributed to the special treatment of capital gains and losses. The distinction between capital and ordinary gain and loss has generated a tremendous amount of litigation. *See* 2 B. BITTKER, *supra* note 10, ¶¶ 50-55.

The distinction remains relevant even under the new regime. Under current law, losses incurred by noncorporate taxpayers from the sale or exchange of capital assets are allowed only to the extent of the gains from such sales or exchanges plus the lesser of (i) the excess of the losses over the gains, or (ii) $3000. I.R.C. § 1211(b) (West Supp. 1987). Gains from the sale or exchange of capital assets are treated as ordinary income with one exception: as noted immediately above, such gains may be useful to offset capital losses that would otherwise be subject to the $3000 annual limitation. *Id. See generally id.* §§ 1200-1254 (rules governing capital gains and losses).

132. I.R.C. §§ 861-999 (West Supp. 1987).

133. The distinction between provisions that simply define and operationalize the tax base and provisions that address social concerns is controversial and difficult to articulate. *See* B. BITTKER, C. GALVIN, R. MUSGRAVE & J. PECHMAN, A COMPREHENSIVE TAX BASE? A DEBATE (1968). At least in extreme cases, however, identification of certain provisions as tax preferences seems warranted. For example, almost everyone would concede that I.R.C. § 107 (1982), the ministers' housing allowance provision, constitutes a tax preference.

134. I.R.C. § 107 (1982) (rental value of parsonages); *id.* § 147(c)(2) (West Supp. 1987) (tax exemption for local government industrial development bonds used to purchase qualifying farmland). *See also id.* § 117 (excluding "qualified scholarships"). The Senate Finance Committee regularly publishes a "tax expenditure budget," which lists preferences and estimates their cost to the fisc. The 1984 Tax Expenditure Budget lists nearly a hundred subsidies by industry and category; many listed subsidies encompass four or five separate statutory provisions. SENATE

comparison to the number of issues surrounding the determination of when particular items of income and expense are recognized for tax purposes. Taxpayers who are able to delay recognition of income and accelerate recognition of expense are able to defer payment of tax. Because of the time value of money, deferral has a high value to the taxpayer and a high cost to the fisc. At a discount rate of 6%, $100 tax due in twenty years has a present cost of about $31; in other words, a taxpayer who is able to defer $100 tax for twenty years can fund the eventual payment by depositing $31 in an interest-bearing account that will provide an after-tax yield of 6%.[135] The graduated rate structure may in some cases increase or decrease the advantage of deferral: The taxpayer may be in a higher or lower bracket in twenty years.[136] But deferral is valuable independent of the rate structure, and in the vast majority of cases the effects of deferral far outweigh the effects of any variation in the marginal rate.

Perhaps the majority of difficult tax issues center around deferral. Deferral-related issues have given rise to complex rules governing the treatment of depreciation and amortization;[137] depletion;[138] long-term contracts and installment sales;[139] accounting methods;[140] insurance products and annuities;[141] nonenterprise tax-free exchanges;[142] and transfers of property to, from, and among corporations,[143] partnerships,[144] and trusts.[145]

C. *Progressivity and the Misdeployment of Capital*

That it reduces work effort and increases complexity are the two most common arguments directed against the progressive tax system. In addition, some critics charge that progressivity adversely affects the

---

COMM. ON FINANCE, 98TH CONG., 1ST SESS., FISCAL YEAR 1984 FINANCE COMM. REPORT UNDER THE CONGRESSIONAL BUDGET ACT (1984).

As we noted above, there is no logical relationship between the number of tax preferences and the effective tax burden borne by differing income classes. *See supra* text accompanying note 7.

135. The formula for determining the present value of a future sum is $PV = S(1 + r)^{-n}$, where PV is the present value, S is the future sum, r is the interest rate, and n is the number of years in which payment is made or received. The present value of a $100 payment received in 20 years at a discount rate of 6% is $31.18. *See* L. LIPKIN, I. FEINSTEIN & L. DERRICK, ACCOUNTANT'S HANDBOOK OF FORMULAS AND TABLES 10 (2d ed. 1973).

136. *See supra* note 113 and accompanying text.

137. I.R.C. §§ 167, 168 (West Supp. 1987).

138. *Id.* §§ 613-617.

139. *Id.* §§ 453, 453A, 453B, 483.

140. *Id.* §§ 446, 447, 455-468A.

141. *Id.* §§ 72, 101.

142. *Id.* §§ 1031-1042.

143. *Id.* §§ 301-306, 312, 316, 317, 331-337, 351-368.

144. *Id.* §§ 704, 706, 709, 721, 731, 734, 736, 743, 752, 754, 755.

145. *Id.* §§ 643-667.

deployment of capital by encouraging income-shifting investments and by increasing tax shelter activities.

1. Investments That Shift Income

We noted earlier that progressivity encourages taxpayers in high brackets to shift income to low-bracket family members.[146] To a lesser degree, progressivity also encourages the use of certain forms of business enterprise and the shifting of income from one period to the next. The presence of these kinds of tax-motivated transactions is often cited as one of the defects of a progressive tax. Blum and Kalven, for example, support their other arguments against a graduated tax with the assertion that it "invites a distorting attention to the tax aspects of any economic transaction."[147] However, Blum and Kalven do not link tax-motivated transactions to specific harms.

By asserting that progressivity is distortionary, Blum and Kalven might be arguing that a graduated tax generates the additional transaction costs associated with tax planning that were discussed above. Alternatively, Blum and Kalven might be arguing that progressivity leads to a misdeployment of capital. This argument would be similar to those voiced against certain other features of the tax law. For example, critics of certain capital recovery rules have argued that such rules distort the balance of investment in short-lived as opposed to long-lived assets,[148] and critics of the tax preference given to home ownership have argued that such preferences lead to overinvestment in housing stock.[149]

In fact, there appear to be few costs of capital deployment that can be attributed to progressivity-related transactions. Most tax planning associated with progressivity consists of shifting capital ownership from

146. *See supra* note 109 and accompanying text.

147. Blum & Kalven, *supra* note 3, at 435.

148. *See, e.g.*, Auerbach, *The New Economics of Accelerated Depreciation*, 23 B.C.L. REV. 1327, 1346-49 (1982). A form of capital recovery generally thought to be nondistortionary is described in Samuelson, *Tax Deductibility of Economic Depreciation to Insure Invariant Valuations*, 72 J. POL. ECON. 604 (1964); *see also* M. CHIRELSTEIN, *supra* note 130, at 127-28 (simplified explanation of "Samuelsonian" depreciation).

149. Taxpayers who purchase and occupy residential housing receive imputed income in the form of free rent. This form of income is not subject to tax. Many expenses of home ownership, however, are deductible. *See* I.R.C. § 163 (West Supp. 1987) (interest expense attributable to qualified residential indebtedness deductible); *id.* § 164 (property tax on home ownership deductible). Moreover, gain from certain sales of principal residences is deferred or excluded from income. *Id.* § 121 (1982) (individuals age 55 and over allowed to exclude first $125,000 gain on sale of principal residence); *id.* § 1034 (West Supp. 1987) (deferral of gain on sale of principal residence by taxpayers who purchase new principal residence within specified time period). The combination of nontaxation of imputed income, deductibility of current expenses, and preferential treatment of sale proceeds is widely thought to distort investment decisions. *See, e.g.*, Hellmuth, *Homeowner Preferences*, in COMPREHENSIVE INCOME TAXATION 163 (J. Pechman ed. 1977); Laidler, *Income Tax Incentives for Owner-Occupied Housing*, in THE TAXATION OF INCOME FROM CAPITAL 50 (A. Harberger & M. Bailey eds. 1969).

high-bracket to low-bracket members of the same family. Such tax planning rarely changes the form of capital investment, or even the party in control of that investment. Parents who use trusts to transfer capital income to their children, for example, almost always retain control over the actual investments.[150] Similarly, parents who organize and donate interests in family partnerships generally exercise control over such closely-held enterprises.[151] Thus, while the form of capital ownership changes, the actual deployment of capital does not.

2. *Increased Tax Shelter Activity*

A number of commentators have asserted that a progressive tax encourages persons to take advantage of tax shelters.[152] Charles Galvin, for example, writes:

> Progressivity thwarts the maximum productivity of goods and services of which our society is capable. The present system tends to prostitute the talents of our most capable citizens. A skilled neurosurgeon cannot devote all his skill to his specialty; he is compelled to deflect his energies and time of concentration to investments in which he can shelter some of his professional income; the talented executive, tied to a particular company with tax-sheltered, qualified or restricted stock options, is deterred from going into the open market where his talents might be used more productively.[153]

The tax shelters referred to by Galvin and others seldom directly minimize the effect of the progressive rate structure; that is, most shelters do not enable taxpayers to shift income or engage in rate arbitrage.[154] But—it is argued—the motivation for investing in tax shelters is attribu-

150. The "grantor trust" rules generally permit donors to exercise managerial authority over trust property even while income from such property is taxed to the donee. *See* I.R.C. §§ 672-678 (West Supp. 1987).

151. The amount of control a donor may retain without paying tax on income attributable to the donated interest is limited by administrative regulations and case law. Commissioner v. Culbertson, 337 U.S. 733 (1949); Treas. Reg. § 1.704-1(e) (as amended in 1986); *see* 1 W. McKee, W. Nelson & R. Whitmire, Federal Taxation of Partnerships and Partners ¶¶ 14.01-.06 (1977 & Supp. 1987).

Ultimately, of course, control does pass from parent to child, or donor to donee. But that change is generally triggered by nontax factors such as the death of the donor or majority of the donee. While the change in control may result in a different deployment of capital, there is no reason to believe that the new deployment will be less efficient. The child who takes control of the family business is as likely to rejuvenate the enterprise as she is to run it into the ground.

152. *See, e.g.*, C. Galvin & B. Bittker, *supra* note 3, at 18; R. Hall & A. Rabushka, *supra* note 57, at 15-16.

153. C. Galvin & B. Bittker, *supra* note 3, at 18.

154. A limited form of rate arbitrage is found in many partnerships, which allocate valuable deductions to high bracket taxpayers. The majority of tax shelters, including most tax shelters operated as partnerships, are built around preferential provisions (such as those governing rehabilitation of historic structures, investment in capital stock, and the like) or time-value-of-money-related arbitrage.

table to the high marginal tax rates that are a product of the progressive rate structure.

This argument suffers from several defects. First, the assertion that high marginal rates encourage tax-motivated transactions carries normative significance only insofar as "tax-motivated" transactions are thought to be undesirable. Generally speaking, however, tax-motivated transactions are those that society has explicitly decided to favor with tax incentives, such as investments in low-income housing or donations to nonprofit organizations. The assertion that progressivity is undesirable because it encourages this kind of tax-motivated investment must be premised in large part on the belief that the use of the tax law to further non-tax goals is inappropriate.[155]

Second, the relationship between progressivity and tax shelter investments is unclear.[156] During the last twenty years, the top marginal rates have declined dramatically.[157] We might therefore have expected a concomitant decrease in tax shelter activity.[158] By most counts, however, the number of tax shelters has increased sharply.[159]

Finally, even opponents of progressivity admit that high marginal rates, rather than progressivity, foster investments in tax shelters. Although switching from the present rate structure to a proportional tax would lower marginal rates for wealthy individuals, who account for a disproportionate amount of total investment, reducing marginal rates by broadening the tax base would be more effective in reducing tax shelter investments because it would lower marginal rates for lower and middle income taxpayers as well. More important, base broadening would directly reduce the number of tax shelters by eliminating the deductions and credits that make such shelters possible. Indeed, this is the approach taken in the Tax Reform Act of 1986, in which, among other reforms,

155. For certain tax shelters, adopting a graduated, rather than a proportionate, rate structure may result in unintended windfall gains to high-income taxpayers. If, for example, a sufficient quantity of tax-exempt bonds is issued so that the interest rate on those bonds is set to attract taxpayers not in the highest marginal bracket, then taxpayers who are in the highest bracket and who purchased those bonds will receive an unintended windfall. *See* M. CHIRELSTEIN, *supra* note 130, at 334-40.

156. A simple theoretical model devised by Cordes and Galper predicts that an across-the-board reduction in marginal rates would reduce the number of tax shelters, but that a reduction in just the top-bracket marginal rates would reduce the number of tax shelters only under certain limited conditions. Cordes & Galper, *Tax Shelter Activity: Lessons From Twenty Years of Evidence*, 38 NAT'L TAX J. 305, 315-16 (1985).

157. Marginal rates ranged from 0% to 91% in 1953; from 0% to 70% in 1973; and from 0% to 50% in 1983; the top current marginal rate is 33%. I.R.C. § 1 (1953); *id.* (1973); *id.* (1982); *id.* (West Supp. 1987).

158. *See supra* note 156.

159. *See, e.g.*, Cordes & Galper, *supra* note 156, at 316-17 (increase in tax shelter activity inferred from examination of partnership statistics).

the capital gains preference was eliminated[160] and the ability of taxpayers to use passive losses to offset other income was reduced.[161]

D. *Effects of Progressivity on Tax Compliance*

Opponents of progressivity often assume that the graduated rate structure decreases the overall rate at which taxpayers voluntarily comply with the tax laws, presumably because taxpayers in high marginal brackets have greater incentive to cheat.[162] In fact, the sponsor of one flat tax proposal has claimed that its enactment would "bring down the underground economy."[163]

An increasingly sophisticated body of literature has explored the determinants of taxpayer compliance. Plausible models of taxpayer behavior developed in this literature suggest that the assumed relationship between high marginal rates and increased tax evasion may be incorrect. One recent model looks at taxpayer compliance as a two-person game involving the taxpayer and the Internal Revenue Service.[164] The model assumes that an increase in tax rates increases the payoff of tax evasion to the taxpayer. However, high marginal rates also increase the payoff of enforcement to the Internal Revenue Service. The model predicts that if each party adopts the strategy that is optimal in light of its opponent's strategy, an increase in marginal rates will lead to a *reduced* level of tax evasion.[165] The effects of the payoff to the Internal Revenue Service dominate the effects of the payoff to the taxpayer.

---

160. Tax Reform Act of 1986, Pub. L. No. 99-514, § 301(a), 100 Stat. 2085, 2216 (1986) (repealing I.R.C. § 1202).

161. *Id.*, 100 Stat. at 2233 (adding I.R.C. § 469).

162. *See, e.g.*, R. HALL & A. RABUSHKA, *supra* note 57, at 3, 28-29; Vickrey, *supra* note 3, at 460; *see also* authorities cited in Graetz & Wilde, *The Economics of Tax Compliance: Fact and Fantasy*, 38 NAT'L TAX J. 355, 362-63 (1985).

163. *Major Tax Reform Options: Hearings Before the Senate Comm. on Finance*, 98th Cong., 2d Sess., pt. 2, at 198 (1984) (testimony of Congressman Jack Kemp); *see also* Bernick, *Merits of Flat Tax Debated*, 16 TAX NOTES 478 (1982) (Hall and Rabushka speculated that enactment of proposal would "flush out income now hidden in the underground economy").

164. Graetz, Reinganum & Wilde, *The Tax Compliance Game: Toward an Interactive Theory of Law Enforcement*, 2 J.L. ECON. & ORG. 1 (1986).

165. The point at which each party has adopted an optimal strategy in light of its opponent's strategy is known as a Nash equilibrium. Under a Nash equilibrium, neither party may improve its position through a unilateral change in strategy. The model predicts that a rise in the level of Internal Revenue Service enforcement generated by high marginal rates would increase the costs of tax collection. *Id.* at 28. The study does not estimate the magnitude of these costs.

The model makes several important simplifying assumptions. First, the model assumes the Internal Revenue Service has unlimited discretion to modify its budget in order to maximize net revenues. Second, the model does not allow for partial noncompliance. Third, the model assumes the Internal Revenue Service can set a fine for evasion at a level that, when added to taxes otherwise due, equals (but may not exceed) the taxpayer's entire income. *Id.* at 24-27 (thoughtfully discussing these and other simplifying assumptions). Changes in these assumptions would not affect the central insight of the article, which is that the study and prediction of tax compliance must consider both taxpayer and Internal Revenue Service incentives.

A second compliance model focuses solely on the taxpayer and challenges the assumption that high tax rates increase tax evasion without regard to Internal Revenue Service enforcement action.[166] The intuition underlying this model can be understood by imagining a taxpayer who would face a rate of 30% under a proportionate tax but who would be in the 40% bracket under a progressive tax. The taxpayer is faced with the decision of whether or not to report $100 of income; if the taxpayer decides not to report the income and is caught, she must pay the amount of tax due plus a penalty of 50%. The expected return from each dollar "gambled" under either tax bracket is proportionately identical. Under the progressive tax, the taxpayer must decide between a tax savings of $40 and a potential cost of $60; under the proportionate tax, the taxpayer must decide between a tax savings of $30 and a potential cost of $45.[167] In all cases in which the penalty is proportionate to the amount of tax evaded, an increase in marginal rates will increase the amount at stake, but will not change the expected payoff per dollar at risk.

Each of the models described above focuses primarily on the monetary costs and benefits of noncompliance. It seems likely, however, that compliance also will be based on moral and social attitudes, on the transaction costs associated with the audit process, and on the possibility of nonmonetary criminal sanctions.[168] The moral and social costs of dishonesty and the transaction costs of enduring an audit may be a more important deterrent to noncompliance than monetary penalties.[169]

The determination of compliance under a more elaborate model thus might depend in part on the ratio of moral, social, and transaction

---

166. Early noninteractive economic models of tax evasion were developed in Allingham & Sandmo, *Income Tax Evasion: A Theoretical Analysis,* 1 J. PUB. ECON. 323 (1972), and in Srinivasan, *Tax Evasion: A Model,* 2 J. PUB. ECON. 339 (1973). Recent refinements of these models are described in Skinner & Slemrod, *An Economic Perspective on Tax Evasion,* 38 NAT'L TAX J. 345 (1985), and Spicer, *Civilization at a Discount: The Problem of Tax Evasion,* 39 NAT'L TAX J. 13 (1986).

167. Under current law, the most severe civil penalty is 75% of the amount of tax due plus 50% of the related interest. I.R.C. § 6653(b) (West Supp. 1987).

168. The importance of nonmonetary factors is emphasized in recent articles by Skinner and Slemrod, and by Spicer. *See* Skinner & Slemrod, *supra* note 166, at 350-51; Spicer, *supra* note 166.

169. In fact, the noninteractive economic model does not seem adequately to account for the relatively high level of tax compliance. The model predicts evasion whenever the expected payoff from evasion is positive. The basic model may be formally written as $\Sigma U = (1 - p)\, U(y + x) + pU(y - Fx)$, where ΣU is the expected utility, U is the utility function, p is the probability of audit and detection, y is the legal after-tax income, x is the amount of undeclared taxes, and F is the penalty rate on the undeclared taxes plus one. Skinner & Slemrod, *supra* note 166, at 347. At a detection rate equal to the 2% average audit rate, and a constant marginal utility of money, the model predicts evasion whenever the penalty rate is less than 5000% of the tax due. The fact that most taxpayers comply with the tax laws notwithstanding much lower penalty levels may be partially attributable to taxpayer misperception of audit rate, taxpayer risk aversion, and the presence of nonmonetary criminal penalties. It seems reasonable, however, to attribute some "unexplained" compliance behavior to the nonmonetary factors described in the text.

costs to a person's income. If moral, social, and transaction costs are fixed, or increase at a slower rate than income, then high tax rates might be expected to increase tax evasion. This is because although the dollars saved from avoidance and the expected monetary penalties if caught each increase proportionately with the tax burden, the indirect costs of evasion remain constant or increase more slowly. As tax rates increase, the indirect costs will become a smaller and smaller disincentive to tax evasion. The existence of fixed or slowly increasing indirect costs may explain the belief that low rates make cheating less attractive.

On the other hand, if tax compliance is determined by the interaction of taxpayer and Internal Revenue Service strategies, the presence of fixed or slowly increasing indirect costs may not affect compliance levels. In such cases, the greater incentive to cheat may be offset by the prospect of greater enforcement.[170] Moreover, even if high rates are positively correlated with tax evasion in the aggregate,[171] it is not clear that switching to a proportionate tax, which generally would decrease the tax burden on the wealthy and increase the tax burden on the poor, would reduce evasion.

A second set of factors not explicitly considered by most current models of taxpayer behavior is the way the report/non-report gamble is framed. Recent literature on risk taking concludes that individuals are more willing to take risks to preserve present wealth than to gain new wealth.[172] This suggests that taxpayers who owe money to the Treasury will be more likely to misreport income on their tax returns than will taxpayers who expect refund checks. An increase in the amount of withholding, which transforms the annual reporting decision from one of retaining wealth to one of obtaining a refund, may increase taxpayer risk aversion and improve compliance.[173]

Finally, current compliance models do not consider the survey literature, including the massive compliance audits conducted by the Internal Revenue Service, which suggests that tax compliance varies dramatically with the level of third-party reporting.[174] Taxpayers accurately disclose income from transactions that third parties report to the Internal Reve-

170. In the Graetz, Reinganum and Wilde model, taxpayer audit costs generally do not affect compliance levels. Graetz, Reinganum & Wilde, *supra* note 164, at 23.

171. The author of one empirical study has reported a positive correlation between high tax rates and tax evasion. Clotfelter, *Tax Evasion and Tax Rates: An Analysis of Individual Returns*, 65 REV. ECON. STAT. 363 (1983). However, the data source used in that study has been criticized in a recent article by Graetz and Wilde. Graetz & Wilde, *supra* note 162, at 360. Graetz and Wilde also point out that low marginal tax rates have not prevented taxpayers from misreporting a substantial portion of long-term capital gain income. *Id.*

172. *See, e.g.*, Kahneman & Tversky, *The Psychology of Preferences*, SCI. AM., Jan. 1982, at 160.

173. A similar point is made in Spicer, *supra* note 166, at 18.

174. *See* Henry, *Noncompliance with U.S. Tax Law—Evidence on Size, Growth, and Composition*, 37 TAX LAW. 1, 4-5 (1983).

nue Service; disclosure of income not subject to third-party reporting is spotty at best. The Internal Revenue Service estimates that taxpayers report more than 90% of legal-source wage income, but less than 50% of income from farms and small proprietorships.[175]

The transaction-based analysis described above suggests that if there is a positive correlation between tax rates and tax evasion, then compliance would be maximized by imposing low marginal rates on taxpayers who are least subject to third-party reporting and therefore most likely to cheat. (Of course, reducing rates on taxpayers most likely to underreport is likely to be thought normatively undesirable.) Here again, the effect of a switch to a more proportionate tax would be ambiguous, since all income classes engage in some transactions not subject to third-party reporting. The wealthy and middle class receive hard-to-trace income from the sale of property, from proprietorships and from farms; the poor often receive unreported cash as an important source of wage income.[176]

The assertion that progressivity contributes to tax evasion thus appears to be weak. Current models of taxpayer behavior suggest that the assumed link between high marginal rates and noncompliance may be incorrect. Under one model, high marginal rates do not change the desirability of tax evasion; under another model, any change in the desirability of tax evasion is offset by changes in Internal Revenue Service behavior. Moreover, even if high marginal rates do contribute to tax evasion, the link between the tax rate structure and tax evasion is unclear since a proportionate tax would raise rates for some taxpayers and lower rates for others. Efforts to better detect evasion and to enforce the Code hold far more promise of improving taxpayer compliance than does a flat tax.

E. Reconsidering the Prima Facie Case Against Progressivity

Critics have levied a plethora of charges against the progressive rate structure. Progressivity is claimed to promote reduced work effort, increased complexity, misdeployment of capital, and reduced compliance. In each of these areas, however, we found that the purported costs of progressivity are overstated and that more focused approaches offer better methods of improving the fairness and efficiency of the tax code than does the adoption of a flat tax. While it must be conceded that progressivity imposes some efficiency costs and tends to increase transac-

175. A 1976 Taxpayer Compliance Management Program audit estimated that 99% of legal source wage income, 81% of proprietorship income, and 49% of farm income was reported. However, this estimate of compliance ratios was revised downward in 1979 and 1982. The 1982 estimate showed 350% greater nonreported income than the original 1976 estimate. *See* Henry, *supra* note 174, at 44-50, 79.

176. *See* Ansberry, *Laid-Off Steelworkers Find That Tax Evasion Helps Make Ends Meet*, Wall St. J., Oct. 1, 1986, at 1, col. 1.

tion costs attributable to professional tax planning, the magnitude of these costs is less than generally asserted and much less than other costs inherent in the present tax law.

In any event, costs attributable to progressivity must be balanced against whatever benefits are derived from the redistribution of billions of dollars per year. In the remainder of this Article we will consider how one might strike this balance.

III
The Costs and Benefits of Progressivity: A Welfarist Evaluation

A progressive income tax imposes certain efficiency costs and redistributes wealth from high-income to low-income individuals. Under a welfarist approach, the changes brought about by a tax structure are judged according to their effect on the welfare of individuals. To make this judgment, it is necessary to clarify the relationship between income, leisure, and individual utility. It is also necessary to specify the way in which the welfare of individuals determines social welfare.

In the past, scholars have not had a reliable method for assessing the level of social welfare associated with any particular rate structure. Moreover, the dependence of any such calculation upon speculative and unverifiable assumptions as to the relationship between income and individual welfare has cast a large shadow over the welfarist enterprise.

The development of a branch of public economics known as optimal taxation resolves the first difficulty and reduces the significance of the second.[177] Optimal tax models can be used to evaluate tax structures under varying assumptions regarding individual and social welfare. These models also account for the impact of the income tax on the labor supply. The capacity of the models to calculate optimal rates under a wide range of assumptions makes it possible to search for robust results—that is, results that remain constant over such a wide range of assumptions.

The optimal tax model described below produces two results of particular interest. First, under a broad spectrum of assumptions, the optimal tax structure is progressive, although not confiscatory. Second, a progressive tax is best implemented through demogrants combined with constant or even declining marginal rates, rather than through constantly rising marginal rates.

177. The field of optimal taxation has been almost entirely ignored in the legal literature on progressivity. Legal scholars may have been exposed to the subject, however, by two brief articles by economists recently published in the National Tax Journal. *See* Hettich & Winer, *Blueprints and Pathways: The Shifting Foundations of Tax Reform*, 38 Nat'l Tax J. 423 (1985); Slemrod, *Do We Know How Progressive the Income Tax System Should Be?*, 36 Nat'l Tax J. 361 (1983).

A. The Mirrlees Optimal Taxation Model

Much of the recent work in optimal income taxation can be traced to James Mirrlees' seminal 1971 article, *An Exploration in the Theory of Optimum Income Taxation.*[178] In that article, Mirrlees considers the following question: If all income is derived from labor, what income tax rate structure maximizes social welfare, given plausible assumptions regarding the utility of income and leisure to individuals?[179]

Answering that question requires the construction of a complex mathematical model. Mirrlees' specific results and analysis have been criticized in the economic literature and are subject to independent criticism here. However, the basic model he uses to calculate the optimal rate structure, referred to here as the "Mirrlees model," has been adopted by optimal tax scholars.[180]

The Mirrlees model requires the specification of both an individual utility function and a social welfare function.[181] An individual utility function specifies the factors that determine an individual's utility or welfare.[182] A social welfare function specifies the factors that determine the welfare of society.[183] Under the Mirrlees model, the goal of the government is to choose a tax rate that maximizes the welfare of society as defined by a social welfare function.[184]

1. Assessing Individual Welfare

The factors that determine a person's welfare are complex and many such factors—good looks, a sunny disposition, or a satisfying family life—could not feasibly be incorporated into a tax structure. Mirrlees therefore assumes a simple utility function in which an individual's welfare depends only on the amounts of consumption and leisure she enjoys. While the measurement of these factors is not without difficulty, income can be used as a rough measure of consumption, and hours worked can provide an estimate of the amount of time a person has remaining for leisure. The individual utility function adopted by Mirrlees may be writ-

178. Mirrlees, *An Exploration in the Theory of Optimum Income Taxation*, 38 REV. ECON. STUD. 175 (1971) [hereinafter *Optimum Income Taxation*]; *see also* Mirrlees, *Labour Supply Behaviour and Optimal Taxes*, in FISCAL POLICY AND LABOUR SUPPLY 7 (Institute for Fiscal Studies 1977); Mirrlees, *The Theory of Optimal Taxation*, in HANDBOOK OF MATHEMATICAL ECONOMICS 1197 (K. Arrow & M. Intriligator eds. 1986); Mirrlees, *Optimal Tax Theory: A Synthesis*, 6 J. PUB. ECON. 327 (1976).

179. Mirrlees, *Optimum Income Taxation*, *supra* note 178, at 175.

180. *See, e.g.*, A. ATKINSON & J. STIGLITZ, *supra* note 12, at 412-22.

181. Mirrlees, *Optimum Income Taxation*, *supra* note 178, at 176-78.

182. *Id.* at 176.

183. *Id.* For a general discussion of social welfare functions, see D. MUELLER, PUBLIC CHOICE 184-206 (1979); Y. NG, *supra* note 54, at 1-17; A. SEN, COLLECTIVE CHOICE AND SOCIAL WELFARE 47-55 (1970).

184. Mirrlees, *Optimum Income Taxation*, *supra* note 178, at 178.

ten as $U = C + L$, where U is utility, C is consumption, and L is leisure.[185]

Optimal tax models make two important additional assumptions regarding individual utility. First, they assume that consumption and leisure have declining marginal utility. Second, they assume that individuals have identical utility functions.[186]

The assumption that the value of an additional dollar to an individual declines as the number of dollars he owns increases ("declining marginal utility") is common in economic analysis.[187] The assumption of identical utility functions is more problematic because individuals obviously do not have the same tastes. Some people value money greatly, enjoying free time only if skiing, dining in expensive restaurants, or touring abroad, while others like nothing more than an afternoon of chess in the public park. Nevertheless, for purposes of determining tax policy, recommendations based on an assumption of identical utility functions may be unavoidable. Politically and administratively feasible tax policy is likely to center on the effect redistribution will have on different income classes. In the absence of evidence to the contrary, it seems reasonable to assume that individuals with particularly strong desires for consumption are distributed in a roughly random way throughout the population. The tax policy recommendations in such a case should not differ greatly from those that would be made if individuals had identical tastes.

Under a utilitarian ethic and in the absence of incentive effects, the assumption that consumption has declining marginal utility and that people have identical utility functions would lead to complete equality of consumption. All incomes above the mean would be taxed at a 100% rate, and all individuals with incomes below the mean would receive grants to bring their income to that level. Put differently, the optimal utilitarian tax structure would consist of a 100% marginal rate on all income and a uniform cash grant, thus ensuring equal consumption for all individuals.[188]

To understand why such a rate structure would be optimal under a utilitarian ethic, consider a society that consists of one individual with an

185. It is also generally assumed that C and L are each greater than or equal to zero (implying that consumption and leisure are never negative) and that U is strictly concave (implying that consumption and leisure have diminishing marginal utility). Mirrlees, *Optimum Income Taxation*, *supra* note 178, at 176.

186. *Id.*

187. *See, e.g.*, L. ATKINSON, ECONOMICS 426-28 (1982); A. BRAFF, MICROECONOMIC ANALYSIS 20-21 (1969); S. CALL & W. HOLAHAN, MICROECONOMICS 32-42 (1980); P. HARDWICK, B. KHAN & J. LANGMEAD, AN INTRODUCTION TO MODERN ECONOMICS 53-56 (1982).

188. *See* Edgeworth, *The Pure Theory of Progressive Taxation*, in ECONOMIC JUSTICE 371, 373-74 (E. Phelps ed. 1973).

income of $30 and a second individual with an income of $50. Since both individuals experience declining marginal utility of income and have identical utility functions, the last ten dollars earned by the higher income individual would produce greater utility in the hands of the lower income individual. Utility is maximized and aggregate sacrifice from taxation is minimized where consumption is equal because additional consumption is always worth less to a person with more of it. The problem, of course, is that the 100% marginal rates needed to equalize incomes would destroy incentives to produce and thus lower utility for everyone.[189]

2. *Choosing a Measure of Social Welfare*

Just as an individual utility function identifies the factors that determine the welfare of an individual, a social welfare function specifies the factors that determine the welfare of a society. The concept of "welfare," however, has a different meaning for a society than for an individual. An individual utility function attempts to measure *objectively* the well-being of each individual. While it is impossible to make a precise assessment of the way in which consumption and leisure affect individual welfare, an individual utility function is value-free in the sense that it attempts to measure what *does* increase an individual's utility rather than what *should* increase utility. A social welfare function, on the other hand, reflects an explicit normative theory of the nature of a good society.

The arguments of a social welfare function may be any factors that might determine the welfare of a society. Under one ethic, social welfare might be determined by the degree to which its members follow a particular set of religious beliefs, while under another ethic social welfare might be determined by the size of the gross national product. The components of social welfare are varied and may include such factors as the amount of individual liberty, the level of democracy, and the way society's rewards are allocated. These factors often are combined with a concern for the well-being of the individuals in the society. Mixed ethics may require a social welfare function whose arguments include all these factors.[190]

---

189. *Id.* at 374-76. Edgeworth was also concerned that such a redistributive tax structure might threaten liberty and lead to other social ills, such as overpopulation. *Id.*

190. The most general form of a social welfare function can be written as $W = w(x_1, x_2, \ldots x_i)$, where the arguments x_i of the function are any arbitrary factors—consumption, population size, behavior in conformity with a particular set of religious beliefs—that are believed to affect social welfare. The idea of social welfare as a function of arbitrarily chosen factors was introduced by Bergson and further developed by Samuelson; such functions are known as Bergson-Samuelson social welfare functions. *See* Burk (now Bergson), *A Reformulation of Certain Aspects of Welfare Economics*, 52 Q.J. ECON. 310 (1938) (stating value judgments required for deriving the conditions of maximum economic welfare); P. SAMUELSON, FOUNDATIONS OF ECONOMIC ANALYSIS 203-53 (1947).

Optimal tax models focus on welfarist theories of distributive justice—that is, ethics under which the welfare of a society is determined solely by the well-being of its members. Under welfarist social welfare functions, social well-being always is positively correlated with improvements in the well-being of any individual in the society. Other features of a society, such as individual liberty and democracy, may be valued under welfarist ethics because of the impact they have on the well-being of individuals, but they are not accorded independent value.[191]

Welfarist theories of distributive justice are of three types: utilitarian theories, weighted utility theories, and leximin theories.[192] Utilitarianism is the least egalitarian of these theories. It accords the utility of each person equal weight, so that social welfare is measured by the unweighted sum of the welfare of the individuals in the society.[193] Proponents of utilitarianism desire to maximize welfare, but do not focus on its distribution.

Weighted utility theories are more egalitarian, weighting the welfare of less well off individuals more heavily than the welfare of those who are better off.[194] One common weighting system assumes that social welfare varies with the *product* of the utilities of the individuals in the society. Adherents of weighted utility theories would accept a reduction in the total amount of welfare in a society in exchange for improving the welfare of society's less well off members.

The most extreme weighting of individual utilities occurs under the "Rawlsian" leximin.[195] Under the leximin, the well-being of the least well off person in society determines that society's social welfare.[196] Any

---

191. *See* Y. NG, *supra* note 54, at 21-22 (arguing that many values are merely elaborations of "basic" values which alone can be used to define welfare).

192. *See supra* text accompanying notes 49-51.

193. A utilitarian social welfare function can be written as $W = w(u_1, u_2, \ldots, u_i)$, or $W = w(\Sigma u_i)$, where u_i is the welfare of the ith member of society.

194. A weighted utility social welfare function can be written as $W = w(a_1u_1, a_2u_2, \ldots, a_iu_i)$, where a_i is the weight given to the utility enjoyed by a person with a utility level of u_i and where a_i decreases as u_i increases.

195. *See* J. RAWLS, *supra* note 29. The leximin is associated with Rawls because of his "difference principle," which states that social and economic inequalities are justified only if the inequalities increase the well-being of the least advantaged members of the society. *Id.* at 75. Rawls' theory of distributive justice is far more complex than suggested by the leximin. Improvement in the level of economic goods is subordinate, for example, to the maximization of the level of basic liberties enjoyed by all citizens. *Id.* at 60-65. Nevertheless, the leximin is consistent with Rawls' theory as it relates to the distribution of material goods.

Rawls suggests, without much analysis, that his principles of distributive justice are consistent with a rate structure that is flat above a certain exemption amount. *Id.* at 274-80. O'Kelley, *supra* note 3, at 727-55, also concludes that a modified Rawlsian analysis leads to a flat tax with an exemption. Optimal tax models that have considered a leximin, however, have found it inconsistent with a proportionate tax. *See infra* text accompanying notes 206 & 220-23.

196. A leximin social welfare function can be written as follows: Let $i(x)$ be the ith worst-off individual of the individuals in social state x. Under the leximin, social state x is preferred to social

reduction in the well-being of someone other than the worst off member of a society is justified if it improves the well-being of the worst-off member. The leximin generally is considered the most egalitarian of the welfarist theories of distributive justice.[197]

3. *Integrating Individual Utility and Social Welfare*

The mathematical techniques used to derive an optimal rate structure in light of particular social welfare and individual utility functions are complex and of little interest to the nonspecialist. A simplified explanation of the methodology is useful, however, in evaluating the findings of optimal tax models.

Imagine a society of individuals whose well-being depends only on the amount of consumption and leisure they enjoy. Each individual wants to maximize her well-being and so works until the utility of the additional consumption she could enjoy from more earnings is exceeded by the loss in utility from the reduction in leisure that would be necessary to enable her to work more. Thus, the amount an individual works depends on the relative value of consumption and leisure to that individual and on the amount of consumption the individual can enjoy by working an additional hour.

The tax structure influences an individual's work effort by reducing the amount of consumption an individual is able to earn by sacrificing an hour of leisure. If the tax structure provides for lump-sum payments or demogrants to individuals, it will also reduce work effort by increasing the individual's nonlabor income, thus reducing her need for the income that could be earned by working. These influences are the substitution and income effects discussed above.[198]

The government will find it difficult to select the combination of taxes and transfers that maximizes welfare because individuals may change their work effort as the government changes the rate structure. Suppose, for example, that the government decides to tax individuals with high incomes at steep rates in order to fund grants to the poor. The

---

state y if and only if there is some r: $1 \leq r \leq n$, such that $Ur(x) > Ur(y)$, and $Ui(x) = Ui(y)$, for all $i < r$. *See* A. SEN, *supra* note 40, at 234.

197. Under some measures of equality a weighted utility social welfare function may be more egalitarian than the leximin. Consider the following two distributions of 100 units of utility: (8,9,10,73) and (7,31,31,31). The former distribution would be preferred under the leximin, but the latter is intuitively more egalitarian and is evaluated as more equal by such measures of inequality as the Gini coefficient and the variance of the logarithms of income.

A more egalitarian social welfare function is possible, but it would not be welfarist. Take, for example, a theory of distributive justice that judges the goodness of a social state according to the amount of equality in the state as indicated by the Gini coefficient of the distribution of income. Such a social welfare function would not be welfarist because it would endorse additional equality even if, because of incentive effects, everyone would be better off with a less equal distribution.

198. *See supra* text accompanying notes 62-65.

government might discover that the tax so reduces work effort that the grants are not feasible. While trial-and-error might eventually lead to a tax structure in which revenues balance expenditures, the results would probably not be optimal.

Optimal tax models provide a means of calculating a tax structure in which revenues equal expenditures and in which social welfare is maximized under the chosen theory of distributive justice. Unfortunately, the complex nature of the optimization problem has limited the ability of optimal income tax researchers to derive important analytical results.[199] It is impossible to show analytically, for example, whether average and marginal tax rates should rise, fall, or remain constant over the range of income.[200] Therefore, the researchers' goal is to calculate the optimal rate structure under various specifications of the distribution of abilities and the determinants of individual utility.

The methodology of optimal taxation can be illustrated by a simple model that calculates the optimal rate structure under two different welfarist ethics in a society of three individuals. For purposes of this model, we will restrict the government's choice to a linear progressive tax structure consisting of a constant marginal tax coupled with a demogrant. We will not, however, alter the core assumptions and methodology of the Mirrlees model.

Imagine a society of three individuals named Alice, Betty, and Cindy. Assume each individual has an identical utility function in which her utility is determined solely by the level of consumption and leisure she enjoys. Further assume that the marginal utility of an additional unit of either income or leisure is inversely proportional to the amount already owned.[201] This can be represented by letting the utility that an

199. The two most significant analytical results are of little practical value in the determination of a rate structure. The first is the rather trivial conclusion that the marginal rate on income should be between 0% and 100%. Mirrlees, *Optimum Income Taxation, supra* note 178, at 184-86. The second is the rather surprising result that for a bounded income distribution the marginal rate of tax on the lowest and highest income should be zero. *See* Sadka, *On Income Distribution, Incentive Effects and Optimal Income Taxation,* 43 REV. ECON. STUD. 261, 266 (1976); Seade, *On the Shape of Optimal Tax Schedules,* 7 J. PUB. ECON. 203 (1977).

The intuition behind the conclusion that the tax on the highest earner should be zero is as follows: Imagine a tax structure where the highest earner faces a positive marginal rate and earns an income of Z dollars. Now imagine that the rate structure is modified so that the highest earner pays no tax on any amount he earns *greater* than Z dollars. Since the individual's after-tax wage rate is increased, he will choose to work more hours and will enjoy a higher level of welfare. No one else in the society will suffer a welfare loss because tax revenues from the highest wage earner are unchanged. Indeed, if the change induces high earners *other* than the highest wage earner to work additional hours because of the prospect of earning untaxed income once their income qualifies for the zero marginal rate, tax revenues will be increased.

200. Mirrlees, *Optimum Income Taxation, supra* note 178, at 184-86.

201. Under such a utility function, the utility gained from an additional dollar of income is ten times as great to a person who has $10,000 than to a person who has $100,000. Similarly, additional

individual enjoys from an amount of consumption or leisure be equal to the logarithm of that amount. If consumption and leisure have equal weight in determining utility, an individual's level of welfare is the sum of the logarithms of the amounts of consumption and leisure she enjoys. This relationship can be expressed as

$$U = ln\ (C) + ln\ (L)$$

where U = utility, C = consumption, and L = leisure.[202]

Each individual's pre-tax income is equal to her working hours multiplied by her hourly wage. Each individual's leisure is equal to the total number of hours available to her (24 in this example) less the number of hours she works. These two relationships can be expressed as

$$z = nh$$

where z = pre-tax income, n = pre-tax hourly wages and h = hours worked, and

$$L = 24 - h.$$

Suppose that Alice, Betty, and Cindy have pre-tax hourly wages of $10, $20, and $40 respectively. Each will choose to work the number of hours that maximizes the sum of the value of her consumption plus the value of her leisure. More formally, each individual will choose to work a number of hours h to maximize the function

$$U = ln\ (nh\ ) + ln\ (24 - h\ ).$$

It turns out that for Alice, Betty, and Cindy the utility-maximizing choice is to work twelve hours. Indeed, for any wage level greater than zero, the utility maximizing choice is to work this amount.[203] Table 1 illustrates the situation that would exist in a no-tax world.

Now consider the role of the government in setting a rate structure. In our model, the government is able to redistribute income through a linear progressive tax consisting of a uniform payment, or demogrant, financed by a constant marginal tax rate. Such a structure effects redistribution because the demogrant will be greater than the amount of tax collected for a low-income individual and less than the amount of tax collected for a high-income individual. If, for example, a rate structure

---

leisure to a person who currently enjoys 10 hours of leisure is worth twice as much as additional leisure to a person who already enjoys 20 hours.

202. It is further assumed that consumption and leisure cannot be negative so that $C \geq 0$ and $L \geq 0$.

203. The first order conditions are $dU/dh = 24n - 2hn = 0$. Solving for h, we find that $h = 12$ for all $n > 0$. An individual's choice to work one-half of all available hours in a no-tax world results from the equal weight given to consumption and utility in the individual utility function. This allocation of weights is arbitrary. If the individual utility function is rewritten in the form $U = a\ (ln\ C) + ln\ L$, the relative weight an individual gives to consumption and leisure can be varied by changing the value of the variable a. If, for example, one believes that individuals would work eight hours per day in a no-tax world, a would have a value of one-half. The decision to use a value of $a = 1$ was made for explanatory simplicity.

TABLE 1
NO-TAX WORLD

Name	Wage	Hours Worked	Pre-Tax Income	Net Tax	Consumption	Leisure	Utility*
Alice	$10	12	$120	$0	$120	12	7.272
Betty	$20	12	$240	$0	$240	12	7.966
Cindy	$40	12	$480	$0	$480	12	8.659
Totals		36	$840	$0	$840	36	23.897

*Utility equals the sum of the logarithms of consumption and leisure.

were adopted with a 20% marginal rate and demogrant of $5,000, an individual with an income of $10,000 would pay a $2,000 tax and receive a $5,000 demogrant for a net gain of $3,000. An individual with an income of $100,000, on the other hand, would pay a tax of $20,000 and receive a demogrant of $5,000 for a net reduction in income of $15,000.

After application of the linear progressive tax, each individual's consumption will equal her earned income minus the tax on that income and plus the demogrant. This can be expressed as:

$$C = nh\ (1 - r) + G$$

where r is the marginal tax rate and G is the demogrant.

Thus, after the implementation of an income tax, an individual will choose to work a number of hours h to maximize the function

$$U = ln\ (nh\ (1 - r) + G) + ln\ (24 - h).$$

In the present example, aggregate income in the no-tax world is $840 and the government might expect that a 20% tax on earned income would raise $168 and finance a demogrant of $56 per person. The government will discover, however, that because of the reduction in work effort caused by the tax, such a rate structure would raise only $147 of revenue, $21 short of the amount needed to finance the demogrant.[204]

In order to enact a tax structure that is both feasible and utility-maximizing, the government must determine the unique revenue-neutral demogrant associated with each tax rate and then calculate the marginal rate and demogrant combination that maximizes aggregate utility. In the case of the 20% marginal rate discussed in the last paragraph, for example, the revenue-neutral demogrant is $49.78, which produces an aggre-

204. An individual will maximize the function

$$U = ln\ (nh(1 - r) + G) + ln\ (24 - h)$$

by choosing to work that number of hours, h, such that $h = 12 - (G/(2n(1-r)))$. For a tax rate of 20% and a demogrant of 56, the revenues raised from the 20% marginal rate on individuals with hourly wages of $10, $20, and $40 are $17, $41, and $89 respectively. Thus, when both the demogrant and the marginal tax rate are considered, the net burden of the tax structure on the three individuals is −$39, −$15, and +$33 for a deficit of $21.

gate utility of 24.058.[205] This represents an increase in total utility as compared to the no-tax world; it is not, however, the utility maximizing tax rate. Instead, utility is maximized by a tax rate of approximately 31% and a demogrant of $70.88. Table 2 illustrates the effects of such a tax structure.

TABLE 2
UTILITARIAN TAX STRUCTURE
Tax Rate: 31%. Demogrant $70.88

Name	Wage	Hours Worked	Pre-Tax Income	Net Tax	Consumption	Leisure	Utility*
Alice	$10	6.86	$ 68.64	−$49.60	$118.24	17.14	7.614
Betty	$20	9.43	$188.64	−$12.40	$201.04	14.57	7.982
Cindy	$40	10.72	$428.64	$62.00	$366.64	13.28	8.491
Totals		27.01	$685.92	$0	$685.92	44.99	24.087

*Utility equals the sum of the logarithms of consumption and leisure.

As compared to the no-tax world, the utility-maximizing tax reduces total work effort by about 25% and total production by about 18%.[206] The utility of the best paid individual declines, but total utility is higher because the utility of the two less well paid individuals increases. Note that better paid individuals still enjoy a higher level of welfare and work longer hours than those who are less well paid.

The method of determining the optimal tax rate would be essentially the same if the government were to adopt a leximin rather than a utilitarian theory of distributive justice. However, under the leximin the government would enact the tax rate and demogrant that maximizes the utility of the least well-off individual, rather than the tax rate that maximizes total welfare. This turns out to be a marginal tax rate of 58% and a demogrant of $96.67. Table 3 shows the distribution of consumption, leisure, and utility under such a tax structure.

205. In the three-taxpayer society examined here, the revenue neutral grant for any given marginal rate r is

$$G = \frac{24r(1 - r)(n_1 + n_2 + n_3)}{3\,(2 - r)}$$

More generally, for a linear progressive tax structure with t individuals, the revenue neutral grant will be

$$G = \frac{\Sigma\, 24r(1 - r)n_i}{t(2 - r)}$$

where n_i is the wage of the ith individual.

206. The decline in productivity is less than the decline in hours worked because much of the reduction in work effort can be attributed to the least productive individual.

TABLE 3
LEXIMIN TAX STRUCTURE

Tax Rate: 58%. Demogrant $96.07

Name	Wage	Hours Worked	Pre-Tax Income	Net Tax	Consumption	Leisure	Utility*
Alice	$10	0.56	$ 5.63	−$ 92.80	$ 98.45	23.44	7.744
Betty	$20	6.28	$125.63	−$ 23.20	$148.83	17.72	7.877
Cindy	$40	9.14	$365.63	$116.00	$249.63	14.86	8.219
Totals		15.98	$496.89	$0	$469.89	56.02	23.840

*Utility equals the sum of the logarithms of consumption and leisure.

The leximin requires a tax structure with a substantially higher tax rate and a larger demogrant than a utilitarian tax structure. The welfare of the lowest paid individual is improved, but total utility is significantly less than under a utilitarian tax system. The high rates and large demogrants reduce the work effort of all individuals, but have the most dramatic impact on the lowest paid. Total hours worked are about 40% less than in the utilitarian case, and total consumption about 28% less. As in the utilitarian case, however, better paid persons enjoy a greater utility level and work harder than lower paid persons.

What can we conclude from our analysis of the optimal linear tax in a three-person world? First, a progressive rate structure is optimal under both utilitarianism, the least egalitarian welfarist theory, and under the leximin, the most egalitarian theory. Second, the level of progressivity depends on which welfarist ethic is adopted. A leximin dictates a much higher marginal rate and a larger demogrant than does a utilitarian ethic. Third, a progressive rate structure decreases total work effort. Fourth, under both utilitarian and leximin ethics, higher-paid individuals work more hours and enjoy a higher level of welfare than do lower-paid individuals. As we will see, these conclusions are consistent with the more complex model developed by Mirrlees.

4. *The Results of the Mirrlees Optimal Tax Model*

The Mirrlees model differs from the simple model described in the preceding section in two important respects. First, it examines a society with a continuous distribution of taxpayers of differing wage levels rather than with just three taxpayers. Second, it permits the government to adopt a tax structure with variable marginal rates rather than limiting the government to a linear structure. Under the Mirrlees model, the government can adopt a tax structure with a demogrant and continuously variable marginal rates rather than a demogrant coupled with a flat rate.

The Mirrlees model calculates the optimal tax structure under both a utilitarian theory of distributive justice like that examined in our simple model, and under a more egalitarian ethic that requires the government to maximize the product of individual utilities. The model also calculates the optimal income tax structure under different assumptions regarding the amount of revenue required by the government for purposes other than redistribution. Finally, the model considers two assumptions regarding the distribution of earning ability.[207]

Like our three-taxpayer model, the Mirrlees model adopts a logarithmic utility function under which the value of an additional unit of consumption is inversely related to the amount already enjoyed. Given this fairly rapid decline in the marginal utility of consumption, Mirrlees expected high rates on the wealthy to be optimal.[208] In fact, his model finds the optimal level of progressivity to be modest. In the utilitarian case, assuming 7% of gross income is required for government purposes other than redistribution, the top marginal rate is 26%.[209] The demogrant is also fairly small, about one-sixth of the median income.[210]

Even more surprising, the highest marginal rate falls on individuals with incomes in the *bottom* 10% of the population and the marginal tax rate thereafter declines. As a result, an individual with an income in the top 1% pays a marginal rate of approximately 17%—about 40% less than the top rate.[211] The falling marginal rates do not, however, prevent the tax structure calculated by the Mirrlees model from being progressive. As Table 4 shows, because of the demogrant the rich pay a higher average tax rate than do the poor, so that the after-tax distribution of income is more equal than the pre-tax distribution.[212] Nevertheless, the level of redistribution is not high.[213]

Mirrlees also finds relatively modest levels of redistribution where

207. Mirrlees, *Optimum Income Taxation*, *supra* note 178, at 200-07.

208. *See id.* at 207.

209. *Id.* at 202 (Table II).

210. The grant to a person who does not work (x_0) is 0.03 units of consumption. Mean consumption is 0.17 units. *Id.* at 202 (Table I). Applying these results to the United States income distribution in 1982, where the mean income for a family of four was $30,924, the demogrant would have been $5,457, far less than the relevant poverty level of $9,862. BUREAU OF THE CENSUS, STATISTICAL ABSTRACT OF THE UNITED STATES 429, 448 (105th ed. 1985).

211. Mirrlees, *Optimum Income Taxation*, *supra* note 178, at 202 (Table II).

212. Various measures have been used to determine the degree of inequality in the distribution of income. In most but not all cases, these measures lead to the same ranking of alternative distributions with respect to their degree of inequality. *See* Hemming & Keen, *Single-Crossing Conditions in Comparisons of Tax Progressivity*, 20 J. PUB. ECON. 373 (1983); *see generally* A. ATKINSON, *supra* note 9, at 53-59; J. MEADE, *supra* note 39, at 112-30.

Table 4 is estimated from figures in Mirrlees, *Optimum Income Taxation*, *supra* note 178, at 202 (Tables I and II).

213. If the amount of revenue required by the government increases, the optimal level of redistribution is slightly reduced, although the main effect is to increase the tax burden on all income classes. *See* Mirrlees, *Optimum Income Taxation*, *supra* note 178, at 202-04 (compare Case 1 with Case 2, and Case 3 with Case 5).

TABLE 4

MIRRLEES MODEL
OPTIMAL TAX STRUCTURE: UTILITARIAN

Elasticity of Substitution = 1.0
Government Expenditures = 7% of goods produced.
Demogrant = 0.03 units. Mean income = 0.17 units.

Income Level	Consumption Pre-Tax	Consumption Post-Tax	Average Tax Rate	Marginal Tax Rate	Income as % of Mean Pre-Tax	Income as % of Mean Post-Tax
10%	0.09	0.10	—	24%	50%	59%
50%	0.17	0.16	6%	22%	94%	94%
90%	0.29	0.25	14%	19%	161%	147%
99%	0.45	0.38	16%	17%	250%	224%

the government attempts to maximize the product of individual utility levels. This result is surprising because the government's goal is quite egalitarian. If utility from consumption alone is considered under such a weighted social welfare function, the value of an additional unit of consumption varies inversely with the *square* of the consumption level of the recipient. Thus, the social value of an additional dollar to an individual with an income of $20,000 is 100 times as great as the social value of an additional dollar to a person with an income of $200,000. A transfer of a dollar from the richer individual to the poorer would improve social welfare so long as the poorer individual gains more than a penny for each dollar lost by the richer individual. When utility from leisure is considered, the additional weight given to increases in the consumption of the poor is less. Nevertheless, the social value of additional income to a poor person will be many times greater than the social value of that income to a wealthy person.[214]

Even when the government wishes to maximize the product of individual utilities, the Mirrlees model produces an optimal top marginal rate of 34% and a demogrant of just 30% of the median income. These represent only modest increases from the levels produced under a utilitarian ethic. Again, the top marginal rate falls on individuals with incomes in the bottom 10% of the population and declines steadily thereafter, so that a person in the top 1% of the population again faces a marginal rate about 40% lower than the highest marginal rate.[215]

214. The inclusion of utility derived from leisure makes the overall distribution of utility more equal because individuals enjoying disproportionately large amounts of consumption are unlikely also to enjoy disproportionately large amounts of leisure. The reduction in inequality from the consideration of the utility of leisure reduces the social gains from redistribution under any social welfare function that assigns additional weight to the utility of the less well off.

215. These figures are for the case in which the government revenue requirement is 2% of gross income. *See* Mirrlees, *Optimum Income Taxation, supra* note 178, at 203 (Tables VII and VIII).

The optimal tax literature provides little explanation for these striking results. Our analysis suggests that the relatively moderate level of progressivity is caused by a confluence of two opposing forces. The assumption of rapidly declining marginal utility of money drives the tax toward steep progressivity. On the other hand, the efficiency costs of progressivity become extremely great at high tax rates. As discussed below, these efficiency costs are exaggerated by the Mirrlees model's unrealistic assumptions regarding the willingness of individuals to substitute leisure for consumption.[216]

The shape of the optimal rate structure—a demogrant plus slowly falling marginal rates—can be explained if we assume that for a given level of redistribution, the marginal rates taxpayers face generally will be lower and the efficiency loss will be smaller under a tax structure with a larger demogrant and declining marginal rates than under a structure with a smaller demogrant and rising marginal rates.[217] Moreover, under a tax structure with falling marginal rates, some individuals may work additional hours in order to reach tax brackets with lower marginal rates.

B. *Modifying the Mirrlees Model*

The development of a method of determining the optimal rate structure in light of a social welfare function and an individual utility function is a remarkable achievement in public economics. Mirrlees also asks the right question: What tax structure is best, given certain normative values and certain assumptions regarding the effect of taxes on behavior? His focus on this issue may be as important a contribution as his model.

The finding that the optimal tax structure consists of a fairly modest guaranteed consumption level plus relatively low marginal rates that peak in the bottom 10% of the population has led Mirrlees to conclude that the income tax alone is a much less effective method of mitigating inequality than is generally believed, and that the optimal rate structure may consist of a demogrant plus a constant marginal rate.[218]

When government revenue requirements are 12% of gross income, the top rate rises to 39%, again in the bottom decile of the population, and the demogrant decreases to about 27% of the median income. *Id.* at 204 (Tables IX and X).

The Mirrlees model finds high marginal rates to be optimal only if both an egalitarian social welfare function and an unrealistically wide dispersion of abilities are assumed. *See id.* at 204 (Tables XI and XII) (spread of abilities with a standard deviation 2 1/2 times greater than best estimate). The adoption of a wider distribution of abilities also has a marked impact on our three-taxpayer model. For example, a change in the hourly wage distribution from $10, $20, and $40 to $7, $20, and $43, respectively, changes the optimal utilitarian tax structure from a marginal rate of 0.31 and a demogrant of $70.88 to an optimal marginal rate of 0.40 and a demogrant of $84.

216. *See infra* text accompanying notes 230-41.

217. *See* Diamond, *Negative Taxes and the Poverty Problem—A Review Article*, 21 NAT'L TAX J. 288 (1968).

218. Mirrlees also states that if the income tax is relatively ineffective in reducing inequality,

The merit of these conclusions depends, of course, on the validity of the optimal tax model. Mirrlees' model requires numerous simplifying assumptions with respect to individual and social welfare and with respect to the structure of the economy. We will examine four of those assumptions that have particular importance to tax policy: the choice of a social welfare function, the treatment of general equilibrium effects, the role of envy and jealousy, and the trade-off between labor and leisure.[219] We find that altering Mirrlees' assumptions regarding the social welfare function, the effect of taxes on pre-tax wages, and the impact of envy and jealousy do not alter the implications of his work for policymaking. On the other hand, we conclude that a more realistic assumption as to the trade-off between consumption and leisure substantially changes Mirrlees' results regarding the appropriate level of redistribution (greatly increasing the optimal marginal rates and demogrant) while leaving his findings about the optimal shape of the tax structure essentially unchanged.

1. The Choice of a Social Welfare Function

Mirrlees' results can be explained by his choice of a utilitarian or weighted utility social welfare function rather than the leximin. Under the leximin, much higher marginal rates are optimal.[220] One study found, for example, that the leximin implies an optimal marginal rate for a linear progressive tax of about 69% and a guaranteed minimum income equal to about 38% of the median income.[221] In our own three-taxpayer

---

efforts should be made to devise redistributive taxes based on ability to earn rather than on actual earnings. Mirrlees, *Optimum Income Taxation*, *supra* note 178, at 208. If it were possible to measure ability to earn and constitutionally permissible to impose such a tax, redistribution could be obtained without any adverse incentive effects by levying lump-sum taxes on individuals with high earning potential. For each of his cases, Mirrlees calculated the optimal tax structure obtainable through such methods, assuming accurate information about each person's earning potential were available. In each case, the level of redistribution is much greater than under an income tax. *Id.* at 202-04.

Mirrlees suggests that measures such as I.Q. scores or hourly wages might be used as indicators of earning ability. The problem, as Mirrlees recognizes, is that even if such measures accurately reflect earning ability, their use in determining tax rates would create an incentive for individuals to conceal their abilities. *Id.* at 208.

219. Optimal tax models adopt other simplifying assumptions that will not be discussed in this Article. For example, optimal tax models generally do not consider the impact of progressive taxation on risk taking, savings, or emigration, and the models typically ignore differences in family size. *See, e.g., id.* at 175-76. In addition, optimal tax models have considered only a small number of different specifications of the individual utility function.

220. *See* A. ATKINSON, SOCIAL JUSTICE AND PUBLIC POLICY 307 (1983) (Table 4); Helpman & Sadka, *The Optimal Income Tax: Some Comparative Statics Results*, 9 J. PUB. ECON. 383 (1978); Stern, *On the Specification of Models of Optimum Income Taxation*, 6 J. PUB. ECON. 123, 144-45 (1976) (Table 4a); Tuomala, *On the Optimal Income Taxation: Some Further Numerical Results*, 23 J. PUB. ECON. 351, 359-61 (1984) (Table 3) (using elasticity of substitution of 0.5).

221. Stern, *supra* note 220, at 145 (Table 4a). Stern's calculations were for a linear progressive

model, the adoption of a leximin increased the optimal tax rate from 31% to 58%.[222] In contrast, the choice of a more egalitarian social welfare function makes little difference in the *shape* of the optimal rate structure. Optimal marginal rates still peak at a relatively low level of income and decline steadily thereafter.[223]

Although the adoption of a leximin leads to high optimal marginal rates, we believe this finding is unlikely to have a large impact on policymaking because the extreme egalitarianism of the leximin is unlikely to be widely endorsed.

2. *General Equilibrium Effects*

The Mirrlees model is based on a partial equilibrium theory. Wage rates are determined exogenously; the tax structure is assumed to have no impact on pre-tax wages. The failure of the income tax to change the relative pre-tax wages of the rich and poor follows from Mirrlees' assumption that labor supplied by unskilled individuals is a perfect substitute for labor supplied by the highly skilled; the talented produce more labor per hour than the less talented but do not engage in a different type of labor.

Using an endogenously determined pre-tax wage rate adds enormous complexity to optimal tax models. To compensate for this additional complexity, optimal tax models that consider general equilibrium effects on the wage rate typically assume only two types of labor, skilled and unskilled.[224] Such models obviously fail to capture the richness of the actual labor market, where workers are far from perfect substitutes, even within income groups. Moreover, the added complexity generated by assuming more than one type of labor often requires the further simplification of the models in other respects, such as limiting the analysis to linear tax structures.

The results of studies in which the pre-tax wage is endogenously determined are varied. Where realistic assumptions regarding the labor supply and production functions have been adopted, Mirrlees' results essentially have been confirmed.[225] Where certain extreme assumptions are adopted, an increase in progressivity can be shown to *decrease* the

tax and used Mirrlees' assumptions with respect to the distribution of abilities and the elasticity of substitution between leisure and consumption.

222. *See supra* Tables 2 and 3 and accompanying text.

223. *See* Tuomala, *supra* note 220.

224. *See, e.g.*, Allen, *Optimal Linear Income Taxation with General Equilibrium Effects on Wages*, 17 J. PUB. ECON. 135, 137 (1982).

225. *See, e.g.*, Feldstein, *On the Optimal Progressivity of the Income Tax*, 2 J. PUB. ECON. 357, 374 (1973) (examining how the general equilibrium effect of a tax on the wage rate influences estimates of optimal tax progressivity).

after-tax income of the poor relative to the rich.[226] The best conclusion we can draw from current research is that the inclusion of general equilibrium effects is likely to reduce the redistributive effects of progressive taxation somewhat but is unlikely to alter the basic results of the Mirrlees model.

3. *Envy and Sympathy: Interdependent Utility Functions*

Mirrlees assumes that an individual's utility level depends only upon her own level of consumption and leisure. The amount enjoyed by others is irrelevant. It seems more reasonable to assume that utility functions are interdependent, that an individual's happiness depends both upon her own consumption and leisure and upon the consumption and leisure enjoyed by others.

Individuals appear to react quite differently to the relative well-being of others. Some people may be entirely selfish, feeling envious of those who are better off and feeling pleasure at having more than those who are worse off. Other people may be unconcerned with their own relative status, but sympathetic to the plight of less well off members of society. Looking at the aggregate population, however, the most plausible assumption seems to be that people generally feel some degree of envy toward those better off and some amount of sympathy toward those worse off, or at least toward those at the very bottom of the economic ladder.

The impact of envy and sympathy is difficult to intuit, and thus little weight can be given to the numerical results of models that attempt to ascribe a quantitative dimension to those factors. The direction in which those factors move the tax structure, however, is readily apparent: The inclusion of envy and sympathy would increase the progressivity of the tax structure.[227]

---

226. *See, e.g.*, Allen, *supra* note 224, at 142-43 (assumes labor supply elasticities are negative and different types of labor are complements rather than substitutes); Allingham, *Inequality and Progressive Taxation*, 11 J. PUB. ECON. 273 (1979) (comparing a 20% flat tax to a 50% progressive tax with the same revenue yield; finds progressive tax more equitable); Carruth, *On the Role of the Production and Consumption Assumptions for Optimal Taxation*, 17 J. PUB. ECON. 145 (1982) (discussing and approving the Allen analysis).

227. If envy and jealousy are considered, the Pareto principle does not necessarily support a policy that would increase the wealth of the rich while leaving the wealth of the poor unchanged. Y. NG, *supra* note 54, at 31-32.

Some scholars argue that the existence of interpersonal utility functions may mean redistribution can improve the welfare of the rich as well as the poor. The argument is that the rich are better off because the utility they derive from the improvement of the welfare of the poor exceeds the loss of utility they suffer from the reduction of their own consumption. Because, under this view, redistribution can be justified by the Pareto principle, this theory is often called "Pareto optimal redistribution." *See* Hochman & Rodgers, *Pareto Optimal Redistribution*, 59 AM. ECON. REV. 542 (1969); Thurow, *The Income Distribution as a Pure Public Good*, 85 Q.J. ECON. 327 (1971).

Under Pareto optimal redistribution, a compulsory tax system is required only because of the

The expected impact of interdependent utility functions has been confirmed by optimal tax simulations. Marginal tax rates and the overall amount of redistribution increase when envy and sympathy are considered.[228] Where envy and sympathy are weighted heavily, extremely high rates are generated even under a utilitarian ethic.[229]

4. *The Overestimation of the Substitutability of Consumption and Leisure*

The capacity of an income tax to redistribute income effectively depends on whether the imposition of the tax causes people to reduce their work effort significantly. If high-income individuals respond to an income tax by sharply curtailing the number of hours they work, the tax will not only reduce the welfare of those individuals, it will also raise little money for redistribution. In extreme cases, more revenue for redistribution may be raised by a lower rate than by a higher rate. In contrast, if the amount of labor individuals provide is only modestly responsive to taxation, steep marginal rates can provide substantial tax revenues for redistribution without significantly reducing work output.

---

freerider problem. Each wealthy individual is willing to contribute if others join in, but is unwilling to contribute alone. If wealthy individuals could reach agreements without transaction costs, they would contract among themselves to transfer income to the poor and government action would be unnecessary. Because the transaction costs of reaching agreement are high, compulsory taxation is required.

Advocates of Pareto optimal redistribution hope to justify redistribution without reliance on interpersonal utility comparisons. If all individuals are made better off by redistribution, there is no need to deal with the thorny problem of weighing the utility gains of one person against the losses of another.

The problem with Pareto optimal redistribution is that no compulsory system of redistribution is likely to make all individuals better off; some individuals are certain to be unconcerned with the plight of the poor. So long as even one person would prefer an increase in her own consumption to an improvement in the welfare of the less fortunate, interpersonal utility comparisons must be made and redistribution cannot be justified on purely Paretian grounds. *See* Canterbery & Tuckman, *Reflections upon the Income Distribution as a Pure Public Good*, 87 Q.J. ECON. 304 (1973); Pasour, *Pareto Optimality as a Guide to Income Redistribution*, 36 PUB. CHOICE 75 (1981); von Furstenberg & Mueller, *The Pareto Optimal Approach to Income Redistribution: A Fiscal Application*, 61 AM. ECON. REV. 628 (1971).

The use of interdependent utility comparisons in the optimal tax field is quite different. In optimal tax models, envy and sympathy are not used to avoid interpersonal utility comparisons, but are simply added to the specification of the utility function; an individual's utility is determined both by his absolute level of consumption and leisure and by the amount of consumption and leisure enjoyed by others. If a person is envious of those who are better off and sympathetic toward those worse off, then the utility of each individual, all else being equal, is improved by a reduction in the level of inequality in the society.

Nevertheless, including envy and sympathy in the utility function does not mean that each person prefers a highly redistributive tax structure, since the utility an individual gains from reduced inequality may be outweighed by the loss in utility she suffers from reduced consumption.

228. *See* Boskin & Sheshinski, *Optimal Redistributive Taxation When Individual Welfare Depends Upon Relative Income*, 92 Q.J. ECON. 589 (1978); Oswald, *Altruism, Jealousy and the Theory of Optimal Non-Linear Taxation*, 20 J. PUB. ECON. 77 (1983).

229. *See* Boskin & Sheshinski, *supra* note 228, at 597-99.

The imposition of an income tax reduces the amount of additional consumption an individual will earn from an extra hour of work. If other variables remain constant, an individual will respond by working less and enjoying more leisure.[230] The key question is: How much less will the individual choose to work?

The answer depends in large part on the substitutability of leisure and consumption. If an individual is almost as well off with a bit more leisure and a bit less consumption, then the individual will work less and enjoy more free time when his effective wage rate is reduced by an income tax. On the other hand, if an individual finds additional leisure a poor replacement for reduced consumption, then his work effort will not be reduced significantly by the tax.

The ability of an individual to maintain the same level of well-being with a different mix of consumption and leisure will depend on the elasticity of substitution between consumption and leisure.[231] A low elasticity of substitution indicates that an individual maintains a uniform ratio of consumption to leisure even if a high tax rate on labor income makes consumption much more expensive. Conversely, a high elasticity indicates that an increase in the price of consumption relative to the price of leisure causes an individual to reduce significantly his work hours in favor of leisure time.

The original Mirrlees model and most other optimal tax models, including our own three-taxpayer model, adopt a utility function that defines individual well-being as the product of individual consumption and leisure or, equivalently, the sum of their logarithms. Thus, a person enjoying 6 units of consumption and 6 units of leisure would have the same level of well-being as a person enjoying 3 units of consumption and 12 units of leisure. This multiplicative utility function implies a constant elasticity of substitution of 1.0 between leisure and consumption; for small changes, an individual's well-being is unchanged if her enjoyment of one good is decreased so long as her enjoyment of the other good is increased by the same percentage. Thus an individual's well-being is unchanged if her consumption is decreased by one percent so long as her leisure is increased by one percent.[232]

230. In this analysis we assume no income effects—that is, the income lost because of the marginal tax is offset by a lump-sum grant. Under a purely redistributive tax, the grant will exceed the tax collected for some people and will be less than the tax collected for others. In the aggregate, however, the amount of the lump-sum grants will be equal to the income tax collected.

231. The elasticity of substitution between consumption and leisure should not be confused with the previously discussed compensated elasticity of the labor supply with respect to the wage rate. *See supra* text accompanying note 66. The former measures the degree to which an individual will alter his mix of consumption and leisure in response to a change in the relative prices of those commodities, while the latter measures the amount an individual will adjust his work hours to changes in the wage rate.

232. More precisely, for infinitesimal changes an individual is equally well off with an increase

The fact that most optimal tax models adopt a utility function with a constant elasticity of substitution of 1.0 is due to the computational advantages of such a function rather than any evidence that it accurately reflects the way in which consumption and leisure shape individual utility.[233] Indeed, Mirrlees makes no attempt to justify his choice of a unitary elasticity of substitution between consumption and leisure. An examination of econometric estimates of labor supply responsiveness suggests that an elasticity of 1.0 does not reflect accurately the tradeoffs individuals make between consumption and leisure.

Econometric models of the labor supply focus on the impact that changes in the wage rate have on work effort. Although typically the results of these studies are stated in terms of the compensated and uncompensated elasticity of labor with respect to the wage rate, at times the elasticity of substitution between consumption and leisure is also calculated and, even when it is not, it often can be estimated on the basis of the other findings.[234] As discussed earlier, most studies find that the compensated elasticity of the labor supply with respect to the wage rate lies between 0.1 and 0.2.[235] These results imply an elasticity of substitution between consumption and leisure of approximately 0.5.[236] Looking at the whole range of econometric studies of the labor supply, the most plausible conclusion is that the elasticity of substitution between con-

in one good and an equal percentage decrease in the other good. For larger changes, the rule that a reduction in the level of enjoyment of one good can be offset by an approximately equal percentage increase in the other is no longer accurate. As noted in the text, a 50% reduction in the amount of consumption from 6 units to 3 units must be balanced by a 100% increase, from 6 units to 12 units, in the amount of leisure.

233. Computational advantages also dictate other aspects of Mirrlees' individual utility function. Mirrlees assumes a Cobb-Douglas utility function in which individual utility is the sum of the logarithms of the levels of consumption and leisure. Mirrlees, *Optimum Income Taxation, supra* note 178, at 180. This utility function is mathematically tractable but may overvalue additional leisure enjoyed by an underemployed person. Consider, for example, an individual who earns $20,000 per year, works 40 hours per week and, after considering time for commuting, sleeping, and performing household chores, enjoys 30 hours of leisure per week. If that individual's utility is the sum of the logarithms of the levels of consumption and leisure, then she would be equally well off if unemployed with 70 hours of leisure per week and an annual income of $8,591. It seems unlikely, however, that many individuals would accept an income barely above the poverty levels in return for the additional leisure that accompanies unemployment.

234. *See* Stern, *supra* note 220, at 135-39.

235. *See id.* at 138 (Table 2); *supra* text accompanying notes 66-92.

236. For the central values used by Stern of a compensated elasticity of labor with respect to the wage rate of 0.12 and an uncompensated elasticity of −0.15, the elasticity of substitution between consumption and leisure is 0.4077. The highest value Stern calculated for the elasticity of substitution was in the case of a compensated elasticity of labor of 0.22 and an uncompensated elasticity of −0.05. In that case the elasticity of substitution between consumption and leisure was 0.7468. *See id.* at 138 (Table 2, col. a).

Even the substantially higher compensated elasticities of labor calculated by some labor supply studies imply elasticities of substitution between consumption and leisure of less than one since the uncompensated elasticity is still found to be negative. *See id.* at 139 (backward-sloping supply curve implies elasticity of substitution of less than one).

sumption and leisure lies between 0.3 and 0.8 and almost certainly is less than the elasticity of 1.0 used in the Mirrlees model.

Using an elasticity of substitution of 0.5 in optimal tax models results in optimal marginal rates and a demogrant that are much higher than those calculated by Mirrlees. In the utilitarian case, with government revenues set at 10% of gross income, the adoption of an elasticity of 0.5 almost doubles the optimal marginal rates throughout the income range and almost triples the size of demogrant.[237] The level of redistribution also becomes large in an absolute sense, with the guaranteed consumption level equaling about 40% of mean income and with a negative net tax burden for individuals with gross incomes less than 80% of the mean.[238] Since the current mean income for a family of four is approximately $31,000, this redistribution corresponds to a tax structure with a guaranteed income of about $12,400 and a negative net tax for families with incomes under about $24,000.[239]

Similar increases in the optimal level of taxation are seen in the case of more egalitarian social welfare functions when a more realistic specification of the tradeoff between consumption and leisure is assumed. For example, when social welfare is the multiplicative product of individual welfare, optimal marginal rates range as high as 68% and the demogrant is about 58% of average income.[240]

Although the assumption of a lower elasticity of substitution significantly changes the optimal level of redistribution, it does not alter the shape of the optimal rate structure. As in the unitary elasticity case, the top marginal rate is levied on individuals in the bottom 10% of the population in income and the rate declines slowly as income increases.[241] Mirrlees' findings with respect to the shape of the rate structure appear quite robust.

In sum, adopting a realistic value for the tradeoff between consumption and leisure leads to the conclusion that even under an ethical theory like utilitarianism, which assigns no additional weight to the welfare of less well off individuals, a substantial degree of redistribution is justified. However, the optimal shape of the tax structure—a substantial demogrant followed by flat or even slightly declining marginal rates—is very different from the steadily rising marginal rates associated with traditional progressive taxation.

---

237. *See* Tuomala, *supra* note 220, at 359 (Table 1).

238. *Id.*

239. Mean money income for a family of four in 1982 was $30,924. BUREAU OF THE CENSUS, *supra* note 210, at 448. The weighted average poverty level based on money income for a family of four in 1982 was $9,862. *Id.* at 429.

240. Tuomala, *supra* note 220, at 360 (Table 2).

241. *Id.* at 359-61 (Tables 1-3).

Conclusion

Traditional legal analysis of progressive taxation is flawed because it is not grounded in a theory of distributive justice. Instead, traditional analysis places the burden of proof on advocates of progressive taxation to justify their position and then attacks those justifications. To the extent that supporters of proportional taxation do offer a positive case for their position, the argument is based almost exclusively on efficiency grounds; proportionate taxation is said to lead to more work effort, less complexity, better compliance, and reduced investment in uneconomic tax shelters.

It is unlikely, however, that eliminating progressivity would produce these anticipated benefits. Only a small portion of the complexity in the tax code is progressivity-related, and there is little evidence that compliance would be improved or tax-motivated investments significantly reduced by adopting a proportional tax. A somewhat stronger case can be made based on the negative impact of progressive taxation on work effort. A progressive tax will tend to have higher marginal rates than a proportional tax, and will therefore cause a greater distortion in the tradeoff between consumption and leisure.

Arguments that the progressive tax should be eliminated on efficiency grounds also are incomplete, since they fail to explain why efficiency gains are desirable. If efficiency is the only objective, a lump-sum tax such as a head tax should be adopted. The rejection of lump-sum taxation by critics of progressivity suggests that fairness as well as efficiency grounds underlie their support for proportional taxation. But critics of progressivity have not claimed that proportional taxation is supported by an appropriate balance of fairness and efficiency. Indeed, traditional legal scholarship offers no theory of distributive justice to justify a proportionate tax.

Optimal tax models, on the other hand, have the great virtue of simultaneously considering normative goals regarding just distribution and the incentive effects of a tax structure designed to further those goals. The rate structures produced by these models vary according to the assumptions made about the determinants of individual utility, the distribution of abilities, and the structure of the economic system. The rate structures produced are also highly dependent on the choice of the social welfare function.

Our analysis nevertheless suggests that under any welfarist social welfare function, and under reasonable assumptions regarding the components of individual utility and the nature of the economy, the optimal tax structure would redistribute income from the rich to the poor, although by means of a demogrant rather than by graduated marginal rates. Although the optimal tax literature does not answer the question of what the exact rate structure should be, it strongly suggests that if a goal of the tax system is to maximize individual welfare, the rate structure should be progressive.

Much additional work needs to be done on the ramifications of the optimal tax model. The social effects of a combination of substantial demogrants and uniform marginal rates raise important and interesting questions. Still more work is needed on the implications of nonwelfarist theories of distributive justice for a tax structure. Based on what we know now, however, the case for progressive taxation appears to be far less uneasy than has been claimed.

[12]

HORIZONTAL EQUITY: MEASURES IN SEARCH OF A PRINCIPLE**

LOUIS KAPLOW*

ABSTRACT

Horizontal equity—the command that equals be treated equally—has received increasing attention, particularly in attempts to assess the desirability of tax reform proposals. It is demonstrated that recent attempts to implement horizontal equity are inconsistent with its stated foundations. More thorough examination raises serious doubts as to whether there is any alternative justification of horizontal equity that would support many common applications of the concept. Examples typically offered to motivate support for horizontal equity are shown to resonate with our intuition only because of the concept's congruence (in such cases) with conventional understandings of risk and vertical equity. Many remaining practical uses of horizontal equity are noted.

1. Introduction

HORIZONTAL equity (HE) is the command that equals be treated equally. The concept arises most frequently in discussions of tax policy alongside the more frequently addressed concerns for equality—denominated as vertical equity (VE)—and efficiency. The structure of analysis is that each of the three criteria has independent significance and must in some way be balanced against the others. (See Atkinson 1980; Feldstein 1976a, 1976b; King 1983).

Despite HE being mentioned in the same breath as VE in Musgrave's (1959) and (although not by name) in Shoup's (1969) pioneering treatises on public finance, HE had long received less serious attention among public finance economists than VE or efficiency, both in theoretical development and empirical elaboration. More recently, there has been a rapidly growing interest in the concept. An often-cited article by Feldstein (1976a) exploring HE in the context of tax reform, joined by an article by Musgrave (1976) that explores all three evaluative criteria, has led the way. Additional work such as that by Brennan (1971), King (1983), Plotnick (1981, 1982, 1984), and Rosen (1978) has focused primarily on refining the measurement of HE.

This rise in prominence may seem surprising since HE, as it has more recently been developed, is in conflict with the social welfare tradition, whereas VE and efficiency are included within it. Moreover, recent applications of HE do not involve the direct use of clearly irrelevant or invidious factors—as in varying tax rates by one's height or race—the sorts of discrimination that motivate the concern for equal protection of the law. Nor do they present arbitrary distinctions in sources or uses of income when defining a tax base, which was the central concern of Simons (1938) when invoking the notion of equal treatment. Rather, the question is whether one should object to *prima facie* reasonable tax reforms, motivated by concerns of efficiency or distribution, because of the incidental, inevitable, and often unavoidable effects of such reforms on the pre-reform distribution of income. Violations of HE are understood as being measured without regard to the origin or justification of the initial distribution of income—including, for example, the possibility that it merely reflects the incidental or even capricious effects of previous reforms.

The thesis of this paper is that recent work on HE has in an important sense jumped the gun. HE is now frequently measured and applied even though there has been virtually no exploration of why one should care about the principle in the contexts and in the manner in which it is now being used. Although the notion of equal treatment of equals is hardly new, it generally has been analzyed and ad-

*Harvard Law School and National Bureau of Economic Research, Cambridge, MA 02138.

vanced in contexts that bear little resemblance to those in which HE is now being avidly discussed. Mosts papers considering HE refer briefly to familiar remarks by Musgrave (1959) or Shoup (1969) without directly considering the connection between the original motivations and current applications.

Two problems arise from the failure to identify the normative justification for current uses of HE. First, if there is no normative basis for a measure of HE, efforts directed toward applying it are misspent and will lead policymakers astray when they are encouraged to sacrifice other values in the pursuit of HE. Second, if there is some normative basis, one cannot properly develop and choose among measures for a concept and methods for weighing it along with other objectives until that basis is specified. It is not always possible to be precise in matters of equity, but neither should ambiguity be accepted without complete investigation, as in some instances ambiguity can be reduced and in others it may indicate that deeper problems remain unresolved.

Section 2 compares traditional definitions and recently offered indexes of HE, suggesting that there exist serious difficulties even before one considers directly the foundations of HE. Section 3 assesses the extent to which the persuasive force often thought to support more recent invocations of HE in the context of tax reform can be understood better in the traditional social welfare framework. This section seeks to illuminate the connection between HE and VE first emphasized by Musgrave and to link the application of HE to the study of risk. Section 4 considers whether recent uses of HE can be defended by attributing normative significance to preserving the status quo or by invoking other theories of justice. Concluding remarks emphasize the practical uses of HE in light of this criticism.

2. Definitions and Indexes of Horizontal Equity

It seems backwards to criticize definitions and indexes of HE before exploring the motivation for the concept. Stiglitz (1982) has aptly characterized some past studies as "ad hoc approaches defining an index of horizontal inequaity and an index of vertical equity, and positing a social welfare function giving trade-offs between the two[, which] seems close to assuming what is to be analyzed." Yet, even before considering foundations directly, it can be demonstrated that traditional definitions of HE are insufficient for current uses, recently developed HE indexes do not follow from these definitions, and such indexes are almost certainly inconsistent with any reasonable normative basis for HE. These defects are not, however, inherent in the concept of HE or in the motivations for extending it; thus, the section closes by offering an index of HE that seeks to capture the relevant features.

2.1. Problems with Simple Definitions of Horizontal Equity

Most generally, and most commonly, HE is said to require the equal treatment of equals. (Musgrave 1959, 1976; Atkinson and Stiglitz 1980.) Feldstein (1976a) defines HE for evaluating tax reform: "if two individuals would have the same utility level if the tax remained unchanged, they should also have the same utility level if the tax is changed." In contrast, VE calls for an appropriate pattern of differentiation (inequality in treatment) among people who are not equals. (See Musgrave 1959, 1976.)

The notion of equal treatment by itself is insufficient. (Similar analysis applies to the expanded version of HE that would require almost equal treatment of those who are almost equal.[1]) First, unless HE is taken to be an absolute constraint,[2] one needs to add some measure of the degree to which HE is violated by any action. Second, HE applies only to equals; it provides no judgment with regard to individuals whose positions are not initially alike, even though the motivations usually suggested for the concept extend more broadly. Related to both of these problems, even an infinitesimal difference in treatment beyond whatever range is deemed "equal treatment" counts as a violation, while further deviations, no matter how significant, are ignored. Thus, once it is recognized that virtually all effects of any action are on individuals who are unequal—either initially or after even modest change—the core definition of HE is inapplicable.[3] All further analysis is *by definition* in the realm of VE, which addresses the appropriate treatment of unequals.

2.2. *Failures of Modified Definitions and Indexes of Horizontal Equity*

Recognizing some of these limitations has led investigators to develop measures of HE that go beyond its traditional definition. Most commonly, indexes measure the number or magnitude of order reversals or the rank correlation between the pre- and post-reform distribution of income. (See Atkinson 1980; King 1983; Plotnick 1982, 1984; and Rosen 1978; also discussed by Feldstein 1976a.) Of course, according to the classic definition, these are really VE judgments since they address the proper treatment of unequals—which suggests that the implicit value judgment must be specified and defended (see Shoup 1969), something that has not been done.

These elaborations are subject to many of the criticisms applicable to the initial definition: Minute movements leading to order reversals count as full violations of HE while substantial disturbances in the initial distribution that result in no order reversal are ignored.[4] The basic problem is that these measures, because they are based on reranking, do not vary continuously with the magnitude of the effect on each individual (or groups of individuals).

To illustrate these shortcomings, consider King's (1983) index, which measures affronts to HE by using a scaled order statistic (s_i) for each individual, defined as follows:

$$s_i = \frac{|y_{pi} - y_{ai}|}{y},$$

where y_{ai} and y_{pi} denote, respectively, "the *ex post* income levels corresponding to the rank of individual *i* in the ex ante and ex post distributions," and *y* denotes the mean income. This measure has some remarkable properties that are not noted by King (or by others taking this approach). First, consider two individuals, A and B, such that A has one cent more income in the ex ante income distribution than B, but two times the income of B in the ex post income distribution. Since there is no rank reversal, $s_A = s_B = 0$. Contrast this with the same situation, except that in the ex ante distribution, A has one cent less than B rather than one cent more. Now, $s_A = s_B = .67$. This large jump (in a two-person example, the maximum value of the indicator is 2) demonstrates how the proposed indicator is discontinuous in ex ante income levels. Moreover, it should be clear that, except at the point of the discontinuity, the indicator is totally unaffected by ex ante income levels. The indicator also has surprising properties in terms of changes in ex post income levels. Until there is a cross-over, $s_A = s_B = 0$. After the cross-over, the s_i's increase smoothly as the gap in income increases, with a discontinuity in the derivative at the crossover point (the derivative jumps from zero to a strictly positive number).[5] The analysis and indexes of many others have reflected a very similar approach.[6] It is hard to conceive of the normative principle that could justify measures with such properties.

2.3. *On the Inconsistency Between Concerns for Horizontal Equity and Economic Mobility*

Before continuing with an analysis of the justification for HE, this section comments briefly on recent indexes of economic mobility (MOB); the striking contrast between analysis of this concept and of HE reinforces the sense of weakness in the conceptual foundations of HE indexes. Despite the substantial sophistication devoted to measuring MOB, little attention has been given to why one cares about the concept in the first place—a problem emphasized in Shorrocks' (1978b) investigation. MOB has been said to be valued for a variety of reasons; these must be distinguished because each implies different definitions and measures. The most relevant interpretation for present purposes,[7] offered by Atkinson (1981), simply would consider MOB to be a good thing in its own right. Basically, this view of MOB is the mirror image to recent implementations of HE. Change from the status quo is preferred (rather than disliked) for its own sake. It turns out that many past attempts to examine MOB more precisely have implicitly adopted this characterization: Measures simply capture changes from the status quo distribution, which are assumed to be desirable.

The most obvious, yet most startling point is simply that, under a variety of interpretations, HE and MOB are direct opposites. The simple example of a reform that gives everyone an equal probability of taking the position of any individual in the income distribution is a massive affront to HE and, at the same time, the maximum possible degree of MOB (according to some measures). This opposition can be seen most clearly by examining King's (1983) article entitled "An Index of Inequality: With Applications to Horizontal Equity and Social Mobility." In one section, he offers and explores a particular index for HE. In the next, he claims to overcome prior difficulties in developing a satisfactory index for MOB by constructing "a normative index along the lines pursued above [i.e., in developing an index for HE]. The only difference is that it is usual *in the context of social mobility* to *favor* changes in the ordering of the distribution." Thus, he simply adopts his HE index as his MOB index, just changing the direction of the effect.[8] If he had attempted to combine VE, HE, and MOB into his total equity index all at the same time, the HE and MOB terms would essentially collapse.

This connection is not as apparent as it might be because King discusses VE and HE in one section, and pairs VE and MOB in the next. Immediately thereafter, he uses his approach to consider optimal taxation and offers an empirical application of his indexes; in both instances he measures overall inequity by using his combined index of VE and HE, making no comment indicating why the just-derived MOB index has been left out of the computation. King's conclusion suggests that his proposed index allows "horizontal equity *or* social mobility to be taken into account," without noting the importance and exclusive nature of the "or" in avoiding normative contradiction.

The idea that there is some connection between HE and MOB has not gone unnoticed by others (Atkinson 1980, Plotnick 1982). But the notion that those writing about HE and those writing about MOB were writing the same things, just switching signs and reversing normative positions whenever switching terminology, seems to have remained quite far from sight. Yet this connection between MOB and HE *measures* should hardly be surprising if some of the simplest motivations for the two *concepts* arise, respectively, from the ad hoc assumption of social preferences for and against changes from the status quo distribution. This suggests that all who use one measure or the other when evaluating proposed reforms are implicitly advocating one of these preferences at the expense of the other, although this underlying value choice typically remains hidden.

2.4. Toward a Working Definition of Horizontal Equity

Having raised doubts about recent applications of HE, the remainder of this investigation examines possible justifications. Initially, however, it is necessary to offer an index with *prima facie* plausibility. To avoid the difficulties specified in subsections 2.1 and 2.2, a measure of violations of HE must in some way reflect the number of individuals affected, weighted by the degree of the effect (i.e., distance of movement). Consider

$$I_{HE} = \frac{1}{2} \sum_i \sum_j [(y_{ai} - y_{aj}) - (y_{pi} - y_{pj})]^2,$$

where y_{ai}, y_{aj}, y_{pi}, and y_{pj} refer to the incomes of individuals *i* and *j* before (ante) and after (post) a reform. This measure sums the (squared) change in distance separating all pairs of individuals.[9]

The following discussion can be simplified by analyzing the five ways a pair of individuals can be affected by a reform. They can:

1. Move further apart (if initially unequal).
2. Move closer together (still remaining unequal).
3. Move apart from an initially equal position.
4. Move together, ending at an equal position.
5. Begin apart, cross over, and end up apart.

Possibility 5 is simply the combination of others (4 and 3).[10] In addition, there seems to be no compelling reason to attach much significance to 3 or 4, as distinguished from 1 or 2, since the latter pair encompass the former except for an infinitesimal movement at either the beginning or the end.

This index thus can be seen to have two central properties. First, in order to avoid the problems of other indexes it was necessary that no particular significance be attached to starting or ending at precise equality or to the cross-over point itself. Second, attaching negative weight to movements in both directions is central to HE. Since unequal treatment of equals most clearly violates HE, moving apart (1 or 3) must be registered by any HE index. But if HE were limited to being an objection to moving individuals further apart in the income distribution, it would solely be an objection to increased income inequality, subsumed in conventional notions of VE. *Hence, the central defining characteristic of HE—and its central force in policy applications—is that it also condemns moving individuals closer together in the income distribution (2 or 4), directly contrary to VE.* Note how distant this core feature is from the original definition of equal treatment of equals that most investigators abandon after introductory remarks—a definition that concerns the preservation of equality rather than opposition to enhanced equality. The next section demonstrates how this aspect of HE, although incorporated in various indexes, has been ignored in past attempts to motivate the concept when assessing the effects of reform on the distribution of income.

3. Horizontal Equity and the Welfarist Approach

Feldstein (1976a) has stated that "equal taxation of equals is implied directly by utilitarianism and does not require a separate principle of horizontal equity" when all individuals are assumed to have the same preferences. (See also Atkinson and Stiglitz 1980, Stiglitz 1982.) In simple examples this is often true because whatever reasons motivate a particular treatment of one individual will require the same treatment of another individual who is equal in all relevant respects.[11] (See Westen 1982.) Requiring HE would be redundant. Yet, in many instances, some incidental unequal treatment will be inevitable. For example, although purely random taxes can be avoided, some randomness in enforcement or mistakes in administration are unavoidable, and often significant. In addition, arbitrary distinctions may be necessary for reasons of convenience (for example, not all fringe benefits that conceptually are income can feasibly be taxed), and individuals with equal incomes may have acted differently, so that they may be differentially affected by a given reform.[12] In such instances, giving weight to HE—understood here to refer to any disruption in the pre-reform distribution of income—is in conflict with the social welfare tradition.[13] The previous section indicated how such an implementation of HE departs from its original motivations. This section suggests that much of the intuitive force behind recent considerations of HE is already accounted for in the economist's traditional use of a social welfare function, which involves evaluating policies based on their effects on individuals' utility.

3.1. Horizontal Equity as an Implicit Appeal to Vertical Equity

Feldstein's (1976a) major example illustrates how the intuitive appeal of HE can be traced to traditional considerations of VE and risk. He considers a tax reform that imposes costs in terms of HE as follows: 1000 taxpayers gain $10 each, at a cost of $1000 to each of 9 taxpayers (a net gain of $1000, but the losses are concentrated). All taxpayers begin with equal incomes and have identical utility functions. He demonstrates that the unequal treatment offsets part of the benefit of the reform; the greater the rate at which the marginal utility of income declines and the lower the initial level of income, the less desirable is the reform. But this result is all too familiar. The reform increases aggregate income but causes inequality in the distribution. The utilitarian framework he employs, like many others, is sensitive to income inequality: The greater is the loss in social welfare due to the resulting inequality, the less desirable is the reform. The only difference is that we generally refer to this effect under the rubric of VE, not HE.[14]

Note that in this example the choice of the status quo—which is the centerpiece of most definitions of HE, including Feldstein's—is clearly irrelevant to the comparative evaluation of the two states. In particular, if one considered the unequal state as the status quo and imagined moving back to what was originally considered to be the initial state, Feldstein's approach would lead to the same evaluation of each state; in this case, the distributive effects of the reform would be seen as desirable. Yet movement back to the initial state equally offends HE using the index I_{HE} offered above, and similar indications would follow from virtually all other definitions and indexes if his example were modified even slightly.[15] This suggests that the persuasive force behind Feldstein's example is captured in the standard social welfare framework whereas his earlier definitions of HE are inconsistent both with that framework and with his example. HE would register a loss from implementing both changes consecutively, while his example (and the social welfare approach more generally) indicate no net effect.[16]

This illustration can be generalized as follows. First, consider two individuals who are moved further apart in the income distribution as a result of a reform. I_{HE} will register some loss, and the loss will vary directly with the significance of the movement. Thus, the greater the increase in inequality caused by the reform, the greater the loss in HE. But, just as was the case with Feldstein's example, we find that HE seems to be measuring just what we are accustomed to considering under the guise of VE. HE and VE have the same sort of measure (distance-related)[17] for the same sort of change (moving apart) and both deem it undesirable.

Next, consider two individuals who are moved closer together in the income distribution as a result of a reform. Just as in the preceding instance, our measure of HE will register some loss, and the loss will vary directly with the significance of the movement. Thus, the more equality is enhanced by the reform, the greater the loss in HE. We again find that HE seems to be measuring just what we are accustomed to considering under the guise of VE. HE and VE again have the same sort of measure (distance-related) for the same sort of change (moving together). But here, HE indicates that the equity impact of the change is negative whereas VE indicates a positive evaluation. But what is the justification for this implication of HE? Examples offered to illustrate violations of HE typically begin with the assumption that all individuals initially have equal incomes, as was the case in Feldstein's illustration as well as those offered by others (e.g., Brennan 1971, Zodrow 1981).[18] This starting point is hardly surprising since the basic definition of HE requires equal treatment *of equals*. The separation of changes into movements together and movements apart, however, suggests that this set of examples has largely missed the issue. By starting with all being equal, all movements are apart; hence, HE yields the same verdict that VE would in any event.[19] It is revealing that those exploring HE, in attempting to motivate their analysis, have not chosen examples involving increased equality, which section 2 has shown to be the relevant application if HE is to have independent significance.

3.2. *Horizontal Equity as an Implicit Appeal to Risk Analysis*

HE arguably could be reinterpreted as an expression of concern for avoiding the imposition of risk. For example, a random tax's arbitrary unequal treatment of equals is welfare reducing, even setting aside for the moment the earlier argument that VE provides a basis for this conclusion. The random tax and a certain tax on each group that raises the same revenues[20] produce the same expected income in the post-reform state, yet the random tax is associated with a lower expected utility precisely because of the risk that is imposed.

Unlike the purely random tax, Feldstein's (1976a) example of the reform producing benefits of $10 to most individuals but a loss of $1000 to a few is similar in its effects to many realistic reforms. Feldstein discovers, however, that he must specify the degree of risk aversion (and the level of ex ante income) in order to evaluate the proposed reform and various modifications thereof. Now one might question whether risk is really implicated here, because it was clear from the beginning who the gainers and losers would be. Yet if an earlier announcement had been made describing the general distributive impact of the reform, but not indicating who the gainers and losers would be, followed the next day by a revelation of the complete proposal and its incidence, our judgment as to the equities or impact on social welfare surely would be unchanged. Thus, most government reforms, which have the characteristic that they impose both benefits and losses, can be analogized, for example, to a change in climate that results in substantial benefits but imposes significant losses through changes in asset values. Whether imposed by the government, nature, or a casino, there is risk all the same. This connection between risk from uncertainty concerning future government policy and other sources of risk is explored in Kaplow (1986, 1987).

Consider further this connection between the imposition of risk and evaluation of the effect of reforms on the distribution of income. It is well known that the statistical measure of variance can be used to describe the probability distribution that characterizes an uncertain prospect or as a summary statistic to describe the distribution of some attribute of a population—e.g., income—after the results of some event (even one not embodying any uncertainty). The frequency interpretation of probability presents a familiar connection between ex ante uncertainty and resulting distributions. One can describe the relevant situations from either an ex ante or an ex post perspective without changing the underlying phenomenon—the former perspective is more in accord with risk analysis, the latter with VE.[21]

Previous discussions of HE contain a number of clues suggesting some connection between HE and risk, although the claim that there is a direct linkage has never, to my knowledge, been asserted. In addition to Feldstein's use of the Arrow-Pratt measure of relative risk aversion, he also sometimes talks of gambles and future risks. Rosen (1978) and Stiglitz (1982) use a random tax as their primary example. King (1983) notes that his HE index bears some resemblance to a risk premium. Hettich (1979) uses a variance measure to capture the loss in HE. Brennan's (1971) discussion of HE frequently refers to variance and related characteristics of probability distributions, and the arguments he uses to motivate his HE measure resemble those often used in motivating statistical measures of dispersion. Moreover, he derives the result that a government choosing among a variety of tax sources—each of which affronts HE to some degree—will always do best by using a combination of all of them, including those causing the greatest affront to HE. Brennan fails to note, however, that this is *precisely* the well known result of standard portfolio theory with regard to how diversification reduces risk. Despite such indications, none of these authors suggests that HE amounts to another way of talking about risk in a particular context.

Risk is a concept that economists (and others) have studied much more carefully than they have studied HE. Using the terminology associated with risk and uncertainty invokes certain intuitions, as well as particular measures, that aid in one's analysis. In contrast, HE is coming to be associated with conflicting indexes that fail to provide even a remotely accurate measure or judgment concerning risk, if that is really the basis for concern.

4. Horizontal Equity Outside the Social Welfare Framework

4.1. Normative Significance of the Status Quo

In order to support more recent applications of HE in the context of tax reform, it is necessary to accord direct normative significance to the status quo distribution of income, independent of the welfare consequences in the post-reform state. After all, HE indexes are measures of the degree to which reform modifies the pre-reform distribution of income. A major justificatory problem posed by any such formulation concerns why the status quo is to be intrinsically valued, thus supporting a preference against all changes in position, when the status quo was itself the product of countless changes throughout history. This cannot be viewed as a mere "definitional" problem, because the very thing to be defined is to be given direct normative significance if HE indexes are to be justified.[22]

The issue is well illustrated by the previous example that involved a reform (moving, say, from state A to state B), followed by a later reform that had the effect of restoring the initial situation. For the latter reform, the status quo is B, producing a double loss in HE from changing and then moving back again. A more extended example reinforces the point. Consider a parent raising two children. One child starts our story with 10, the other with 8. The parent periodically has some discretionary income that can be used to benefit the children—by purchasing books, sending them to summer camp, taking them to the dentist, and the like. As it turns out, the discretionary income usually becomes available 4 at a time, and most relevant purchases are lumpy, also costing 4 each. On the first occasion, the parent decides to spend the 4 on the child who started with 8, thinking that such treatment is more fair since that child is then less well off and the resulting distribution is more equal than if the opposite choice is made. Sometime later when 4 more is available, it is spent on the other child, for the same reasons. This pattern continues. I doubt anyone would describe the parent's decision rule as remotely inequitable. Yet the effect at each stage is a loss in HE by any reasonable measure.

The most obvious response if one hopes to defend HE measures is to describe this not as a number of separate actions but rather as a single action: the adoption of a decision rule for the period during which the children are cared for by the parent. This recharacterization essentially treats the situation (10,8) as the status quo throughout. But how is this definition to be justified? Which "reforms" should be combined? Why not all reforms, past and future? Note that any such combinations would require a wholly different application of HE indexes than has been conventional. Does it matter how much time passes between the periods? Not that much time passes between many reforms—the recent sequence of major tax reforms being but one example. Would we feel the same way if the status quo, instead of being (10,8), were (100,1)? Or if the status quo, regardless of the income levels, has arisen as a result of theft? Or if one of the children was extremely sick and needed medical care for five periods in a row? Should the notion of HE count as a reason against rectifying theft or caring for a sick child first? Moreover, even if all these problems were overcome, one still would have to determine which point in the past decade, century, or era corresponds to the place of (10,8) in the above example. Thus, one must determine why it is that some pre-existing (or never-existing) "status quo" is important and then analyze what relationship such a hypothetical state bears to the actually existing status quo.

Even if some of these questions seem to demand excessive precision, it must be emphasized that some sort of answer to each is required before HE, understood as a desire to maintain the status quo distribution of income, could be assessed in the context of a particular tax reform. In the literature, such assessments are never attempted. Moreover, there remains the question of the independent weight to be given to the status quo. Returning to the illustration, once the parent has evaluated the relative needs of the two children, their merits, relevant considerations of equality, and the like, one must then ask why and when (if ever) the parent should make a different decision than indicated by these factors on the ground that the otherwise desirable result incidentally changes the existing distribution of welfare between the two children. (Furthermore, recall that, as developed in section 2.4, if one is to decide differently on this account, one's decision should change regardless of whether this incidental effect is in the direction of further inequality or further equality. VE objects to inequality and favors equality whereas HE constitutes an objection to change itself.)

Another alternative to attaching direct significance to the status quo would involve attempting, in the manner of Nozick (1974), to portray the status quo as the result of an intrinsically justified *process*. Thus, the status quo can be defined as the distribution that results from this process. This gambit, however, is subject to essentially the same problems just described. There must be some prior "status quo" from which that process began, again raising the foundational problem. In dealing with the neverending sequence of changes that occur in any society, one would have to isolate all those that violated the just process and recompute what the world would have been like had those changes never occurred, modified by any desire to accord some respect to actions that arguably were justified given the imperfect circumstances in which they were made.[23]

Thus, the status quo as conventionally defined and as traditionally used in measuring HE—which consists of the income distribution moments before the pending reform, and shortly after countless previous reforms—would only by the most extreme of repeated historical coincidence be very relevant under this process approach. The appropriate comparison would much more closely resemble the comparison of the post-reform state with some externally specified distribution, or at least results that could be speculatively derived therefrom. Finally, even if the external distribution from this process perspective were specified, it is not clear how violations of HE would be measured. Arguably, all reforms would have to be prohibited (which apparently is Nozick's (1974) position)—an extreme approach criticized in note 2, and one in contradiction with prior attempts to develop indexes of HE. Moreover, in an imperfect world where such an absolute constraint had often been violated, it might be thought appropriate to adopt reforms that made the resulting distribution conform more closely to the ideal. But such an approach also has little to do with recent implementations of HE. The status quo is now devalued; reforms can increase HE. These problems are pursued further in the next subsection's examination of broader attempts to justify HE outside of the traditional social welfare framework.

4.2. Horizontal Equity and Distributions External to the Status Quo

The difficulties just described arose from our attempt to give intrinsic significance to the status quo itself. It may not be the status quo that we care about after all, but rather some other distribution that is capable of independent justification. (A pre-existing normatively significant status quo could be viewed simply as an instance of this more general class.) Some authors discussing HE in the context of tax reform in fact use as their reference point not the status quo, but some other distribution such as that existing if the ideal tax system were in place or if there were no taxes.[24] Departures from the status quo would no longer be deemed relevant, and some reforms could be seen as increasing HE.[25]

Yet any approach relying upon an external distribution is hard to reconcile with the traditional concept and measures of HE. The status quo generally would be irrelevant; social welfare—including all equity concerns—would be measured solely by reference to the final distribution. In addition, there would be no particular reason to expect the idea of equal treatment to have special significance. If the post-reform state is not ideal, there would be no *a priori* implication following from the fact that the shortcoming arose from unequal treatment of equals rather than, for example, equal treatment of unequals. Of course, it might well be an improvement if two "ideal world equals" that were formerly treated in a less than ideal manner, and unequally, were instead treated equally, by taking the average treatment that both received. But gains from moving individuals closer together are already encompassed in VE and, in many instances, by considerations of efficiency.[26]

There also is only a modest connection between more complex measures of HE that have been developed and an externally specified ideal. To be sure, an index of HE such as that suggested in subsection 2.4 (where the external distribution is substituted for the status quo distribution) would tend to be positively correlated with the degree to which a state fell short of the external ideal. But it would be more natural (and more accurate) to measure the degree to which one failed in achieving the ideal by reference to the objectives used in generating the external distribution. More fundamentally, even if an index of HE were useful as a proxy, such an index would hardly be indicating a value to be traded off *against* optimal achievement of the objectives that generated the external distribution. Rather, it indicates the degree to which these other stated goals *are being achieved*. Finally, to the extent one's reference distribution was derived in a second-best framework that balances a number of factors—as is often the case—it would be inappropriate to base a measure of inequity on deviations from that second-best distribution rather than from the unattainable first best.

All these considerations indicate that HE as embodied in recent indexes would be a totally derivative concept, not an independent normative consideration. To the extent HE departs from such a role, it is not only outside of the traditional social welfare framework, but inconsistent with more general notions of optimally achieving any set of stated objectives. In sum, the closer one gets to a plausible justification, the further one moves from recent implementations of HE. It thus seems appropriate to consider more carefully various concepts of equity that appear to merit attention and develop pragmatic measures tailored directly to those concepts.

5. Concluding Remarks

The familiar definition of HE is inconsistent with attempted applications, and more elaborate indexes often produce paradoxical results. In addition, the illustrations that have been offered to motivate recent implementations of HE involve precisely those instances where traditional concerns for risk and VE are sufficient to explain the intuition against the distributive effects that arise. Finally, it is doubtful that current approaches could be based upon attempts to attribute normative significance to the status quo or derived from other intrinsically valued distributions. In either case, the command for equal treatment was seen to be a *by-product* of the optimization process, not an independent factor to *trade off against* whatever normative principle is represented by the posited distribution. It thus appears that the desire to capture our intuitive sense of justice cannot be met by continued attempts to derive ever more complex measures of HE that are not grounded in the original motivation of the concept or some other principles that are identified and defended.

In the tax reform contexts in which HE

indexes are applied, pre-reform equals in the income distribution are often equal by happenstance or as a result of undesirable aspects of the status quo that the reform is designed to change. Post-reform inequality thus may be an appropriate result, there being relevant differences between individuals that justify unequal treatment. Much unequal treatment is, however, more incidental. Yet, so long as such inequality is not capricious and is justified—often by the excessive administrative cost or other adverse effects of attempting to remedy it—there is no obvious affront to the principles of justice originally offered to motivate the HE concept. After all, HE demands equal treatment only when there is no legitimate basis for inequality. To be sure, unequal treatment does raise concerns for overall economic inequality and may involve the imposition of risk (as when there is the prospect of reform that will produce "windfall" gains and losses). When that is the case, such effects should be identified and subject to the sort of analysis that has been developed to address these concerns, rather than being measured by an index not designed for this purpose.

From a practical perspective, it will often be useful to pay particular attention to the unequal treatment of equals, even though the measures offered by HE indexes are not of independent normative significance. First, to the extent that equal treatment of equals is often implied by the maximizaton of any quasi-concave objective function, unequal treatment may indicate the potential to improve upon the existing situation. For example, in much of the tax reform debate, discovering violations of HE entails identifying wedges that create inefficiency or making appropriate relative income determinations among individuals that are necessary to determine the degree of inequality for application of VE norms.

Second, violation of HE on a repeated basis might have adverse effects on incentives. And, independent of the effects on behavior, the simple imposition of risk (or increase in dispersion of the income distribution) is generally undesirable, so we should be attentive to unequal treatment to the extent it is connected to these effects. These and related issues are studied in the context of assessing transition policy in Kaplow (1986, 1987).

Third, Atkinson (1980) and Jenkins (1986) have noted that in attempting to measure the degree of equality (VE) resulting from a reform, one can be misled by examining the post-reform averages for groups of pre-reform equals to the extent equals are not treated equally.

Fourth, the status quo orientation of HE could be motivated by intuitions relating to endogenous preferences—for example, that utility is determined not only by the absolute level of income or wealth, but changes in that level.[27] The rationale might be that, over time, individuals and households make investments in tangible assets, human capital, and information that are most valuable at a certain level of well-being, making unanticipated adjustment costly. Alternatively, support may be found in various psychological interpretations of the sources of utility, particularly those—such as Veblen's (1899) original formulation or more recent interpretations such as Yitzhaki (1982)—that emphasize relative incomes within reference groups.[28] Empirical evidence concerning disparities in offer and asking prices that exceed what can be explained by wealth effects, such as that offered by Knetsch and Sinden (1984), as well as asymmetric treatment of gains and losses in situations involving uncertainty, as documented and modeled by Kahneman and Tversky (1979), similarly suggest modifications in the typical formulation of the utility function. Of course, even if different utility functions were deemed appropriate to employ in welfare analysis, the resulting formulation is still within the welfarist tradition. Moreover, the most direct implication of such modifications is that welfare analysis should not treat all individuals—particularly those at different income levels—as if they have the same utility functions, since the function itself would depend upon current income or wealth.[29] These implications, although arising from justifications for giving independent weight to the status quo distribution, are not aspects of HE as generally understood and implemented.

Fifth, as suggested by Atkinson (1980) and Plotnick (1984), political advisors would certainly care about HE. This is true, of course, since how people are treated is highly relevant to how they will react.[30] It is a bit surprising, however, that this justification for the concept would be offered without further explanation amidst what appear to have been intended as normative discussions.

Finally, quite apart from the effects of violating HE on individuals, imposing requirements of equal treatment as a constraint might limit actions by imperfect government institutions that do not in fact advance social welfare. For example, Stiglitz (1982) suggests on these grounds that permitting unequal treatment may make arbitrary discrimination favoring certain interest groups more likely. He is correct that this view implies that analysis of HE such as that "contained in Feldstein, Rosen and King may not be focusing on the critical issues" since his argument, like the others noted in this section, relates to determining the likely effects of government action, not to evaluating them. (This application is considered further in note 2.)

That violations of HE can have so many implications helps to explain the attention the concept has received. It must be emphasized, however, that these reasons have one thing in common: They are not reasons why HE in itself is valued in any normative sense. Rather, each are reasons why unequal treatment may provide information as to the actual motivations for or effects of a given reform, whether such effects are to be evaluated by a maximizer of social welfare (who cares about risk, incentives, and VE), a politician on the move, or anyone else using whatever criteria are justified in a particular context. Each rationale may warrant further analysis in some instances, but none supports implementations of HE of the sort now in use.

ENDNOTES

**A prior version appeared as NBER Working Paper No. 1697. Comments from Lucian Bebhuk, Martin Feldstein, John Parsons, Steven Shavell, Lawrence Summers, and the anonymous referees are gratefully acknowledged. Support was received from the John M. Olin Foundation through the Harvard Program in Law and Economics.

[1]The problems raised in the text would arise at whatever boundaries were to be drawn to separate the almost equal from the not sufficiently equal. As will be clear in section 2.2, these problems inhere in any measure that is not continuous in the degree of change caused by reform.

[2]Atkinson and Stiglitz (1980) suggest that imposing HE as a constraint that cannot be violated in reaching other objectives may in fact be the most appealing interpretation of HE. This lexicographic preference, in addition to being subject to the criticism developed in the text, has little appeal as applied to the context considered here. It seems implausible that the slightest inequality in treatment of status quo equals would be thought more important than even substantial gains in overall welfare levels (including to the individuals treated unequally) and significant improvements in equality or other objectives. Similarly, this lexicographic approach would accord no weight to inequitable treatment of whatever magnitude to individuals that were not precise equals in the status quo. Finally, typical reform proposals inevitably involve at least *some* violation of HE—and, admitting various differences among individuals (see Feldstein 1976a) or unavoidable administrative error, this would be true of all reforms. Similarly, it is necessary to rely on enforcement strategies that have random aspects in virtually all policy contexts. HE used as a constraint thus virtually forbids reform—and the enforcement of most existing laws and policies.

Interpreting HE as a side constraint may have some force in terms of prohibiting arbitrary discrimination, for example among individuals of different race. See Musgrave (1976). Justification for such an approach would probably rest on assumptions concerning the fallibility of human institutions, since nondiscrimination would typically be implied by social welfare maximization in any event. The criticism that the side constraint imposes an unjustifiable lexicographic ordering and that the constraint is generally violated by making virtually any reform would be less powerful since the constraint would typically be satisfied in such cases at no—or little—cost in social welfare. It is the application of the side constraint approach to any change in income or wealth that results directly or indirectly from any change in government policy that leads to crippling implications.

Shleifer and Waldmann (1985) have defended HE as a constraint on the ground that it might assist in addressing the time consistency problems of the sort developed by Kydland and Prescott (1977). They examine the well-known problem that, ex post, it is optimal to adopt a complete capital levy, which, ex ante, will destroy investment incentives. Since in their basic model HE prohibits any reform, assuming adherence to HE does imply that a capital levy will not be employed ex post. (For an alternative approach to this problem, see Kotlikoff, Persson, and Svensson (1986).) Despite their contrary claim, however, this approach is little different than simply positing specific abilities to commit. HE is broader, as they argue, but precisely because it rules out all desirable ex post actions as well. (See also Mueller (1979) discussing HE as a constraint on government revenue-raising capacity.)

[3]For example, Schmalensee (1984) admits that his measure of horizontal inequity is zero if no two individuals are exactly alike, yet attributes significance to the magnitude of inequality in treatment among those who are identical, and insists that this magnitude is of a different normative order than similar differences arising between individuals who initially are different, regardless of how small that initial difference might be.

[4]Part of this problem has been noted by Plotnick (1982) and Rosen (1978). Yet Rosen's distance-sensitive measure has some bizarre properties—for example, a complete reversal in the income distribution registers no loss in HE. Only the absolute value of the distances, measured before and after the reform, not the total change in distance, is used; his approach sharply differs from a direct distance measure when there are crossovers.

[5]Essentially, negative weight is attached only to any "overshooting," i.e., movements apart after the reform has reached the point of equality in ex post income. This might be viewed as a sort of VE measure since, as will be discussed in subsection 3.1, HE and VE give the same indications when individuals are moved further apart in the distribution. This does not fully hold, however, since movement apart absent a cross-over is ignored by King's index, and the index also places no beneficial weight on movements together up to the cross-over point.

[6]For example, Feldstein (1976a) simply asserts that "the introduction of a tax should not alter the *ordering* of individuals by utility level" (emphasis added) and later criticizes one possible measure of order reversals because it "would be distorted . . . if the utilities were altered by a nonlinear function" that preserved ranking perfectly, not noticing the somewhat bizarre judgments implicit in such criticism. Feldstein's implicit defense of a discontinuous index is most surprising in light of his criticism of Rawls' (1971) difference principle on the basis of its discontinuity.

Plotnick explicitly advocates the need for distance measures (1982, page 383 and note 17, page 388; 1984, page 5). But elsewhere, Plotnick (1984, note 7) states that: "Useful measures will *not* be concerned between initial and actual final levels of well-being, nor between initial and final rank-preserving levels. These comparisons may also be of interest, but they are not appropriate for assessing horizontal inequity." (See also 1984, page 11.) He never resolves this tension. Four of the five indexes Plotnick (1984) examines exhibit precisely the character of King's index. The fifth, based on the Spearman rank correlation coefficient, takes no account of distance, which he agrees makes it less satisfactory.

[7]There exist others as well. MOB may be desired because, as stated by Atkinson (1981), "it is instrumental in leading to greater efficiency." From this perspective, MOB is seen primarily as a symptom of a freely functioning economy or as a policy instrument that can be directly manipulated (increased) in order to improve the efficiency of the economy, either interpretation being wholly consistent with the traditional social welfare framework and thus of no further interest here. This should be contrasted with a decision to place intrinsic value on greater equality of opportunity. Of course, observed MOB would only be a symptom of such equality, as MOB can also be generated, for example, by arbitrary fiat or random events, neither of which would indicate that opportunities are more equal in the relevant sense. This interpretation of MOB, therefore, calls more for a direct evaluation of the processes by which individuals' positions are endogenously determined before and after a reform, rather than measurement of the actual change in welfare positions directly resulting from a reform. In particular, equal opportunity in this sense can be understood as a preference for equality in ex ante positions, where ex ante refers not to before a particular reform, but to before the processes permitted as a result of any reforms have produced particular outcomes for different individuals. MOB also can be interpreted as a dynamic analog of VE, the idea being that the greater the movement within the income distribution over an individual's lifetime, the more likely highs and lows average out in some manner. See Shorrocks (1978a).

[8]Compare conditions 1–3 (1983, pages 105–06) with conditions 1′–3′ (page 109); equation 23 with equation 30; and Theorem 2 with Theorem 3.

[9]It may be noted that the expression for I_{HE} includes the terms for where $i = j$, but since those terms equal zero, they can be ignored. Simple manipulation shows that

$$I_{HE} = \sum_i (\Delta y_i)^2 - (\Delta y)^2,$$

where Δy_i is the change in income of individual i caused by the reform and Δy is the change in total income caused by the reform. One could weight the index by the inverse of the population to compare relative inequality among societies of differing sizes. With this final modification, this function is in the class axiomatized by Cowell (1985, expression 59). See also Russell (1985).

[10]This is not to say that any particular measure will be separable in that each of the two movements can be weighed without regard to the magnitude of the other. Rather, my claim is that the *character* of the measure—i.e., whether a movement is good or bad and why—in instance 5 can be understood from how one evaluates instances 3 and 4.

[11]Exceptions to this general proposition due to diversities in tastes (see Feldstein 1976a, Musgrave 1976), offsetting the incentive to substitute labor for leisure (see Weiss 1976), or nonconvexities in the feasible set (see Stiglitz 1982) are not relevant for present purposes.

[12]See also note 11. With respect to the latter instances, which account for a large portion of the unequal treatment that is the focus of attention when measuring the HE brought about by tax reform, one might simply say that the individuals are not equal in all relevant respects and thus the concept of HE, as traditionally understood, is inapplicable. So long as the inequality in treatment is rationally based on the differences in circumstances, there is no inequity. Thus, it becomes clear that many of the problems discussed in the text are not in the original motivation for HE, but rather in recent attempts to equate changes in the pre-reform income distribution with inequity,

regardless of the cause of the distributive effects.

In some instances, resulting unequal treatment could be rectified by a complex compensation or grandfathering scheme. For present purposes, this is assumed to be prohibitively costly. More generally, the issue arises so long as perfect compensation involves some cost, for then it would be necessary to consider the magnitude of the HE violation and the weight to be attributed to HE in order to determine whether the compensation was justified.

[13]Technically, HE can be seen as violating the social welfare tradition in two ways. First, it introduces nonwelfare information (see Sen 1977)—in this case positions in the distribution of income in a state (the status quo) other than the one being evaluated. In social choice theory discussions, this would be termed a violation of the anonymity condition. Second, as discussed in note 26, increases in an individual's welfare, ceteris paribus, can reduce social welfare. Analysis in section 4 suggests, moreover, that existing conceptions of HE also seem inconsistent with the notion of optimization more generally.

[14]This example is interpreted further in section 3.2 as illustrating the imposition of risk. It will then be argued that both of these interpretations are interchangeable since both arise from the assumed concavity of the utility function. Feldstein (1976a) claims that "[t]he concavity of the utility functions *together with the assumption* that everyone should be treated as if they had the same utility function and the same initial income imply that the optimal tax change may be smaller than if horizontal equity is ignored." The important point here is that concavity alone is what drives his conclusion—i.e., the concept of HE is superfluous. To prove that it is a necessary condition, simply consider (1) where utility functions are linear, in which case his social welfare measure simply reflects the net gain of $1000, independent of the distribution, and (2) where utility functions are convex, in which case the unequal treatment actually would improve welfare under his measure. Concavity will often be sufficient as well, for even if individuals had different initial incomes or different utility functions, the unequal incidence would tend to lower social welfare. The exception would be where the losers happened to be those with the lowest marginal utility of income and the gainers those with the highest—which typically would be a redistribution from the rich to the poor. But that is precisely what is captured by VE. The assumption that all should be treated as if they have the same utility function is usually justified either as an approximation for an unmeasurable reality or as dictated by egalitarian principles, which are directly linked to economists' references to VE. (The "as if same initial income" assumption is discussed further in the text that follows.)

Yet, in addition to the fact that this equal income assumption does not really drive the analysis, the assumption is inappropriate, particularly in the context of tax policy. Feldstein's argument that, for example, courts often ignore unequal income seems beside the point for tax policy, which is explicitly concerned with the allocation of tax burden according to income level, is not wholly true; e.g., damage awards do reflect the income level of the victim; and, where true, is typically capable of independent justification (ignoring the income level of the injurer is often supported by administrative concerns) or simply may be wrong.

[15]Consider, for example, moving back to Feldstein's initial situation, but overshooting by 1 cent for each person. There would be a complete order reversal between the two groups.

[16]Consider the well known example in which there exist two groups of individuals with different abilities. The utilitarian solution may well entail a reversal in ranking from the pre-tax status quo. (See Atkinson and Stiglitz 1980, Mirlees 1971, King 1983.) Achieving VE in this example clearly affronts HE. Plotnick (1984) advances the general argument that "[u]nless the socially optimal distribution is one of full equality, those earning more initial well-being should surely have greater final well-being than those earning less." Yet one might ask why the status quo distribution should be given normative weight. Since it is assumed in the example that individuals did not determine their own abilities, it seems no more unfair for the less able to be better off due to accident of birth than for the more able to be better off due to the same accident. The problem of justifying normative weight being attributed to the status quo is pursued further in subsection 4.1.

[17]Both HE and VE could be interpreted as being concerned not with absolute changes, but relative changes, measured for example by proportions relative to the mean. Similar analysis would apply.

[18]A modification with very similar effects is when the population is divided into large groups, all perfectly equal within each, as is the case in White and White (1965).

[19]At most, HE can be said to give added weight to this preference, but when there are no movements together being considered and no explicit formula is offered to combine the HE judgments with other factors, the difference in weighting has no operational significance.

[20]A strictly random tax might not, but one can similarly imagine a tax that is random as to each individual but designed to raise a specified amount of revenue overall. Incentive effects are ignored here.

[21]That the same phenomena can be interpreted equally well in terms of risk or VE should hardly be surprising. At least in the utilitarian framework, concerns for VE traditionally have been justified by reference to the decreasing marginal utility of income, which is precisely the source of risk aversion. In fact, Harsanyi (1953, 1977) has modeled the VE issue by using the methods of decisionmaking under uncertainty, taking as the starting point a hypothetical situation in which individuals do not know which person they will be in any possible social state. This framework suggests that each would choose states by maximizing expected utility, implying unanimous agreement upon the utilitarian criterion. States with greater inequality (lower in VE) are opposed because of the risk to each that they would be one of the individuals at the low end of the income distribution. In addition, Harsanyi (1955, 1977) has shown that acceptance of the axioms for rational choice under uncertainty for both social and individual preferences also leads to the utilitarian criterion.

[22]Plotnick (1981) advocates using the status quo—despite philosophical objections—"on pragmatic grounds [since] it may not be too bad. If, despite the contrary arguments that can be offered, most persons

tacitly accept the fairness of the preredistributive rankings when making judgments on redistributive equity, a useful measure of [horizontal] inequity must also accept this ranking." But redistributive judgments usually reject the preredistributive situation—almost by definition. In addition, by this analysis, violations of HE from past reforms are ignored. Thus, if a reform were enacted over Plotnick's objections on HE grounds, even that post-reform distribution would be given normative significance in evaluating the next reform—including the repeal of the reform just (inappropriately) enacted. Finally, whatever norms provide the *basis* for any such tacit acceptance of the fairness of the status quo should provide the foundation for equity measures, as discussed later in this section.

Plotnick (1984) discusses how different initial positions should be selected for analyzing various policies. He concedes "that whatever the initial measure selected by the analyst, he or she is implicitly assuming the initial ranking to be fair." The problem, however, is that in each of his examples a different initial position is selected, and thus the set of implicit fairness assumptions are directly contradictory. He does not explain how inconsistent normative assumptions can simultaneously be maintained in analyzing a single normative concept.

[23]Nozick (1974) is often referenced for a process defense of the status quo. Yet his process theory is applicable only if original entitlements and all subsequent transfers have been in accord with his justifications. If not, he supports rectification to account for past injustice, and willingly notes that such reparations could justify substantial government action that disturbs the status quo distribution (1974, pages 152–53, 230–31). The argument in the text suggests that most process approaches one can envision would be subject to precisely these limitations in attempting to justify giving weight directly to the status quo distribution.

[24]For examples of the latter, see Brown (1983), King (1983), Plotnick (1982). The latter approach raises the distinction sometimes made in the HE literature, traced to Feldstein (1976a), between tax *design* and tax *reform*. Reform, which has been referred to throughout, defines the status quo as that which exists prior to the change. Subject to the numerous problems noted in the text, this admits of some definition, even if lacking in normative significance. By contrast, design takes as the reference point not the status quo itself, but a hypothetical world in which no tax exists. Choosing the perspective of design versus reform is not a matter that should be taken lightly since the two definitions can lead to contradictory results—i.e., design A can have better HE than design B, yet reforming from B to A can only diminish HE by the reform-oriented definition. Similarly, one would not simultaneously advocate that, in the case of a "reform," the status quo (in particular, characterized by the existing tax system) has great normative significance whereas in the case of greater change—tax (re)design—the normative significance of the status quo would disappear altogether (to be replaced by some other reference point). Any of the choices suggested by the tax *design* way of thinking are purely arbitrary in normative terms, except to the extent they refer to some independently justified ideal and the corresponding distribution thereby implied, in which case the discussion in the text would apply.

[25]As he operates in this context, it is not clear why Hettich (1979) claims that his index is a measure of HE and not VE. His external reference distribution is chosen based on preferences concerning progressivity and his index measures departures from that distribution. (See also Hettich 1983.) His argument that partial expansions of a less-than-comprehensive tax base may rationally be rejected based on pursuit of the goals of HE and VE can surely be supported based on VE considerations alone. (His argument is a simple application of the theory of second best.) In fact, his index registers a substantial loss in HE when equals are treated perfectly equally, but unequals are taxed in proportions that deviate from the optimal distribution of the tax burden, which clearly is a VE concern. If his measure were truly to capture VE, however, it would measure VE directly rather than measuring departures from a distribution derived in part based on VE considerations. Hettich's (1979, 1983) conclusion that VE and HE cannot be separated in making policy judgments is not a "result," but rather an interpretation of his arbitrarily selected aggregate equity index that was not derived from any clear statement of the basis for or meaning of VE and HE concerns.

[26]It is not clear why upward deviations are deemed undesirable in the HE context. With VE, this is the case only to the extent that others at lower points in the income distribution are made worse off. In contrast, the HE concept would attach independent *negative* weight to gains regardless of their adverse effects on others. Hettich (1983) is typical: "With regard to [horizontal] equity, no cancellation occurs, *of course*. According to the principle of equal treatment of equals, paying too little [tax] is as undesirable as paying too much." No further motivation or justification for this normative approach is offered.

[27]As a simple, though extreme illustration, it can be demonstrated that, for a reform that does not change total income, but only the distribution, the index I_{HE} presented in subsection 2.4 corresponds to the traditional utilitarian social welfare function in the case where individual utility is a quadratic function of the *change* in income—i.e., $U = \alpha + \beta\Delta y - \gamma\Delta y^2$.

[28]Within each reference group, the relevant concept is VE—i.e., unequal treatment of equals involves increasing the degree of inequality in the group, and increasing equality within the reference group is considered to be desirable, contrary to the dictates of HE.

[29]Implementing such an approach in practice would be even more complex than suggested by the discussion in the text. For such concerns, it would surely matter whether the effects of a reform were permanent, what the trend of income was over time, and if additional prospects affecting the same individuals were on the horizon.

[30]Since the concept of equal treatment of equals has so much surface appeal, the unequal treatment in itself may have intrinsic political significance even if it lacks intrinsic normative significance. People are often quite attached to the status quo, regardless of the degree of justice entailed in producing it. Independently, the cry of unequal treatment derives much rhetorical power from its force in unrelated contexts, such as those involving racial discrimination.

REFERENCES

Atkinson, A. B., 1980, "Horizontal Equity and the Distribution of the Tax Burden," in: H. Aaron and M. J. Boskin, eds., *The Economics of Taxation* (Brookings Institution, Washington, D.C.), 3–18.

Atkinson, A. B., 1981, "The Measurement of Economic Mobility," in: A. B. Atkinson, *Social Justice and Public Policy* (MIT Press, Cambridge), 61–75.

Atkinson, A. B. and J. E. Stiglitz, 1980, *Lectures on Public Economics* (McGraw-Hill, New York).

Brennan, G., 1971, "Horizontal Equity: An Extension of an Extension," *Public Finance* 26, 437–456.

Brown, E., 1983, "Comment: Bequests and Horizontal Equity Under a Consumption Tax," *National Tax Journal* 36, 511–513.

Cowell, F. A., 1985, "Measures of Distributional Change: An Axiomatic Approach," *Review of Economic Studies* 52, 135–151.

Feldstein, M., 1976a, "On the Theory of Tax Reform," *Journal of Public Economics* 6, 77–104.

Feldstein, M., 1976b, "Compensation in Tax Reform," *National Tax Journal* 29, 123–130.

Harsanyi, J. C., 1953, "Cardinal Utility in Welfare Economics and in the Theory of Risk-Taking," *Journal of Political Economy* 61, 434–435.

Harsanyi, J. C., 1955, "Cardinal Welfare, Individualistic Ethics, and Interpersonal Comparisons of Utility," *Journal of Political Economy* 63, 309–321.

Harsanyi, J. C., 1977, *Rational Behavior and Bargaining Equilibrium in Games and Social Situations* (Cambridge University Press, Cambridge).

Hettich, W., 1979, "A Theory of Partial Tax Reform," *Canadian Journal of Economics* 12, 692–712.

Hettich, W., 1983, "Reforms of the Tax Base and Horizontal Equity," *National Tax Journal* 36, 417–427.

Jenkins, S., 1986, "Reranking and the Analysis of Income Redistribution," University of Bath Papers in Political Economy 86/01.

Kahneman, D. and A. Tversky, 1979, "Prospect Theory: An Analysis of Decision Under Risk," *Econometrica* 47, 263–291.

Kaplow, L., 1986, "An Economic Analysis of Legal Transitions," *Harvard Law Review* 99, 509–617.

Kaplow, L., 1987, Optimal Transition Policy: Replacing Horizontal Equity with an Ex Ante Incentives Perspective (dissertation, Harvard University).

King, M. A., 1983, "An Index of Inequality: With Applications to Horizontal Equity and Social Mobility," *Econometrica* 51, 99–115.

Knetsch, J. L. and J. A. Sinden, 1984, "Willingness to Pay and Compensation Demanded: Experimental Evidence of an Unexpected Disparity in Measures of Value," *Quarterly Journal of Economics* 99, 507–521.

Kotlikoff, L. J., T. Persson, and L. E. O. Svensson, 1986, "Social Contracts as Assets: A Possible Solution to the Time Consistency Problem," *American Economic Review* 78, 662–677.

Kydland, F. E. and E. C. Prescott, 1977, "Rules Rather than Discretion: The Inconsistency of Optimal Plans," *Journal of Political Economy* 85, 473–491.

Mirlees, J., 1971, "An Exploration in the Theory of Optimal Income Taxation," *Review of Economic Studies* 38, 179–208.

Mueller, D. C., 1979, *Public Choice* (Cambridge University Press, Cambridge).

Musgrave, R. A., 1959, *The Theory of Public Finance* (McGraw-Hill, New York).

Musgrave, R. A., 1976, "Optimal Taxation, Equitable Taxation and Second-Best Taxation," *Journal of Public Economics* 6, 3–16.

Nozick, R., 1974, *Anarchy, State and Utopia* (Basic Books, New York).

Plotnick, R., 1981, "A Measure of Horizontal Inequity," *Review of Economics and Statistics* 63, 283–288.

Plotnick, R., 1982, "The Concept and Measurement of Horizontal Equity," *Journal of Public Economics* 17, 373–391.

Plotnick, R., 1984, "A Comparison of Measures of Horizontal Inequity Using Alternative Measures of Well-Being," Institute for Research on Poverty Working Paper 752–84.

Rawls, J., 1971, *A Theory of Justice* (Harvard University Press, Cambridge).

Rosen, H. S., 1978, "An Approach to the Study of Income, Utility, and Horizontal Equity," *Quarterly Journal of Economics* 92, 307–322.

Russell, R. R., 1985, "A Note on Decomposable Inequality Measures," *Review of Economic Studies* 52, 347–352.

Schmalensee, R., 1984, "Imperfect Information and the Equitability of Competitive Prices," *Quarterly Journal of Economics* 99, 441–460.

Sen, A., 1977, "On Weights and Measures: Informational Constraints in Social Welfare Analysis," *Econometrica* 45, 1539–1572.

Shleifer, A. and R. Waldmann, 1985, "Horizontal Equity as a Socially Valuable Taboo," mimeo.

Shorrocks, A. F., 1978a, "Income Inequality and Income Mobility," *Journal of Economic Theory* 19, 376–393.

Shorrocks, A. F., 1978b, "The Measurement of Mobility," *Econometrica* 46, 1013–1024.

Shoup, C. S., 1969, *Public Finance* (Aldine Publishing Company, Chicago).

Simons, H. C., 1938, *Personal Income Taxation: The Definition of Income as a Problem of Fiscal Policy* (University of Chicago Press, Chicago).

Stiglitz, J., 1982, "Utilitarianism and Horizontal Equity: The Case for Random Taxation," *Journal of Public Economics* 18, 1–33.

Veblen, T., 1899, *The Theory of the Leisure Class* (Macmillan, New York).

Weiss, L., 1976, "The Desirability of Cheating Incentives and Randomness in the Optimal Income Tax," *Journal of Political Economy* 84, 1343–1352.

Westen, P., 1982, "The Empty Idea of Equality," *Harvard Law Review* 95, 537–596.

White, M. and A. White, 1965, "Horizontal Inequality in the Federal Income Tax Treatment of Homeowners and Tenants," *National Tax Journal* 18, 225–239.

Yitzhaki, S., 1982, "Relative Deprivation and Economic Welfare," *European Economic Review* 17, 99–113.

Zodrow, G., 1981, "Implementing Tax Reform," *National Tax Journal* 34, 401–418.

[13]

HORIZONTAL EQUITY, ONCE MORE**

RICHARD A. MUSGRAVE*

ABSTRACT

This paper reconsiders the proposition, drawn from the Pigovian tradition, that vertical equity is the primary norm for tax design, with horizontal equity a mere derivative therefrom. This is an unlikely conclusion once a broader view of distributive justice is taken: Horizontal equity stands up under alternative approaches, whereas that of vertical equity undergoes drastic change. Even in the utilitarian context there is a good case for viewing horizontal equity as an independent norm. Vertical equity, in that context, is interpreted as minimizing the aggregate welfare cost of taxation. This does indeed mean that horizontal equity is met as well, but only in a perfect policy setting. For the more realistic case of limited policy options, vertical and horizontal equity goals may conflict so that a trade-off will be needed. Independent values must then be assigned to each, confirming the standing of horizontal as well as vertical equity as a primary norm.

THE call for equity in taxation is generally taken to include a rule of horizontal equity (HE), requiring equal treatment of equals, and one of vertical equity (VE), calling for an appropriate differentiation among unequals. HE appears non-controversial. Not only does it offer protection against arbitrary discrimination but it also reflects the basic principle of equal worth. The United States Constitution provides for "equal protection under the law." Similarly, to quote an eminent utilitarian, "in laying down the law, no less than carrying it out, all inequality affecting the interests of individuals which appears arbitrary, and for which no sufficient reason can be given, is held to be unjust" [Sidgwick, 1874]. Or to quote Henry Simons, the high priest of HE, "it is generally agreed that taxes should bear similarly upon all people in similar circumstances" [Simons, 1950]. While there is room for how "similar circumstances" is to be defined—e.g., accretion or consumption, annual or lifetime—the principle of equal treatment of equals is generally accepted. VE, on the contrary, is inherently controversial. An appropriate pattern of differentiation must be chosen but people will disagree on its shape. Whereas HE is a minimal rule of fairness, VE is a matter of social taste and political debate; hence the strategy of the 1986 tax reform over the middle-upper income range, which was designed to draw on common support for improving HE, while remaining neutral on the controversial issue of VE.

Notwithstanding the apparent priority given to HE, the literature on tax equity has stressed VE as primary and denied the significance of HE as an independent norm. Compliance with VE, so it is argued, already assures compliance with HE, whereas HE by itself does not assure compliance with VE. Hence VE is seen as the basic rule, with HE but a consequence thereof. This conclusion has been supported in Kaplow's recent contribution to this journal (1989), and I suggested a similar inference some decades ago:

> Perhaps the most widely accepted principle of equity in taxation is that people in equal positions should be treated equally. This principle of equality, or *horizontal equity,* is fundamental to the ability-to-pay approach, which requires equal taxation of people with equal ability and unequal taxation of people with unequal ability. Beyond this, the principle of equality is accepted by many who do not lay much store in the ability-to-pay approach. Indeed, it has been suggested that the rule of horizontal equity is valid, even though little can be said about the matter of *vertical equity* or about how the taxation of people in different positions should differ.
>
> This is hardly justified. The requirements of horizontal and vertical equity are but different sides of the same coin. If there is no specified reason for discriminating among unequals, how can there be a reason for avoiding discrimination among equals? Without a scheme of vertical equity, the requirement of horizontal equity at best becomes a safeguard against

*H.H. Burbank Professor of Political Economy, Emeritus, Harvard University, and Adjunct Professor of Economics, University of California at Santa Cruz, CA 95064.

capricious discrimination—a safeguard which might be provided equally well by a requirement that taxes be distributed at random. To mean more than this, the principle of horizontal equity must be seen against the backdrop of an explicit view of vertical equity [Musgrave, 1959, p. 160].

Repeated at a later time [Musgrave, 1976], I now find this to be in need of reconsideration. The independent role of HE becomes apparent once focus on an optimal outcome is replaced by comparison of second-best solutions.

Tax Equity in Distributive Justice

Kaplow rightly insists that meaningful measures of tax equity must be grounded in a view of entitlement and distributive justice. Depending on how these priors are seen, the content of tax equity will differ. This therefore is where our analysis has to begin.

Entitlement to Earnings

Natural law, according to Locke [1689], entitles a person to keep what is earned in the market. A common claim exists only to gains from natural resources, but not beyond. Supposing this common claim to have been settled by some "base-line agreement" [Nozick], there remains no case for redistribution. Taxes will still be needed to pay for social goods, but the entitlement logic calls for payment in line with benefits received.

How then do HE and VE enter into benefit taxation, and what does the benefit principle imply regarding the tax treatment of equals and unequals? In a world of private goods, individuals are entitled to that level of welfare which they can secure by purchasing at uniform market prices. Given a positive income elasticity of demand, high income consumers will purchase more and derive a larger surplus, and to this they are entitled. Provision for social goods differs in that all consumers must partake in the same amount. Assuming equal tastes, those with equal incomes will assign equal values to the marginal unit of the public good, and should thus pay the same tax. HE is thereby satisfied. But higher income consumers now attribute a higher monetary value to the marginal unit. By analogy to entitlement in the private goods context, where prices are equated with marginal utility, they should pay more. The burden distribution will be regressive, proportional, or progressive, depending on whether income elasticity falls short of, equals, or exceeds price elasticity of demand for social goods. While entitlement rules out redistribution, VE as well thus retains a place in the context of benefit taxation. But based on income and price elasticities of demand, its rationale differs wholly from that in the utilitarian context.

Ability to Pay

Adam Smith in his earlier philosophical work [1759] sustained the entitlement doctrine, if with some degree of unease. But when dealing with tax equity later on [1776], he replaced the benefit rule with a principle of fair taking. His first maxim of taxation accordingly held that "the subjects of the state ought to contribute towards the supply of government, as nearly as possible, in proportion to their respective abilities . . ." Income was seen as the relevant measure of ability and proportional taxation as the fair way of distributing the burden. Though he did not break down his equity rule into HE and VE components, contribution in line with ability-to-pay satisfied both dimensions.

Smith thus came to be seen as an ability-to-pay theorist, but this seems to contradict the second part of his maxim, continuing with ". . . that is in proportion to the revenue which they respectively enjoy under the protection of the state." In combination, the two parts seem to contain an uneasy mix of ability-to-pay and benefit components. Smith might have indeed wanted to have it both ways, or he might have been aware (if not stating so explicitly) that the ability and benefit doctrines may be linked via the income elasticity of demand for public goods. His ability-to-pay rule could then be viewed as a prescription for benefit taxation.

This ambiguity disappeared with J. S. Mill, who separated the analysis of tax equity from the expenditure side of the budget, a separation which for better or for worse (and mostly worse) has dominated tax analysis ever since. Expanding on the spirit of Smith's ability-to-pay doctrine, Mill [1848] then translated equal ability into equal sacrifice terms. Given the premise of identical utility functions and declining marginal utility of income, individuals with equal incomes should pay the same while those with higher incomes should pay more. Fairness, according to Mill, required tax differentials which impose *equal absolute* sacrifice across unequal incomes. While he noted, if mistakenly so, that total sacrifice would be minimized thereby, *least total* sacrifice was not his basic rule. Tax taking was to be arranged in a fair fashion, and this he defined as equal absolute sacrifice. Once more, the requirements of both HE and VE were met.

Maximum Welfare

Both Smith and Mill took pre-tax incomes to be given by entitlement to earnings, and then addressed how limited revenue requirements should be met by taxing in an equitable fashion. Bentham's utilitarian model dropped entitlement and proposed a principle which arranges the entire distribution in an optimal fashion. Viewing happiness as the goal of human activity, and postulating that the happiness of all individuals be valued equally, maximum aggregate welfare emerged as *the* goal of government. To this goal all rational people should subscribe [Bentham, 1789]. Considering the optimal distribution of a fixed total income and postulating equal and declining marginal income utility schedules, total satisfaction would be maximized by an egalitarian distribution [Bentham, 1802]. The basic case for viewing VE as calling for progressive taxation was thus made, although Bentham hastened to qualify it in various respects. Allowance had to be made for detrimental taxation effects on the level of income and on other components of satisfaction, such as security and freedom.

Resuming Mill's discussion, Edgeworth [1897] and Pigou [1928] distinguished between equal absolute, proportional, and marginal sacrifice rules. Among them, equal marginal sacrifice emerged as the correct version, not because of its immediate fairness appeal, but as an instrument to achieve the utilitarian goal of least aggregate sacrifice or maximum welfare. There can be no question, so Pigou concluded, that least aggregate sacrifice is an ultimate principle of taxation, following directly as it does from the supreme goal of maximizing total satisfaction [Pigou, 1928]. While recognizing that tax equity "in its barest form" calls for equal treatment of equals, he hesitated to endorse Sidgwick's claim that HE should also be considered an ultimate principle of distributive justice [Sidgwick, 1874]. Since HE is implied already in the least aggregate sacrifice rule, so he argued, no independent normative role for HE is needed.

Before long, Pigou's utilitarian calculus encountered two objections. For one thing, there was no ready way by which to measure the rate at which the marginal utility of income falls as income rises. For another, the conventional assumption of equal and comparable utility functions was questioned [Robbins, 1938]. The traditional view of the social welfare function thus collapsed, giving way to a disaggregated version. Each individual may have his/her own view of what the income distribution should be like and thus have a personalized image of the social welfare function [Bergson, 1938]. Earlier objections to the social welfare approach were thus set aside, but at the cost of losing the essential policy linkage. Individual social welfare functions need be combined into a representative one if a basis for policy choice is to be provided.

For this purpose, society must agree on a decision rule so that a representative function can be determined. Provided that difficulties in defining an unambiguous decision rule [Arrow, 1951] can be overcome, this offers a contractarian solution, but the resulting status of VE no longer reflects the compelling criterion of an objectively based measure of aggregate satisfaction, such as the utilitarian model had visualized. Rather it is reduced to a compromise of individual views on fair distribution. The ethical premise taken to be commonly accepted by the utilitarian model—that the satisfaction of others be valued as one's own—is lost in the process. Any one person's view of fair distribution may be shaped by his/her own earnings potential, a premise appropriate to the entitlement but not to the utilitarian model.

The Veil Construct

As suggested by Vickrey [1945] and Harsanyi [1953], the premise of equal worth was reinstated in a "neo-utilitarian" model. This model postulates a social contract under which individuals will choose among alternative patterns of distribution from behind a veil, so as to be ignorant of their own earning capacities and their own position in the final (post-redistribution) outcome. Given similar utility functions, expressed as degrees of risk aversion, individuals will then agree on a preferred pattern of distribution so as to maximize the sum or mean of individual utilities [Harsanyi, 1957]. Given a fixed amount of income available for distribution, an egalitarian distribution will result. But taxation for purposes of redistribution reduces taxable income, since it induces substitution of leisure for income. Taking this into account, the resulting state of distribution under the neo-utilitarian model will fall short of an egalitarian outcome.

Like the neo-utilitarian model, John Rawls' [1971] view of justice as fairness rejects the entitlement premise and calls for rearrangement of earnings. The argument again begins with the premise of impartial choice and a veil construct. But unlike the former, Rawls adds a postulate of infinite risk aversion. Individuals who do not know what their position in the outcome will be thus opt for a solution which assigns maximum income to the lowest recipient. Since taxation reduces taxable income, this again falls short of an egalitarian solution, but redistribution will be carried further than under the neo-utilitarian model. This, however, is an extreme assumption. Confronted with choosing between a more certain but slight gain at the bottom and a large but less certain gain at the top, individuals may well prefer the latter.

Restoring impartiality via the veil construct—be it in the neo-utilitarian or Rawlsian formulation—is appealing to the economist's fascination with uncertainty, but also raises problems. While risk aversion provided a useful way of testing the shape of the income utility function, the uncertainty construct is open to a distorting note if risk aversion allows for gambling likes and dislikes. Gambling likes and dislikes should hardly merit a central role in arriving at distributive justice. More important, the veil construct involves an awkward inconsistency by first assuming individuals to enter into a social contract for impartial choice and then leaving them free to obstruct the outcome by substituting leisure for income in response to taxation. The veil construct thereby leaves an uneasy mix between entitlement and fairness principles, especially with regard to maxi-min. Comparison with the position of the lowest may well be postulated directly as a premise of social ethics, and such an approach is built into the Rawlsian formulation as well, but its derivation from the veil construct is unconvincing.

We return to the role of HE and VE in the veil approach. In both the neo-utilitarian and Rawlsian version, people with equal incomes will once more pay equal amounts, while those with higher incomes will pay more. Conformity with both equity rules is again assured, but the contexts of VE as defined by the veil models differ, and neither is the same as under the classical utilitarian formulation.

Conclusion

As this brief survey shows, the requirement of HE remains essentially unchanged under the various formulations of distributive justice, ranging from Lockean entitlement over utilitarianism and fairness solutions. That of VE, on the contrary, undergoes drastic change under the various approaches. While HE is met by the various VE outcomes, this does not mean that HE is derived from VE. If anything, it suggests that HE is a stronger primary rule. As a matter of social ethics, HE not only emerges with a normative basis of its own, but one which is more firmly rooted than that of VE. Not surprisingly, it also has more popular appeal.

HE vs. VE in Second-Best Settings

This is not the place in which to rank the various models of distributive justice or combinations thereof, if this can at all be done in an "objective fashion." Values are involved on which individuals may differ. Instead, we return to the economist's standard approach of the utilitarian model, assume a social welfare function to be given, and consider how the equity of tax systems may be evaluated in that context. To simplify, we initially assume the level of pre-tax income to be invariant to taxation, and take welfare to be a function of income only. Assuming uniform utility functions, people with equal incomes are thus taken to be in equal positions. These assumptions are reconsidered later on.

Measures of Tax System Quality

Various indices may be defined by which to measure and to compare the HE and VE quality of tax systems.

Welfare Cost and VE Performance. To begin with, we determine the aggregate actual welfare cost or ΣWC_a which the system imposes. That cost is measured by applying a concave social welfare function. We then compare the cost under the actual burden distribution with the minimum cost which would have resulted under an optimal distribution. The excess cost, expressed as a percent of the actual cost, gives an index of WC performance defined as

$$\frac{\Sigma WC_a - \Sigma WC_m}{\Sigma WC_a} \times 100$$

where ΣWC_a is the aggregate welfare cost imposed on the entire group of taxpayers under the actual burden distributions and ΣWC_m is the minimum cost which would have been imposed under the optimal distribution. Equal to zero for perfect performance, the index rises with the degree of imperfection.

The same index may also be taken to measure VE performance in the utilitarian context. Since perfect VE is defined in terms of least total cost, both purposes are served by the same formulation.

Horizontal Equity Next we turn to performance in HE terms. Applied to any one group of equals, HE performance is measured by the excess of the combined actual welfare cost for that group over what it would have been with equal division of liability within the group, taken as a percent of the actual. The index is thus given by

$$\frac{\Sigma WC_{ea} - \Sigma WC_e^*}{\Sigma WC_{ea}} \times 100$$

where ΣWC_{ea} is the welfare cost for the particular group of equals under the actual distribution among its members and ΣWC^*_e is that which would have resulted with equal distribution. The expression thus measures the excess cost due to HE failure expressed as a percent of actual cost. An index of zero once more reflects perfect compliance and then rises with the degree of imperfection. Thus a distinct measure of excess cost, due to imperfect HE, may be obtained for each group of equals.

But HE measures which are applicable to particular groups of equals do not suffice. To assess the HE quality of the entire system and to permit comparison with other burden distributions, an overall measure of HE is needed. The construction of such an index is awkward, since HE, by its very nature, relates to comparison among equals only. Nevertheless, a combined measure might be provided by extending the approach taken for each group of equals. A simple average of the HE indices for the two subgroups will not do since a more explicit allowance for the respective welfare losses due to non-compliance with HE is needed. Our HE index for the entire group is thus given by

$$\frac{\Sigma WC_a - \Sigma WC^*}{\Sigma WC_a} \times 100$$

where ΣWC_a is the actual welfare cost for the entire group and ΣWC^* is that which would have resulted had there been an equal division of actual combined liabilities within each group of equals. Thereby an overall picture is given while inappropriate comparisons between unequals are avoided. Once more perfect compliance with HE is shown by an index of zero, with its weight increasing with the degree of imperfection.

Note that this measure of HE does *not* focus on changing differentials among unequals, as has been the case with various indices proposed in recent years. Measures of tax-induced mobility among income levels [Atkinson, 1980] and of resulting changes in Gini coefficients [King, 1983] are of interest, but they do not measure changes in HE. The same holds for changes in ranking which have been featured as constituting an essential part of the HE concept [Feldstein, 1976]. A comparison of pre- and post-tax income differences across all individuals [Kaplow] is superior to ranking in that it allows for changes in the magnitude of differentials which may occur without switching in rank, but again involves border crossings which mix HE and VE issues. A distinction need be drawn between (1) differentiation in the treatment of equals, viewing each group of equals by itself, and (2) differentials in the treatment of unequals. The first deals with HE and the second with VE. Given a setting of imperfect HE in both the L and H groups, the differentials between pairs of L and H units (say between H_1 and L_1 as compared with that between H_2 and L_2) may differ as well, but these differentials (and changes therein) reflect a mix of HE and VE features and confuse the two basic issues.

A further concern may be noted. The reader may object that by measuring the quality of HE performance in terms of excess welfare costs, we proceed in the spirit of the utilitarian framework but do not directly address the HE norm on its own grounds. The welfare cost due to noncompliance has to be considered since the principle of equal treatment and departure therefrom involves not merely dollar differentials but also their social utility. Our formulation may thus be seen as a first step of measuring effective differentiation, to be followed by applying a demerit scale thereto, needed also where a trade-off with VE deficiencies is called for.

Vertical Equity Adjusted. Returning to our earlier measure of VE in terms of ΣWC, we concluded that no separate VE index is needed, as the purpose is served already by that for welfare costs incurred. Since the standard of VE in the utilitarian context is given by adherence to the least cost rule, that index may also be taken to measure VE. It does so, however, by also including the VE implications of departures from HE within the sub-groups of equals.

To correct for this overlap it might be useful to define an adjusted VE index which is unaffected by HE deficiencies. This is in line with our preceding proposition that the measure of HE should avoid border crossing so as not to overlap with VE. For this purpose, an adjusted index or VEA may be defined similar to that previously given for welfare cost, except that the actual costs incurred by the various taxpayers is now replaced by that which would have resulted had the combined actual tax paid by each group of equals been distributed equally among them. The VEA index is thus given by

$$\frac{\Sigma WC^{**} - \Sigma WC_m}{\Sigma WC^{**}} \times 100$$

where ΣWC^{**} is the aggregate welfare cost for the entire group assuming the actual distribution among but equal division of the burden within each group of equals, and ΣWC_m is the minimum cost for the entire group under the optimal solution. The VEA index, viewed in conjunction with the HE index, has the advantage of separating VE performance from HE deficiencies, but also carries the disadvantage of referring to a hypothetical situation, overlooking thereby the fact that HE performance also affects ΣWC outcomes, and vice versa.

The indices used here have been chosen so as to make our point in its simplest form. More complex formulations may be developed. It should be noted, however, that the outcomes and even rankings are sensitive throughout to the shape of the social welfare function over the relevant range [Hettich], as well as to the amount of revenue to be raised. This is in the nature of the problem and should not be surprising.

Comparison Between Tax Systems

These indices may now be applied to compare the quality of alternative tax systems. For this purpose, a numerical illustration will be helpful. As shown in the Table, we consider a distribution among four individuals, including two with low incomes, L_1 and L_2, receiving \$5 each and two with high incomes, H_1 and H_2, with \$10 each. Out of the total income of \$30, an amount of \$8 is to be raised by income tax. Columns I to IV show alternative tax patterns and after-tax incomes. To translate tax payments into welfare costs such as appear in the various indices, use is made of an assumed social welfare function which assigns a value of \$10 to the first dollar of income, of \$9.1 to the second, of \$8.19 to the third, and so forth, the social weight declining by 10 percent for each successive dollar of income. The particular shape chosen is arbitrary, but meets the essential condition of being concave, as generally (and conveniently!) assumed in economic analysis. We also assume for the time being that taxation does not affect the level of pre-tax income, an unrealistic assumption to be reconsidered below.

Given such a social welfare function and assuming pre-tax income to remain unchanged, aggregate welfare cost ΣWC is minimized in column I where the burden is divided equally between H_1 and H_2. By the same token, L_1 and L_2 are treated equally as well, so that HE is met throughout. All indices record a perfect score (zero value) with column I the first best solution on all grounds.

But optimal solutions are hardly available in a real world setting. Tax policy is subject to many pressures—political, technical, and administrative—which limit what can be done. Policy choices therefore are limited to imperfect arrangements, such as illustrated in columns II to IV. We begin by ranking these outcomes in terms of ΣWC (line 6) and overall HE (line 9). Comparing II and III, both are equally defective regarding ΣWC, but II is superior on HE grounds. Without a normative basis for HE, this would render the choice between II and III a matter of indifference, but HE matters and II is accepted as superior. Comparison between III and IV shows IV to win on both grounds, but conflict re-emerges if the choice is between II and IV with II superior on HE terms and IV on ΣWC grounds. To establish a ranking, a trade-off between the HE advantage of II and the ΣWC advantage of IV is needed.

Substituting VEA for ΣWC as our measure of vertical equity, we now compare line 6 and 10. We find that III now outranks II on vertical grounds and the VE advantage of IV over II and III is increased. Given that HE is already consid-

RANKING OF SECOND-BEST SOLUTIONS

	Initial Income	I		II		III		IV	
		Tax	Net	Tax	Net	Tax	Net	Tax	Net
1. L_1	5	0	5	1	4	0.4	4.6	0	5
2. L_2	5	0	5	1	4	1.3	3.7	0	5
3. H_1	10	4	6	3	7	2.5	7.5	3	7
4. H_2	10	4	6	3	7	3.8	6.2	5	5
5. Total	30	8	22	8	22	8.0	22.0	8	22
Indices									
6. ΣWC	—	0		6.2		6.2		1.7	
7. HE L	—	0		0		2.3		0	
8. H	—	0		0		3.5		1.6	
9. Total	—	0		0		2.1		1.6	
10. VEA	—	0		6.2		5.4			

ered on its own terms, there may well be a case for preferring the use of VEA, which neutralizes the HE feature.

Similar considerations apply where new revenue is added to an already existing and inequitable tax system. We assume further that the latter cannot be changed, while the new tax is added. Based on the underlying social welfare function, policy may then have to choose between minimizing the additional ΣWC and improving the overall level of HE. Returning to column III of the illustration and assuming an additional revenue of \$3 to be needed, minimizing additional ΣWC will call for \$2.15 to be collected from H_1 and \$0.85 from H_2. Horizontal equity may be met in various ways, for instance by collecting \$0.60 from L_1, \$0.55 from H_1 and \$1.85 from H_2. Policy choice in a second best setting once more involves a trade-off between HE and VE.

Conclusion

Additional illustrations might be added but this suffices to make our central point: when having to choose among second-best arrangements, differences in HE might be a decisive factor. Choice then calls for normative values to be attributed to HE as well as VE. HE enters as an "end state principle" and not, as has been suggested [Plotnik, 1987], as a rule of fair process only. Such is the case even in an otherwise utilitarian context, not to mention that of other approaches to distributive justice as discussed in the initial section. Pigou's widely accepted conclusion to the contrary is thus in need of correction. Perfect compliance with VE does indeed imply compliance with HE, but it does not follow that HE lacks independent merit. This becomes evident once the choice is between second-best solutions. Trade-offs between HE and VE imperfections are then needed, calling for a specified trade-off matrix. This admittedly poses a complex task but the problem is not solved by addressing it on the unrealistic premise of perfect settings.

Further Issues

In presenting the argument, a number of simplifying assumptions have been made which do not affect our main conclusion regarding the independent status of HE, but which should be noted briefly.

1. To begin with, we have dealt with departures from HE in terms of differentials in rates of tax imposed on equal levels of statutory income. In practice, inequities arise because the tax base is defined imperfectly, thus causing equal statutory rates to generate differential effective rates on equal levels of "true" income. For the income tax, the state of imperfections in HE and VE must thus be reinterpreted with regard to people's level of "true" income, i.e., accretion. Or, in the case of an expenditure tax, the same holds for a correct definition of the expenditure base. The factors which give rise to horizontal inequities may differ for the two bases [Zodrow], and so forth. All this complicates presentation but does not change our basic finding. We need only add that differentiation due to base preferences complicates the linkage between VE and HE. Various types of preferences change in weight when moving up the income scale, a crucial factor in tax politics and the trade-off problem.

2. Next, we have assumed the level of pre-tax income to be unaffected by taxation, thus bypassing the issue of leisure-income substitution, the inclusion of leisure utility in the social welfare function, and of dead-weight losses in the measure of tax burden. All this need be allowed for in a fuller analysis.

The various indices must then be redefined accordingly and the optimal tax distribution which minimizes ΣWC becomes less progressive as the dead-weight burden rises with the marginal tax rate. All this complicates matters but does not invalidate our central proposition, that VE and HE policy goals may conflict in an imperfect policy setting and may have to be traded off against each other.

Allowance for income change raises the further question of how equal position should be defined. Assuming HE compliance and equal utility functions, individuals with equal income Y_z in a zero-tax setting respond equally to the same tax and will be left with equal (if reduced) before-tax incomes Y_b or net incomes Y_n after the tax is imposed. This is no longer the case with imperfect HE. Subjected to different tax treatment, Y_z equals will respond differently and be left in different Y_b and Y_n positions. The prevailing departure from HE should then be measured with regard to Y_z not Y_b equals. Strictly speaking, this would call for individuals to be regrouped into equals in Y_n terms, thereby requiring income responses to be known.

As the assumption of equal utility functions is dropped, individuals in equal Y_z income positions need no longer be equal in utility terms since they may differ in leisure. Exposed to the same tax rate, they may now incur differing welfare losses. Similar difficulties arise if consumer preferences are allowed to differ. A perfect HE concept would then call for tailoring amounts of tax to the preferences of each individual [Rosen, 1978], and the same would hold for implementing VE.

3. The analysis has focussed on the equity of a particular tax, the income tax only. A similar argument need be applied to other taxes. Inequities of both the HE and VE type imposed by any one tax may be offset or accentuated by those of another and the merit of alternative systems should be appraised in terms of their joint or net equity. While this is done generally with regard to VE, it should also be applied to HE.

4. Our focus has been on situations where a trade-off between HE and VE is needed because structural, political, or other obstacles preclude an optimal solution. It remains to note that a conflict between HE and the utilitarian rule of minimizing ΣWC—and, for that matter, with Pareto optimality—may arise even without such impediments. This may be the case with non-concave income utility functions and where similar individuals are confronted with different prices [Stiglitz, 1982], with special application to urban planning [Wildasin, 1986]. As with second-best solutions due to faulty policy, it does not follow that HE should be set aside because it conflicts with utilitarian doctrine. Rather, the case is again for a social welfare function which covers both concepts and provides for a trade-off between them.

5. Finally, a note on the proposition [Feldstein, 1976; Musgrave, 1959] that horizontal equity is of minor importance because departures therefrom are self-correcting. As the return to income derived from a particular asset is reduced by imposition of a differential tax, its gross return will rise to restore equality of net returns with tax-free assets. Assuming equal abilities and factor mobility, the argument is extended to apply to differential treatment of wage income in different occupations. More questionably so, it is extended even to differential treatment across wage and capital income [Feldstein]. Tax differentials may continue to offend against VE and leave lasting efficiency costs, but the problem will no longer be one of deficient HE. Removal of old differentials may indeed cause new offenses against HE.

These conclusions, however, do not void concern with HE. For one thing, they rely on strong assumptions regarding the perfection and speed of market adjustments, so that continuing concern with HE can hardly be discarded. For another, the initial inequity caused by the introduction of differential taxes is not annulled by the adjustment process. Rather, the loss or gain is capitalized, falling entirely on the initial party [Musgrave, 1951, p. 385]. Capitalization, therefore, does not remove the need for concern with the HE quality of tax changes, and the resulting HE/VE trade-offs in a second-best system.

ENDNOTE

*I am pleased to contribute this paper in the memory of Morris Beck, and to acknowledge support from the Morris Beck Fund in its preparation. I would like to thank Walter Hettich, Carl Shoup, Peggy Musgrave, Melvin White, and George Zodrow for helpful suggestions.

REFERENCES

Arrow, K. J., 1951. *Social Choice and Individual Values*, New York.

Atkinson, A. B., 1980. "Horizontal Equity and the Distribution of the Tax Burden," in H. Aaron and M. J. Boskin, eds., *The Economics of Taxation*, Brookings, Washington, D.C.

Atkinson, A. B., and Stiglitz, J. E., 1980. *Lectures on Public Finance*, New York, McGraw-Hill.

Bentham, J., 1789. *The Principles of Morals and Legislation*, Hafner Press, New York, 1948.

Bentham, J., 1802. *Principles of the Civil Code*, as given in C. B. Macpherson, ed., *Property*, University of Toronto Press, 1978, p. 47.

Bergson, A. "A Reformulation of Certain Aspects of Welfare Economics," *Quarterly Journal of Economics*, February, 1938.

Edgeworth, F. Y., 1897. "The Pure Theory of Taxation," *Economic Journal*, 1897, reprinted in *Papers Relating to Political Economy*, Vol. II, Macmillan, London, 1925.

Feldstein, M., 1976. "On the Theory of Tax Reform," *Journal of Public Economics*, 6.

Harsanyi, J. C., "Cardinal Utility in Welfare Economics," *Journal of Political Economy*, LXI (1953). Reprinted in J. C. Harsanyi, *Essays on Ethics, Social Behavior, and Scientific Explanation*, 1976, Reidl, Boston. "Cardinal Welfare, Individualistic Ethics, and Inter-Personal Comparison of Utility," *Journal of Political Economy*, LXIII (1957). Also included in above volume.

Hettich, Walter, "Reforms of the Tax Base and Horizontal Equity," *National Tax Journal*, XXXVI, No. 4.

Kaplow, Louis, "Horizontal Equity: Measures in Search of a Principle," *National Tax Journal*, XLII, 1989.

King, M. A., 1983. "An Index of Inequality With Application to Horizontal Equity and Social Mobility," *Econometrica* 51.

Locke, John, 1689. *Two Treatises of Government*, ed. Laslett (1960), Mentor Books, New York, p. 327.

Mill, J. S., 1848. *Principles of Political Economy*, W. G. Ashley, ed., Longman's, 1921, Book 5, Chapter 2, p. 804.

Musgrave, R. A., 1959. *The Theory of Public Finance*, McGraw-Hill, New York, pp. 161 and 385.

Musgrave, R. A., "ET, OT, or SBT," 1976. *Journal of Public Economics*, vol. 6, no. 1, 2, p. 4.

Nozick, R., 1968. *Anarchy, State and Utopia*, Basic Books, 1978, p. 178.

Pigou, A. C., 1928. *A Study in Public Finance*, 3rd ed., 1951, Macmillan, p. 50.

Plotnick, Robert, 1982. "The Concept of Measurement of Horizontal Equity," *Journal of Public Economics*, 17.

Rawls, J., 1972. *A Theory of Justice*, Harvard University Press, Cambridge.

Robbins, L., "Interpersonal Comparisons of Utility," *Economic Journal*, 1938.

Rosen, H. S., "An Approach to the Study of Income, Utility and Horizontal Equity," *Quarterly Journal of Economics*, 92.

Sidgwick, 1874. *The Methods of Ethics*, University of Chicago Press, 1962, p. 267.

Simons, H., 1950. *Federal Tax Reform*, University of Chicago Press, p. 8.

Smith, Adam, 1759. *The Theory of Moral Sentiments*, E. G. West, ed., Liberty Classics, 1969.

Smith, Adam, 1776. *The Wealth of Nations*, Book IV, Chapter II, Part II.

Stiglitz, Joseph, 1982. "Utilitarianism and Horizontal Equity. The Case for Random Taxation," *Journal of Public Economics*, 18-1.

Vickrey, W. C., 1945. "Measuring Income Utility by Reactions to Risk," *Econometrica*, 13.

White, M. and White A., 1965. "Horizontal Inequality in the Federal Income Tax Treatment of Homeowners and Tenants," *National Tax Journal*, p. 142.

Wildasin, David, 1986. "Spatial Variation of the Marginal Utility of Income and Unequal Treatment of Equals," *Journal of Urban Economics*, 19.

Zodrow, G. R., "The Choice Between Income and Consumption," Unpublished Manuscript.

[14]

FLORIDA TAX REVIEW

VOLUME 1 *1993* *NUMBER 10*

Horizontal and Vertical Equity: The Musgrave/Kaplow Exchange

Paul R. McDaniel and James R. Repetti***

Over the past several years, Professors Richard Musgrave and Louis Kaplow have engaged in an exchange over the question whether the concept of horizontal equity has any independent significance apart from vertical equity.[1] Kaplow answers that question in the negative, Musgrave in the affirmative. The purposes of this comment are (1) to sort out the issues raised in the Musgrave-Kaplow exchange, and (2) to set forth a somewhat different perspective from which to view those issues.

I. CONCEPTUAL ISSUES

A. *The Definitions*

Kaplow and Musgrave define horizontal equity (HE) as the requirement that equals be treated alike. Both define vertical equity (VE) as requiring an "appropriate" pattern of differentiation among unequals.[2]

B. *Synopsis of the Arguments*

The starting point was a statement by Musgrave in 1959 that the requirements of horizontal and vertical equity are but different sides of the same coin. Musgrave asked rhetorically "[i]f there is no specified reason for discriminating among unequals, how can there be a reason for avoiding

---

* Professor of Law, New York University School of Law.

** Associate Professor of Law, Boston College Law School. The authors thank Emily Powers, a second year law student at Boston College Law School, for helpful research assistance.

1. Louis Kaplow, Horizontal Equity: Measures in Search of a Principle, 42 Nat'l Tax J. 139 (1989) [hereinafter Kaplow I]; Richard A. Musgrave, Horizontal Equity, Once More, 43 Nat'l Tax J. 113 (1990) [hereinafter Musgrave I]; Louis Kaplow, A Note on Horizontal Equity, 1 Fla. Tax Rev. 191 (1992) [hereinafter Kaplow II]; Richard A. Musgrave, Horizontal Equity: A Further Note, 1 Fla. Tax Rev. 354 (1993) [hereinafter Musgrave II].

2. Kaplow I, supra note 1, at 140-41; Musgrave I, supra note 1, at 113.

discrimination among equals."[3] His rhetorical question can be rephrased as a statement: If we cannot explain why we discriminate among unequals, then we cannot explain why we fail to discriminate among equals. Thus, in 1959, Musgrave viewed HE and VE as inextricably linked. He explained:

> Without a scheme of vertical equity, the requirement of horizontal equity at best becomes a safeguard against capricious discrimination—a safeguard which might be provided equally well by a requirement that taxes be distributed at random. To mean more than this, the principle of horizontal equity must be seen against the backdrop of an *explicit view of vertical equity* (emphasis added).[4]

Musgrave also felt in 1959 that HE and VE, by themselves, were inadequate for formulating tax policy because they are dependent upon the determination of some measure for distinguishing equals and unequals. He stated: "An objective index of equality or inequality is needed to translate either principle into a specific tax system."[5]

Subsequently, in 1989, Kaplow examined the current use of HE in tax policy analysis.[6] He concluded, like Musgrave in 1959, that HE is not a useful tool because it has no normative content and has no significance apart from VE.[7] Compliance with VE will always assure compliance with HE, Kaplow stated, "because whatever reasons motivate a particular treatment of one individual will require the same treatment of another individual who is equal in all relevant respects."[8]

In response to Kaplow's critique of HE, Musgrave reexamined his own 1959 critique of HE.[9] He surveyed various formulations of distributive justice and concluded that HE has a normative basis of its own that is more firmly planted than VE.[10] He stated:

> the requirement of HE remains essentially unchanged under the various formulations of distributive justice, ranging from Lockean entitlement over utilitarianism and fairness solutions. That of VE, on the contrary, undergoes drastic change

3. Richard A. Musgrave, The Theory of Public Finance 160 (1959).
4. Id.
5. Id. at 161.
6. Kaplow I, supra note 1, at 139-40.
7. Id.
8. Id. at 143.
9. Musgrave I, supra note 1.
10. Id. at 117.

> under the various approaches. While HE is met by the various VE outcomes, this does not mean that HE is derived from VE. If anything, it suggests that HE is a stronger primary rule.[11]

As discussed below, Musgrave argued that it is necessary to compare proposed tax changes that differ in their VE and HE outcomes. Where VE results are similar, then the change that produces better HE results is to be preferred.[12]

But Kaplow then responded: "Musgrave does not attempt to offer an example involving HE violation that any relevant distributive theory would count as decisive against an otherwise desirable policy."[13] As an example of the insignificance of HE, Kaplow stated:

> [A]ssume that the only administratively feasible way to redistribute wealth from the rich to the poor involves omitting some of the rich from the tax base or excluding some of the poor from receiving transfers (perhaps because some individuals live in remote areas). Clearly, neither a maximum welfare perspective nor a Rawlsian approach (derived from a veil construct) would oppose such redistribution because it violated HE. (They would indicate that the distributive objective is satisfied incompletely.)[14]

In a subsequent response, Musgrave agreed with Kaplow that in an ideal world, arrangements which satisfy VE also satisfy HE.[15] Moreover, in the real world, Musgrave stated that it is unreasonable "to limit considerations of departure from HE to individuals with identical incomes only, while disregarding the relative treatment of individuals with more or less similar incomes."[16] Musgrave argued, however, that this did not mean that HE is a useless concept since HE and VE concerns must be traded off in assessing proposed tax changes in the less than ideal world in which those changes must be considered.[17]

---

11. Id. at 116-17.
12. Musgrave II, supra note 1, at 356-58.
13. Kaplow II, supra note 1, at 192.
14. Id. (footnote omitted).
15. Musgrave II, supra note 1, at 355.
16. Id. at 358.
17. Id. at 359.

C. *Analysis of the Exchange*

In analyzing the above exchange, it is necessary to return to the HE and VE definitions employed both by Musgrave and Kaplow. Recall that HE is the requirement that equals be treated alike. One might think that VE, then, simply is a requirement that unequals be treated differently. Stated in this way, it is clear that neither concept has any normative content. The response to each definition is "why"? Neither definition, in itself, provides any answer.

Thus, both Kaplow and Musgrave use a definition of VE which is different from the above, i.e., for both it is a requirement that there be an "appropriate" pattern or system of differentiating among unequals. The word "appropriate" is not self-defining, so where do the two go to provide it with content?

Theoretically, VE could apply to a tax system that is progressive, proportional or regressive. Which of these designs is chosen depends upon one's underlying theory of justice and decisions about some key economic assumptions.

For example, one can be a thoroughgoing utilitarian and reach any of the three tax equity designs noted above. The reason for this is that the utilitarian must make a decision about the slope of the marginal utility of income. If she thinks that the slope declines, the tax paid will rise with income. However, whether the rate schedule should be regressive, proportional or progressive will depend on the rate of decline of the slope (i.e., the elasticity of the marginal utility of income with respect to income).[18]

Perhaps somewhat surprisingly, the same conclusion about possible tax system designs (i.e., progressive, proportional or regressive) is true for a believer in distributive justice as articulated by Rawls. For Rawls, the demands of justice are met by a society that provides maximum liberty for everyone and in which the advantages of the more fortunate promote the well-being of the least fortunate.[19] In the context of taxation, Rawls concluded that the best tax system for his theory of justice may be a flat tax rate on consumption.[20] By design, a tax on consumption only exempts capital income from tax and capital income is concentrated in the upper income levels. Economists commonly argue that, under certain assumptions,

18. The tax design will be progressive, proportional, or regressive depending on whether the elasticity of the marginal utility of income with respect to income is, respectively, greater than, equal to, or less than one. Richard A. Musgrave & Peggy B. Musgrave, Public Finance I, Theory and Practice, 200 (1973). Although most economists agree that the slope of the marginal utility of income declines, there is far less agreement about its rate of decline (its elasticity).

19. See John Rawls, A Theory of Justice 60-61, 83 (1971).

20. Id. at 278-79.

such a tax is the equivalent of a tax on wage income only.[21] Given the facts that lower income earners have mostly wage income and that they consume a higher percentage of total income then do upper income individuals, the optimal tax design favored by Rawls is regressive to income (although not to consumption).

With this background, what is the VE to which Kaplow refers? Kaplow infuses VE with content by adopting a progressive income tax system as the "appropriate" differentiation in the tax treatment of unequals. For example, in his analysis of various HE indexes, he suggests that VE favors moving individuals closer together.[22] Similarly, he subsequently states that "VE objects to inequality and favors equality."[23] and that "gains from moving individuals closer together are already encompassed in VE."[24]

Kaplow's appeal to progressivity in defining VE is entirely understandable. VE lacks normative content and is derivative, because in order to determine what the "appropriate" differential among unequals should be, one has to refer to economic assumptions and some theory of distributive justice.[25] For example, if one believes that the marginal utility of income declines in such a manner as to permit the use of a progressive tax rate in order to impose equal burdens on taxpayers, then a tax provision based on the belief that marginal utility *increases* is "bad." It is not "bad" because it failed to make a distinction among unequals. It is "bad" because one disagrees as to whether it is an "appropriate" distinction. In order to determine what is "appropriate," one has to refer to additional concepts. Thus, the concept of VE, as defined, is itself entirely derivative.

---

21. Musgrave, supra note 3, at 262, 266-67. Rawls would use progressive rates to prevent excessive accumulations of wealth that could impair the liberty of others. Rawls, supra note 19, at 279. For some, this concession might consume the rule for the reasons described in the text. To make sure that no one would think he was making use of any of the tools of utilitarianism (which he rejects totally), Rawls added:

> It is evident also that the design of the [system of taxation] does not presuppose the utilitarian's standard assumptions about individual utilities. . . . The aim of [tax] is not, of course, to maximize the net balance of satisfaction but to establish just background institutions. Doubts about the shape of utility functions are irrelevant.

Id. at 280.

22. Kaplow I, supra note 1, at 143. He states: "Hence, the central defining characteristic of HE—and its central force in policy applications—is that it also condemns moving individuals closer together in the income distribution . . . directly contrary to VE." See also id. at 144 (stating that the impact of moving two individuals closer together in income distribution as a result of a tax reform is measured under VE).

23. Kaplow I, supra note 1, at 147.

24. Id. at 148.

25. Joseph Bankman & Thomas Griffith, Social Welfare and the Rate Structure: A New Look at Progressive Taxation, 75 Cal. L. Rev. 1905, 1910 (1987).

With respect to HE, given the economic and justice judgments which Kaplow appears to make, he clearly is correct that HE will always merge into VE and will not survive as an independent normative criterion. A system which seeks to impose equal burdens on all taxpayers should, by definition treat equally the subset of taxpayers that have equal income. Similarly, a system that seeks to equalize the income of all taxpayers will, of course, treat taxpayers with equal income equally.[26]

Thus, Kaplow correctly asserts that HE never will prevail to prevent enactment of a provision that would otherwise be appropriate on grounds of administrative efficiency or VE. As Kaplow has noted, Musgrave has not provided any such example and indeed he cannot. The reason Musgrave cannot, however, has nothing to do with his defense of HE. The reason is that Musgrave has accepted Kaplow's definition of VE and, in that definition, HE is subsumed into VE. Thus, neither Musgrave nor anyone else can respond to Kaplow's challenge on his terms. Musgrave properly, in our view, subsequently pointed this out by observing that Kaplow is correct only "if the relevant norm is defined in [prescribed] VE terms."[27]

Even where the "appropriate" form of differentiation among unequals for VE purposes does not involve a progressive rate structure, HE will lack normative content.[28] In order to determine whether equals are treated equally, the measure of equality has to be defined, i.e., in tax terms the tax base must be determined. Once that definition is properly articulated, it necessarily follows they will be treated alike. In a different, but relevant, area of the law, Professor Westen stated:

> The formula "people who are alike should be treated alike" involves two components: (I) (sic) a determination that two people are alike; and (2) a moral judgment that they ought to be treated alike. The determinative component is the first. Once one determines that two people are alike for purposes of the equality principle, one knows how they ought to be treated.[29]

26. Musgrave II, supra note 1, at 358.

27. Id. at 356.

28. There has been a debate over whether equality has any normative content in the context of the administration of justice. That discussion is relevant to our analysis. See, e.g., Peter Westen, The Empty Idea of Equality, 95 Harv. L. Rev. 537 (1982); Erwin Chemerinsky, In Defense of Equality: A Reply to Professor Westen, 81 Mich. L. Rev. 575 (1983); Anthony D'Amato, Comment: Is Equality a Totally Empty Idea. 81 Mich. L. Rev. 600 (1983); Kenneth L. Karst, Why Equality Matters, 17 Ga. L. Rev. 245 (1983); Kenneth W. Simons, Equality As a Comparative Right, 65 B.U.L. Rev. 387 (1985).

29. Westen, supra note 28, at 543.

The first component is satisfied in the context of taxation by a selection and definition of a tax base. Thus, with respect to HE, once one has decided on the tax base (say, income), then all that is required is a definition of income.[30] However, once income is defined, those with equal amounts of income will, by definition, be taxed equally. If a particular item which constitutes "income" is not taxed or a consumption cost is allowed to be deducted, we know that the provision is "bad" and applying HE adds nothing to that analysis.

Musgrave resorts to external resources to support his assertion of the independence of HE. For example, he refers to the fact that it reflects "a basic premise of social mores"[31] and is "almost universally accepted."[32] And, in his assertion that it is necessary to conceive of a "meta principle" by which trade-offs between VE and HE may be weighed in assessing a particular tax revision, he relies on "the public's sense of equity."[33] We do not imply that Musgrave is inappropriately calling on these principles to justify HE. We only point out that in this process, he is doing exactly what both he and Kaplow do in asserting a normative content for VE.

In summary, we believe that Musgrave/Kaplow exchange reveals the following: (1) Musgrave in 1959 demonstrated that there is no independent content to VE and resort must be had to economic assumptions and a theory of justice to provide that content; (2) we read Kaplow as agreeing with that view and he, in fact, does infuse VE with just such content; and (3) given Kaplow's now content-infused VE, he has demonstrated (and Musgrave agrees in an ideal world) that HE is subsumed within it and has no independent normative content

For us, however, both HE and VE at best become surrogates to describe consistency with or departures from the underlying decisions about the tax base and rate structure. The question is whether they are useful surrogates or whether they confuse or obscure the real issues that should be addressed in assessing proposed or actual changes in tax structure. We address those issues in III, below. But first we turn to the indexes of HE discussed by Kaplow and Musgrave.

30. Musgrave, supra note 3, at 161.
31. Musgrave II, supra note 1, at 355.
32. Id. at 356.
33. Id. at 358.

II. Measurement Issues

A. *The Kaplow/Musgrave Exchange*

If one agrees with our conceptual analysis, it follows that any attempt to develop an index to measure the extent to which a tax change violates HE or VE is futile. However, economists, including Musgrave,[34] have sought to develop such indexes.

Kaplow asserts that the inadequacies of HE as an independent normative concept become apparent when one seeks to measure it. He states that two major problems exist. First, unless HE is viewed as an absolute constraint, it is necessary to assign some measure of the degree to which it is violated.[35] Second, since by definition HE applies only to equals, it does not address individuals whose positions initially differ.[36] Thus, Kaplow observes, that "even an infinitesimal difference in treatment beyond whatever range is deemed 'equal treatment' counts as a violation, while further deviations, no matter how significant, are ignored."[37]

Kaplow analyzes the efforts of investigators who have sought to deal with these problems by measuring changes in HE. He states that several economists have sought to measure the HE impact of a tax law change by comparing the pre-change ranking of taxpayers to the post-change ranking of taxpayers.[38] If the rankings change, HE is said to be violated.[39] For example, assume that prior to a tax law change the ranking of individual[40] taxpayers A, B, and C, based on after-tax income is:

34. See Musgrave I, supra note 1, at 117-20; Musgrave II, supra note 1, at 357-58.

35. Kaplow I, supra note 1, at 140.

36. Id.

37. Id. at 140-41.

38. The rankings are based on measures of economic well-being. See, e.g., Robert Plotnick, A Comparison of Measures of Horizontal Equity, in Horizontal Equity, Uncertainty, and Economic Well-Being 239, 246-47 (Martin H. David & Smeeding Timoth eds., 1985). Economists have suggested or actually employed various definitions of income or utility in ranking the economic well-being of taxpayers. See, e.g., A.B. Atkinson, Horizontal Equity and the Distribution of the Tax Burden, in The Economics of Taxation 3-19 (Henry J. Aaron & Michael J. Boskin eds., 1980); Martin Feldstein, On the Theory of Tax Reform, 6 J. Pub. Econ. 77 (1976); Mervyn A. King, An Index of Inequality: With Applications to Horizontal Equity and Social Mobility, 51 Econometrica 99 (1983); Harvey S. Rosen, An Approach to the Study of Income, Utility, and Horizontal Equity, 92 Q. J. Econ. 307 (1978).

39. See Kaplow I, supra note 1, at 141, 146-48. See also King, supra note 38 at 99-115; Robert Plotnick, The Concept and Measurement of Horizontal Equity, 17 J. Pub. Econ. 373, 373-91 (1982).

40. Usually, individual taxpayers are not ranked but rather groups of similar taxpayers are ranked. This example uses individuals for illustrative purposes.

Ranking	Taxpayer	Income
1	A	100
2	B	99
3	C	50

while after the tax change the ranking of taxpayers based on their after-tax income is:

Ranking	Taxpayer	Income
1	B	99
2	A	98
3	C	50

HE is deemed violated by the change because B and A have changed ranks.

Kaplow argues that the ranking studies suffer from essentially the same defects as the concept of HE itself because a small change in income (A's income dropped only by 2 in the above example) as a result of a tax law change may result in a rank change while a large change in income might result in no rank change.[41] This is illustrated by the following example.

Consider again taxpayers who have the following after-tax income and rankings prior to a tax law change:

Ranking	Taxpayer	Income
1	A	100
2	B	99
3	C	50

As discussed above, if A's after-tax income were to decrease by 2 to 98 as the result of a tax law change, while the income of B and C remain the same, the ranking studies would show a violation of HE because A and B have switched ranks.

Contrast this result with the consequences where the tax change causes A's income to increase to 147, B's income to decrease from 99 to 51, and C's income stays at 50.

Ranking	Taxpayer	Income
1	A	147
2	B	51
3	C	50

41. Kaplow I, supra note 1, at 141.

Note that the rankings have not changed and, therefore, that no change in HE would be registered by the ranking analysis although the disparity between A's and B's income has increased markedly. Also note that Kaplow correctly states that the indexes are not measuring the treatment of equals (HE), but really are measuring the treatment of unequals (VE) since the ranking process begins with individuals (or groups) with different incomes.[42]

Lastly, Kaplow asks why the ranking of taxpayers prior to the tax law change is the starting point for this form of HE analysis.[43] The use of changes in the ranking of taxpayers to measure the impact of a tax law change on HE must in effect assume that the pre-change ranking achieved HE. Yet, Kaplow observes, the pre-change ranking is itself the result of several prior tax law changes that may or may not have achieved HE.[44]

Musgrave also proposes an index that seeks to measure HE. Rather than using a ranking system such as that described above, Musgrave devised an index with two parts. The first part, the HE component, would measure the difference between the welfare cost of the tax system if equals were treated equally and the welfare cost of the system when equals are not treated equally.[45] The second component, the VE component, would measure the difference between the welfare costs of the tax system assuming that VE had been achieved and the welfare costs of the tax system where VE is not achieved.[46] Musgrave uses the term welfare costs to represent the burden imposed on all taxpayers by the tax system. In his examples, he calculates welfare cost by assuming that the marginal utility of income declines as income increases.[47] He argues that his system of employing two components to isolate the welfare costs arising from the failure to achieve HE or VE is superior to ranking studies because his system measures changes in the allocation of tax burdens that might be considered significant but that might not result in a rank shift.[48]

42. Id.

43. Id. at 146-47.

44. Id. Kaplow notes that some authors have attempted to deal with this problem by determining what the distribution of income would be if the ideal tax system were in effect and then comparing the effect of the tax reform on the distribution of income to the ideal distribution. Id. at 147-48. However, Kaplow argues that the distribution analysis is really focusing on VE since it is analyzing the impact on unequals.

45. Musgrave I, supra note 1, at 117-18; Musgrave II, supra note 1, at 357-58.

46. Musgrave I, supra note 1, at 117-18; For this purpose, Musgrave assumes that VE has been achieved with a tax distribution that minimizes aggregate welfare costs.

47. Musgrave assumes a social welfare function that assigns a value of 10 to the first dollar of income, of 9.1 to the second dollar of income, of 8.19 to the third dollar of income, etc., with the social welfare of each successive dollar of income declining by 10%. Musgrave I, supra note 1, at 119.

48. Id. at 118.

A simple version of Musgrave's index will illustrate Musgrave's thesis. Consider four individuals L1, L2, H1, and H2. L1 and L2 have low incomes, each receiving $5, and are grouped together in the low rank category L. H1 and H2 have high incomes, each receiving $10, and are grouped together in the high rank category H. Two proposals to implement an income tax for the first time ever are being considered. The impact of the two proposals on the after-tax income and rankings of the individuals is illustrated below.

	Initial Income	Initial Group Rank	First Tax Proposal Tax	First Tax Proposal Net Income	First Tax Proposal Group Rank	Second Tax Proposal Tax	Second Tax Proposal Net Income	Second Tax Proposal Group Rank
H1	10	1	4	6	1	2.5	7.5	1
H2	10	1	4	6	1	3.8	6.2	1
L1	5	2	0	5	2	.4	4.6	2
L2	5	2	0	5	2	1.3	3.7	2

Note that although the two tax proposals have a disparate impact on the members of the two groups, L and H, the reforms do not register a rank change so long as only two ranking groups are used because H1 and H2 still have after-tax incomes that place them in the highest ranking group and L1 and L2 still have incomes that place them in the lowest group. Thus, using the ranking analysis, each proposal is consistent with HE although after-tax incomes differ markedly depending upon which proposal is adopted.

Musgrave's index attempts to capture the HE movement which the ranking studies miss. In addition, Musgrave's index attempts to measure VE differences. Thus, under Musgrave's approach, the two systems would register different welfare impacts, as illustrated below.[49]

	Initial Income	First Tax Proposal Tax	First Tax Proposal Net Income	Second Tax Proposal Tax	Second Tax Proposal Net Income
H1	10	4	6	2.5	7.5
H2	10	4	6	3.8	6.2
L1	5	0	5	.4	4.6
L2	5	0	5	1.3	3.7
VE Welfare costs as result of not achieving VE		0		6.4	

49. This example is obtained from Musgrave II, supra note 1, at 357.

HE welfare costs as result of not achieving HE	0	2.3

Note that the first tax proposal has no excess welfare cost under Musgrave's approach,[50] but the second tax reform registers both excess HE and VE costs.[51] Thus, the first tax proposal would be preferable.

Kaplow criticizes Musgrave's two-component index because it devotes one entire component (the HE component) to the few persons who just happen to be equal while all other persons are lumped together in the VE component. In terms of the above example, if L1 and L2 had not started with identical incomes of 5 but had instead had initial incomes of 5 and 4.9, and H1 and H2 had not started with initial incomes of 10 each, but had initial incomes of 10 and 9.9, no HE measure would be applied to the treatment of H1, H2, L1, and L2. Instead, the treatment of H1, H2, L1, and L2 would be measured solely by the VE index. Kaplow asks why a separate index, the HE index, should be devoted solely to the measurement of the impact of individuals who start out as equals when all other taxpayers are lumped into the VE index.[52] Moreover, Kaplow asks what weight should be assigned to VE and HE costs. For example, if one proposed tax law change results in an excess VE cost of 6 and HE cost of 0 while the other result in an excess VE cost of 3 and HE cost of 3, both will have the same aggregate welfare cost of 6. Kaplow queries which tax proposal should be selected. He asserts that since both HE and VE derive from the same normative base,[53] it is difficult to see why they should have a different normative import.

In a subsequent article, Musgrave admits that in a complex world it is unrealistic "to limit considerations of departure from HE to individuals with identical incomes only, while disregarding the relative treatment of individuals with more or less similar incomes."[54] But he maintains that this does not mean that HE is a useless independent concept.

B. *Analysis*

In our view, Kaplow's analysis of the defects of ranking studies to analyze HE is correct. As noted above, to the extent that ranking studies use

50. That is, equals are treated equally, and there is an "appropriate" differentiation between H and L.

51. That is, equals are not treated equally, and there is not an "appropriate" distinction in the treatment of unequals.

52. Kaplow II, supra note 1, at 195.

53. See supra text accompanying notes 3-7.

54. Musgrave II, supra note 1, at 358.

the distribution of income existing prior to a tax law change as a base to measure the HE impact of the change, the studies are in effect assuming that the pre-change distribution achieved HE, an assumption that appears to be extremely weak. Moreover, because in the real world the ranking studies compare the impact of the change on taxpayers or groups of taxpayers who start with different incomes, Kaplow is correct in asserting that ranking studies really involve a VE analysis.

We also believe that Musgrave's effort to defend the vitality of his indexes for measuring HE and VE ultimately must fail. We believe that his concession quoted above that the HE component cannot be limited to taxpayers with identical incomes is in fact a reversion to his 1959 assertion that HE folds into VE once a system that makes appropriate distinctions among unequals is adopted. Moreover, the VE component gives no information in addition to the economic assumption made by Musgrave that the marginal utility of income declines. Finally, it follows that the index will not assist in identifying relevant trade-offs in assessing proposed tax changes because VE and HE both are derivative concepts. Because HE and VE derive their normative base from economic judgments, values based on some theory of justice and efficiency concerns, the relevant trade-off is between or among those potentially conflicting fundamental judgments and values.

If it is agreed that objective indexes of HE and VE are not likely to be developed, the question remains as to whether HE and VE concepts may have some utility in the real world.

III. HE AND VE AS SURROGATES FOR BASIC ECONOMIC AND JUSTICE DECISIONS

A. *Kaplow's Suggestions*

Although Kaplow rejects both the proposition that HE contains any normative content and the validity of indexes of measures of HE, he nonetheless concludes his 1989 article by suggesting some practical, if limited, uses for which HE may be employed. Two of those uses are:

(1) HE analysis may reveal provisions (or the absence thereof) that are the source of inefficiencies or which need adjustment in order that VE norms may be applied properly.[55]

55. Kaplow I, supra note 1, at 149.

(2) Repeated violations of HE could have adverse effects on (presumably labor and investment) incentives and undesirably impose the element of risk.[56]

B. *Analysis*

Kaplow concludes that none of these uses demonstrates any normative content to HE (and, we would add, the same is true for VE). Instead, according to Kaplow, they serve as signals that something is amiss that needs investigation. The question is whether attention to HE in the above situations (and others he describes) adds anything to the analytical process.

To take Kaplow's first example, would application of HE analysis have added anything to the analysis of the need for the time value of money rules enacted in 1984? Indeed, the more troubling question is whether a focus on HE concerns would have masked the source of the problems and hence the need for the changes. That is, were not principles of income definition and allocation of income and expenses to proper accounting periods sufficient to indicate the need for changes?[57] After applying the principles, what further could HE analysis have provided that would have led to any different conclusions about the appropriate legislative responses?

In the case of Kaplow's second example, if legislative changes impose undesirable elements of risk, it is the identification of the undesirable risk effects (undesirability measured in terms of risk, not HE) that will be determinative. HE adds nothing to the analysis and waiting for HE analysis to reveal the risk effects may postpone identification of problems that would have been revealed if risk analysis were used to begin with.

Similar lines of analysis lead to the conclusion that Kaplow's other suggested uses of HE are better served by an examination of the fundamental concerns that underlie each problem.

Because Musgrave sees a broader role for HE than the practical uses suggested by Kaplow, he presumably does not object to these lesser suggestions. We suggest, however, that the questions raised as to the more limited uses require further exploration. In the end, we believe, any use of HE is going to be driven by more fundamental concerns. The question for advocates of even limited use of HE is why should analysis not begin and end in terms of those more fundamental concerns. The risk is that relying on HE or VE analysis might lead policymakers and the public astray if those

56. Id.

57. In 1959, Musgrave observed that once the appropriate income definition is agreed upon, most of the HE concerns have been resolved. Musgrave, supra note 3, at 161.

concepts in fact do not accurately or adequately reflect underlying principles in a given situation.[58]

C. *The Effect of Tax Expenditure Analysis on HE and VE*

Even if one believes that HE and VE analyses do or should have a role to play, it is important to keep in mind the kind of provision being assessed. If the provision is a tax expenditure, HE and VE notions should not play a role in assessing a change. As McDaniel demonstrated in an earlier article,[59] the introduction or removal of a tax expenditure has no impact on tax equity, whether HE or VE. This counter-intuitive result flows from the tax expenditure construct itself: a taxpayer is deemed to pay tax based on economic income and is then given a Treasury check in an amount equal to the subsidies run through the tax system for which he or she qualifies. Obviously, in the real world two checks are not exchanged. Instead, the taxpayer nets his or her "economic tax check" amount with the "tax subsidy" check amount and remits the difference (or gets a refund). But focusing on the economic tax check portion of the analysis reveals that a tax expenditure is not the object of traditional tax HE or VE concerns. Indeed, if those concerns are applied to tax expenditures (as frequently they are), policy-makers can be led astray (e.g., "no new taxes" as a call to oppose repeal of a tax expenditure). Of course, there are equity concerns to address in assessing tax expenditures. But those concerns are those that are involved in assessing the outlay side of the budget (which may or may not be identical to tax notions of HE and VE).

Use of tax expenditure analysis also is consistent with our criticisms of HE and VE. That is, tax expenditure analysis avoids HE and VE altogether and focuses directly on the issues of why, for example, an item of income is untaxed and what the economic and distributional effects of that omission are.

IV. CONCLUSION

The Kaplow/Musgrave exchange has raised issues of considerable theoretical and practical interest. Our analysis of this exchange leads us to the following conclusions: (1) neither HE nor VE has any independent normative content, and that content must be supplied by reference to economic assumptions and a theory of justice; (2) Kaplow has demonstrated convincingly the inadequacies of efforts to develop indexes that will measure

58. See Westen, supra note 28 (making a similar point in his broader analysis of equality).

59. Paul R. McDaniel, Identification of the "Tax" in "Effective Tax Rates," "Tax Reform" and "Tax Equity," 38 Nat'l Tax J. 273, 277 (1985).

movements in HE as a result of tax law changes; and (3) it is not likely that HE and VE add anything to the need to analyze tax changes in terms of basic tax policy objectives and indeed may conceal problems or lead policymakers astray as particular tax changes are considered.

[15]

REALIZATION, RECOGNITION, RECONCILIATION, RATIONALITY AND THE STRUCTURE OF THE FEDERAL INCOME TAX SYSTEM

Patricia D. White *

TABLE OF CONTENTS

Federal income tax reform is much talked about these days. No longer the sole province of the person with a professional interest in the tax system, tax reform is discussed, at some level or other, by people in every walk of life. This recent popularity is due largely to the widespread unpopularity of the current system. This popularity is also responsible, unfortunately, for making large-scale, reflective, and systemically coherent reform highly unlikely, and for ensuring that frequent, politically motivated, piecemeal legislative change will continue. The Tax Reform Act of 1986 probably illustrates the most

* Visiting Professor of Law, University of Michigan. B.A. 1971, M.A. 1974, J.D. 1974, University of Michigan. — Ed.

I want to thank Charlotte Crane, Martin Ginsburg, Patrick Gudridge, Robert Haft, Daniel Halperin, Douglas Kahn, Jeffrey Lehman, Elliott Manning, George Mundstock, and Frederick Schauer for their helpful comments on earlier drafts of this paper. I would also like to thank June Jones, William Sider, and Aaron Stauber for their able research assistance.

to be hoped for in the present climate.[1] Nonetheless, talk of real reform will surely persist, and theoreticians of tax policy will continue to do the hard work that ought to underlie tax reform.

Despite the skepticism revealed by the above remarks, this article, too, is a plea for reform. It is not, however, directed at the ills that have stirred public discontent and made tax reform such a popular topic. Instead, it addresses the conceptual features that characterize the federal income tax system as a system. I am interested in changing the way we think about certain fundamental aspects of any income tax system and thereby in clarifying the way we describe, explain, understand, and argue about our own system, whatever it may look like at a particular time. Call this an argument for conceptual reform.

Serious normative discussion about our tax system typically falls into one of two broad spheres. The first is concerned principally with the interpretation of existing law. Such discussions are normative because they attempt to establish how a particular circumstance or sort of circumstance *ought* to be treated by the tax law as it in fact exists. This sort of normative discussion is very common, since a salient characteristic of federal income tax law is the frequent opportunity for disagreement about the details of its application. Arguments about the actual intent or content of the Code, Regulations, administrative positions, and case law fall within this category.

The second sphere of discussion is more obviously normative, encompassing accounts of what the tax law ought to be. Usually these fall under the broad rubric of discussions of "tax policy." In this group I include discussions of the hard questions surrounding social and economic goals, political expediency, administrability, and other questions concerning the proper role in society of the tax rules, their effects, or both. I conceive of policy questions as those focusing on what makes a *good* system or *good* rule or set of rules within a system. Policy discussions can concentrate on asking what the goals of the set of tax rules ought to be as well as on asking how best to implement particular goals.

The distinction between discussions that purport to be about how existing law should be interpreted and those that purport to be about

1. For a brief and characteristically wise account of the nature of the reform achieved by the Tax Reform Act of 1986, see Bittker, *Tax Reform — Yesterday, Today, and Tomorrow,* 44 WASH. & LEE L. REV. 11 (1987). For a lively account of the background to the 1986 legislation, see Chirelstein, *Back from the Dead: How President Reagan Saved the Income Tax,* 14 FLA. ST. U. L. REV. 207 (1986). For an analysis of the prodigious rate of recent tax reform. see Doernberg & McChesney, *On the Accelerating Rate and Decreasing Durability of Tax Reform,* 71 MINN. L. REV. 913 (1987).

what the law ought to be is rough at best,[2] and it is not my intention to make overmuch of it. Indeed, discussions within each sphere often make use of arguments from the other. Thus, for example, it is common practice to invoke fairness in an argument for reading the Code (or legislative history of administrative pronouncements or case law) one way rather than another. Similarly, an argument that something constitutes good policy may make persuasive use of the claim that current law can be interpreted in a particular way.

Normative discussions of both sorts sometimes rely on claims about the internal coherence of the tax system itself. Arguments for or against a particular interpretation or policy frequently are based on concerns for the internal coherence or rationality of the system. Professor Wayne Barnett's celebrated *amicus* brief in *Commissioner v. Tufts*[3] provides an instructive example.

In *Tufts* the Supreme Court was asked to determine the amount realized by a taxpayer who had sold property subject to a nonrecourse mortgage whose face value exceeded the fair market value of the property. The United States Court of Appeals for the Fifth Circuit had held that the amount realized was limited to the fair market value of the property. The government argued that the amount realized for the asset included the full face value of the assumed mortgage. The government's argument was based on the view that the *Crane*[4] rule's inclusion of an assumed loan's face value in a seller's amount realized and its corresponding inclusion of the amount of a purchase money mortgage in an asset's basis should be generalized to apply to the unusual case where the value of the property is less than the outstanding amount of the mortgage.[5] The Supreme Court overruled the Fifth

2. Some might deny even the possibility of such a distinction on the ground that law can be read or interpreted to say almost anything the interpreter desires, but that sort of analysis seems ill-suited to interpretation of the Internal Revenue Code.

3. Brief for *Amicus Curiae*, Commissioner v. Tufts, 461 U.S. 300 (1983) (No. 81-1536). Barnett's position was rejected by the Court but was accorded respect unusual for an *amicus* brief. The majority opinion devotes a footnote to describing his argument and says that, "[a]lthough this indeed could be a justifiable mode of analysis, it has not been adopted by the Commissioner." Commissioner v. Tufts, 461 U.S. 300, 310-11 n.11 (1983). Justice O'Connor, concurring, endorsed Barnett's view in theory, saying, "were we writing on a slate clean except for the decision in *Crane v. Commissioner*, 331 U.S. 1 (1947)," she would take Barnett's approach. *Tufts*, 461 U.S. at 317 (O'Connor, J., concurring). Barnett's brief has also provoked unusual interest among commentators. *See, e.g.*, M. GRAETZ, FEDERAL INCOME TAXATION 234 (1985); Andrews, *On Beyond* Tufts, 61 TAXES 949 (1983); Lurie, *New Ghosts for Old —* Crane *Footnote 37 Is Dead (Or Is It?)*, 2 AM. J. TAX POLY. 89 (1983).

4. Crane v. Commissioner, 331 U.S. 1 (1947).

5. Whether the *Crane* rule should be generalized to apply to this kind of circumstance was put into doubt in footnote 37 of the *Crane* opinion itself. There, in a celebrated piece of dictum, the Court wrote:

> Obviously, if the value of the property is less than the amount of the mortgage, a mortgagor who is not personally liable cannot realize a benefit equal to the mortgage. Consequentiy, a

Circuit and adopted the government's position.

Barnett's *amicus* brief argued that the issue had been miscast by the government and that it was a mistake to view the case simply as presenting the question of how much the seller had realized for the asset upon its sale. Instead, he argued, the transaction should be viewed as *two* dispositions and the "amount-realized" question should be asked for each. Thus, the seller is indeed selling the property, but he is also disposing of a liability. Each disposition has an associated gain or loss. Any gain associated with the asset is capital gain, subject, at the time of *Tufts* (and probably soon again), to a preferential tax rate, while any gain associated with relief from the liability is ordinary income. The *Tufts* facts suggest a capital loss on the sale of the asset and an ordinary gain as a result of the liability relief.

Barnett's argument is interesting in part because he maintains that the law, properly interpreted, *does in fact* require the kind of bifurcation he describes and because he gives as evidence for that claim an argument that appeals to the coherence and rationality of the system:

> *A rational system* for measuring income *also requires,* however, that all receipts and expenditures be accounted for at some time and hence that those that are not finally accounted for when they occur be kept in a suspense account so that proper account can be taken of them at another time. In the case of an asset, the amount that needs to be kept track of (the unaccounted-for prior expenditures) has by statute been given a name — it is the taxpayer's "basis" for the asset (§ 1012) — and the *necessity* of having such an account is therefore familiar. But *there is obviously just as much need* to keep track of a taxpayer's unaccounted-for prior receipts with respect to a liability, and that amount too needs to have a name.[6]

Thus, Barnett appeals to the coherence and rationality of the system as a justification for his interpretation of the law. Yet, only if one assumes that the tax system *is* in fact consistently coherent and rational, or if a tax system (or at least our tax system) *ought* to be coherent and rational, can the requirements of rationality be a reason for accepting Barnett's interpretation. The first proposition is clearly false. The second is a normative claim and itself requires justification. An appeal to internal systemic coherency or rationality does not, by itself, provide a reason — sufficient or otherwise — either for inter-

---

different problem might be encountered where a mortgagor abandoned the property or transferred it subject to the mortgage without receiving boot. That is not this case.

Crane, 331 U.S. at 14, n.37. The first case directly to address the issue was Millar v. Commissioner, 577 F.2d 212 (3d Cir.), *cert. denied,* 439 U.S. 1046 (1978), which held that the taxpayer's gain was not limited by the fair market value of the abandoned property. *Millar,* 577 F.2d at 215-16. For a brief, but clear and illuminating, discussion of this part of the background to *Tufts,* see Andrews, *supra* note 3, at 950-52.

6. Brief for *Amicus Curiae, supra* note 3, at 3-4 (emphasis added).

preting the tax law in a particular way or for making a policy judgment. Moreover, any argument for the claim would itself be an instance of a normative discussion about what the law should be rather than a discussion about how the law as it is should be interpreted. As it happens, Barnett neither makes nor acknowledges the need for such an argument.[7]

Barnett is not unusual in this respect. Even people who rely on claims about systemic coherence or rationality when arguing for a particular interpretation of tax law or for some tax policy do not directly confront the question whether the system *should* be rational or coherent. Yet given the obvious lack of consistency and coherence among the hundreds of provisions in the current Internal Revenue Code and the piecemeal character of tax legislative activity, it is an argument that must not seem self-evident to those who formulate our tax law. To what extent, if any, should internal coherence and rationality be goals of an income tax system?

Having asked the question, this article does not purport to answer it.[8] It does, however, try to do some of the work that a serious answer would require. To that end, it focuses on the underlying structure on which the content of the tax law hangs. By isolating the structure of tax systems generally, perhaps we can come to understand and describe our own system better, and to begin to develop a more useful and richer conceptual vocabulary that is independent of concerns about the content of the tax base. Only then can we be more self-conscious about exactly what coherence and rationality in our tax system might mean, and about the possible tradeoffs between that value and other values that we might want the system to embody. Further, we should gain a better understanding of the structure of our arguments about the content of the income tax system.

I begin, then, with the observation that systemic coherence and rationality are not necessary qualities of a tax system. Are there, nonetheless, any structural features that must, as a matter of logic, underlie *any* tax system? On examination, there *are* a few structural requirements that are necessarily common to any tax system. In Part

7. This may be somewhat unfair to Barnett since he only speaks here of rationality and not of coherence. If it is rational — as indeed it might be — to talk about its being rational for a tax system to be comprised of an incoherent collection of rational parts, then Barnett need only argue that the component parts of the tax system ought to be rational. He does not make this argument either. Moreover, at another point in his brief he writes, "And that, of course, is just as it *should and must be:* given the treatment of the 'opening' transaction as an independent liability-creating transaction, no other treatment of the 'closing' transaction would be *coherent.*" *Id.* at nn.7-8 (emphasis added).

8. Nor does it argue for or against particular applications or interpretations of current federal income tax law, nor make recommendations about what the content of the tax law ought to be.

I of this article I examine those requirements. I show that by isolating the necessary structure of a tax system from its particular content or goals, we can better understand the role played within the federal system of certain of its most characteristic features. In particular, I trace the function of the realization requirement for the recognition of income and distinguish it from another sort of function that could lead to the recognition of income within an income tax system. This second function is a corrective one, and it is achieved in the federal system by a mechanism I call "reconciliation."

Reconciliation has considerable descriptive power within the federal system. I show this in Part II by examining, as examples, three general circumstances that are well described as instances of reconciliation. Two of the three lead to the recognition of income, yet neither can be properly described in terms of realization.[9]

Finally, in Part III, I argue that the notion of reconciliation can play an important role in normative discussions about the federal income tax system. This role has two parts. First, reconciliation describes actual phenomena within the federal system with more coherence and rationality than traditional vocabulary and concepts allow. Those who accept coherence within a tax system as a value will attach some value to that description. Second, describing those phenomena in that way implies certain further descriptions of other parts of the tax system. Sometimes, however, these further descriptions do not fit the law as it actually is, and so the overall coherence of the system will turn out to be less than it would have been if the law had been otherwise. In such cases, a desire for coherence above all else would indicate that the law ought to be changed. However, other, sometimes competing, values such as administrability or equity, can be relevant to determining whether the law really should be changed. When values compete, one will have to choose between particular aims on the one hand and the coherence and rationality of the system on the other. My purpose here is not to recommend a particular choice among these options, but rather to establish that self-conscious articulation and exploration of those values and their importance should be a goal of normative discussion about our income tax system. In Part

9. My interest in this sort of inquiry stems from my observation of our current system's inability to account easily for amounts that it includes in taxable income under the rubric of the tax benefit rule. The system seemed to struggle unduly to describe in its own terms what seemed to be a reasonably plausible, common-sense principle. It appeared to be missing the explicit conceptual apparatus that it should have for that task. In an earlier paper I suggested a conceptual framework within which the tax benefit rule could be more easily understood and described as a feature of the federal income tax system. *See* White, *An Essay on the Conceptual Foundations of the Tax Benefit Rule*, 82 MICH. L. REV. 486 (1983).

III, I illustrate this argument by showing that, in contrast to the usual description, reconciliation allows us to describe the tax treatment of simple borrowing in a way that is internally consistent and coherent. I discuss the implications of this coherent description for the analysis of purchase money mortgages and for the central issue in *Tufts.* Ironically, although my analysis does suggest the kind of transactional bifurcation advocated by Barnett, the requirements of rationality turn out to be somewhat different from what he claims, and to come closer to the current system than we might expect. There are important respects, however, in which the analysis is not consistent with current practice. Instead of arguing that the law ought either to be reformed or differently interpreted, I explore one significant administrative cost of implementing the analysis and suggest that a full articulation of the issue in *Tufts* would be more complicated than indicated by either Barnett or the Supreme Court.

I. The Basic Structure of Any Tax System

Any tax system must make some effort to determine what is potentially taxable. If it is a system that purports to tax income, it need not define "income," but it must nonetheless offer some means of identifying that which might be taxed.[10] Once something has been deemed potentially taxable, a system has three possible responses: it can tax the item or amount currently, it can tax it later, or it can exempt it from taxation.[11]

No tax system need employ all three basic responses, much less any of their variations.[12] The simplest system would first determine

10. I use the phrase "potentially taxable amount" rather than the word "income" to designate that which falls within the purview of a taxing system. This is because all that is logically required of the structure of any income tax system, as of any tax system of whatever description, is some means of dividing the world into those items that might possibly be taxed and those items that could not be.

11. Actually, there is a fourth general possibility — some combination of the other options — but since it is clearly a derivative of the others, I shall not isolate the idea of an allocation scheme in the following discussion.

12. Items that satisfy the threshold criterion (whatever that may be) must be reacted to by the system in one of the three basic ways. Those items that do not (and there need not be any of them), simply elicit no reaction (although this effect, of course, is equivalent to being excluded). A system with a clear definition of "income" might use that definition as the threshold criterion for dividing the world. Any system (like the federal income tax system) with no clear definition of "income," could employ other criteria to make the division — or it could employ none, and make no division at all. A system might well operate with some implicit sense of what should be included in "income," and its reactions to the items it considers could be arranged so as to tax only those items deemed to be "income." (In fact, the federal income tax system may operate to some extent in this last way. In the federal system, taxable income is determined in part by deducting from gross income those expenses that it is thought appropriate to net against revenue included in gross income. For an interesting criticism of the idea that tax accounting should accept this sort of matching as a central principle, see Gunn, *Matching of Costs and Revenues as*

that something is potentially taxable and then immediately tax it. Perhaps some sort of periodic accounting convention would be instituted for administrative ease, but the principal inquiry in such a system would be *what* to tax.[13] The only significant additional complications in such a system would involve the quantification and valuation of what was to be taxed.[14]

A more complicated system might allow either of two reactions to the determination that something is potentially taxable: tax it now or tax it later. As before, if something were deemed to be within the aegis of the tax system it would be taxed, but in this sort of a system the timing could vary. Various sorts of criteria might be used to determine which reaction was appropriate: random choice, alternating reactions, or reactions designed to bring about a particular state of affairs. The many examples of the latter include the desire to maximize revenue, administrative ease, social welfare, aid or comparative advantage to some group or other, and economic parity among taxpayers. Here the system must answer both the questions *what* to tax and *when* to tax it.

A system that admits of the third possible response and reacts to the determination that something is potentially taxable by taxing it currently, taxing it later, or by not taxing it after all is significantly more complex than either of the first two types. The same range of criteria is available to guide its choices as in a system with two possible reactions, but, because exclusion is now a possibility, everything that is potentially taxable need not eventually be taxed. This means that the system can use exclusion to tailor its tax base and that the determination that something is potentially taxable is not necessarily determina-

a Goal of Tax Accounting, 4 VA. TAX REV. 1 (1984). *But see* Crane, *Matching and the Income Tax Base: The Special Case of Tax Exempt Income*, 5 AM. J. TAX POLY. 191, 204 n.18 (1986).) In any event, however, labeling everything that falls within the scope of some income tax system "income" for the purpose of the system would be misleading. Moreover, the term itself is so fraught with meaning that it seems ill-advised to use it schematically.

13. A system could answer the question "what is potentially taxable?" in an infinite variety of ways. Possible potentially taxable items include: salary, free time, bagels consumed, use of one's own winter jacket, and impacted wisdom teeth. Moreover, the *what* to tax question is inextricably tied to the question of *whom* to tax. Thus, the examples might include: a taxpayer's own salary, a taxpayer's spouse's free time, bagels consumed by the taxpayer's family, use of any jacket by a taxpayer's nephew, and incidents of impacted wisdom teeth on the taxpayer's block (or on some block which the taxpayer has never seen). *See infra* note 39 and accompanying text; *see also* McIntyre, *Implications of US Tax Reform for Distributive Justice*, 5 AUSTL. TAX F. 219, 239-40 (1988).

14. Quantification is a different issue from valuation. It arises because the world is not naturally described in numerical amounts, and a tax system would seem to require some common denominator for quantifying whatever is to be taxed. Valuation involves the actual assignment of value to whatever is to be taxed. Quantification and valuation issues can both be intractable, and I have no intention of minimizing either their importance or their difficulty.

tive of what will in fact be taxed. The increased flexibility offered by the possibility of exclusion would serve no purpose if the determination of what was potentially taxable fully satisfied the normative goals for the tax base. As a result, a system that makes use of exclusion in addition to deferral must answer an additional question: *whether* to tax that which it has deemed potentially taxable. The *what* to tax question is no longer fully answered by the determination of what is potentially taxable; instead, it is only answered as the *whether* to tax question is answered. Indeed, it may only be completely answered after the timing issues implicit in the *when* to tax question are fully resolved. The federal income tax system is a good example of this phenomenon. It does not, although its authors could have allowed it to, rely on a definition of "income" (perhaps a Haig-Simons standard)[15] to determine what is potentially taxable and then use current taxation, deferral, and exclusion as mechanisms for departing from the standard established by the definition. Instead, it uses the responses themselves (particularly deduction and exclusion) to achieve something very loosely approaching a standard for income.

The crucial observation is that the three possible responses to what has been deemed potentially taxable provide a crude model for a tax system of whatever degree of complexity. By themselves, they neither prescribe nor proscribe any criteria for their application. Nor do they entail any requirement that the criteria chosen be applied consistently.[16] Thus, whatever treatment an income tax system ultimately accords anything it identifies as potentially taxable can be described in terms of current taxation, deferral, or exclusion. A system need not determine at the point of the item's characterization as potentially taxable which of the three treatments it will receive. That decision may be deferred, but ultimately the item will either be taxed or excluded.[17]

Any criteria could be employed by an income tax system to decide whether to tax currently something deemed potentially taxable, to defer its taxation, or to exclude it from taxation. A system could be more or less systematic in its selection and articulation of these criteria. Doubtless at some point the taxing mechanism would cease prop-

15. The Haig-Simons definition of income is an ideal much favored by economists. Henry Simons' classic statement of the definition: "Personal income may be defined as the algebraic sum of (1) the market value of rights exercised in consumption and (2) the change in the value of the store of property rights between the beginning and end of the period in question." H. SIMONS, PERSONAL INCOME TAXATION 50 (1938).

16. Two distinct sorts of consistency might be required. The first is that the criteria treat the same item in the same way in identical circumstances, the second is that similar items or circumstances be accorded at least similar treatment. A *system* would seem to require consistency of the first sort. It is consistency of the second type that I am referring to in the text.

17. *See infra* text accompanying notes 38-60.

erly to be called a "system" if the choices about recognition were thoroughly *ad hoc*, but there is an enormous range within which a system could operate.[18] In the United States and elsewhere there might, of course, be constitutional or other legal constraints on the content of an income tax system, but such limitations bear on the system's legitimacy, not on its status as a system.[19]

A system might well include some means of keeping track of how potentially taxable amounts have been treated.[20] This would seem particularly desirable if the system were designed so as not to tax any potentially taxable amount more than once. Income tax systems generally are characterized by this feature and, indeed, it may usefully distinguish an income tax from a wealth tax, a property tax, or a receipts tax. In the federal income tax, basis is the mechanism used to keep track of what has been taxed and what has not been.[21] Nonetheless, a tracking mechanism is not a necessary feature of a tax system — even of an income tax system.

The essential structure of an income tax system, then, requires only a mechanism or mechanisms for identifying what is potentially taxable and a mechanism or mechanisms for determining whether that amount is to be recognized at the point of its identification, to have its recognition deferred, or to be given permanent nonrecognition treatment. The system could, of course, provide that all potentially taxable amounts are to be treated in the same specific way. In that case, there would not be any need for any separate mechanisms to determine whether or when to tax them. It is easy to lose sight of this fundamental structural simplicity when confronting a system as complex as the one embodied in the current Internal Revenue Code. Nevertheless, for

18. For example, a system could provide for the immediate recognition of everything potentially taxable, yet exclude (or permit the deduction of) all (potentially taxable) salary earned by an employee of an American automobile manufacturer (or, better yet, by a university professor). Or it might provide for a ten-year deferral of the recognition of one third of all potentially taxable amounts credited to each taxpayer born on the same day as the Commissioner of the Internal Revenue Service (a date that would doubtless vary from Commissioner to Commissioner) and for the nontaxation of all potentially taxable amounts attributed to 100,000 (or 1000 or 10) taxpayers chosen, freely with no constraints whatever, by the head elephant keeper at the National Zoo.

19. *See generally* Bittker & Kaufman, *Taxes and Civil Rights: "Constitutionalizing" the Internal Revenue Code*, 82 YALE L.J. 51 (1972); Norton, *The Limitless Federal Taxing Power*, 8 HARV. J.L. & PUB. POLY. 591 (1985).

20. I am indebted to Charlotte Crane for forcing me to focus on this point at this point.

21. I.R.C. § 1012 (1988) defines a property's "basis" as its "cost" to the taxpayer. I.R.C. § 1016 (1988) sets forth rules for adjusting basis upward or downward to reflect additional costs incurred by the taxpayer with respect to the property or returns to the taxpayer of the costs previously included. *See infra* note 101. Adjusted basis is the operative amount wherever the Code makes use of basis. William Andrews aptly describes adjusted basis as reflecting "the whole history of the tax treatment of an item." Andrews, *supra* note 3, at 954; *see also* Crane, *supra* note 12, at 217-23.

reasons that I trust will become increasingly clear, it is instructive to examine the underlying fundament.

A. *The Role of Realization*

In the federal income tax system, one mechanism used for determining that a potentially taxable amount will be currently recognized is the notion of realization. Articulating the exact content of the concept may well be impossible (if indeed there is a single coherent concept),[22] but its function in the structure of the system is apparent. Simply put, our system[23] generally regards the realization of a potentially taxable amount as the occasion for its recognition. It does not, however, always recognize potentially taxable amounts when they are realized.[24] Nor, as long as a system has some means of determining how to treat potentially taxable amounts, is there any systemic reason why realization as intended by the federal system need play any role in the recognition/deferred recognition/nonrecognition determination.

These observations about the general structural requirements of an income tax system seem almost too obvious to be worth making. They become important, however, because they were so little understood in the early evolution of our system. As a consequence, that system became enormously complex without the degree of structural self-consciousness that one might have hoped for. This complexity, in turn, obscures both the actual relationships between central features of the

22. *See, e.g.*, 1 B. BITTKER & L. LOKKEN, FEDERAL TAXATION OF INCOME, ESTATES AND GIFTS § 5.2 (2d ed. 1989); M. CHIRELSTEIN, FEDERAL INCOME TAXATION ¶ 5 (5th ed. 1988); R. MAGILL, TAXABLE INCOME pt. I (rev. ed. 1945).

23. I emphasize "our" because an income tax system need not rely on or even have a realization requirement.

24. Several Internal Revenue Code provisions *defer* the taxation of realized amounts. *See, e.g.*, I.R.C. § 351 (West Supp. 1990) (exchange of appreciated property for stock or securities of equal value in a corporation controlled by the transferor); I.R.C. § 354 (1988) (exchange of appreciated stock or securities in a corporate reorganization); I.R.C. § 721 (1988) (exchange of appreciated property for partnership interest); I.R.C. § 1031 (West Supp. 1990) (like-kind exchanges of appreciated business or investment property); I.R.C. § 1033 (1988) (involuntary conversion of appreciated property); I.R.C. § 1034 (1988) (sale of appreciated principal residence combined with purchase of new principal residence); I.R.C. § 1035 (1988) (certain exchanges of life insurance and annuity contracts); I.R.C. § 1036 (1988) (certain exchanges of stock for stock in the same corporation); I.R.C. § 1041 (1988) (transfers of appreciated property between spouses or incident to divorce). Elliott Manning observed to me that, as Andrews points out, some of these deferral provisions allow us to finesse difficult realization issues by postponing the question of whether income has been realized until it is no longer difficult. *See* Andrews, *A Consumption-Type or Cash Flow Personal Income Tax*, 87 HARV. L. REV. 1113, 1130-31 (1974).

Other Code provisions *exclude* realized amounts from taxation altogether. *See, e.g.*, I.R.C. § 71(c) (1988) (child support payments); § 101 (certain death benefits); § 102 (gifts, inheritances, devises); § 103 (interest on certain government obligations); § 104 (certain compensation for personal injury and sickness); § 112 (certain armed forces combat pay); § 117 (certain scholarships); § 119 (meals or lodging furnished for an employer's convenience); § 121 (gain on sale of principal residence by an individual aged 55 or older); § 132 (certain employee fringe benefits).

Code and the fact that there are a few structural requirements. One of these requirements is the need for a mechanism or mechanisms whereby a system can determine when and whether to tax that which it deems potentially taxable. I am not, in this article, going to address directly the issues surrounding the choice of what to deem potentially taxable, but it is through its response to the determination that something is potentially taxable that any system prescribes whether and, if so, when, the item will be taxed.

Realization was first articulated by the Supreme Court as a condition of taxability in 1920 in *Eisner v. Macomber.*[25] Few transactions are as famous as Mrs. Macomber's receipt of a stock dividend from Standard Oil, and no one who has borne with me thus far can have avoided acquiring more than passing acquaintance with that case.[26] It is repeatedly cited both as the case that held that the Constitution imposed limitations on what could be deemed to constitute income[27] and as the case that actually tried to spell out a definition of "income."[28] Both the notion of defining income for tax purposes and the notion of grounding that definition in the Constitution now strike us as quaint, and the case seems to be preserved largely for its antiquarian value.[29] I think, however, that its actual legacy is greater than is commonly thought.

25. 252 U.S. 189 (1920).

26. On January 1, 1916, Standard Oil Corporation issued a 50% stock dividend to Mrs. Macomber and the other Standard Oil stockholders as a result of its transfer of an equivalent par amount from its surplus account to its capital account. Of this amount, 18.07% represented surplus earned between March 1, 1913 (the effective date of the sixteenth amendment), and the date of distribution. Therefore, when Mrs. Macomber received 1100 shares of the new common stock in the distribution, the Commissioner of Internal Revenue assessed income tax on her "income" of $19,877, an amount equal to 18.07% of the par value of the total stock she received. Mrs. Macomber paid the tax under protest but lost her appeal to the Commissioner. She then sued for a refund, contending that the Revenue Act of 1916, which provided that stock dividends constituted income taxable under the Act, was unconstitutionally taxing her Standard Oil stock dividend as income.

The Supreme Court agreed and held that the stock dividend was not income within the meaning of the sixteenth amendment because a mere growth of value in a capital investment did not constitute income. To be income, the gain had to proceed from capital, be severed from it, and be received by Mrs. Macomber for her own separate use or benefit. Since the stock dividend represented undistributed corporate earnings, the Court declared that the Revenue Act of 1916 unconstitutionally required that stock dividends be taxed as income.

27. *Macomber,* 252 U.S. at 211. *See, e.g.,* W. ANDREWS, BASIC FEDERAL INCOME TAXATION 123-24 (3d ed. 1985); B. BITTKER & J. EUSTICE, FUNDAMENTALS OF FEDERAL TAXATION OF CORPORATIONS AND SHAREHOLDERS ¶ 7.60 (1980 & Supp. 1989); M. GRAETZ, *supra* note 3, at 201.

28. *Macomber,* 252 U.S. at 207. *See, e.g.,* W. ANDREWS, *supra* note 27, at 212; M. CHIRELSTEIN, *supra* note 22, at 8-9; M. GRAETZ, *supra* note 3, at 110.

29. The *Macomber* result is encompassed today by § 305 of the Code. However, § 305 limits the extent to which stock dividends are nontaxable. For example, a stock dividend is fully taxable if the shareholder can elect whether to receive it either in stock or property. I.R.C. § 305(b)(1) (1988).

The task the Court set itself in *Macomber* was to discover what "income" meant in common parlance. The Court interpreted the sixteenth amendment as using the word in its ordinary sense and thought its task was to give "only a clear definition of the term 'income,' as that used in common speech, in order to determine its meaning in the Amendment."[30] This general view had been articulated two years earlier by Learned Hand in *United States v. Oregon-Washington Railroad and Navigation Co.*[31] The meaning of "income" in the sixteenth amendment, Hand wrote, is "to be gathered from the implicit assumptions of its use in common speech."[32] The *Macomber* Court attempted to do so:

> Here we have the essential matter: *not* a gain *accruing* to capital, not a *growth* or *increment* of value *in* the investment; but a gain, a profit, something of exchangeable value *proceeding from* the property, *severed from* the capital however invested or employed, and *coming in,* being *"derived,"* that is *received* or *drawn by* the recipient (the taxpayer) for his *separate* use, benefit and disposal; — *that* is income derived from property. Nothing else answers the description.[33]

Here, the *Macomber* Court was making not as much a constitutional claim as a linguistic one. To be sure, the decision gave constitutional status to the requirement that gain from property be realized, but that status was presumably derived from the Court's finding about the ordinary meaning of "income," rather than the other way around. If the ordinary understanding of the word had been different, the content of *Macomber's* constitutional requirement should have differed accordingly. Realization was important to the Court because they viewed it as part of what people *meant* when they spoke about income. Thus, it would seem that the content of the concept of realization could, in principle at least, evolve as the language evolved.

Although *Eisner v. Macomber* has long since ceased to be important as a source of a definition of income or as constitutional interpre-

30. *Macomber,* 252 U.S. at 206-07. The Court noted that economists distinguish between "capital" and "income" in various terms, including likening "capital" to a tree or a piece of land with the resulting fruit or crop constituting the "income." However, the Court viewed the case at hand as requiring only an "ordinary" definition of income. The Court cited as examples of its "ordinary" definitional approach two earlier excise tax cases, *Stratton's Independence, Ltd. v. Howbert,* 231 U.S. 399, 415 (1913), and *Doyle v. Mitchell Bros.,* 247 U.S. 179, 185 (1918), in which the Court had rejected "theoretical" distinctions between capital and income for a definition in its "natural and obvious" sense. *Macomber,* 252 U.S. at 207.

The Court relied on this same "common speech" approach in subsequent cases as well. *See, e.g.,* Merchants' Loan & Trust v. Smietanka, 255 U.S. 509, 519 (1921) (income given its "commonly understood meaning," not as defined by "lexicographers or economists").

31. 251 F. 211, 212 (2d Cir. 1918).

32. 251 F. at 212.

33. *Macomber,* 252 U.S. at 207.

tation,[34] the sense that realization is intimately tied to the *meaning* of "taxable income" has survived. Although some writers are careful to refer to realization as an administrative rule intended to establish the time for taxation,[35] others write of it, at least implicitly, as a *requirement* of taxability.[36] Possibly because the effort to define income for purposes of the tax system has been dropped, often no clear line is drawn between the part of the phrase "taxable income" that is concerned with *what* might be taxed (the potentially taxable amounts) and the part that is concerned first with *whether* and then with *when* it is taxed. From the point of view of understanding the structure of an income tax system, the difference is crucial.

As a theoretical matter, of course, unless a requirement of realization is built into an income tax system's very conception of taxable income, a potentially taxable amount need not be realized to become taxable income.[37] It may be, however, that amounts which are potentially taxable within the system must be realized to be taxed. If a system conditions taxability on realization (or on anything else for that matter), while nonetheless maintaining that the basic notion of potential taxability is independent of realization (or independent of that "anything else"), it necessarily has a concept of taxable income distinct from its concept of potential taxability. My discussion throughout reflects this distinction.

The taxonomy of the relationship in the federal income tax system between the determination of a potentially taxable amount and the determination of whether and when to tax it is more complex than appears at first blush. It begins with the identification of an item as within the aegis of the system (that is, as potentially taxable).[38] The identification can be complicated by questions of *whose* potentially tax-

---

34. *See, e.g.*, B. Bittker & L. Lokken, *supra* note 22, at § 5.1; M. Chirelstein, *supra* note 22, ¶ 5.01, at 68-69; M. Graetz, *supra* note 3, at 110, 202.

35. *See, e.g.*, M. Chirelstein, *supra* note 22, ¶ 5.01, at 68; H. Simons, *supra* note 15, at 207-08; Andrews, *supra* note 24, at 1140-48; Kahn, *Accelerated Depreciation — Tax Expenditure or Proper Allowance for Measuring Net Income?*, 78 Mich. L. Rev. 1, 7-9 (1979).

36. *See, e.g.*, B. Barton, R. Campfield, *et al*, Taxation of Income 1988-1989, at ¶ 2511 (1988); D. Posin, Federal Income Taxation of Individuals 146-48 (1983). Perhaps the clearest current counterexample to this view can be found in I.R.C. §§ 1271-1275 (1988). These provisions set forth the rules for taxing original interest discount, a form of unrealized income.

37. Even the federal income tax system occasionally taxes unrealized amounts. *See, e.g.*, *supra* note 36; I.R.C. § 1256 (1988) (relating to certain regulated futures contracts, foreign currency contracts, nonequity options, and dealer equity options).

38. It is important to notice that the status of being potentially taxable within the federal income tax system is not equivalent to any of the categories identified by the Code. The broadest category specified by the Code is I.R.C. § 61 (West Supp. 1990) gross income. However, some amounts are statutorily excluded from gross income (*e.g.*, I.R.C. § 102 (1988) (amounts received as gifts, bequests, inheritances, and devises); *see supra* note 24 for other examples) and their exclusion would be unnecessary if they were not potentially taxable.

able amount it is[39] and questions about the point at which it became potentially taxable (a different set of questions from questions about whether or when it should be taxed). The initial identification of something as potentially taxable very often does happen to coincide with the identification of an amount that has been realized by the taxpayer. In simple terms, something often becomes potentially taxable (although maybe not taxable income) in the eyes of the tax system at the same time that the taxpayer realizes it in the eyes of the tax system. For example, in the federal income tax system, a cash basis taxpayer's receipt of his paycheck marks both the receipt of a potentially taxable amount and its realization. But its status as potentially taxable is independent of the fact that it was realized.[40] It is clear, moreover, that amounts identified as potentially taxable are not always realized at the time of their identification. One obvious example in the federal income tax system is the so-called unrealized appreciation of an asset. Presently the federal system does not tax the appreciation of an asset until the taxpayer disposes of it and realizes its increase in value.[41] There seems to be widespread sentiment among tax commentators however, that Congress could, if it chose to, tax appreciation currently.[42] This view reflects the sense that a potentially taxable amount need not be realized to become taxable income.

Once something has been identified within the system as a potentially taxable amount, it becomes relevant to ask whether and when it should be taxed; to ask, in other words, whether it should be recognized, have its recognition deferred, or be excluded altogether from taxation (receive permanent nonrecognition treatment). These three basic responses to a potentially taxable amount are the only ones available to any income tax system. It is easy to think of examples of each

39. The question of attribution in the context of ascertaining potential taxability is likely the same as the question of attribution in the context of ascertaining actual taxability ("taxable income" in the federal system). This is because once an amount has been identified as potentially taxable to *X*, the response of the system can be to tax it (to *X*) now, to tax it (to *X*) later, or to exclude it from taxation (to *X*). If the last option is selected and the amount is instead taxed (now or later) to *Y*, then the amount can be construed as having been reidentified as potentially taxable to *Y*. Indeed, the amount may be taxed to *Y* even if it is also being taxed to *X* (and perhaps to others as well). This simply means that the same amount has been identified as potentially taxable to more than one taxpayer. In fact, because the federal system does not explicitly isolate the question of potential taxability at all, it is difficult to tell in which context an attribution question is being asked.

40. Although here it is the receipt that constitutes the realization, receipt is not a necessary condition of realization.

41. *See, e.g.*, Surrey & McDaniel, *The Tax Expenditure Concept: Current Developments and Emerging Issues*, 20 B.C. L. REV. 225, 228 (1979).

42. *See, e.g.*, M. CHIRELSTEIN, *supra* note 22, ¶ 5.01, at 68-9; M. GRAETZ, *supra* note 3, at 201; Musgrave, *In Defense of an Income Concept*, 81 HARV. L. REV. 44, 49 (1967); Shakow, *Taxation Without Realization: A Proposal for Accrual Taxation*, 134 U. PA. L. REV. 1111 (1986).

in the context of the federal income tax. The paycheck received by the cash basis taxpayer above probably will be recognized currently,[43] the compensation put into an Individual Retirement Account by a taxpayer has its taxation deferred,[44] and the amount received by a taxpayer as a bequest is excluded from his income tax permanently.[45]

Although a system that provides for the possibility of exclusion can only tax (now or later) or not tax amounts that it deems within its scope, it need not make the choice when it identifies those amounts as potentially taxable. Of course, if the choice is deferred, taxation at the time of identification is no longer an option and any subsequent decision to tax will have resulted in a deferral of the amount's recognition. Our system does exactly this when refusing to recognize the unrealized appreciation of an asset. Such appreciation is potentially taxable within the system and is not taxed currently, but its ultimate treatment is not settled until some later time (often the time the asset is disposed of). If, for example, appreciated stock with a basis in the hands of the taxpayer of $10 has a fair market value of $50 on March 3, the taxpayer has a potentially taxable $40 that the system could tax currently. Instead the system does nothing. This leaves open both the possibility that the amount will be taxed later and the possibility that it will be excluded altogether. If the price of the shares remains at $50 until April 2, when it drops to $45, and if the taxpayer sells the shares on April 2 for $45, he will normally recognize $35. Thus, from the perspective of the situation on March 3, he has deferred the recognition of $35 and excluded $5 altogether. If, instead, the taxpayer were to die on April 2, holding the appreciated shares with a fair market value of $45, current federal income tax law would exclude both the $35 of potentially taxable, but untaxed, appreciation that the taxpayer held at his death and the potentially taxable $5 that he had held on March 3 but that he no longer held on April 2.

Other examples are less straightforward. Suppose the stock price fluctuates between March 3 and April 2. If the price were $48 on March 4, $47 on March 5, $52 on March 6, and $50 from March 7 until the stock was sold for $50, we cannot simply compare the sale price with the price on March 3 and say that, from the perspective of the situation on March 3, the taxation of the $40 identified on that

43. I.R.C. §§ 61(a) and 446 (1988).

44. A qualified individual may contribute up to a specified amount (currently $2000) to an Individual Retirement Account and deduct that amount from her gross income. I.R.C. § 219 (West Supp. 1990). Any distributions from the I.R.A. will be included in the taxpayer's gross income, so the deduction has the effect of deferring taxation on the contributed amount until a distribution is made. *See* I.R.C. § 408 (1988).

45. I.R.C. § 102(a) (1988).

date as potentially taxable had been deferred. Instead, it would seem as if $2 of that amount had been lost on March 4 and another $1 of it lost on March 5. Those lost amounts are permanently excluded from taxation. Five additional dollars were earned on March 6, and two of them were lost (and hence excluded) on March 7. Thus, from the perspective of the $40 identified on March 3 as potentially taxable, the sale of the stock for $50 should represent the (deferred) recognition of $37 and the exclusion of $3. The remaining $3 recognized as taxable income was identified as potentially taxable on March 6, along with $2 that was subsequently excluded.[46]

This last example raises a question about the first one. What does it mean to say "from the perspective of the situation on March 3"? Unless the entire $40 of appreciation present on that date was first identifiable on that date, it, no less than the appreciation measured on April 2, represents a net figure established over the life of the investment. In the absence of special circumstances, the choice of March 3 as a time to measure the unrealized appreciation of the stock is arbitrary. At least some of the amount identified on that date as potentially taxable likely could have been identified earlier and traced forward to March 3, just as it was traced beyond March 3 in my examples. The point of the examples is to show that the federal income tax system sometimes defers the determination of whether and when to tax a potentially taxable amount until some time after it has identified the amount as potentially taxable. It is not necessary, for this purpose, actually to specify when the identification could first have been made.

46. The federal income tax system allows some losses to be deducted from a taxpayer's gross income. In contexts where losses are fully allowed, the potentially taxable amounts that are permanently excluded from taxation because of downward fluctuations in the value of the asset would not have been taxed even if they had been recognized. Thus, in the example in the text, the $35 gain recognized from the sale of the shares on April 2 for $45 is the same amount that would ultimately have been recognized if the shares had been sold and repurchased each time that their value had changed and the attendant losses and gains had been recognized.

Date	*Basis*	*Sale & Repurchase Price*	*Gain or (Loss)*
March 3	$10	$50	$40
March 4	$50	$48	(2)
March 5	$48	$47	(1)
March 6	$47	$52	5
March 7	$52	$50	(2)
April 2	$50	$45	(5)
Net gain = $35			

The result would not be the same, however, in contexts where losses are not fully allowed. *See, e.g.*, I.R.C. § 165(c) (1988) (limitation on losses deductible by an individual to those incurred in a trade or business or in a transaction entered into for profit or from casualty or theft); I.R.C. § 267 (1988) (disallowance of losses with respect to transactions between related taxpayers); I.R.C. § 1091 (1988) (disallowance of losses from wash sales).

It is sufficient that the amount has been identified and that its ultimate treatment has not yet been decided.

If a decision is made not to recognize currently an amount identified by a tax system as potentially taxable, at least three general types of nonrecognition are possible. One is to exclude the amount from taxation.[47] Within the federal income tax system this result is achieved both by provisions cast explicitly as exclusions[48] and by provisions cast as deductions.[49] It is also achieved preliminarily by the realization requirement itself. Since the system normally conditions taxation on realization, much that is potentially taxable is excluded because it is lost before it is realized. This effect is illustrated by the downward fluctuations in the unrealized appreciation of the stock in the earlier examples.[50]

A second possible kind of nonrecognition is deferral. A decision not to recognize currently a potentially taxable amount could be a decision to defer its recognition until some future date or event. This means, of course, that the amount would be recognized, but later. Parenthetically, it should be noted that in a pure deferral, the amount of the later recognition would be at least the amount identified as potentially taxable at the time of the decision to defer its recognition. To the extent that the later recognition were contingent upon the occurrence of a subsequent event[51] or upon the taxpayer's surviving until some later date,[52] "pure deferral" would be something of a misnomer, but it is one with which I propose to live for the moment. I am not

47. This response is possible, of course, only in a system that is sufficiently complex to include exclusion as a potential reaction.

48. *See supra* note 24 for examples.

49. *See, e.g.*, I.R.C. § 163 (1988) (deduction for certain interest payments); I.R.C. § 164 (1988) (deduction for certain taxes).

50. *See* Grauer, *The Supreme Court's Approach to Annual and Transactional Accounting for Income Taxes: A Common Law Malfunction in a Statutory System?*, 21 GA. L. REV. 329, 393-97 (1986) (characterizing the realization requirement as an example of transactional accounting).

51. For example, I.R.C. § 1034 (1988) provides that a taxpayer will recognize current gain on the sale of his principal residence only to the extent, if any, that the adjusted sales price exceeds the cost of a newly purchased principal residence. The taxpayer's basis in his new residence is reduced by any nonrecognized gain. This basis adjustment serves to defer recognition of the earlier gain until the new residence is sold. The recognition is still contingent, however, on the new residence's being sold for more than its adjusted basis, on the taxpayer's not buying yet another principal residence for more than the sale price of the second one (thus falling once again within the nonrecognition provided by § 1034), and on the taxpayer's not qualifying and electing under I.R.C. § 121 (1988) (a one-time exclusion of up to $125,000 of gain on the sale of a principal residence by a taxpayer age 55 or older) to exclude all or part of the previously deferred gain.

52. I.R.C. § 1014(a) (1988) provides that a person who inherits property takes it with a basis equal to its fair market value at the date of the decedent's death. Because no Code provision requires that either the decedent or his estate recognize any difference between the decedent's actual basis in the property and its fair market value, any previously deferred gain which was reflected in the decedent's basis (under § 1034 for example) will be permanently forgiven.

certain in fact that there are any examples of genuinely pure deferral within the federal income tax system.[53]

A third general sort of nonrecognition is the result of a decision to ignore an event that ordinarily would trigger recognition. A decision to ignore in this context is obviously similar to the choice, discussed above,[54] to defer the decision about whether or when to tax something identified as potentially taxable.

In our current tax system, this phenomenon is illustrated by provisions tying nonrecognition to a carryover basis. There are many such provisions,[55] but a single example should illustrate the point. If taxpayer *A* buys a building for $20,000 and its value appreciates to $100,000, we call her gain unrealized as long as *A* continues simply to hold the building. If the building is destroyed by fire and *A* receives insurance proceeds of $100,000, she has realized $80,000 gain. The federal tax system generally regards the realization of gain as an occasion for the recognition of income. Section 1033 of the Internal Revenue Code allows *A* to avoid recognition of that gain if she reinvests it within a specified time[56] in "similar" property.[57] If the cost of the similar property is $100,000, the replacement property will have the same basis as the original property.[58] Here the Code appears to indulge in a bit of metaphysical fiction and treats the replacement property *as if it were* the original, undiminished by fire. If that is indeed what is happening, then section 1033 is properly characterized as a provision that ignores the realization that the receipt of the insurance proceeds represented. That moment of realization, under this analysis, cannot be regarded as an occasion for deferral or forgiveness of the

53. I.R.C. § 1363(d) (1988) may come close to being an example of pure deferral. That section requires a corporation that converts from C status to S status to recapture the amount of any excess of its inventory valued as of the end of its last tax year as a C corporation using a first-in-first-out cost flow assumption, over its last-in-first-out value. The tax is paid in four equal installments and its amount is independent of any subsequent value of the inventory. The first installment is due on the due date for the S corporation's last return as a C corporation and the remaining three are due on the due dates of the S corporation's return for the three succeeding years. If the S corporation fails to survive for three years, liability for the uncollected amount would presumably pass through to its shareholders under I.R.C. § 1366 (1988).

54. *See supra* text accompanying notes 45-47.

55. *See, e.g.*, I.R.C. § 351 (1988) (exchange of property for stock or securities in corporation controlled by transferor); I.R.C. § 354 (1988) (exchange of stock or securities in a corporate reorganization); I.R.C. § 721 (1988) (exchange of property for partnership interest); I.R.C. § 1015 (1988) (gifts); I.R.C. § 1031 (1988) (like-kind exchanges of business or investment property); I.R.C. § 1033 (1988) (involuntary conversions of property); I.R.C. § 1035 (1988) (certain exchanges of life insurance and annuity contracts); I.R.C. § 1036 (1988) (certain exchanges of stock for stock in same corporation); I.R.C. § 1041 (1988) (transfers of property between spouses or incident to divorce).

56. I.R.C. § 1033(a)(2)(B) (1988).

57. I.R.C. § 1033(a) (1988).

58. I.R.C. § 1033(b) (1988).

amount realized. Taxation of the realized gain is not being deferred because the amount of gain taxed upon the final disposition of the second property is a function solely of the difference between the amount received for the second property and its basis and is in no way affected by the amount of the earlier realization. The gain is not being forgiven or permanently excluded because if the value of the replacement property persists, the appreciation of the original property *will* be recognized when the replacement property is disposed of.[59] The provisions that are commonly referred to as deferral provisions in the federal income tax system are in fact nonrecognition provisions of this sort.[60]

B. *The Role of Reconciliation*

Because a tax system of any complexity will provide for various possible treatments of potentially taxable amounts, it makes sense to ask whether the choices that the system makes are irrevocable. For example, if a system included only the possibilities of immediate recognition (current taxation) and permanent exclusion from taxation, could it later include the previously excluded amount or exclude the item taxed earlier? The same question arises with respect to the characterization of items. The federal income tax system provides for differing tax results depending on the characterization of potentially taxable amounts as, for example, capital gain, passive income, or ordinary income. Clearly nothing inherent in the structure of an income tax system requires either that its particular choices, once made, be permanent or that they be susceptible to change.

A system that opted for revocable choices could incorporate any of a number of features to facilitate flexibility. For example, it could provide for reconsideration of earlier choices at pre-set intervals,[61] it could institute some form of open-ended transactional accounting as a means of aggregating amounts identified as potentially taxable, or it could incorporate an amendatory mechanism for correcting earlier responses that later seemed inappropriate. The most likely motivation

59. Of course, if the value of the property fluctuates, as in the earlier stock example, *see supra* note 46 and accompanying text, the amount of the realized gain that is lost will thereby have been forgiven.

60. *See, e.g.*, I.R.C. §§ 721-723 (1988) (exchange of appreciated property for partnership interest); I.R.C. § 1031 (1988) (like-kind exchanges of appreciated property); I.R.C. § 1034 (1988) (sale of appreciated principal residence combined with purchase of new one); I.R.C. § 1035 (1988) (certain exchanges of life insurance and annuity contracts); I.R.C. § 1036 (1988) (certain exchanges of stock for stock in the same corporation); I.R.C. § 1037 (1988) (certain exchanges of U.S. obligations); I.R.C. § 1041 (1988) (transfers of appreciated property between spouses or incident to divorce).

61. It probably could not allow for criterion-less reconsideration at will and still remain a system.

for making the responses of a system revocable would seem to be the desire to prevent mistakes within the system from becoming permanent. It is important to note, however, that any such device is a mechanism whereby a system can determine whether and when to tax that which it deems potentially taxable and, to that extent at least, plays a role not unlike that played by realization in the federal income tax system.

Two general sorts of corrective devices are available to any tax system. The simplest way to correct a mistake is simply to undo it. Life seldom affords us that opportunity, but a tax system might come close. If, for example, a taxpayer within an income tax system includes in taxable income something that the system, its rules correctly applied, treats as excludable, the system could allow him to go back and recalculate his taxable income after he discovers his mistake. It could allow him to make whatever future adjustments are necessary to put him in precisely the position he would have been in had he initially made an accurate calculation. The federal income tax system provides for something like this kind of "return amendment" within three years of the filing date of the original tax return.[62]

On the other hand, some kinds of mistakes cannot be undone. Sometimes we make decisions that turn out to be mistaken because things did not turn out as we reasonably had expected them to. I decide to drive to work and not to walk because I am in a hurry. I arrive at my office much later than I would have had I walked, because I was involved in an automobile accident on the way. Or I decide to go to Kauai for my vacation, and it is unexpectedly devastated by a typhoon while I am there. In cases like these, it would not be enough to be given the opportunity to return to the original point of decision. The decisions themselves were entirely reasonable when they were made. Only unforeseeable subsequent events cause these choices to be mistakes.

Analogous errors can be made in the context of a tax system. Assume, for example, an income tax system that allows the exclusion (through a deduction) of all potentially taxable amounts spent on food consumed by the taxpayer. Assume, too, that the system requires taxpayers to calculate and report their taxable income on a monthly basis and that it requires them to deduct money spent on food in the period

62. I.R.C. § 6511(a) (1988) allows a taxpayer to file an amended return which claims either a credit or a refund within the later of three years from the time the original return was filed or two years from the time the tax was paid. The amount of any credit or refund is limited to the tax paid within the applicable period plus interest. I.R.C. § 6511(b)(2) (1988); I.R.C. § 6611(a) (1988).

in which it is spent, even if the food will be consumed later. If a taxpayer in this system spent $100 in May on meat that she planned to eat in June but did not eat because she discovered in June that the meat was tainted, two mistakes would have occurred. First, it was obviously a mistake for the taxpayer to have spent $100 on tainted meat, but second, her deduction of the $100 in May has turned out to have been a mistake too. If the taxpayer could have known when she bought the meat that it was spoiled or that it would spoil before she would eat it, then she likely would not have taken the May deduction.[63] This mistake, at least, would be amenable to the kind of corrective measure provided by return amendment. If, however, the taxpayer could not have known in May about the taint (perhaps because it came about as a result of a power outage in June), then her second mistake is analogous to my mistaken decisions to drive to work and to vacation on Kauai. Return amendment would not be an appropriate antidote because the mistake did not lie in the return. The return only became an inaccurate account of the taxpayer's income because of what happened in June.[64] But the May return *did* nonetheless present an incorrect picture of what happened in May since the taxpayer did not in fact spend $100 for meat that she eventually consumed.

Mistakes of this sort are possible in any tax system that both is capable of giving more than one possible response to amounts identified as potentially taxable and requires periodic accounting.[65] A system could simply accept such mistakes as a cost of the enormous

---

63. Assume that no deduction is allowed in this system for the tainted meat.

I cannot forbear noting here, in anticipation of the discussion (*see infra* text accompanying notes 77-97) of the tax benefit rule, that there is a curious difference between the scienter requirement of provisions, like the hypothetical one in the example and, more importantly, like I.R.C. § 162 (West Supp. 1990) (business expense deduction), which condition deductibility on the intended and predicted use of the purchased item, and provisions, like I.R.C. § 164(a)(3) (West Supp. 1990) which provides for the deductibility of state income taxes paid, which condition deductibility simply on whether the expense was in fact incurred or accrued (as the case may be) regardless of the taxpayer's knowledge that he will later receive a refund of the expenditure.

64. *See, e.g.*, Stradlings Bldg. Materials, Inc. v. Commissioner, 76 T.C. 84 (1981), for a good example of exactly this sort of inaccuracy. In *Stradlings* the taxpayer deducted prepaid intangible drilling expenses pursuant to a binding contract with a company called Thor. In a subsequent year Thor breached the contract by not drilling. The Tax Court upheld the original deduction:

> The determination and payment of income taxes is based on annual accounting periods. This determination is based on the facts as they exist with respect to the particular year involved. . . . We do not see how respondent [the IRS] could have expected petitioner to foresee that Thor would breach his contractual commitment subsequent to June 30, 1973, the end of petitioner's 1973 fiscal year.

76 T.C. at 89-90.

65. Such mistakes might also arise where there has been transactional accounting if a transaction that was apparently closed (and had therefore been accounted for within the tax system) later reopened.

administrative benefits that come from periodic accounting. Consistent with this position, it would include no corrective devices designed to address this kind of mistake. The taxpayer who bought the meat in May would be allowed her deduction, and the fact that it spoiled in June would have no tax consequences for her. But a system might utilize a second general sort of corrective device. It is to that device that I now turn.

If a mistake cannot be undone effectively (either because of the nature of the mistake or because the system does not include a corrective mechanism of the first sort), it might still be mitigated by making an adjustment to the current period's accounting.[66] Consider, once again, the example of the tainted meat. The income tax system could respond to the fact that the meat is disposed of in June without being consumed by the taxpayer by adding some amount to June's reported income. I say "some amount" because the determination of the measure of the corrective adjustment in a case like the example raises a set of issues of its own. Put these aside briefly and focus instead on the nature of the adjustment. It is an adjustment that seeks to reconcile the present[67] with the past to make them compatible. Clearly such adjustments have considerably greater feasibility within the quantifiable context of a tax system than they do within most of the nonquantifiable contexts in which mistakes occur. But, to return to my hurried drive to work and my vacation in Kauai, it is as if I could see these calamities through somewhat rose-colored glasses — it was not bad, after all (and unpredictably), that I did not arrive at the office when I would have, had all gone as expected, and I am not unhappy that I got to experience a typhoon at close range on my vacation.

The second general sort of corrective device available to a tax system, then, is reconciliation.[68] The federal income tax system makes enormous use of this mechanism,[69] both by itself and in combination with return amendment. Although the applications of reconciliation

66. There are three other logical possibilities. The adjustment could be made to a future period's accounting, made to some other past period's accounting, or allocated in some way between the accounting of multiple periods. Nothing said in this article about adjusting the current period's accounting is inconsistent with the possibility of adjusting a past or future period's accounting instead or as well. None of these other sorts of adjustment would be as conceptually satisfying and none is much relied on by the federal income tax system. *But see* I.R.C. § 6511(d)(2) (1988) (establishing a period of limitation and procedures for adjusting for overpayments attributable to net operating loss carrybacks or capital loss carrybacks).

67. Or the future, if the adjustment were to a future accounting period.

68. *See* White, *supra* note 9.

69. Though not in *Stradlings Bldg. Materials, Inc. v. Commissioner*, 76 T.C. 84 (1981), discussed *supra* note 64, because the only year at issue was the year in which the deduction had been taken.

are familiar, they are seldom all viewed as instances of the same phenomenon. Nor is there any sense of the role of that phenomenon in the overall structure of the system.

II. The Descriptive Power of Reconciliation

Reconciliation itself is not, of course, a necessary feature of a tax system. A system might not provide for the sort of correction afforded by reconciliation. But a system might in fact allow for the possibility of nonamendatory revocability, and, if the foregoing account is correct, any such change *will* be an instance of reconciliation whether or not it is so described. Thus, I do not argue that each of the following examples of the operation of reconciliation within the federal income tax system is widely perceived as such.[70] None of them is. Indeed, as far as I know, "reconciliation" in this context is my own term.[71] Instead, I am interested in exposing the structural framework that must underlie *any* tax system and hence any income tax system. Once the necessary features of the structure are understood, we can begin to give a much richer description of the details of our particular system.

A. *The Claim of Right Doctrine*

Perhaps the easiest context within the federal income system in which to see reconciliation operating as a corrective device is the so-called claim of right doctrine. Sometimes a taxpayer, in good faith, includes an amount in the taxable income of one year only to discover in a later year that the amount did not properly belong to him and must be returned. Sometimes a taxpayer claims in one year that he is entitled to an amount even though his claim is being disputed and in a later year may be resolved against him. Broadly stated, the claim of right doctrine requires a taxpayer to include in his or its taxable income any amount otherwise currently taxable and acquired or held under a claim of entitlement.[72] Thus, in both circumstances, the tax-

70. Nor do I claim that any of these examples currently represents a fully consistent application of reconciliation. Still less do I wish to argue that good tax policy necessarily requires a consistent application of this (or any other) principle.

71. White, *supra* note 9, at 496. The term seems now to have been adopted in the context of the tax benefit rule by Chirelstein as well. M. Chirelstein, *supra* note 22, ¶ 10.03, at 217.

72. The claim of right doctrine has its genesis in *North American Oil Consolidated v. Burnet*, 286 U.S. 417 (1932). A dispute arose between North American and the U.S. government concerning profits earned in 1916 from certain government-owned oil properties, from which the government was seeking to oust the company. The disputed profits were placed in the hands of a receiver appointed to operate the property and hold the income until the dispute was resolved. In 1917, the government's case was dismissed, and the receiver paid the money to North American. Meanwhile, the government pursued appeals without success until 1922. North American reported the income for the tax year 1916 through an amended return filed in 1918. The Com-

payer correctly includes the amount in the earlier year's taxable income but, as a result, may fail to meet the system's standards of accuracy for measurement of that year's taxable income. The tax system could, of course, make no effort to respond to the inaccuracy. Or it could require the taxpayer to amend its original return in the light of later events. In this context, the federal income tax system has developed a different response — it adjusts the current (later) year's taxable income.[73] The current situation, *i.e.*, the one in which the earlier included amount has been relinquished, is reconciled with the earlier one.

The notion of transcending strict adherence to annual accounting to reconcile the present with the past does not necessarily require that the reconciliation be complete. Thus, the *amount* of the corrective

missioner assessed a deficiency for North American's failure to report the income for 1917, the year the company actually received the income, rather than for 1916.

The Court held that the disputed profits became income to the company in 1917, when it first became entitled to them and when it actually received them, regardless of whether the company's return was filed on a cash or accrual basis.

> If a taxpayer receives earnings under a claim of right and without restriction as to its disposition, he has received income which he is required to return, even though it may still be claimed that he is not entitled to retain the money, and even though he may still be adjudged liable to restore its equivalent.

286 U.S. at 424.

The Court rejected North American's claim that the income was reportable in 1916, either by North American or by the receiver, who held the profits. The income was not taxable to the receiver because he was the receiver of only a part of the properties operated by the company and, therefore, was not required to file a return. The amount was not income to North American in 1916, because the company was not required to report as income an amount that it might never receive. Consistently with the position it had taken, the Court similarly rejected North American's alternative claim that the income was reportable in 1922 when the Government's last appeal failed and the dispute was finally resolved. The Court, however, did say, in *dicta*, that if the Government had prevailed in the final appeal, North American would have been entitled to a deduction from its 1922 income, since it would have paid the money to the Government in that year. This approach was subsequently adopted by the federal income tax system. *See infra* note 73.

The claim of right doctrine has been applied to require inclusion in income during the tax year in which the payment was received even if the payments were based on erroneous computations or were obtained illegally. The fact that the taxpayer might have to relinquish the money to a superior claimant in later years does not affect the income's taxability in a tax year when the taxpayer has unrestricted use of the income. *See, e.g.*, James v. United States, 366 U.S. 213 (1961) (embezzled monies income to embezzler regardless of duty to repay); United States v. Lewis, 340 U.S. 590 (1951) (compensation based on erroneously computed employer's profits includable in income under claim of right rule although later repayment of erroneous amount required). *See generally* B. BITTKER & L. LOKKEN, *supra* note 22, at ¶ 6.3; Lister, *The Use and Abuse of Pragmatism: The Judicial Doctrine of Claim of Right*, 21 TAX L. REV. 263 (1966).

73. This approach consists of two components, one of judicial origin and the other statutory. The judicially created aspect provides for deduction from gross income in the tax year in which repayment is made, rather than for amendment of the prior year's tax return. This result was suggested in dicta in *North American*, 286 U.S. at 424. *See supra* note 72. However, *United States v. Lewis*, 340 U.S. 590 (1951), is the case in which the Supreme Court first actually applied this approach.

The statutory component of this approach is embodied in I.R.C. § 1341 (1988). That section provides for the special computation of the tax due from a taxpayer who is deducting the restoration of an amount previously included in income under a claim of right.

adjustment is not dictated by the fact of the use of reconciliation. Two methods of measuring that amount have figured in the development of the claim of right doctrine. In *United States v. Lewis,*[74] the Supreme Court held that a taxpayer who had received a cash bonus in 1944, reported the amount as income on his 1944 return, was later notified that the bonus was greater than it should have been, and repaid half of the amount in 1946, could not reopen his 1944 return to reflect what had happened in 1946 but must instead be content to deduct the repayment amount in 1946. The taxpayer in *Lewis* had a higher effective tax rate in 1944 than he had in 1946, and so the deduction in 1946 did not fully correct for the tax overpayment of 1944. If his tax rate for 1946 had been higher than his rate for 1944, he would have been better off taking the deduction in 1946 than amending his 1944 return, but reconciliation would still have been an imperfect corrective device because it would have overcorrected for the earlier inclusion.

In 1954, Congress reacted to the *Lewis* side of this imbalance with section 1341 of the Code.[75] That provision allows a taxpayer in Lewis' situation to choose, instead of taking a deduction in the year of repayment, to lower his tax bill for the repayment year by an amount equal to the tax that would have been saved in the earlier year had the amount later repaid not been included in the first place.[76] Although

---

74. 340 U.S. 590 (1951).

75. It seems clear that I.R.C. § 1341 (1988) was enacted solely to cure the unfair situation present in *Lewis*. The House Report on § 1341 contains the following reference to the case:

> If the taxpayer included an item in gross income in one taxable year, and in a subsequent taxable year he becomes entitled to a deduction because the item or a portion thereof is no longer subject to his unrestricted use, and the amount of the deduction is in excess of $3,000, the tax for the subsequent year is reduced by either the tax attributable to the deduction or the decrease in the tax for the prior year attributable to the removal of the item, whichever is greater. Under the rule of the *Lewis* case, the taxpayer is entitled to a deduction only in the year of repayment.

H.R. REP. No. 1337, 83d Cong., 2d Sess. A294, *reprinted* in 1954 U.S. CODE CONG. & ADMIN. NEWS 4017, 4436 (citation omitted); *see also* S. REP. No. 1622, 83d Cong., 2d Sess. 451, *reprinted in* 1954 U.S. CODE CONG. & ADMIN. NEWS 4621, 5095; H.R. CONF. REP. No. 2543, 83d Cong., 2d Sess. 72, *reprinted in* 1954 U.S. CODE CONG. & ADMIN. NEWS 5280, 5333.

76. The provisions of I.R.C. § 1341 (1988) are applicable to a cash basis taxpayer in the tax year "in which the item of income included in a prior year under a claim of right is actually repaid" or in the year or years that the taxpayer relinquished his right to receive the income if the income was only constructively received in the prior year. Treas. Reg. § 1.1341-1(e) (as amended in 1978). For an accrual method taxpayer, § 1341 applies "to the year in which the obligation properly accrue[d] for the repayment of the item included under a claim of right." Treas. Reg. § 1.1341-1(e) (as amended 1978).

"Income included under a claim of right" means an item included in gross income because it appeared from the facts available in the year that the amount was included in gross income, that the taxpayer had an "unrestricted right" to the income. Treas. Reg. § 1.1341-1(a) (as amended in 1978). The deductible amount is considered "restored" for § 1341 purposes if its repayment results because it is established after the close of the prior tax year that the taxpayer did not have an unrestricted right to the income, as he had earlier believed. Treas. Reg. § 1.1341-1(a) (as amended in 1978).

There are certain limitations and exceptions to § 1341. For example, the section applies only

this provision clearly protects taxpayers from suffering poor Lewis' fate, it does not provide a perfect corrective either. Under section 1341, a taxpayer will not recover the costs to him (if any) associated with having actually paid the tax in the earlier year. Nor does section 1341 prevent the overcorrection that occurs when the effective tax rate in the year of deduction is *higher* than that for the earlier year of inclusion.

B. *The Tax Benefit Rule*

A tax system might also include some mechanism by which to correct the mistakes that result from *deductions* or *exclusions* that were properly taken in one year but turn out in a later year, usually (but not necessarily) because of the recovery of some (or all) of the amount deducted or excluded, not to reflect what the system deems to be the taxpayer's appropriately taxable amount. Here too, the federal income tax system reconciles the later and earlier situations. The general name given to our system's response to this kind of circumstance is the "tax benefit rule." Roughly speaking, the tax benefit rule applies to include the reclaimed amount in the later year's taxable income to the extent that the earlier deduction or exclusion resulted in an actual tax benefit.[77] Despite its obvious mirror-image-like relationship to what today passes as the claim of right doctrine, the tax benefit rule originated quite independently of its "converse." It has been an acknowledged feature of the federal income tax system since 1927, when the Board of Tax Appeals upheld the Commissioner's claim that a taxpayer who collected on accounts that had been listed on an earlier year's return as deductible worthless accounts, had to include the amount of the collections in income for the year of collection.[78] As

if the amount of income repayable (because the taxpayer does not have an unrestricted right to it) exceeds $3000. I.R.C. § 1341(a)(3) (1988). Section 1341 does not generally apply to repayments of amounts initially included in gross income by reason of the sale or other disposition of inventory by the taxpayer, such as sales returns and allowances. I.R.C. § 1341(b)(2) (1988); Treas. Reg. § 1.1341-1(f)(1) (as amended in 1978). In addition, the regulations provide that § 1341 does not apply to deductions attributable to bad debts or legal fees and expenses incurred by the taxpayer in contesting the restoration of an item previously included in income. Treas. Reg. § 1.1341-1(g), (h) (as amended in 1978). Further, § 1341(b)(4) and (5) provide special rules regarding the treatment of net operating losses and capital losses.

77. For an extended discussion of the tax benefit rule, see White, *supra* note 9; *see also* M. CHIRELSTEIN, *supra* note 22, at ¶ 10.03.

The tax benefit rule has two aspects. The "inclusionary" component requires the inclusion in income of an amount equal to the amount deducted in an earlier year. The "exclusionary" component conditions inclusion on there having been a tax benefit as the result of the earlier deduction. The exclusionary aspect is currently set forth in I.R.C. § 111 (1988).

78. Lee v. Commissioner, 6 B.T.A. 541 (1927), *affd. sub nom.* Carr v. Commissioner, 28 F.2d 551 (5th Cir. 1928); *see also* Excelsior Printing Co. v. Commissioner, 16 B.T.A. 886 (1929) (recovery of debt earlier charged off as worthless held to be taxable income for year of recovery). In these early cases the principle was limited to its inclusionary aspect and was not typically given a

with any essentially nonstatutory rule, the contours of the tax benefit principle within the federal income tax system have evolved over time. Most recently, the Supreme Court, in *Hillsboro National Bank v. Commissioner,*[79] dealt squarely, and at some length, with the tax benefit rule.[80]

The conventional description of what is happening when the tax benefit rule is applied to require inclusion of the amount of an earlier deduction in a taxpayer's income for a later year[81] is straightforward. It is couched in terms of basis and realization. The item whose cost was deducted[82] has a basis in the taxpayer's hands equal to its after-tax

---

name. The exclusionary component first surfaced in 1932 when it was rejected by the Board of Tax Appeals. Lake View Trust & Sav. Bank v. Commissioner, 27 B.T.A. 290 (1932). Congress codified the exclusionary aspect in 1942. Revenue Act of 1942, ch. 619, § 116, 56 Stat. 798, 812-13 (1942) (current version at I.R.C. § 111 (1988)). The phrase "tax benefit rule" was used by the Board of Tax Appeals by 1942 primarily, if not exclusively, to refer to the rule's exclusionary component. *See* Haughey v. Commissioner, 47 B.T.A. 1, 4 (1942). Legal commentators from the same period varied in their use of the phrase. *See, e.g.,* Lassen, *The Tax Benefit Rule and Related Problems,* 20 TAXES 473, 473 (1942) (applies "tax benefit rule" to both components); Plumb, *The Tax Benefit Rule Today,* 57 HARV. L. REV. 129, 130-31 (1943) (refers to inclusionary aspect as a "general rule" without naming it). Current use of the phrase encompasses both the inclusionary and exclusionary components.

For further background on the history of the tax benefit rule, see generally Bittker & Kanner, *The Tax Benefit Rule,* 26 UCLA L. REV. 265 (1978); Note, *The Tax Benefit Rule, Claim of Right Restorations, and Annual Accounting: A Cure for the Inconsistencies,* 21 VAND. L. REV. 995, 999-1010 (1968).

79. 460 U.S. 370 (1983).

80. *Hillsboro* was a consolidation of two cases presenting rather different fact situations. In *Hillsboro,* Hillsboro National Bank paid a state property tax on behalf of its shareholders in 1972. *Hillsboro,* 460 U.S. at 373. Because the validity of the tax was under question, the state placed the collected amounts in escrow. *Hillsboro,* 460 U.S. at 373. When the tax ultimately was declared invalid, the state paid the amounts collected from the bank directly to the shareholders on whom the tax had been imposed. *Hillsboro,* 460 U.S. at 374. The Bank deducted its payment of the tax under § 164(e), which allowed a corporate deduction for shareholder taxes paid by a corporation, and it neither made any adjustment nor reported any income when the tax refund was made to the shareholders by the state. *Hillsboro,* 460 U.S. at 373-74. The Commissioner sought to use the tax benefit rule to include the amount of the refund in the bank's income. *Hillsboro,* 460 U.S. at 374. The bank argued that since it had not recovered the amount, the tax benefit rule did not apply. *Hillsboro,* 460 U.S. at 381.

The second case was originally known as *United States v. Bliss Dairy, Inc. See infra* text accompanying notes 87-91 for a summary of the facts.

The Court rejected the view that economic recovery is required before the tax benefit rule can apply. *Hillsboro,* 460 U.S. at 381-83. It went on to hold that when a later event is "fundamentally inconsistent with the premise on which the deduction was initially based," the tax benefit rule applies. 460 U.S. at 383. As articulated by the Court, the test is whether the later event would have foreclosed the deduction if the two had occurred within the same taxable year. 460 U.S. at 383-84. Curiously, despite its articulation of the tax benefit rule, the Court did not frame its consideration of whether the tax benefit rule actually applied to Hillsboro National Bank or Bliss Dairy, Inc. in terms of fundamental inconsistency. It held that the rule did not apply to the bank because of the legislative history of § 164(e) and that it did apply to the Dairy. *See* White, *supra* note 9, at 499-500.

81. One example would be the inclusion of a taxpayer's state income tax refund in her federal taxable income for the year received if she deducted it from her federal taxable income when she paid the state tax in an earlier year.

82. The "item" in the example in note 81 *supra* is the state income tax paid.

cost — zero if the entire cost was deducted. Thus, when the item is recovered by the taxpayer, the amount realized is offset against its basis in the taxpayer's hands and the difference is treated as a realized gain.[83]

The conventional account, while adequate for many descriptive purposes, does not capture a significant subset of the circumstances in which the tax benefit rule has been applied. Nor, more importantly, does it *explain* the role that the tax benefit rule has within the structure of the federal income tax system. A couple of examples can illustrate the first problem. The second will itself require a bit of explanation.

The statutory portion of the tax benefit rule is set forth as section 111 of the Internal Revenue Code. That provision currently excludes from income any recovered amounts that did not produce a tax benefit when they were deducted in an earlier year.[84] It represents the statutory expression of what has long been known as the exclusionary aspect of the nonstatutorily developed tax benefit rule.[85] The adjusted basis of any item that was expensed in the earlier year will be zero, however, even if the deduction did not in fact yield a tax benefit. The limitation on the inclusion of the recovered amount to the actual amount of the earlier tax benefit is not simply the result of offsetting the amount of the recovery against the basis.

Another, quite different, sort of example of the failure of what I have called the "conventional account" to describe some core applications of the tax benefit rule is the Supreme Court's opinion in *Hillsboro.*[86] *Hillsboro* was the name under which two cases were consolidated. My point is best illustrated by the facts of the case originally known as *United States v. Bliss Dairy, Inc.*[87] Bliss Dairy, Inc. bought cattle feed for use in its business operations and deducted the full cost of the feed in the same year.[88] Two days into the next taxable year, the company liquidated under section 336.[89] The assets distrib-

83. *See, e.g.*, M. CHIRELSTEIN, *supra* note 22, at ¶ 10.03.

84. I.R.C. § 111(a) (1988) currently provides: "Gross income does not include income attributable to the recovery during the taxable year of any amount deducted in any prior taxable year to the extent such amount did not reduce the amount of tax imposed by this chapter."

85. *See supra* note 77.

86. 460 U.S. 370 (1983).

87. *See supra* note 80 for a description of the facts of the case originally known as *Hillsboro Natl. Bank v. Commissioner.*

88. *Hillsboro*, 460 U.S. at 374.

89. *Hillsboro*, 460 U.S. at 374. At the time that Bliss liquidated, I.R.C. § 336(a) (1982) provided in pertinent part that "no gain or loss shall be recognized to a corporation on the distribution of property in complete liquidation." That section was substantially changed by the Tax Reform Act of 1986 to make nonrecognition the exception rather than the rule.

uted to its shareholders by Bliss in liquidation included unused, though previously expensed, cattle feed.[90] Bliss did not include the value of the unused cattle feed in its income for the second year on the ground that the tax benefit rule required an actual recovery of a previous tax benefit.[91] The Supreme Court applied the tax benefit rule to Bliss Dairy saying, "[t]he purpose of the rule is not simply to tax 'recoveries.' "[92] Instead, the rule "ordinarily applies to require the inclusion of income when events occur that are fundamentally inconsistent with an earlier deduction."[93] The Court has been much criticized for its failure fully to spell out when a later event is "fundamentally inconsistent" with an earlier deduction.[94] Instead, the Court left both the content of the notion and the conditions of its application somewhat vague. The emphasis throughout the opinion however is on the *relationship* between the later year's circumstances and the prior year's report of taxable income. The Court makes no explicit effort to specify precisely the conditions that trigger the comparison, much less to tie the rule's application to the current realization of some amount. Thus, although the amount included in taxable income under the tax benefit rule may well equal the difference between a current valuation and a previously established basis,[95] it is at least unhelpful to describe the rule solely in terms of an amount realized against which the adjusted basis is offset.

As a general matter, a tax system could build the possibility of understatement into its operating rules by allowing taxpayers to deduct or exclude amounts on the assumption (tacit or explicit) that certain future events would or would not occur. So long as the future is contingent, such a system includes the possibility that the taxpayer has understated his taxable income — at least that she would have stated it differently had she known then what she knows now. She has made a mistake akin to the ones I made when I took my vacation trip to Kauai or drove to my office. A system with this feature might or might not include a mechanism or mechanisms to correct the mistakes

---

90. *Hillsboro*, 460 U.S. at 374.

91. *Hillsboro*, 460 U.S. at 381; Brief for the Respondent Bliss Dairy, Inc. at 5, *Hillsboro* (No. 81-930).

92. 460 U.S. at 381.

93. 460 U.S. at 372.

94. *See, e.g.*, 460 U.S. at 417-18 (Stevens, J., concurring in *Hillsboro* and dissenting in *Bliss*); Blum, *The Role of the Supreme Court in Federal Tax Controversies* — Hillsboro National Bank *and* Bliss Dairy, Inc., 61 TAXES 363, 366-67 (1983); White, *supra* note 9, at 495-99; Comment, *An Asset-Based Approach to the Tax Benefit Rule*, 72 CALIF. L. REV. 1257, 1270-78 (1984).

95. *But see* the example discussed *supra* text accompanying note 86.

it will inevitably breed. The federal income tax system does. The tax benefit rule is an example of one such mechanism.

The principal role of the tax benefit rule within the federal income tax system is corrective. It serves as an exception to the administrative requirement of annual accounting when annual accounting distorts a taxpayer's taxable income in a manner favorable to the taxpayer. Obviously, it does not apply in all instances where a taxpayer's income for some year has been understated,[96] but it *only* applies in instances where that has happened. Moreover, as *Hillsboro* tells us, the tax benefit rule only applies when the understatement occurs because a later year's events are "fundamentally inconsistent" with the picture of the future upon which the original deduction (or deductions) was premised. The rule applies to reconcile the past prediction of the future with the actual outcome. This is the principal function of the tax benefit rule, and it is this central feature that the "conventional" description of the rule fails to capture.

Finally, it should be noted that the notion of an understatement or distortion of a taxpayer's taxable income is a relative one. In this discussion, I am giving a schematic account of the structure of any tax system, and I began with a set of observations that emphasized the independence of the determination of *what* constitutes a potentially taxable amount within a system from the determination of *whether* and *when* to tax it. Although, for example, a system could certainly seek to employ a notion of potentially taxable amount identical to the economists' sense of income (whatever that sense is) and could further attempt to structure its taxing mechanisms so as to tax all amounts thus construed as soon as they became the taxpayer's, there is no necessary identity between a taxpayer's taxable income for any year and his income in the economist's sense for the same year.[97] Further, since a system could adopt *any* notion of potentially taxable amount and *any* standards for determining whether and when to tax it, an understatement of taxable income can only result within a system's own framework.

C. *Recapture Provisions*

My third example of reconciliation operating within the federal income tax system is, in a way, a variant of the tax benefit rule. The Internal Revenue Code includes a number of recapture provisions

96. In some circumstances return amendment is the appropriate antidote, in others the statute of limitations (normally three years after a tax return is filed; *see* I.R.C. § 6501(a) (1988)) operates to allow a taxpayer to ignore the earlier understatement.

97. *See supra* text accompanying notes 18-19.

whereby an amount is included in a later year as an adjustment for a deduction or credit taken in an earlier year.[98] Section 1245 historically has been the most important[99] of these provisions, and, although its current importance has been much reduced by the Tax Reform Act of 1986,[100] it illustrates reconciliation well. Another reason for using section 1245 as illustrative of recapture provisions generally is that its intimate connection with depreciation invites a look at depreciation, which itself illuminates the nature of reconciliation.

When an asset is depreciated for tax purposes, a deduction is taken from the taxpayer's taxable income and the taxpayer's basis in the asset is adjusted downward by the amount of the deduction.[101] If, as usually happens, the fair market value of the asset has not in fact decreased by an amount as large as the depreciation deduction, a subsequent sale of the asset will result in gain to the taxpayer even if the fair market value of the asset has not increased during the period that the taxpayer has held it. Section 1231 of the Code provides for long-term capital gain treatment for net gain from the sale of depreciable assets. Until it was repealed by the Tax Reform Act of 1986, section 1202

---

98. *See, e.g.*, I.R.C. § 1245 (1988) (recapture as ordinary income of gains from certain depreciable property); I.R.C. § 1250 (1988) (recapture as ordinary income of gains from certain depreciable realty); I.R.C. § 1252 (1988) (recapture as ordinary income of certain amounts deducted under I.R.C. § 175 (1988) (soil and water expenditures) and I.R.C. § 182 (1988) (land clearing expenditures)); I.R.C. § 280F(b)(3) (1988) (recapture of excess depreciation of listed property not in fact predominantly used in a qualified business use); I.R.C. § 1254 (1988) (recapture as ordinary income of gains from disposition of certain oil, gas, or geothermal property).

99. At least as measured by frequency of application. The disposition of any tangible depreciable property connected with manufacturing, transportation, or any other business enterprise historically has been likely to trigger § 1245.

100. Section 1245 and other recapture provisions that transform capital gain into ordinary income have, temporarily at least, lost much of their importance because of the elimination of the capital gains preference. The statutory structure for distinguishing between ordinary income and capital gains remains intact, but both are currently subject to the same tax rates. ("The current statutory structure for capital gains is retained in the Code to facilitate reinstatement of a capital gains rate differential if there is a future tax rate increase." H.R. REP. NO. 841, 99th Cong., 2d sess. II-106, *reprinted in* 1986 U.S. CODE CONG. & ADMIN. NEWS 4075, 4194 (Conference Report accompanying Tax Reform Act of 1986)).

101. I.R.C. § 1001(a) (1988) provides that the gain or loss realized from the sale or other disposition of property is measured as the difference between the amount realized on the disposition and the property's adjusted basis.

I.R.C. § 1011(a) (1988) provides that the adjusted basis for purposes of § 1001(a) is the basis, as determined under the appropriate basis section of the Code (*see, e.g.*, I.R.C. § 1012 (1988) (basis equals cost unless another basis provision applies); I.R.C. § 1014 (1988) (basis of property acquired from a decedent); I.R.C. § 1015 (1988) (basis of property acquired by gift); I.R.C. § 332 (1988) (basis of property received in corporate liquidation); I.R.C. § 722 (1988) (basis of contributing partner's partnership interest) (adjusted as provided by I.R.C. § 1016 (West Supp. 1990)).

Section 1016(a) provides for a reduction in basis for various items including deductions taken for exhaustion, wear and tear, obsolescence, amortization, and depletion deducted under sections of the Code such as I.R.C. § 167 (West Supp. 1990). The reduction amount required is the greater of the amount (1) allowed as a deduction to the extent the deduction resulted in a tax benefit or (2) the amount allowable under the Code for the applicable years. *See also* Treas. Reg. § 1.1016-3 (1960).

provided for a deduction from gross income of 60 percent of a taxpayer's net capital gains, thus providing for what was in effect a lower capital gains tax rate. Section 1245 was designed to prevent a taxpayer from taking advantage of this lower capital gains rate with respect to any gain that arose simply because of depreciation in excess of the actual diminution in value of the asset. Thus, if an asset were purchased for $20,000 and depreciation deductions of $6800 were taken over a three-year period, the asset's adjusted basis would be $13,200. If the asset had then been sold before January 1, 1987, for its fair market value of $16,000, section 1245 would have prohibited the taxpayer from characterizing the $2800 gain as section 1231 gain subject to the long-term capital gain rate and would have required her to treat it as ordinary income. If the asset's actual value had appreciated as the asset had been depreciated, and if the asset had been sold before 1987 for $25,000 (rather than $16,000), the entire amount of the earlier depreciation deductions ($6800) would have been treated as ordinary income and the rest of the gain ($5000) would have received the benefit of the lower rate prescribed by section 1202. The amount of gain converted by section 1245 into ordinary income is said to have been "recaptured." Without the adjustment required by section 1245, the taxpayer would have received the full benefit of three years of depreciation deductions from ordinary income and then, in effect, have recovered the entire (or partial, in my first example) amount of the earlier deduction at the lower capital gains rate.[102] Section 1245 ensures that the recovery (or recapture) occurs at ordinary income rates.

The practical motivation for a provision like section 1245 is clear enough — to prevent a taxpayer from both receiving capital gains treatment on the sale of a business asset and recovering his cost for the asset out of ordinary income.[103] This motivation arose because of the

102. *But cf.* Kahn, *supra* note 35, at 46-53 for an argument that the assumptions that underlie recapture are misguided.

103. The legislative history of I.R.C. § 1245 confirms this underlying motivation. Testifying before the Senate Finance Committee before the section was adopted, the Secretary of the Treasury, Douglas Dillon, said:

> The President recommended that capital gain treatment be withdrawn from gains on the disposition of depreciable property, both real and personal, to the extent of prior depreciation allowances.
>
> Such gain reflects depreciation allowances in excess of the actual decline in value of the asset and under the President's proposal would be treated as ordinary income. Any gain in excess of the cost of the asset would still be treated as capital gain. This reform would eliminate an unfair tax advantage which the law today gives to those who depreciate property at a rate in excess of the actual decline in market value and then proceed to sell the property, *thus, in effect, converting ordinary income into a capital gain.* It is particularly essential at this time in view of the impending administrative revision of depreciation guidelines.

Revenue Act of 1962: Hearings on H.R. 10650 Before the Senate Comm. on Finance, 87th Cong.,

special rate for long-term capital gains and goes away without it.[104] But even though the practical motivation for a special recapture provision seems to hinge on the rate differential brought about by a capital gains preference, the function of the provision within the structure of the income tax system is somewhat broader and can be described quite independently of that difference. Section 1245, together with the provisions which set forth the procedures for reducing basis to reflect deductions taken for depreciation,[105] is a corrective device. When a taxpayer recovers the cost (or a portion of it) of an asset which it acquired for business purposes by taking depreciation deductions,[106] it has taken a deduction — fully authorized by the federal income tax system — which, in rough theory at least, presumes a future outcome;[107] namely, that the taxpayer will use the asset (for business purposes) and that it will ultimately consume at least as much of the value of the asset through that use as it has deducted through the mechanism of depreciation.[108] As with any presumption about the future,

2d Sess. 87-88 (1962) (emphasis added). *See also* 2 B. BITTKER & L. LOKKEN, *supra* note 22, at ¶ 55.1; M. CHIRELSTEIN, *supra* note 22, at ¶ 18.02(b); Kahn, *supra* note 35, at 43-46.

104. Actually, I.R.C. § 1245 retains some practical effect in several circumstances. For example, capital gains are still offset by capital losses while ordinary income is offset only to a very limited extent, *see* I.R.C. § 1211 (1988). Thus, characterization of gain as ordinary income by § 1245 can increase a taxpayer's taxable income by reducing the deductibility of his losses. *See also* I.R.C. § 170(e) (1988) (reducing the amount of a charitable contribution of property by the amount that would not have been long-term capital gain if it had been sold for fair market value); I.R.C. § 453(i) (1988) (recognizing § 1245 recapture income in the year of the disposition of property sold in an installment sale).

105. *See supra* note 101.

106. The historic function of depreciation was to recover the cost of the property being depreciated over the period of its economically useful life. Indeed, the phrase "cost recovery" is often substituted for "depreciation." *See, e.g.*, I.R.C. § 168 (1988) ("Accelerated Cost Recovery System"). A depreciation deduction has been a part of the federal income tax system since 1909. *See* Tariff Act of 1909, ch. 6, § 38, 36 Stat. 11, 113. It has been explained by the Supreme Court as follows:

> The depreciation charge permitted as a deduction from the gross income in determining the taxable income of a business for any year represents the reduction, during the year, of the capital assets through wear and tear of the plant used. *The amount of the allowance for depreciation is the sum which should be set aside for the taxable year, in order that, at the end of the useful life of the plant in the business, the aggregate of the sums set aside will (with the salvage value) suffice to provide an amount equal to the original cost.* The theory underlying this allowance for depreciation is that by using up the plant, a gradual sale is made of it. The depreciation charged is the measure of the cost of the part which has been sold. When the plant is disposed of after years of use, the thing then sold is not the whole thing originally acquired. The amount of the depreciation must be deducted from the original cost of the whole in order to determine the cost of that disposed of in the final sale of properties.

United States v. Ludey, 274 U.S. 295, 300-01 (1927) (emphasis added).

See also Fribourg Navigation Co. v. Commissioner, 383 U.S. 272 (1966). *See generally* B. BITTKER & L. LOKKEN, *supra* note 22, at ¶ 23.1.1; M. CHIRELSTEIN, *supra* note 22, at ¶ 6.08. For a historical account of depreciation policies, see Lischer, *Depreciation Policy: Whither Thou Goest*, 32 SW. L.J. 545, 546-71 (1978).

107. Crane v. Commissioner, 331 U.S. 1, 3-4 (1947).

108. *See supra* note 106. The original goal of tax depreciation seems to have been to devise methods by which the actual economic depreciation of the asset would be deducted as it oc-

this one can turn out to be mistaken. A capital gains preference exacerbates the mistake;[109] it does not cause it.

A fine-tooled analysis of depreciation is itself a complicated and controversial undertaking. Depreciation for tax purposes is a mechanism for spreading the deduction of an item's cost over multiple tax periods. Even in a world with a currency unaffected by inflation or deflation, where the single goal of depreciation was to deduct as much of an item's cost in any period as was consumed in that period, it would still be exceedingly difficult to allocate cost to use accurately. Much of the difficulty stems from the problem of measuring consumption. We would need to know a variety of things, including the value of the item at the beginning and end of each accounting period and how much of that value represented the original cost unaffected by fluctuations in the market price.[110] The project is complicated still further if additional goals are introduced into the design of the depreciation mechanism. The federal system has in fact used depreciation schedules as a tool for directing investment behavior since at least 1954,[111] and a vast literature addresses the complex questions surrounding both the desirability of that practice and its implementation.[112] It might well appear, therefore, that reconciliation would ill-describe what has happened when depreciation is recaptured, because the amount of depreciation actually taken on an asset is often neither intended nor believed to be an accurate estimate of the cost that has in fact been consumed. Indeed, most theorists view the Accelerated Cost

curred. *See* M. GRAETZ, *supra* note 3, at 391-92. The goal of accuracy eroded over time as depreciation began to be seen as a vehicle by which investment behavior could be stimulated and directed. The Code introduced so-called accelerated depreciation methods in 1954, and the Accelerated Cost Recovery System was added to the Code as I.R.C. § 168 in 1981. ACRS shortened the period over which cost recovery would occur even beyond the period permitted by the earlier accelerated methods. In adding § 168, Congress made it clear that its intent was to stimulate capital investment. *See* S. REP. NO. 144, 97th Cong., 1st Sess. 47, *reprinted in* 1981 U.S. CODE CONG. & ADMIN. NEWS 105, 152. Nonetheless, the general notion persists that depreciation's basic justification is as a form of spreading the deductible cost of an asset over time.

109. Measuring the amount of the mistake is a separate and difficult issue.

110. For two quite different views about how, in theory, consumption should be measured, see M. CHIRELSTEIN, *supra* note 22, ¶ 6.08, at 137-39 (arguing that sinking fund depreciation is the only theoretically proper method for measuring the economic cost of an asset's use) and Kahn, *supra* note 35, at 30-43 (arguing that only some form of accelerated depreciation can accurately measure the cost of an asset's use); *see also* Blum, *Accelerated Depreciation: A Proper Allowance for Measuring Net Income?!!*, 78 MICH. L. REV. 1172 (1980), and Kahn, *Accelerated Depreciation Revisited — A Reply to Professor Blum*, 78 MICH. L. REV. 1185 (1980).

111. *See supra* notes 106 and 108.

112. *See, e.g.*, Auerbach, *The New Economics of Accelerated Depreciation*, 23 B.C. L. REV. 1327 (1982); Bradford, *Issues in the Design of Savings and Investment Incentives*, in DEPRECIATION, INFLATION, AND THE TAXATION OF INCOME FROM CAPITAL (C. Hulten ed. 1981); Hulten & Wykoff, *Economic Depreciation and Accelerated Depreciation: An Evaluation of the Conable-Jones 10-5-3 Proposal*, 34 NATL. TAX J. 45 (1981).

Recovery System, for example, as accelerating the rate of deduction beyond the rate of consumption.[113] That was certainly the intention of Congress.[114] In light of all this, it hardly seems appropriate to characterize accelerated depreciation deductions as "mistakes."

In my earlier discussion of the distinction between mistakes that can be undone and mistakes that cannot be, I contrasted choices that *could have been* recognized as mistakes when they were made because *all* the data necessary for a fully informed decision was at least theoretically available by the time the choice was made with those whose ultimate resolution was in some sense contingent on the future.[115] These latter choices could not, even in theory, have been decisively identified as mistakes when they were made. I illustrated the second kind of mistake with the example of my vacation trip to Kauai and the unexpected typhoon.[116] But this kind of example does not really capture what has happened when a taxpayer takes fully authorized depreciation deductions in Year 1, only to sell the asset for more than its adjusted basis in Year 3. The amount of the allowable deduction is in no way affected by the taxpayer's reasonable belief (or even his knowledge) about the likelihood of his disposing of the asset for more than its adjusted basis.[117] Neither predictions about the particular taxpayer's circumstances and plans nor predictions about the actual rate at which the taxpayer will consume the asset are relevant to determining the allowable deduction under the Accelerated Cost Recovery System, since the allowable deduction does not presume to represent an accurate assessment of an asset's rate of consumption. Thus, a more apt analogy would be my choosing to go to Kauai because I want to see a good friend who lives there even though I believe, correctly as it turns out, on the basis of apparently reliable weather forecasts, that a typhoon will strike.

Sometimes we choose to satisfy one goal (seeing my friend) at the likely expense of satisfying another (avoiding typhoons). When it turns out that we did in fact have to sacrifice the one goal (I was caught in the typhoon), we might look for some way to mitigate the situation (some might say "to have our cake and eat it too"). In some sorts of circumstances, like the typhoon, that may be difficult. But in

113. *See, e.g.*, M. CHIRELSTEIN, *supra* note 22, ¶ 6.08.

114. *See* S. REP. NO. 144, 97th Cong., 1st Sess. 48, *reprinted in* 1981 U.S. CODE CONG. & ADMIN. NEWS 105, 153.

115. *See supra* text accompanying notes 62-65.

116. *See supra* text accompanying notes 62-65.

117. Indeed he is *required* to adjust his basis downward even if he does not avail himself of an allowable depreciation deduction. I.R.C. § 1016(a)(2) (1988).

others, it might be easier to make an adjustment, after the fact, which goes some way toward reconciling the conflicting goals. The recapture of depreciation is one of these easier adjustments.

Annual accounting sets short-term goals for taxpayers, whereas the fundamental goal of depreciation is a long-term one — to allow taxpayers to deduct the full cost of that portion of long-lived assets which they actually consume for business purposes but to require that they allocate that cost over multiple tax years. Since the allocation procedures established by the Code are not a function of either the particular taxpayer's actual consumption of the asset or his likely plans for disposing of it, there is the clear possibility of a conflict between his satisfying the depreciation requirements of annual accounting and the long-term goal of deducting the cost of only that portion of the asset that he has actually consumed. Whatever our expectations, we can only quantify the full extent of the conflict after the entire history of the taxpayer's ownership of the asset has been determined. The federal income tax system responds to this quantification by making an adjustment to a taxpayer's income in the year that he actually does dispose of a not-fully-consumed depreciable asset. The corrective is not perfect, but it does go some distance toward reconciling the conflict. Whether we call the quantification a "mistake"[118] is of no real importance, but it does not seem an inappropriate label if we are clear about the sense of the word that I intend. The adjustment that is made after the "mistake" has been determined *is* an instance of what I mean by reconciliation. Like the tax benefit rule, this adjustment seeks to reconcile the present with the past presumption (not prediction) about the future (rate of consumption of the depreciated asset) to make them compatible with one another.

By itself, in fact, section 1245 only addresses the increment of the mistake that results from the preferred treatment given to capital gains. Alone, it does not remedy the central problem. That is corrected, to the extent that it is,[119] by adjusting the basis of an asset each time a depreciation deduction is taken[120] and using the asset's adjusted basis to measure the asset's value when it is sold or otherwise converted.[121] Let us return to the examples that illustrated the operation of section 1245: first, an asset bought for $20,000, depreciated for

118. Albeit a mistake that has in many instances been voluntarily built into our tax system.

119. Recapture in a later year of the excess depreciation of earlier years does not take into account the time value of the amount by which the taxpayer's earlier taxes were reduced by the excess depreciation. That amount has, in effect, been loaned to the taxpayer without interest.

120. I.R.C. § 1016(a) (1988). *See supra* note 101.

121. I.R.C. § 1001(a) (1988). *See supra* note 101.

three years by $6800, and sold for $16,000; second, the same asset sold for $25,000 instead of $16,000. In both of these examples the adjusted basis of the asset is $13,200. The amount taken into taxable income upon the first sale is the difference between $16,000 and $13,200 or $2800; upon the second, the difference between $25,000 and $13,200 or $11,800. In the first case the entire $2800 represents so-called excess depreciation. In the second case $6800 of the $11,800 does. In both cases the inclusion of the amount that represents excess depreciation is an instance of reconciliation.

III. The Normative Role of Reconciliation

As I have shown, reconciliation is a general corrective device, available to any tax system that chooses to provide for the possibility that a reporting decision may be revoked in some way other than by return amendment. It, like realization, is a mechanism that a tax system might use to determine whether and when to tax amounts it views as potentially taxable. Each of the preceding examples of phenomena within the federal income tax system is an instance of reconciliation. On the other hand, each traditionally has been described in terms that do not include reconciliation. What distinguishes the descriptions that make use of reconciliation from those that do not is that they are not purely descriptive. Recognizing reconciliation allows us to give a unified explanation of a number of features of the federal income tax system, an explanation that relates these features both to one another and to a schematic functional account of all tax systems.

Another feature of the federal income tax system that profitably can be discussed in terms of reconciliation is its treatment of loans.[122] Conceiving of the tax treatment of simple borrowing in terms of reconciliation allows us to give a more coherent account of an important feature of the federal income tax system than is allowed by the traditional conceptual vocabulary. To the extent that coherence is a desirable feature of a tax system, this account is therefore preferable to others. However, conceiving of the tax treatment of simple borrowing in terms of reconciliation has implications for one's conception of the tax treatment of other kinds of loan arrangements as well. In this part of the article I shall explore those implications in the context of purchase money mortgages. It turns out, however, that the treatment of purchase money mortgages that is implied by the coherent account of simple borrowing is not consistent with the facts of current law. If

122. Although he might not want to associate himself with my actual product, the discussion of loans which follows was inspired by a remark of Martin Ginsburg's.

coherence is an overriding value, reform of current law would be warranted. If, on the other hand, coherence is allowed to compete with other values (assuming that it is a value at all), those values should be identified and their relative strengths assessed before a justified call for specific reform could be made.

My choice of the tax treatment of simple borrowing and the implications of coherence for the tax treatment of mortgages as examples is not accidental. Early in this essay, I referred to Barnett's *amicus* brief in *Tufts* as an example of an argument that relies on rationality as a sufficient reason for interpreting the law as having certain requirements.[123] Barnett's argument is about the tax treatment of purchase money mortgages upon the disposition of the asset they were used to purchase. Ironically, given the importance that he ascribes to the rationality of the tax system, Barnett's own argument seems tacitly to accept the traditional account of the tax treatment of simple borrowing.[124]

A. *Simple Borrowing*

A system might treat borrowed funds as potentially taxable or not potentially taxable. The federal income tax system, of course, does not regard loan proceeds as taxable income to the borrower.[125] This might mean that the federal system chooses to exclude loans from taxation, even though it regards them as potentially taxable amounts, or it might mean that it does not regard them as potentially taxable at all. The familiar justification for the rule that loan proceeds are not included in taxable income is that the borrower's obligation to repay offsets the amount borrowed and leaves her net worth unaffected.[126] As she repays, her liability diminishes by the amount of the repayment and her net worth remains the same. By contrast, however, the federal system *does* include borrowed amounts in the basis of any asset they are used to buy.[127] This treatment is inconsistent with the view that

123. *See supra* text accompanying notes 3-7.

124. *See* Brief for *Amicus Curiae, supra* note 3, at 4-5.

125. *See, e.g.*, Shuster v. Helvering, 121 F.2d 643, 645 (2d Cir. 1941); Matarese v. Commissioner, 34 T.C.M. 791 (CCH) (1975); Gatlin v. Commissioner, 34 B.T.A. 50 (1936); Stayton v. Commissioner, 32 B.T.A. 940 (1935), *nonacq.*, 1936 C.B. 44; Dilks v. Commissioner, 15 B.T.A. 1294 (1929), *affd.*, 69 F.2d 1002 (7th Cir. 1934); Fisher v. Commissioner, 7 B.T.A. 968, 969 (1927), *acq.*, 1928 C.B. 11. One exception to this rule is I.R.C. § 77 (1988), which permits taxpayers to elect to include loans from the Commodity Credit Corporation in gross income.

126. *See, e.g.*, Brief for *Amicus Curiae, supra* note 3, at 3; B. BITTKER & L. LOKKEN, *supra* note 22, at ¶ 6.4.1; M. CHIRELSTEIN, *supra* note 22, ¶ 3.01, at 44; M. GRAETZ, *supra* note 3, at 216; Coven, *Limiting Losses Attributable to Nonrecourse Debt: A Defense of the Traditional System Against the At-Risk Concept*, 74 CALIF. L. REV. 41, 63 (1986); Popkin, *The Taxation of Borrowing*, 56 IND. L.J. 43, 43 (1980).

127. Crane v. Commissioner, 331 U.S. 1, 11 (1947). Borrowed amounts are generally includ-

loan proceeds are not taxable income, since basis is supposed to be a measure of the after-tax cost of an asset,[128] and the borrowed dollars have neither been taxed nor repaid and, cannot, consistently with the view that they are not taxable income, be taxed. Despite the inclusion of untaxed loan proceeds in its measure, basis is nonetheless the amount used to calculate depreciation deductions.[129] This means, ob-

able in basis whether the debt is recourse or nonrecourse. 331 U.S. at 10-11; *see also* Commissioner v. Tufts, 461 U.S. 300, 307 (1983) (nonrecourse mortgage to be treated as "true" loan); Estate of Franklin v. Commissioner, 544 F.2d 1045, 1049 (9th Cir. 1976) (absence of personal liability does not deprive debt of its bona fide character). In *Tufts*, the Supreme Court emphasized that *Crane* had upheld the Commissioner's *choice* to treat nonrecourse debts as he treated recourse debt ("The Commissioner might have adopted the theory . . . that a nonrecourse mortgage is not true debt . . . . Because the taxpayer's investment in the property would not include the nonrecourse debt, the taxpayer would not be permitted to include that debt in basis." 461 U.S. at 308 n.5) and indicated that it was now merely reaffirming *Crane* ("We express no view as to whether such an approach would be consistent with the statutory structure and, if so, and *Crane* were not on the books, whether that approach would be preferred over *Crane*'s analysis." 461 U.S. at 308 n.5 (citations omitted)).

However, the Commissioner may attack nonrecourse indebtedness as lacking in economic substance if, at the time the debt is incurred, the foreseeable value of the property that secures it is less than the indebtedness amount, an indication that the borrower will not repay it. *See* Rice's Toyota World, Inc. v. Commissioner, 81 T.C. 184 (1983) (nonrecourse debt invalid since foreseeable value of encumbered property less than principal amount of debt), *modified* 752 F.2d 89 (4th Cir. 1985); Hilton v. Commissioner, 74 T.C 305 (1980) (foreseeable value of the encumbered property must make abandonment imprudent for nonrecourse debt to exist), *affd.*, 671 F.2d 316 (9th Cir. 1982); Estate of Franklin v. Commissioner, 64 T.C. 752 (1975) (for debt to exist, nonrecourse borrower must have economic incentive to make capital investment in unpaid amount), *affd.*, 544 F.2d 1045 (9th Cir. 1976) .

Inclusion in basis may also be denied if the indebtedness is adjudged contingent on its face. *See, e.g.*, Fox v. Commissioner, 80 T.C. 972 (1983) (notes payable out of proceeds too contingent), *affd. sub nom.*, Barnard v. Commissioner, 731 F.2d 230 (4th Cir. 1984); Lemery v. Commissioner, 52 T.C. 367 (1969) (contingent on profits), *affd. per curiam*, 451 F.2d 173 (9th Cir. 1971); Albany Car Wheel Co. v. Commissioner, 40 T.C. 831 (1963), *affd. per curiam*, 333 F.2d 653 (2d Cir. 1964); Rev. Rul. 80-235, 1980-2 C.B. 229 (1980) (limited partnership nonrecourse note payable out of cash flow too contingent).

128. *See* I.R.C. §§ 1001(a), 1011(a), and 1016(a) (1988), described *supra* note 101, for the statutory structure from which this observation is derived. *See also supra* note 21 and accompanying text. There are notable exceptions to the general conception of basis as representative of after-tax cost. When a corporation exchanges its own stock (in which it has no basis) for property it recognizes no income. I.R.C. § 1032 (1988). Yet I.R.C. § 362 (1988) provides that the corporation's basis in the acquired property will be the same as it was in the hands of the transferor, increased in the amount of gain recognized to the transferor on such transfer. A similar rule governs the basis of property received by a partnership in exchange for a partnership interest. I.R.C. § 723 (1988). *See generally* Manning, *The Issuer's Paper: Property or What? Zero Basis and Other Income Tax Mysteries*, 39 TAX L. REV. 159 (1984).

129. I.R.C. § 167(a) (1988), the basic authorization provision for depreciation deductions, provides for the deduction of a "reasonable allowance" for the exhaustion, wear and tear, and obsolescence of property used in a trade or business or for the production of income. Section 167(g) provides that this deduction must be based on the adjusted basis provided in § 1011. *See supra* note 101. Tangible property placed in service after 1980 and before 1987 is subject to the Accelerated Cost Recovery System rules of old § 168. Under this provision, depreciation deductions are based on the taxpayer's "unadjusted basis" in the property as defined in old § 168(d). Property placed in service after December 31, 1986 is subject to the rules of current § 168, which relies on the definition of adjusted basis in § 167(d).

The at-risk rules of I.R.C. § 465 (1988) have the effect of placing some limitations on the deductibility of depreciation on assets purchased with nonrecourse financing. In general, § 465 limits a taxpayer's annual deductible loss for certain activities engaged in as a trade or business or

viously enough, that borrowed funds can produce significant tax benefits (not to mention the significant economic benefit of being able to invest the entire borrowed amount while deferring its repayment)[130] before they are taxed.[131] For my present purposes, however, the more important observation is that borrowed funds are a sort of hybrid in the federal income tax system. For some purposes (*e.g.*, calculating taxable income) they are not treated as taxable income, while for other purposes (*e.g.*, cost recovery) they are treated as if they had been taxable income.

The apparent hybrid character of the tax treatment of loan proceeds suggests that the concern with net worth that characterizes the justification for noninclusion might not in fact function within the federal income tax system as a factor for distinguishing potentially taxable amounts. Rather, for good reasons or bad, it may function within the system as an indicator of *when* to exclude potentially taxable amounts from taxation. Otherwise, if "no change in net worth" is taken as seriously meaning "not within the scope of the system" (as opposed to "excluded from taxable income"), the inclusion of untaxed loan proceeds in basis represents a genuine systemic incoherence. To pose the question in terms of the simple structural model of an income tax system suggested in Part I of this article:[132] Are loan proceeds not taxed at receipt because they are not even within the purview of the system, or are they potentially taxable amounts that are excluded from taxation? If they are conceived of as potentially taxable amounts that are excluded from taxation (probably *because* of the offsetting obligation and the resultant sameness of net worth) on the presumption that repayment will be made, systemic coherence can be preserved. A description of the account that would be given under this analysis of loan arrangements should illustrate the point.

---

for the production of income to the amount for which the taxpayer is economically at risk. When the at-risk rules were added to the Code in 1976, they classified nonrecourse debt as amounts for which the taxpayer was not at risk. This restriction was considerably modified in 1986. For post-1986 losses with respect to real property, an exception is now provided for "qualified nonrecourse financing." I.R.C. § 465(b)(6) (1988). Generally, qualified nonrecourse financing is nonrecourse financing which has both been provided by an organization that is in the business of lending and is secured by real estate used in the activity. For an argument that the at-risk concept is wrong in principle, see Coven, *supra* note 126.

130. *See, e.g.*, Popkin, *supra* note 126, at 44-45.

131. "By holding that nonrecourse liabilities are includable in the taxpayer's basis for property, *Crane* laid the foundation stone of most tax shelters . . . ." Bittker, *Tax Shelters, Nonrecourse Debt and the* Crane *Case*, 33 TAX L. REV. 277, 283 (1978). *See, e.g.*, M. CHIRELSTEIN, *supra* note 22, at ¶ 13.01; Ginsburg, *The Leaky Tax Shelter*, 53 TAXES 719 (1975); McKee, *The Real Estate Tax Shelter: A Computerized Exposé*, 57 VA. L. REV. 521 (1971); Popkin, *supra* note 126.

132. *See supra* text accompanying notes 16-17.

If a taxpayer borrows $1000 at a standard rate of interest[133] in Year 1 and pays back the principal per the loan agreement in a lump sum five years later, he is not taxed on the $1000 that he borrowed (although he may well have repaid the loan with funds that have been taxed, their treatment is entirely a function of their *own* source). The suggested analysis would simply describe the taxpayer as having excluded the loan proceeds from taxation on the presumption that repayment in full would be made in the future. If the loan were forgiven in Year 2, the taxpayer would be taxed on the amount of the forgiven principal in Year 2. The suggested analysis would explain this result in terms of reconciliation. The loan proceeds were excluded in Year 1 on the assumption of their future repayment. When that proves false, the earlier exclusion is corrected by reconciling it with the current situation and including the forgiven amount in Year 2's taxable income. Year 2's taxable income is *not,* under this account, a new potentially taxable amount entering the purview of the income tax system for the first time because of the increase in the taxpayer's net worth. Reconciliation allows us to account coherently for the current treatment of simple borrowing and discharge of indebtedness.

B. *Purchase Money Mortgages, Footnote 37 and the Issue in* Tufts

This analysis of simple borrowing, consistently applied, implies an analysis of purchase money mortgages. If the $1000 loan in the above example were a purchase money mortgage, and the asset acquired were sold later for an amount that included the assumption of the mortgage liability, the implied analysis of the loan relief would be stated similarly in terms of reconciliation.

1. *The Implications of Coherence*

Consider, then, a range of illustrative cases. In each of these examples assume, unless otherwise specified, that the asset held by the taxpayer is nondepreciable, that the sale takes place in Year 3, and that the outstanding principal on the loan remains $1000.

133. Assume here, and throughout the discussion *infra* of examples A-M(NR), that the interest payments are based on a fixed rate and are unconditionally payable during the term of the loan at six-month intervals. This assumption will allow the discussion to proceed schematically without the added (but unnecessary for my purposes) complexity introduced by the original issue discount rules of I.R.C. §§ 1271-75 (1988 & West Supp. 1990). For a detailed analysis of how the original issue discount rules work see McCawley, *Time Value of Money: OID and Imputed Interest,* 333-3d Tax Mgmt. (BNA) (1990).

EXAMPLE A

Mortgage Liability	*Asset*
Face value = $1000	Basis = $1000
	FMV = $1200

Purchaser assumes the mortgage liability and pays an additional $200 to acquire the asset.

This transaction, like any sale, has two conceptually distinct components to be accounted for by each taxpayer — the amount received and the amount given up. Here the seller has given up an asset with a basis of $1000 and has received relief from a liability of $1000 plus $200 in cash.[134] Each of these components can be separately analyzed.

1. *The asset given up:* The taxpayer receives value of $1200 for an asset in which he had a basis of $1000. He realizes $200 gain.

2. *The liability relief received:* At the time the loan was incurred the taxpayer had excluded the amount of the proceeds ($1000) from his income on the presumption that he would later repay that amount in its entirety. Here the taxpayer is giving up an asset worth $1200 to receive relief from the $1000 liability plus $200 in cash. Put another way, the taxpayer is repaying the $1000 liability in full, as per the earlier presumption, and so no corrective measure is appropriate.

EXAMPLE B

Mortgage Liability	*Asset*
Face value = $1000	Basis = $1000
	FMV = $900

Purchaser assumes the mortgage liability and acquires the asset plus an additional $100.

1. *The asset given up:* The taxpayer receives value of $1000 in exchange for an asset in which he had a basis of $1000 and an additional $100 in cash. He received $900 for the asset alone and thus he realizes a loss of $100.

2. *The liability relief received:* The taxpayer is giving up an asset worth $900, along with another $100 in cash, in exchange for relief from a $1000 liability. Thus he is repaying the liability in full, consistent with the presumption behind the original exclusion of the $1000 loan proceeds.

134. For an analysis of this and the next three examples from the purchaser's perspective see *infra* text accompanying notes 151-57.

EXAMPLE C

Mortgage Liability	*Asset*
Face value = $1000 $800 = cost to discharge at time of sale [or amount one could now borrow on the same terms] (*i.e.*, the prevailing interest rate for similar loans has gone up)	Basis = $1000 FMV = $1000

Purchaser assumes the mortgage liability and pays an additional $200 to acquire the asset.

1. *The asset given up:* Perhaps somewhat counter-intuitively, the seller only receives $1000 of value for the asset. This can be seen if one focuses on the value of the assumed mortgage liability from the purchaser's perspective. Because interest rates have risen in the three years since the original loan was taken out, it would cost an additional $200 now to borrow $1000. This means that a promise now to abide by the repayment terms of the earlier loan would only finance a loan of roughly $800 and that it would therefore cost the purchaser an additional $200 simply to relieve the seller of the liability of $1000.

2. *The liability relief received:* The taxpayer gives up an asset worth $1000 in order to be relieved of a $1000 liability and receive $200 in cash. When he originally excluded the $1000 loan proceeds he did so on the presumption that he would repay the full amount. In fact he is satisfying his entire liability for only $800. The premise behind the earlier exclusion has therefore turned out to be mistaken. The mistake can be ameliorated by reconciling the current year's repayment of $800 with the earlier year's presumption of repayment and consequent exclusion of $1000. This results in $200 being included in the current year's taxable income.

At least two things should be noted about this analysis. First, although its practical consequences are less in a system without a special tax rate for long-term capital gains than they would be in one whose rate structure distinguished between kinds of taxable income,[135] the $200 gain to the taxpayer *results from* the sale of the asset but does not represent *gain from* that sale associated with the appreciation of the asset. The analysis therefore implies that if the asset were a capital

135. *See supra* note 101.

asset, the $200 would *not* be long-term capital gain. This is in contrast to current federal income tax law. Current federal law does not, in fact, bifurcate transactions of this sort as the analysis suggests.[136] Instead, relying on *Crane*'s[137] inclusion of the *face value* of any mortgage liability assumed by the purchaser as part of the seller's amount realized (and ignoring the fact that the cost to discharge the mortgage liability has changed), it simply focuses on the asset. Thus, the asset in Example C has a basis of $1000 and the seller has received $1200 (face value of the mortgage liability assumed plus the additional $200) for it.[138] The gain is characterized as *gain from* the sale of the asset — capital gain if the asset was a capital asset.

Second, under the suggested analysis, the $200 gain does not represent a newly realized potentially taxable amount. Rather, it represents an amount that was excluded from taxable income when it was first identified as potentially taxable but which, in the light of the future that has come to be, should not be excluded after all. Its current recognition is not a function of its being newly realized but of the current reconciliation of the present situation with mistaken past presumptions.

EXAMPLE D

Mortgage Liability	*Asset*
Face value = $1000	Basis = $1000
Cost to discharge = $1100	FMV = $1000
(The prevailing interest rate for similar loans has gone down.)	

Purchaser assumes the mortgage liability and acquires the asset plus $100.

1. *The asset given up:* For reasons analogous to those given in this part of the discussion of Example C, the purchaser could borrow roughly $1100 at Year 3's lower interest rate for the same total cost that he would have incurred to borrow $1000 three years earlier. This means that in an arm's length transaction he would require $1100 of value in exchange for his assumption of the three-year-old mortgage liability. Here, he receives $100 in cash and the asset, which must be

136. However, if the lender conditioned the purchaser's assumption of the mortgage liability on the modification of its terms, I.R.C. § 1274(c)(4) (West Supp. 1990) and Prop. Treas. Reg. § 1.1274-1(c), 51 Fed. Reg. 12,082 (1986), appear to bifurcate the transaction in a highly stylized way by treating the modified mortgage liability as a new mortgage liability which was exchanged for the original mortgage liability.

137. Crane v. Commissioner, 331 U.S. 1 (1947).

138. I.R.C. § 1001(b) (1988); Treas. Reg. § 1.1001-2(a) (1980).

valued at $1000. Since the seller-taxpayer's basis in the asset is $1000, he has no gain or loss with respect to the asset.

2. *The liability relief received:* The seller gives up both an asset worth $1000 and an additional $100 to be relieved of a $1000 liability. He has thus fully repaid the $1000 which was earlier excluded from his taxable income on the presumption of later repayment. There is no mistake to correct, and hence no reconciliation is needed. He has, of course, spent an additional $100 in order to procure the liability relief. A system could choose to characterize that expenditure as deductible or not.

Again, current federal income tax law yields a different result. It ignores the fact that the cost required to discharge the mortgage has changed, and simply treats this transaction as the exchange of cash and an asset with a total basis of $1100 for mortgage relief of $1000. The result is a $100 asset loss. The bifurcation of the transaction into its "asset given up" side and its "liability relief received" side is a logical consequence of the suggestion that the apparent incoherence of the federal system's exclusion from tax of borrowed amounts and its concurrent inclusion of them in the basis of assets that they are used to acquire could be cured by conceiving of borrowed amounts as having been excluded from taxation on the presumption that full repayment would be made in the future. The inclusion in income of forgiven loan amounts could therefore be accounted for as instances of reconciliation.

As I indicated earlier, Barnett, in his *Tufts amicus* brief conceives of cases of this sort as *requiring* bifurcated analysis.[139] In his view, it is irrational to ignore the fact that the value of a liability can vary just as the value of any asset can. Thus he posits the general rule that "the gain or loss realized by a purchase of relief from a liability is equal to the difference between the adjusted basis of the liability and the amount expended for the relief."[140] According to Barnett, the amount of "the obligor's prior receipt for accepting the liability [is] his basis for the liability."[141] Barnett values systemic rationality highly. There is some evidence that he regards it as a sufficient reason for interpreting the law as in fact providing one thing rather than another.[142] Nonetheless, his own analysis does not proceed from concern that the federal system's basic treatment of simple borrowing is systemically incoherent. Indeed, he seems to accept the net worth rationale with-

139. *See supra* text accompanying note 6.

140. Brief for *Amicus Curiae, supra* note 3, at 5.

141. *Id.*

142. *See supra* text accompanying notes 5-7.

out question.[143] As a result, Barnett's bifurcated analysis is somewhat different from the one I am spelling out here. In each of the preceding examples, Barnett would analyze the liability relief received in terms of the taxpayer's basis in the liability (its face value in these examples) and the amount expended to procure relief. When the taxpayer, like the taxpayer in Example C, gives up assets worth less than the face value of the liability, he will realize liability gain in the amount of the difference between the face value of the liability and what he gave up for the liability relief alone, $200 of ordinary income in Example C. This amount, and its characterization, should always be the same as that yielded by my analysis even though the descriptions of what has happened differ. However, when the taxpayer, like the taxpayer in Example D, gives up assets worth more than the face value of the liability in exchange for relief from the liability, the two analyses yield interestingly different results. Under Barnett's analysis, such a taxpayer would realize a liability loss in the amount of the difference between what he gave up in exchange for relief from the liability and his basis in the liability (face value). This would be a $100 liability loss in Example D. My reconciliation analysis, by contrast, does not regard the taxpayer as having suffered a *loss.* He has simply spent $100 more to procure liability relief than he expected to.

Example D is related to Example B just as C is to A. The form of the transaction in D is identical to that in B, just as that of C is identical to that in A. The difference in the analyses of the hypotheticals within each pair is entirely a function of whether either the value of the asset has changed from Year 1 to Year 3 or the prevailing interest rate for a purchase money mortgage of $1000 is different in Year 3 from what it was in Year 1. One of the two variables remains constant in each of the four hypotheticals. In the next four hypotheticals, *both* the value of the property and the prevailing interest rate have changed.

EXAMPLE E

Mortgage Liability	*Asset*
Face value = $1000	Basis = $1000
Cost to discharge = $800	FMV = $1100

(The prevailing interest rate for similar loans has gone up.)

Purchaser assumes the mortgage liability and pays an additional $300 to acquire the asset.

1. *The asset given up:* For precisely the same reasons as those

143. Brief for *Amicus Curiae, supra* note 3, at 3.

given in this part of the discussion of Example C, the seller here has received $1100 of value for the asset; $800 associated with the loan assumption and $300 in cash. Since the asset's basis was $1000 he realized a $100 gain.

2. *The liability relief recovered:* The taxpayer repays a total of $800 of the previously excluded $1000 loan. He gives up an asset worth $1100 in exchange for relief from $1000 of liability plus an additional $300 in cash. Reconciliation would square the previous assumption with the actual resolution of the debt and include $200 in Year 3's taxable income.

For the reasons discussed above, Barnett's analysis would yield the same results. Federal income tax law currently lumps the asset gain and the liability gain together and characterizes all $300 as asset gain.

By now the pattern of the analysis should be clear.

EXAMPLE F

Mortgage Liability	*Asset*
Face value = $1000	Basis = $1000
Cost to discharge = $800	FMV = $900

(The prevailing interest rate for similar loans has gone up.)

Purchaser assumes the mortgage liability and pays an additional $100 to acquire the asset.

1. *The asset given up:* The taxpayer has received value of $800 (mortgage liability assumed) plus $100 (cash), or $900. Loss on the asset equals $100.

2. *The liability relief received:* $1000 of relief received at a cost of $900 (asset) less $100 (cash received) equals $800. Reconciliation gain is $200.

Barnett's result would be the same. Federal law offsets the gain against the loss and calls it $100 asset gain.

EXAMPLE G

Mortgage Liability	*Asset*
Face value = $1000	Basis = $1000
Cost to discharge = $1100	FMV = $1100

(The prevailing interest rate for similar loans has gone down.)

Purchaser assumes the mortgage liability in exchange for the asset.

1. *The asset given up:* The taxpayer receives value of $1100 (mortgage liability assumed). Gain on the asset equals $100.

2. *The liability relief received:* $1000 of previously excluded loan receipts are repaid with the equivalent of $1100. No reconciliation is called for (see the discussion in part 2 of Example D).

Barnett's analysis would differ exactly as it did in Example D and treat this as $100 asset gain and $100 liability loss. Under current law *no* gain or loss would be recognized.

EXAMPLE H

Mortgage Liability	*Asset*
Face value = $1000	Basis = $1000
Cost to discharge = $1100	FMV = $900
(The prevailing interest rate for similar loans has gone down.)	

Purchaser assumes the mortgage liability and acquires the asset plus an additional $200.

1. *The asset given up:* The taxpayer receives value of $1100 (mortgage liability assumed) less $200 (cash paid), or $900. Loss on the asset equals $100.

2. *The liability relief received:* $1000 of relief is received at a cost of $900 (asset) plus $200 (cash) equals $1100. No reconciliation is called for.

Barnett would treat the seller as sustaining $100 asset loss and $100 liability loss. The federal income tax treats the seller as having a $200 asset loss.

A central tenet of federal income tax law ever since *Crane* was decided in 1947 has been that it does not distinguish between recourse and nonrecourse borrowing.[144] Thus, *Crane* held that the amount realized by someone who sells mortgaged property includes the face amount of the mortgage, regardless of whether the seller is personally liable for the debt. A corollary of this holding has been that the taxpayer's basis in the property includes the amount of any purchase money mortgage. However, the analysis of purchase money mortgages implied by the "reconciliation" analysis of simple borrowing suggests distinguishing between recourse and nonrecourse mortgages in some contexts.

If the purchase money mortgage is a nonrecourse loan, secured by the asset whose fair market value has dropped, the taxpayer would have no economic motivation to compensate a purchaser by paying him the difference between the face value of the loan and the fair mar-

144. *See supra* notes 5 and 131. For a concise and informative history of the tax treatment of nonrecourse debt in the federal income tax, see Shaviro, 44 TAX L. REV. 401, 420-27 (1989).

ket value of the asset. He does not need the purchaser in order to satisfy his obligation, but can simply turn the asset over to the lender/secured-interest holder. This fact suggests an important distinction between the *presumptions* that underlie recourse and nonrecourse purchase money mortgages.

Under the analysis that I have suggested, when someone borrows money, excludes it, but nonetheless includes the amount of the loan in the basis of the asset that it is used to acquire, a presumption is made. When the loan is a recourse loan, the presumption is that its face amount will be repaid in full. As Examples C, E, and F have illustrated, sometimes loans can be discharged for less than their face value. When this occurs, the analysis suggests that an adjustment might be made to the taxpayer's current ordinary income to reconcile actual events with the earlier presumption about the resolution of the loan.

But, when the loan is a nonrecourse loan, the presumption is slightly different: the face amount of the loan will be repaid in full as long as the fair market value of the property that secures it does not drop below the face amount of the loan. Otherwise, the loan will be repaid to the extent of the fair market value of the underlying property. The presumption, therefore, has two parts. First, like the case of a recourse loan, a presumption is made about the future cost of discharging the obligation. If this turns out not to be accurate, reconciliation might be appropriate. Second, and unlike the case of a recourse loan, an additional presumption is made about the future value of the asset acquired with the loan proceeds. The presumption is that the full face amount of the loan represents the appropriate amount to include in the asset's basis, because the fair market value of the asset will not fall below that face amount and the amount of after-tax investment in the asset (attributable to the loan) will thus turn out to be the face amount of the loan rather than a lesser amount. If this presumption turns out to be inaccurate,[145] the remedy might be to adjust the taxpayer's amount realized *for the asset* to reconcile actual events with

145. Current federal income tax doctrine distinguishes between "true" debt and contingent debt. A number of courts have upheld the Internal Revenue Service's contention that an inadequately secured nonrecourse loan is too contingent to be characterized as debt includable in the basis of the asset which secures it. Rev. Rul. 77-110, 1977-1 CB 58; *see, e.g.*, Brannen v. Commissioner, 722 F.2d 695 (11th Cir. 1984); Rice's Toyota World, Inc. v. Commissioner, 752 F.2d 89 (4th Cir. 1985); *see also* Estate of Franklin, 544 F.2d 1045 (9th Cir. 1976). My analysis of the two-part presumption underlying the inclusion of a nonrecourse loan in the securing asset's basis involves a different kind of contingency. Traditional contingent loan concerns center on uncertainty about the value of the securing asset *at the time that it is acquired.* This is hardly surprising since the issue invariably arises in the context in which the lender and the seller of the asset are the same taxpayer. The contingency which characterizes my presumption involves uncertainty about the value of the securing asset *at the time that it is sold.*

the earlier presumptions that the fair market value of the asset would not drop below the face amount of the loan that it secured.

Consider three more hypotheticals. ("NR" indicates that the loan is nonrecourse.)

EXAMPLE I (NR)

Mortgage Liability	*Asset*
Face value = $1000	Basis = $1000
Cost to discharge = $1000	FMV = $900

No purchaser would reasonably assume the mortgage liability. Taxpayer abandons the asset to mortgagee and is thereby relieved of his obligation.

1. *The asset given up:* The taxpayer's basis in the asset is the amount of the loan that it is presumed will be repaid. Precisely speaking, that amount should be the lesser of $1000 or the fair market value of the asset at the time of its disposition or abandonment. Less precisely speaking, the basis is presumed to be $1000. The basis has, in effect, been "rounded up" to the only determinable amount available at the time that the asset is acquired. When the fair market value of the asset drops to $900 and the taxpayer abandons the asset to the mortgagee, it becomes apparent that the presumption of $1000 has turned out to be incorrect, even though the more precisely stated presumption was correct. The current situation could be reconciled with the earlier presumption either by adjusting current income directly or by making an adjustment to the taxpayer's current basis in the asset. Adjusting basis to reflect the fact that the fair market value of the asset at the time of its disposition turned out to be less than the face amount of the loan would result, here, in a basis of $900, and there would be no gain or loss on the abandonment of the asset.

2. *The liability relief received:* The taxpayer has been relieved of a liability equal to the lesser of $1000 or the fair market value of the asset that secures it. He has achieved this relief by giving up the securing asset. He has thus repaid the liability in full, consistent with the repayment assumptions behind the original exclusion of the loan proceeds.

Example I(NR) is similar to Example B. Because his loan was a recourse liability, however, the seller in B could not simply abandon the devalued asset to the mortgagee without further consequence. Thus, he had to pay an additional $100 to a purchaser to be rid of the obligation.

Example I(NR) is familiar to tax lawyers as the case whose outcome was left in doubt by the Supreme Court in its famous footnote 37 to the *Crane* decision:

> Obviously, if the value of the property is less than the amount of the mortgage, a mortgagor who is not personally liable cannot realize a benefit equal to the mortgage. Consequently, a different problem might be encountered where a mortgagor abandoned the property or transferred it subject to the mortgage without receiving boot. That is not this case.[146]

Thirty-six years later in *Tufts,*[147] the Supreme Court finally returned to that case. Its answer was somewhat anticlimactic. Since *Crane* does not distinguish generally between recourse and nonrecourse loans, and since *Crane* always includes in a seller's amount realized the face amount of any recourse liability assumed by a purchaser, the face amount of any nonrecourse debt assumed or forgiven (the practical effect of abandonment) should be included in a seller's amount realized as well.[148] The result in Example I(NR) is that the taxpayer recognizes no gain or loss on the abandonment of the asset because he is conceived as having realized $1000 for an asset in which his basis is also $1000. Although the rationale is different, the same result is suggested by the above analysis. Barnett's result would be the same as well.

EXAMPLE J (NR)

Mortgage Liability	*Asset*
Face value = $1000	Basis = $1000
Cost to discharge = $800	FMV = $800

(The prevailing interest rate for similar loans has gone up.)

Purchaser assumes the mortgage liability in exchange for the asset.

1. *The asset given up:* The taxpayer's basis in the asset should be described in exactly the same way as the taxpayer's basis in the asset in Example I(NR) was. Since the fair market value of the asset at the time of its disposition had dropped to $800, the original basis was, in effect, overstated by $200. As seller, the taxpayer is receiving value of $800 (current cost to discharge the mortgage) for an asset whose basis is $1000 but whose adjusted basis, as things turned out, should be $800. Reconciliation could correct for the basis overstatement by disallowing the $200 asset loss that would otherwise be indicated by this bifurcated form of analysis.

2. *The liability relief received:* The taxpayer has satisfied an obli-

146. Crane v. Commissioner, 331 U.S. 1, 14 n.37 (1947).

147. Commissioner v. Tufts, 461 U.S. 300 (1983).

148. *Tufts,* 461 U.S. at 307-10.

gation to repay the lesser of $1000 or the fair market value of the asset that secures it, for the latter amount. There is no mistake to correct, nor is there any gain or loss to recognize.

Once again, this result is consistent with *Crane* and *Tufts*. The taxpayer would recognize no gain or loss on the transaction because he would have exchanged an asset with a basis of $1000 for relief from a $1000 liability. Barnett's analysis, on the other hand, since it does not distinguish between recourse and nonrecourse loans, would treat the taxpayer as having realized a $200 asset loss and a $200 liability gain.

EXAMPLE K (NR)

Mortgage Liability	*Asset*
Face value = $1000	Basis = $1000
Cost to discharge = $800	FMV = $900

(The prevailing interest rate for similar loans has gone up.)

Purchaser assumes the mortgage liability and pays an additional $100 to acquire the asset.

1. *The asset given up:* The taxpayer has received value of $900. The basis was thus overstated by $100, and there is no gain or loss.

2. *The liability relief received:* $900 of liability satisfied for $900 (fair market value of asset) less $100 (cash received) equals $800. Gain is $100.

This is the same set of facts as those in Example F, except that the loan is nonrecourse. Since neither Barnett nor (in this context) current federal practice distinguish between recourse and nonrecourse loans, their analyses of Example K(NR) would not differ from their analyses of Example F.

It is important not to lose sight of the point of the suggested analysis. This analysis follows from an account of simple borrowing that can account for the hybrid treatment of loan proceeds by the federal income tax system without inherent incoherency. Since loan proceeds used to purchase a depreciable asset are included in the asset's basis, they are treated, for that purpose at least, as taxable income within the federal system. This flies in the face of any account of loans, like the net worth account, that explains their nontaxation by *distinguishing* them from taxable income.

Tufts forces us to confront the incoherence directly. It involves an asset whose original basis included the face amount of a purchase money mortgage, whose adjusted basis reflected depreciation deductions, and whose fair market value at the time of its sale was less than the face value of the loan assumed by the purchaser. The following two hypotheticals are representative of facts like *Tufts'.* Example L assumes a recourse loan. Example M(NR) assumes a nonrecourse loan.

EXAMPLE L

Mortgage Liability	*Asset*
Face value = $1000	Original basis = $1000
Cost to discharge = $800	Depreciation deductions taken = $200
Adjusted basis = $800	FMV = $800

(The prevailing interest rate for similar loans has gone up.)

Purchaser assumes the mortgage liability in exchange for the asset.

1. *The asset given up:* The current cost to discharge a $1000 mortgage at Year 1's interest rate is $800. The value received by the seller is therefore $800, and he realizes no gain or loss.

2. *The liability relief received:* The taxpayer-seller has repaid a $1000 loan with an asset worth $800. Thus, the $1000 loan proceeds that were excluded in Year 1 on the assumption that they would be repaid in full, have been repaid with only $800. Reconciliation corrects for the mistake and prescribes a $200 gain.

EXAMPLE M (NR)

Mortgage Liability	*Asset*
Face value = $1000	Original basis = $1000
Cost to discharge = $800	Depreciation deductions taken = $200
Adjusted basis = $800	FMV = $800

(The prevailing interest rate for similar loans has gone up.)

Purchaser assumes the mortgage liability in exchange for the asset.

1. *The asset given up:* The original basis of the asset turns out to have been, in effect, overstated by $200. If one ignores for the moment the added complications of the effect of that overstatement on the depreciation deductions taken, reconciliation would suggest that the adjusted basis should be thought of as $600, and a $200 asset gain would seem to have been realized. Depreciation, however, complicates the answer in two ways. First, if we assume that there is no need to reconcile for the extra depreciation that resulted from the overstatement in the original basis, the gain that reconciliation suggests might well be treated as properly characterized in accordance with the applicable rules for the recapture of excess depreciation.[149] Theoretically anyway, all excess depreciation should be taken into income, characterized just as it was when it was taken out. Second, there is the issue of

149. For a schematic description of the role of a recapture rule see *supra* text accompanying notes 101-02.

how to adjust for the fact that the actual depreciation was based on an inflated basis. If a goal of reconciliation is to be wholly corrective, then the proper way to think of the new adjusted basis is as it would have been had the original basis been $800 and had depreciation deductions been calculated and taken accordingly. This would result in a revised adjusted basis of something more than $600. On the one hand, this would reduce the asset gain subject to the recapture of depreciation rules by the amount of adjusted basis in excess of $600. On the other hand, it would introduce the need to reconcile for the fact that exactly this much extra depreciation was taken as a result of the inflated basis.

2. *The liability relief received:* The taxpayer-seller has repaid his loan in accordance with the presumptions that governed its terms — *i.e.*, with the lesser of $1000 or the fair market value of the underlying asset at the time of its disposition. No gain or loss is realized, and no reconciliation is appropriate.

Tufts held that the taxpayer in this situation should be treated as having realized asset gain equal to the difference between his adjusted basis ($800) and the face value of the mortgage liability relief he received ($1000). This $200 would likely be characterized either as capital gain or section 1231 gain, depending on the nature of the asset. Any portion of the gain that represented excess depreciation would presumably be recaptured in accordance with the applicable rules.[150] This is very nearly the *same* result as that yielded by the suggested analysis. Barnett's bifurcation analysis, on the other hand, results in no asset gain or loss and a $200 liability gain.

If we are serious about systemic coherence, and insist on it throughout our analysis of borrowed funds, its implications turn out to be different in some circumstances, including *Tufts* itself, from those claimed by Barnett. And although the *results* of our coherent analysis differ from current federal income tax law in the context of many recourse loans, they are remarkably similar in the context of nonrecourse loans.

2. *A Significant Cost of Coherence*

Systemic rationality and coherence may well be desirable for a tax system to have. Most of us are doubtless inclined, at least, to think so. But other features might be desirable for our tax system as well. Unless we can show generally that systemic coherence trumps all other values — an argument that does not get made, even by those, like

150. *See Tufts*, 461 U.S. at 303 n.2.

Barnett, who seem to think that systemic rationality and coherence provide sufficient reason for interpreting the law one way rather than another — normative arguments about a tax system must articulate and weigh a variety of values. Hence, even if the implications of coherence are as described in the previous section, I have not yet made the case for reforming current law to conform to my rationale and results.[151] Indeed, it is not my aim here to make that case, but rather to show something about how recognizing the necessary functions of any tax system can help both in describing our own income tax system and in structuring normative arguments about it. In any case, one should note that the administrative cost of the preceding analysis of purchase money mortgages would be considerable. Just how considerable can begin to be seen by revisiting Examples A through D above, this time analyzing them from the perspective of the purchaser.

EXAMPLE A_P

Mortgage Liability	*Asset*
Face value = $1000	Basis = $1000
Cost to discharge = $1000	FMV = $1200

Purchaser assumes the mortgage liability and pays an additional $200 to acquire the asset.

1. *The asset purchased:* The purchaser has purchased an asset at a cost of $1200. His basis in the asset should be $1200.

2. *The liability incurred:* The purchaser has, in effect, borrowed $1000 of his $1200 purchase price. The borrowed $1000 is not currently taxed on the assumption that the taxpayer will repay it in the future.

EXAMPLE B_P

Mortgage Liability	*Asset*
Face value = $1000	Basis = $1000
Cost to discharge = $1000	FMV = $900

Purchaser assumes the mortgage liability and acquires the asset plus an additional $100.

1. *The asset purchased:* The purchaser has bought an asset for a net cost of $900 and, accordingly, his basis in the asset should be $900.

2. *The liability incurred:* The purchaser has borrowed $1000 which he has used to acquire $1000 of value (an asset worth $900 plus

151. Since my results conform fairly well to both *Crane* and *Tufts*, such reform is not impossibly impractical.

$100 in cash). This amount is not currently taxed on the assumption that it will be repaid in the future.

EXAMPLE C_P

Mortgage Liability	*Asset*
Face value = $1000	Basis = $1000
Cost to discharge = $800	FMV = $1000

(The prevailing interest rate for similar loans has gone up.)

Purchaser assumes the mortgage liability and pays an additional $200 to acquire the asset.

1. *The asset purchased:* The purchaser has acquired an asset worth $1000. One would, therefore, expect the purchase price to have been $1000. In fact, it was, since he paid $200 cash and agreed to pay an amount equivalent to the amount he would have to pay had he borrowed $800 for the same term at current interest rates.[152] If basis represents cost, the purchaser's basis in the asset should be $1000. But the face value of the mortgage is $1000, and that amount plus the additional cash which he paid would appear to give the purchaser a $1200 basis.

2. *The liability incurred:* By undertaking the mortgage obligation the purchaser has achieved a current purchasing power of $800. This amount is not currently taxed on the assumption that it will be repaid in the future. But, once again, it must be noted that the face value of the liability is $1000. If the value of the liability were measured by its purchasing power at the time it was undertaken ($800), then the face value of the loan ($1000) would not be the standard against which future dispositions of the loan would be offset. If, for example, two years later, the asset was still worth $1000 and the face value of the unpaid mortgage was still $1000[153] but its cost to discharge was now also $1000,[154] the sale of the asset by the person I have called "the purchaser" for relief from the liability would seem to result in no gain or loss on the asset but in a $200 loss on the liability. In effect, the purchaser would have spent $1000 (his basis in the asset) in order to be relieved of what, in his hands, had started out to be an $800 debt. On the other hand, if the value of the liability were measured by its face value, regardless of fluctuations in its purchasing power, then the

152. *See supra* discussion of Example C.

153. Perhaps because its terms required periodic interest payments with a balloon payment of the principal at some future date.

154. Perhaps because current market interest rates for similar loans had returned to those originally set forth by the terms of the loan.

purchaser's basis in the asset would be $1200 and the transaction in this example would result in neither gain nor loss on the liability, but in a $200 loss on the asset.

EXAMPLE D

Mortgage Liability	*Asset*
Face value = $1000	Basis = $1000
Cost to discharge = $1100	FMV = $1000
(The prevailing interest rate for similar loans has gone down.)	

Purchaser assumes the mortgage liability and acquires the asset plus an additional $100.

1. *The asset purchased:* The purchaser has bought an asset worth $1000 and has been given $100 as well. Clearly, a fair price for this package would be $1100. Because the purchaser agreed to pay back an amount equivalent to the amount he would have to repay had he borrowed $1100 for the same term at current interest rates, it would be reasonable to assign him a basis of $1000 in the asset (his cost less the $100 he received with the asset). If the face value of the mortgage is determinative of basis, the buyer's basis in the asset would be $900 ($1000 obligation assumed less $100 cash received).

2. *The liability incurred:* The purchaser here is in a position analogous to that of the purchaser in Example C_P. He has undertaken to pay back an amount equal to the amount he would have to repay had he borrowed $1100. This gives him a current purchasing power of $1100. He is not taxed currently because it is assumed that he will repay in the future. This example, no less than Example C_P, illustrates how the standard against which future dispositions of the loan are measured can differ from the loan's face value if the acquired asset is given a basis equal to its value and actual cost (here $1000) and the loan assumption is viewed as having contributed its actual purchasing power (here $1100) to the transaction.

Bifurcation of transactions that involve both the exchange of an asset and the exchange of a liability would seem to require that the value of the liability be adjusted to reflect its current cost to discharge. If face value were always used as the measure of the value of the liability, then there could be no fluctuation in the value of any given liability[155] and bifurcation would have no effective role. All gains and losses would be represented as attaching to the exchange of the asset.

155. Of course, the amount of the liability could change as it was partially paid or as additional amounts were borrowed, but such changes are not fluctuations in the value of a given liability.

The seller in Example C would be said to have sold the asset for $1200 (even though its fair market value was only $1000 and even though someone who paid fair price in any currency other than the assumption of the outstanding mortgage liability would be treated as having paid $1000) and thereby as having realized a $200 gain on the asset. Consistently with that result,[156] the buyer in Example C_P would be given a $1200 basis in the asset. As the preceding discussion has shown, on the whole, the current federal income tax system in fact operates in this manner. It tends to treat the increase or decrease in the value of any liability relinquished or assumed in connection with an asset sale as if it had been assimilated into the price of the asset itself.[157]

The actual purchasing power of a particular liability can fluctuate, however, as a result of differences in the prevailing interest rates. As long as these fluctuations are not accorded any special significance by the tax system, the system can operate using the dollar as a fungible standard for measuring gain, loss, and income. If bifurcation of the sort spelled out in Examples A through M(NR) were adhered to, and for tax purposes, the value of a liability were not automatically pegged to its face value but face value nonetheless governed the relationship between debtor and creditor, then accounting for the tax consequences of satisfying assumed obligations would become a different enterprise. Essentially, the face value of the dollar paid to satisfy an obligation would cease to function as the measure of the amount paid to satisfy the obligation. The complications arise because bifurcation allows a value *different* from the face value to be assigned to a liability for tax purposes, even though face value will necessarily continue to represent the amount that the borrower is contractually due to pay to the holder of the note. Thus, in Example C_P, if, three years after he had assumed it as part of his purchase price for the asset, the buyer were to pay off the entire outstanding mortgage liability of $1000 as per the terms of the original note, his tax treatment would vary in accordance with the purchasing power of the dollar. If its purchasing power at the end of three years were the same as it had been anticipated at the beginning of Year 1 that it would be, then paying off the debt with 1000 Year-3 dollars would not have any tax consequences, even though the loan

156. Consistency in the treatment of buyer and seller seems, at the least, a desirable feature. Coven apparently thinks that it is a necessary one. *See* Coven, *supra* note 126, at 77; *see also* Brief for *Amicus Curiae, supra* note 3, at 20. Without such consistency it would be possible for a seller to be treated as having received a different amount from the buyer for the asset from what the buyer is credited (through his basis) with having paid.

157. An exception to this way of proceeding is suggested by Bowers v. Kerbaugh-Empire Co., 271 U.S. 170 (1926).

had been treated in Year 1 as having a purchasing power of only $800. This result is a straightforward consequence of the fact that the purchasing power ascribed to the loan assumption in Year 1 *assumed* a payback of $1000 at the end of Year 3 and necessarily made certain assumptions about what the value of 1000 Year-3 dollars would be. Things would become more complicated, however, if the purchasing power of a Year-3 dollar differed from what had been anticipated in Year 1. In that case, the satisfaction of the mortgage for $1000 at the end of Year 3 would mean either that the buyer had not paid back the entire amount that he had borrowed and therefore had, in effect, benefitted from the discharge of some of his debt, or that he had paid back more than he had borrowed. Under either description, the payback might well trigger a response by the income tax system.

Embarking on a path that allows for the possibility that the face value of the dollar will not always be treated by the tax system as a fungible unit of measurement opens up a veritable Pandora's box of practical and theoretical difficulties. Any system, like the federal income tax system, that ever measures what is taxed by comparing current value with previous value needs some standard to serve as a common denominator. The dollar has traditionally served that purpose. As the preceding examples and discussion have shown, the bifurcation of a transaction that involves both the exchange of an asset and the exchange of a liability into two distinct transactions does not allow the dollar to play this role, nor does it suggest a ready substitute.

But this analysis has not attempted to articulate the practical or policy issues surrounding the specific choices that the federal income tax system might make with respect to the taxation of transactions involving purchase money mortgages, much less to resolve them. It *is* an effort, however, to provide a general conceptual framework within which those issues can be identified, articulated, understood, and debated.

IV. Postscript to Parts II and III: When To Reconcile

Each of the foregoing examples of reconciliation within the federal income tax system illustrates *how* it functions as a corrective device. Reconciliation involves the comparison of the actual current circumstances with a position taken on an earlier return with respect to some potentially taxable amount. When it operates, it adjusts the current year's taxable income if the comparison reveals that the earlier position presumed a future that is relevantly different from what actually occurred. In this way it prevents at least some of the system's earlier choices about the treatment of potentially taxable amounts from being irrevocable. At the same time, it determines whether and when to tax that potentially taxable amount.

Although none of the foregoing examples focuses directly on the question of *when* reconciliation might be appropriate, they certainly suggest the beginnings of an answer. In each example, reconciliation is invoked only when events have shown, once and for all, that some presumption about the future that characterized an earlier year's treatment of a potentially taxable amount has proved incorrect.[158] The relevant future has in some sense been resolved.

Not surprisingly, given the connection between reconciliation and the ultimate resolution of a contingent event, the identification of a mistake that triggers reconciliation often coincides with the realization of another potentially taxable amount. This is easily illustrated by my discussion of section 1245 recapture.[159] There, the event that made it certain that the earlier years' depreciation had been excessive was the sale of the depreciated asset. Any increase in the value of the asset was realized at the same time. Similarly, in Examples A through M(NR),[160] the final disposition of the loan made it certain that the earlier year's report of taxable income hinged on a mistaken presumption about the future. That disposition occurred at the same time the property securing the loan was sold or abandoned. In each instance, the event triggering reconciliation was also the event marking the realization of any potentially taxable amounts arising from the appreciation of the asset.

The frequent identity of a reconciliation event and a realization event has obscured the fact that reconciliation is different from realization and functions within our system as a separate and distinct means for determining whether and when a potentially taxable amount will be recognized. This is doubtless at least a part of the reason why the conceptual vocabulary of the federal income tax system has not included reconciliation. Instead the system has struggled unsuccessfully to account for all instances of taxation in terms of realization. This aggrandizement of realization has, in turn, necessarily led us to ignore the straightforward structural requirements common to any tax system, including one that purports to tax income. This essay is an effort to begin to look directly at those requirements and their implications for the structure of the federal system.

158. *See* White, *supra* note 9, at 502-05.

159. *See supra* text accompanying notes 98-121.

160. *See supra* section III.B.1.

CONCLUSION

I have claimed here that there are certain necessary questions that any tax system must ask. At the least, a system must make some determination about whether it considers an item within its aegis, and for each such item, must determine whether to tax it, and, if so, when.[161] If this observation is correct, and I do not see how it cannot be, then any tax system, including the federal income tax system, can be described in terms that relate its particular features to the necessary functions. We can expect that any system will have some means of determining what falls within its province (even if that means is not terribly systematic)[162] and some means of determining whether things within its compass will be taxed and when. In a simple system the initial division will obviate the later *whether* question, and only the *when* (now or later) question will remain.[163] This paper begins to describe the federal income tax system in terms that relate its features to these necessary functions.

The federal system is complex and does not neatly divide the world, first into a pile of things that are potentially taxable and a pile of things that are not, and then go about the task of deciding *when* to tax the things in the first pile. Instead, it conceives of exclusion (whether by initial exclusion or by deduction) from the tax base as a possible response to those items included in the first pile. This means that it asks the question *whether* to tax any item as well as the question *when* to tax it after it has made some initial attempt at dividing the world into two piles.[164] More importantly, it also means that the normative goals that determine the federal system's tax base are not fully specified by the criteria of initial division. Indeed, no criterion of initial division is ever really articulated by the system because it relies on the answers to the *whether* and, to a lesser extent, the *when* questions to determine the content of the tax base.[165]

Any tax system, including the federal income tax system, will have

161. *See supra* text accompanying notes 10-21.

162. *See supra* text accompanying note 19.

163. Actually in the simplest sort of system there is no *when* question either; once an item is identified, it is taxed. *See supra* text accompanying notes 13-14.

164. Some attempt at division seems to have been made, since our system does not *ask* the *whether* and *when* to tax questions of everything in the world (my left big toe, for example). Or perhaps it does include everything as within its scope and can be conceived instead as determining not to tax my big toe in answer to the *whether* question. If so, everything in the world that is untaxed can be regarded as being potentially taxable and as having been excluded from the system. The criteria for inclusion in the system's tax base would be identical to the criteria for determining whether to tax. The general structural model is unaffected by this possible interpretation of the federal system.

165. *See supra* text accompanying notes 14-17.

mechanisms for answering the *whether* and *when* to tax questions which may be more or less systematic. The federal system explicitly identifies realization as playing a central role in its determinations of whether and when to tax. In fact, however, the federal system also relies importantly on another, unarticulated, mechanism to make these determinations. I call this mechanism "reconciliation."

Reconciliation has considerable descriptive and explanatory power. Distinguishing it allows us to give a more coherent account of a number of phenomena in the federal income tax system than we can give with the traditional conceptual vocabulary. But it is important to realize that coherence and rationality are only one (two?) of a variety of aspirations that we might have for a tax system. Thus, whenever a coherent account of an actual phenomenon within a system has implications for the description of certain other parts of the system, and the further descriptions turn out *not* to fit the facts, we cannot simply assume that the best course would be either to reform or to interpret the law so as to increase its coherence. Sometimes other, often competing, values, such as administrability, equity, economic growth, or political expediency are relevant to the question of what the law ought to be or how it should be interpreted. Self-conscious articulation and exploration of those values and their importance ought to be a goal of normative discussion about the content of the income tax system.

The federal income tax system has become grotesquely complex. On the one hand, the temptation to declare that it no longer has any structural foundations is great. On the other hand, the importance of a structure that can be looked to to help us understand what we have and to provide us with a conceptual apparatus within which to focus our critical and reforming efforts is also great. This paper is borne of the belief that there is reason to pursue the latter course.

Name Index